Also in the Variorum Collected Studies Series:

JOHN W. WATT
The Aristotelian Tradition in Syriac (CS1074)

PEREGRINE HORDEN
Cultures of Healing
Medieval and After (CS1073)

DAVID LUSCOMBE
Peter Abelard and Heloise
Collected Studies (CS1072)

STEPHAN KUTTNER, edited by PETER LANDAU
Gratian and the Schools of Law, 1140–1234
Second Edition (CS1071)

JACQUES van der VLIET
The Christian Epigraphy of Egypt and Nubia (CS1070)

PETER MEREDITH, edited by JOHN MARSHALL
The Practicalities of Early English Performance: Manuscripts, Records, and Staging
Shifting Paradigms in Early English Drama Studies (CS1069)

MEG TWYCROSS, edited by SARAH CARPENTER and PAMELA KING
The Materials of Early Theatre: Sources, Images, and Performance
Shifting Paradigms in Early English Drama Studies (CS1068)

SEYMOUR DRESCHER
Pathways from Slavery
British and Colonial Mobilizations in Global Perspective (CS1067)

DAVID JACOBY
Medieval Trade in the Eastern Mediterranean and Beyond (CS1066)

GILES CONSTABLE
Medieval Thought and Historiography (CS1065)

GILES CONSTABLE
Medieval Monasticism (CS1064)

For more information about this series, please visit: www.routledge.com/Variorum-Collected-Studies/book-series/VARIORUM

VARIORUM COLLECTED STUDIES SERIES

Holocaust Studies: Critical Reflections

Steven T. Katz

Holocaust Studies

Critical Reflections

LONDON AND NEW YORK

First published 2019 by Routledge

2 Park Square, Milton Park, Abingdon, Oxon, OX14 4RN
605 Third Avenue, New York, NY 10017

Routledge is an imprint of the Taylor & Francis Group, an informal business

First issued in paperback 2020

Copyright © 2019 Steven T. Katz

The right of Steven T. Katz to be identified as author of this work has been asserted by him in accordance with sections 77 and 78 of the Copyright, Designs and Patents Act 1988.

All rights reserved. No part of this book may be reprinted or reproduced or utilised in any form or by any electronic, mechanical, or other means, now known or hereafter invented, including photocopying and recording, or in any information storage or retrieval system, without permission in writing from the publishers.

Notice:
Product or corporate names may be trademarks or registered trademarks, and are used only for identification and explanation without intent to infringe.

British Library Cataloguing-in-Publication Data
A catalogue record for this book is available from the British Library

Library of Congress Cataloging-in-Publication Data
Names: Katz, Steven T., 1944– author.
Title: Holocaust studies : critical reflections / Steven T. Katz.
Description: Abingdon, Oxon ; New York, NY : Routledge, 2019. | Series: Variorum collected studies series ; CS1075 | Includes bibliographical references and index.
Identifiers: LCCN 2018054360 (print) | LCCN 2018058702 (ebook) | ISBN 9780429018701 (ebook mobi) | ISBN 9780429018718 (ebook epub) | ISBN 9780429018725 (ebook adobe) | ISBN 9781138579606 (hardback) | ISBN 9780429507908 (ebook)
Subjects: LCSH: Holocaust, Jewish (1939–1945)—Study and teaching. | Holocaust, Jewish (1939–1945)—Historiography.
Classification: LCC D804.33 (ebook) | LCC D804.33 .K38 2019 (print) | DDC 940.53/18072—dc23
LC record available at https://lccn.loc.gov/2018054360

ISBN: 978-1-138-57960-6 (hbk)
ISBN: 978-0-367-78650-2 (pbk)

Typeset in Times New Roman
by Apex CoVantage, LLC

VARIORUM COLLECTED STUDIES SERIES CS1075

To a wonderful daughter
Tamar Chaya Zippora
and her very special family:
husband Eitan, and children
Abraham, Aaron, Meira, Efraim, and Gabriella

CONTENTS

	Acknowledgments	xi
	Introduction	xiii
1	On the Holocaust and comparative history	1
2	Mass death under Communist rule and the limits of "otherness"	27
3	Auschwitz and the *Gulag*: A study in dissimilarity	57
4	Children in Auschwitz and the *Gulag*: Alternative realities	73
5	On the definition of genocide and the issue of uniqueness	90
6	Exploring the Holocaust and comparative history	110
7	Extermination trumps production: On the issue of Jews as slave laborers	121
8	The murder of Jewish children during the Holocaust	150
9	Thoughts on the intersection of rape and *Rassenschande* during the Holocaust	171
10	Irving Greenberg on history and *Halakha*: The implications of the Holocaust	201
11	Exploring the concept of *Kol Yisrael Arevim Zeh L'Zeh*	215

12 Thinking about Jewish resistance during the Holocaust	233
13 Elie Wiesel: The man and his legacy	267
14 The issue of confirmation and disconfirmation in Jewish thought after the *Shoah*	291
15 Jewish theologians respond to the Holocaust	335
Index	349

ACKNOWLEDGMENTS

All "Updates" (at the end of each chapter) are previously unpublished

Introduction – previously unpublished

Chapter 1 "On the Holocaust and comparative history" was originally published as the 1993 Leo Baeck Memorial Lecture and is reproduced courtesy of the Leo Baeck Institute, New York.

Chapter 2 "Mass death under Communist rule and the limits of otherness" was originally published in Robert S. Wistrich (ed.), *Demonizing the Other: Antisemitism, Racism and Xenophobia* (Amsterdam, 1999), pp. 266–92; reprinted by permission of Taylor & Francis, UK.

Chapter 3 "Auschwitz and the *Gulag*: A study in dissimilarity" was originally published in Alan Berger (ed.), *Bearing Witness to the Holocaust, 1939–1989: Proceedings of the Holocaust Scholars Conference* (Lewiston, ME, 1992), pp. 71–89; reproduced by permission of Edwin Mellen Press.

Chapter 4 "Children in Auschwitz and the *Gulag*" originally appeared in Rachel Millen (ed.), *New Perspectives on the Holocaust* (New York University Press, 1996), pp. 19–38; reprinted by permission of NYU Press.

Chapter 5 "On the definition of Genocide and the issue of uniqueness" is taken from the Introduction to Steven T. Katz, *The Holocaust and New World Slavery: A Comparison*, 2 vols. (Cambridge UK, 2019); reproduced by permission of Cambridge University Press.

Chapter 6 "Exploring the Holocaust and comparative history" is reprinted from *Holocaust Scholarship: Personal Trajectories and Professional Interpretations – Festschrift in Honor of Milton Shain*, eds. Christopher Browning, Susannah Heschel, and Michael Marrus (London, 2015), pp. 84–98; reprinted with permission of Palgrave Macmillan.

Chapter 7 "Extermination trumps production: On the issue of Jews as slave laborers" originally appeared in Roni Stauber (ed.), *Holocaust and Antisemitism: Essays Presented in Honor of Dina Porat* (Jerusalem, 2015), pp. 71–100; reprinted courtesy of Yad Vashem Publications in association with Tel Aviv University.

ACKNOWLEDGMENTS

Chapter 8 "The murder of Jewish children during the Holocaust" originally appeared in *Continuity and Change: A Festschrift in Honor of Irving Greenberg's 75th Birthday*, edited by Steven T. Katz and Steven Bayme (Lanham, MD, 2010), pp. 167–88; reprinted by permission of Rowman & Littlefield.

Chapter 9 "Thoughts on the intersection of rape and *Rassenchande* during the Holocaust" was originally published in *Modern Judaism*, 32.3 (October 2012); reproduced by permission of Oxford University Press.

Chapter 10 "History and *Halakha*" appears in *Yitz Greenberg and Modern Orthodox: The Road Not Taken*, eds. Adam Ferziger, Steven Bayme, and Miri Freud-Kandel (Boston, MA, forthcoming 2019); included courtesy of Academic Studies Press.

Chapter 11 "Exploring the concept of *Kol Yisrael Arevim Zeh L'Zeh*" was originally given at a conference entitled *Aspects of Jewish Solidarity during the Shoah*, held at Yad Vashem in 2014. The conference volume is forthcoming. The paper is included courtesy of Yad Vashem.

Chapter 12 "Thinking about Jewish resistance during the Holocaust" – previously unpublished.

Chapter 13 "Elie Wiesel: The man and his legacy" originally appeared in *Yad Vashem Studies* 44.2 (December 2016) pp. 11–42; reprinted by permission of Yad Vashem Publications.

Chapter 14 "The issue of confirmation and disconfirmation in Jewish thought after the *Shoah*" was originally published in Steven T. Katz (ed.), *The Impact of the Holocaust on Jewish Theology* (New York, 2005), pp. 13–60; reprinted by permission of New York University Press.

Chapter 15 "Jewish Theologians respond to the Holocaust" was originally published as the Introduction to Part III, "European and American Responses during and following the War" in *Wrestling with God: Jewish Theological Responses during and after the Holocaust*, eds. Steven T. Katz, Shlomo Biderman and Gershon Greenberg (New York and Oxford, 2007), pp. 355–67; reprinted by permission of Oxford University Press.

INTRODUCTION

I

The present collection of essays comprises twelve previously published and three never-before-published essays written over the past three decades.[1] By choosing to republish those that previously appeared, I am indicating that I still endorse, in the main, the views expressed and believe that the research embodied in these articles can continue to contribute to the scholarly discussion of which they have been a part since their initial appearance. The three papers published in this volume for the first time are, I believe, works of scholarly substance that represent a "sample" of my more recent interests.

The form of the present work requires a comment before I start to analyze substantive conceptual and historical matters. When the proposal suggesting this project was accepted by Robert Langham, senior editor at Routledge in London, he rightly pointed out that a number of the essays had appeared several decades ago. He therefore correctly reasoned that, in most instances, there must be a more recent relevant discussion of the topics under consideration, and furthermore, that I might have had additional thoughts on the subjects and controversies raised in my initial research. In consequence, it was agreed that I would add an "Update" at the end of each paper, representing my current view, as well as the more recent work of significance of others, on the topic being analyzed. In the case of the previously unpublished essays – "Exploring the concept of *Kol Yisrael Arevim*" and "Thinking about Jewish resistance during the Holocaust," along with the recently published pieces "On the definition of genocide" and the article on Elie Wiesel, there is little to add to what is in the papers themselves. In consequence, the Updates to these four articles are very brief. On the other hand, many of the other Updates are substantial, even in those instances where the original publication was quite recent, for instance, relative to the essays on "Extermination trumps production," "Rape and *Rassenschande*," and the still

---

[1] Two earlier collections of my essays have appeared under the titles *Post-Holocaust Dialogues: Critical Studies in Modern Jewish Thought* (New York, 1983), and *Historicism, the Holocaust and Zionism: Critical Studies in Modern Jewish Thought and History* (New York, 1992).

unpublished "History and *Halakha*." At the same time, I would note, explicitly, that none of these Updates are meant to be exhaustive. Rather, it is hoped that they will contribute to the ongoing scholarly discussion and that readers will find them both interesting and useful.

The contents of the essays included in this collection fall into three broad categories: (a) the Holocaust and comparative history; (b) "Jewish issues," mostly related to the Holocaust; and (c) meta-historical reflections. The first of these, comparative history, requires that one understand that comparison is a crucial, highly informative, scholarly method of analysis. Whenever I take up issues involving comparisons – something that I have done at considerable length in regard to both the Holocaust and comparative mysticism[2] – I am reminded of two sound pieces of advice that I have received, one from a teacher, one from a friend. From the great scholar of medieval Jewish philosophy, Harry Wolfson, came the wisdom that "before you compare two things you should know something about at least one of them." And from my friend Moshe Lewin, an outstanding student of Stalinism and Russian history, I learned that "not to compare is to limit what one knows."

Comparative study, because of all the substantive and methodological issues involved in its pursuit, is a highly demanding form of research. Comparative work on the Holocaust requires not only that one master the complexities connected with the murder of European Jewry but also that one securely controls the historical details and interpretive challenges related to the other cases with which one is comparing the "Final Solution." Judging by the overall quality of the by now very sizable secondary literature that involves comparisons of other historical events with the Holocaust, this standard is rarely met. The authors of many of these comparative studies know what conclusion they want to reach before they begin to do their research and, therefore, spend inadequate time actually investigating in what ways the comparison being proposed is accurate and in what ways it is not. In consequence, the authors of many comparative studies reveal that they know too little about the subjects that they wish to explain and regarding which they often make very strong, but unjustifiable, claims. And their working hypotheses almost always involve a presumption of similarity, of likeness, usually facilitated and advanced through vague and confused employments of the problematic concept of "genocide."

The term "genocide" has, in all too many instances, become a moral term indicating that the case under review is among the worst type of mass crimes rather than, as it is technically meant to be employed, indicating that a specific type of crime, as defined in law, has been committed. Thus, much of the work one sees in this area of study is not impressive and should be seen as suspect. All conclusions offered relative to asserted comparisons between the "Final Solution" and other mass crimes require independent checking and investigation, both of the evidence introduced to support these proposed judgments and the method and logic employed to make the comparative argument being advanced.

---

2 See sources provided in note 3 below.

INTRODUCTION

As to the Jewish material included here, much of which is related to theological matters and the link between theology and the Holocaust, it should be emphasized for those who are not familiar with sophisticated theological reflection that this activity makes very high hermeneutical and logical demands. Not only does speaking about, or inquiring into, or describing the ways of God require intelligence and learning, as do all other academic disciplines, but it deals with metaphysical issues for which there is no certain evidence. And the objects or subjects of its concern, most specifically God, have many meanings, none of which are demonstrable. Consider, as a paradigmatic case in point, the perplexing question: can we still attribute omnipotence to God after Auschwitz? If we do, then we need to ask why God did not intervene in the death camps – or did He? And if we deny the attribute of omnipotence, what happens to the coherence of the Jewish tradition? As readers will see, while I value the determined efforts by distinguished colleagues to deal with, and resolve, these highly challenging theological puzzles, I do not find the proposals and the "solutions" offered satisfactory, either individually or as a group. My methodological – and existential – predicament is that I believe I can show the flaws in all the main positive, i.e., affirmative, post-Holocaust Jewish theological positions, as well as deflect all the negative, i.e., God-denying, arguments. Therefore, I go on arguing about these fundamental issues with others as well as with myself.

I would add that theology requires not only conceptual acuity but also special sensitivities to the complexities of life. Having spent most of my time over the past three decades studying mass death and human evil in its many different forms I have come to realize, as I did not adequately recognize in the earlier decades of my academic career, that deconstructing the human predicament, and the role that transcendent forces might play in it, requires a wisdom that transcends logic and philosophical argument alone. This does not mean that I have lost interest in rigor and lucidity, or faith in the necessity of the rule of the "excluded middle." And I still refuse to endorse non-cognitive positions like those made famous by Tertullian, Pascal, and Kierkegaard. Subjectivity is not "truth" and believing things that are false, however "passionately," does not make them "true." Reason still makes demands that *must* be met. Evidence still matters, though I now appreciate much more fully that the complexity that inhabits and defines theological conversation arises to a considerable extent from trying to decide – and defend – what counts as evidence and confirmation. Moreover, these epistemological and evidentiary matters are both more tangled and more obscure than I had earlier allowed, and dealing with them is more philosophically challenging than I had earlier understood. As a result of my work on religious experience and mysticism in the world's great religious traditions,[3] I have become much more cognizant of, and much more

---

3 See, for example, my articles in the following volumes (that I also edited): *Mysticism and Philosophical Analysis* (New York and Oxford, 1978); *Mysticism and Religious Traditions* (New York and Oxford, 1983); *Mysticism and Language* (New York and Oxford, 1992); *Mysticism and Sacred Scripture* (New York and Oxford, 2000); and *Comparative Mysticism: An Anthology of Original*

xv

sensitive to, the problems that arise when one attempts to agree – and disagree – as to what counts as evidence.

Regarding the essays that I describe as "meta-historical," it is necessary to understand that in these papers I am not trying to write history in the sense most familiar to students of history. My purpose is not to take a collection of material and reveal the story – the dates, names and places – that it records and reports. Rather, in this work I am attempting to interrogate the historical sources that I work with in order to explore the philosophical, theological, and interpretive issues that arise from reflecting on the historical data. Representative here is my engagement with such issues as verification, the definition of genocide, and my concern with the question of the Holocaust's uniqueness. Likewise, I am not interested, for example, only in the mountain of details connected with the murder of Jewish children by the Führer state. Instead, my concern is to uncover the *intent* behind the Nazi assault on all Jewish women and all Jewish youngsters and the special light that this shines on the Third Reich in its ideological entirety. Similarly, I am curious not only about the use of Jews as slave laborers in Nazi-occupied Europe but also about the implications, the meaning, of the way in which the Third Reich, because of its racial-metaphysical principles, utilized Jews.

In all of my research I have tried to be faithful to the methodological principle of reading the primary sources for myself, holding secondary sources, however valuable, at a distance until I could independently either confirm or disconfirm what they had to say. As I have inquired into various controversial subjects this principle has proven significant, yielding substantive consequences. In this connection I would call attention to my reading of wartime sources on the subject of Jewish resistance. If I had only read Raul Hilberg, the greatest historian of the Holocaust, and those who have followed his lead on this subject, I would not have come to the position I presently hold on this topic that essentially repudiates his interpretation.[4] Similarly, my own reading of the sources tells me that Hannah Arendt's presentation of the issue of Jewish

---

Sources (New York and Oxford, 2013). In these works, I have set out a new way to read mystical texts and to "contextualize" religious experience.

4 Hilberg's final position is set out in *The Destruction of the European Jews*, 3rd ed., 3 vols. (New Haven CT, 2003), vol. 2. It was, however, already stated in the 1st edition of this classic work published in 1961. I criticize his interpretation of this critical issue in my Introduction to the reprint of *Documents on the Holocaust: Selected Sources on the Destruction of the Jews*, 8th ed., edited by Yisrael Gutman and Yitzhak Arad (Lincoln, NE, 1999), pp. v – xi. Raul and I discussed the issue at length after my comments appeared in print several times. He was a hard man to persuade to change his mind – especially because he said Isaiah Trunk, the author of the major study, *Judenrat* (1972), told him he agreed with his interpretation of the matter. As a result, I was not very successful in getting him to alter his view. He did, however, admit that, especially in light of the evidence and arguments made by me and by a number of Israeli scholars – who he could not read as he was not a Hebrew speaker – that he needed to think about the issue again. But this was never evident in any of his later publications or in the third edition of his *Destruction* published in 2003.

leadership in her *Eichmann in Jerusalem* is a radical distortion of the actual historical situation in which the Jews and the *Judenräte* found themselves. My own independent inquiries have convinced me that her presentation and explanation of Adolf Eichmann's behavior was, is, seriously misleading.[5] The same is the case relative to my disagreement with the views of Raphael Lemkin, Leo Kuper, and others, on the comparability between the murder of European Jewry and the massive depopulation among the aboriginal peoples of the New World following the arrival of Columbus and his Spanish heirs. Which is to say that the colonial Spanish empire, despite the extraordinary loss of life that undoubtedly took place, was not the Holocaust, and not a genocide if by the employment of this term one means the intentional murder of an entire people. The influential claims to the contrary advanced by David Stannard and his acolytes like Ward Churchill are radical misinterpretations of the reality that was – a fact that I only discovered by immersing myself in sixteenth and seventeenth century Spanish New World history.[6] Again, the claims comparing New World slavery and Nazi concentration camps made by historians of slavery like Stanley Elkins,[7] and Holocaust scholars like Richard Rubenstein,[8] are far wide of the mark, a truth that became evident to me only after years of study of the history of slavery in the Americas.[9]

In my publications I have also decided not only to describe the relevant historical and meta-historical circumstances as I understand them but, in addition, to confront directly those interpretations of the material under review that I saw as mistaken in serious ways. Readers will encounter this sort of critical response in what I have to say about authors like A. Dirk Moses, Donald Bloxham, and Dan Stone on the matter of the uniqueness of the Holocaust,[10] and David Stannard regarding the comparisons he advances between the Holocaust and the treatment of Native Americans and African slaves in the New World.[11] The point that I want to make by offering these responses is not criticism for its own sake but, rather, a concern to warn readers not to be taken in by erroneous interpretations, scholarly mendacity, and false conclusions.

---

5 Hannah Arendt, *Eichmann in Jerusalem* (New York, 1963).
6 This judgment will be explained and defended fully in a forthcoming study devoted to this subject.
7 Stanley Elkins, *Slavery: A Problem in American Institutional and Intellectual Life* (3rd ed. revised; Chicago, 1976), pp. 98–139.
8 See his *The Cunning of History: The Holocaust and the American Future* (New York, 1975; paperback 1987), pp. 36–47.
9 My understanding of this comparison is set out at length in my study of *The Holocaust and New World Slavery: A Comparative History*, 2 vols. (Cambridge, 2019).
10 See the essay "On the definition of genocide and the issue of uniqueness" in this volume.
11 In my *The Holocaust and New World Slavery* readers will find a lengthy, critical, Appendix on Stannard's work, with many further errors made by him identified in the notes to that study. This critical evaluation of Stannard's views will be extended still further in the analysis offered in my forthcoming comparative study of Spanish Colonial America, i.e., the treatment of the native population after the Spanish Conquest as compared to the Holocaust.

INTRODUCTION

II

In the course of putting this collection together I have had the help of a number of special individuals. Ms. Lilka Elbaum helped with various computer-related tasks and, as usual, was always there to assist, no matter the challenge. Abby Brockman, a graduate student at Boston University, kindly assisted with the production of the manuscript by keying in a number of the earlier essays. Whenever her help was requested she responded with great courtesy and a continual smile. I am also indebted to the librarians at Mugar library, Boston University; Widener library, Harvard University; and Baker-Berry library at Dartmouth College for assistance with bibliographical issues. And, as always, I owe more than I can say to my wife Rebecca who has helped with this volume in so many ways.

Baker-Berry Library,
Dartmouth College

1

ON THE HOLOCAUST AND COMPARATIVE HISTORY

(Leo Baeck Memorial Lecture, 1993)

I

The special opportunity offered by the Leo Baeck Memorial Lecture is an appropriate occasion to reflect on the fate, and the meaning of the fate, of European Jewry under the Third Reich. Emerging out of the conflict and confusion of the Weimar years, Hitler came to power first in Germany and then in almost all of western and central Europe, creating in turn the Nuremberg racial laws to disemancipate the German Jews, ghettos in which to incarcerate the Polish and Baltic Jews, *Einsatzgruppen* to murder the Russian Jews, and in the end, death camps to exterminate all the remaining Jews of Europe. East and west, north and south, male and female, young and old, six million out of nine-and-a-half million European Jews were consumed, with active designs existing for the annihilation of the remainder of world Jewry, beginning with the Jews of Britain, the Sephardic communities of North Africa, and the growing community of the *yishuv* (the Jewish settlement in the Land of Israel).

This is what we know as the Holocaust. The ideologically driven plan to make the world *Judenrein*. But it is not only as a Jewish phenomenon that this event has entered into the contemporary consciousness. Given its uncompromising project of genocidal elimination coupled with its technological-bureaucratic characters, directed by a capacious racial-Manichean dogmatic, the *Shoah* has become one of the defining symbols of our age. And as such, given its iconic status, an intense debate has emerged regarding its singularity. This is not least because to the degree that it has become the symbol of evil in our time, it has been co-opted as the standard, the model, by which, through which, and over against which, the writing of other histories of persecution and mass death now take place.[1] In consequence, the historiographical placement of this event cannot be avoided. Or, to put the question very simply and directly: to what degree is the destruction of European Jewry a unique historical event?

---

1 For a description of this phenomenon as it pertains to the writing of medieval history see my essay, "Misusing the Holocaust Paradigm to Mis-Write History: Examples from Recent Medieval Historiography," in Dina Porat and Shlomo Simonsohn (eds.), *Michael: On the History of the Jews in the Diaspora*, vol. 13 (Tel Aviv, 1993), pp. 103–30.

In trying to answer this vexing and by now much discussed question I would begin with three hermeneutic principles.[2] (1) The *Shoah* can and must be historicized, i.e., it must be held to be a subject open to historical investigation free of *a priori* theological and metaphysical judgments that would "mystify" it by definition. (2) The *Shoah* is not individuated as a historical happening by the number of Jewish victims, either as regards the absolute number of dead or the percentage of loss these deaths represent. As to the aggregate, at least four cases surpass Jewish losses during World War II, namely, New World Indian deaths in the sixteenth century, the depopulation of the USSR under Stalin, Chinese casualties during the Taiping Rebellion of the 1850s, and the long series of bloody occasions in China in the twentieth century that, according to at least one recent estimate, has claimed a total of one hundred million persons.[3] As to the percentage of decline – a loss of 40 percent of world Jewry and 60 percent of European Jewry – these figures are matched or exceeded by, for example: the Native American catastrophe following conquest that claimed up to 96 percent of the total indigenous population within a century; by the Armenian massacres of World War I that were in the range of 40 percent (higher on many projections, though I disagree with these higher figures); and by the decimation of the Australian aborigines following European contact. And other examples could be provided. (3) When making historical comparisons and distinctions of the kind I will offer in my analysis this evening I am not making moral comparisons. Nor again, in defending uniqueness, am I simultaneously endorsing the injudicious claim that the Holocaust is *more evil* than alternative occurrences of extensive and systematic persecution, organized violence, and mass death. The character of the uniqueness that I am prepared to champion is not tied to a scale or a hierarchy of evil (i.e., of event X being more or less malevolent than another event Y, or all previous events E^1 to E^{11}).

II

I have elsewhere described why it is that the comparison regularly made between the Holocaust and medieval forms of persecution, including medieval antisemitism, are in fact incorrect.[4] Here let me only summarize this complex issue by saying that in no case of medieval persecution – not the Church's persecution of the Jews, nor of witches, nor again in the Crusade against Albigensians and Cathars, and finally against sodomites – was it the intention of the Church or Christian State to carry out a policy of physical (not cultural) genocide. In every

---

2 R. J. Rummel, *China's Bloody Century: Genocide and Mass Murder since 1900* (New Brunswick, NJ, 1991).
3 For a full presentation of my argument, with supporting evidence, consult vol. 1 of my *Holocaust in Historical Context: The Holocaust and Mass Death before the Modern Age* (New York, 1994).
4 For a full presentation of my argument, with supporting evidence, consult volume 1 of my *Holocaust in Historical Context: The Holocaust and Mass Death before the Modern Age* (New York, 1994).

instance theological doctrines and practical necessities intervened to constrain the form of the persecutory campaign tool. Those who regularly, if confusedly, see medieval anti-Jewish bigots as Nazis, who misunderstand the attempt to destroy heresy as the equivalent of racial immolation, who mistake the violence against women incarnate in the witch craze for physical genocide, and lastly, those who liken the rhetoric again homosexual acts with the actuality of gas chambers, are both constructing fictions and manipulating the symbol of the Holocaust in ways that are unwarranted by the historical evidence.

The reality is that most Jews survived the outbursts of medieval anti-Judaism. For example, the Crusades, for all their real and terrible violence, probably claimed only 3,000 to 4,000 Jewish lives; relatively few Jews were killed by the *Flagellants* in 1348–49; and the Inquisition murdered only a very small number of *conversos*, certainly only a small percentage of the *converso* population in a statistical sense. It should also be clearly understood that most women in the medieval era survived the misogynistic clerics who pursued witches – on my figures 99.9+ percent of women so survived. Likewise, the overwhelming majority of Christian heretics were able to successfully abjure and re-enter the Catholic Church after the destruction of the heretical centers of southern France. The same social and theological logic prevailed in the case of the hundreds of thousands of Huguenots who preferred to remain in France rather than go into exile after the revocation of the Edict of Nantes. Finally, very few sodomites were killed for their sexual deviance, though a small number were put to death in sixteenth-century Spain and Italy. Thus, the likening of the Holocaust to these medieval precedents, given their actuality, has produced very little by way of substantive historical insight.

III

As regards the modern period the situation is more complex not least because of the occurrence of a number of instances in which there has been large-scale loss of life. Here one immediately thinks of at least seven relevant cases: the massive losses experienced in the sixteenth century by the native peoples of North and South America (counted as two); the millions of blacks who died in the enterprise of slavery; the large Armenian losses during World War I; the millions consumed by the *Gulag*; the tens of millions who lost their lives in the Chinese Civil War and the so-called Cultural Revolution; and more recently, the one million or so Cambodians murdered by their own government in the bizarre episode that went by the name of Kampuchea. Each of these events has, with some good reason, been called a Holocaust and likened to the destruction of European Jewry. And this inventory could easily be extended to include the Nigerian Civil War, the tribal conflicts in Burundi and Rwanda, the decimation of Indonesian Communists, the Civil War in Pakistan/Bangladesh, and, for some – though incorrectly – Yugoslavia today (in 1993), and this brief list by no means exhausts the catalogue of possible candidates.

However, I would like to make a bold historical and phenomenological counterclaim: none of these events is, at least on what I will call the *genocidal criteria*, comparable to the Holocaust; efforts by historians and others to make the contrary case are in error. Here I would introduce two elements that will help individuate the phenomenological character of the *Shoah*: (1) the intention of the victimizers including, in particular, the complete physical extermination of the targeted victim population; and (2) the multi-layered category of mediation present in other cases but not in the Holocaust, as I shall explain as I proceed.

As regards the former, note that in none of the modern cases mentioned as putative parallels do we find comparable genocidal intent, that is, the intention to totally extirpate the victim community. Though we have several cases where the losses experienced in these other historic tragedies exceed the rate of loss – as well as the absolute number – of Jewish victims during the *Shoah*, in no case other than the Holocaust do we have evidence that the killer was single-minded about murdering all the members of the victim group. The Conquistadors needed native slaves and did not seek to murder the indigenous population of the New World. Blind pathogenic forces did this work *against* the will of the European conquerors. Europeans involved in the black slave trade, which came about because of the unintended death of the indigenous population, participated in this vile traffic in order to make a profit: dead slaves brought no profit. The *Gulag* was a vast slave empire created in large part to finance the modernization of Russia. Stalin needed his *Gulag* population if only so that he could exploit them – he did not set out purposely to murder them. The *Khmer Rouge* hated the old Cambodia and its bourgeois elements, but it aimed at creating a new Kampuchea in which seven-eighths of the pre-revolutionary population would continue to live, if now in dramatically altered circumstances. This is to say, the intent to murder an entire people, even amidst the vast slaughters that have marked the modern historical epoch, is an historical exception.

IV

I would support this repercussive claim by considering in some detail what many consider the closest historical parallel to the *Shoah* – the destruction of the Armenian community of Turkey during World War I. There are many good reasons to argue for this comparison but, ultimately, it is incorrect. While intending no diminution to the Armenian tragedy, and in no way denying the enormous proportions of the Armenian massacres, I would contend that the intentionality of the two victimizers – and hence, the character of the two historic events – was, in fact, *fundamentally dissimilar* and does not provide grounds for an argument as to the convergence of the Armenian and Jewish circumstance. Despite the intense, almost millenarian, talk of "total liquidation" and "total extermination of all non-Turkish elements" to be found in the diverse Turkish materials of the 1915–1916 period, the actual, systematic nature of the savage Turkish assault reflects a distinctive policy determination that was significantly different from that operative in the German context. The controlling ambition, the collective civic agenda, behind Turkish inhumanity was primarily nationalist in character and, in practice, limited in scope and purpose. The Armenian massacres were an indecent, radicalized, manifestation of a most primitive jingoism activated by the exigencies of war without and the revolutionary collapse of the Ottoman Empire from within. Turkish nationalism, the extreme nationalist elites in control of the Turkish state, now under the violent cover of war, envisioned and pursued the elimination (*not* the murder) of *all* non-Turkish elements – and most especially and specifically the eradication of the Armenian community – from the national context. The anti-Armenian crusade was, as a result, for all its lethal extravagance, a delimited political crusade. Of course, mixed into the noxious brew that represented itself as national destiny were other obsessions: a loathing of Christians if not all non-Muslims, xenophobia, greed, jealousy, fear, desire, and the like. But, above all else, the "war against the Armenians" was a vulgar and desperate manifestation of raw nationalist politics.

As a direct and immediate consequence, anti-Armenianism is not expressed in the baroque language of metaphysical evil, not does it require – paraphrasing Himmler's asserting that "all Jews without exception must die" – the complete annihilation of *every* Armenian man, woman, and child. It does not represent a racial collision as that term came to be understood in the ornate ontological schema of Nazism. There is no assertion of primordial reciprocity between power and being, between intra-human aggression and meta-historic causations, between biological contingencies and noumenological principles. Rather, the elemental rational almost universally cited by the Turks in defense of their actions is political: the Armenians are secessionists, Russian spies, fifth-columnists, divisive nationalists, who would subvert the Turkish people's revolution and destroy Turkish national and political integrity. For example, this explanatory tack, this nationalist warrant, is already determinative in the pre-war Turkish interpretation of the Armenian massacres at Adana in April 1909 and it reappears in full force in the explanation of the events of 1915–16. Repeated Turkish reference to the Armenian Revolution at Van in 1915 is perhaps the outstanding example of this "legitimating" mode of moral-political reasoning.

Operating within the confines of this dominant political logic, the invocation of communal "self-defense" against Armenian sedition, actual and possible, explains nearly all that needs to be explained about Turkish behavior during this critical moment of potential national dissolution.

What was here intended was a particular political goal. Certainly, the Armenians had long been despised as religious outsiders and feared as economic rivals, but as Lord Bryce told the House of Lords on October 6, 1915:

> There was no Moslem passion against the Armenian Christians. All was done by the will of the Government, and done not from any religious fanaticism, but simply because they wished, for reasons purely political, to get rid of a non-Moslem element which impaired the homogeneity of

the Empire and constituted an element that might not always submit to oppression.⁵

Though I am conscious that I am here telescoping a great deal of complex religious, social, cultural, and historical material into the "political" – as Bryce and others before me – there is no real evidence that anything but a ferociously nationalist political dogmatic was responsible for the evils of 1915–18 (and up to and including the events of 1922). As Winston Churchill observed in 1929: "There is no reasonable doubt that this crime was planned and executed for political reasons."⁶

In this context it is important to remember that the Young Turks were, in the main, atheists who cynically manipulated Islamic loyalists for their own doctrinal purposes. Accordingly, they employed the rhetoric of theological confrontation and ancient tribal and religious antipathies for purposes other than the narrowly denominational. For the Young Turks, World War I presented an "historic" opportunity, "justified" by Armenian disloyalty, to definitively settle a long-standing struggle over sovereignty with the Armenians – a geopolitical issue that has no parallel in the Nazi-Jewish context – and, as part of the same process, to put an end to largely self-serving foreign intervention in Turkish affairs by the Great Powers on behalf of the oppressed Armenian minority. As Cemal Pasha, a leading member of the *Ittihadist* regime, noted in his memoirs: "Our sole objective [in our Campaign against the Armenians] was to free ourselves from all the governmental measures [imposed on us] in this war [by the Great Powers] and which constituted a blow to our internal independence."⁷ For the Young Turks it was the restitution of Turkish national honor and the protection of Turkey's geographical integrity that were at the center of this brutish campaign.

If the Young Turks were ardent nationalists, the Armenians were perceived, not without cause, as being intensely concerned to purpose their own separatist national agenda in the now to be dismembered Ottoman territory. In the heated circumstance that prevailed after Turkey's entry into World War I there was sufficient anti-Turkish Armenian military and political activity to lend credibility – especially for those predisposed to believe it – to this root anxiety. Thus, while such early Armenian sympathizers as Johannes Lepsius, Herbert Gibbons, and Bertha Papazian sought to justify the wartime relations between the Armenian community and the Russian government and to defend against charges of Armenian disloyalty during the war, Richard Hovannisian has felt obligated to conclude his more recent appraisal of Armenian behavior with the telling admission that:

---

5 Arnold Toynbee, *Armenian Atrocities: The Murder of a Nation* (London, 1915), p. 7.
6 Winston Churchill, *The World Crisis: The Aftermath* (London, 1929), p. 405.
7 *Hatiralar* (1977), p. 438, cited from Vahakn N. Dadrian, "Genocide as a Problem of National and International Law: The World War I Armenian Case and Its Contemporary Legal Ramifications," *Yale Journal of International Law*, 14.2 (Summer, 1989), p. 259.

Although most Armenians maintained a correct attitude vis-à-vis the Ottoman government, it can be asserted with some substantiation that the manifestations of loyalty were insincere, for the sympathy of most Armenians throughout the war was with the Entente, not with the Central Powers. By autumn 1914 several prominent Ottoman Armenians, including a former member of parliament, had slipped away to the Caucasus to collaborate with Russian military officials.[8]

To this manifest disloyalty should be added, as causes for Ottoman concern, the zealous anti-Turkish war enthusiasm of the Armenian population in Russia; the anti-Turkish activity of Armenian factions and supporters in Western Europe and America; Turkish Armenian relations with the Entente powers aimed at the partition of Turkey and the establishment of an independent Armenian state; the diverse pro-Russian activity of the Armenian populace residing in Turkish territory; the 1914 Dashnak rejection of a request for assistance against Russia on the grounds of neutrality; and the fact that the "Russian Imperial Army with Armenian volunteer units from the Caucasus (totaling 150,000 Armenians in all) had occupied most of the eastern provinces of Van, Bitlis, Erzerum, and Trebizond in 1916."[9] Moreover, these invading forces had carried out atrocities against the local Turkish population in retaliation for earlier Turkish crimes.

In addition, and consequential, the Turks had suffered a humiliating defeat at the Battle of Sarikamish (that began on December 25, 1914) to a Russian force comprised in some identifiable measure of Armenian volunteer units. During this crucial campaign the Turkish Third Army, commanded by Enver Pasha, lost over 80 percent (75,000) of its men in the short space of two weeks. Such was the magnitude of this debacle that it markedly shaped subsequent perceptions on both sides of the military front, as well as on both sides of the Armenian Question. One need not accept the apologetic Turkish reading of this critical military engagement to recognize that something dramatic, of far-reaching consequence, involving the direct collusion of Turkish and Armenian national interests, had occurred at Sarikamish. Many, if not most, Armenians had now openly sided with the cause of Turkey's enemy – in the midst of a life and death conflict for the *Ittihadist* regime. Even if the Armenian contribution to the Russian military cause was ultimately negligible, as measured by the overall size of the military forces engaged in the hostilities, and even if it was exaggerated for ulterior and heinous purposes by the Young Turks (as it was also exaggerated for their own domestic reasons by Armenian nationalists), the reality was that many Armenians had been actively disloyal in time of war.

The statist implications of Armenian action – for both nationalities – can be seen even more clearly in connection with the revolt at Van in April 1915. Whatever

---

8 Richard Hovannisian, *Armenia on the Road to Independence* (Berkeley, 1967), p. 42.
9 R. Hovannisian, "Genocide and Denial," in Israel W. Charney (ed.), *Toward the Understanding and Prevention of Genocide* (Boulder, CO, 1984), p. 88.

one's final interpretation of this event, what is salient from our point of view is that both sides agree that the sizable Armenian population at Van, with direct Russian military assistance, did revolt. Whatever the initial provocation they, at least at first, succeeded in defeating the Turkish forces and establishing, if only briefly, an incipient Armenian state within the territorial boundaries of pre-war Turkey. The Armenians had temporarily won a great military victory carrying extraordinarily important nationalist implications. No *ex post facto* minimizing of Armenian nationalist aspirations, or of the wider meaning of this particular success, can negate this salient act. As Henry Wood, the pro-Armenian American United Press correspondent wrote belatedly from Constantinople on August 14, 1915:

> *The Armenians are in open revolt* [and] actually in possession of Van and several other important towns, [and] may meet with fresh successes . . . The Armenians . . . are seeking to establish an independent government.[10]

All this is to argue that contrary to, for example, Helen Fein's contention that the Armenians were "enemies by definition,"[11] i.e., on *a priori* ideological or racial grounds – thereby allowing her erroneously to equate the action against Jews and Gypsies in World War II with that against the Armenians in World War I – the Armenians were "enemies," to the degree that they were enemies in this context, on practical and political grounds. That is, on grounds that centered around long-standing policies of internal colonialism, the implications – and machinations – of national self-determination, and the provocative issue of loyalty in time of war. Accordingly, the objective of Turkish action, when it came in 1915–16, was the destruction, once and for all, of Armenian national identity. The criminality of the Armenians did not require – as I shall show in detail in a moment – the biological extinction of every Armenian man, woman and child – especially if such individual and collective survival took place outside Turkish national boundaries and therefore made no claims upon Turkish sovereignty or national territory.

This is not to ignore the magnitude of the crime perpetrated against the Armenian people, the misery and death entailed by the mass deportations, the continual abuse of Armenian women, the mix of ideology, sadism, and self-interest in the massacre of Armenian men, and the theft and murder of infants and children. It is, however, to insist that these deliberate acts of despoliation and near-unlimited cruelty be deciphered aright. And this means recognizing that even this vast, inhumane carnage involved limits. Being a political-national assault against a political enemy the Young Turks could achieve their preeminent goal – the protection of the nation as they defined it – without requiring the complete physical extirpation of every person of Armenian heritage. To this degree – and here I make only this

---

10 Reprinted in Lord Bryce, *The Treatment of the Armenians in the Ottoman Empire 1915–1916* (London, 1916), p. 2.
11 Helen Fein, *Accounting for Genocide* (New York, 1979), p. 30.

limited and very precise claim – the intentionality behind, as well as the actualized structure of, the Turkish program for the eradication of Armenian national existence was *unlike* the biocentric war that Nazism carried on against the Jews. And this is because the "Armenian Question" differed in its quintessential character from the "Jewish Question." The former had been a conflicted political issue for nearly a century, had created manifold pressures and functional comprises for the Ottoman state, and now could be, once and for all, resolved by the annihilation of the organized Armenian *community* within Turkey. In contrast, the "Jewish Question," which had likewise been a central, exceedingly controversial, political concern in Europe since the beginnings of Jewish emancipation in the eighteenth century, was categorically transformed by Hitler into an inescapable metaphysical challenge – "blood" in the Nazi universe of discourse being understood as the elementary vehicle by which ontological values become incarnate in history – that could only be solved by an uncompromising genocidal assault. The Third Reich therefore insisted not only on the elimination of Jewish collective identity and communal existence but also on the murder of *every* Jewish person of whatever age and gender.

Three additional seminal factors that strengthen the morphological *dis*analogy between the Armenian tragedy and the Holocaust need to be introduced into our argument at this juncture. They are: (1) the possibility of Armenian Christian conversion to Islam as a way of avoiding deportation and worse; (2) the specific character of the forced deportations; and (3) the *non-totalistic* nature of the anti-Armenian crusade.

As regards the mediating role of conversion to Islam, the eyewitness accounts of the tragedy repeatedly mention this life-saving though communally destructive possibility. Both "willingly" and unwillingly, large numbers of Armenians became Muslims. There appears, in particular, to have been extensive forced proselytization of Armenian women and children. It is difficult to ascertain just what role official *Ittihadist* ideology played in these coerced prophylactic rituals, though it is clear that the C.U.P. (Committee of Union and Progress, the party of the "Young Turks") devoid as it was of a racist ideology, did not oppose such recreative, death-deflecting, actions. Indeed, to the degree that Islamicization constructively reinforced the Young Turks normative political agenda – Islam being a fundamental buttress of Turkification (while Christianity was the key element in Armenian self-identity) – this survivalist (flagrantly inhumane) program was consistent with C.U.P. ambitions. And it found wide instantiation. So wide in fact that Lepsius again and again excoriates the Turkish government for allowing, even encouraging, this tyrannical policy, while Toynbee accusingly refers to "survival being purchased by apostatizing to Islam."[12] Likewise, the German, American, British (and other) governments are on record as protesting this unwelcome practice.

---

12 Arnold Toynbee, *The Murderous Tyranny of the Turks* (pamphlet: New York, 1917).

In that neither Islam nor Turkism was predicated on inelastic biologistic concepts, both possess absorptive capacities that create existential as well as socio-political possibilities unavailable in Nazism. Accordingly, the "other" is not only defined differently by the *Ittihad* elites than in Hitler's Reich – not genetically and without reference to metaphysical canons of ontic pollution and decadence – but the required response to the "other" allows for the remaking of the "other," primarily through the mysterious rite of conversion, so as to obviate still more complete – that is exterminatory – forms of overcoming. Thus, for example, children in Christian orphanages were converted *en masse*. And it was not only women and children who were forcibly converted. Lepsius, for instance, records that the entire male medical staff of the German Mission Hospital in Urfa was coerced into becoming Muslim, as were Armenian army physicians at Sivas.[13] In Aleppo, the entire Armenian labor battalion was converted in February 1916, and further large-scale conversions of Armenian males occurred in March and April 1916. Lepsius also reports that "all Armenian villages in the Samsun area and in Unich have been Islamicized. No favors were granted to anyone, apart from renegades."[14] In fact, Lepsius conservatively estimates that 200,000 men, women and children, approximately 12 to 13.5 percent of the entire Armenian community, were forcibly converted and thereby saved,[15] however objectionable the instrument of their salvation. In this respect, Turkish policy reproduces medieval procedures of cultural homogenization, not modern procedures of physical genocide. As such, it kept Armenians, if not Armenianism, alive.

Second, the Armenian deportations were not uniformly events of total annihilation. Though these Armenian removals, carried out under the most brutal conditions, were regularly occasions of mass death – that sealed the fate of hundreds of thousands – several hundred thousand Armenians did survive these horrific journeys. Lepsius, for example, (under)estimates the remnant at 200,000 individuals. Toynbee cites a total of 600,000 Armenian survivors – the combined total of those who lived through the deportations and those who fled into Russian territory – up to 1916.[16] He summarizes that:

> in general wastage [death during the deportations] seems to fluctuate, with a wide oscillation, on either side of 50 percent; 600 out of 2,500 (24 percent) reached Aleppo from a village in the Harpout district; 60 percent arrived there out of the first convoy from the village of E. (near H.), and 46 percent out of the second; 25 percent arrived out of a convoy from the village of D. in the same neighborhood. We shall certainly be well

---

13 Johannes Lepsius, *Deutschland und Armenien, 1914–1918* (Potsdam, 1919), p. 283.
14 *Ibid.*, p. 160.
15 *Ibid.*, p. LXV.
16 Arnold Toynbee in Bryce, *The Treatment of the Armenians*, pp. 648–50.

within the mark if we estimate that at least half of those condemned to massacre or deportation have actually perished.[17]

Supporting these large estimates of the number of those who were *not* killed during these forced evacuations are the figures for Armenians who found refuge in Arab countries and then later in Western Europe and America. Richard Hovannisian, writing of their acceptance in the Arab world, indicates: "Many of the deportees suffered a cruel fate at the hands of certain Bedouin tribes in the Syrian desert, but most were accorded sympathetic asylum by the Arab peoples, who had themselves endured four centuries of Ottoman domination. In all, the number of Armenian deportees who found refuge in Arab lands, by 1925, is estimated at well over 200,000,"[18] and this figure excludes the 50,000 who found refuge in Iran. More specifically, Hovannisian breaks these refugee figures down as follows: Syria accepted 100,000 Armenian refugees, Lebanon 50,000, Palestine and Jordan 10,000, Egypt 40,000, Iraq 25,000, and Iran 50,000, making a total of 275,000 survivors. These numbers are supported by later governmental statistics issued by the respective Arab countries. Census data released between 1931 and 1945 by the individual Middle Eastern states indicates that Syria had an Armenian population of 125,550 (1945), Lebanon 72,797 (1944), Palestine 3,802 (1931), and Egypt 19,596 (1937). And to these aggregates Justin McCarthy adds the following estimates for Armenian refugees in various European and North American locations (to what degree these overlap with Hovannisian's figures for the Arab world, for there must have been such overlap, is unclear. McCarthy [p. 129, Table 7.6] makes no such allowance): France 30,000, Czechoslovakia 200, Switzerland 250, Greece 34,000, Cyprus 21,500, Bulgaria 20,000, Hungary 15, Austria 270, Yugoslavia 543, Italy 603, Canada 1,244, and the United States of America 34,136. If we therefore put the number of survivors of these inhumane transfers at between 300,000 and 400,000, we shall be on secure grounds – or at least grounds that are as secure as possible given all the statistical uncertainties – remembering that Hovannisian's total of 275,000 does not include any survivors in Russia, Europe, or the United States of America. This translates into somewhere between a 17.7 percent (300,000 out of 1,700,000, the maximum Armenian population) and 26.6 percent (400,000 out of 1,500,000 the minimum Armenian population) survival rate. Then, too, beyond the mathematics alone, these substantial statistics indicate that the Turkish oppressor did not require, did not demand, the death of all Armenians. The Turks had all these individuals, this entire defenseless population, within their control and could have murdered them all – despite the practical difficulties involved in murdering an entire people in a country as large as Turkey – had they so desired. But, evidently, this was not necessary.

17 *Ibid*, p. 650.
18 Richard Hovannisian, "Ebb and Flow of the Armenian Minority in the Arab Middle East," *Middle East Journal* 1.28 (Winter, 1974): 20.

Third, the enacted policy of deporting Armenians was not universally applied even within the borders of Turkey. The Armenians of Constantinople numbering up to 200,000 and the Armenians of other large cities, e.g., Smyrna (where between 6,000 and 20,000 Armenians lived), Kutahia, and to some degree Aleppo, were not uprooted *en masse* during the entire war period. Lepsius estimated (and in his own word perhaps "overestimated") that the number of Armenians so protected represented 1/7 to 1/9 of the total Armenian population, or some 204,700 persons (out of what he projected as an original Armenian population of 1,845,450).[19] Though recent studies[20] require that we temper Lepsius's figures, and indicate that up to 30,000 Armenians were in fact deported from Constantinople, the need to modify all generalizations as to Turkish intentions given the very real limitations placed upon evictions from Constantinople and elsewhere stands. To gain a full picture of all the relevant statistics bearing upon the question of Armenian survival we must also add in the 300,000 or so Armenians who retreated with the Russian army back into Russian territory after the final defeat at Van in the summer of 1915 and the 4,200 who survived the famous battle of Musa Dagh and were rescued by the French in mid-September 1915. Accordingly, the comprehensive demographic picture regarding casualties and survival is indicated in the table below.

	Minimum	Maximum
1914 Armenian population	1,500,000	1,700,000
Converts to Islam	200,000	300,000
Survive deportations outside Turkey	300,000	400,000
Survive in large Turkish cities	170,000	220,000
Survive in Russia	250,000	300,000
Survivors of Musa Dagh	4,200	4,200
Total survivors	924,200	1,224,200
Total deaths (1915–18)	476,000	776,000

This is not the Holocaust.

V

I would now like to consider, however briefly, a second hard case that has recently gained a new prominence as a consequence of the corrupt thesis of the so-called German Revisionists led by Ernest Nolte.

---

19 J. Lepsius, *Deutschland und Armenien*, pp. LXII – LXIII.
20 See Vahakn N. Dadrian's important qualification regarding the Armenians of Constantinople, *Genocide as a Problem of National and International Law*, p. 262, n. 131; and again, V. Dadrian, "The Documentation of the World War I Armenian Massacres in the Proceedings of the Turkish Military Tribunal," *International Journal of Middle East Studies*, 23.4 (November, 1991): 570, n. 26. According to Dadrian's reconstruction, based on the testimony of German Ambassador Wolff-Metternich on December 7, 1915, who gave as his source the Turkish Chief of Policy, 30,000 Armenians were deported from Constantinople, and more deportations were feared.

Nolte argues that the *Shoah* is not a singular event, having been modeled after Stalin's *Gulag*. In lieu of a more extended rebuttal of this erroneous claim, I would say only this: while there are many good reasons to abhor the *Gulag* and the vast evil that it perpetrated, the reality is that this comparison of the Soviet work camps and Auschwitz is deeply flawed. I have argued elsewhere[21] that it is necessary to understand the *Gulag* as a cross between a penal institution and slavery that was utilized by Stalin both to eliminate his political enemies and, even more importantly, to create an unfree labor pool whose labor could be tapped to support the much needed modernization of Russia. I will not repeat these arguments at length here. Instead, in support of my thesis regarding the need for scrupulous care in the writing of comparative history, I would draw attention to several phenomenological characteristics that I believe clearly indicate the primal difference that separate Auschwitz from Kolyma.

I begin with a small but significant detail: the Russian convoys to Siberia and the Arctic carried a doctor or medical officer. Ignore, for the moment, the indifference of these medical officers, even their criminal complicity in the terror, and concentrate instead on the structural fact of their presence itself: medical officers accompanied the convoys. Does this unexpected element, this sign of at least a utilitarian discipline, not suggest that the comparative judgment as to the larger meaning(s) of these alternative events – that is, Auschwitz and the *Gulag* – has to be varied? That, in fact, the Soviet convoys, however wretched, should be likened phenomenologically more exactly to the Middle Passage than to the train shipments organized by Eichmann and the SS? Slave vessels also carried ships' surgeons whose job was more than perfunctory, and whose remuneration, in part, depended on the successful crossing of their cargoes, i.e., they received a bonus for bringing their slave cargoes in alive.[22] One could not make a profit from dead slaves, and one could not mine the Kolyma or fell the needed export timber of the northern forests with dead men. By comparison, the *Reichsbahn* and the SS had no similar incentive, for their substantive enterprise was predicated on an antithetical rationality. The *Reichsbahn* was paid whether their "shipments" arrived alive or dead; when its Jewish cargo arrived as corpses the SS had already done their primary job without taxing the ovens and incinerators.

This detail, the importance of which is not to be exaggerated, points to a larger elemental truth: the *Gulag*, in its vastness, exists to meet *real*, economically significant, quotas – to extract minerals necessary for the national good; to mine gold needed by the national treasury; to fell timber for export; to supply labor that could be exploited in the name of rapid industrialization. In this environment utilitarian motives, however base, count against ideological fantasies and death.

---

21 See my essay "Auschwitz and the Gulag: A Study in Dissimilarity," in Alan Berger (ed.), *Bearing Witness to the Holocaust 1939–1989. Proceedings of the Holocaust Scholars' Conference* (Lewiston, ME, 1992), pp. 71–89. (Reprinted as essay 3, pp. 57–73 below.)

22 I present the full evidence on the relevant aspects of the Middle Passage vis-à-vis the *Shoah* in *The Holocaust and New World Slavery: A Comparative History* (New York, 2019), Vol. 1, pp. 68–128.

Collective gain, wealth, production, industrialization, and socialist modernization are the justification for the violence. It is this immanent, practical, economic and industrial design that defines the *Gulag*. In contrast – and I make this comparative observation not to diminish the Soviet camps and the experience of their inmates, but to distinguish them – the evil(s) of Auschwitz, Treblinka, Sobibor and Chelmno had almost no linkage to utilitarian norms, to production goals, national wealth, industrialization, required modernization, or even to self-enrichment; Auschwitz and the other Death Camps existed essentially as a negation of utilitarianism and in contradiction to the ethos of survival. The SS did not seek to exploit the Jew but to transform the Jew into an *Untermensch*, and then into a corpse.[23]

If we now pursue the structural disparity between the *Gulag* and Auschwitz, if only schematically, we will discover that the victims of Stalin's regime were subjected to a less total rupture with their past than was the case with Jews during the *Shoah*. Gustav Herling, for example, tells of the *Dom Svidanyi*, the House of Meeting, at Kargopol in the early 1940s "where prisoners were allowed to spend between one and three days with their relatives who had come from all parts of Russia to Kargopol Camp for this short visit."[24] Such renewing, pain-filled encounters, while difficult to arrange – and recognizing all the manipulation by the authorities that they were heir to – were, in many cases at least, a possibility once a year. Solzhenitsyn confirms this,[25] as do Roeder[26] and other chroniclers of the *Gulag*.[27] And even when this was not possible, or between visits, mail[28] was allowed into and out of the Camps, even "care" packages,[29] including food,[30] and the sending of money,[31] though an uncommon occurrence, was permitted. In contrast, Jews neither visited nor corresponded. Their loved ones were either already ashes or living in another segment of the Kingdom of Night.

It might be objected that I here exaggerate the structural and existential differences between Nazi death camps and the *Gulag*, for in the latter such family meetings were rare occurrences and letters and parcels were likewise exceptional.

---

23 The industrial plant established at Auschwitz – that did not exist at Treblinka, Sobibor or Chelmno – does not contradict this conclusion though it does complicate it, if only marginally. And this is because these industrial operations were organized in such a way that all the Jewish workers in these plants were intended to be killed through their work regimen in a very short period of time. That is, this work should be understood as another aspect of the genocidal program. I provide a fuller analysis of this issue in *The Holocaust and New World Slavery*. And see essay 7 below.
24 Gustav Herling, *A World Apart* (New York, 1951), p. 86.
25 Alexander Solzhenitsyn, *Gulag Archipelago* (New York, 1975), vol. 2, p. 225.
26 Bernhard Roeder, *Katorga* (London, 1958).
27 See Vladimir Tchernavin, *I Speak for the Silent: Prisoners of the Soviets* (Boston, 1935), p. 306.
28 See, e.g., Vladimir Petrov, *Soviet Gold* (London, 1951), pp. 184–85; and Erica G. Wallach, *Light at Midnight* (New York, 1967), pp. 279–80.
29 Note, for example, Varlem Shalamov's comments in *Graphite* (New York, 1981), pp. 270–71; and E. Wallach, *Light at Midnight*, pp. 281–83 and 319–22.
30 Reported by Joseph Scholmer, *Vorkuta* (London, 1954), pp. 82–83; and Lev Kopelev, *To Be Preserved Forever* (Philadelphia, 1977), p. 253.
31 Helene Celmina, *Women in Soviet Prisons* (New York, 1985), p. 196.

Such objections, however – true enough on the face of it – would miss the essential matter – namely, that between some visits, no matter how intermittent, and some mail, no matter how rare, and no visits, and no mail, i.e., the systemic denial of all human contact outside of the camp, and the complete negation of one's historic community, there exists a qualitative metaphysical abyss.

Here I note, too, the odd presence in the Soviet camps of the so-called KVCH – the Cultural and Educational Section. Not surprisingly, these centers were hopelessly run, poorly staffed, and provided with extremely limited facilities. As Solzhenitsyn announces: "If anybody should ever try to tell you with shining eyes that someone was re-educated by government means through the KVCH . . . you can reply with total correctness: Nonsense."[32] And, of course, he is right. With his accustomed biting wit, he dismantles any pretense regarding this uncommon program of "re-education." Yet *its very existence* is of some interest, whatever its monumental lack, even if by design, of accomplishments. For by merely being there it informs us of the distinctive political consciousness that was implicated in the organization of the *Gulag* which made class and status transformation – as compared to an uncompromising program of physical genocide – an ideological, if not a practical, goal.

The KVCH organized classes, lectures, movies, plays, and concerts. In contrast, the Nazis permitted Jews none of these things. Even the pretense of "re-education" – re-educate lice? – is absent. When one reads of rabbinical leaders offering courses to their fellow Jews in the death camps it must be remembered that this was done solely on *their* initiative, against orders, as an act of overwhelming fidelity, *despite* the Nazis. The official SS ideology permitted no such activity, severely punished it when discovered, and did everything it could to see that it did not take place. Possession of any Jewish cultural or religious artifact could easily mean "selection," any sign of Jewish commitment would make one the special target for verbal and physical abuse, for "*sportmachen*," often ending in death. That Jews celebrated, prayed, remembered their liturgical calendar, "learned," even in Auschwitz, is a testimony to their remarkable courage and faith; it was not the design of the camp's creators.

Touching upon the most intimate matters of human subjectivity and identity the evidence for differentiation and distinction becomes still more convincing. "There was," we are correctly informed by Terence Des Pres, "more sexual activity in the Soviet camps because there was more opportunity, but also because conditions were less openly horrible."[33] This significant observation regarding the availability and extent of sexuality in the *Gulag*, and the immediate reasons for it, is borne out by all the detailed autobiographical accounts.[34] There existed a Hieronymous Bosch-like underworld in the *Gulag* that exhibited a sexually explicit, surrealistic,

---

32 A. Solzhenitsyn, *The Gulag Archipelago*, vol. 2, p. 468.
33 Terence Des Pres, *The Survivor* (New York, 1976), p. 190.
34 See, for example, Michael Solomon, *Magadan* (Toronto, 1971), pp. 140–56; and E. Wallach, *Light at Midnight*, p. 317.

salaciousness that finds no authentic analogue in the Nazi ecology. Not that the latter was devoid of all sexuality, or perversion, or sexual exploitation, but rather that the immediate parameters, both spatial and temporal, for such carnal activity were far more controlled and constrained – and the moderating effects of these functional limits were compounded by the sheer debilitation of Jewish physical strength. There was simply less possibility in the Nazi death camps of enacting the lurid, obscene, sexual rituals that played a fundamental part in the daily life of the Soviet camp empire.

But there is, there was, something more fundamental at issue. One knows that Jewish women, as women in the *Gulag*, were exploited sexually, and that they, like their Russian counterparts, tried on occasion to trade sex for life – though for the most part the technological and bureaucratic forms that governed the "Final Solution" created far fewer opportunities for such sexual exploitation. But with the SS this trade, even momentarily "accepted," almost never meant survival. It was not functional, it had no value relative to the future. It was a futile act that could not alter one's fate. The luciferian biocentrism of the Nazi system precluded the possibility that such exchanges – which constituted a racial crime – could have any but very temporary results. The SS would sexually assault Jewish women and then murder them. They were obligated to murder them.

Even more revealing, more informative, is the fate of children in the *Gulag* and during the *Shoah*. Olga Lengyel tells us of Auschwitz:

> One day we decided we had been weak long enough. We must at least save the mothers. To carry out our plan, we would have to make the infants pass for stillborn . . .
>
> Unfortunately, the fate of the baby always had to be the same. After taking every precaution, we pinched and closed the little tike's nostrils and when it opened its mouth to breathe, we gave it a dose of a lethal product. An injection might have been quicker, but that would have left a trace and we dared not let the German suspect the truth.
>
> We placed the dead infant in the same box which had brought it from the barrack, if the accouchement had taken place there. As far as the camp administration was concerned, this was a stillbirth.
>
> And so, the Germans succeeded in making the murderers of even us. To this day the picture of those murdered babies haunts me. Our own children had perished in the gas chambers and were cremated in the Birkenau ovens, and we dispatched the lives of others before their first voices had left their tiny lungs.[35]

---

35 Olga Lengyel, *Five Chimneys: The Story of Auschwitz* (New York, 1947), pp. 110–11.

These murdered infants stand for an entire generation of doomed Jewish children. *No* Jewish child was to be allowed to live; over one million Jewish children were actually killed.

By comparison, Elinore Lipper writes as follows of pregnancy and childbirth even in the severe conditions of Magadan, in the Kolyma region:

> The new prisoners would be sent to chop wood. That was not allowed from the sixth month of pregnancy on. In winter they (pregnant women) could do no snow shoveling or field work in the spring. During the last month of pregnancy, the women would be relieved of work and placed in the highest ration category.[36]

And when it was time for the birth of the child:

> The children come into the world in the prison hospital. For a week mother and child stay together. Then the mother is dismissed from the hospital and the child is taken to the children's house, or "combine," as it is called. The mother is not obliged to work for the first month after the birth of the child. Then she is sent to work at a place fairly near the children's combine, for it is Russian custom that the mother has the right to nurse her baby for nine months. At certain times the nursing mothers, who are called *mamki*, are assembled and taken under guard to the combine."[37]

And Lipper's testimony is in no sense unique in the literature of the *Gulag*. There is abundant evidence[38] that pregnant women were accorded privileges in this time and place, however meager these privileges may appear to us.

Mother and child had a legitimate, if wretched, place within the system. The Soviet state, even under Stalin, even in the northernmost slave-labor camps after 1937, recognized some obligation to these mothers and to these infants. Lipper's particular description of this natural cycle in the midst of this unnatural environment may be too mechanical as well as too benign, the reality far more punishing, unquestionably less ideal, but whatever the humanizing exaggerations of her account, it belongs to an altogether different history, and results in a radically alternative reality, than that played out at Auschwitz.

The most significant fact is that both the Russian mothers and the Soviet state, whatever their mixed motives, whatever the pain involved, *wanted* the babies produced in the *Gulag*. Despite the terrible material conditions into which and

---

36 Elinore Lipper, *Eleven Years in Soviet Prison Camps* (London, 1951), p. 120.
37 *Ibid.*, p. 120. The same policy is reported by Karlo Stajner, *Seven Thousand Days in Siberia* (New York, 1986), p. 89.
38 Consult, e.g., Margarete Buber, *Under Two Dictators* (New York, 1949), p. 81; and Michael Solomon, *Magadan*, pp. 155–56.

under which they came into the world there is no presumption of inherited and accusing guilt. The innocence of these newborn, whatever the crime of their mothers, is acknowledged. Being born in the *Gulag* will have terrible and life-long ramifications – but one of them is not necessarily the sentence of death.

Only under the Third Reich were Jewish mothers and children *intentionally, systematically, unrelentingly*, and *without exception murdered*. (Not in the Soviet slave empire, not in ancient or modern slavery, not in the medieval wars of religion, not in the conquest of the New World, not in World War I Turkey, not in Sudan, Rwanda, Burundi, not in Indonesia, China, or Cambodia, indeed nowhere else in history did such an uncompromising imperative exist. I now feel prepared to affirm this categorically.)

If I might generalize, I would say that all the truly important differences between the Stalinist and Nazi camp-worlds are a consequence of the fact that in the former the prisoners were still, in principle, considered juridically, ideologically and metaphysically fellow human beings. Despite their "crimes" – even if "class enemies," "wreckers," deviationists," "capitalists," "rootless cosmopolitans," "enemies of the people," and "Zionists" – these criminals against the socialist order remained, theoretically at least, inhabitants of the same moral universe as their accusers and jailers.

Consider, as one example which stands for many, the interesting and puzzling system of "wages" for camp prisoners that was kept at all labor camps.[39] This phenomenon in particular, insofar as it carries anthropological and ethical implications, supports our measured (not naive!) understanding of the Soviet conception of who its camp inmates were. The policy of tracking and recording the productivity of prisoners in order to pay them for their work that was standard procedure in the *Gulag* unmistakably indicates – despite all the abuses and dishonesty that this bureaucratic procedure lent itself to – that the prisoners were still fellow persons, beings whom the socialist state was still obligated to deal with in some legal (economic) fashion. As such, their labor could not be completely stolen[40] – whatever the daily reality.

---

39 See Gustav Herling's comments on this in *A World Apart*, p. 43. Herling is writing of 1939 and subsequently, though the system existed earlier. He refers to the occasion – that took place only once in his presence – during which "a camp's pay officer [came] to [the] barracks with statements of our earnings" (p. 43). See also Elinore Lipper, *Eleven Years*, pp. 136, 194–97.

40 Prisoners who accomplished their assignment were given "premium compensation" in special SPU scrip – manual laborers three to four roubles a month, specialists of exceptional qualification up to 25 and even 35 roubles. With this money they could buy "premium products," in the GPU stores from a list which changed every month. In 1931 one could buy, during a month, about 200 grams of sugar, 100 grams of biscuits, two to three packages of low grade tobacco, two to three boxes of matches, and sometimes 200 grams of melted lard; in 1932 sugar, biscuits, and lard were omitted from the list. Furthermore, the prisoner could purchase on his premium card 200 extra grams of bread per day, but even this extra ration – highly valued by the prisoners – could not be relied upon since the stores were often short of bread. Nevertheless, however small this premium compensation might be, it was a powerful incentive to hungry prisoners" (V. Tchernavin, *I Speak for the Silent*, p. 305). Dimitri Panin reports using his camp account to buy an extra bread ration, *Notebooks of Sologden* (New York, 1976), p. 165; while P. Yakrit tells us: "Passengers kept looking into our compartment

ON THE HOLOCAUST AND COMPARATIVE HISTORY

One is struck in this connection by the "voluntary" war bond subscriptions, aimed at the camp earnings of prisoners, carried out among the *Gulag* slave laborers during World War II. This was certainly, on the most fundamental level, a Kafkaesque performance in which what was voluntary was compulsory and the meaningful possibility of authentic human autonomy was altogether absent. However, on a second, and different, level it again points towards at least a theoretically maintained conception of the humanity of the camp population. And this in three ways: first, these inmates were entitled to wages for work done; second, even these Siberian prisoners were entitled, recognizing all the practical, legal and contextual constraints that were here operative, to do as they would with the money they earned. Even Soviet legality, wherein putative historical necessities trampled human freedoms and positive law, recognized this right. And so they must agree – the need of their agreement being the legal-ethical condition that makes the situation both interesting and paradoxical – to contribute part of what they had earned to the national war effort. Third, even such slaves were believed capable of selfless patriotism – and it was expected of them.

Now no one should take these transactions at face value – surely neither the camp personnel nor the prisoners did so. Yet intrinsic to this historical scene, necessary for this peculiar civic dialogue to continue at all, is a lingering metaphysical belief, if only in an attenuated vestigial form, that somehow these presently mutilated individuals were still moral subjects. One certainly must tread carefully in interpreting such realia for the descriptions of such scenes as the sale of war bonds in the *Gulag* have a fantastic quality about them. But that such events took place at all, that the state felt the need for them to take place, that the state staged them, this too has a phenomenological valence that is not to be ignored.

I must content myself with these broad observations. They will, I hope, at least suffice to warn others of making too easy a linkage between Hitler's death camps and Stalin's labor camps and, in any case, support the complete rejection of the apologetic and dishonest German revisionist reading of these two grotesque but fundamentally alternate historical circumstances.

VI Conclusion

There is much more to be said, many additional cases, issues and categories to be explored in the comparative investigation of the Holocaust. But let what has already been argued stand as an introduction to a vast topic – and as support for

---

with a certain amount of surprise: two kids under escort was not a common sight. All around, as is usually the case with railway carriages, people were getting out their parcels and in fact one person had already started eating. We too were very hungry. We put this to the escort commander. He said that our journey would only last for two and a half hours, but if we had any money, then we could buy something to eat at the station. We had in fact been given all that we had in our account. After we left the next station some food appeared on the little table in our compartment: bread, butter, sausage and even some vodka. The guards ate with us. (Piotr Vakir, *A Childhood in Prison* [New York, 1973], p. 103)

our larger thesis as to the uniqueness of the Nazi Kingdom of Night. Still more generally, let it be understood that the close, painstaking work of comparative historical analysis will show, as we have shown in our analysis of the Armenian tragedy and the *Gulag*, that fundamental, defining, distinctions – necessarily varying from case to case and context to context – will need to be made in every instance in which the *Shoah* is said to be like another historic event of mass death. For in the final analysis the destruction of European Jewry stands alone not as a moral but as a phenomenological and historical *novum*.

UPDATE

My research on the Holocaust and comparative history began in the early 1980s with the publication of an essay entitled "The Unique Intentionality of the Holocaust," that appeared in the first number of *Modern Judaism* in May 1981. In the opening paragraph of that paper I described Nazism as having, "as an integral part of its purpose and behavior the total eradication of world Jewry." I then asked the following question: "In so doing was Nazism 'unique'? Indeed, does the uniqueness of Nazism lie in its genocidal intent against the Jewish people?"

To try and answer this question I very briefly commented on the historical occasions that suggested comparability to the Holocaust and, therefore, refuted the claim to "uniqueness" that I was seeking to establish. Most of these historical cases were already being discussed in what was then a small but growing literature on the Holocaust in comparative terms and the separate, but related, issue of "genocide." Thus I made mention, very cursorily, on topics arising from Jewish history that I already knew quite well, for example, the Assyrian Conquest in 722–721 B.C.E.; the Babylonian Conquest of 586 B.C.E.; the destruction of the First Temple in Jerusalem; the abuses by Antiochus IV, and the Hellenistic kings of Syria in the second century B.C.E.; the Roman conquest at the end of the "Great Revolt" of 66 to 70 C.E. that concluded with the destruction of the Second Temple; the failed revolt of Bar Kokchba against Rome in 132–135 C.E. with its disastrous consequences; Christian antisemitism beginning with the polemical writings of Paul and the severe condemnation of Jews and Judaism in the New Testament; and Islamic anti-Judaism.[41]

Among the many cases of mass violence in non-Jewish history that I discussed were: the terrible treatment of American and Brazilian Indians by European colonizers; the horrific murder of Armenians during 1915–1916 in the midst of World War I; and the killing of gypsies by the Hitler state. In retrospect, what is now striking is that, while I also mentioned the Nigerian Civil War, I did not refer to the crimes of Stalin in either the Ukraine or the *Gulag*. In any case, this brief and very limited review completed, I then concluded:

> Much additional research has to be done to draw a complete phenomenological description of each of the historical episodes we have quite briefly reviewed, as well as the many we have not had the space to comment upon. Yet, while recognizing this need for further analysis, I believe enough evidence has been marshaled to suggest that in and through the category of "intention" we can begin to perceive at least one seminal individuating characteristic of the Holocaust.[42]

---

41 I returned to examine all these historical events in much greater detail and with a careful review of the relevant primary and secondary sources in *The Holocaust in Historical Context*, vol. 1, *Mass Death Before the Modern Age* (hereafter *HHC*) (New York, 1994).

42 The essay, "The Unique Intentionality of the Holocaust," was republished in my *Post-Holocaust Dialogues: Critical Studies in Modern Jewish Thought* (New York, 1983), pp. 287–317. I here cite p. 310.

For the past four decades I have been pursuing this "additional research" in order to test my original thesis. This study has led me in many fascinating directions and has taught me a great deal about important subjects regarding which I was, in 1981, woefully ignorant. As I carefully began this work in the 1980s and 1990s I began to reduce my ignorance, both as regards the historical events I was trying to understand as well as concerning the thicket of hermeneutical and methodological issues that I felt needed to be sorted out if I was going to do comparative study seriously and with the needed scholarly accuracy and integrity. This, in turn, led to the publication of a series of essays that more deeply probed the relevant instances of mass death that challenged the claim that the Holocaust was unique. In addition, it led to a more encompassing investigation of essential issues like the definition of "genocide," the significance – and limits of the significance – of high casualty counts, and the major importance of the concept – the issue – of intention. A number of the individual essays that were written during this period are now reprinted here, beginning with the Leo Baeck lecture given in 1993. In that lecture my main foci were the previously neglected subject of the *Gulag* and the heinous murder of Armenians during World War I by the Young Turks, then in control of the remnants of the Ottoman Empire.

In the lecture I argued that while both circumstances were horrific, and no distinction should be made morally between them and the murder of European Jews – or, as I began to understand, vis-à-vis the suffering of the victims in all three circumstances – there were what I began to identify as "phenomenological" differences between them. The organizing structure and the energizing intentions of Stalin's crimes, the barbaric actions of the Turkish leadership and their cause(s), and the Holocaust, were all very different. Not least in significance, in the cases of the *Gulag* and the Armenian massacres the victimizers did not intend the total eradication of the victim groups, as *was* the case in the Holocaust.

Since I made this presentation, the literature on all aspects of Holocaust studies, genocide studies, and comparative history has exploded, and I have attempted to keep up with it. Interestingly, during these years, original research on the Armenian tragedy has continued to be published and the claim that this new literature most often advances is that what occurred in wartime Turkey represents a legitimate comparison to the Holocaust. I note in this regard that when Leo Kuper published his wide-ranging study, *Genocide: Its Political Use in the Twentieth Century*,[43] he felt it appropriate to call the Armenian case "the forgotten genocide of the twentieth century." This is certainly no longer the case. So one finds, for instance, that, next to the Holocaust, the systematic destruction that occurred in wartime Armenia has been the second-most discussed subject in the prestigious American Holocaust journal *Holocaust and Genocide Studies*, published by the United States Holocaust Memorial Museum. And almost every recent collection of essays on the subject of "Genocide" includes analysis of the Armenian massacres and overwhelmingly

---

43 (New Haven, CT, 1982), p. 195.

accepts that the term "genocide" appropriately applies to this event. Thus, one is not surprised to learn that, for example, when Manus J. Midlarsky set out to study the three paradigmatic cases of genocide in the twentieth century, he chose as his subjects the Armenian massacres, along with the Holocaust and the killings of the Tutsi (and others, including Hutu and Twa) in Rwanda.[44]

I, however, have continued to insist on the structural differences between Armenia and Auschwitz, the main reason for my doing so being my interpretation of the empirical evidence. On my reading, what took place in Turkey in 1915–1916 was not "genocide" as I understand the technical meaning of this legal concept. I use the term, having in mind the Holocaust, to indicate the "intention to murder *all* members of a group."[45] In this I am at odds with the United Nations' Genocide Convention[46] that I believe is too loose in its criteria. I agree that, by employing the U.N. definition, one can label the Armenian tragedy as "genocide." On my tighter definition, however, this is not the case. The Turks did not set out to murder all Armenians, either in the Ottoman Empire or elsewhere, nor did they have any need to do so. Therefore, relative specifically to the issue of the "uniqueness" of the Holocaust, i.e., independently of all other considerations, I abide by my original judgment that the Armenian case does not compare phenomenologically (not morally) to the "Final Solution."

---

44 Manus Midlarsky, *The Killing Trap: Genocide in the Twentieth Century* (Cambridge, UK, 2005), p. 34.
45 For a fuller explanation see my argument in the paper, "On the definition of genocide and the issue of uniqueness," in this volume, and my more detailed review in *HHC*, pp. 125–39, where I have explained at length my reasons for not accepting, for purposes of scholarly work, the U.N. definition of "genocide." I here reprint my main (but not only) objection to the U.N. definition:

> "as to the 'degree' of violence done to a group required for said violence to qualify as genocide [according to the U.N. Convention] (i.e., as regards the extremely vague and problematic notion that genocide is to be defined as any act 'committed with *intent* to destroy, in whole or *in part*, a national, ethnical, racial, or religious *group*'), I demur. It is logically and practically impossible to employ these criteria both meaningfully and with control. For the intended destruction of what percentage, what 'part,' of a group constitutes sufficient intent? Any part at all? One percent, 20 percent; one-half, three-quarters? Therefore, this definition, whatever its functional value in the political arena, must give way to something tighter and more exact. For myself, I shall use the following rigorous definition: the concept of genocide applies *only* when there is an actualized intent, however successfully carried out, to physically destroy an *entire* group (as such a group is defined by the perpetrators). . ." Therefore, "the intention to physically eradicate only part of a group – in contradistinction to the U.N. Convention and most alternative definitions proposed by others – I will not call genocide." (pp. 127–29).

46 Reprinted, among many other places, in Alexander Hinton, *Genocide: An Anthropological Reader* (Oxford 2002), pp. 43–47. See also Mark Levene, *Genocide in the Age of Nation States*, vol. 1: *The Meaning of Genocide* (London, 2005); Adrian Gallagher, *Genocide and Its Threat to the Contemporary International Order* (Houndmills, 2013), chapter 2, "Words Matter: Genocide and the Definitional Debate," pp. 18–39; and Martin Shaw's confused efforts to redefine the term "genocide" in his *Genocide and International Relations* (Cambridge, UK, 2013).

Unfortunately, the scholarly issues related to the Armenian case have been overtaken by both American and international politics. The Turkish government has resisted, and continues to resist, all public pressure to accept the accusation of "genocide," while the U.S. government has rejected applying this term for reasons of its own.[47] Alternatively, many individual scholars and groups, like the International Association of Genocide Scholars, have sought to intervene on behalf of the Armenian position and to defend the claim that what happened was, without doubt, "genocide."[48] The application of Turkey to join the International Holocaust Remembrance Alliance, the most prestigious international Holocaust organization, comprising thirty-one countries and organizations such as the United Nations, the Council of Europe, and UNESCO, has also been kept at bay until such time as the Turkish government makes some meaningful acknowledgment regarding this issue. In this *political* context I recognize that there is virtue in criticizing the actions and attitudes of the Turkish government but, at the same time, it is imperative to understand that the problematic political position adopted by the current Turkish state does not bear upon the scholarly matters of concern. Scholarship as scholarship needs to respect the fundamental difference between advocacy and research.

Consider, in defense of this distinction between research and public protest, that the crucial issue of the number of Armenians killed, on which many of the central academic-historical questions turn, is still unresolved. The Armenian community and its supporters claim the number of victims was between 800,000 and 1,500,000.[49] Alternatively, according to scholars supporting Turkish claims, the number was approximately 400,000. My own position is that there was a total of approximately 1,500,000 Armenians in the Ottoman Empire in 1915 and of these 476,000 to 776,000 were killed.[50] To date I have seen no evidence that requires that I change my mind. Moreover, this death toll, and the percentage of the Armenian community in Turkey that it represents, given the absolute vulnerability of the Armenian community in this context, tells us something important about the Turkish agenda that precipitated this lethal campaign: that is, the numbers of dead supports the interpretation that the Turkish ambition was to decapitate Armenian nationalism, not kill all Armenians in the state (and certainly not outside the Turkish state). This could be accomplished by uprooting the Armenian community in the Empire, and murdering a percentage of the Armenian population that

---

47 The subject has been discussed by Samantha Power, *"A Problem from Hell": America and the Age of Genocide* (New York, 2013).
48 This observation should not be misunderstood. There is a justified place for public protest of the serious misdeeds of political regimes and national states. But such protests, and the positions staked out in these protests, should not be mistaken as the equivalent of technical scholarly analyses and should not be taken as defensible scholarly argument.
49 Rouben Adalian recycled the high number of 1.5 million in his 2009 essay, "The Armenian Genocide," in Samuel Totten and William Parsons (eds.), *Century of Genocide: Critical Essays and Eyewitness Accounts*, 3rd edition (New York, 2009), p. 71.
50 The explanation of these numbers can be found in the present essay, pp. 10–12.

harbored its own nationalistic goals. It did not require the complete extermination of this Christian minority. Alternatively, it is relevant to observe that this territorial nationalism, and the specific agenda it entailed, was altogether absent in the assault, and the reasons for the assault by the Third Reich against European Jewry.

It is often argued that Hitler's *Weltanschauung* was profoundly nationalist and his campaign against the Jews was a consequence of this. This is a serious, if common, error. Hitler was not a nationalist in any usual sense of this term. Instead, and very different, he was an ardent racist who divided the world by racial criteria. His murder of the Jews, his effort to make Europe *Judenrein*, has little to do with the concept of nationalism and everything to do with the racial re-engineering of the human family. Just consider the realities that existed in the Third Reich. An Austrian (Hitler) became Chancellor of Germany and took it as his most basic political and moral obligation to deport all the Jews from places as separate and distinct as Greece, Bulgaria, Norway, Denmark, France, Poland, Lithuania, and Latvia, among still other places, to camps in Poland created solely for the purpose of annihilating them by gas and other means. What sort of nationalism is this?

The differing ambitions of Young Turks vis-à-vis Armenians and German National Socialists vis-à-vis Jews is evidenced by the fact that roughly one-third of Armenians in Turkey were murdered compared to more than 90 percent of Jews in locations such as Lithuania, Poland, and Greece. And with regard to the latter, the murderous action was propelled by the intention that the Jewish death rate in these contexts should be 100 percent. It is not of minor significance, for instance, that the essay, "The Armenian Genocide" by Donald Bloxham and Fatma Müge Göçek in the *Historiography of Genocide*, edited by Dan Stone,[51] mentions this crucial subject of losses but makes no attempt to resolve the competing narratives, and does not even supply a footnote referring to any literature on the issue.[52]

As for the *Gulag*, while the study of Stalin's regime has continued in a productive way among those interested in the history of Russia, in the larger conversation among comparativists there is far less emphasis on the world of the Siberian labor camps and the *Gulag* and less insistence on the claim that they represent authentic counterparts to Auschwitz. Thus, to refer again for evidence to Midlarsky's *The Killing Trap*, it is to be noted that while he discusses Stalinist crimes throughout his study he chooses not to include them as paradigm examples of "state-sponsored systematic mass murder" (p. 34). Likewise, Adam Jones, in his edited volume *New Directions in Genocide Research*,[53] provides a description of

---

51 (Houndmills, 2008), pp. 344–72.
52 Amongst useful and informative studies that have appeared since the publication of my Leo Baeck lecture, see: Fatma Müge Göçek, Norman Naimark, and Ronald Gregor Suny (eds.), *A Question of Genocide: Armenians and Turks at the End of the Ottoman Empire* (New York, 2011); Benjamin Lieberman, *Terrible Fate: Ethnic Cleansing in the Making of Modern Europe* (Chicago, 2006); and Ronald Grigor Suny, *"They can Live in the Desert but Nowhere Else;" A History of the Armenian Genocide* (Princeton, 2015).
53 (London, 2012).

five "Cases" (of Genocide), one of which offers a "Fresh Understanding of the Armenian Genocide,"[54] but does not include a chapter on Stalinist crimes.[55]

There has of course, independently of the matter of "genocide," continued to be important research published on all the main aspects of the Stalinist regime: the collectivization of agriculture and the persecution of the Kulaks; the deportations to, and life within, the *Gulag*; the exile of the minority nations; and the catastrophic famine in the Ukraine.[56] But while all these impressive works add significant details to our knowledge of the operation of the *Gulag*, and have taught me many new things about Soviet Russia, they have not required that I change my view that Stalin was not interested in physical genocide and did not pursue such a policy against any of his "enemies."[57]

There is no doubt that both the killing of the Armenians and Stalin's victimization of many different groups present specific, and distinctive, methodological and historical challenges that must be confronted by anyone who would pursue comparative study of twentieth-century history and the place of the Holocaust within it. But, at this juncture, in light of what I now know about these two great tragedies, each involving evil intentions and mass death, I am still prepared to defend the conclusion originally offered in my Leo Baeck lecture as to the singularity of the Holocaust.

---

54 *Ibid.*, pp. 198–214.
55 This is not to ignore the learned additions to the literature on Stalin's crimes and the issue of genocide. See, for example, the relatively long discussion in Ben Kiernan's *Blood and Soil: A World History of Genocide and Extermination from Sparta to Darfur* (New Haven, CT, 2007), pp. 486–511; Benjamin Valentino's analysis in his *Final Solution: Mass Killing and Genocide in the Twentieth Century* (Ithaca, 2004), pp. 91–117; Nicolas Werth's essay "The Mechanism of a Mass Crime: The Great Terror in the Soviet Union, 1937–1938," in Robert Gellately and Ben Kiernan (eds.), *The Specter of Genocide: Mass Murder in Historical Perspective* (Cambridge, UK, 2003), pp. 215–40; *idem*, "The Crimes of the Stalin Regime: Outline for an Inventory and Classification," in *The Historiography of Genocide*, ed. Dan Stone (Houndmills, 2008), pp. 400–419; and Norman Naimark, *Stalin's Genocides* (Princeton, 2010). It should also be said that this decline in references to Stalin's crimes as comparable to the Holocaust is a sign of better scholarship. It is a conclusion for which I argued early – before it became more widely accepted – in several essays republished in this collection, see "Mass death under Communist rule and the limits of otherness"; "Auschwitz and the Gulag: A Study in Dissimilarity"; and "Children in Auschwitz and the Gulag."
56 On the *Gulag* consult: Anne Applebaum, *Red Famine: Stalin's Non-War on the Ukraine* (New York, 2017); Norman Naimark, *Fires of Hatred: Ethnic Cleansing in Twentieth Century Europe* (Cambridge, MA, 2001); and J. P. Pohl, *Ethnic Cleansing in the USSR, 1937–1949* (Westport, CT, 1999). On the collectivization of agriculture take note of R. W. Davies and S. G. Wheatcroft, *The Years of Hunger: Soviet Agriculture 1931–1933* (New York, 2004); and S. Courtois, N. Werth, J.-L. Paine, et al. (eds.), *The Black Book of Communism* (Cambridge, MA., 1999). On the Ukraine see the discussion in Chapter 2 in this volume, "Mass death under Communist rule and the limits of otherness." pp. 33–39.
57 See my further analysis of Stalin's actions in Chapter 2.

2

MASS DEATH UNDER COMMUNIST RULE AND THE LIMITS OF "OTHERNESS"

Mass death is not a new reality. Over the centuries this tragic phenomenon has manifest itself in many times and places. An integral feature of this history of large-scale violence is what I shall call, "otherness." That is, the victimizer stigmatizes and stereotypes the victim in various ways in order to legitimate the violence that is then unleashed.

What is worthy of note is that this distancing process takes many forms. The historical record reveals cases where the "Other" is created on the grounds of class, sex, color, race, religion, ethnicity, and nationality. So, for example, the majority of Stalin's victims were identified as "class enemies." The most notorious example of such class war was directed at the Kulaks, though his entire massive campaign against the peasantry as represented by his forced drive to collectivize agriculture, was based on the notion of class (and his desire for national modernization). Likewise, the extraordinary event that was Kampuchea was defined by the application of a radical Communist ideology in which class was everything. In addition, nationalism – connected usually to other factors such as religion, ethnicity, race, or color – has also played its part in justifying oppression and death – as a decisive ingredient in Stalin's exile of the minority nationalities during World War II and in his assault on the Ukraine in the early 1930s.

The Kulaks

Let me begin, then, with the category of class as it was applied in Stalin's infamous campaign against the Kulaks.[1] Two fundamental facts about this defining event of the Stalinist era can be highlighted at the outset of our analysis: A) Stalin

---

[1] In the actual campaign that unfolded after January 1928, the term "Kulak" was used in a variety of ways and, in general, lost much of its technical meaning, becoming equivalent in practice to any peasant whom the regime wished to persecute. For further consideration of this definitional issue see Moshe Lewin, "Who Was the Soviet Kulak?," in his *The Making of the Soviet System: Essays in the Social History of Inter-war Russia* (New York, 1985), pp. 121–41; and Dorothy Atkinson, *The End of the Russian Land Commune, 1905–1930* (Stanford, 1984), pp. 281–84. At the Fifteenth Party Congress in 1927, Molotov defined a Kulak as a peasant who hired labor and rented land,

murdered only a minority of the Kulaks. He could have murdered them all, but he explicitly, consciously, chose not to do so; B) Stalin's primary target in this violent confrontation, for all its deadly severity, was a contingent, "socially alien," identity that, by definition, could be altered.[2] Whatever neurotic fears energized and accompanied this convulsive anti-peasant policy, elemental in this unstinting war were the Kulaks' self-interested class loyalties that had to be broken down. This coercive policy was judged necessary for the general good, as defined by socialist theory, to prevail. (Stalin was not alone in holding this position. It was the view of almost the entire Bolshevik elite, including Trotsky – differences existed only as to how best to accomplish this "progressive" policy.)

The need for this policy was the immediate consequence of three related socialist imperatives. First, there was the axiomatic requirement that called for the elimination of all "capitalist" classes which threatened socialist hegemony. Second, only the collectivization of agriculture, following upon the shortages and economic chaos of 1927 and the 1928 confiscations of grains – which Stalin interpreted as pointing the correct way to future policy – could end the severe grain crisis that led to food rationing in the cities in 1928–29. In 1928, grain acquisitions by the government, despite the new use of coercion, fell 2 percent below the poor levels of 1927. This failure was symptomatic of the enduring and recurring structural weakness of Soviet agriculture. There was the decline/absence of draft power (horses and oxen, and later, tractors), the inherent limits of communal land tenure, and the inefficiency of subsistence farming; the variety of problems posed by the need for assured acquisition of grain by the state, faulty pricing mechanisms, inadequate distribution and marketing networks; finally, there was the "capitalist greed" on the part of the Kulaks. As Stalin came to understand this weakness he was convinced that only the complete and permanent collectivization of agriculture could remedy this deeply unsatisfactory situation. Only the forced collectivization of the Kulaks and other peasants could provide the needed capital, primarily in the form of grain exports that were to be squeezed out of the newly created collective farms. This capital was required for the massive and rapid industrialization of Russia called for by socialist theory. This had indeed been the governing ideological understanding of Trotsky and the so-called "left" throughout the 1920s, but

---

calculating that 3.7 percent of the peasants belonged to this category. See here also the statistics on the Kulak proportion of the peasantry worked out by Stephan Merl, *Die Anlange der Kollektivierung in der Sowjetunion* (Wiesbaden, 1985), pp. 138–41. His figures for the size of the Kulak population for 1927 and 1929 are 3.9 and 2.2 percent respectively. His Table 29, p. 140, entitled "Verlinderung der Kulakenwirtschaften zwischen 1927 and 1929 nach Regionen" (Changes in Kulak Commerce between 1927 and 1929 according to Region) gives an idea of the nature and size of Kulak market activity between 1927 and 1929. Lynn Viola has also pointed to the many other sorts of "class" enemies undone as part of the program of dekulakization, "The Second Coming: Class Enemies in the Soviet Countryside, 1927–1935," in *Stalinist Terror: New Perspectives* (eds.) J. A. Getty and R. T. Manning (Cambridge, UK, 1993), pp. 65–98.

2 I borrow this expression from M. Lewin, "The Social Background of Stalinism," in *Making of the Soviet System*, p. 122.

now it was adopted by Stalin as his own point of departure. In addition, ideological compulsions aside, the leadership acted to overcome the national economic crisis that now directly involved both rural and urban sectors. Inflation, which was due in large part to a shortage of grain, dramatically eroded real urban wages between 1928 and 1932, while farm wages declined by nearly half in the same period. Though the Bolshevik leadership had in large measure created the present crisis, something dramatic had to be done to overcome it.

At the Sixteenth Party Congress held in April 1929, against the background of another grain crisis, the First Secretary's demand for collectivization (a demand typical of Stalin's Bolshevik voluntarism) became Party policy. This transformed the situation, as Stalin later said, from "a policy of limiting the exploiting activities of the Kulaks to a policy liquidating the Kulaks as a class."[3] There would now be an end to accommodations and vacillation. Stalin had convinced the Party Congress – and there were considerable segments within the Party that required little convincing – that there was only one reasoned option that it could choose and that there could be no turning back once this course was selected. The uncompromising treatment of the Kulaks, their exemplary victimization, would set the pace for the collectivization of the whole of the peasantry. This decision would send the appropriate message to the entire agricultural sector, particularly the middle peasantry: the State would not countenance any deviation from or interference with its grand political objective. "We must deal the Kulak such a blow," Molotov announced, "that the middle peasant will snap to attention before us."[4] The country was ill-prepared for the draconian measures that were about to ensue, as was the state apparatus that had to carry out these extraordinary initiatives. But they would come to pass. Between late 1929 and March 1930, in a mere five months, the percentage of all peasants living on collective farms rose from 4.1 percent to 58 percent, i.e., from approximately 1.1 million households to 15 million households (12 percent of the total population). By 1934 the percentage of peasants

---

[3] Vasily Grossman's provocative claim that "Just as the Germans proclaimed Jews are not human beings, thus did Lenin and Stalin proclaim, 'Kulaks are not human beings,'" cited with at least implicit approval by Robert Conquest, is simply an error. Conquest's self-correcting awareness of its incorrectness is, I believe, indicated by the fact that having used the quote he does nothing more with it and quickly moves on. That is, were this putative similarity more than a rhetorical device, Conquest would be obliged to analyze this entire issue more fully. Grossman's remarks are made in his *Forever Flowering* (New York, 1972), p. 144, cited by Robert Conquest, *Harvest of Sorrow* (New York, 1986), p. 129. More recently Alan Bullock, basing himself I suspect on Conquest's view (though no attribution is given) repeats this erroneous description – "Like the Jews under the Nazis the Kulaks [were] – declared sub-human," *Hitler and Stalin* (New York, 1992), p. 308. The larger principle to be borne in mind in any close analysis of why individuals are killed, is that, contra Conquest and Bullock, one does not have to be "sub-human" to be persecuted or murdered. Human beings are perfectly capable of doing horrendous things to other human beings. The Nazi classification of Jews as "sub-human" (*Untermenschen*) is a technical notion, not a metaphor, predicated on pseudo-scientific racial theories that have no parallel within the Stalinist (or Marxist-Leninist) orbit.

[4] This assumed, however much it was ignored in practice (though far from completely ignored as we shall see), that one could separate a Kulak's status from his person.

living on collectivized farms had risen to 75 percent. Thus, through the harsh intrusion of the OGPU (Secret Police), a massive metamorphosis of Soviet peasant life, though *not* its genocidal demise, had occurred.

There was no fully genocidal intention behind the assault on the Kulaks as becomes clear from the policy directives governing the entire action against them. Stalin did intervene to stiffen the guidelines recommended by the special Politburo Commission on Dekulakization that reported in December 1929. But his own more radical version of this transformational program, published in the name of the Central Committee on January 5, 1930 under the title "On the Tempo of Collectivization and Measures of State Assistance in Collective Farm Construction," still allowed for a tripartite distinction among Kulaks. The first category of Kulaks was held to be composed of hardened, unrepentant reactionaries and anti-Soviet counter-revolutionaries. Such individuals were to be separated out, jailed, or exiled to the Gulag, and if necessary, shot. Their families were also to be exiled. It is estimated that 50,000 to 63,000 households (averaging between 4.2 and 6 persons per family, a maximum of 300,000 to 378,000 persons) fell into this class. The second category to be established recognized the existence of less recalcitrant, though still "potentially" dangerous Kulaks and their families who were also to be exiled, though to less distant and less harsh conditions. Approximately 112,000 households (672,000 persons at a maximum) were identified as belonging to this second subdivision. The third and largest group established by Stalin's edict was comprised of the less affluent, less politically active Kulaks who constituted the majority, estimated at 75 percent, of all Kulak families. There were between 650,000 and 800,000 households (between 3,900,000 and 4,800,000 persons at a maximum) in this category. They were to be settled in their own *raion* (area), but, on Stalin's insistence, outside of the collective farms. In any event, this three-part organizational plan that involved the active participation of tens of thousands of armed personnel, provided the national blueprint for the program of collectivization.

When the Kulak relocation program actually took place, elements of a class war were unleashed, involving "a positive orgy of violence which were later referred to as 'excesses.'"[5] At the same time, the conditions of exile and resettlement were much harsher than those proposed, however cynically, in the relevant official legislation. As a result, the removals actually carried out amidst the chaotic conditions extant in the countryside (often by overzealous and ill-disciplined district level authorities) created more exiles dispatched to more distant northern locations, more deportations to labor camps, and more "executions" than originally envisioned. Officially, it was at first reported that a total of 240,757 Kulak families, approximately 25 percent of Kulak households,

---

5 Lenin's many compromises during the so-called New Economic Policy (NEP) were now to be seen as only temporary concessions to historic circumstance overtaken by new socio-economic actualities. Zhores Medvedev's conclusion in his *Soviet Agriculture* (New York, 1987) that NEP was still a viable option is a minority scholarly position.

some 1 to 1.5 million people, had been exiled. Later this total was revised upwards to 381,000 families, or nearly (at a maximum) 2.3 million persons. The final number, when all the deportees are included, was most likely more than double this estimate, involving upwards of 5 million individuals. These deportations were also the cause, directly and indirectly, of between 1 and 2 million deaths, with a disproportionate number of the dead being children who were unable to survive the appalling living conditions (including severe food shortages and wretched weather that existed during the transport and the first years of resettlement).

These horrors and the enormous damage they did to the agricultural infrastructure of the country brought about a public outcry and monumental disorder in the countryside, including the accelerating slaughter of animals with the greatest losses taking place in February and March 1930. Even Stalin, in direct contradiction to his own desire to force the tempo of collectivization, felt constrained to criticize the deportations in his hypocritical essay, "Dizziness from Success."[6] In addition, new guidelines were issued limiting the number and types of Kulaks to be deported. However, this respite from forced collectivization was temporary. A second wave of dekulakization now occurred with the result that while "only 26 percent of peasant households participated as Kolkhoz members in the spring sowing of 1930 . . . between January and March 1931 . . . the figures rose sharply from under 30 percent to 42 percent."[7] And this process continued throughout the second half of 1931 so that "over half the peasant households of the Soviet Union were collectivized by the end of the 1931 sowing, and more than 60 percent by the end of the harvest season.[8] By the spring of 1933 collectivization was a fait accompli and Stalin ordered the cessation of any further forced deportations in support of it.

As a result of these extreme governmental actions, the Minister of Agriculture was able to announce by 1931 that the Kulak population (using the term very broadly), in *terms of class membership,* had declined from 5.4 million in 1928 to its then present size of 1.6 million. Four years later, in 1935, an official document described this class constriction in even more dramatic terms: the 1928 Kulak population of 5,618,000 had been reduced to 149,000 by

---

6 C. Ward, *Stalin's Russia* (London and New York, 1993), p. 42. This new round of shortages was accompanied by significant free-market price rises of grains and other foodstuffs creating further dislocations throughout the national economy.

7 Analyzed in detail by Moshe Lewin, *Russian Peasants and Soviet Power: A Study of Collectivization* (London, 1968), pp. 214–50, 383–405; Naum Jasny, *The Socialized Agriculture of the USSR* (Stanford, 1949), p. 204; H. Holland, "Soviet Agriculture with and without Collectivization, 1928–1940," *Slavic Review* 47.2 (1988): 206–08; Dorothy Atkinson, *The End of the Russian Land Commune, 1905–1930,* 313–45; S. Merl, *Die Anfonge der Kollektivierung in der Sowjetunion* (Wiesbaden, 1985), pp. 230–41, particularly on the issue of tractors, Table 70, p. 237.

8 M. Lewin, "'Taking Grain': Soviet Policies of Agricultural Procurements before the War", in *Essays in Honour of E. H. Carr,* ed. C. Abramsky, C. Williams, and E. H. Carr (London, 1974), pp. 169–73; and L. Volin, *A Century of Russian Agriculture* (Cambridge, MA, 1970), pp. 250ff.

January 1, 1934. It must be stressed, however, lest serious misunderstanding of what was occurring should arise, that this precipitous drop in class affiliation, involving approximately 5.4 million individuals, does not equal a corresponding loss of life, i.e., every lost unit of class membership is not equivalent to a death. The number of Kulak deaths, from all causes, as a consequence of these tyrannical removals is estimated, as already noted, at between 1 and 2 million. This is to recognize that despite the ferocity of the attack upon the approximately 5.4 (to 5.6) million persons identified as Kulaks in 1928, somewhere between 63 and 81.5 percent of this original group – some 3.4 to 4.4 million individuals – *remained alive*. This statistical conclusion is in line with Stanisaw Swianiewicz's researches. He estimates that of the Kulaks who were deported, one-third perished, and this is consistent with Robert Conquest's more recent calculation that 25 to 30 percent of the Kulaks died in or, as a consequence of the deportations.

But millions of Kulaks and other peasants were deported and lived. Millions of others were not deported at all. In other words, the Kulaks were not subject to a state orchestrated campaign of physical genocide. Consider, in support of this judgment, the overall aggregates of peasant population: in 1929 it is estimated that there were circa 25,900,000 peasant households throughout the Soviet Union with an average of 4.2 persons (at a minimum) per household, or 108,700,000 peasants. By 1938 the number of peasant households had declined to circa 19,900,000, or (at an average of 4.2 members) 83,600,000 individuals, a deficit of 36 million persons. But, of this 36 million decline, nearly 24.5 million are projected to have changed their status by moving to the cities or towns, in itself a major testimony against genocide, leaving a net loss of about 11.5 million or approximately 7.5 to 8 percent, up to 1937. Even when another 3 to 3.5 million peasant dead are added to the figure of 11.5 million to account for those imprisoned in this period but who died after 1937, making a total of up to 15 million peasant casualties, the loss rate comes to only 11 to 12 percent of the total peasant population. Or put the other way around, 88 percent of the peasants, even on the highest responsible estimates of loss, survived. This constrained, very carefully calibrated interpretation of Stalin's crusade against the Kulaks is not intended to lessen the evil nature of his campaign. Nor again, does it challenge the identification of Stalin as a mass murderer of unrivalled proportions. The criminality of Stalin's behavior towards the Kulaks, and against Russia's peasantry more generally, remains a supreme example of political malevolence. At the same time, however, its discrete empirical morphology and ideological particularity cannot be ignored – despite the temptations of facile historical and phenomenological comparisons – without making truth a casualty. For the class war against the Kulaks never escalated into total annihilation, a war of all against all. The dialectic of history, in Stalinist terms, required the forcible social transformation of the Kulak as a necessary part of its internal and immanent self-development and as an unavoidable imperative in class evolution, but it did not require more than this.

The case of the Ukraine

The next substantial category, relative to the creation of "Otherness," that I would like to discuss at some length is nationalism. This is important in itself as a cause of large-scale violence in the modern era. Here, two instances of persecution and mass death generated by nationalist ambitions and their suppression during Stalin's reign are highly instructive: the famine in the Ukraine in 1932–33, and Stalin's deportation of seven national groups during World War II.

There are two main lines of scholarly interpretation concerning what actually happened and why in the Ukraine.[9] The first of these emphasizes the nationalist dimensions of the event. On this reading, both the indigenous Ukrainian population and the Soviet ruling class knew that the Ukraine, as recently as 1918, had been independent and that it wished to be politically independent again. Accordingly, the confrontations after 1918 in this region are seen as defined by the collision of two competing claims to sovereignty, one nationalist and the other putatively internationalist, though increasingly a cover for Russian national chauvinism.[10] For Stalin, the ultimate objective is assumed to have been the full integration

---

9 For an introduction to this event see Bohdan Krawchenko and Roman Serbyn (eds.), *Famine in Ukraine, 1932–1933* (Edmonton, AB, 1986); Bohdan Krawchenko, "The Great Famine of 1932–1933 in Soviet Ukraine: Causes and Consequences," *Critique* 17 (1986): 137–46; Iwij Borys, *The Sovietization of the Ukraine* (Edmonton, AB, 1980); the report to the U.S. Congress, prepared primarily by James Mace, *Investigation of the Ukrainian Famine 1932–1933; Report to Congress* (Washington, D.C., 1988); R. Conquest, *Harvest of Sorrow* (New York, 1987); and for further sources, Alexander Pidhaina, "A Bibliography of the Great Famine in the Ukraine, 1932–1934," *New Review: A Journal of East-European History* 4 (1973): 32–68. The post-Stalinist work on the famine and its causes is reviewed in the *U.S. Commission on the Ukraine Famine* (Washington, D.C., 1998), pp. 37–68. As one would expect, until the post-Gorbachev era Soviet scholarship on this subject was intensely apologetic in tone.

10 This conflict has been analyzed by Tares Hunczak (ed.), *The Ukraine, 1917–1921: A Study in Revolution* (Cambridge, MA, 1971); Hryhory Kostiuk, *Stalinist Rule in the Ukraine* (New York, 1961); John Reshatar, *The Ukrainian Revolution: A Study in Nationalism* (Princeton, 1952); Arthur Adams, *Bolsheviks in the Ukraine: The Second Campaign, 1918–1919* (New Haven, 1963); Basil D. Mytryshan, *Moscow and the Ukraine, 1918–1953: A Study of Russian Bolshevik Nationality Policy* (New York, 1956); Bohdan Krawchenko, *Social Change and National Consciousness in Twentieth-Century Ukraine* (New York, 1985); James E. Mace, "Politics and History in Soviet Ukraine, 1921–1933," *Nationality Papers* 1 (1982): 157–80; idem, "Famine and Nationalism in Soviet Ukraine," *Problems of Communism* 33.3 (1984): 37–50; idem, "The Man-Made Famine of 1933," in *Famine in Ukraine*, ed. R. Serbyn and B. Krawchenko, pp. 1–14; W. Kosyk, "Der Hungergenozid in der Ukraine 1932–1933," in *Jahrbuch der Ulcrainekunder* (1983): 89–126; Steven L. Guthier, "The Popular Base of Ukrainian Nationalism in 1917," *Slavic Review* 38.1 (March 1979): 30–47; Andrew P. Lamis, "Some Observations on the Ukrainian National Movement and the Ukrainian Revolution, 1917–1921," *Harvard Ukrainian Studies* 2.4 (December 1978): 525–31; Orest Subtelny, *Ukraine: A History* (Toronto 1988); a number of the essays dealing with Ukrainian history in Anthony Smith and Tamara Dragadze (eds.), *National Identity in Russia, the Soviet Union, and Eastern Europe* (London, 1992); George O. Liber, *Soviet Nationality Policy* (Cambridge, UK and New York, 1992), and idem, *Communism and the Dilemmas of National Liberation: National Communism in Soviet Ukraine, 1918–1933* (Cambridge, MA, 1983). For a comprehensive study of Soviet politics in relationship to the "Ukrainian Question,"

of the Ukraine into the larger, ideally homogenized Soviet state. Anything less was dangerous. In practical terms it would interfere with the Bolsheviks' control of the agricultural market – including the essential issue of grain collection and distribution, a circumstance that often divided the local leadership. There was also danger from the geopolitically divisive character of all nationalist aspirations. Accordingly, Stalin on this reading consciously decided on a deadly campaign – most accurately described by the political category of internal colonialism – to eradicate this recurring threat to Soviet hegemony. Beginning with the purge of Ukrainian academics, as well as political and cultural leaders that began in April 1929, Stalin set in motion a movement that would eventually consume millions of Ukrainians.[11]

The object of the entire terror campaign was allegedly to bring about the complete annihilation of Ukrainian nationalism – a goal that was also consistent with the larger policy of the socialization of agriculture. Much like Hitler's later strategy in Poland for example (and elsewhere in Eastern Europe), Stalin sought to expunge local autonomy and all manifestations of cultural or political independence in order to facilitate continued domination from Moscow. Here, as in many other cases (e.g., Cambodia, Nigeria, Sudan, and more recently in Rwanda) the purpose of state-organized violence is the maintenance of political control.

Given the importance of the economically autonomous peasantry in the Ukraine's socio-economic structures, the First Secretary's plan for the extermination of Ukrainian identity also required a crusade against the national intellectuals and "proto-capitalist" strata that supported them.[12] As Semen O. Pidhainy has described it, Stalin had to move against both intellectuals and "Ukrainian nationalism's social base – the individual land-holdings."[13] Above all, "[o]nly a mass terror throughout the body of the nation – that is, the peasantry – could reduce the nation to submission."[14] As long as the *selianyn* (free peasants) existed, nationalist (and capitalist) sentiment would remain: both needed to be crushed.

The dominant method used to achieve this collective submission to socialism and the elimination of the base of Ukrainian national sentiment, was once more to be

---

though relatively weak and under-informed on the famine of 1932–1933, see Robert S. Sullivant, *Soviet Politics and the Ukraine, 1917–1957* (New York, 1962).

11 On Soviet opposition to Ukrainian culture and cultural elites see George S. Luckyj, *Literary Politics in the Soviet Ukraine: 1917–1934* (New York, 1956); and H. Kostiuk, *Stalinist Rule in the Ukraine*, 47–59.

12 The Ukrainian *selianyn* should not be equated with a Russian peasant or serf. The *selianyn* was "a free Cossack-farmer before the Russian occupation of Ukraine. For this historical reason Ukrainian farmers had a much stronger sense of private ownership and deeper feeling of freedom and independence," Miron Dolot, *Execution by Hunger: The Hidden Holocaust* (New York, 1985), p. xiv.

13 Semen O. Pidhainy, et al. (eds.), *The Black Deeds of the Kremlin: A White Book* (Detroit, 1955), vol. 1, 205.

14 Conquest, *Harvest of Sorrow*, p. 219. Repeated in the *U.S. Commission on the Ukraine Famine*, p. xiii: "crushing the Ukrainian peasantry made it possible for Stalin to curtail Ukrainian national self-assertion."

the forced collectivization of the agricultural sector. At the same time, such a centralized agrarian policy gave the Communist Party, in the form of the All Union Commissariat of Agriculture, control over the region's grain supply. It was the task and responsibility of this Commissariat, in conjunction with Soviet planners, to calculate, coordinate, and organize the yearly grain harvest and to set the state exactions to be levied and collected. When this direct control was expressed in an overly demanding target for grain exports from the region – ostensibly justified by the increased program of industrialization that was to be financed by the agricultural surplus – it effectively translated into a man-made famine in the Ukraine in 1931 that grew worse in the next two years. For example, in 1931 the procurement quota for the region was set at 7 million tons out of a total of 18.3 million tons (much of which had been lost to inefficient collective harvesting).[15] Such a level of national procurement certainly spelled trouble for the local community.

Matters of food supply only got worse in 1932 when the procurement total was again set at 7 million tons while that year's harvest, due to drought, inefficiency and a decline in the number of acres sown – the latter partly in protest to Stalinist policy – came in at the very reduced level of 14.7 million tons. The local leadership, in the face of the total decline in tonnage, managed to persuade Moscow, at great cost to itself in the suspicions of disloyalty and nationalism that this awakened, to reduce the quota to 6.6 million tons.[16] But even this reduced sum was still far too high to make it possible to avoid massive starvation. Stalin, however, despite the mounting death toll, did not believe that the harvest was too small both to feed the Ukrainian people and to provide sufficient grain for export. Instead, already intensely suspicious of Ukrainian separatism and fearful of local disloyalty, he chose to interpret the failure to meet the inordinate quotas set by the central agencies as deliberate acts of "sabotage." The peasants, he concluded, were no better than "wreckers" of the socialist dream. In a deliberate act intended to punish the population of the Ukraine – which he justified as socialist self-defense – he

---

15 Conquest, *ibid.*, pp. 221f puts the 1931 procurement at 7.7 million tons, with 7 million tons actually collected. This total already indicates a severe decline from the 23.9 million tons harvested in 1930.
16 On the ambiguities inherent in all these grain statistics, see the pertinent observations of R. W. Davies, "A Note on Grain Statistics," *Soviet Studies* 21.3 (January 1970): 314–29; and *idem*, *The Socialist Offensive*, vol. I, 65–68. On the trustworthiness (or otherwise) of Russian statistics see also Steven G. Wheateroft's essay, "The Reliability of Russian Pre War Grain Output Statistics," *Soviet Studies* 25.2 (April 1974): 157–80; *idem*, "A Reevaluation of Soviet Agricultural Production in the 1920s and 1930s," in *The Soviet Rural Economy*, ed. Robert C. Stuart (Totowa, NJ, 1983), pp. 37–38; Abram Bergson, *Soviet National Income and Product in 1937* (New York, 1953), pp. 7–9; Naum Jasny, "Intricacies of Russian National Income Indexes," *Journal of Political Economy* 55.4 (August 1947): 299–322; *idem*, "Soviet Statistics," *Review of Economics and Statistics* 32.1 (February 1950): 92–99; Vladimir G. Trevel and John P. Hardt (eds.), *Soviet Economic Statistics* (Durham, NC, 1972); and Gregory Grossman, *Soviet Statistics of Physical Output of Industrial Commodities: Their Compilation and Quality* (Princeton, 1960). Joseph S. Berliner has, likewise, revealed the tremendous fraud in factory statistics in his *Factory and Manager in the USSR* (Cambridge, MS, 1957), pp. 160–81. Cf. also A. Solzhenitsyn's devastating critique of Soviet statistics in his *Gulag Archipelago* (New York, 1974–78), vol. 2, p. 69.

continued to export grain from the region (if at a lower rate):[17] 1.73 million tons in 1932 and 1.68 million tons in 1933, compared to 5.2 million tons in 1931. It was this export of grain, given the greatly reduced supplies, which turned an already grave situation into the catastrophe of mass death.

Increased pressure was now also applied against the peasant "class enemy" and against local party officials. Over a third of the new Ukrainian Communist Party members and candidate members were purged (37.3 percent) and 75 percent of local Soviets and members of local committees were replaced, with many being arrested for failing to produce the required quota. Pressure was also applied against those involved in local agricultural middle management with 3 percent of these officials arrested in the second half of 1932 for sabotaging Bolshevik policy;[18] and there was pressure against all channels of Ukrainian self-sufficiency – economic, cultural, and nutritional. On December 14, 1932 the Central Committee of the All Union Communist Party accused the leadership of the Ukrainian Communist Party "of tolerating a Ukrainian nationalist deviation in its ranks," and then proceeded, on January 24, 1933, to replace it with a new ruling clique headed by Pavel Postyshev.[19] At the same time, it is argued, all available food aid to the stricken population was consciously denied, existing grain reserves in the region and elsewhere were not made available, the importation of food was stopped at the border of the Ukraine. Meanwhile Stalin, in an act of depravity, continued as already noted, to export more than 3 million tons of grain in 1932 and 1933. As a result, there was massive intentional starvation throughout the Ukraine which peaked in 1933 and 1934. Of a peasant population of more than 25 million, about 20 percent (up to 5 million), plus 500,000 to 750,000 persons in the urban areas of the Ukraine, died from lack of food and related medical problems in this period.[20] In some areas the death rate was as low as 10 percent, in others the rate was

---

17 Robert Conquest takes the view that Stalin and his bureaucrats knew that it would be impossible to meet the new targets. They understood, he argues, that the notion that the peasants were hoarding grain and that they controlled large stockpiles of food which they refused to release to the market was "a myth" (*Harvest of Sorrow*, p. 221). Walter Laqueur has alternatively argued, on the basis of post-*Glasnost* evidence, that: "the punishment thesis has not been proved. There seems to have been no plan to destroy Ukrainian agriculture and to cause the death of millions of people." See his *Stalin, The Glasnost Revelations* (New York, 1990), p. 282 for an assessment.
18 Conquest, *Harvest of Sorrow*, pp. 227 ff.
19 Cited from G. O. Liber, *Soviet Nationality Policy*, p. 166. On these political activities, interpreted from a radical Ukrainian perspective, see H. Kostiuk, *Stalinist Rule in the Ukraine*, pp. 18–37; for a less ideological perspective, consult R. S. Sullivant, *Soviet Politics in the Ukraine*, pp. 195–208.
20 This figure concurs with R. Conquest's estimate, *Harvest of Sorrow*, pp. 303, 306. He gives a "conservative" aggregate of 7 million famine-related deaths in 1932–33 for all areas affected by the disaster, 5 million of which occurred in the Ukraine. Cf. also James Mace's calculations in his essay "The Famine of 1933: A Survey of the Sources," in *Famine in Ukraine, 1932–1933*, ed. R. Serbyn and B. Krawchenko (Edmonton, AB, 1986), p. 50. Serhii Pirozhkov, "Population Loss in Ukraine in the 1930s and 1940s," in *Ukrainian Past, Ukrainian Present*, ed. B. Krawchenko (London, 1993), p. 89, argues that Conquest overestimates the losses. This would also appear to be the conclusion of V. V. Tsaplin who has calculated excess deaths in the Soviet Union in 1933

nearly 100 percent, the variations depending largely upon local agricultural and ecological conditions, such as the ability to find fish, wildlife, or other sources of nutrition. In many places this also led to cannibalism and infanticide in a desperate effort to cope with the lost grain harvests.

This is the *nationalist version* of the Ukrainian famine, interpreted as an intentional, man-made "genocide." It views Stalin as killing 5 million or more Ukrainians, plus hundreds of thousands of additional individuals belonging to other ethnic groups such as the Volga Germans and Kuban Cossacks. The goal was to simultaneously decapitate opposition to agricultural collectivization and to eradicate Ukrainian and other nationalist aspirations.

If we accept this nationalist interpretation of Ukrainian history, at least for the sake of argument, what are we to conclude about these events as an instance of genocide? This is certainly neither irrelevant nor a trivial question given the scale of the human losses involved and the evil will which directly caused these losses. There can be no doubt about the horror of this vast collective tragedy. But even 5 million deaths do not constitute in this case the technical crime of genocide and, for all of its murderous ferocity and demographic enormity, the event is not comparable to the Holocaust. The ruthless campaign against Ukrainian nationalism that destroyed a majority of the indigenous Ukrainian cultural and political elite (as well as a significant segment of the peasant population of the region) is better categorized as an instance of nationalist conflict and internal colonialism.[21] Stalin did not intend to exterminate the entire population of the Ukraine.

This conclusion finds support from the relevant statistical indicators. Though the human carnage was enormous (approaching the number of Jewish victims during the Second World War) the portion of the Ukrainian peasant population lost was somewhere in the region of 20 percent, while the losses for the Ukrainian population as a whole were in the area of 15 percent.[22] These demographic results resemble the figures for population decline in those Eastern European

---

at between 3 and 4 million. (I cite this figure from S. Fitzpatrick, *Stalin's Peasants* [New York, 1994], p. 342, n. 88). Alternatively, the figure of 4.5 million to 5 million actual deaths due to the famine in the Ukraine in 1932–33 is supported by the recent (1990) demographic research of S. V. Kulchytskyi, called to my attention by G. Liber, *Soviet Nationality Policy*, p. 237, n. 23; and by G. Simon, who refers to "at least 8 million people starved" and "at least 4.5 million deaths" in the Ukraine, *Nationalism and Policy toward the Nationalities in the Soviet Union* (Boulder, 1991), p. 99. These figures are, as all figures in this article, subject to revision.

21 This is not to deny the logical possibility that nationalist conflicts can become genocidal. It is only to assert that this is not what actually occurred in this particular historical instance.

22 R. Conquest gives the slightly higher figure of 18.8 percent of the total population of the Ukraine, *Harvest of Sorrow*, p. 306. However, he does not give sufficient weight to various life-saving factors, especially migration, in his tabulation. The total Ukrainian population in this era was circa 32–35 million, some of it resident outside the Ukraine proper since the terror and famine of 1928. A more detailed reconstruction of Ukrainian population statistics will be found in Robert Lewis et al., "The Growth and Redistribution of Russia and the USSR: 1897–1970," in *Ukraine in the Seventies*, ed. Peter Potychnyj (Oakville, ON, 1975), 151–75; and S. Pirozhkov, "Population Loss in Ukraine in the 1930s and 1940s," pp. 90–95.

countries overrun by the Nazis, and in both cases the numbers do not indicate that a policy of total population eradication was pursued. Had Stalin in the Ukraine sought to pursue a genocidal war, given the destructive possibilities that lay open to him, more than 15 percent of the population would have been done away with. But more people were not killed because amidst the murderous toll there was still some restraint. The fact is that Stalin did not want to eradicate the people of the Ukraine, he wanted to exploit them. Eliminating the whole of a vanquished "helot" population makes no more sense than slaughtering one's slaves. However, eliminating a conquered people's controlling elite, leaving it leaderless, anxious, and vertiginous, is a rational, functional strategy. This is a policy long pursued by conquerors to achieve enduring subordination of the subjugated and the political stability of an empire. It is certainly not a humane imperial strategy, nor a program to be recommended as a form of empire maintenance, but neither is it genocide.

This judgment is confirmed, ironically, by the heartrending condition of the children, especially infants and the newborn. Throughout the Ukraine, youthful corpses lay strewn across the landscape – the entire territory had become a necropolis for children under 11 and 12 who were unable to obtain enough nourishment to stay alive. Yet, even here in the midst of the most intense human suffering, the relevant population statistics require careful decipherment. The latest demographic data indicates that fewer than 760,000 children died, largely from starvation, from 1932 to 1934.[23] This represents, depending on one's estimation of other relevant demographic variables, between 6 percent and 33.5 percent of the age cohort, and a significant percentage of the total population decline.[24] But, recognizing the great tragedy that occurred here, even the maximum loss of 33.5 percent does not support a genocidal reading of this event. For, on these numbers, at least 66.5 percent of Ukrainian children survived. Moreover, once the famine passed its peak in May 1933, the surviving two out of three children were not singled out for further harassment and worse. Most of those who managed to live through the crisis of 1932–33 survived.

This historical outcome regarding children is not trivial. What makes the Ukrainian case non-genocidal and different from the Holocaust is the fact that the majority of Ukrainian children *were permitted to survive*.[25] Even the mountains

---

23 Conquest's maximum total of child deaths of 4 million (3 million as a result of the famine, 1 million due to the program of dekulakization), based on currently available evidence, appears to be too high, *Harvest of Sorrow*, p. 297. Moreover, this total includes non-Ukrainian children, e.g., those of Kazakhstan, thus significantly reducing the number and percentage of child losses in the Ukraine, even on Conquest's numbers.

24 S. Pirozhkov calculates that, "the unborn and dead children accounted for 54.4 percent of total losses (that is, the potential demographic losses of children were approximately 3.1 million people) and direct losses of children and youths aged under 25 represented 13 percent, or 760,000 people," "Population Loss in Ukraine in the 1930s and 1940s," p. 89.

25 M. Maksudov estimates that for the entire period 1926–39, of the 12 million Ukrainian children born, 1.4 million died, "Ukraine's Demographic Losses 1927–1938," *Sucasnist* 10 (1983): 37.

of evidence pertaining to Stalin's evil actions produced by the proponents of the nationalist genocide thesis (for example James Mace and Robert Conquest) does not indicate either any intent or motive that would plausibly justify the extermination of the general Ukrainian biological stock. The number of Ukrainian children who died (or on the intentionalist reading were murdered) was as high as or even higher than the number of Jewish children who were exterminated in the Nazi Holocaust. But their deaths represented something different from what the murder of Jewish children at Auschwitz and Treblinka represented and intended. In the Ukrainian case, the aim of the violence and death was national enfeeblement and political dismemberment. In the *Shoah* the focused object, given its racial determinants, was physical genocide. Stalin intended that after the famine there should still be Ukrainians, though not Ukrainianism. Hitler intended that after Auschwitz there would be neither Jews nor Judaism. The loss of every child in both contexts was, to echo the Talmudic Sages, the loss of a world. The death of each child was an act of equal immorality. Nonetheless there is an important, non-reductive, phenomenological difference to be drawn between mass murder (including children) and complete group extinction; between a war for political and territorial domination (including children) and a war of unlimited biological annihilation.

Deported Minorities in the Soviet Union

The case of the deported Soviet national minorities is also instructive as to the nature of massive state violence and its limits. The post-1940 removals of seven national groups en bloc in the USSR under the turbulent and catalytic circumstances of a world war (swelling the demographic pool of Gulag inmates by over 1.3 million) requires separate analysis in the present context.[26] Do these deportations – an organized state action against identifiable collectives – qualify as acts of physical genocide?

The deportation of the four northern Caucasian peoples, the Karachay, Balkars, Chechens, and Ingushi, can be analyzed as a unit. All shared four defining attributes in addition to geographical contiguity: (a) all belonged to non-Russian ethnic groups; (b) all were Muslim; (c) each had a considerable history of opposition to Tsarist and Russian rule and would have preferred political independence from the Russian state[27] (the overt political uprisings of the Chechens, Ingushi, Balkar and

---

[26] The seven are: the Kalmyks, the Chechens, the Ingushis, the Volga Germans, the Balkar, the Crimean Tatars, and the Karachay. The so-called Meskhetians (a mixed Turkicized-Muslim population from Georgia) were an eighth category of persons now often included in the lists of deported national minorities. They were not, in fact, a single, identifiable people with a discrete national territory and identity before they were subject to removal. See B. Nahaylo and V. Swoboda, *Soviet Disunion: A History of the Nationalities Problem in the USSR* (New York, 1989), p. 97.

[27] See, on these nationalist aspirations, Serge Zenkovsky, *Pan Turkism and Islam in Russia* (Cambridge, MA, 1960); Edige Kirimal, *Der nationale Kampf der Krimturken* (Emsdetten, 1952); Gerhard von Mende, *Der nationale Kampf der Rußlandturken* (Berlin, 1936); Alan Fisher, *The Crimean Tatars* (Stanford, 1978), pp. 94–108; Edward Lazzerini, "Godism at the Turn of the

Tatar populations in 1929–30 and again in 1939–40 speak decisively to this cardinal issue); (d) each experienced various forms of persecution and coercion under both the Tsars and the Soviets. In addition, each of these national communities was relatively small in size compared to the larger national blocs that comprise the Soviet Union and in comparison with the Jewish population of Europe in 1939. It is worth recalling that Khrushchev, in his famous anti-Stalinist speech at the Twentieth Party Congress, acknowledged the importance of the *size* factor when discussing the fate of the Ukrainians under Stalin who, unlike the small Muslim nations, could not be deported because they were too numerous.

The second group of national deportees, comprising Kalmyks, Tatars, and Volga Germans, was more ethnically and religiously diverse, though their historical and socio-political experience under the Tsars and their Soviet successors was much the same as that of other exiled peoples. National and religious prejudices, continued misrule, occasional severe eruptions of violence and the suppression of ethnic or national aspirations marked their internal colonial status within the Empire. The Kalmyks were ethnically Mongols and practicing Buddhists. On the other hand, the Tatars were an ancient and historically independent Turkic-speaking Muslim people annexed to the Tsarist Empire in 1783. The Tatars had a strong national self-consciousness and harbored fervent national aspirations. The Volga Germans, by contrast, were a distinct ethnic community that had settled in Russia in the second half of the eighteenth century in return for economic advantages. Clearly separate in ethnic and religious identity from the surrounding people among whom they lived, they too sought national autonomy, achieving this valued status under the Soviet reorganization that established the autonomous German Volga Soviet Socialist Republic in 1924. (A similar political concession had been made to the Kalmyks in 1920, the Balkars, Chechens, and Karachay in 1922, and the Ingushi in 1924.) The national position of the Volga Germans was obviously anomalous and especially sensitive during the Nazi occupation of their territory after 1941.

Between 1941 and 1944 all seven of these national groups were forcibly relocated and their autonomous republics effectively dissolved.[28] In addition, the more disparate Greek population of the Black Sea and Sea of Azov regions was dispersed and resettled in stages during the 1940s.

The rationale employed by Stalin to justify the exile of these national populations involved four major elements: (a) they were said to have resisted and to

---

Twentieth Century: A View from Within," *Cahiers* (April – June 1975): 245–77; Alexandre Bennigsen and Chantal Lemercier-Quelquejay, *La presse et le mouvement national chez les musulmans de Russie avant 1920* (Paris, 1964); and G. E. von Grunbaum, "Problems of Muslim Nationalism," in *Islam and the West*, ed. Richard Frye (Gravenhage, 1957), pp. 7–29.

28 The Volga Germans were the first group deported. Their removal was authorized by a decree on August 28, 1941. The Karachay and Kalmyks were deported in October – November 1943 and December 1943, respectively, while the Chechen and Ingushi were exiled in March 1944. The Crimean Tatars were not removed until the Soviet reoccupation of the Crimea. The actual date of the beginning of their removal was May 18, 1944.

have continued to oppose the forced socialization of agriculture; (b) they harbored unacceptable minority nationalist aspirations; (c) they were *in potentia*, if not also in fact, pro-Nazi,[29] and (d) they were targeted, as part of Russia's expansionist industrial and agricultural plans, to supply part of that laboring population which could be redeployed in underdeveloped, geographically isolated areas of the Soviet Empire. Another, not implausible, reason has also been advanced for at least some of the removals in the area of the Crimea – namely that Stalin harbored sinister geopolitical designs on Turkish territory after the war. The Muslim and Turkic populations of the borderlands were perceived as a threat to this expansionist ambition.

Regarding the truth of these differing charges and pretexts, the following details should be noted.

(A) Collectivization

All seven of these minority nationality groups opposed the injudicious policy of collectivization from its beginnings in 1929, suffering substantively, even abysmally, as a consequence. The programmatic confiscations of property and the rigorous socialist remaking of the countryside (which included the exile of many individuals from these ethnic blocs to Siberia and the camps of the Gulag) won few friends for the revolutionary agricultural effort in these communities. Throughout the inhospitable mountain terrain of the North Caucasus region, minority uprisings in opposition to this vast, transformational schema occurred. They were put down with great ferocity by the Red Army. As early as 1929, 40,000 Balkars were either exiled or died of famine as a direct result of compulsory collectivization. In this same period, as an integral part of the same violent confrontation, 30,000 to 40,000 Tatars and approximately the same number of Chechen-Ingushi were deported. This was only the beginning of the terror. In the partially government-induced famines of 1932–33, tens of thousands of the minority populations would die. (Some scholars have suggested that this desolate event can also be seen as an immensely hostile governmental act to punish and break minorities unreconciled to implacable socialist imperatives.) Yet, even after such punishing measures, these minority peoples continued, if in a less activist mode, to resist the collectivization program. After the Nazi invasion of Russia in 1941 this opposition, at least in certain border areas, once again became more direct and explicit. In response, Stalin, under the banner of national self-defense in time of war, finally put an end to resistance against what had become the hallmark of his commitment to the socialist transformation of Russia.

---

29 On this sensitive question see Joachim Hoffmann, *Deutsche and Kalmyken 1924 bis 1945* (Freiburg, 1974); Patrick von zur Malden, *Zwischen Hakenkreuzund Sowjetstern: Der Nationalismus der sowjetischen Orientvollcer im Zweiten Weltkrieg* (Dusseldorf, 1971); and Norbert Faller, *Wehrmacht and Okkupation 1941–1944* (Berlin, 1971).

(B) The nationalist issue

The undisguised desire for autonomy and independence by these minorities threatened the dismemberment of the Soviet state. With the Nazi occupation of large parts of the USSR, its dissolution became more than an idle and distant possibility. Though the Soviets had sought to limit and control earlier geopolitical threats through the creation of "autonomous" national republics in the 1920s, this compromise did not remove incremental pressures for more complete independence. Nor did it strike a workable, satisfactory balance between "center" and periphery. As a result, the nationality issue would not go away, nor was the unequal and unfair distribution of power between the majority and the minorities appreciably altered.

Transfiguring the meaning and significance of this territorial threat was Stalin's instinctive and parochial Russian nationalism. The dying Lenin, as early as 1923, had privately recorded his extreme unhappiness with Stalin's illiberal approach to the nationality question. The minorities, he wrote, suffered "from invasion of their rights by this typical Russian man, the Chauvinist, whose basic nature is that of a scoundrel and oppressor."[30] The defining considerations in this critical situation, cannot however, be reduced to one of individual psychology, however perverse. Socialist theory recognizes the absolute *moral* priority of class over national interests. "There are cases," Stalin wrote, "when the right of self-determination conflicts with another, a higher right – the right of the working class.... In such cases – this must be said bluntly – the right of self-determination cannot and must not serve as an obstacle to the working class in exercising its right to dictatorship."[31] In the event, under the cover of this ideological justification, almost the entire national minority leadership was purged in the 1930s and 1940s. For example, the political leadership of the Chechen-Ingushi Republic was destroyed in 1937, with many of the Republic's 14,000 "leaders" arrested and murdered. Similar repression occurred in the Balkar, Karachay, and Tatar areas, and among the Kalmyks.[32]

Such a proletarian, anti-nationalist ideology logically aspires in its maximalist form to ethnocide (or perhaps a more accurate term would be "politicide"). If national identity threatened the class unity of the international working class and its champion, the Soviet Union, then such divisive self-consciousness, with all its attendant features of language, religion, national literature, particularistic calendars, and schooling, must be forfeit. At its most radical, this was precisely what Stalin's systematic design of national expatriation sought to accomplish.

---

30 V. I. Lenin, *Works*, vol. 40 (Moscow, 1950), p. 356. Further consideration of Lenin's position on the nationality issue is provided by B. Nahaylo and V. Swoboda, *Soviet Disunion*, pp. 50–59.
31 J. Stalin, *Works*, vol. 5, 270, cited by Robert Conquest, *The Soviet Deportation of Nationalities* (London and New York, 1960), p. 105.
32 Conquest, *Soviet Deportation*, pp. 84–87.

The Stalinist program of complete cultural conversion through migration (to the extent that there was such a conscious plan) directly and indirectly caused up to 500,000 deaths. It is therefore a paradigmatic instance of ethnocide facilitated through mass murder. But it was neither intended, nor did it become in practice, an example of physical genocide, i.e., the complete physical extermination of a minority nation. The intent was to destroy a variety of minority cultures and the political ambitions built upon them, rather than to murder all the members of a specific people. The growth in the minority populations after removal and the initial period of transition is incontrovertible evidence as to the non-genocidal intentions of the Stalinists.

Two additional aspects of Stalin's assimilationist, "internationalist" agenda, with regard to the national minorities (despite his arbitrary, chauvinistic equation of socialism with Russian national culture) throw light on the non-genocidal character of these deportations. First there is the much discussed Stalinist project of forced Russification of indigenous cultures. Such a far-reaching scheme could be proposed and pursued precisely because the indigenous peoples were not to be eradicated. By comparison, the Nazis had no comparable program for Jews because there was no need to re-educate a people who are about to disappear. There was no point in recreating their linguistic base if they were all shortly to be corpses, no need to convert them religiously and to remake them culturally, if they were soon thereafter to be immolated. Stalin's efforts at acculturation, his ideal of assimilation, was precisely the reverse of Nazi policy towards the Jewish People. Jewish assimilation was seen as an enormous threat by Hitler to be fought without compromise for it allowed the Jew to conceal his real nature and to disguise his unalterable bio-metaphysical characteristics. It made the Jew all the more dangerous in the socio-political, economic and sexual realm, with all the attendant negative racial consequences. For this reason, Hitler's anti-Jewish crusade necessarily entailed complete Jewish *disassimilation*. For example, every Jew had to insert the name Sarah or Abraham into their given name and mark their often-indistinguishable appearance through the wearing of the yellow star. Any sexual contact and intermarriage with non-Jews were strictly prohibited.

If we consider the persecution of the intellectual and leadership elites among the Soviet national minorities, both before and after deportation, then the objective of ethnocidal domination rather than unrestrained physical genocide becomes even more clear. In the case of the Kalmyks there was an assault against the Buddhist religious leadership.

> The purge destroyed the entire Kalmyk intelligentsia, which had never been large. The majority were charged with bourgeois nationalism, or with working with foreign countries. As many as 5000 persons were liquidated. The entire priesthood, the most highly educated section of the

population, which in 1926 numbered about 3,000 persons . . . was liquidated. All Buddhist temples and all sacred treasures were destroyed.[33]

For the Chechens and Ingushis this entailed:

> Arrests [that] continued until the beginning of 1938. The chief sufferers were the new national intellectuals. The leading Party members among the North Caucasians, including all members of the Party oblast committees, the national parliament, the government, scientists, writers, journalists, etc., were among those arrested. The leading national intellectuals were charged with organizing a "counter-revolutionary and bourgeois nationalist center" in Chechen-Ingushetia, whose members were alleged to have engaged in preparation for an armed uprising against the Soviet regime in 1922–23, in sabotage, in organizing terrorism, etc. All of the 137 persons accused of belonging to the counter-revolutionary center were members of the Communist Party, and 60 percent of them had been educated in special Communist training schools.[34]

In the particular instance of the Balkars and Karachay, "the NKVD struck first at the remnants of the pre-revolutionary non-party intellectuals."[35] Then at their national cultural institutions:

> On the pretext of liquidating "the consequences of the sabotaging activity of these enemies of the people," meaning the "bourgeois nationalists," the "Pan-Turks," "the Pan-Islamites," and the Trotskyite and Bukharinite elements in the North Caucasus, the entire national literature, both original and in translation, was destroyed, including all school textbooks and teaching aids; all fiction, including translations from the Russian and world classics; almost all scientific, technical, and agricultural literature; all historical and philological literature; all works of reference and dictionaries; and all Party and Soviet literature, including translations of Marx, Engels, Lenin, and Stalin. By the first half of 1938 everything in the North Caucasus under the name of "culture, national in form and socialist in content" had been destroyed. So that no trace might remain of this "form," the Kremlin in 1939 "recommended" to the peoples of

---

33 Dorza Akbakov, "The Kalmyks," in *Genocide in the USSR: Studies in Group Destruction*, ed. Nikolai K Deker and Andrei Lebed, trans. Oliver J. Frederiksen (New York, 1958), p. 34. On the religious anti-Buddhist aspect, more specifically, see the papers by Nicholaz N. Poppe, "Attempted Distribution of other Religious Groups," and Shamba Balinov, "The Kalmyk Buddhist," in *Genocide in the USSR*, pp. 181–92 and 193–96 respectively.
34 R. Karcha, "The Peoples of the North Caucasus," *Genocide in the USSR*, p. 39.
35 *Ibid.*

the North Caucasus and later to all the Turkic and Moslem peoples of the USSR that they adopt the use of the Russian alphabet instead of the Latin.[36]

A similar tale could be told in the case of every national bloc that was deported, as well as in the case of other minority nationality groups that were not uprooted but subjected to other forms of state pressure.

What these measures demonstrate is that though Soviet cultural hegemony recognized few limits to its chauvinistic self-aggrandizement, Stalinist extirpation of the cultural and political elites was the converse of a program of total extermination. Stalinism annihilated the leadership in order to preserve the mass, if in a culturally altered state.

The continued existence in reduced circumstances of hundreds of thousands of these uprooted peoples is certain proof that Stalin did not intend their complete liquidation. In their new eastern environments, they were put to work primarily, though not exclusively, in agriculture. A considerable minority segment of this now available manpower was enlisted in ongoing mining and industrial projects, such as the difficult task of building the railroad system in the Lake Issyk-Kul region. The explanation for this pragmatic outcome is to be found in Stalin's *Weltanschauung*. Marxist-Leninist socialism, even when crudely interpreted by Stalin, imputed the criminality of the class enemy to an acquired false consciousness created by objective economic and social structures. The threatening "otherness" of the other, having been learned, can also be unlearned. Hence the doctrinal basis for the centrality of political re-education in Marxist-Leninist theory, whatever the deplorable abuses of this dogma in Soviet practice. Even when the internal opposition is most dangerous, and its insidious perversions threaten the world-historical victory of the working class, the prime source of danger is the result of an ideological misreading of events, a normative misperception of "what is to be done." For this reason, the criminality of the "class enemy," or of the "bourgeois nationalist," however destabilizing and reactionary, is a threat of an altogether different order from that represented by the "racial enemy." In the Manichean biocentric ontology of Nazism where individuals are seen as the biological carriers of essential genetic and metagenetic attributes, their negative behavior (and being) can never, by definition, be unlearned. The Nazi racial ideology of conflict therefore produces physical genocide rather than repression, socio-economic re-education, the Gulag, national deportations, or mass death.

The stark disparity between Nazi and Stalinist analyses of the type of danger represented by their "opponents," and hence the alternative type of actions deemed appropriate in response, is revealed in the post-exilic history of the deported Soviet national minorities. Stalin possessed the police power and

---

36 *Ibid.*, pp. 40–41.

necessary ruthlessness to carry out a program of physical genocide against the minority peoples had he so intended. The decisive fact is that he chose instead a policy of compulsory resettlement and colonial expansion in underdeveloped and underpopulated regions of Russia. As a result, three years after Stalin's death, there were sufficiently large numbers of the deported minority peoples in existence to make their "rehabilitation" both an empirical possibility as well as a Soviet political necessity. Nikita Khrushchev's speech to the Twentieth Party Congress in February 1956 was the highly dramatic beginning of a public recantation of Stalin's past "errors." He spoke of "gross violations of the basic Leninist principles of the nationalities policy of the Soviet state," referring to the national deportations of the Karachay, Chechens, Ingushi, Balkars, and Kalmyks. This was the start of a series of practical reforms relating to the minority groups, including the official reestablishment of most of their autonomous republics. As a result:

> Of the seven deported nations three resumed their old constitutional status. One has been downgraded; and one was downgraded for a time then restored to its old status[37] and two others, numbering at least 584,000 in 1936, have had no rehabilitation at all.[38]

The number of minority peoples available for repatriation under this change of policy, allowing for all the imprecision in the relevant demographic statistics, was, in 1953, somewhere between a minimum of 280,000 and a maximum of 603,400, excluding the Volga Germans and Tatars.[39] If we add the German and

---

37 These five include the Karachay, Chechens, Ingushi, Balkars, and Kalmyks.
38 The two were the Volga Germans and Crimean Tatars. The Meskhetians were also not repatriated. However, the Volga Germans were granted cultural privileges such as the opening of two German newspapers, German language radio broadcasts, and the teaching of the German language, B. Nahaylo and V. Swoboda, *Soviet Disunion*, p. 126; Conquest, *Soviet Deportations*, p. 143.
39 1959 is the first year for which census data are available following Stalin's death in 1953. W. Kolarz, *Russia and Her Colonies* (New York, 1952), p. 75, puts the Volga German population in 1941 at 480,000. Of these, 200,000, or about 40 percent, were exiled by the Russians while the Germans during their occupation of the region deported the remaining 280,000, or about 60 percent, to Germany. A. Sheehy and B. Nahaylo give the higher estimate of 400,000 Soviet deportations. Interestingly, in response to continued protests from this German community within its borders, the Soviets allowed 55,000 Soviet Germans to leave Russia between 1970 and 1979. A. Sheehy and B. Nahaylo, *The Crimean Tatars, Volga Germans and Meskhetians*, 3rd. ed. (London, 1980), p. 5. I arrive at these numbers as follows. For the maximum, I use the 1959 Russian census figures: for the Chechens, 418,000; the Ingushi, 106,000; the Kalmyks, 106,000; the Karachay 81,000; and the Balkars 42,000. These total 758,000 less 20 percent for natural increase (a rough, perhaps too high, concession to population growth) between 1953 (the year of Stalin's death) and 1959. For the lower figure, I have used R. Conquest's estimate of an absolute minimum less the same 20 percent, though Conquest himself, in his final reckoning, favors the less severe tally of 490,000 survivors rather than the extreme figure of 350,000 (in 1959) that I have employed. See Conquest, *Soviet Deportations*, p. 170. According to NKVD archives the total number of Chechen, Ingushi, Karachay, and Balkar deportees between 1943

Tatar population the figures increase dramatically.[40] The 1959 census lists the total Soviet German population at 1,619,000.[41] Though the number of surviving Crimean Tatars is difficult to estimate with precision, their population by the late 1950s was considerable. Roy Medvedev, in trying to reconstruct their national odyssey, suggests that 50 percent of the original 200,000–250,000 deportees died, but this is certainly too high a figure.[42] A loss rate of about 30 percent (plus or minus 5 percent) appears more in keeping with the data that we have. Building from this post-removal base of between 140,000 and 175,000 their population advanced until it again numbered in the region of 200,000 to 250,000 by 1953. At the same time, the Tatar population in the Soviet Union as a whole grew in the 1950s reaching, according to 1959 estimates, 4,967,700. This was an increase of 15 percent over what it had been in 1939. These aggregates for the Tatar community are all subject to revision, but they indicate the continued existence of this minority group, even under the rigors of exile. When all these population estimates from 1959 are added together, and the required backward demographic extrapolations are made, the resultant sum of survivors reveals that a large percentage of the resettled minorities were *not* murdered by Stalin. Indeed, the total population of the five main minority peoples – excluding the Volga Germans and Tatars – was only 20 percent smaller in 1953 (on the maximum estimate cited above) than it had been in 1939, just two years before the forced deportations began. If we include the numbers for the Volga Germans and Crimean Tatars, the population of the seven deported national groups was in fact greater in 1953 than

---

and 1949 was 608,749 of whom 184,556 "disappeared [*ubylo*] due to various causes"; figures reported by N. F. Bugai, "The Truth About the Deportation of Chechen and Ingush Peoples," *Soviet Studies in History* 30.2 (Fall 1991): 78.

40 The Volga Germans and Crimean Tatars were not included in the policy of return decreed in 1957 because their war record was considered to have been so reprehensible. However, in August 1964 the Volga Germans were politically rehabilitated. Finally, in 1967 the Tatars were partially rehabilitated though their Crimean territory was not returned to them. Consult for the particulars of the 1957 act and for developments during the 1960s, A. Sheehy, *The Crimean Tatars, Volga Germans and Meskhetians*, p. 13. On Tatar resistance to continued Soviet oppression following the institution of Khrushchev's policy of rehabilitation for the other deported minorities, see Borys Lewytzkyj, *Politische Opposition in der Sowjetunion 1960–1972* (Munich, 1972); and A. Sheehy and B. Nahaylo, *The Crimean Tatars, Volga Germans and Meskhetions*. Further information on the contemporary fate of the German population in the Soviet Union is provided by Sidney Heitman, *The Soviet Germans in the USSR Today* (Cologne, 1980); and Isabelle Kreindler, "The Soviet Deported Nationalities: A Summary and Update," *Soviet Studies* 38.3 (July 1986), pp. 387–405.

41 The 1970 Soviet census gives their total number at 1,846,000.

42 Roy Medvedev, *Let History Judge* (Oxford, 1989), p. 492. This is consistent with the Tatars' own estimate of casualties that has been put at 46 percent during the removals and during their first 18 months in their new surroundings, Sheehy and Nahayalo, *Crimean Tatars, Volga Germans and Meskhetians*, p. 8. Soviet figures suggest a smaller percentage of casualties, certainly for the deportation phase itself. This Soviet claim is supported by the demographic estimates of A. Fischer who calculated that the Tatar population in 1978 was 450,000 (*Crimean Tatars*, p. 700) a figure that certainly could not have been reached if the loss among the original population of 200,000 to 250,000 was anywhere near as high as 50 percent.

it had been in 1939.[43] In effect, there were many hundreds of thousands, even millions of minority individuals that Stalin could have killed but did not, as a result of his restraining ideology.

Kampuchea

Let us consider one final case of mass death as a species of class war: Kampuchea. Between 1975 and 1978 Cambodia was a living hell. In many ways the people of Cambodia were the main victims of the Vietnamese war. The radical instability caused and sustained by that misconceived, ineffectively managed adventure spilled over into Cambodia and undermined its native institutions. This made possible the victory, in an extended civil war, of the fanatical Communist Khmer Rouge in April 1975. The exact details of what happened next are still uncertain and subject to widely different interpretations. Yet there is no doubt that an astonishing, if unconscionable, revolutionary transformation of the existing social order was attempted, with thousands upon thousands of casualties in its wake.

In making its singular vision real, the Khmer Rouge held that not only must existing class modalities be destroyed but the individuals who had inhabited these outmoded and perfidious structures must be either fundamentally reformed or killed.

In the eyes of Pol Pot, there were three types of enemies: the "capitalists," shopkeepers and traders; the "feudalists," Buddhists, intellectuals, and royalty; and finally, the largest category of all – the "imperialists." They included ethnic minorities who dressed or spoke differently from the Khmer, as well as so-called agents of the CIA, the KGB, or the Vietnamese.

These groups – that is, the persons who comprised them – were, by definition, "enemies of the people" and therefore had to be socially reeducated and remade into productive agricultural labor, or else eliminated. No third way was permissible. Any compromise was a betrayal of the revolution and hence itself a capital crime. Total revolution, the absolute recreation of the civic and cultural order, the reduction of the body-politic to only peasants and party members, was not a task easily accomplished, and it produced its carnal sacrifices, even in the hundreds of thousands.

Nevertheless, certain distinctive features of this situation need be understood. First, the overwhelming majority of victims came from the majority population. They were not singled out for belonging to specific ethnic stock as in tribal wars in Africa; or for membership in a particular religion as in the Huguenot wars, the

---

[43] In reaching this conclusion I have employed the following statistics for 1953: Crimean Tatars 200,000; Volga Germans, 600,000; the five main minority peoples, 603,400; making a total of 1,403,400. This exceeds the original deportations for these seven groups, on Conquest's numbers, by about 67,000.

Pakistan-Indian conflict, the wartime Croatian massacres of Serbs, the Turkish slaughter of Armenians, or the various persecutions of Jews. True, the Vietnamese, Chinese, and Cham communities in Cambodia were persecuted for being what they were. However, great care must be taken in labeling the persecution of these ethnic minorities as genocide, for they do not appear to have been marked out for complete physical annihilation.

The Khmer Rouge, for example, ordered the eviction of 150,000 (out of about 200,000) ethnic Vietnamese living in Cambodia – no matter how long their residence had been – rather than murder them. The later murder in 1978 of most of the remaining ethnic Vietnamese came in the wake of intense Cambodian-Vietnam political tensions between 1976 and 1978 and the attempted assassination of Pol Pot by Cambodian troops believed to be linked to the Vietnamese regime. Again, the undeniable persecution of the large Chinese community (numbering up to 425,000 in 1975) half of whom are said to have died between 1975 and 1978, is not explicable simply as racial prejudice. As Ben Kiernan has shown, it was directly related to class status, i.e., the role of the ethnic Chinese community as an urban "middle class.[44] And even then, "[The] Chinese . . . were targeted in an indirect way, as the archetypal urban dwellers (and therefore "exploiters"), and they suffered far more from enforced starvation and disease."[45] This conclusion is supported by the fact that the location to which individual Chinese were deported directly impacted on their chance for survival. If they were deported to the now overpopulated northwest region, where conditions were chaotic, food in short supply, due to the massive influx of 230,000 people from Phnom Penh in 1975 – overwhelming the original population of 170,000 – then the death rate was high. If, however, the Chinese were deported to the Southwest or Eastern Zones, the rates of survival were far higher. This disparity makes clear that there was no central program of Chinese extermination but rather a massively cruel policy in general, that fell disproportionately on city dwellers ill-equipped for their new life in the rugged countryside – among whom the Chinese were again disproportionately represented. Moreover, "there was no noticeable racialist vendetta against people of Chinese origin in Democratic Kampuchea," and the "tragedy of Kampuchea's Chinese was not that they were singled out for persecution by an anti-Chinese regime, but rather that a pro-Chinese regime subjected them to the same brutal treatment as the rest of the country's population."[46]

The case of the Muslim Cham people is still more ambiguous. There is no doubt that many Cham were killed by the Khmer Rouge. However, the larger Khmer Rouge governing strategy towards the Cham appears not to have required the death

---

44 Ben Kiernan, "Kampuchea's Ethnic Chinese Under Pol Pot," *Journal of Contemporary Asia* 16.1 (1986): 26–27. Kiernan gives the figure of 425,000 Chinese in Kampuchea in 1975, and a death rate of 50 percent: 18.
45 *Ibid.*, 18.
46 *Ibid.*, 20.

of all Cham, though it certainly required uprooting the distinctive Cham culture and its social and political manifestations. Ben Kiernan has identified the persecution of the Cham, which appears to be rooted in class distinctions as much as racial or religious ones, as an instance of physical genocide that claimed 90,000 victims out of 250,000 Cham. Michael Vickery, however, has questioned this description noting that, "unfortunately Kiernan has tinkered with the statistics in a tendentious manner in an attempt to prove the case for genocide."[47] Rather than a roughly 34–35 percent loss rate (based on a population of 250,000 in 1975), the actual rate of loss allowing for some natural growth in the Cham population between 1975 and 1979, is approximately 10 percent – and not genocidal. Though one must be cautious here, and no hard evidence exists to support Vickery or Kiernan, these debates should be taken as a warning not to proceed too quickly or casually. Support for Vickery's position comes from the presence of Mat Ly, a Cham, on the standing committee of the People's Representative Assembly since April 1976 and from the fact that many Cham once resettled on the agricultural collectives – their distinctive Islamic culture shattered – were not then singled out to be murdered. Certainly, such acts as forcing Cham women to cut their customarily long hair, forcing Cham men and women to adopt a more conventional manner of dress, to abandon their own language, to eat pork, to give up their copies of the Koran, and the disbursement of Cham villages, are all acts of ethnocide. I note in support of this judgment that in his paper, "Orphans of Genocide," Kiernan acknowledges that: "the documentary case [for physical genocide] is weak."[48] Moreover, and this is not unimportant, the murder of the Cham appears to have varied from location to location. "In parts of the Center and East in particular, there were apparently massacres of Cham as such, but Chams from the Northwest and North assert that they were not the object of any special attention by the authorities and that they survived in the same proportion as other people."[49]

The majority of those murdered in Kampuchea were identified as *ideological* enemies (along class and military lines) and they were eradicated as political opponents. However, even with regard to class enemies there is reason to question

---

47 Michael Vickery, "Comments on Cham Population Figures," *Bulletin of Concerned Asian Scholars* 22.1 (1990): 31–33. An accusation to which Kiernan replied, "The Genocide in Cambodia, 1975–79," *Bulletin of Concerned Asian Scholars* 22.2 (1990): 35–40. The earlier Finnish Commission cited a decline of 75 percent in the Cham population, from 200,000 in 1975 to 50,000 in 1979. But the basis of these figures was unreliable, and more Cham survived than the 50,000 here indicated, K. Kiljunen (ed.), *Kampuchea: Decade of the Genocide* (London 1984), p. 34.
48 Ben Kiernan, "Orphans of Genocide: The Cham Muslims of Kampuchea under Pol Pot," *Bulletin of Concerned Asian Scholars* 20.4 (October–December 1988): 2. See his summary of the evidence for cultural genocide, *ibid.*: 32–33. David Hawk's more recent statement, almost completely derived from Kiernan's work, is even more confused regarding the issue of the appropriateness of the charge of genocide – which he applies. See his essay, "International Human Rights Law and Democratic Kampuchea," in *The Cambodian Agony*, ed. D. Ablin and M. Hood (New York, 1990), p. 129.
49 M. Vickery, *Cambodia: 1975–1982* (Boston, MA, 1984), p. 182.

the completeness and thoroughness of the purge by the Khmer Rouge. Undoubtedly many bureaucrats, intellectuals, civil servants, artists, and entrepreneurs were executed. But, at the same time, one must take into account the number of individuals – in the hundreds of thousands – coming from these hated classes, who survived both within Cambodia and as refugees in neighboring Vietnam and Thailand. Thus, it is open to serious doubt whether every member of these "socially unprogressive" and "parasitic" groups was marked out for extermination. The brutal "re-education camps" established by the new regime – though places of mass death – are significant counter-indicators to those who argue for genocide. These camps did have survivors. The Khmer Rouge did feel themselves successful in at least some small way in transforming the enemy class consciousness of the former bourgeoisie, and so permitted individuals who belonged to "counter-revolutionary classes" to take their place in the new order. For example, it appears that there were considerable numbers of Buddhist monks – there were approximately 80,000 monks in 1975 when the CPK took power – who fell into this category. The same appears to apply in the case of agricultural engineers and doctors who, after time in these "reduction camps," were integrated into the regular agricultural collectives. As a result, 50 percent of the physicians remaining in Cambodia in April 1975 survived the Khmer onslaught against society. This, of course, means that 50 percent of physicians died – but in their totality these figures indicate the complexity, the compromise, the mediation that is here at issue. Even the Khmer Rouge did not insist on the death of *all* its class enemies, now remade into farm laborers. The evil of class could be shed, transformed, and a productive individual remade out of the former economic oppressor. This is significantly different from the ineradicable stigma of *racial* distinctiveness attached to those, like the Jews, earmarked for extermination under Nazi rule.

UPDATE

This second essay focuses on three cases of mass murder committed by Communist regimes. The first of these concerns Stalin's deportation of a variety of groups, most specifically the Kulaks and the several national minorities that he found ideologically and politically threatening. The second is the Holodomor, the lethal famine in the Ukraine in the first half of the 1930s. The third is the extraordinary violence perpetrated by the Khmer Rouge in Cambodia. My interest in these events does not reside in their historical details per se – though one must always get the details right – but, rather, in how and if they might be said to compare to the "Final Solution."

Close study of these three events, each peculiar in its own way, suggests that while all of them involved nightmarish brutality and each was exceedingly costly in human lives, none can be correctly described as genocidal.[50] And this because the number of deaths involved in the deportation of the Kulaks, the losses caused by the Ukrainian famine in the early 1930s, and the data on the deported national minorities – the Balkars, Karachay, Checken, Inguslu, Volga Germans, Kalmyks, and Tatars[51] – all indicate that, while Stalin had ideological reasons related to the matters of class and national identity for pursuing the deadly policies that he did, he did not intend to completely destroy the groups he targeted. He permitted the majority of the Kulaks to survive on collective farms, and the majority of the national minorities to continue to exist. (I use the term "permitted" after much careful reflection on its appropriateness.) As for Cambodia, the statistics related to the "revolution from below" show that Pol Pot's persecutions left room for many of the victim groups he persecuted to go on living, if not as they had, or in exile from Cambodia.

To begin our analysis, consider the ideologically inspired revolutionary, class-related, chaos that overtook Cambodia in the 1970s. Since then, there has been intense debate regarding how this extreme political event should be understood and classified. Distinguished scholars, like David Chandler,[52] have been cautious about labeling it "genocide," while Ben Kiernan has made a career of doing just this.[53] Why this has proven such a complex and uncertain task is, once again,

---

50 As I define this term.
51 Recent work that speaks to this issue includes Pavel Polian, *Against Their Will: The History and Geography of Forced Migrations in the USSR* (Budapest, 2003); Norman Naimark, *Fires of Hatred: Ethnic Cleansing in Twentieth-Century Europe* (Cambridge, MA, 2001); M. Pohl, "'It Cannot Be that Our Graves will be Here': The Survival of Chechen and Ingush Deportees in Kazakhstan, 1944–1947," *Journal of Genocide Research* 4.3 (2002): 401–30; and Nicholas Werth, "Handling an Awkward Legacy: The Chechen Problem, 1913–1958," *Contemporary European History*, 5.3 (2006): 342–66.
52 David Chandler, *Brother Number 1: A Political Biography of Pol Pot* (Boulder, 1992); and idem, *The Tragedy of Cambodian History: Politics, War, and Revolution since 1945* (New Haven, CT, 1993).
53 Ben Kiernan, *The Pol Pot Regime: Race, Power and Genocide in Cambodia under the Khmer Rouge, 1975–82*, 2nd edition (New Haven, CT, 2002); and see the relevant chapter in *idem, Blood*

a matter of definition. Employing the confused and confusing understanding of the UN. *Convention on Genocide*, Kiernan has argued that the "Khmer Rouge committed genocide against the Cham minority group, the ethnic Vietnamese, the Chinese and Thai minority groups, and the Buddhist monkhood."[54] But the fact is, whatever the U.N. definition, the Khmer Rouge, activated by its "purist" Communist ideology, did not seek, and was not required to seek, the death of *all* members of these "enemy" groups in the way that the Hitler state sought, on its racist-metaphysical principles, to murder *all* Jews, everywhere.

Among its radical, insistent, state actions, the Khmer Rouge forcibly transported between 40,000 and 60,000 Buddhist monks to the countryside as part of their war against traditional religion and the old regime, but they did not see the need to kill them. Rather, the monks were forced to work in the labor brigades. Thus, though many of them died from the appalling material conditions and the overwhelming hunger, they were not intentionally killed. The same pattern of persecution was essentially followed vis-à-vis the Muslim Cham people. The 250,000 Cham were forced into the labor brigades in the villages where many died, but their deaths were not an intentional act of total mass murder as is indicated by a survival rate of 64 percent among this national community.[55] As for the 175,000 Vietnamese living in Cambodia at the time when Pol Pot came to power, the great majority, up to 150,000, were forced to leave the country. This was a major act of ethnic cleansing, but it was not an instance of mass murder. As for the Thai and Chinese who were resident in the country and identified as enemies of the regime, 40 percent of the Thai were killed, and 50 percent of the Chinese lost their lives.[56] Given their absolute vulnerability, the Khmer Rouge could have exterminated all the Thai and Chinese individuals resident in Cambodia but they did not choose to do so.

As for deconstructing Stalin's many mass crimes, I believe, in spite of the literature that has been produced in the past three decades, that my analysis of the *ideological* reasons that provoked and justified this monumental effort to politically refashion and economically modernize the Soviet state is still accurate. Stalin did not wish, nor intend, to murder all Kulaks – the majority survived – nor to exterminate all of the Ingushi, Volga Germans, or Tatars, nor, under very different circumstances, all Ukrainians. And I still hold the view, with increased confidence in light of recent scholarship, that the brutality shown by Stalin in the Ukraine was necessarily linked to the pressing matter of nationalism. Thus, one could decapitate Ukrainian nationalism without decapitating all Ukrainians. When this essay, "Mass death," was originally written, as readers can see, I was not certain that the "nationalist" interpretation, that laid the blame for the hunger in the Ukraine between 1932 and 1934 squarely on

---

and Soil: A World History of Genocide and Extermination from Sparta to Darfur (New Haven, CT, 2009), pp. 539–70.

54 Ben Kiernan, "Documentation Delayed, Justice Denied: The Historiography of the Cambodian Genocide," in *The Historiography of Genocide*, ed. Dan Stone (Houndmills, 2008), pp. 47–49.

55 Norman Naimark, *Genocide: A World History* (Oxford, 2017), p. 102.

56 *Ibid.*

Stalin's shoulders, was altogether correct. Thus, I wrote of accepting the "nationalist interpretation of Ukrainian history, at least for the sake of argument" (p. 37). Today, the substantial research that has been done over the last thirty years has removed all doubts as to whether this interpretation is the correct one.

The new documentation on the Holodomor (killing by hunger) supports, first of all, an estimate of 4 to 5 million deaths. As such, it confirms the earlier estimate of Robert Conquest,[57] and others. Some recent accounts put the total upwards at 7 to 8 million, but this is beyond the consensus estimate. Second, the evidence now available makes it absolutely certain that it was Stalin's actions and decisions that caused the famine to become as consequential as it became. That is, the famine was, for Stalin, a cynical means by which to destroy Ukrainian national ambitions and identity. In effect, what transpired is that, over the opposition of the local Communist Party leaders, who Stalin concluded were colluding with the peasants, the First Secretary ordered the export of grain from the Ukraine in spite of the obvious hunger that dominated the region. A situation caused, in the first instance, by a shortfall in overall agricultural production in 1931 and 1932, due to the program of collectivization. Though informed of the dire food shortage Stalin did not believe the reports regarding the famine, holding instead that the peasants were hoarding grain and intentionally subverting the collectivization of agriculture.

Because of the number of deaths that the famine caused, that approaches the 6 million Jews extirpated by the Nazi regime, the Holodomor is regularly part of the scholarly conversation of comparative issues related to the Holocaust and the issue of genocide. As regards this conversation, I will not enter into a discussion as to the meaning of genocide here as this is discussed elsewhere in this volume.[58] Furthermore, my concern at present is *not* the subject or the meaning of "genocide" *per se* but rather the issue of the comparison of the national Ukrainian tragedy to the Holocaust and the subject of uniqueness. Regarding this topic, I continue to hold that however one wishes to identify the Ukrainian famine – i.e., as a "genocide" or not – the murder of European Jewry has a different and distinctive phenomenological structure that fundamentally differentiates it from the Holodomor, most especially due to the singular, uncompromising, exterminationist goals of National Socialism.

Significantly, even recent advocates of the application of the term "genocide" to the Ukrainian famine agree on this divergence. Norman Naimark, in his study of the Holodomor, has asked, "Can the Ukrainian famine be considered genocide?" and answered: "It would seem so."[59] Yet he recognizes that, "Of course, Stalin did not want to kill all Ukrainians or deport them all to Siberia, the Far North, or Central Asia." Rather, his ambition was "to destroy them as the enemy nation he

---

57 Robert Conquest, *Harvest of Sorrow: Soviet Collectivization and the Terror Famine* (London, 1986).
58 I briefly mention this issue in my essay "On the Holocaust and comparative history" (Chapter 1), and discuss it again, in some detail, in the article entitled "On the definition of Genocide and the issue of uniqueness" (Chapter 5).
59 *Stalin's Genocides* (Princeton, 2010), p. 74.

perceived them to be."⁶⁰ Instead, of mass annihilation he intended, as Naimark tells us, "to transform them into a Soviet nation that would be completely reliable, trustworthy and denationalized in all but superficial ways."⁶¹ Hitler, in contrast, did not want to transform Jews. Because of their race they could never, under any circumstances, be made "reliable, trustworthy, and denationalized." He wanted only to eliminate them. This very distinctive intention creates an unclosable theoretical – and then ontological – gap between what took place in the Ukraine and what took place in Nazi-occupied Europe.⁶²

The statistics that I cite in the present essay regarding the death rate among Ukrainian children are here relevant and, among other implications, they reinforce my methodological principle that the fate of children in the cases of mass death is a telling indicator of what is determinative in a given situation. Thus, when one compares the rate of loss among Ukrainian children one learns that, on the most negative estimates, 33 percent of children in the region died during the famine. This represents, without any question, an immoral outcome of the highest order. Yet, in an investigation of the similarity of the Holodomor to the Holocaust, one finds that in the latter, in locations like Lithuania, Belorussia, Thessaloniki (Greece), the Ukraine and Poland, the death rate of Jewish children was 95 percent or more. This is not to make a moral comparison, i.e., to mistakenly claim that what occurred in the Holocaust was morally worse than what took place in the Holodomor, but to point out that the purpose, the agenda, driving the Ukrainian losses was very different than the *Weltanschauung* that caused the death of almost all Jewish children in Eastern Europe.

Nicolas Werth has recently made the same case as Naimark vis-à-vis the Holodomor. He, too, describes the Ukrainian famine as "genocide" but once again identifies it as being "very different from the Holocaust" because it did not aim to physically eradicate the entire Ukrainian nation. He observes: "It was not based on direct murder of the victims but was motivated and planned on the basis of a political rationale, not ethnic or racial themes."⁶³ Werth does, however, note the comparable number of victims in the two cases. However, it needs to be pointed out that numbers per se do not define an event as "genocide."⁶⁴

Norman Naimark has made the same point in concentrating on the fate of children in Auschwitz and the Holodomor.

> Yet from a historical perspective, which is not necessarily the same as that of the victim or the perpetrator, it seems evident, as stated above,

---

60 *Ibid.*, p. 78.
61 *Ibid.*
62 Among the victims of the famine, the population in Kazakhstan lost the largest percentage of its population, 38 percent. N. Naimark, *Stalin's Genocides*, pp. 75–76. The full story of the terrible reality created in Kazakhstan is ably retold by Isabelle Ohayon, *Due nomadisme au socialisme: Sédentarization, collectivization et acculturation des Kazakhs en USSR, 2918–1945* (Paris, 2006).
63 Nicolas Werth, "The Crimes of the Stalin Regime: Outline for an Inventory and Classification," in *The Historiography of Genocide*, ed. Dan Stone (Houndmills, 2008), p. 415.
64 This crucial methodological issue has been more thoroughly analyzed in *The Holocaust in Historical Context*, pp. 65–99.

that the Holocaust is the most extreme case of genocide in human history. This comes from the apocalyptic nature of the Nazi racial utopia, the complete helplessness of the Jews in face of the attack on their very existence as a people, the sheer extent of the killing, and the industrial nightmare of the gas chambers and ovens of the elimination camps. As Richard Evans writes, "There was no Soviet Treblinka, built to murder people on their arrival." Therefore, Courtois's comparison between the death of a child by starvation in the Warsaw Ghetto and that of a child caught up in the Ukrainian famine is a false one when comparing the larger dimensions of the Holocaust to Soviet mass killing. The legitimate comparison is between the fate of the child in Auschwitz or Treblinka and that of a child in famine-stricken Ukraine or in the Gulag. The Ukrainian child in the Soviet countryside or the child in the Gulag had a chance to survive; the Jewish child in the death camps was condemned to death, even if there were scattered exceptions.[65]

In the most recent major study of the Ukrainian famine, *Red Famine: Stalin's War on the Ukraine*, Anne Applebaum concludes her work by directly taking up the comparison between the Holodomor and the Holocaust, and then offering this unambiguous judgment: "Stalin did not seek to kill all Ukrainians, but Stalin did seek to physically eliminate the most active and engaged Ukrainians, in both the countryside and the cities."[66] And going still further, she strikingly observes that the events in the Ukraine do not even conform to the U.N. definition of genocide.[67] In Applebaum's view: "it is now difficult to classify the Ukrainian famine . . . as genocide in international law."[68] The most up to date scholarship on the Holodomor, in fact, makes my point as to uniqueness thirty years after my initial claim.[69]

---

65 Norman Naimark, *Stalin's Genocides*, pp. 122–23.
66 Anne Applebaum, *Red Famine: Stalin's War on Ukraine* (New York, 2017), p. 347.
67 Compare here Raphael Lemkin's alternative conclusion in his 1953 lecture "Soviet Genocide in the Ukraine," referred to by Applebaum, *Red Famine*, p. 349.
68 Applebaum, *ibid.*, p. 350.
69 Besides the studies of Naimark, Werth, and Applebaum that have been referred to, the most important recent works on the Ukrainian famine are: Terry Marten, *The Affirmative Action Empire: Nations and Nationalism in the Soviet Union 1923–1939* (Ithaca, 2001); R. W. Davies and Stephen Wheatcroft, *The Years of Hunger: Soviet Agriculture, 1931–1933* (New York, 2004); and Andrea Graziosi, "Les famines soviétique de 1931–1933 et le holodomor ukrainien. Une nouvelle interpretation est-elle possible et quelles en seraient les circonstances," *Cahiers du monde russe* 46.3 (2005): 453–72, available in English translation as "The Soviet 1931–1933 Famine and the Ukrainian Holodomor: Is a New Interpretation Possible and What Would Its Consequences Be?" in *Hunger by Design: The Great Ukrainian Famine and its Soviet Context*, ed. Halyna Hryn (Cambridge, MA, 2009). All the essays in this volume are informative and relevant to the present conversation. See also Michael Ellman, "Stalin and the Soviet Famine of 1932–1933 Revisited," *Europe-Asia Studies*, 59.4 (2007): 663–93; and on the differing explanations of how to account for the famine, consult Roman Serbyn, "The Ukrainian Famine of 1932–33 as Genocide in Light of the UN Convention of 1948," *Ukrainian Quarterly*, 62.2 (2006): 87–106. Bohdan Klid and Alexander Motyl have edited an informative collection of sources under the title, *The Holodomor Reader: A Sourcebook on the Famine of 1932–1933 in Ukraine* (Edmonton, AB, 2012). It includes both scholarly articles and eyewitness accounts and memoirs.

3

AUSCHWITZ AND THE *GULAG*: A STUDY IN DISSIMILARITY

I

Scholars and others have, for various reasons, been likening Auschwitz and the *Gulag* since the 1940s, and the comparison has become "canonical" since its powerful employment by Hannah Arendt in *The Origins of Totalitarianism*, first published in 1951.[1] Today this linkage is again at the center of the historical and normative discussion due to its vital role in the "Historical Debate" generated in Germany by the obscene nationalist apologetics of Ernest Nolte and his supporters.[2] But is this accepted historical piety correct? I think not. In contradistinction to Arendt and Nolte,[3] and others, I want to argue that the usual analogies drawn between these two evil phenomena are largely and essentially misleading, even fundamentally incorrect.

Before proceeding, however, let me be very clear about what I am and am not saying. The disjunctiveness that I will argue for is not moral – that one environment was more evil than the other (though this may also be the case) – but phenomenological, that is that the two contexts were created by, organized through, and employed in and for vastly different purposes, with nearly wholly different regulative ideologies. In their design, empirical facticity, intentionality, and teleology, they are radically alternative forms of manipulation, violence, and death. Both Auschwitz and the *Gulag* perpetrated monstrous acts of inhumanity and it is the recognition of this fact that leads to the intuitive assertions regarding their commonality. But on other than ethical grounds, and the unsparing moral condemnation of both, the comparison is misleading. That is to say, the awareness of this primal ethical similarity must serve as the beginning of a conversation not its conclusion if we are not to lapse into intellectual barrenness, into that type of conceptual sterility

---

[1] Hannah Arendt, *The Origins of Totalitarianism* (New York, 1951; revised edition New York, 1966).
[2] Fuller details of this debate are provided by Charles Maier, *The Unmasterable Past: History, Holocaust, and German National Identity* (Cambridge, MA, 1988); and *Historikerstreit: Die Dokumentation der Kontroverse um die Einzigartigkeit der Nationalsozialistischen Judenvernichtung* (Munich, 1987).
[3] In mentioning these two individuals together I do not mean to equate Arendt's employment of this connection with that of Nolte.

that is a corollary of an inability to make necessary, if hard, distinctions. And it is to the making of such repercussive phenomenological discriminations as a moral obligation, as a debt to the truth, that we must now turn, inquiring in what ways the *Gulag* is comparable to Auschwitz, in what way it is not.

II

The intriguing, not altogether transparent, exposition of the larger social-historical contexts out of which Nazism and Stalinism respectively grew is where we must begin.[4] Nazism emerged out of the turmoil of the post-World War I years, out of the inability of Germany to admit its own responsibility for defeat, out of the lack of viable democratic traditions in Germany, exacerbated by the inherent weaknesses of the Weimar state,[5] and out of the economic chaos created by the combination of reparations required by the Versailles Treaty and the "Great Depression." Yet it occurred in a highly modernized, technologically and culturally advanced society.[6] By contrast, Stalin came to power in the wake of a violent revolution wrought by an ideological, urban minority whose achievement of political control was in direct violation of those very Marxist theories in whose name it seized power. The Revolution and Stalin's eventual triumph occurred in a society which was generally backward[7] and underdeveloped in every sense and, importantly, that was accustomed to harsh autocratic government maintained by force, secret police agencies, and detention camps, chronicled so powerfully by Dostoevsky:[8] a society without any tradition of political freedom or human rights. It was therefore not altogether unexpected that Bolshevism should, once it had seized political power, replace one menacing dictatorship with another.[9] Certainly

---

4 The particulars of the Nazi onslaught against Jewry is described and analyzed exhaustively in my study, *The Holocaust in Historical Context* (Oxford, 1994).

5 On the growth and importance of antisemitism in the Weimar Republic, consult my essay, "1918 and After: Antisemitism in Weimar," in *Antisemitism in Times of Crisis*, eds. Steven T. Katz and Sander Gilman (New York, 1990).

6 The many complex issues of the post-1918 situation in Germany will be analyzed in much greater detail, especially as they bear upon questions of German and Nazi antisemitism, in a future volume of my project, *The Holocaust in Historical Context*.

7 For example, only 33 percent of the population could read in 1920. See, for more, Jean Elleinstein, *The Stalin Phenomenon* (London, 1976), pp. 15–16.

8 Note especially his *The House of the Dead* (1861–62). See also D. Dallin and B. Nicolaevsky, *Forced Labor in Soviet Russia* (New Haven, CT, 1947), pp. 299–305; and particularly Richard Pipes' extreme view of the origin of and continuity between the Soviet police state and its Czarist predecessor, *Russia Under the Old Regime* (New York, 1974). The work of Solzhenitsyn is, of course, relevant here as well.

9 We note that the White Russian army and its short-lived terror were not very much different. Consider, for example, the pogroms in the Ukraine that caused thousands of casualties. It was a case of terror on the right and terror on the left. For fuller analysis of the Ukrainian situation see James Mace, *Communism and the Dilemmas of National Liberation: National Communism in Soviet Ukraine, 1918–1933* (Cambridge, MA, 1983); and J. Borys, *The Sovietization of the Ukraine* (Edmonton, AB, 1980).

the revolutionary leadership was not averse to the use of force to maintain itself, as the Kronstadt[10] uprising and its suppression showed; or again, as the coming into being of the Checka revealed. Indeed, Lenin seems to have felt such repression was a necessary condition for the maintenance of a proletarian revolution.[11] Thus, the ground for the bureaucratic, centralized, dictatorial, if not murderous, regime was established,[12] to be exploited to its full potential for evil, as well as transmuted in unprecedented[13] ways, by Lenin's successor, Comrade Stalin.

Stalin, with his immense energy, uncanny cunning, total unscrupulousness, and eccentric psychology, which included considerable native intelligence, would exacerbate, in central areas even recreate and transmogrify through a quantitative radicalness, all existing problems.[14] His parochial Russian nationalism[15] would bring him into conflict with Russia's minorities; his uncompromising drive towards rapid industrialization would produce the terrible, ravaging collision with the peasants (not only the wealthy Kulaks); and his egomaniacal hunger for absolute power would cause his paranoic fear of any and all holders of power, no matter how marginal or delimited, within the state, and lead thereby to the many bloody party and army purges that mark his tenure as the leader of the Soviet

---

10 The entire Kronstadt experiment has been described in the recent excellent study by Israel Getzler, *Kronstadt 1917–1921: The Fate of the Soviet Democracy* (Cambridge, UK, 1983); and the earlier work by Paul Avrich, *Kronstadt, 1921* (Princeton, 1970).
11 Cf. Lenin's 1917 essay, *Can Bolshevites Retain State Power?* For discussion of the early history of the *Checka* and *GPU* see Ronald Hingley, *The Russian Secret Police: Muscovite, Imperial Russian and Soviet Political Security Operations 1565–1970* (London, 1970); Boris Lewytzkyj, *Die rote Inquisition: die Geschichte der sowjetischen Sicherheitsdientse* (Frankfurt A.M, 1967); Simon Wolin and Robert M. Shesser, *The Soviet Secret Police* (New York, 1957); and Elleinstein, *The Stalin Phenomenon*, pp. 20–29. Reference should also be made to Solzhenitsyn's treatment of, and quotation from, Lenin in *The Gulag Archipelago*.
12 On the meaning of the Civil War for later Soviet policies, see Sheila Fitzpatrick's interesting study, *The Civil War as a Formative Experience* (Washington, D.C., 1981). See also on this important issue Ronald Gregor Suny, *The Baku Commune 1917–18* (Princeton, 1972); David Lane, *The Roots of Russian Communism* (Assen, the Netherlands, 1969); Robert Service, *The Bolshevik Party in Revolution, 1917–1923: A Study in Organizational Change* (New York, 1979); T. H. Rigby, *Lenin's Government, Sovnarkom 1917–1922* (Cambridge, UK, 1979); and Sheila Fitzpatrick, *The Russian Revolution* (Oxford, 1982).
13 There can be no doubt that Stalinism, in its use of mass murder, transcends the Czarist past. Czarist policy was oppressive in the extreme but judging by all available statistics *not* murderous to any marked degree, as A. Solzhenitsyn points out in his *Gulag*. In the 50 years before the revolution the Czarist regime, with all the provocation of the anarchists and other revolutionaries, executed fewer than 15,000 individuals. On this issue see also R. Conquest, *Kolyma* (New York, 1979), pp. 229–30.
14 This claim, of course, depends on how one understands the relation of Stalin and "Stalinism" to previous events in Russian history both Czarist and Bolshevik, an issue too complex to enter into in detail here.
15 Stalin's Russian nationalism represented something very different from Lenin's attitude to other nationality groups. The brief encouragement of minority national identities under Lenin (d. 1924) and for a brief period thereafter, e.g., the brief flourishing of Ukrainian, Armenian, Muslim, Tatar, and Yiddish cultures, was soon eclipsed by a militant, homogenizing Russian cultural imperialism.

Union.[16] Together these factors, always combined with his heightened political instincts and total lack of political morality, would sweep away all real and imagined opposition, leaving him not only the undisputed ruler of Russia, but the greatest murderer, in quantitative terms, history has ever known.[17]

---

16 On these purges, see Robert Conquest, *The Great Terror: Stalin's Purge of the Thirties* (New York, 1968), and the additional sources cited in the next note.

17 For a more detailed investigation of this highly complex problem see, among many relevant sources, Robert Conquest, *The Great Terror, idem, Kolyma, idem,* "Forced Labor Statistics: Some Comments," *Soviet Studies* 34.3 (July 1982): 434–39; *idem, The Harvest of Sorrow: Soviet Collectivization and the Great Famine* (New York, 1986); Josef G. Dyadkin, *Unnatural Deaths in the USSR, 1928–1954* (New Brunswick, 1983), to be used with care, cf. the review by Michael P. Sacks in *Slavic Review* 43.1 (Spring, 1984): 119–20; Frank Lorimer, *The Population of the Soviet Union: History and Prospects* (Geneva, 1946); Mikhail Heller and Aleksander Nekrich, *Utopia in Power: The History of the Soviet Union from 1917 to the Present* (New York, 1986); Jerry Hough and Merle Fainsod, *How the Soviet Union is Governed* (Cambridge, MA, 1979); Moshe Lewin, *Russian Peasants and Soviet Power* (Evanston, 1968); Robert A. Lewis, Richard H. Rowland, and Ralph S. Clem, *Nationality and Population Change in Russia and the USSR: An Evaluation of Census Data, 1897–1970* (New York, 1976); Murray Feshbach, "The Soviet Union: Population Trends and Dilemmas," *Population Bulletin* 37.3 (August, 1982): 3–44. The most intense debate on the issue has been carried out since 1981 between Steven Rosefielde who favors very high mortality estimates for the Stalinist era: "Collectivization, Gulag forced labour and the terror apparatus that sustained the Stalinist system appear to have claimed the lives of 21.4 to 24.4 million adults and 7.2 to 8.0 million children. An additional 14.4 million unrealized births unrelated to the war may also be included in this inventory, bringing the total population deficit attributable to Stalin's forced industrialization policies to 43.8 to 46 million people; figures more than double the 20 million civilian and military casualties incurred during the war," in "Excess mortality in the Soviet Union," (full bibliographical citation below), and Stephen G. Wheatcroft who has been aggressive in defending much lower estimates. For the acrimonious dialogue between these two see Steven Rosefielde, "The First 'Great Leap Forward' Reconsidered: Lessons of Solzhenitsyn's *Gulag Archipelago*," *Slavic Review* 39.4 (December, 1980): 593–602; *idem,* "An Assessment of the Sources and Uses of Gulag Forced Labor 1929–1956," *Soviet Studies* 33.1 (January 1981): 51–87; Stephen G. Wheatcroft, "On Assessing the Size of Forced Concentration Camp Labour in the Soviet Union, 1929–56," *Soviet Studies* 33.2 (April, 1981): 265–95; *idem,* "Towards a Thorough Analysis of Soviet Forced Labour Statistics," *Soviet Studies* 35.2 (April, 1983): 223–37; Steven Rosefielde, "Excess Mortality in the Soviet Union: A Reconsideration of the Demographic Consequences of Forced Industrialization 1929–1949," *Soviet Studies* 35.3 (July, 1983): 385–409; *idem,* "Excess Collectivization Deaths 1929–1933: New Demographic Evidence," *Slavic Review* 43.1 (Spring 1984): 83–88; Stephen G. Wheatcroft, "New Demographic Evidence on Excess Collectivization Deaths: Yet Another *Kluvkva* from Steven Rosefielde," *Slavic Review* 44.3 (Fall, 1985): 505–508; and Steven Rosefielde, "New Demographic Evidence on Collectivization Deaths: A Rejoinder to Stephen Wheatcroft," *Slavic Review* 44.3 (Fall, 1985): 509–16. A further evaluation of the issues discussed by Rosefielde and Wheatcroft, favoring Wheatcroft's position in general, can be found in Barbara A. Anderson and Brian D. Silver, "Demographic Analysis and Population Catastrophe in the USSR," *Slavic Review* 44.3 (Fall, 1985): 517–36. In this context one should also read Stephen Wheatcroft's two complementary papers, "Famine and Factors Affecting Mortality in the USSR: The Demographic Crisis of 1914–1922 and 1930–33" and "Famine and Factors Affecting Mortality in the USSR: The Demographic Crisis of 1914–1922 and 1930–33, Appendices," both published in *The Soviet Industrialization Project Series*, pamphlet numbers 20 and 21, University of Birmingham, UK. The basic work done in Russia has been that of B. Urlanis, whose major demographic studies are, unfortunately, still not translated.

Of great importance is the fact that the historical context, the political culture and socioeconomic realities, out of which Stalinism emerged and in which it functioned, were markedly different[18] from that of Nazism. In Nazi Germany, because of its virulent antisemitic legacy (shared with most of Europe), and, even more, due to its own contemporary ideological constructions which led to genocide, the Jews were singled out for "metaphysical," i.e., racial and Manichean, reasons. There was, neither in 1933 nor subsequently, any fundamental political or economic[19] gain in persecuting them, despite much widespread misunderstanding to the contrary. In Russia the Terror was, in contrast, a function of politics and economic policy (industrialization) plus Stalin's mental instability – a murderous quirkiness[20] he shared with Hitler.

Put another way, Hitler could have pursued all the dominant goals in his political revolution, e.g., national renaissance, *lebensraum*, even the dis-emancipation of western Jewry, without the "Final Solution" – assuming for the moment that killing Jews *per se* was not his major goal, as it seems finally to have been.[21] In contrast, Stalin could not have succeeded in his push towards rapid collectivization and the transformation of the fundamentals of the Soviet economy as part of the overall socialist transmogrification of Russian society without a direct clash with the peasantry as well as a deadly collision with the remaining elements of the pre-revolutionary socioeconomic structure that still survived.[22] He could,

---

18 Hannah Arendt's attempt in *The Origins of Totalitarianism*, and the derivative efforts of those many others who have followed her lead, to portray Stalinism and Nazism as two forms of a common political reality called "Totalitarianism" is seriously flawed and leads to more distortion than illumination in the final analysis of these two movements.

19 The "economics" of antisemitism are complex, but I would argue that economic justifications are "bad reasons for what people believe on instinct." Jews did *not* control the German national economy as the antisemites claimed, and their purge would not "free" the economy in any appreciable way.

20 Robert Tucker has described both Stalin and Hitler as "warfare personality" types, a category he defines as follows:

> The warfare personality shows paranoid characteristics as psychologically defined, but what is essential from the standpoint of our discussion is that it represents a *political* personality type. The characteristically paranoid perception of the world as an arena of deadly hostilities being conducted conspiratorily by an insidious and implacable enemy against the self finds systematized expression in terms of political and ideological symbols that are widely understood and accepted in the given social milieu. ("The Dictator and the Totalitarian," *World Politics* 17.4 [July 1964]: 555–83)

21 See his "Last Testament," for example.

22 The intimate relationship between modernization and conflict in the Stalinist era has been amply studied. Among the more reasoned analyses are N. Valentinov, *The NEP and the Party Crisis* (Stanford, 1971); Cyril E. Black (ed.), *The Transformation of Russian Society: Aspects of Social Change Since 1861* (Cambridge, MA, 1967); Alex Inkeles, *Social Change in Soviet Russia* (New York, 1971); E. H. Carr and R. W. Davies, *Foundations of a Planned Economy, 1926–1939*, 3 vols. (New York, 1969–71); Nicholas Lampert, *The Technical Intelligentsia and the Soviet State* (New York, 1971); Alexander Ehrlich, *The Soviet Industrialization Debate, 1924–1928* (Cambridge, MA, 1960); and R. V. Daniels, *The Conscience of the Revolution: Community Opposition in Soviet Russia* (Cambridge, MA, 1960). On the economic situation under NEP see V. N. Bandera, "The New Economic Policy (NEP) as an Economic System," *Journal of Political Economy* 71.3 (June 1963): 265–79.

of course, have taken a different tack on economic policy, as Lenin and others had thought the better course, but once he decided on radical socialization and industrialization, or as he might argue in his own self-defense, with some modest justifications, once these policies were forced by events upon him, extensive, pervasive conflict was inevitable. Isaac Deutscher has thoughtfully described the inherent confrontation in these terms:

> It would be easy for the historian to pass unqualified judgement on Stalin if he could assume that in his fight against Bukharin, Rykov, and Tomsky he pursued only his private ambition. This was not the case. His personal ends were not the only or the most important stakes in the struggle. In the tense months of 1928 and 1929 the whole fate of Soviet Russia hung in the balance.

On the face of things, the opening of the crisis was so undramatic as to appear irrelevant. The peasants had failed to deliver a few million tons of gain to the towns. Prosaic as the event was, there was real drama in it. In refusing to sell food, the peasants had no clear political motives. They did not aim at the overthrow of the Soviets, although some of the politically minded elements among the well-to-do peasantry hoped for such an ending. The mass of the peasants was driven to apply that peculiar form of "sabotage" by economic circumstances. Most of the small farms did not produce more than was needed to feed their owners. After more than ten years the agricultural upheaval of 1917 was now taking its revenge. The splitting up of large estates into tiny holdings had given the Bolsheviks the support of the peasantry in the Civil War; but in consequence the productivity of farming, or rather its capacity to feed to the urban population, deteriorated. The big farmers, on the other hand, demanded high prices for food, prices intolerably burdensome to the townspeople; and they also pressed for further concessions to capitalist farming. Stalin was, indeed, confronted with a most complex dilemma. If he yielded more ground to the peasants he would dangerously antagonize the urban working classes, which, on the whole, now again stood behind the Government, especially after the Government had, about 1927, succeeded in rebuilding industry to its pre-war condition. But the refusal to yield to the peasantry also entailed the threat of famine and unrest in the towns. The problem demanded a radical solution. If the Government had begun to curb the big farmers and to encourage gradual collectivization earlier, as Trotsky and Zinoviev had counselled, it might not have needed now to resort to drastic emergency measures in orders to obtain bread. As things stood, Stalin acted under the overwhelming pressure of events. The circumstance that he was not prepared for precipitated him into a course of action over which he was liable to lose control.[23]

Survival, economic and national, not ontological fantasies, was the key determinant. That is to say, the contextual consideration of the terror in Russia suggests that

---

23 Isaac Deutscher, *Stalin: A Political Biography* (New York, 1949), pp. 317–18.

Stalin was confronting, to some degree at least, real[24] enemies both politically and in class terms during the 1920s, and possibly up until 1934–36.[25] By contrast, the Jews of Germany (and Europe) were not, except by definition, an authentic, political "enemy."

Still more, despite scholarly claims to the contrary,[26] Stalinism is not a complete *novum* in Bolshevik (and earlier Russian) tradition; it is, for all its radicalness, even recognizing its innovativeness, intimate with the Russian past. Not so the Nazi death camps. Auschwitz was unpredictable before it occurred, while having occurred it is not accounted for, not explained, by precedents, despite the many terrible antisemitic precedents that do exist. A student of Czarist coercion and Leninist ideology would not be totally surprised, as the vast secondary literature proves, to encounter the phenomenon of the *Gulag*, though its sheer magnitude would still ravage one's sensibilities. By contrast, no study of pre-1933 German or modern Western European history would suggest, or *ex post facto* explain, Treblinka and *Einsatzgruppen*. Looking back one can find "roots," but no amount of such "backward looking" historiography is sufficient to the reality. What occurred not only so exceeds what was "predictable," but in its qualitative dimensions is so discontinuous with it immediate pre-history as to represent its antithesis. The uncompromising, revolutionary evil of Auschwitz as compared to the massive, unceasing, primitive immorality of the *Gulag*, therefore conjures a different mood, a dissimilar cognitive response. The Holocaust remains always "beyond comprehension," an event as much revealed as mysterious, much as we must insist that it be open to scholarly investigation and ordinary rules of historical and philosophical enquiry. It is these very qualities that lead to the constant temptation – *to be resisted* – to remove it altogether from history. By contrast, the *Gulag* generates rage and dread, anger and sorrow, but not mythification. One is prepared, alas, to find it all too believable.

III

It may be that this impression, this disjunctive response, rests ultimately on the assimilability of the *Gulag* to two not unfamiliar historical categories, penal detention and slavery, that mix together in a particularly better way to create the Stalinist camps. Penal institution, including the use of special incarceration centers for political "dissidents," is an all too common historical phenomenon.[27]

---

24 "Real" does not mean I approve, nor that Stalin was the "good" guy and the enemies the "bad" guys. It means only that Stalin had cause to be concerned with, for example, Trotsky and his faction on the one hand and the peasants on the other.

25 See A. Ulam, *Stalin*, p. 295, for more on this issue.

26 Consider, for example, the argument of S. Cohen, "Bolshevism and Stalinism," *Dissent* (Spring 1977). See also Robert Tucker's revisionist thesis in the same general direction though much more subtly and dialectically stated, and therefore also perhaps embodying a more profound contradictoriness, "Stalinism as Revolution from Above," in *Stalinism: Essays in Historical Interpretation*, ed. R. Tucker (New York, 1977), pp. 77–110.

27 The history and character of such penal institutions has been described in Michel Foucault's interesting, but limited, *Discipline and Punish: The Birth of the Prison* (New York, 1977); U. R. Q. Henriques, "The Rise and Decline of the Separate Systems of Prison Discipline," *Past and Present*

For example, the Nazi use of internment camps from 1933, e.g., Dachau, for political enemies such as Communists and liberals, is a parallel occurrence belonging to this general history and need not detain us.[28] The same may be said of the schematic role and temporal evolution of Czarist prison institutions into Bolshevik ones. Dostoevsky's *The House of the Dead* leaves us no innocent illusions on this subject. The relation of Stalin's *Gulag* to the normative structures of slavery,[29] however, requires a closer, adequately nuanced, look. The basic, compelling comparability of the two oppressive configurations lies in their purposeful, aggressive exploitation of human labor, i.e., both are rooted in and maintained by specific economic and social needs that are held to be best met by unfree labor.[30] Stalin's policy of the forced acceleration of industrialization was "aided"[31] by reducing a significant percentage of Russia's population into, effectively, "slaves," if by another name. Through this coercive labor policy, rooted in the Czarist past,[32] the inmates of the camps were made to provide crucial cheap labor for all forms of Soviet industrialization ranging from the mining of raw materials to the building of transportation networks.[33] Representing, at its peak, on some accounts, more than one-sixth[34] of the male adult population, this

---

54 (1972): 61–93; and George Ruschke and Otto Kirchheimer, *Punishment and Social Structure* (New York, 1939).

28 It should, however, be remembered that so-called "concentration camps" are to be clearly distinguished from death camps, i.e., places created primarily, if not solely, to kill people. The existence of industrial complexes at Auschwitz should not be misunderstood, i.e., as mitigating their overall genocidal charge, for all their workers were scheduled to die as a result of their work. Also, Treblinka, Belzac, Sobibor and Chelmno had no work camps.

29 The salient, complex comparative questions raised by the historical institution of slavery are taken up in detail in *The Holocaust in Historical Context*, vol. 1 (*Roman Slavery*) and my two-volume study, *The Holocaust and New World Slavery*.

30 A sad story with many earlier chapters. One such abuse which is paradigmatic of many is that of sixteenth-and seventeeth-century galley slavery on which see Paul Bamford, *Fighting Ships and Prisons: The Mediterranean Galleys of France in the Age of Louis XIV* (Minneapolis, 1973).

31 I use this term in quotation marks in light of the counter-claim advanced in many recent studies, particularly of the agricultural sector, that contend that this policy was counter-productive even on the basis of strict economic rationality. For myself, I am not altogether convinced by these arguments against the strictly economic benefits of this activity, which, vis-à-vis industrialization, seem positive and meaningful. It seems to me that while this collectivized labor was not efficient it did produce modest results when all elements are factored in, which were exaggerated enormously by Stalin and the ruling elite. This however, of course, does not mean that I would agree that this was the best way to achieve such results.

32 The use of criminal proceedings and institutions to assure needed labor is an old policy not only in Russia but elsewhere in Europe.

33 A full list of camps and the type of work carried on in them is given in David J. Dallin and Boris Nicolaevsky, *Forced Labor in Soviet Russia*, pp. 58–72.

34 All demographic statistics provided in this paper are provisional and the subject of great scholarly debate. For an introduction to the problematic aspects of this basic issue see: Dallin and Nicolaevsky, *Forced Labor in Soviet Russia*, who give a figure of 5–6 million slave workers in 1937 and 8 million "slave" workers in 1941; Steven Rosenfielde, who provides very high estimates of 8 million *Gulag* workers in 1937, 10 million in 1940, and 12–15 million in 1946–50; "An Assessment of the Sources and Uses of Forced Labor, 1929–1956," *Soviet Studies* 1 (January, 1981): 51–87;

"enslaved" group comprised the largest single industrial working class in Russia. Moreover, this captive class was able to be set tasks that were: (a) necessary to the economy as a whole, yet which were situated in places where labor on the free market would have been very costly to procure;[35] and (b) that could be accomplished by the calculated substitution of a large work force in place of expensive machines, machines that could only be procured through foreign currency that the Soviet Union did not have.[36]

What requires particular recognition is that this slave labor system was not created as the result of the devastation wrought by World War I, nor the consequences of special short-term problematics, aberrations, in the life of the Stalinist regime, though the numbers of such workers did vary from period to period. Rather, and unmistakenly, it was inherent, as Solzhenitsyn has so dramatically emphasized, in the very fabric of Stalinism *per se*.[37] The abiding constitutive excess which was a dominant feature of Stalinism was predicated upon, enacted within, an already grotesque, authoritarian, order. Not only in the *Gulag* empire, but throughout the Soviet economy, coercion was the norm after 1929. The brutalities of agricultural collectivization form an essential ingredient in our schematic deconstruction, and to them must be added the extensive reorganization of (regular) industrial labor in 1930 that led, for example, in December 1938, to the system of industrial passports and in October 1940 to the introduction of severe penalties for lateness and absenteeism, and curtailment of the workers' freedom in job selection.[38] Even more significant, analogous in intent to slave labor, is the

---

Stephen Wheatcroft concludes that "some four to five million is the maximum number of concentration camp labourers who could have existed in 1939," "On Assessing the Size of Forced Concentration Camp Labor in the Soviet Union, 1931–1956," *Soviet Studies* 2 (April, 1981): 286, the entire essay covers pp. 265–95; *idem*, "Towards a Thorough Analysis of Soviet Forced Labor Statistics," *Soviet Studies* 2 (April, 1983): 223–37; R. Conquest, *The Great Terror*; and *idem*, "Forced Labor Statistics: Some Comments," *Soviet Studies* 3 (July, 1982): 434–39. Conquest puts the figure of slave laborers at 8 million or above, *Great Terror*, Appendix A. On Soviet manpower note, in addition, Warren W. Eason, "Forced Labor," in *Economic Trends in the Soviet Union*, ed. Abram Bergson and Simon Kuznets (Cambridge, MA, 1963), pp. 38–93; N.S. Timasheff's much lower estimate (2.3 million) of forced labor in 1937 in his "The Post War Population of the Soviet Union," *The American Journal of Sociology* 54 (1948): 148–55; and N. Jasny "Labour and Output in Soviet Concentration Camps," *Journal of Political Economy* 59.5 (October, 1951): 405–91, who gives a lowish figure of 2.5 million *Gulag* workers in 1941.

35 More details in support of this view can be found in Roy Medvedev, *Let History Judge*, p. 394.
36 Dallin and Nicolaevsky, *Forced Labor in Soviet Russia*, pp. 88–90, discuss this issue more fully. Also note the comments of Robert Conquest, *Kolyma*, p. 39; and the observations of A. Ciliga, *Sibërie, terre de l'exil de l'industrialisation* (Paris, 1960).
37 It may well be that part of this problematic is structural, i.e., it is part of the larger problem of trying to re-form Russia on the basis of a Marxist theory ill-suited to the industrial and agrarian realities of Russia in the 1920s. Ulam suggests: "One cannot find out from Marx how to build socialism in a prevailing agrarian society, any more than one can learn how to build a nuclear reactor by reading the works of Newton," *Stalin*, p. 294.
38 This labor reorganization and its implications are analyzed by Solomon M. Schwarz, *Labor in the Soviet Union* (New York, 1952), pp. 209f. This issue and relevant sources were called to my

system of State Labor Reserves[39] established by Stalin in October 1940 which, in effect, created large-scale pools of young, *unfree* industrial workers. According to this scheme, as many as 1 million male teenagers, the majority off the farms, would be "drafted" into technical industrial apprenticeships deemed necessary by the State economic planners. After a training period lasting between six months and two years depending on the job for which one was being prepared, the young man would be assigned to a task to which he was legally bound for four years. In this way a novel method of industrial serfdom was instituted. The Fourth Five-Year Plan called for 4,500,000 such recruits, a major percentage of all industrial employees. And, as in the *Gulag*, such unfree labor was expected to provide, in particular, 70 to 80 percent of the new workers in the heavy industries, e.g., coal mining, the mining of ferrous metals, and machine building.[40] In this sense, then, the *Gulag* can be identified as the endpoint of a spectrum of Soviet labor exploitation rather than as a discontinuous and radical alternative to the "normal" Stalinist social order.

Upon reflection it becomes unarguably clear that those who project a mythical "Stalinism without excess" are twice deluded, once because the notorious extremes were built into a normative, abiding structure that, in and of itself, was barbarously abusive. Hitler, or perhaps more precisely Himmler and Speer,[41] would create, during the war, a somewhat comparable slave empire comprised of captured prisoners of war, overrun Slavic peoples, and even citizens of conquered countries in Western Europe, not to mention the industrial complexes utilizing Jewish labor at Auschwitz and elsewhere. However, Hitler's use of slave labor, whatever its overall qualitative comparability to Stalin's, differed with respect to the expropriation of Jewish labor. Jewish manpower resources were not utilized as slave labor either in the classical, or Stalinist, sense,[42] but rather as, in Benjamin Ferencz's telling phrase, "less than slave [labor]," i.e., the German intent was not to foster economy efficiency, or substantive production gains, but instead, sought to establish the disutilitarian equation that balanced labor utilization with

---

attention by Barrington Moore Jr., *Terror and Progress – USSR* (Cambridge, MA, 1954), pp. 54–55.

39 On this program see Harry Schwartz, *Russia's Soviet Economy* (New York, 1950), pp. 449f.

40 Solomon M. Schwarz, *Labor in the Soviet Economy*, pp. 77–83.

41 Himmler's entrepreneurial ambitions are described in Speer's study entitled *Infiltration: How Heinrich Himmler Schemed to Build an Industrial Empire* (New York, 1981).

42 Jerzy Gliksman, an inmate in the *Gulag*, gives us this accurate understanding of the Stalinist slave-labor system:

> The Soviet *lagers* are in fact institutions practicing slave labor. They are closely tied to various industrial or other enterprises which, in turn, are part of the over-all Soviet economy. They are expected to fulfill their part in the general economic plan and are a tremendous source of cheap labor for this plan. Openly and cynically, without any trace of concern for appearances, the camp inmate is therefore treated simply as a forced supplier of needed work (*Tell the West* [New York, 1948], p. 244).

necessary guarantees that Jewish workers be worked to death in a very specific, highly inelastic period of time.[43]

Stalin's system, in contrast, theoretically at least and more often than not in practice, was predicated on a fixed period of forced labor, the dominant concern of the regime being the realization of the labor quotas, while at the same time being callously, cynically *indifferent* to the survivability of its prisoner labor force. Whether Kolyma workers lived or died was a matter of little moral or practical import, aside from its bearing on productivity, to Stalin or the camp bureaucracy. If inmates could survive under the prevailing execrable conditions, well and good, but their individual fate was not primary – *neither that they survive nor that they die*. The *Gulag*, in the main, during most of the Stalinist era, vis-à-vis the majority, was uncaring, its state-dictated attitude towards its wards expressed in a skeptical, perverse disinterest in their particularity. Without doubt there was in the organization of the *Gulag* much malice, sadism, murder. Brutality was normal, the norm brutal. What was absent, however, was a specific, unambiguous, national policy of mass murder. That is to say, despite the high death toll in the *Gulag*, with the exception of that exception year 1938, the major causes of death in this environment were corollaries of the dolorific natural condition and the official attitude of unconcern which had the impact of ramifying the negative consequences of the ecological habitat. No less a critic of Stalin's Camps than Robert Conquest has summarized these circumstances in the following terms:

> Previous years [pre-1938] had seen, on occasion, massive casualties. But these had been due to inefficiencies in supply, attempts to carry out assignments in impossible conditions, and in fact – if in exaggerated form – the normal incompetence and brutality of Soviet life. When the difficulties could be overcome, conditions, as we have seen, were tolerable. But above all, prisoners were not subjected to lethal conditions on purpose.[44]

Even in that cruelest year, 1938,[45] when Stalin and his new chief henchman for the Kolyma region, Major Garanin, ordered an unprecedented wave of shootings, increased every manner of abuse, and saw to it that conditions went from bad to unbearable, even then, for the entire year, the whole Kolyma district witnessed "only" 40,000[46] shootings, i.e., planned, directly sponsored, intentional, official murders.[47] And, even now, 1938, executions were still coupled to work quotas[48] –

---

43 Raul Hilberg, *The Destruction of European Jewry* (Chicago, 1967), pp. 334–45, discusses the relation of slave labor to survival in detail. His important conclusion: "The Polish Jews were annihilated in a process in which economic factors were truly secondary" (p. 345).
44 R. Conquest, *Kolyma*, p. 47.
45 On these events see R. Conquest, *Kolyma*, pp. 49–66.
46 R. Conquest, *Kolyma*, p. 58.
47 By comparison, the Nazis were killing more Jews in one week at Auschwitz in late 1943 and 1944 than is represented by this *Gulag* total for the entire year 1938.
48 Further details of this deadly activity are provided by R. Conquest, *Kolyma*, pp. 51–52.

and generally unconnected to any other ideological or normative category, e.g., Kulaks, old Bolsheviks, or Jews. This is not to argue that Stalin's new ferocity towards the *Gulag*'s population did not take its considerable, if more oblique, toll during this year. Figures are uncertain, but estimates ranging from 200,000 to 400,000 deaths caused by cold, starvation, and overwork are commonly accepted. For this one year, under these exceptional conditions, the *Gulag* approached Auschwitz *asymptotically*. Asymptotically because even in this worst of years the *Gulag* did not operate under the same equation of life[49] and death as did Auschwitz. The priorities of labor versus death, of productivity vs. dehumanization, did shift towards a heretofore unprecedented near equality; yet even at its nadir, the demands of life, even if translated and reduced to economic units, still had at least equal weight.[50] In this matrix, exploitation and annihilation certainly became too casually contraposed while the original dominant economic drive saw itself paralleled by a corrupt desire to debase, even destroy, many of the Camp inmates. However, even amidst this rueful reevaluation of purposes, at no time was the equation so wholly inverted that death was all; the highest, supreme unchallenged good. Moreover, and elemental to the Nazi vs. *Gulag* comparison, the *Gulag* killed people distributively, i.e., taking its toll on all groups, singling none out for "special treatment."[51] Then again, the powerful streak of harsh realism in Stalin's perception of reality caused him to recognize the need for "compromise" between actual economic requirements and the primitive desire to "punish" real or imagined enemies, while his Marxist-Leninist ideology allowed for such mediation. Alternatively, Hitler's severe biocentric "idealism" encouraged no comparable compromise on the Jewish Question, while his immolating racial metaphysics permitted none.

As a consequence, Himmler's SS empire manifested no such mediating dispositions, nor did it represent similar, primarily utilitarian, priorities, at least not where the *Judenfrage* was concerned. In this arena it was primordially committed not only to Jewish submissiveness, to the exploitation of brutally controlled Jewish labor, but also, and more rudimentarily, to the un-enigmatic biological extinction of each and every Jew trapped within its parameters. Hitler and his Aryan elite were neither skeptical about nor disinterested, *contra* the controlling rationality of the *Gulag*, in the date of "their" Jews – they were, rather, passionate advocates of the universal imperative that all Jews *must* die. Under no conditions, no matter how economically advantageous their efforts and no matter how politically

---

49 This conclusion becomes incontrovertible when one examines in detail the day-to-day conditions in the two environments; i.e., matters of "selections," work assignments, health care, living conditions, sex, women, children, and release, all reveal fundamental differences.

50 Even Robert Conquest, in his most telling indictment of the Stalinist enterprise, does not claim more than this: "All in all, these conditions reflected one main truth. In the minds of its creators and organizers the conscious purpose of Kolyma, which had originally been the production of gold, with death as an unplanned by-product, had become the production, with at least equal priority, of gold and death" (*Kolyma*, p. 124).

51 I.e., in the generality of the *Gulag* life itself.

co-operative Jewry proved itself to be, could it be left to survive. *Mere* Jewish survival was the active enemy. Compared to 40,000 shooting in total in the Kolyma in 1938, 10,000 Jews a day died at Auschwitz in 1944, Treblinka consumed 1.5–2 million Jews in 18 months, and the *Einsatzgruppen* efficiently murdered at least 1.5 million Jews in about the same period of time.

IV

In pointing out the sociological, historical, economic, and ideological factors that operated distinctively and disjunctively in the *Gulag* and Auschwitz we have no desire to relativize one at the expense of the other, nor to deny the immense evil of both. However, evil comes in many forms and it is the task of scholarship, painful and difficult as it might be, to study these variegated forms and to recognize differences as well as similarities between them. When one looks closely at the *Gulag* and Auschwitz in all their destructive complexity, one cannot but be profoundly aware of how very dissimilar they are.[52]

---

52 The full examination of these differences may be found in *The Holocaust in Historical Context*.

UPDATE

The present essay, and the one that follows it, again deal with questions of comparative study relative to the issue of the singularity of the Holocaust and the *Gulag*. Now the focus is on: (a) the differences in the agendas of Stalinism and Nazism; and (b) the way that these differences worked themselves out in practice vis-à-vis the issue of labor. They thus begin to explore a subject, the Nazi use of Jewish labor, that has grown increasingly significant in my research, as readers will clearly see in the essay entitled "Extermination trumps production" in this volume (Chapter 7).

As noted in my "Update" to chapter 1, there has been a good deal of valuable new research on the *Gulag* spurred by the fall of the Soviet Union and the opening of KGB and other state archives. This research, based on new sources, has made possible a much closer, more detailed, examination of such fundamental matters as Soviet decision making, the role of bureaucratic initiatives in the expansion of Stalinist policy, the role of specific individuals in the upper levels of the Soviet regime, and the way in which state violence was carried out and the policy of terror was pursued.

What this new research reveals is that the number of individuals imprisoned in the *Gulag* was smaller than previously thought – about 18–20 million – and that the number who died in its camps was lower than prior accounts had estimated. Of the tens of millions incarcerated in the *Gulag*, the now much more complete demographic record indicates that there was a total of 1,800,000 deaths.[53] As a percentage of the total of those held captive, this represents a loss of less than 10 percent. These numbers, both in absolute and percentage terms, persuasively indicate the fundamental difference between being imprisoned in the *Gulag* versus Jewish imprisonment in both Nazi work camps and death camps.

In the Soviet universe of camps, "Apart from 'politicals' who were invariably sentenced to a minimum spell of ten years, nearly always extended, the other detainees spent an average of five to six years in a camp, if they survived that long."[54] The majority of Russian camp inmates lived through the horrific experience to which they were subjected, and returned to mainline Soviet society. I would specifically note that millions of *Gulag* prisoners (over one million) were liberated during World War II and immediately taken into the Red Army, and that, following Stalin's death, millions more were set free.[55] In contrast, most

---

[53] The relevant demographic data has been provided by Anne Applebaum, *Gulag: A History* (New York, 2003); Nicolas Werth, *Cannibal Island: Death in a Siberian Gulag* (Princeton, 2007); Lynne Viola, *The Unknown Gulag: The Lost World of Stalin's Special Settlements* (Oxford, 2007); Steven Barnes, *Death and Redemption: The Gulag and the Shaping of Soviet Society* (Princeton, 2011); Oleg Khlevniuk, *The History of the Gulag: From Collectivization to the Great Terror* (New Haven, CT, 2004); and M. Khlusov, *The Economics of the Gulag and Its Part in the Development of the Soviet Union in the 1930s: A Documentary History* (Lewiston, NY, 1999).

[54] Nicolas Werth, "The Crimes of the Stalin Regime: Outline for an Inventory and Classification," in *The Historiography of Genocide*, ed. Dan Stone (Houndmills, 2008), p. 403.

[55] *Ibid.*, p. 402.

Jewish prisoners sent to Auschwitz, Treblinka, Sobibór, Bełżec, and Chełmno were murdered on or soon after arrival at a rate of 90 percent (or more), with the governing intention that even those selected for slave labor – approximately ten percent of arrivees at Auschwitz, fewer at the other killing centers – would soon be dead. Accordingly, this recent reevaluation of the relevant demographic data on the *Gulag* has confirmed my judgment that there was a fundamental, purposeful difference between the intentions guiding the Soviet and National Socialist systems respectively.

This conclusion, and my confidence in it, has gained further support from the research done, since 1989, on Stalin's collectivization of agriculture and his assault, in the 1930s, on the Kulaks as a class. Those individuals and families moved or deported under this draconian policy – some ten million persons were uprooted and two million were deported – suffered terribly during and after their exile. In the course of this action, depending on the year and the location to which individuals were sent, the loss rate appears to have averaged in the region of 20 to 25 percent.[56] But this also means that 75 to 80 percent of those subjected to this state-sponsored onslaught survived, with the agreement of the Soviet state that they should do so.

In total, as a result of all forms of punishment, of the 767,000 individuals arrested as being members of the most dangerous of the three different classes of Kulaks defined by the Soviet state, 387,000[57] were killed. Most of those defined as Kulaks, however, who were identified as belonging to the second and third category of Kulaks, were not killed. This was not the "Final Solution." Likewise, to extend an essential point already made in earlier updates, Stalin did not intend, and did not act to carry out, the total murder of the deported minorities and other groups that were assaulted by the Soviet state. Accordingly, Norman Naimark and other historians of Soviet Russia now use the term "ethnic cleansing" to describe Stalin's project, thereby making evident the difference between what took place in Stalin's Russia and what transpired in Hitler's Third Reich. So, for example, when the 228,000 Tatars (and others) were deported from the Crimea in 1944, they suffered the loss of 45,000 individuals or 20 percent of their community over the next four years. The same sort of loss was experienced by the Chechens and Ingushi who were also deported in early 1944. There is, therefore, no question that these actions were certainly immoral, inhumane, and unjustifiable. However, as these statistics indicate, they were not, and were not intended to be, acts of genocide.

As for the "Great Terror" of 1937–38,[58] which represents Stalin's last major push against his political and class adversaries, it needs to be comprehended that

---

56 See for more details, Lynne Viola, *Peasant Rebels under Stalin: Collectivization and the Culture of Peasant Resistance* (New York, 1996); Andrea Grazioni, *The Great Soviet Peasant War: Bolsheviks and Peasants, 1917–1933* (Cambridge, MA, 1996); and Lynn Viola et al., *The War Against the Peasantry, 1927–1930: The Tragedy of the Soviet Countryside* (New Haven, CT, 2005).
57 Nicolas Werth, "The Crimes of the Stalin Regime," p. 402.
58 On the 1937–1938 "Great Terror" see J. Arch Getty and Oleg Naumov, *The Road to Terror: Stalin and the Self-Destruction of the Bolsheviks, 1932–1939* (New Haven, CT, 2010); David Priestland,

this "group" of supposed "enemies" was thoroughly mixed insofar as the identity of those who composed it was concerned. Defined by its constituent parts, it was a composite drawn from a wide variety of ethnic, social, political and economic groups. It was *not* an attack on one or two particular targets but, rather, a very broad-based effort to "cleanse" the Soviet Union of all undesirable social and political elements. Hence, it falls outside of all sensible notions of "genocide" despite its eventuating in the murder of 800,000 individuals.[59]

Stalinism and the Politics of Mobilization: Ideas, Power and Terror in Interwar Russia (Oxford, 2007); Robert Conquest, *The Great Terror: A Reassessment* (Oxford, 2007); Wendy Goldman, *Inventing the Enemy: Denunciation and Terror in Stalin's Russia* (Cambridge, UK, 2011); Vadim Rogovin, *1937: Stalin's Year of Terror* (Oak Park, MI, 1998); and idem, *Stalin's Terror of 1937–1938: Political Genocide in the USSR* (Oak Park, MI, 2009).

59 More complete recent descriptions of this event can be found in David Shearer, *Policing Stalin's Socialism and Repression and Social Order in the Soviet Union, 1924–1953* (New Haven, CT, 2009); Wendy Goldman, *Terror and Democracy in the Age of Stalin: The Social Dynamics of Repression* (Cambridge, UK, 2007); and Paul Hagenloh, *Stalin's Police: Public Order and Mass Repression in the USSR, 1926–1941* (Washington, D.C., 2009).

4

CHILDREN IN AUSCHWITZ AND THE *GULAG*: ALTERNATIVE REALITIES

Contrary to the widespread tendency to relativize the Holocaust and to employ it as a universal metaphor of evil, I would insist that the destruction of European Jewry is an unprecedented (phenomenologically, not morally) singular form of evil. Though many have sought, in various ways, to deny the uniqueness of the *Shoah*, the closer that one examines its detailed structure, and the intentionality of its creators, the more obvious it becomes that Auschwitz and Treblinka have no real historic parallels.

In this chapter, I support this conclusion through a close and careful comparative analysis of the treatment, the fate, of children (not infants) in the *Gulag* and the Nazi Death Camps. In contradistinction to those who would assimilate these two environments and treat both as if they represented one common mode of oppression and destruction, it will be seen that, based on the relevant historical evidence and the testimony of survivors of both systems, Auschwitz and the *Gulag* were radically dissimilar.

"THOU SHALT NOT KILL CHILDREN"

What happened to children in the *Gulag* and at Auschwitz? In order to answer this question, we must first recall an important distinction that operated within Soviet culture vis-à-vis young people, between those who were orphans and those who were juvenile criminals. The lot of the former has been described as follows:

> The waifs were taken from the streets – not from their families – into the colonies for juvenile delinquents (there was one attached to the People's Commissariat of Education as early as 1920; it would be interesting to know, too, how things went with juvenile offenders before the Revolution), into workhouses for juveniles (which existed from 1921 to 1930 and had bars, bolts, and jailers, so that in the outworn bourgeois terminology they would have been called prisons), and also into the "Labor Communes of the OGPU" from 1924 on. They had been orphaned by the Civil War, by its famine, by social disorganization, the execution of their parents, or the death of the latter at the front, and at that time justice

really did try to return these children to the mainstream of life, removing them from their street apprenticeship as thieves. Factory apprenticeship began in the labor communes. And this was a privileged situation in the context of those years of unemployment, and many of the lads there learned with a will.[1]

Such juveniles were not part of the criminal population of the *Gulag*.

By comparison, the latter's presence in the *Gulag* was the harsh product of a developing view in Soviet law[2] that made children twelve and over subject to

---

1 Aleksandr Solzhenitsyn, *Gulag Archipelago* (New York, 1975), part 3, pp. 447–48. Stefan Knapp describes a similar situation in 1941:

> We were building a children's village: these villages were called Children's Corners and they are important party inventions. A great many children are in the care of the state, either because they are illegitimate, and their mothers have abandoned them . . . or because their parents were killed or imprisoned for political or other reasons. So, the children were taken to these special villages – outsize orphanages, in a sense – which are run as a combination of boarding school and military camp. They work half the day and are given their schooling in the other half. In a great many ways, they are well looked after – decently fed, for instance – on strictly military lines. These Arctic regions were uninhabited, apart from the camps. The idea was to accustom the children to the climate from their early youth and make them the nucleus of a new population (*The Square Sun*, [London, 1965], pp. 75–76)

The representative accounts of Solzhenitsyn and Knapp relating to the state care of orphan children find corroboration in the evidence pertaining to the terrible years 1938–40, supplied by E. Lipper, *Eleven Years* (London, 1951), pp. 121–22. See also E. Ginzburg who tells us:

> The children's home was also part of the camp compound. It had its own guardhouse, its own gates, its own huts, and its own barbed wire. But on the doors of what were otherwise standard camp hutments there were unusual inscriptions: "Infants' Group," "Toddlers' Group," and "Senior Group." After a day or two I found myself with the senior group. The very fact of being there restored to me the long-lost faculty of weeping. For more than three years my eyes had smarted from tearless despair. But now, in July 1940, I sat on a low bench in a corner of this strange building and cried. I cried without stopping, sobbing like our old nurse Fima, sniffing and snuffling like a country girl. I was in a state of shock. The shock jerked me out of a paralysis that had lasted for some months. Yes, this undoubtedly was a penal camp hut. But it smelled of warm semolina and wet pants. Someone's bizarre imagination had combined the trappings of the prison world with simple, human, and touchingly familiar things now so far out of reach, that they seemed more than a dream . . . Some thirty small children, about the age my Vasya was when we were separated, were tumbling and toddling about the hut, squealing, gurgling with laughter, bursting into tears. Each of them was upholding his right to a place under the Kolyma sun in a perpetual struggle with his fellows. They bashed each other's heads unmercifully, pulled each other's hair, bit each other. (*Within the Whirlwind* [New York, 1967], p. 3)

This is not to subtract or detract from the intense misery and terror of the *Gulag*, but to recognize that within its crushing, hegemonic parameters there were post-revolutionary countervailing socio-political and ideological valences that contravened an all-inclusive genocidal criminality. The sustenance and protection of children were among these contrapuntal values.

2 The 1926 Penal Code, article 12, sentenced children twelve years and older to exile and prison but made certain allowances for their age. These mitigating reservations were removed by the

exile and slave labor and which after 1935 did so without any allowance for their age.[3] As Solzhenitsyn sums it up: "The conclusion we draw is that from 1935 to 1948 children *were* sentenced for taking apples."[4] The myriad abuses, the uncamouflaged exploitation, present in the numerous penal institutions established for such youthful inmates, from beatings to sexual exploitation, can all too easily be imagined. This was no place for children! Yet in disentangling the governing principles that operated in these brutal and brutalizing penal environments, we discover one constraining moral rule that was in force and generally respected: *the children were to be kept alive*.[5] They received, for example, as mandated by the system that had imprisoned them, *additional* rations[6] – though, inevitably, in a manner subject, like all else in the *Gulag*, to corruption.[7] All allowances for

---

Decree covering youthful offenders issued on April 7, 1935. And even this law was stiffened to include "carelessness" rather than only intentionally criminal acts according to the Decree of July 7, 1941. This latter decree was finally softened and some sentences commuted by the Decree of April 24, 1954.

3 Every commentator, both first and third person, remarks on the shame that the entire nation experienced when the age of imprisonment was unconscionably lowered by Stalin so that children under twelve could be *exiled* if found guilty of political crime under Article 58 of the Criminal Code. And who can wonder at this? See, for details, Robert Conquest, *The Great Terror* (New York, 1968), pp. 86–87. He makes the important observation that though this law was actually enforced, as we know from Solzhenitsyn and others, the real purpose of the legislation was to allow Stalin to "threaten oppositionists quite 'legally' with the death of their children as accomplices if they did not carry out his wishes" (p. 87). Alexander Orlov's *Secret History of Stalin's Crimes* (New York, 1953) reveals how often and effectively this strategy was employed and with what success.

4 A. Solzhenitsyn, *Gulag*, vol. 2, p. 450.

5 There were exceptions, e.g., the fourteen-year-old son of Nestor Lakoba, the Georgian Communist, was executed. Robert Conquest, "Introduction," in *A Childhood in Prison*, Pyotr Yakir (New York, 1973), p. 11.

6 P. Yakir reports: "At eight o'clock in the morning rations [in jail] were brought round. At that time adults got 600 grammes of bread, but I was brought a larger ration, as juveniles were entitled to 800 grammes" (*A Childhood in Prison*, pp. 36–37). Yakir's position might have been somewhat anomalous, i.e., his treatment more benign, given the fame of his father, Army Commander Iona Yakir. However, there is nothing said explicitly in this remark or as regards its context that would suggest this, and he specifically speaks not only of himself but of "juveniles" – apparently meaning all juveniles – in this passage. Moreover, Eugenia Ginzburg, writing of the younger children, tells us that:

> It would be wrong to say that the children were kept on a starvation diet. They were given as much to eat as they could manage, and by my standards at the time the food seemed quite appetizing. For some reason, though, they all eat like little convicts: hastily, with no thought for anything else, carefully, wiping their tin bowls with a piece of bread, or licking them clear. (*Within the Whirlwind*, p. 4)

7 As A. Solzhenitsyn writes:

> And what did he see in the children's colony? "There was even more injustice than in freedom. The chiefs and jailers lived off the state, shielded by the correctional system. Part of the kid's ration went from the kitchen into the bellies of the instructors. The kids were beaten with boots, kept in fear so that they would be silent and obedient." (Here it is

corruption made, with all necessary skepticism, the inescapable fact of the extra rations remains. National requirements and fundamental morality – *permitted by the regnant doctrine* – conspired to moderate the rigid social organization and the resultant existential experience of these youngsters. Though alienated and violated in many ways, these young criminals were *not* murdered:

> The kids knew their strength very well. The first element in their strength was unity, and the second impunity. It was only on the outside that they had been driven into here on the basis of the law for adults. But once in there, in the Archipelago, they were under the protection of a sacred taboo. "Milk, chief! Give us our milk!" they would howl and beat on the door of the cell and break up their bunks and break all the glass in sight – all of which would have been termed armed rebellion or economic sabotage among adults. They had nothing to fear! Their milk would be brought them right away!
>
> Or say that they were marching a column of kids under armed guard through a city, and it seems even shameful to guard children so strictly. Far from it! They had worked out a plan. A whistle – and all who wanted to scatter in different directions! And what were the guards to do? Shoot? At whom? At children? . . . And so, their prison terms came to an end. In one fell swoop 150 years ran away from the state. You don't enjoy looking silly? Then don't arrest children![8]

They do not shoot children in the *Gulag*, even youthful criminals, even while these juvenile offenders contravene the system, abuse its overseers, and finally flee from its incarcerative embrace. The victimization of teenagers has real limits, at least one real limit: the requirement that, in almost any circumstance, their life be preserved.

Pay close attention to the key clause in Solzhenitsyn's text: "they were under the protection of a sacred taboo," in other words, *thou shalt not kill children*. This singular moral law applies even in the *Gulag*, restrains even Stalinist behavior,[9]

> necessary to explain that the ration of the youngest juveniles was not the ordinary camp ration. Though it sentenced kids to long years of imprisonment, the government did not cease to be humane. It did not forget that these same children were the future masters of Communism. Therefore they added milk and butter and real meat to their rations. So how could the *instructors* resist the temptation of dipping their ladle into the kids' pot? And how could they compel the kids to keep silent, except by beating them with boots? Perhaps one of these kids who grew up in this way will someday relate to us a story more dismal than *Oliver Twist*? (*Gulag*, vol. 2, p. 453)

8 A. Solzhenitsyn, *Gulag*, vol. 2, 454.
9 P. Yakir, e.g., tells of a hunger strike of juveniles in prison and its outcome:

> Having organised ourselves into an egalitarian commune, we quickly concluded that a hunger strike should be declared in defence of our rights. So one morning we refused to take any food and set forth our demands as follows:
>
> 1. That we should be permitted to receive parcels and to use the prison shop.

and is acknowledged as a binding ethical imperative even when it is confronted by the meta-historical truth embodied in the proletarian revolution. A "future novelist (one who spent his childhood among the kids) will describe to us a multitude of kids' tricks" – our own great chronicler of the Stalinist nightmare records. He will tell us, how the kids "ran riot in the colonies, how they got back at and played nasty tricks on their instructors. Despite the seeming severity of the terms meted out to them and the camp regimen, the kids developed a great insolence out of the impunity."[10] *Thou shalt not kill children.*

Just how far this animating impunity extended is attested to, for example, in this precise report of a gang rape of a camp nurse:

> Some excited and frightened children ran to the nurse of a children's colony and summoned her to help one of their comrades who was seriously ill. Forgetting caution, she quickly accompanied them to their big cell for forty. And as soon as she was inside, the whole anthill went into

---

2. That we should be allowed to send for the interrogators to have our cases explained to us.

After we had issued this statement, the duty warden and the block chief came running up every few minutes. At first they tried to use persuasion, then they began to shout and threaten us. Towards evening on the first day, the prison governor arrived and began shouting: "We'll have you wretches in court! What are you on about? Have you got something against the authorities? Aren't you getting enough kasha? Isn't the boiling water hot enough for you? I'll show you which side your bread's buttered!" We were unmoved. The next morning when we were brought our bread ration, we refused to accept it. Apart from water nothing passed our lips. Forty-eight hours passed without anyone coming to call. The hunger strike was going perfectly. I argued with my cousin, who said that everything that was being done was right and proper. It was right and proper that we should be in prison. Our parents had been rightly and properly arrested and shot, and Stalin was a genius. I was against what was happening and saw the root of the evil in the sadist who was sitting on the throne. On the fourth day everyone began to grow weak. To help keep all their spirits up I danced the "Tsyganochka" in one of my father's shirts, which came down to my knees. At lunch time on that same day the door to the cell opened and a group of bigwigs came in. The duty warder, the block chief, the prison governor and a man in civilian clothes who introduced himself as a city procurator. The procurator did the talking. He asked us to repeat our demands. We repeated them. He replied that the interrogators would come to see us without delay, that we could use the prison shop, but as far as parcels were concerned there was nothing he could do, as they had been instructed in a circular from Moscow that persons under investigation were not to have parcels. I was the spokesman for the cell in these talks. I said that we would not call off the hunger strike, because Moscow could not have forbidden parcels to juvenile prisoners, and eventually Moscow would have to deal with people who had no respect for the law. "All right, go ahead, starve yourselves to death," the prison governor erupted. They left. On the following day the block chief came to see us and said that our demands had been accepted. Our relations had already been informed and would bring parcels that very day.(*A Childhood in Prison*, pp. 51–52)

A second hunger strike, Yakir reports, brings forced feeding and a five-year sentence in a corrective labor colony (*ibid.*, pp. 59–61), but even for this second serious offense, this collective organization against camp authority, Yakir is not murdered.

10 P. Yakir, *A Childhood in Prison*, p. 455.

action! Some of them barricaded the door and kept watch. Dozens of hands tore everything off her, all the clothes she had on, and toppled her over; and then some sat on her hands and on her legs; and then, everyone doing what he could and where, they raped her, kissed her, bit her. It was against orders to shoot them, and no one could rescue her until they themselves let her go, profaned and weeping.[11]

To fully comprehend the immediacy of this sexual assault, the kisses, the bites, the perversion, it is necessary to understand that it is preceded by a substantive understanding on the part of these youngsters that, however violative their collective behavior, they possess an irreplaceable value to the state that transcends any consideration of their murder by the state. And after such an unbridled assault there may or may not be some punitive response, but this too occurred within ethico-political bounds that at least implicitly acknowledged their ontic primacy, the unsurpassed worth of their being, whatever utilitarian or societal ends the Stalinist regime envisioned for them in their adulthood.

Such unrestricted behavioral latitude created young monsters who equated "good" with self-interest and "bad" with all that obfuscated or thwarted it. Their uninhibited conduct, their quasi-solipsistic ethical comportment, was an added torment to the rest of the camp population, as the offended memory of many a camp inmate makes plain. Aino Kuusinen remembers her journey from Moscow to Kotlas:

> The "Stolypin" carriage was hitched to a train and in pitch darkness we set out for an unknown destination. The worst feature of the journey was the juveniles, who were given the upper berths and perpetrated all kinds of indecencies – spitting, uttering obscene abuse and even urinated on the adult prisoners.[12]

Yet, for all their bestiality, for all their anarchic miscreance, the youthful humanity of these urinators was respected by the system. They were neither harmed nor hung, but lived above the law while they proceeded to injure and kill others.[13] And they did so consciously, as *zoon logon archon* in

---

11 *Ibid.*, p. 455.
12 Aino Kuusinen, *Before and after Stalin: A Personal Account of Soviet Russia from the 1920s to the 1960s*, trans. Paul Stevenson (London, 1974), p. 150.
13 Johan Wigmans writes of the teenagers in Karabas:

> A completely separate problem in Karabas was that of the *maloletki*, the younger people aged between twelve and seventeen. Before they were finally sent to this camp, these children had hung around the city streets in bands of varying size and from an early age the boys had lived by theft and the girls by prostitution . . . In Karabas two hundred boys were housed in hut 4 and one hundred and fifty girls in the adjacent hut 5. Two Russian guards, both of them convicts, were under orders to see to it that the division between the two

Aristotle's formulation,[14] for they knew the curious, outrageous rules under which they lived. Rules that they could lavishly manipulate in light of the constitutive ethical relationship, grounded not least in self-interest that existed between themselves and those in control of the political order. Put another way, they insisted that, insofar as they represented the future of the Society polity they possessed, despite the brutal daily circumstances of their existence, some real power that, in its turn, was able to modify the determinate immoral-statist assault against them. The *need*(s) of the rulers, the very needful character of their opposition, empowered – however peculiarly and within limited parameters – these youngsters.

Things, however, were vastly different under the Nazi occupation as one of the *Gulag*'s smarter fifteen-year-old kids tells Solzhenitsyn in the course of a revealing conversation:

> Before the war, at the age of nine, Slava began to steal. He also stole "when our army came," and after the war, and, with a sad, thoughtful smile which was so old for fifteen, he explained to me that in the future, too, he intended to live only by thievery. "You know," he explained to me very reasonably, "that as a worker you can earn only bread and water. And my childhood was bad, so I want to live well."
>
> "What did you do during the German occupation?" I asked, trying to fill in the two years he had bypassed without describing them – the two years of the occupation of Kiev. He shook his head.
>
> "Under the Germans I worked. What do you think – that I could have gone on stealing under the Germans? They shot you on the spot for that."[15]

This alert teenage boy knew the "secret" that those who liken the *Gulag* and Auschwitz too casually dare not face: the Nazis "shot you on the spot," or worse.[16]

> groups was strictly enforced; but they did not take too much notice of that and for a piece of bread or a handful of tobacco they would close their eyes to everything. The barbed-wire between the two huts presented even less of an obstacle and the inevitable result was a lively traffic, especially towards the evening . . . The majority of these youngsters probably did not really mind having to live in these camps. Officially they were supposed to work but in practice that was the last thing they ever did. At the same time they had the benefit of regular meals and ample opportunity of learning from their cronies much that would come in useful once they were let loose.(*Ten Years* [London, 1964] pp. 90–91)

14 Things (animals) capable of reason (*logos*).
15 *Gulag*, vol. 2, 457.
16 E. Ginzburg was so profoundly moved by the children of the *Gulag* that she wrote,

> When one calls to mind Elgen's gray, featureless landscape, shrouded in the melancholy of nonexistence, the most fantastic, the most satanic invention of all seems to be those huts with signs saying, "Infant's Group," "Toddler's Group," and "Senior Group." (*Within the Whirlwind*, p. 11)

The technical dichotomy between waifs or orphans and criminals did not exist for Nazism where Jewish children were at issue. There was no categorical distinction between "unfortunates" to be cared for by the State, to whom the State had an obligation, and juvenile delinquents who needed incarceration, and who, despite their crimes, the state still had an interest in. All Jewish children of whatever age, sex, background, and personal virtues were incorrigible criminals of the worst sort – racial criminals. All stood "legally" condemned to the severest punishments decreeable by the omnipotent Aryan state. No Jewish children either separately or together had any meaningful impunity, any delineated protection juridical or moral, from anything[17] – not least from a violation of the elemental taboo: *thou shalt not kill children*. Being Jews, if still immature ones, they too were carriers of that cosmic contagion that threatened death to all. As such they had to be "cleansed"[18] not only out of their body-politic, but out of history and nature as well. "The baby's mother went up to one of the friends and implored him: 'Let the child go. He hasn't done anything: he's only a baby!' But the heart of the stone was not moved. He replied, 'He's a baby now but he'll grow up to be a Jewish man. That's why we have to kill him.'"[19]

In support of this stringent argument for differentiation I cite the following symptomatic incidents, among a vast array of homicidal occurrences that challenge the limits of our imagining: beginning first with the *regular* use of Jewish children in medical experiments at the Neuengamme and other camps that specialized in "scientific" research.

In November 1944, the SS brought a transport from Auschwitz to Neuengamme containing twenty-five children between six and twelve years of age. Dr. Heissmeyer in Berlin had previously selected those children for experiments for the

---

But she still had the keen sense, the deep honesty, to recognize that:

> They are never to be forgotten, those Elgen children. I'm not saying that there is any comparison between them and, say, the Jewish children in Hitler's empire. Not only were the Elgen children spared extermination in gas chambers, they were even given medical attention. They received all they needed by way of food. It is my duty to emphasize this so as not to depart from the truth by one jot or tittle. (*Within the Whirlwind*, pp. 10–11)

17 The eternal witness to the truth to which I here refer were the biopsies, castrations, sterilizations, and other medical "experiments" carried out on Jewish children.
18 The term "ethnic cleansing" so much in the news during 1993–94 due to the savage situation in the former Yugoslavia should not be confused with my use of the term "cleansing" vis-à-vis the Nazi *Weltanschauung*. In the Bosnian case, fully recognizing the hideous indecency of Serbian behavior, and the thousands killed in this ethnic conflict, the Serbs had as their primary objective political and territorial ambitions related to the exchange of populations and the conquest of Muslim territory. In the case of the Third Reich, the ends desired were metaphysical and entailed not the exchange or the expulsion of the resident Jewish Community of Europe (and elsewhere) but its complete physical annihilation.
19 This testimony of a young girl of fifteen who was eight when these incidents occurred is recorded in Benjamin Tennenbaum, *Ehad Ba'eer U'Shnayim Ba'Mishpacha* (in Hebrew), translated into English in A. Eizenburg, *Witness to the Holocaust* (New York, 1981), p. 310.

"benefits of progress in medicine." The doctors placed the children in isolated blocks under the care of prisoner professors and Dutch orderlies. All the children showed some evidence of tuberculosis.

The researchers started the experiment three weeks after the arrival of the children. The project's originator, Dr. Heissmeyer, came from Berlin every ten days to work with the children. He made incisions in the skin and rubbed cultures of tubercular bacilli into the skin of the left or right arm. After a few days redness and swelling appeared on the arm and the auxiliary glands enlarged; the child's temperature rose sharply for a few days, and then returned to normal in a week. The process was repeated several times. After administering local anesthetic such as novocaine, a doctor made a long incision under the armpit to remove the lymphatic nodes of each child, an operation lasting about fifteen minutes. He then plugged and dressed the wound and sent the sterile test tubes, numbered and named, to Berlin. There, technicians bred new cultures of tubercular bacilli, made an emulsion, and sent the mixture back to the camp. Every two weeks each child was given an injection of the vaccine from his own lymphatic node. After four or five months the majority of the children ran high temperatures. In the third month, enlarged lymph nodes appeared in 80 percent of the children. The doctors noted serious lung changes in almost every child.

While secretly giving sweets and toys to the children, adult prisoners had an opportunity to observe the experiment. Dr. Kowalski, one of these prisoners, provides us with descriptions of the disposition of the tubercular children. In April, when the Allies were nearly at the gates of Neuengamme, Dr. Heissmeyer proposed that the children be transferred to a subcamp of Neuengamme called Bullenhausendamm. He wanted all traces of the experiment eliminated, including the children. General Pohl gave the order and the doctors moved the children to Bullenhausendamm, where they were taken down to the basement. After administering morphine, the doctors put ropes around the children's necks and hanged them, as one prisoner observed, "like pictures hung up on a wall on hooks."[20] Such experiments, including Mengele's infernal activities at Auschwitz, assume the complete absence of inherent value in these youngsters. Answering to a "higher" racial law, these physicians were able, in the name of the Aryan people, to violate every inherited cultural decency, to mock every law of natural morality, to perpetuate absolute evil, against the living bodies of these Jewish children.

Then there is the fate of the Jewish children of Zhitomir:

> Children up to the age of twelve were brought to the execution place in wagons, naked and unshod. The air shook from the wails of the children. I met one man who was witness to the executions. He had once been a stevedore of the Baranovka cooperative. He told me that he saw many

---

20 Feig Konnilyn, *Hitler's Death Camps* (New York, 1981), p. 212.

Jewish children thrown into the ditches and buried alive. In the town of Lubar, Zhitomir region, we were shown graves of Jews murdered in the Peshchana field. At the order of the chief of the Zhitomir Gestapo, children up to the age of twelve were not shot but were thrown into ditches and buried alive. For several days the earth trembled above the infants. Their blood seeped up to the surface.[21]

The senseless terror of this merciless scene is overwhelming – and every elemental question, the impotence of really understanding such an infernal ritual of death, emerges anew over against it. Why did they need to bury the children alive? Why? Was it to economize? Though offered as an explanation, it is an absurd suggestion. Such utilitarian justifications could only suggest themselves, and even then not convincingly, as crude rationalizations to a mind, to a spirit, so corrupt that the suffering of a child – not to speak for the life of a child – would not be felt to be worth a penny (more or less). Was it for the sake of "convenience?" But surely it is more convenient to kill someone, even a child, cleanly than to force it into an open grave and bury it alive. For conscience's sake? Obviously not. Then why?[22] Any explanation that meets even the minimal demands

---

21 *Black Book: The Nazi Crime Against the Jewish People* (New York, 1981; reprint of 1946 edition), pp. 355–56.
22 Yitzchak Greenberg has called our attention to an analogous situation regarding young children thrown into open crematorium furnaces or fiery pits at Auschwitz in 1944, as testified to during the Nuremberg trials:

> WITNESS: . . . women carrying children were (always) sent with them to the crematorium. (Children were of no labor value so they were killed. The mothers were sent along, too, because separation might lead to panic, hysteria – which might slow up the destruction process, and this could not be afforded. It was simpler to condemn the mothers too and keep things quiet and smooth.) The children were then torn from their parents outside the crematorium and sent to the gas chambers separately. (At that point, crowding more people into the gas chambers became the most urgent consideration. Separating meant that more children could be packed in separately, or they could be thrown in over the heads of adults once the chamber was packed.) When the extermination of the Jews in the gas chambers was at its height, orders were issued that children were to be thrown straight into the crematorium furnaces, or into a pit near the crematorium, without being gassed first.
> SMIRNOV (Russian prosecutor): How am I to understand this? Did they throw them into the fire alive, or did they kill them first?
> WITNESS: They threw them in alive. Their screams could be heard at the camp. It is difficult to say how many children were destroyed in this way.
> SMIRNOV: Why did they do this?
> WITNESS: It's very difficult to say. We don't know whether they wanted to economize on gas, or if it was because there was not enough room in the gas chambers. (Yitzchak Greenberg, in *Auschwitz: Beginning of a New Era*, ed. Eva Fleischer [New York, 1977], pp. 9–10)

Emil Fackenheim doubts, as do I, the economic explanation offered by the Polish guard. "Much evidence," he writes, "could be adduced to the effect that the Pole's opinion should not be taken as

of conceptual adequacy will have to include a profound awareness of such happenings as chthonic ministrations, as solemnities of Aryan consecration, in which the murder of such Jewish children is the sacrificial act *par excellence*. For the Gestapo chieftain who orchestrated this monstrous rite, these young deaths were an exaltation, a confirmation of his (the Third Reich's) deepest pieties. They affirmed his Aryan manhood: he was no shirker, the Jews, Jewish children, must suffer, must die, and he was willing to participate, without pity and without evasion, directly in their annihilation.

Or consider the different meaning of child's play, of sport, in the *Gulag* and in the Nazi Death Camps. In the former:

> The kids' actions were unpremeditated, and they didn't mean to cause hurt or offense. They weren't pretending; *they simply did not consider anyone a human being* except themselves, and the older thieves. This is how they came to perceive the world, and how they clung to that view. At the end of work, they would break into a column of adult zeks who were utterly fagged out, hardly able to stand, sunk in a kind of trance or reverie. The kids would jostle the column, not because they had to be first – this meant nothing – but just for the fun of it. They used to talk noisily, taking the name of Pushkin in vain. ("Pushkin took it!" "Pushkin ate it!") They used direct obscene curses at God, Christ, and the Holy Virgin, and they would shout out all sorts of obscenity about sexual deviations and perversions, not even shamed by the presence of elderly women standing there – let alone the younger ones . . . During their short camp stay they attained the peak, the summit, of freedom from society! During the periods of long roll calls in the camp compound the kids used to chase each other around, torpedoing the crowd, knocking people into one another. ("Well, peasant, why were you in the way?") Or they would run around a person, one after the other, as they might around a tree – and the person was even more useful than a tree, because you could shield yourself with him, jerk him, make him totter, tug him in different directions.[23]

What different sport the children of Janowski Camp were part of:

> *Obersturmführer* Wilhaus especially enjoyed this form of sport. He was in the habit of standing on the balcony of his camp office and taking potshots at the prisoners working below to amuse his wife and nine-year-old daughter. Sometimes Wilhaus would order someone to throw three- or four-year-old children into the air while he shot at them. His daughter

---

authoritative. Doubtless, in the new way of murdering children, utilitarian considerations played a role. But utility, in this case, was synthesized with idealism – [as Jean Amery has remarked regarding the ideal SS man] 'becoming great in enduring the suffering of others'" (*To Mend the World: Foundations of Future Jewish Thought* [New York, 1982], p. 132).

23 A. Solzhenitsyn, *Gulag*, vol. 2, p. 460. Italics in original.

would clap her hands and cry: "Do it again, Papa, do it again." And he would go on shooting.[24]

Again, and still more brutal, if any measures still apply, was the following incident:

> "Cover the accursed Jewish blood!" the officer ordered. Several days later, they took us to the Golosayev woods. The woods were brightly lit up with huge bonfires. We saw sumptuously set tables. At the tables sat officers in parade uniforms. Near the bonfires were many small children trembling with fear . . . I heard one German officer explain to the soldiers how the game was to be played. From a distance of twelve meters, they were to toss the children in such a manner that their heads would strike a trunk of the tree. For every cracked skull they would receive a glass of schnapps. This gruesome pastime lasted for several hours. The woods were filled with the cries of the children.
> "Now there isn't a Jew left in all of Kiev!" the German officers yelled, as they tossed the children into the ditch. "We will do the same all over the world. We will annihilate all the Jews."[25]

It cannot be believed though it did happen. And it happened because the humanity, the justifying ethical claim, of the Jewish three- or four-year-old, unlike that of the Soviet youngster, had been nullified altogether. The defining conditions of the "relationship" between Obersturmführer Wilhaus and his Jewish wards, or again, that between the German soldiers and the Jewish children whose heads would be crushed for fun in the Golosayev woods, was so alienated, so distorted, so untouched by either ethical or utilitarian constraints, by even the most minimal ties of interpersonal reciprocity, that everything and anything was possible.

Children in the *Gulag* received an extra food ration – it was a demand of the system. These children were the future of the Soviet regime. In Kharkov, the Germans issued no food to children, for the Jewish children had no future.

Little children were dying. They looked emaciated; they begged for bread in thin, weak voices. The mothers appealed to the officers, but loud laughter was their only answer. The commandant promised to help the children. He fulfilled his promise very soon. In the dim lantern light the Gestapo searched out the children and smeared their lips with some kind of liquid. Shortly after, the barracks resounded with dreadful cries. The children were in agony, threw themselves on the earthen floor. In the morning mountains of children's bodies were loaded onto

---

24 *Black Book*, p. 246, citing the Extraordinary State Committee Report of 1944. Another use of Jewish children as targets is reported in Lvov as well. "Little children were condemned to a horrible death. They were turned over to the Hitler Youth, who used them as live targets during rifle practice" (*Black Book*. p. 310).
25 *Black Book*, p. 364–65.

wagons.[26] And if, by some quirk of fate, they did have something to eat, this too only meant death:

> [a] witness recalled seeing a little boy jump off an incoming truck of Jewish children. He held an apple in his hand. Boger, one of the SS terrors, and another officer were talking nearby: the child was standing next to the car with his apple and was enjoying himself. Suddenly Boger went over to the boy, grabbed his legs, and smashed his head against the wall. Then he calmly picked up the apple. And Draser told me to wipe "that" off the wall. About an hour later I was called to Boger to interpret in an interrogation and I saw him eating the child's apple.[27]

Three incidents further illustrate the brutality:

> "With my own eyes," continued Magidov, "I saw Germans kill Jewish children. One cold rainy night the children were dragged out of their homes, their clothes torn off their bodies and chased around the settlement. The Germans flogged their naked bodies with rubber knouts. At the hospital a fearful scene took place: a German held a child by its feet, shouted: 'One!' A second German struck the child on the head with an iron rod. Covered with blood, the child was thrown into the pit. No one knew whether he was alive or dead. Most of the children drew their last breath on the damp earth, saturated with their own blood."[28]

After a young woman gave birth, SS officer Gustav Franz Wagner ordered the baby to be thrown into the latrine. Later prisoners found the baby floating in excrement.[29]

> Eugenia Glushkina took along her two children aged twelve and seven. The third, who was a one-year-old infant, she left behind in his cradle, thinking that perhaps the beasts would spare him. But after the shooting, the Germans returned to the ghetto to pick up the rags. They saw little Alek in his cradle. One German dragged the child out into the street and smashed his head against the ice. The chief of the detachment ordered the body of the infant cut into pieces and given to his dogs.[30]

What is one to make of such *regular* and *regulative* happenings? A newborn infant drowned in excrement. A child cut into pieces and served up as dog food.

---

26 *Ibid.*, p. 369.
27 K. Feig, *Hitler's Death Camps*, p. 346.
28 *Black Book*, pp. 338–39.
29 This incident occurred at Sobibor and is reported in K. Feig, *Hitler's Death Camps*, p. 289.
30 *Black Book*, p. 343.

All children sentenced to death by poison, shootings, drownings, beatings, starvation, torture, medical experimentation, overwork, hunger, burial while still alive, immolation, hangings, and gassing. A sentence of death so universal that it included every fetus, every newborn, every infant. "The particular bestiality [of the Nazis]," the villagers of Tartarsk reported in 1943, "was reserved for the children, whom they seized, blackjacked and, dead or half dead, threw into the pits."[31] And why? Because of the inexorable, noncontradictable racial necessities that the Führer, in his transcendental uniqueness, had discerned at the center of the law of historical and meta-historical being. Unless these biocentric laws were respected, society, even civilization as a universal norm, would be undone and communal anarchy – and with it the (Aryan) individual's descent into servitude and despair – would ensue. Killing all Jewish fetuses, murdering Jewish children by every means available was the prophylactic non-metaphorical sacrifice, the propitiative nonsymbolic offering that would keep this individual and social chaos at bay. This is not the world of the *Gulag*, even when the devouring demands of ruthless class warfare are fully factored in – it is a world apart.[32]

Of the Jewish child, of the million Jewish children, whose lives were snuffed out we shall say no more – can one ever say enough – but, with regard to the killers, the recognition of a further, onto-psychic[33] dimension harboring within the barbaric act is required. For the slayers, to the extent that such outrages flowed not from bureaucratic-technological dispassion but from a sense of self, of commitment, of basic values shared with the regime, as a true believer, as confirmation

---

31 *Black Book*, p. 340.
32 In advancing this strong conclusion, I am not simultaneously making the erroneous claim that the *Gulag* belongs to history and can be judged by usual ethical categories while the Holocaust, in some mysterious ontological manner, stands outside of time and defies all standard ethical judgments. As made clear in my discussion in *The Holocaust in Historical Context*, vol. 1 (New York, 1994), especially in my unqualified endorsement of the "historicization of the *Shoah*" (pp. 25–26), and in my detailed criticism of what I have called the mystification of the *Shoah* (pp. 42–51), I hold that the destruction of European Jewry was an immanent historical event that is, and must be, fully subject to the rigorous canons of historical research, and the exacting rules of linguistic and moral description and decipherment. Moreover, it is this very insistence on the historical character of the *Shoah* that sustains my entire comparative enterprise, of which this extended analysis of the *Gulag* is an important part. Then again, my historicized understanding of the death camps is precisely what makes them relevant to succeeding generations. Though they are "a world apart" from the *Gulag*, both belong within our capacious human experience. Alternatively, to repeat a cardinal point made at length elsewhere (see, e.g., *The Holocaust in Historical Context*, vol. 1, pp. 1–2 and 28–31), in advancing a claim for the uniqueness of the *Shoah*, in this case for the uniqueness of the *Shoah* vis-à-vis the *Gulag*, I am not proposing any theological claims. The uniqueness of the "Final Solution" does not derive from the uniqueness of its victims (i.e., the classical theological claim made on behalf of the Jewish People) but rather from the unprecedented and unparalleled genocidal ideology of those who perpetrated it.
33 I use this hybrid term to indicate that the act of killing as understood by the Nazi killers was not, in their own self-construction, merely a subjective, psychological act. Rather, for them, it also carried a fundamental ontological significance that had epic meaning both for the Aryan collective and for their own personal lives.

of his or her Nazi beliefs and credentials, this murder was not murder alone, but an act of becoming.[34]

> SS Sergeant Moll tore a child away from his mother, took him over to the crematorium, and threw him into the boiling fat of recently cremated victims. Then he turned to a colleague and said, "I have done my duty. I am satisfied."[35]

This self-authenticating "(pseudo) ethicization" of homicide, this sense that what one had done was not evil after all, was achieved through the sacramentalization of the outrage. The *Endlösung* in its totality, and all specific abusive and destructive acts within it, no matter how scandalous when judged by inherited moral categories, are transubstantiated by the racial mystery whose depth the Führer alone has plumbed. All ethical language of reproach, all juridical categories that define the act as murder, as a criminal deed, are altogether inappropriate; they need to be replaced by the semiotics of Aryan mythography and the meta-legal biocentric axiology of Nazi ritual. Accordingly, Hitler, in his *Last Will and Testament*, speaks in the vocabulary of religion when he talks of Jews "atoning" for their "guilt," just as Sergeant Moll does when, after immolating the living child in the bubbling remains of other Jews, he lionizes his act in the prescriptive, Kantian-sounding pronouncement: "I have done my duty."[36]

Conclusion

The fate, the alternate fate, of children in Auschwitz and the *Gulag* eloquently, if tragically, testifies against those who would relativize, and thereby reduce, the Holocaust. This is not to deny or misrepresent the horrors of the Stalinist camps, but to insist that both Auschwitz and the *Gulag* be accurately deciphered so that the evil that each represents can be understood properly. Moral outrage must be accompanied by conceptual precision and hermeneutical exactitude if the enterprise of comparative scholarship on the literature and phenomenology of mass death is not to degenerate into incorrect banalities.

---

34 This comment raises basic issues as regards the differing forms that the self-consciousness of the Nazi murderers took. It is a question of major importance that, however, is beyond the scope of this essay.
35 Cited in K. Feig, *Hitler's Death Camps*, p. 346.
36 Interestingly, Adolf Eichmann used a similar idiom at his trial.

UPDATE

In the course of my research it has become increasingly apparent that one of the decisive issues in the study of the Holocaust, as well as the study of genocide – and the related matter of the uniqueness of the Holocaust – is the treatment of children (and women). If one intends to physically eliminate a people then murdering the children of the target group will, necessarily, be part of one's plan of action. In this essay, I take up this basic issue at some length in the comparative context of the murder of Jewish and Russian children in the Holocaust and Stalin's Russia respectively.[37]

The many sources emanating from both personal records and state archives in the Soviet Union that bear on this issue tell us that when responsibility for the children of Kulaks, deported nationalities, and other groups defined as "enemies" of the Russian state was taken over by the state institutions, many children died. However, most of these children, numbering in the millions, survived and were cared for by various official state agencies and organizations.

I emphasize this documented, empirical, outcome because the main point that I sought to make when the present essay was first published was that, while the Nazi state defined all Jewish children – including fetuses – as dangerous racial criminals who had to be killed, the Soviet view of children under the state's control was markedly dissimilar. Though Russian children were punished along with their parents by being sent to the camps that together comprised the world of the *Gulag*, once they arrived at their new homes they were not killed. In fact, they had a relatively privileged position in the camps – though still one that was marked by hunger, cruelty, deprivation, and personal trauma.

The most important new study on this topic, *Children of the Gulag* by Cathy Frierson and Semyon Vilensky, informs us that:

> Leaders recognized that the enormous numbers of child victims of revolutionary events and policies threatened the new order, yet they dreamed that the Soviet system could mold children into the primary agents of socialist transformation. Furthermore, success in transforming childhood to produce socialist children was essential to the Soviet self-image. "The happy child" was "the icon of socialist transformation."[38]

---

37 I have already introduced this subject in the context of the analysis of the Holodomor in the essay "Mass death under Communist rule" (Chapter 2). I have, in addition, made a special effort to investigate the treatment of black slave children, along with the issue of slave reproduction in the Americas, in my recently published study, *The Holocaust and New World Slavery* (New York, 2019), and a similar enquiry relative to Native American children is forthcoming.

38 Cathy Frierson and Semyon Vilensky, *Children of the Gulag* (New Haven, CT, 2010), p. 6. Other works of value that address the issue of children in Stalinist Russia are: Lisa Kirschenbaum, *Small Comrades: Revolutionizing Childhood in Soviet Russia, 1917–1932* (New York, 2001); Catriona Kelly, *Children's World: Growing Up in Russia, 1890–1991* (New Haven, CT, 2008); also consult the more general histories of the *Gulag* by Anne Applebaum and Oleg Khlevniuk cited in the update to the essay "Mass death under Communist rule" (Chapter 2).

In principle, Stalinism, class conflict, and the struggles created by the demand imposed regarding the alteration of class identity, did not require the eradication of the children from the "wrong" classes, i.e. those derived from ethnic-national groups that Stalin objected to and acted against. The self-understanding of the leaders of the Communist Revolution, and the subsequent Soviet state, required the reorganization of the national economy and the reconstitution of the social order along Marxist principles, not the killing of children. As a result, political "re-education," however inefficiently and bizarrely pursued, was the governing directive.

5

ON THE DEFINITION OF GENOCIDE AND THE ISSUE OF UNIQUENESS[1]

Explanation of the meaning of "genocide"

In *The Holocaust in Historical Context* (pp. 58–62), a revised definition of the difficult concept of "genocide" was put forward. This definition, and the explanation that was offered for adopting it has, not surprisingly, engendered much comment. The nature of the criticism directed at my definition indicates that many readers did not fully grasp the meaning that I assigned to this term, nor my purpose in defining the term as I did. Therefore, so that readers of the essays in the present volume will not be confused and will know what I mean when this basic term is used in the present study, let me once again set out my position.[2]

Due to irremediable problems in the United Nations' definition of "genocide" that was included in its "Convention on the Prevention and Punishment of the Crime of Genocide" and unanimously adopted without abstentions by the General Assembly on December 9, 1948, I have chosen to offer a revised, more restrictive, definition for the purpose of my own work. Accordingly, as was previously done and as will be done again in the present collection, the notion of "genocide" will be seen as applying to, and only as applying to, "the actualization of the intent, however successfully carried out, to murder in its totality of any national, ethnic, racial, religious, political, social, gender, or economic group, as these groups are defined by the perpetrator, by whatever means." The implementation of such intent, which is very specific, is most usually carried out by states, but this is

---

1 This essay was written only recently and forms part of the Introduction to my two-volume study *The Holocaust and New World Slavery* (Cambridge, UK, 2019).
2 Because of the problematic nature of the United Nations definition of "Genocide," there have been many further attempts to provide a better definition over the past twenty years. Collectively, these efforts highlight a number of relevant matters that require a thorough analysis. Many of these attempts raise considerations of salience with regard to fundamental issues like the question of what constitutes a "group," whether genocide is always state-related, how should one apply the Genocide Convention's notion of "in whole or in part," and the role of, and necessity for, the presence of "intent." However, I do not believe that any of these revisionist attempts materially alters the value of my definition as stated. I will return to this issue, and the more recent body of suggestive proposals for improvement, at length in a future publication.

not required by my definition. As an empirical matter, government power is very often employed in actual (and putative)[3] genocides, but this need not always be the case.[4] In the absence of centralized state power, it may be possible for groups within the body-politic to carry out genocidal assaults against other segments of the population. Which is to recognize that genocide is possible in socio-political situations where you have direct state intervention or state collusion as well as in those where you have a weak central authority that is unable to prevent genocide from happening within given borders. Recognition of this variable precludes the criterion of state intervention as a necessary condition for the definition of "genocide."[5] In the argument that follows, any form of mass murder that does not conform to the definition of "genocide" provided here will not be identified by me as an occasion of this very particular phenomenon.

My revised definition emphasizes that *intent*,[6] that is, the intent to murder a group in its totality (possibly linked to a variety of national, utilitarian, political, ideological, racial, retributive, religious, sexual, social, and economic ends), is a necessary condition of "genocide." Those who find this requirement problematic on the grounds that the notion of *intention* is ambiguous should recognize that, whatever ambiguities attend this concept, it is a widely and successfully employed

---

3 The term *putative* is being used to indicate that many of the cases referred to and classed by others as "genocide" are, in my view, not instances of genocide but cases of mass murder.

4 Dan Stone, for instance, ties "genocide" to state action, what he describes as "state-led mass murder," in *History Today* 60.7 (2010): 5. Similarly, Meredith Hindley refers to "state sponsored mass murder," "Executing the Twentieth Century," *H-Net Reviews* (December 2004). Both of these citations were drawn to my attention by Dan Michman, "The Jewish dimension of the Holocaust in Dire Straits? Current Challenges of Interpretation and Scope," in *Jewish Histories of the Holocaust: New Transnational Approaches*, ed. Norman Goda (New York, 2014). Also relevant in this context is Zygmunt Bauman's *Modernity and the Holocaust* (Ithaca, 1989), that emphasizes that modernization and the nation state are central to genocide; and Mark Levene's two interrelated projects that highlight international political and economic competition between nations, as indicated by the title of his 2005 two-volume study *Genocide in the Age of Nation States* (London, 2008); and his more recent two-volume work *The Crisis of Genocide* (New York, 2013).

5 Frank Chalk's effort at definition does not recognize this nuance adequately; see his "Definitions of Genocide and Their Implications for Prediction and Prevention," in *Remembering for the Future: Working Papers and Addenda*, vol. 3, *The Impact of the Holocaust and Genocide on Jews and Christians*, ed. Yehuda Bauer et al. (Oxford, 1989), pp. 70ff.

6 The presence of "intent" is a requirement for genocide as this crime is defined in international law. This necessity has been reconfirmed by a series of discussions and debates among legal scholars. To pursue this issue further turn to John Quigley, *The Genocide Convention: An International Law Analysis* (Burlington, VT, 2006); Alexander Greenawalt, "Rethinking Genocidal Intent: The Case for a Knowledge-Based Interpretation," *Columbia Law Review* 99 (1999): 2259–94; William Schabas, *Genocide in International Law: The Crimes of Crimes* (Cambridge, UK, 2000); Otto Triffterer, "Genocide, Its Particular Intent to Destroy in Whole or in Part the Group as Such," *Leiden Journal of International Law* 14.2 (2001): 399–408; and the analysis offered in the proceedings of the Yugoslavian trials of the International Tribunal *Prosecutor v. Krstić*, IT 98-33-T (see n. 19 below for further information on this trial).

legal concept,[7] for instance, in the distinction between premeditated murder and lesser forms (legally defined) of murder. As such, it has proven its functionality and practical usability. Therefore, there is no good reason not to utilize it. In consequence, I employ the notion of "intention" as being crucial to the definition of "genocide"[8] in the essays published in this study. This axiomatic usage will, in fact, be one of the essential characteristics that distinguish[9] "genocide" from other forms of mass death, for example, those related to the unintended consequences of pandemics. My insistence on involving the notion of "intent" in the definition of "genocide" reflects, among other things, an awareness of the fact that not every cause represents or implicates an intentional act, that is, an act of a will.

It needs, in addition, to be noted that the original draft of the Genocide Convention prepared in 1947 by the U.N. Commission on Human Rights included in its definition the broad idea of what can properly be labeled "cultural" genocide, understanding this category to mean the "destruction of the specific characteristics of the persecuted group by means, including forced exile, prohibition of the use of the national language, destruction of books, and similar acts."[10] Though this clause was dropped from the final formulation as being too indefinite for

---

7 The objection to including "intent" and "intention" in the definition of genocide has, by now, a long history. It was made, for example, by Isidor Wallimann and Michael Dobkowski in 1987, in their edited volume, *Genocide in the Modern Age: Etiology and Case Studies of Mass Death* (New York, 1978), pp. XVI – XVIII. The paper by Tony Barta, "Relation of Genocide: Land and Lives in the Colonization of Australia," in the Wallimann and Dobkowski volume, pp. 237–52, similarly advanced an argument that would eliminate the notion of "intention" from the concept of "genocide" but makes a series of logical and historical errors in doing so. This methodological suggestion was, likewise, proposed by Henry Huttenbach, "Locating the Holocaust on the Genocide Spectrum," *Holocaust and Genocide Studies* 3.3 (1988): 289–304. Unfortunately, his argument was thoroughly misleading and, therefore, found almost no supporters. More recently a redefinition along this line has been championed by Martin Shaw in *What is Genocide*, 2nd ed. (London, 2015); idem, *Genocide and International Relations: Changing Patterns in the Transitioning of the Late Modern World* (Cambridge, UK, 2013); idem, *War and Genocide: Organized Killing in Modern Society* (Cambridge, UK, 2003). What Shaw's multiple efforts show is that a faulty argument can be repeated over and over again.
8 I well understand that ascertaining the *intent* of a particular action or series of actions, especially as the cause of an action or actions that eventuate in mass death or genocide, is not a simple matter. This is one of the main reasons why I have studied the relevant occasions suggested as instances of genocide in close detail.
9 Here no misunderstanding should arise. My intention in drawing and defending this distinction between genocide and other forms of mass murder is not to lessen the moral and criminal responsibility involved in these other crimes. There are many forms of "crimes against humanity," as well as crimes of a more usual political and socioeconomic type, that should be prosecuted to the fullest extent possible, and in regard to which other national and international legal statutes exist (e.g., those involving homicide, national and group self-determination, and human rights). It is unnecessary, as well as contrary to good sense, to force all manner of state and collective criminality under the rubric of genocide and the stipulations of the U.N. Genocide Convention.
10 Nehemiah Robinson, *Genocide Convention: A Commentary* (New York, 1960), p. 19. This is Robinson's explanation of the meaning of the term *cultural*. See also his discussion of why the concept was deleted from the final draft, pp. 64–65.

purposes of international law, by recalling it, we can differentiate – following the precedent of the U.N. discussion, if not of its final draft – between cultural genocide and physical genocide. Cultural genocide is defined as "the actualization of the intent, however successfully carried out, to destroy the national, ethnic, religious, political, social, or class *identity* of a group, as these groups are defined by the perpetrators."[11] This difference between cultural and physical genocide is self-evidently important and should be, as a matter of method and substance, always respected. For it entails the essential recognition that identifying an event as an instance of "cultural genocide" and identifying a different event as an instance of "physical genocide" is, in effect, to describe two dissimilar realities.

Use of the terms "unique" and "uniqueness"

The employment of the terms "unique" and "uniqueness" in relation to the Holocaust and, by implication, the significance that these notions might have in relation to other events of mass death that have been identified as instances of "genocide," has engendered a good deal of discussion. Because much of this conversation has been critical of the use of these concepts, a number of distinguished Holocaust scholars interested in this issue have altered their earlier positions and now avoid the employment of these terms. Instead, they now utilize other descriptors, e.g., the terms singular, paradigm, and paradigmatic, as in the description that "the murder of European Jewry is the paradigmatic genocide." This change of nomenclature serves to signal that the Holocaust, while highly significant in itself and in relation to an analysis of the concept of "genocide," is not the only historical instance of a specific "class" of events. Moreover, this revisionist strategy has the added advantage of removing a considerable amount of the heat that all too often surrounds the consideration of the Holocaust in comparative analyses.

The appeal of avoiding the terms "unique" and "uniqueness" is, therefore, obvious. Before endorsing this decision, I would, however, make six points.

(1) My own use of the terms "unique" and "uniqueness" is never meant, as has been continually and consistently insisted, to indicate a preference or priority of any sort.

(2) When I use the term "unique" it is solely in a logical-descriptive way. By recourse to this locution, I intend to suggest the following: Event X is A, B, C, D ... Y. Any other event to which the predicates A, B, C, D ... Y apply would be comparable to X. Alternatively, an event that lacks one or more of the predicates A, B, C, D ... Y is different from – though *not* necessarily inferior in any moral, emotional, or evaluative sense – to X. This means

---

11 Obviously, *cultural* genocide cannot include the subcategories of racial or gender obliteration without becoming *physical* genocide.

that X could be, in theory, replicated. If this is so then the substitution of the term "unprecedented" (by Yehuda Bauer, seconded by Timothy Snyder)[12] or other alternative descriptions, e.g., singular (utilized by Christopher Browning)[13] or paradigmatic (used as a second possibility by Yehuda Bauer), would not yield any real conceptual or hermeneutical gain; though it might provide some advantage in terms of "political correctness."

(3) When scholars challenge the claim that "the Holocaust is unique" and assert that other events, whatever events they choose for this purpose, compare to the Holocaust, it is incumbent on them as a methodological obligation to undertake the following test: do the predicates A, B, C, D . . . Y that describe the Holocaust apply to these other historical contexts as well. If not, for example, they possess the qualities A, B, C . . . E . . . Y or A, C, D, E . . . Y, then they are not like the Holocaust. Their structure and character are different from that of the "Final Solution" and, therefore, they do not, *per se*, falsify the claim that the "Holocaust is unique."

(4) To provide a simpler explanation of my position, it needs only to be said that I have maintained that the Holocaust is "unique" because it is the only historical case in which the perpetrators sought to murder *all* members of the target group: the Jewish People. There are those who object to this claim on the grounds that, as Kurt Jonassohn and Karin Björnson have argued, "Hitler did not intend to murder the Jews in their totality. There were many exceptions

---

12 Bauer now prefers the term "unprecedented" to "unique." So, for instance, in a speech given at UNESCO in January 2012 he made this point very clearly. I thank Professor Bauer for sharing this still unpublished essay with me. Working in the same direction, Timothy Snyder refers to the "radical defense of the unprecedented character of the Holocaust" in his essay "The Holocaust as a Regional History: Explaining the Bloodlands," in *Jewish Histories of the Holocaust*, ed. Norman Goda, p. 49. And in n. 12, p. 51, Snyder adds regarding his description that: "Yehuda Bauer's formulation of the Holocaust as 'unprecedented' seems well chosen."

13 Christopher Browning, in describing the Holocaust, has written that the Final Solution "gained an autonomy priority, *significantly* apart from all other persecutory and genocidal policies of the Nazi regime. Its goal was the total and systematic extermination of every Jew – man, women, and child – within the Nazi sphere of power, and was therefore a genocidal project that ultimately had no geographical limit," "The Nazi Empire," in *The Oxford Handbook of Genocide Studies*, ed. Donald Bloxham and A. Dirk Moses (New York, 2009), pp. 420–21, emphasis added. Saul Friedländer has argued relative to this issue: "the absolute character of the extermination of the Jews, not only within the general framework of Nazi persecution, but even within the wider aspects of contemporary ideological-political behavior such as fascism, totalitarianism, economic exploitation and so on . . . the Holocaust does not fall within the framework of explanatory categories of a generalizing kind." "On the Possibility of the Holocaust: An Approach to Historical Synthesis," in *The Holocaust as Historical Experience*, eds. Yehuda Bauer and Nathan Rotenstreich (New York, 1981), pp. 2, 6. David Cesarani, in a variation of this same idea, has employed the term "singular" to describe the Holocaust in a number of his publications. See his *Final Solution: The Fate of the Jews, 1939–1945* (New York, 2016). Similarly, Michael Marrus has described the Holocaust as: "Unlike the case with any other group, and unlike the massacres before and since, every single one of the millions of targeted Jews were to be murdered. Eradication was to be total." *The Holocaust in History* (London, 1987).

to this intent."[14] But this counter to my description only reveals the limited and inaccurate knowledge that Jonassohn and Björnson possess regarding the Holocaust. They, like others,[15] who misread the details of the Holocaust, mistake very temporary exemptions of a small group of Jews from immediate annihilation – usually in relation to the use of Jews as slave laborers – for meaningful, structural, "loopholes" in the National Socialist genocidal program *contra* the Jews. In reality, in contrast to this misinterpretation, the aim of Nazi policy was, given the ideological first principles of the Third Reich, that all of the Jews who had been temporarily exempted from the rule that the world must be made *Judenrein* were soon to be murdered. Many of these Jews were, in fact, subsequently murdered and every one of them would have been annihilated had the Third Reich won the war.

(5) Yehuda Bauer, despite his plea for the use of the term "unprecedented" (and "paradigmatic") instead of "unique," openly acknowledges, in fact, actually insists, that the Holocaust was "the most extreme case of genocide so far."[16] Indeed, consistent with the claim made for the unique character of the *Shoah* in (4), the "extreme" nature here referred to by Bauer is due to his awareness of the total war on Jewry undertaken by the Third Reich. All Jews, it insisted, must be exterminated. But if this were the case then the question again arises relative to the issue of uniqueness whether, because of the radical, i.e., "extreme," nature of the assault mounted by the Führer state, the "Final Solution" represents a circumstance that differs from other events only in degree. Or, alternatively, was it an event that differs, that was singular, in quality, i.e., in its phenomenological character, its ideological foundations, and its projected ontological consequences?

(6) In attempting to answer this last question about whether the Holocaust is qualitatively distinctive – "unique" – among cases of mass murder, several historical happenings of consequence that have occurred since 1994, the date of the publication of *The Holocaust in Historical Context*, need to be investigated. These cases include the massacre of the Tutsi by their Hutu neighbors in Rwanda in the period between April and July 1994. The killings in Bosnia-Herzegovina in 1995, and those in Darfur (Sudan) beginning in 2003 and continuing after that.[17] All three of these events have, using the

---

14 Kurt Jonassohn and Karin Solveig Björnson, *Genocide and Gross Human Rights Violations: In Comparative Perspective* (New Brunswick, NJ, 1998), p. 132.
15 See, for example, D. Stannard's comments in "Uniqueness as Denial: The Politics of Genocide Scholarship," in *Is the Holocaust Unique?* ed. A. Rosenbaum (Boulder, 1996), pp. 162–208. And those of Adam Jones who makes the same misleading argument in his edited volume, *Gendercide and Genocide* (Nashville, 2004), p. 19. Some of the voluminous evidence that disconfirms this position is presented in the papers on Jewish women and children, and the essay (Chapter 7) on Jewish labor, that are included in the present volume.
16 *Ibid.*, p. 8.
17 In addition to the more recent events mentioned here there are a number of other cases that have occurred since the end of World War II that are regularly referred to in the scholarly literature on

United Nations' definition, been identified as "genocide" by international bodies, including the United Nations, as well as by many individual scholars. In my view, this characterization is highly problematic relative to the cases of Bosnia and Sudan. As regards the horrific events in the former Yugoslavia, no less an authority than the International Criminal Tribunal for the former Yugoslavia in The Hague tried the perpetrators of the mass murder in Bosnia for the crime of genocide and found them guilty as charged. During a meeting I had, on November 20, 2011, with the five justices who sat on of this court, I asked them, given the distinctive facts in this demographically limited case, how they could find for the verdict they reached. In response, they explained that they had created an idiosyncratic method, designed to apply to what transpired in Srebrenica, in order to reach this conclusion. The novel definition that they invented was predicated on revising the United Nation Genocide Convention's description that refers to "destroying a group in whole or in part." The last element – "in part" – was crucial for them. And given the rules under which they were operating, which accepted this Convention as the basis of international law, this decision was, even though it required a considerable "stretch" in its logic, possible. But, I would strongly contend that the loss of 7,000 to 8,300 individuals – or on the count of the court up to 15,000[18] – in Srebrenica in July 1995, out of a community of 60,000 individuals on the court's own statistics,[19] plus the failure to prove the "intent" to destroy the entire victimized group,[20] did not justify reaching the judgment that an act of "genocide" had been committed.

---

genocide. These include the killing of Communists in Indonesia in 1965, the murder of Mayans in Guatemala in the 1960s and 1970s, the violence connected with both the Nigerian Civil War and the Pakistan/Bangladesh Civil War, and the large-scale killing in East Timor. In all of these locations mass murder was undoubtedly committed and, were this the sole criterion for identifying acts and events as genocidal, all of these historical happenings would count as "genocide." However, given my definition of this term, I do not classify any of them as instances of genocide. All fall short of the definition's requirement that the perpetrators intended to murder *all* victims in the target group. On the United Nations' definition, however, a number of these events would be correctly classified as genocide. All these cases require closer inspection whether one finds them to be instances of genocide or not. I will, therefore, return to them individually, and at length, in future publications. Here I would add, in light of recent events in Myanmar, that the world community should react as vigorously to "Crimes Against Humanity" and "ethnic cleansing" as to instances of *genocide*. It should not be necessary for criminal state (and other) actions to be [mis] identified as "genocide" in order to arouse the conscience of the civilized world community. Thus, the case of the *Rohingya*, which is clearly a case of *ethnic cleansing*, not *genocide*, should be as vigorously prosecuted as one which is correctly identified as involving "genocide." "Genocide" is a legal, *not* a moral, term!!

18 Section 546 of the Trial Record of *Prosecutor v. Radislav Krstić* by the International Tribunal for the Prosecution of Persons Responsible for Serious Violations of International Humanitarian Law committed in the Territory of Former Yugoslavia since 1991, case No. IT-98–33-T, August 2, 2001.
19 *Ibid.*, section 565 of the Trial Record.
20 The court has explained both the method it created to justify its conclusion – that this was an instance of genocide – and its reliance on the notion of "in part" in the U.N. Convention on

The horrific violence in Darfur was indisputably criminal. But, now that we can, with hindsight, see this event clearly, it is evident that it did not constitute genocide on my definition. However, given the looseness of the United Nations definition – allowing murder "in part" to qualify as genocide – there are those who argue that this event meets this very vague standard. It might be considered to meet this standard. But to so conclude is to extend the meaning of the term "genocide" in ways that essentially undermine its significance as a description of a distinctive type of crime.

Alternatively, though there are significant differences between what took place in Rwanda in 1994 and the Holocaust, the murderous conditions that did obtain in this heinous circumstance though, unlike the Holocaust, geographically limited to one country, appear to go a long way towards meeting my criteria for identifying a historical experience as genocide. In this event, one appears to be confronted with the "intention" to kill an entire group, in this instance "the entire group" being those Tutsis who resided within the boundaries of Rwanda, i.e., not Tutsis universally. The lethal violence in this immediate context began with the killing of the Tutsi elite in Kigali, the nation's capital, on April 6–7, 1994, and then spread throughout the country. The Hutus, claiming that they were defending the country from a Tutsi insurrection and the breakup of Rwanda, unleashed a ferocious and indiscriminate rampage, with the asserted objective of creating a homogeneous Hutu state, that claimed approximately 800,000 victims in three months.

Genocide in its *Judgment* issued in the case of *Prosecutor v. Radislav Krstić*. When the initial finding for "genocide" was appealed the court defended its logic this way: "If a specific part of the group [being oppressed] is emblematic of the overall group . . . that may support a finding that the part qualifies as substantial" (*Prosecutor v. Radislav Krstić*, ICTY Appeals Chamber Judgment, 19 April 2004, paragraph 12). And it went on to argue:

> Srebrenica was important due to its prominence in the eyes of both the Bosnian Muslims and the international community . . . The elimination of the Muslim population of Srebrenica, despite the assurances given by the international community, would serve as a potent example to all Bosnian Muslims of their vulnerability and defenselessness in the face of Serb military forces. The fate of the Bosnian Muslims of Srebrenica would be emblematic of that of all Bosnian Muslims.(paragraph 16)

This, however, transforms the notion of "genocide" beyond all recognition and makes it over into a symbolic action rather than an actual occasion of murder of such a specific character as to be included within the category of genocide. A fuller critical analysis of this case, that differs from mine, has been offered by Robert Hayden, "Mass Killings and Images of Genocide in Bosnia, 1941–1945," in *The Historiography of Genocide*, ed. Dan Stone (New York, 2008), pp. 487–516. I would like to thank Judge Theodor Meron, President of the Court, for meeting with me in The Hague to discuss this case and for subsequently providing me with the relevant documents. I would, in addition, note that the issue of "genocide" was debated in the appeal launched by Radislav, Krstić's legal team. The discussion of the appeals court can be found in *Prosecutor v. Radislav Krstić*, case No. IT-98–33-A, 19 April 2004, sections 14–58. On the issue of killing "part of a group" as constituting genocide, see sections 43–44, pp. 102–103, of the "Partial Dissenting Opinion of Judge Shahabuddeen" in the record of the appeal.

Given what I now know about the events in Rwanda, including what I learned from my conversations in a country visit in 2014, I would characterize them as a second instance of "genocide" according to my definition of this concept.[21] That is to say; my definition may now apply to two cases, not just one.[22] However, the many crucial phenomenological differences between what transpired in Rwanda and the Holocaust still allow for the conclusion that there were a number of singular aspects related to the murder of European Jewry that need to be recognized, and that distinguish the two events, one from the other. Among these significant differences are: the role of technology and bureaucracy, the definition of the "victim" on racial criteria, the governing ideology, i.e., the national vs. ontological teleology, the unlimited assault on children, and especially the international character of the campaign against Jews, being five of the most important such elements.

Seriously misunderstanding the claim for uniqueness

A serious misinterpretation of my reason(s) for defending the claim that the Holocaust is unique has been widely circulated by A. Dirk Moses. His view needs to be addressed and corrected both because it is totally false in itself and because other scholars not investigating the topic for themselves have repeated it. Moses, in discussing my views on uniqueness, has correctly noted that I "profess not to posit a hierarchy of victims or to claim that individual Jewish victims suffered more than non-Jewish ones." Yet, he concludes that "the burden of [Katz's] argument, nonetheless, is that Jewish victims are sacred and those of other genocides are not because only the Jews as a group were singled out for total extermination."[23] This is a complete misrepresentation that has been advanced without *any* relevant supporting evidence. I have *never* advanced such a claim. In fact, I have continued to contest any such argument. I have never, in contradistinction to Moses' assertion,[24] referred to either the Holocaust or the victims of the Holocaust as "sacred." In point of fact, I assign no specific theological meaning to the Holocaust.[25] Furthermore, I have never said anything at all about other occasions of

---

21 Note here Mark Levene, *Genocide in the Age of the Nation-State*, vol. 1, *The Meaning of Genocide* (London and New York, 2005), p. 40, who, more than a decade ago, linked the events in Rwanda with my criteria regarding the application of the term "genocide."
22 The literature on Rwanda is extensive and will be cited when I return to examine the Rwandan case in detail in a future study.
23 A. Dirk Moses, "Conceptual Blockages and Definitional Dilemmas in the 'Racial Century': Genocides of Indigenous Peoples and the Holocaust," in *idem* (ed.), *Genocide: Critical Concepts in Historical Studies*, vol. 1, *The Discipline of Genocide Studies* (London, 2010), pp. 164–165. This was first published in *Patterns of Prejudice* 36.4 (2002): 7–19.
24 *Ibid.*, p. 164. Quoting from Steven Katz, *Post-Holocaust Dialogues: Critical Studies in Modern Jewish Thought* (New York, 1983), pp. 142–43.
25 I neither endorse nor deny any particular theological opinion as a consequence of my conclusion as to uniqueness – a position I explained in *The Holocaust in Historical Context*, pp. 28–31, 45–46; and earlier articulated in my *Post-Holocaust Dialogues*.

mass death/genocide and the presumably profane, i.e., "non-sacred," character of their victims.

Because of the unfortunate influence that Moses' inaccurate interpretation of my work has had, I reproduce the key passage in his analysis here.

> Elie Wiesel has made the logical connection between trauma, group identity and the insistence of uniqueness:
>
>> I always forbade myself to compare the Holocaust of European Judaism to events which are foreign to it. Auschwitz was something else. The Universe of concentration camps, by its dimensions and its design, lies outside, if not beyond, history. Its vocabulary belongs to it alone.
>
> Accordingly, he has expressed alarm that other victim groups are "stealing the Holocaust from us . . . we need to regain our sense of sacredness." Renowned scholars such as Lucy Dawidowicz, Steven T. Katz, and Bauer do not differ from Wiesel and survivors in this regard, even if they locate the Holocaust in history. Bauer himself has pointed out the traumatizing effect of the Holocaust on Israeli society, demonstrated, above all, by its instrumentalization by all sides in public debate for partisan political purposes. And with characteristic forthrightness, Katz insists on its centrality for Jewish identity:
>
>> To understand ourselves [as Jews] requires ineluctably that we come to some grasp of these events [the Holocaust] and our relation to them . . . Those who would enquire what it means to be a Jew today must ask not, or even pose primarily, vague and unformed questions about Jewish identity and the relation of Judaism and modernity and Judaism and secularity, but must rather articulate the much more precise and focused question through which all other dimensions of our post-Holocaust identity are refracted and defined: "What does it mean to be a Jew after Auschwitz?" Auschwitz has become an inescapable *datum* for all Jewish accounts of the meaning and nature of covenantal relation and God's relation to man. Likewise, all substantial answers also need to be open and responsive to the subtleties of the dialectical alternation of the contemporary Jewish situation: that is, they must also give due weight to the "miracle" which is the state of Israel. They must thoughtfully and sensitively enquire whether God is speaking to the "survivors" through it and if so how.

Based on this text, Moses goes on to conclude that:

> Because Katz and Bauer locate the Holocaust at the centre of Jewish life, they are forced to insist on its uniqueness, for to do otherwise would undermine their personal identity and concept of collective Jewish existence. The significance Katz and Bauer attach to the Holocaust cannot be sustained if it is "merely" another case of the mass killing that punctuates human history, for the problem of evil – the mystery of undeserved suffering – cannot be faced without the sense of a cosmic meaning subtended by the division of the world into sacred and profane domains.[26]

But this argument is completely nonsensical. As readers will immediately see, the term "sacredness" comes from Elie Wiesel, not me. Yet, Moses' analysis moves forward first by completely ignoring this basic fact and then, secondly, by conflating Wiesel's position and my own. The reality, however, is that Elie Wiesel and I often discussed this issue in private conversation and held very different views on the matter.[27] Contrary to Moses' assessment that: "Steven T. Katz . . . does not differ from Wiesel and survivors in this regard," the truth is that I "do differ from Wiesel and survivors fundamentally in this regard." As evidence in direct support of this important claim regarding my difference from the position articulated by Elie Wiesel I note that in *The Holocaust in Historical Context*, in a section entitled "Clarifying Disclaimers," I wrote: "One must be open to the philosophical possibility that the *Shoah* is transcendentally unique, [but] I shall not advance this and like claims as my own."[28] Explicating my position, I explained that "I am not proposing or endorsing any particular theological conclusions. It is not clear to me that there is a direct, preferred, theological meaning to be drawn from the exceptionality of this event." Moreover, I contended that both religious radicals and conservatives have "run ahead of the available evidence . . . to posit conclusions that are not epistemologically or intellectually persuasive."[29] After which I concluded that: "We remain, therefore, satisfied with a more modest phenomenological, *contra* transcendental, definition of the historical *novum* that is the Sho'ah."[30] That is I have always rejected all views which claim that the Holocaust is "sacred" and opposed all comparisons that would advance metaphysical and theological truths predicated on the *Shoah*. Because of this agnosticism, I have explicitly and repeatedly emphasized that: "I reject

---

26 A. D. Moses, "Conceptual Blockages," pp. 452–53.
27 See here my critical comments on the apophatic interpretation of the Holocaust in *The Holocaust in Historical Context*, pp. 42–53. I have written about my close relationship with Wiesel in an essay entitled "Elie Wiesel: The Man and His Legacy" which first appeared in *Yad Vashem Studies* 44.2 (2016): 11–41, and is reprinted in the present collection.
28 S. Katz, *The Holocaust in Historical Context*, p. 36.
29 *Ibid.*, pp. 28–30.
30 *Ibid.*, p. 37.

the metaphysical mystification of the Sho'ah,"[31] and have very publicly observed that "I oppose ... an analogy between the Sho'ah and religious experience."[32]

As for Moses' linking of my views with those of Professor Yehuda Bauer the same methodological error is made, but even more so. Though there is a similarity of view on many points in Bauer's work and my own, to evaluate my views one has to consider what I wrote not what Bauer wrote. Professor Bauer and I have never worked together to write anything in common, and most definitely, have never jointly composed anything that bears on the topic of uniqueness. In point of fact, there are significant differences between our views on this matter. Therefore, if Moses wants to discuss Katz let him discuss Katz rather than an invented, i.e., nonexistent, Katz-Bauer thesis. This erroneously asserted connection leads only to confusion and error, for it inevitably leads Moses to attribute things to me that I have never said and assigns meanings to my work that are without foundation. I may well have written things that are incorrect, and misinterpreted the historical evidence with which I work, but you cannot "prove" this by quoting the views of Yehuda Bauer and imputing them to me.

Here I would add, parenthetically, that Professor Bauer does not believe in God, and was for several years the President of *The International Federation of Secular Humanistic Jews*. He is the last person who would introduce the term "sacred" into the analysis of Holocaust victims. This was one of his long-standing differences with Elie Wiesel whose writings he strongly felt were too theological. Furthermore, the citation of Bauer's position employed by Moses is given a completely distorted meaning. He quotes Bauer to the effect that:

> All these universalizing attempts [regarding the Holocaust] seem to me to be, on the Jewish side, efforts by their authors to escape their Jewishness. They are expressions of a deep-seated insecurity; these people feel more secure when they can say "we are just like all the others." The Holocaust should have proved to them that the Jews were, unfortunately, not like the others. Obviously, it did not.[33]

And then interprets this statement as proof that Bauer is addressing, as Moses describes it, the "sacredness of the Holocaust."

> The link between the ongoing maintenance of group identity and the sacredness of the Holocaust could hardly be made more explicitly than in this extraordinary statement.[34]

---

31 *Ibid.*, p. 45.
32 *Ibid.*
33 A. D. Moses, "Conceptual Blockages," pp. 14–15.
34 Ibid., p. 15. Lest anyone think it possible that Professor Bauer spoke about Jewish Holocaust victims as "sacred," I call to attention his sharp theological argument: "In retrospect, we must admit

But this is absurd. Bauer is not talking about the "sacredness" of the Holocaust and its Jewish victims but, rather, about what he takes to be the historical singularity of antisemitism and Jewish self-hate. As readers will have no difficulty recognizing, Bauer never mentions anything to do with religion or "sacredness."

Then, too, I would add, so that there will be no confusion regarding the significance of holding the Holocaust central to post-Holocaust Jewish identity (what I referred to as "an inescapable datum"), that making this claim about the post-Holocaust consciousness of contemporary Jews is not equivalent to saying anything regarding "sacredness." It means only that in discussing the nature and meaning of Judaism in the post-war era it is *necessary* to consider what implications, if any, the *Shoah* may have for Judaism after Auschwitz. So, for instance, Richard Rubenstein explored these issues and came to the radical conclusion that there was no God, no covenant, and no revelation at Sinai or subsequently. Which is to say that all that is being insisted upon when one refers to the extermination of European Jewry as "an inescapable datum" is that one must wrestle with the possible meaning(s) of the Holocaust in our contemporary circumstance. My own position has continually been non-committal as to specific theological proposals based on the experience of the Holocaust. I would also repeat that I have never said anything about the religious status of the victims killed during other occasions of mass death, and I certainly do not posit, as Moses falsely asserts (*ibid.*, p. 64), a typological distinction between Jewish victims of the Holocaust being "sacred" and victims of other occasions of mass death being profane. This claim is simply untrue.

This altogether mistaken argument about "sacredness" has unfortunately been recycled by Dan Stone in an essay, "On the Holocaust and Genocide.".[35] Stone, in discussing my work on the issue of the uniqueness of the Holocaust, tells us that the "historical grounds for defending the Holocaust's uniqueness are in fact ideologically driven attempts to maintain the Holocaust as a kind of 'sacred entity' . . . it stems from a historically explicable, but by now harmful, belief that Jewish identity would be massively threatened if one of the mainstays (the fact that all Jews were potential victims of Nazism) were to lose its 'sacred' aura, and also, unconsciously a belief that the Holocaust status as unique constitutes a bulwark against revivified antisemitism."[36] This explanation, that readers will recognize as a repetition of Dirk Moses' erroneous reading, is no more correct when it is repeated than when it was first articulated. Insofar as it relates, or is said to relate, to my use of the terms "unique" and "uniqueness" and seeks to explain my position, I need only repeat that I do not believe that the Holocaust is a "sacred entity," nor that it has a "sacred

---

that belief in God in our generation has been transformed into an elementary absurdity of logic," and again, and even more radical: "If there is God [after the Holocaust, S.K.], then He is Satan. If He is not Satan, then He does not exist". "Returning to the Source of Human Morality," in Steven Katz (ed.), *Wrestling with God* (New York, 2007), p. 295.

35 This essay, "On the Holocaust and Genocide," appeared in Dan Stone's volume *History, Memory and Mass Atrocity: Essays on the Holocaust and Genocide* (London, 2006), pp. 236–51.

36 *Ibid.*, pp. 237–38.

aura." It is not an accident that Stone provides no citation from my publications, not a single sentence or even a part of a sentence, that would indicate that I have ever said anything like this. I see nothing "sacred" in the murder of 1,400,000 (or more) Jewish children, the use of Jewish women in ghastly medical experiments, a million and a half Jewish men and women killed by *Einsatzgruppen* and millions more gassed in death camps. Nor do I hold now, nor have I ever held, that the *Shoah* needs to possess a "sacred aura" in order to serve as a prophylaxis against antisemitism. This interpretation, in its totality, is simply fallacious.

Donald Bloxham has, likewise, repeatedly objected to identifying the Holocaust as unique. In 2005 he called the issue of "uniqueness" "an obstacle to historical understanding," though unlike Dirk Moses he agreed that "it itself [is] an acceptable contention for a historian to make." But he, nonetheless, critically observed that it "can never be more than a contention for the simple reason that it is not possible to prove. It is a matter of opinion, not fact." As he understands it, this concept belongs to a Holocaust "metanarrative" that rests on weak historical foundations. Furthermore, he asks:

> Since the intent and extent of the killing are the salient issues both in judging "uniqueness" and indeed in establishing genocide, at what point, are we entitled to ask, [when] did genocide become genocide, and this uniqueness thereby manifest itself? Thousands of Jews had already perished under Nazi rule, particularly in the Polish ghettos, before the beginning of the "Final Solution" as many historians have understood it (that is, before the invasion of the Soviet Union crystallized or precipitated mass direct killing as a policy tool). And even when killing of Soviet Jews on a genocidal scale had demonstrably begun – say by the end of August 1941 – did this equate to the sort of total, utterly all-encompassing genocide that Bauer and Katz have in mind in their *ex post facto* judgments?[37]

But this critique is nothing more than a series of logical and conceptual errors. Bloxham is correct that the "Final Solution" went through and, in its totality, represented a developmental process, but this fact does not eliminate the specific question about the outcome of the process and its "uniqueness." Obviously, the claim for uniqueness is being made looking back at the event as a whole, and, as I use the relevant term(s), does not deny that there were many steps along the way. Which is to say that, in making these arguments and working towards my conclusions, I have employed the same type of analysis as that utilized by other scholars to describe, characterize, and evaluate other (all other) historical events. To the degree that this common method considers past events from a future position that

---

37 Donald Bloxham and Tony Kushner (eds.), *The Holocaust: Critical Historical Approaches* (Manchester, UK, 2005), p. 67.

is capable of viewing them in their entirety, it allows for judgments relative to all historical matters including the Holocaust. Bloxham is correct that the claim for "uniqueness" is an "*ex post facto* judgment" and represents what he now labels a "metanarrative." However, insofar as it is a judgment about a historical event, it *must* be a "metanarrative." This is true of *all* judgments, whether phenomenological or moral, or otherwise – including Bloxham's judgments – about *all* historical events. Thus, we can either give up all historical judgments or learn to cope with "metanarratives."

Second, in asserting that the "uniqueness of the Holocaust" cannot be proven one has to ask what type, what form, of "proof" Bloxham is requesting. It is certainly reasonable to assert that the claim regarding "uniqueness" is not verifiable in the way that scientific propositions are verified. But, at the same time, it is necessary to insist that this contention is open to "proof" in the same way that all other historical evaluations are: that is, by marshaling evidence that one hopes will make a persuasive case. Similarly, disconfirming the claim happens in the same way that falsifying all historical conclusions occurs, i.e., by way of superior counter-arguments and reference to relevant evidence. Accordingly, the claim that "the Holocaust is unique" is comparable to other historical judgments. And this not least to the contrary position that Bloxham endorses: that the Holocaust is not unique. What sort of evidence will Bloxham produce to defend and verify this claim, this "metanarrative," that is different from the type of evidence – and method – that I, and others, have employed to make the contrary case. To show that X is unique, understanding "unique" to mean different from all other items or events, one measures X and all the other items or events against the same criteria to see if X is like or unlike all of these other possibilities to which it is compared. There is no mystery or metaphysics here. This method is, as I invoke it, strictly historical and phenomenological.

In his more extended study, *The Final Solution: A Genocide*, published in 2009, Bloxham returned to the issue of "uniqueness." The book's subtitle "A Genocide," is meant to indicate that the Holocaust is just one event in a series of like-events, all the events in the series being instances of genocide. Thus, he writes that, "even the most extreme genocide, the murder of the Jews, retains some of the shape of other genocides." (p. 10). But this standard setting sentence entails that the "Final Solution" was not only like other genocides but that it had properties, attributes, a "shape" that it did not share with other events identified by Bloxham as genocides. Therefore, it appears to be *different* – the "most extreme genocide" – even on Bloxham's accounting. He emphasizes this by noting that among Nazi crimes, such as the 13 million forced laborers made to work for the Nazis, and the assault on the Roma, "none [of these crimes] was pursued with quite the same zeal as the Jewish genocide" (p. 10). So, at a minimum, within the context of World War II and Nazi violence, the murder of the Jews was distinctive, and destructive in such a way including a special "zeal" – that is significant. Otherwise, its destructiveness would not need to be called to attention.

Bloxham then continues to explain why, in his view, certain scholars have identified the Holocaust as "unique." In doing so, he attributes the reason to "identity politics" that he defines as "the need to give a special significance to past suffering of Jews in the name of present communal identity."[38] There is, in a general sense, truth to this. But there is a crucial distinction that he ignores between the question of "uniqueness" *per se*, i.e., is it the case or is it not the case that the Holocaust is "unique," and the *use* of the answer given to this query. The "uniqueness" or "non-uniqueness" of the Holocaust as an event is completely separate from the instrumental *use* that individuals may make of the answer to this question. Furthermore, insofar as Bloxham attributes this instrumental purpose to my work, he is unable to cite a single sentence that I have written as evidence that I have such an agenda. The reality is that I have never advanced such an argument.[39]

Bloxham refers to my work as developing "uniqueness" into a philosophical proposition. I am described as seizing upon the "Nazi racial imperative that all Jews must die, and they must die here and now,"[40] as the grounds for a philosophical argument for the singularity of the Holocaust. But Bloxham finds this highly problematic and argues that:

> While the scale, determination, and intensity of the Nazi pursuit of Jews across Europe is exceptional even within the annals of genocide, we have seen earlier in this book that the murder was not perpetuated mindless of economic, political, or logistical cost, and that up to the last stage, it was paralleled by less destructive forms of ethnopolitics against other groups. We have also seen that the idea that Hitler (and Himmler) actively sought to murder every last Jew everywhere is open to question. It is far from clear that even Hitler himself was overly concerned with the fate of the Jews of Norway or Rhodes.[41]

But this counter-argument is defective. For we know that the Führer state, with Hitler in charge, was, in fact, concerned enough with the complete extermination of the Jewish People to deport the Jews of Norway and Rhodes to death camps; and to kill almost the entire Jewish population of Thessaloniki. While, the "exceptions" to the Nazi plan to murder all Jews, that Bloxham refers to, were little more than very *temporary* exemptions. See the papers on the killing of Jewish women and children, and also on Jewish workers in this collection that make this very clear. Nor should we ignore Bloxham's self-contradictory observation that the murder of the Jews was "exceptional even within the annals of genocide," and at "the last stage," was *not* paralleled by any other actions of the Third Reich. So, indeed, the

---

38 *The Final Solution*, p. 315.
39 *Ibid.*, p. 318.
40 *Ibid.*
41 *Ibid.*, p. 316.

Nazi assault on the Jewish People was, in fact, "exceptional." This sounds very much like a "metanarrative" defending the "uniqueness" of the Holocaust.

It is notable that Bloxham does not enter into any conversation regarding my detailed case-by-case comparisons and does not attempt to correct or refute them. Instead, he repeats Dirk Moses' objection that:

> Whether the similarities [between the Holocaust and other genocides] are more significant than the differences is ultimately a political and philosophical, rather than a historical question . . . Uniqueness is not a category for historical research; it is a religious or metaphysical category.[42]

But this claim is false no matter how many times it is repeated. "Uniqueness" can be a meaningful historical category if the conditions of its employment are appropriately defined. I note that Bloxham does not hesitate to refer to "the exceptional character of the Holocaust." Is the term "exceptional" less metaphysical and more subject to proof than the term "uniqueness"? Bloxham further asserts that "it is possible to go further still [i.e., beyond Moses' criticism]. The claim of uniqueness must mean unique from any perspective." This, however, is still another logical mistake. To utilize the concept of "uniqueness" appropriately requires only that one employs it according to the notion as defined; X is "unique" in terms of the criteria A, B, C . . . Z given.

Bloxham concludes with the requirement that "the study of the Holocaust should be no different to the study of any given genocide."[43] This is a principle I agree with. In *The Holocaust in Historical Context*, when discussing the topic of historicization, and the critical claim that Holocaust scholarship tends not to be sufficiently historicized, I stressed that:

> Like Martin Broszat I accept the sensible argument that the Holocaust must be open to historical investigation. However, *contra* the conventional wisdom on this subject (i.e., in opposition to the false dichotomy championed by Broszat and others between historicization and uniqueness), it is my intention to establish the uniqueness of the *Sho'ah* precisely by historicizing it. This, in fact, is the cardinal objective of the extensive comparative historical exploration undertaken in volumes 1 and 2 of this study.[44]

Historicization is the necessary condition for establishing, in a logically and methodologically valid way, the uniqueness of the *Shoah*. This is precisely what my research is primarily about. In consequence, adhering to this methodological requirement will not disconfirm my use of the term "unique" and "uniqueness." It would be a conceptual mistake to conclude otherwise.

---

42 This citation from Moses appears in *ibid.*, p. 317.
43 *Ibid.*, p. 319.
44 *The Holocaust in Historical Context*, p. 25. The reference to Volume 2 is to *The Holocaust and New World Slavery* (2019).

Finally, in a third attempt to explain his rejection of "uniqueness," Bloxham, in a paper published in 2016,[45] entitled a subsection of his discussion: "The Uniqueness Issue Revisited – It is Hoped For the Last Time."[46] Given his faulty argument, now repeated yet again, I too hope it is the "Last Time." As previously, self-contradiction is introduced early in this latest version of Bloxham's critique by his acknowledgment that "I have always recognized the extremity of the Holocaust relative to other genocides."[47] But is "extremity" – like his use of the term "exceptional" – more provable and non-metaphysical than "uniqueness"? Then he again introduces the bogus claim that the use of the term "unique" necessarily creates a "hierarchy that hinders the integrated study of genocide."[48] But he does not recognize that this asserted "hierarchization" may well not be the actual meaning of what defenders of "uniqueness" write (or "intend") but, rather, the outcome of a serious misreading, based on stilted *a priori* assumptions, by those who dislike this particular idea. To say "X" is not "Y" is not to rank "X" higher than "Y." Here he refers for support to "Moses's seminal article on the subject."[49] But, as already shown, Moses' article is not "seminal" but fictional. Bloxham, Stone, and others, would have done well to make sure of the correctness of Moses' interpretation before endorsing and employing it. Furthermore, his explication of what the use of the term "unique" means, relative to my work, is inaccurate. He writes:

> By "unique" is meant not the mundane uniqueness of every historical event, but a special quality whereby the particular characteristics of the Holocaust are promoted to the exclusion of its commonalities with other genocides, and whereby comparative studies – which is concerned with similarities as well as differences – is, therefore, a distorted pursuit.[50]

But, I have never attributed a "special quality" to the Holocaust. (Readers should note that there is no corroborating citation from my work.) Rather, the purpose of all my critical reading and detailed historical work is to show that, using "uniqueness" in the "mundane sense" of "every historical event," the extermination of European Jewry was "unique."

The criticisms of the concept of "uniqueness," which have just been discussed, have a common character. Individually and collectively they attempt to disconfirm the claim for the Holocaust's uniqueness and substitute instead a relativizing thesis that the murder of European Jewry is like other instances of genocide, of which, it is asserted, there was quite a number. The arguments made to defend

---

45 "Holocaust Studies and Genocide Studies: Past, Present and Future," in *Genocide Matters: Ongoing Issues and Emerging Perspectives*, ed. Joyce Appel and Ernesto Verdeja (London, 2016), pp. 59–81.
46 *Ibid.*, p. 63.
47 *Ibid.*
48 *Ibid.*
49 *Ibid.*
50 *Ibid.*

this position, however, and in particular, the exposition of my views, have been more than questionable. None of my critics can cite anything I have written that might justify their claims, but they feel, nevertheless, justified in asserting that I made the claims they erroneously attribute to me. In place of evidence all three of my critics depend on invented, fabricated, religious, psychological, and sociological theories that do not rightfully, accurately, apply, and put forward arguments that are essentially a series of non-sequiturs. What all scholars have a legitimate right to require is that academic criticism be fair and based on a reasoned investigation of the position being rebutted. In the present instance, this requirement for basic intellectual honesty has not been met.

UPDATE

This essay was prompted by my continued wrestling with the issues related to the definition of genocide that are unavoidable as I pursue my research on the issue of the "Uniqueness" of the Holocaust. As stated in footnote 1, the material republished here is part of the Introduction to my two-volume study entitled *The Holocaust and New World Slavery* (Cambridge, UK, 2019). Because of its topicality I am re-using a version of it in the present collection.

I am confident that proposing new definitions of "genocide" will continue to be a growth industry. I am not confident, however, based on the efforts in this direction that already exist, that most of these attempts will shed much new light on the subject. In many cases, this specific enterprise has to date yielded only very modest "added value" to the existing conversation that centers around the definition adopted by the United Nations Convention on Genocide, though there have been some contributions of significance (see here my comments in n. 2 of this essay). What I will now try to do, having reviewed this potpourri of proposals in detail, is to respond critically in a new essay to these various revisions of the concept of "genocide." But based on what I already know about this vexing issue of definition, I am prepared even now to suggest that the most significant way forward would be for a new, or heavily revised, international definition to be formulated by the United Nations. However, there is no sign of this happening.

6

EXPLORING THE HOLOCAUST AND COMPARATIVE HISTORY[1]

(Talk given at a conference in Cape Town honoring Professor Milton Shain)

I am delighted to be part of this wonderful occasion in honor of Milton Shain. Milton and I have been friends for more than 30 years and I have had the pleasure of visiting the Kaplan Center under his auspices several times. He has done a masterful job making the Jewish Studies and Holocaust program at the University of Cape Town an integral part of the world academic community, as indicated by the stellar roster of his friends who have come together from near and far to honor him at this conference.

The assignment given to speakers for this meeting was to speak personally about our own intellectual odyssey while explaining why our scholarly concerns are not just our own private interests but also legitimately enrich Holocaust scholarship more generally. So, let me start at the beginning of my own involvement with Holocaust studies. At Cambridge, during my doctoral studies, I did not involve myself in the study of the Holocaust in any way. And even during the first eight years that I taught at Dartmouth College in the U.S. when I returned from Cambridge, I did not teach anything dealing with the *Shoah*, nor did I publish anything bearing on or about it. Even my serious reading generally avoided the subject. This evasion was due partly, as I now realize looking back, both to my own profound ignorance of the subject and because I was well aware, as a non-tenured Assistant Professor, of the jaundiced view that some of my colleagues had regarding it. I was reminded more than once by both Jewish and non-Jewish colleagues that: "there is no business like *Shoah* business." In addition, this avoidance was at least partly due to my own Yeshiva education that still exerted some influence on my philosophical views and had taught me to see the Holocaust as – in the classic interpretation given of the cause of antisemitism in the *midrash* – just another, if more intense, case of "Esau hates Jacob."

This all changed suddenly and unexpectedly in 1981 when I was asked to give the annual Jewish lecture to the Theology Department at Notre Dame University. After accepting the invitation, I had to find a subject, but this presented a serious

---

[1] This essay, written in 2012, was originally published as "On the Holocaust and Comparative History." I have changed the title for the purposes of this volume so as not to confuse it with my Leo Baeck lecture (1993) which also bore the same title but deals with different topics (see Chapter 1).

conundrum: what Jewish topic could I talk about that would make sense to a Catholic audience at Notre Dame. While wrestling with this problem, and seeking some guidance, I asked my hosts at Notre Dame what the previous year's speaker had talked about. I was told that the speaker had been Elie Wiesel and that he had spoken about his view of the unique and apophatic nature of the Holocaust. Armed with this information I decided, even though I had not heard or read Elie's lecture, that I knew, based on our friendship and many conversations, what he would have said, and so I decided that I would present the opposite view to his: the Holocaust was *not* unique.

But then came my research. For six months I probed and explored and looked at what would now be identified as the early comparative literature on mass murder and genocide that then existed. After this intensive study I realized that I was wrong and Elie Wiesel was right, but he was right for reasons other than the ones he gave. That is to say, by this point in my research I had come to realize that to make the academic case for the Holocaust's uniqueness one had to do rigorous and in-depth historical study and had to be willing to historicize every aspect of the "war against the Jews." It was, as I was beginning to understand, if only "through a glass darkly" at this early stage, that one had to submit the Holocaust to the most detailed historicization and to reject apophatic claims if one wanted the argument for uniqueness to be academically valuable and a claim that could, and would, be accepted as a respectable position within the world of the academy.

And so, I gave the lecture at Notre Dame on "The Uniqueness of the Holocaust" or some such title, incorporating the insight into the issue that I thought I had gained. And, at the same time I called a friend, Arthur Samuelson, then editor at Schocken books and asked him if he wanted a short study on the subject of my lecture that would be ready in six months. The more general interest in the Holocaust was then taking off, and he said "sure," he would be delighted to have the monograph. Six months later I called him back and, with considerable embarrassment, told him that there would be no book as I had come to realize that I did not even know how to begin to do the historical and conceptual work that needed to be done to make a reasonable, coherent, knowledgeable, case for my conclusion.

Now more than thirty years later, and having written many thousands of pages in manuscript, with only a fifth of this material so far in print, I am beginning to grasp what the right questions are and have some, at least minimal, grasp of the methodological and hermeneutical issues that confront – and challenge – this scholarly undertaking.

Let me conclude these brief opening biographical comments by simply observing that all of this labor over the past three decades has been energized by my unwavering sense of the academic and ethical significance of the study of the *Shoah*. As many of you know, I have also written and edited books and essays on Jewish philosophy, and Jewish history, like volume 4 of the *Cambridge History of Judaism* on the rabbinic era, and have worked in detail on comparative mysticism – but no subject has so gripped my imagination and dominated my intellectual life, because of the absolute seriousness of the subject, as the destruction of European Jewry.

Now, what have I learned that is of more than personal interest? I will describe what I think is important about my work under three headings, beginning with the issue of *method*.

I Method

I have come to understand that one must never make *moral* comparisons between mass tragedies. The death of an Armenian woman or child or Native American woman or child or black woman and child caught up in New World slavery, or women and children trapped in the Gulag or East Timor, or Rwanda are all morally and humanly equal. I know of no way to quantify evil such that one could create a moral hierarchy of evils. Likewise, and related, one should never engage in conversations about comparative suffering for this too is a subject beyond quantification and legitimate comparison.

I have also learned that before you compare two things, you should know something about at least one of them. I emphasize this point because most of the comparative work done, much of it – indeed too much of it – by sociologists, is historically uninformed and full of both historical errors and false generalizations. One needs, to do the required comparative work properly, to be the master of all the details and subtleties of not only the Holocaust but also the tragedies to which the Holocaust is compared. Otherwise you get the gross distortions found, for example, in David Stannard's and Ward Churchill's work on the history and tragedy of Native Americans. In their historical reconstruction they completely ignore, among other critical things, the missionary aspects of Spanish (and Portuguese) colonialism, the unintentional character of the main killer of the native peoples, disease, and misrepresent the nature of American government policy form Jefferson to the twentieth century, including the Indian wars and the crucial subject of reservations. Here it is necessary to know that by 1887 there were 138 million acres of land devoted to reservations. Then there is the ideologically driven, monumental historical ignorance of Mary Daly, Andrea Dworkin, and others who have argued that there were 9,000,000 women killed during the European witch craze and therefore one can, and should, create a new subject of study called "genocide." I will return to this issue in more detail in a moment.

Or again, we have the repeated misrepresentation of the Armenian tragedy in World War I by numerous authors who fail to appreciate that the largest Armenian community in the Ottoman Empire, numbering some 250,000 persons, was not violated by the Young Turks (with minor exceptions that took place at the end of the war), that several hundred thousand Armenians were forcibly converted to Islam – a terrible act but a contra-genocidal one – and that approximately 50 percent of the population that was forced marched across Mesopotamia survived. Or again, there are scholars like Richard Rubenstein who mistakenly compare the *Shoah* and New World black slavery and do not appear to know that 400,000 African men, women and children were imported into the United States over the centuries and that by 1860 and the Emancipation Proclamation there were over

4 million blacks in America. Thus whatever else slavery as an institution was in the United States, it was not genocidal. This inventory of ignorance that passes for scholarship could be extended, almost without end, to include those who do not know that most Albigensians and Cathars were not murdered by the medieval Church, that most *conversos* were not killed by the Inquisition, that most Kulaks and the majority of the populations of the deported national minority groups were *not* killed by Stalin, and that he had no intention of killing them, and that, contrary to A. Dirk Moses' extraordinary misrepresentations of the Holocaust, the crimes of New World colonialism are phenomenologically distinct from those committed by the Third Reich.

II On the dialectic of mass murder

The second important lesson gained is an understanding, however partial and still incomplete, regarding the structures of almost all historical instances of mass murder relative to the structure of the Holocaust. And this has taught me that there is a defining dialectic that operates in the many non-Holocaust cases that we are all familiar with and that explains the nature and morphology of these terrible historical events, but which did not exist in the Holocaust.

What I here refer to is this: usually the ideology, the central idea, that causes the violence and mass death in a given instance, also, perhaps ironically, limits it. Consider, for example, the very interesting and challenging example of the witch craze that has already been mentioned.

This craze, that spread across Europe and to the Americas in the sixteenth and seventeenth centuries, was rooted in Christian misogynism. And this misogynism was newly energized by the breakdown of medieval Christendom and the need to explain why "the body of Christ," which was the Christian Community, was unraveling. This is to say, here an explanation was at hand in the theological traditions of Eve and Lilith, i.e., the stereotypical image of women as embodiments of inexhaustible negativity, that explained who the enemies of Christ and Christendom were. Women, in league with the Devil, were the cause of the societal and religious disarray that was occurring. As Augustine had taught, women were *non posse non peccare* (incapable of not sinning). Just as Eve at the beginning of time was the subtle, insidious tool of Satan in the Garden of Eden, so every generation knows the unsanctified alliance of its womenfolk with the Devil. Playing upon congenital feminine weaknesses, Lucifer involves them in unholy ritual intercourse with himself, violates them, and draws them into his cabal against Christendom. Thus, the witch craze is a justified defensive action by the Church. And it claims up to 50,000 (or so) female victims.

This angry, menacing description of women, however, is only a partially accurate account of the medieval Christian image of women, and it ultimately fails to be a true portrait because it altogether ignores the more encompassing ideology that governed and defined the real position of women in medieval society. The whole truth comes into focus only by recognizing that the adversarial conception of women as witch, as sorcerer, as numinous being was juxtaposed, and profoundly mediated in medieval and Reformation Christendom, by a whole series of countervailing understandings and their institutionalization whose purpose was to fully integrate women in a "non-terrifying" way into the larger communal fabric.

Women, in effect, were perceived to lose their sybaritic indecency by entering into, by being absorbed within, various anodyne structures whose very existence – as understood by the Church – was tied to their ability to assure just such a transmutational result. From sensual and devouring creatures of ordinary and extraordinary ability, women become domesticated (i.e., sexually controlled and subordinated) by entering into societal arrangements meant to insure just this austere transformation. So, the institution of the family – of women as wives and mothers and economic partners in nearly every trade and task – and the institution of the nunnery, with its idealized sublimation of female sexuality for non-married women, particularly of the upper and middle classes, came into being and had their sacred function. These culturally defined roles acted to neutralize women's inherently anarchic libido, to subdue the undesirable qualities of feminine nature, and hence to curtail the feminine threat to the divine order.

Within socially constructed parameters, women were to be protected and loved. Marriage, even if viewed as an exchange of women by men, was, in society's estimation, a divine blessing, having the status of a sacrament. Later, for Luther and the reformers, though marriage was no longer a sacrament *per se* – Protestantism having eliminated such sacraments – it was a great good, "the commonest, noblest state." Sexuality when expressed within matrimony was a sacred action blessed by God with children and the cycle of responsibility and care that such procreatic activities engendered. Medieval philosophers and mystics alike saw motherhood in positive terms and described it through such affirmative attributes as generation and sacrifice, love and tenderness, nurturing and selflessness.

In sum, the family unit was intended to serve as the medium through which female nature, female sexuality, was controlled and transformed. And it appears, largely, to have succeeded in this ambition. The roles of mother and wife had the desired prophylactic impact and guaranteed both the proper control of women by men as well as the creation of bonds of mutual affection that served to protect women in moments of societal crisis. Insofar as nearly all women entered into, and performed, these pre-established, publicly defined roles, they were, with very small statistical exceptions, so protected. The system worked.

Complementing the integrative function of the family was the socio-doctrinal role of the nunnery, predicated upon the dominant critical Christian view of sexuality, coupled with the transcendental meaning of the virginity of Mary, "the Mother of God." As a result of this two-sided Christian view of women, I estimate that less than one twenty-seventh of one percent of the late medieval female population was executed as witches. Christian safeguards were socially effective.

This same type of dialectic of theologically rooted aggression and limit also applied in the cases of medieval antisemitism – remember Jews survived about

1500 years of Christian domination despite the dark image of the Jew that runs from the *Adversus Judaeos* writings of the Church Fathers into Protestantism through Luther's invective, and despite the pogroms, blood libels and other manifestations of prejudice. Here the dialectic that creates this possibility of survival lies in the Pauline roots of Christianity and its theology of Israel in *Romans* 9:11 and elsewhere and Augustine's teaching on Jews that demanded of Christians that they *not* destroy the Jewish People. And the same, if in a different way, was true of the Church's response to heretics. This, too, was created as well as limited by Christian beliefs and values. In a manner that appears to us as paradoxical, the *mentalité* of the medieval Church sought the conversion of the nonbeliever and the abjuration of the heretic rather than their death. Indeed, even for those entire communities that proved unassimilable, unconvertible, like the Jews, the ultimate medieval solution was expulsion. And this because, for all real and symbolic violence manifest in this civilization, the social order was controlled and constrained by a heteronomous, Christian, moral vision that – however often forgotten, ignored, abused, or contorted – neither encouraged nor permitted physical genocide.

A dialectic, that is the inseparable linkage of aggression and restraint of the sort that I have here pointed to vis-à-vis major persecutions of the medieval era, is also present in the various modern cases usually raised in discussions of historical comparisons to the Holocaust. I include here, for example, the Armenian tragedy in 1915–16; Stalin's war on the Soviet Union's peasantry; and the four-centuries-long crime of New World black slavery. (And, if time and space allowed, I could illustrate my argument with many other cases.)

The dialectic embodied and played out in the Ottoman Empire during World War I centers around the *cause* of this tragedy: nationalism. Though there are real and significant similarities between the Armenian tragedy and the *Shoah*, there is a decisive difference that results from the nationalist rather than racial priority in the former event. The Young Turks persecuted and sought to uproot the Armenians out of fear of Armenian nationalism that they believed had led to treason and revolution in a time of war. The primary intentionality behind Turkish inhumanity was essentially a profound concern with further dismemberment and diminution of the Ottoman Empire/Turkey. This led, under the exigencies of war, to the attempted destruction of Armenian nationalism that, of course, also meant killing Armenians – but within limits.

The importance of recognizing the political-cum-nationalist configuration of this historical event lies in the fact that it provides the proper and necessary frame of reference for analyzing and evaluating Turkish behavior. It allows one to recognize that the Young Turks had no argument against Armenians per se, or put more appropriately, against "Armenianism," for example, the Armenian population of Russia or the U.S. Rather they objected to Armenians on Turkish soil, seeing them as a vital source of the betrayal of Turkish destiny and integrity. Therefore, and this is the essential matter in this context, one could satisfy Turkish interests through several processes that, though destructive and immoral, did not require murdering all Armenians resident in Turkey. The most salient of these in terms of their life-saving significance were:

(A) Deportations of Armenians. The cruelty of these forced marches and evacuations is not to be underestimated. Yet the principle of deportation logically allowed for continued life at the journey's end and indeed several hundred thousand Armenians survived such journeys. The Armenian populations throughout the Middle East – in Paris and Boston, among other places – are proof enough of this. Had the Turks intended a total Armenian genocide, the deportations, as well as their "destinations," would have been different.
(B) The forced conversion of Armenians. Hundreds of thousands of Armenians were converted as all the Western Christian powers complained. This was an ugly, but life-saving, phenomenon.
(C) The non-attack on Constantinople's 250,000 Armenian population.

Thus at least 50 percent, if not up to 65 percent of the Turkish Armenian population, despite contrary Armenian claims and ignoring Turkish falsifications, survived the onslaught against them.

And, in relation to Stalin's crimes, particularly regarding the Kulaks, the dialectic turns on issues of class. But class, unlike race, allows for "conversion" and so all members of the "offending class" do not need to be murdered. And the majority of such class enemies, though subject to brutal, violent, persecution, were *not* murdered in the Soviet Union between the late 1920s and Stalin's death in 1953. And this holds, I would specifically add, for the Ukrainian tragedy between 1932 and 1935. In this context too, the issue was Ukrainian nationalism and this Stalin could decapitate within limits – though certainly horrifically high limits of approximately 4–5 million that was equivalent to 10 to 12.5 percent of the Ukrainian population. It even applied in the Gulag where economics was more important than politics. The main purpose of the Gulag was producing raw materials not exterminating the labor force.

III The issue of "mediation"

The third element that I have learned is significant is what I call "mediation." That is, searching out those factors in historical contexts of mass murder that work against, and restrain, genocide. Here, for example, consider the issues of the value of reproduction, the significance of miscegenation and the connection between sex and manumission in the universe of black slavery; or again the possibility of, and actual historical role of, expulsion rather than extermination in the cases of medieval antisemitism; the case of the forced migration of five Southern Indian Tribes under President Jackson; and the deportation of the minority nationalities under Stalin. Only in the *Shoah* – and with recognition of the killings in Rwanda – was "mediation" essentially absent. This was true even with regard to Jewish labor during the Holocaust – a large subject that I do not have time to explore here.

IV Understanding the Third Reich

My study of the Holocaust, and its singularity, has given me a way of interpreting the phenomenon of Nazism more generally. While recognizing that monocausal explanations of Nazism are inadequate, the Holocaust points to the absolute centrality of racial antisemitism in the construction of the Third Reich and the policies it pursued.

I would here mention six major issues illuminated in fundamental and distinctive ways as a result of the concentration on the unique Nazi assault against world Jewry.

(1) At the center of the Nazi *Weltanschauung* stood a massive project of racial engineering and population restructuring, at the core of which was an unyielding racial antisemitism that was at the apex of this racial hierarchy. In this schema the Jew was the main source of all national and international political, social and economic problems. As such, Jews had to be removed without remainder in order to "liberate" history from their controlling, deforming, and destructive presence. According to Hitler's worldview, that became the blueprint for the building of the Third Reich, all other interests, motives, policies, agendas, intentions, and goals were secondary to this absolute requirement. The extraction and elimination of "der Jude" was the necessary precondition for all other cultural, socio-economic and political progress. This cardinal belief impacted, directly or indirectly, on just about everything that was significant in Nazi Germany and within all the territories conquered by the armies of the Hitler state. It was now insisted that all normative values, and all practical undertakings, be brought into conformity with this foundational racial belief. Anything else was treason against the natural order, and against the National Socialist state that was created to pursue and defend this natural order. And when the lethal ends dictated by this unshakable obsession clashed with other ends or ambitions, it was almost always the other goals, the alternative objectives, that had to give way. Making Europe free of Jews was far more important to the Führer, and hence to the workings and predetermined teleology of the Third Reich, than more mundane political or economic aims.

(2) In the long-running, and consequential, debate between "intentionalists" and "functionalists" that, despite the view of many contemporary scholars, is neither unimportant nor transcended by more recent scholarship, the "functionalist" position must be judged erroneous, even dysfunctional. The key to events in World War II from the German side were almost always the result of a decision or series of decisions made by the Nationalist Socialist leadership in Berlin – what happened was the consequence of decisions and choices made at the "center" of the Reich rather than at its "periphery," even while all that occurred at the periphery is recognized as being significant for an understanding of the entire historical narrative. Moreover, in every significant instance where decisions were made in Berlin and elsewhere, and choices decided, the role and implications of racial antisemitism were preeminent factors. If conflicts arose between the cardinal racial imperatives held by the Hitler state and other interests and goals of the state, it

was the former that almost always held sway, and the course of action taken was consistent with its requirements.

(3) I would remind everyone of the following in support of this claim:

(a) The assault on Jewry was pan-European.
(b) The formation and activities of the *Einsatzgruppen* was the result of plans made in Berlin.
(c) The events leading up to and away from the Wannsee Conference – i.e., the fateful decision on the "Final Solution" and its implementation – are a testament to centralized planning, predicated on the dominant, foundational antisemitic beliefs of the leadership of the Third Reich.
(d) The creation of approximately 1,000 ghettos, across all areas of Poland, the Baltic States, and the conquered territories in Belorussia and the Ukraine was not the result of a decision made at the periphery by local actors. Similarly, the liquidation of the ghettos beginning in 1942 came about directly as a result of an order by Himmler.
(e) Then there is the last great paroxysm of violence of the *Shoah*: the murder of Hungarian Jewry in the spring and early summer of 1944. Contrary to the absurd views of Götz Aly and Christian Gerlach it was the arrival of Adolf Eichmann, with his *Sonderkommando*, on the Führer's orders – and for ideological reasons only – in March 1944 that led inexorably to the movement of over 437,000 Jews, primarily to Auschwitz, where about 90 percent of these individuals were gassed.
(f) And, finally, there are the death camps. These have become the symbol *par excellence* of what Nazism was, what, above all else, it stood for and what it most distinctively achieved. Their coming into existence was not the result of local decisions made by marginal actors. They were, rather, the incarnation of Hitler's (and Himmler's) most cherished beliefs.

In regard to all of these major, central, matters, recognition of the *unique* role of racial antisemitism and the unique project that was the "Final Solution" helps explain the nature of the Third Reich as nothing else does.

Thus, contrary to much foolishness written about studying the Holocaust in comparative perspective, and after decades of close study, I am still willing to defend the uniqueness of the *Shoah* as an historical event. I would conclude that the comparative approach, and the study of the Holocaust – and Nazism and World War II – within a comparative frame of reference, sheds light on the events under consideration in a particular, distinctive, and especially helpful way.

I would, therefore, recommend it to others.

UPDATE

The shape of this essay may well seem odd to readers so the occasion for which it was written should be explained. In 2012, Milton Shain, a distinguished historian of antisemitism in South Africa, was nearing retirement from the University of Cape Town where he had directed the Kaplan Center for Jewish Studies for many years. To honor his work, as well as his person, a group of friends and colleagues, all of whom could be broadly defined as Holocaust scholars, came together in Cape Town, in the summer following his retirement, to hold a conference in his honor.

Prior to the conference it was agreed by those of us presenting papers that instead of just offering the usual academic lecture, the speakers would also say something about their own schooling, families and careers. And, as for their scholarly work, they would identify larger themes that their research had addressed and explain why their publications were, and remained, valuable. Thus the reason for the biographical details at the start of this essay, and then a concentration on broad conceptual issues in the remainder of the paper.

The central point I attempted to make in reporting on the nature of my research on comparative history was that the dialectic that usually operates in cases of mass murder, and that limits the number of individuals in the targeted group of victims who are killed, was absent in the Holocaust. This fact, and I take it to be certain, illuminates in a powerful and distinctive way both the dominant structural circumstance to be found in cases of mass murder and genocide (according to the U.N. definition) other than the murder of European Jewry and the peculiar morphology of the *Endlösung*. This is to say, there was, in contradiction to other cases of mass murder, no restraining ideological or utilitarian factor that limited the murder of Jews.

To further explain what I mean by the "dialectic that usually operates in cases of mass murder" I will refer to my work on New World black slavery and my research on Spanish Colonial America. In the context of slavery in the Americas, I would emphasize that economic considerations both caused and limited the violence that slavery incarnated as an institution. Profit was the aim of the slave trade on both sides of the Atlantic, and of slave ownership in the Western hemisphere. It was both the chief cause, and the primary goal, of slavery as an institution in the United States, the Caribbean sugar islands, and Brazil. This pursuit of monetary gain, however, required limits on the maltreatment permitted, including lethal injury – as dead slaves produce no economic benefit. Likewise, in colonial Spanish America, the lust for wealth not only was responsible for the exploitation of the aboriginal peoples but, as represented by the ameliorating interventions of both the Crown and the Church, was the reason for restraint relative to this exploitation. Indian labor was required to take advantage of the New World's natural and mineral resources. Moreover, for the

Crown, living Indians were required in order to collect tribute while, for the Church, the presence of native peoples was required if there was to be meaningful proselytization. Alternatively, in the Holocaust, Hitler wanted only that Jews become corpses (allowing for some small *temporary* exclusions related to the use of Jews as slave laborers).[2]

---

2 These temporarily exempted Jews were, of course, also already marked for death, if not immediately. See my further comments in the essay on "Extermination trumps production" in this volume (Chapter 7).

7

EXTERMINATION TRUMPS PRODUCTION: ON THE ISSUE OF JEWS AS SLAVE LABORERS

German historians Götz Aly and Susanne Heim, as well as others, have made the provocative claim that the Holocaust was a rational event, the consequence of an analysis by National Socialist technocrats concluding that the pressing issue facing Germany after its military conquests in Poland and the Soviet Union was overpopulation. To put it simply, this problem could be "solved" by the "rational" process of murdering the Jews of Eastern Europe.[1] In the present essay, I wish to examine this claim by analyzing the crucial issue of the use – and misuse – of Jews as slave laborers by the masters of the Third Reich. Moreover, I will ask whether, in fact, the utilization – or non-utilization – of Jews as potential or actual workers was "rational," or rather it represented a wasteful, non-utilitarian, and ultimately dysfunctional policy when measured by criteria other than racial ideology.

By 1941, if not earlier, the Third Reich found itself short of workers for its war economy. According to Ulrich Herbert's data, in September 1941, the Nazi hierarchy projected that 2,600,000 additional workers were needed.[2] So here we come up against two interrelated facts: by late 1941 the Nazi war economy was very short of workers and Poland had been conquered and was now part of the National Socialist empire. Therefore, the three million Jews of Poland were available to be moved, as were nationals of other conquered countries, to wherever they were needed as workers for the Third Reich. Given their portability – and the fact that millions of citizens of other nations were

---

1 Götz Aly and Susanne Heim's full argument is presented in their *Architects of Annihilation* (Princeton, 2003), ch. 3.
2 Ulrich Herbert, "Arbeit und Vernichtung: Ökonomisches Interesse und Primat der 'Weltanschauung' im Nationalsozialismus," in *Ist der Nationalsozialismus Geschichte? Zu Historisierung und Historikerstreit*, ed. Dan Diner (Frankfurt am Main, 1987), p. 213. Heim and Aly have responded to Herbert's work and his critique of their views in their essay, "Wider die Unterschätzung der nationalsozialistischen Politik: Antwort an unsere Kritiker," in *Vernichtungspolitik: eine Debatte uber den Zusammenhang von Sozialpolitik und Genozid im nationalsozialistischen Deutschland*, ed. Wolfgang Schneider (Hamburg, 1991), pp. 165–75. But their attempt to deflect and rebut Herbert's well-targeted criticism, especially insofar as it centers on the shortage of labor, is unsuccessful.

transferred to Germany and elsewhere – the Jews of Poland did not, per se, represent an "oversupply" of workers. Had the National Socialist state been primarily concerned with matters of production and efficiency, it would have moved Jews, or at least those capable of work, as it moved millions of other nationals, to other parts of its empire to live as slave laborers. But it did so only very partially and temporarily – essentially up to the latter part of 1942, with a few further exceptions into 1943.

The "temporary" nature of the arrangements governing the use of Jewish labor is confirmed by the report of the main Division of Labor in the *Generalgouvernement* for December 1943, which refers to the fact that during 1942 there were 1,426,495 Jewish laborers, of which "980,000 were employed for a short time."[3] Based on these statistics, two-thirds of Jewish workers in the region had been extirpated during that year. Richard Korherr, Himmler's personal statistician, supplied further data of relevance when announcing that his research showed that 1,274,166 Jews had, in his code-language, been "evacuated" by the end of 1942. In addition, it should be remembered that at the Wannsee Conference held on January 20, 1942, the State Secretary of the *Generalgouvernement*, Dr. Josef Bühler announced that there were still 2,500,000 Jews in occupied Poland. By January 25, 1944, according to Hans Frank, the governor of this territory, there were approximately 100,000 Jews still alive.[4]

What seems more than probable is that by the fall of 1941, Himmler, after conversations on the matter with Hitler, already had plans for instituting the Final Solution. Accordingly, Jewish labor would necessarily, completely – and soon – disappear, eliminating the possibility that Jews might make any contribution to the German war economy. To help realize this momentous project Himmler, rather than accommodate those who wanted, as a practical concession, to preserve Jewish lives, ordered Rudolf Höss to begin constructing Auschwitz and initiated the construction of Chełmno and Bełżec extermination camps.[5] Over the next year – up to the end of September 1942 – Jews killed in the new death camps and by the *Einsatzkommando*, concomitant with the invasion of Russia in the summer of 1941, could have provided – even when deducting the number of Jewish children and elderly who were murdered – a considerable number of the workers that

---

3 Cited in Albert Speer, *Infiltration* (New York, 1981), p. 282.
4 *Ibid.*, pp. 281–82.
5 Himmler ordered Odilo Globocnik, the *SS-und Polizeiführer* in the Lublin District, to begin the construction of the Bełżec extermination camp on October 13, 1941. A comprehensive analysis of anti-Jewish events in Lublin and their role in an evaluation of the Final Solution is provided by Bogdan Musial, "The Origins of 'Operation Reinhard': The Decision-Making Process for the Mass Murder of Jews in the Generalgouvernement," *Yad Vashem Studies* 28 (2000): 113–53. The exact date on which Himmler ordered Rudolf Höss to begin the erection of Auschwitz is the subject of debate. However, this order was certainly given by late 1941.

Germany needed.[6] However, this utilitarian option was significantly underutilized and in many places and instances, ignored altogether, and the Jews of Poland and millions of potentially valuable Jews from elsewhere – in the Baltic States, Belorussia, Ukraine, among others – were exterminated. For the goals of the Final Solution, recognizing that there were some short-term accommodations was ultimately not about issues arising from the supply, or *over*-supply, of available workers.[7] Neither the actual undersupply nor the asserted oversupply of laborers was relevant to the Führer's decision to annihilate the Jews of Poland and, in due course, the Jews of Europe.

In support of this conclusion, it should be recalled that, despite Hermann Göring's insistence, as the Plenipotentiary for the Four-year Plan, that German and Polish agriculture continue its crucial production and, therefore, that all evacuation orders in Poland of labor to Germany be carefully scrutinized so that "useful manpower does not disappear,"[8] he did not oppose the ongoing deportation of potential Jewish agricultural laborers from Germany, or their disappearance from Western Poland (Wartheland). Again, in mid-February 1941, Göring demanded that an additional 250,000 Polish workers be sent to work in the Altreich. But this was to be accomplished without Jewish workers, whose deportation to the East was reaffirmed in a directive of February 7, 1941.[9] In February and March 1941,

---

6 R. Korherr, Himmler's personal statistician, also provided the following information:

Table 1 The "Evacuation" of the Jews to the East, up to the end of 1942

Origin	
Reich territory, Protectorate, Białystok	170,642
New eastern territory	1,449,692
France	41,911
Netherlands	38,571
Belgium	16,886
Norway	532
Occupied eastern territories	633,300
Croatia	4,927
Slovakia	56,691
Total	2,413,152

Source: R. Korherr Report (n.d.), BA NS 19 neu/1570. Cited from B. Kroener, Rolf-Dieter Müller, and Hans Umbreit (eds.), *Germany and the Second World War*, vol. 5, *The Global War* (Oxford, 2000), p. 342, table I, vi. 4.

7 Aly and Heim, *Architects of Annihilation*, ch. 3, "Demographic Economics: The Emergence of a New Science," pp. 58–72.
8 Göring made this assertion in his speech of February 12, 1940, "Sitzung über Ostfragen unter dem Vorsitz des Ministerpräsidenten Generalfeldmarschall Göring," in *Trials of Major War Criminals before the Nuremberg Military Tribunal* (TMWC), vol. 36, pp. 299–307, document No. 305-EC.
9 The directive of February 7, 1941 is discussed by Phillip T. Rutherford in *Prelude to the Final Solution: The Nazi Program for Deporting Ethnic Poles, 1939–1941* (Lawrence, KS, 2007), pp. 198–99.

9,000 Jews were deported to the *Generalgouvernement* from the Wartheland. Then in late 1941/early 1942, as the German labor situation worsened, most of the Jews of the Wartheland, contrary to all "rational" labor utilization standards, were killed in the gas vans that operated at the Chełmno death camp.

A second example of the ruling dysfunctional attitude towards Jewish labor occurred when Arthur Greiser,[10] the *Gauleiter* of Posen, offered German industry 73,000 Jews as forced laborers, with the approval of Göring, in February and March 1941. Several corporations that were short of workers expressed interest in utilizing them, but Hitler rejected the idea on April 7, 1941, and the proposal was dropped.[11] Then, too, at exactly the same moment that Reinhard Heydrich, in December 1941, was creating a Working Group on Foreign Labor (*Ausländer-Arbeitskreis*) in order to address the critical shortage of workers in German industry, Göring – with Heydrich's active and direct assistance – was busy organizing the original date for the Wannsee Conference on the Final Solution.[12] A third example of National Socialist irrationality was manifest in the fall of 1941 when a number of government offices involved in matters of war production, including agricultural output, expressed concern about the need to bring forced laborers to Germany. They would, in fact, bring Polish and other workers to fill the existing labor gap, while Göring, on November 7, 1941, ordered that German Jews, rather than being sent to work, be deported to Minsk and Riga where they were murdered by *Einsatzkommandos*.[13]

The priority given to the murder of Jews rather than to their much needed employment as slave laborers was also evident in Hitler's instruction to Fritz

---

10 Arthur Greiser is the subject of a thorough study by Catherine Epstein, *Model Nazi: Arthur Greiser and the Occupation of Western Poland* (Oxford, 2010). The earlier studies of Czesław Łuczak, *Arthur Greiser: hitlerowski władca w Wolnym Mieście Gdańsku i w Kraju Warty* (Poznań: PSO, 1997), and Czesław Madajczyk, *Die Okkupationspolitik Nazideutschlands in Polen 1939–1945* (Berlin, 1987) are also of relevance. So, too, is the essay by Ian Kershaw, "Arthur Greiser – Ein Motor der 'Endlösung'," in *Die Braune Elite*, vol. 2, no. 21, *weitere biographischen Skizzen*, ed. Ronald Smelser, Rainer Zitelmann, and Enrico Syring (Darmstadt, 1993), pp. 117–27.

11 Staatsarchiv, Nuremberg Document NG-363, Cited in Raul Hilberg, *The Destruction of the European Jews*, 3rd ed., 3 vols. (New Haven, CT, 2003), vol. 2, p. 461.

12 The Wannsee Conference was originally planned for December 9, 1941, but because of the attack on Pearl Harbor, among other factors, it was postponed until January 20, 1942. The invitation sent by Adolf Eichmann to attend the conference, and the explanation of the purpose of the gathering, has been republished in Kurt Pätzold and Erika Schwarz (eds.), *Tagesordnung, Judenmord: die Wannsee-Konferenz am 20. Januar 1942: eine Dokumentation zur Organisation der "Endlösung"* (Berlin, 1992), pp. 88–89. The discussions at the conference and the plans agreed upon there are summarized in the document known as the Wannsee Protocol, prepared by Adolf Eichmann. A translation of this document can be found in Jeremy Noakes and Geoffery Pridham (eds.), *Nazism 1919–1945*, vol. 3, *Foreign Policy, War and Racial Extermination: A Documentary Reader* (4 vols.), rev. ed. (Exeter, UK, 1988), pp. 535–41. This document was partially translated and entered into evidence at Nuremberg as NG-2686-G, Prosecution Exhibit 1452, *Trials of War Criminals* (TWC), vol. 13, p. 210, "Extracts from the Minutes of the Wannsee Conference, 20 January 1941."

13 Ulrich Herbert, "Labour and Extermination: Economic Interest and the Primacy of Weltanschauung in National Socialism," *Past & Present* 138 (February 1993): 168.

Sauckel,[14] General Plenipotentiary for Labor Mobilization, given between September 20 and 22, 1942, to deport all Jews working in the armaments industry in Germany, despite the compromise reached on this critical issue a week earlier by *SS-Gruppenführer* Oswald Pohl, head of the *Wirtschafts und Verwaltungshauptamt*, the SS Central Office for Economics and Administration, and Albert Speer, minister of armaments.[15] It was also manifest in Poland when the agreement that Hitler made with Sauckel, over and against Himmler's wishes, to temporarily retain Jewish workers in the *Generalgouvernement* so as to aid in reducing the slave manpower shortage that existed[16] was trumped by Himmler's order to eliminate all the ghettos in this territory that still housed hundreds of thousands of Jews[17] by the end of December 1942.

The predominance of racial ideology over an economic-labor policy was then further evidenced when, on November 26, 1942, Sauckel – knowing that Hitler had ordered the deportation of Jewish workers from Germany in September and that Himmler's genocidal obsession essentially knew no limits – required that all Jews still working in Germany be removed from their jobs in the armaments industry, despite the loss in productivity that would inevitably result. This goal was achieved mainly by the so-called Factory Action that began at the end of February 1943 and which saw 10,948 German Jewish workers deported during the first week of March 1943 to Auschwitz where most were gassed on arrival at the

---

14 Fritz Sauckel was appointed by Hitler to be the Third Reich's *Generalbevollmächtigter für den Arbeitseinsatz*, General Plenipotentiary for Labor Mobilization, on March 21, 1942. Albert Speer tells us that at the meeting at which Sauckel was given his new position Hitler told him "to bring in the needed workers by any means whatsoever." Albert Speer, *Inside the Third Reich: Memoirs* (New York,, 1970), p. 219. As a result, Sauckel delivered 2,800,000 foreign workers to Germany over approximately 15 months, until June 1943. This meant that by July 1943, 6,500,000 foreign workers had been brought to toil in Germany. Of these, 4,950,000 were civilians; the remainder were prisoners of war. These figures are drawn from Adam Tooze, *The Wages of Destruction* (New York, 2008), p. 517. This drafting of foreign workers continued into 1944.

15 On September 15, 1942, an agreement was reached between Pohl and Speer regarding the use of Jews as slave workers in the armaments industry. See, for details, the report Pohl sent to Himmler about this meeting on September 16, 1942; republished in Falk Pingel, *Häftlinge unter SS-Herrschaft: Widerstand, Selbstbehauptung und Vernichtung im Konzentrationslager* (Hamburg, 1978), pp. 276–78. According to a document submitted to the Nuremberg Tribunal, R-124, dated September 29, 1942, "The Führer accepts Sauckel's suggestion that for the present skilled Jewish workers should remain in the Generalgouvernement, but he stresses the importance of removing the Jews from the armament industry in the Reich."

16 It is relevant to recall here that the Governor of Galicia – Galicia had been made part of the *Generalgouvernement* in November 1941 – ordered a limitation on the "uncontrollable" violence against Jews then occurring in his area of responsibility on the grounds that it was contrary to "rationality and productivity." This call, however, was essentially ignored. Document issued by Governor Lasch on November 28, 1941. Cited in United States Holocaust Memorial Museum (USHMM) Archives, RG 31.003M, file 35/6/581.

17 The report of Richard Korherr, Himmler's personal statistician, prepared in spring 1943, indicated that by the end of 1942, of the 2,300,000 Jews originally in the *Generalgouvernement* only 298,000 were still living in ghettos and another 300,000 plus were still alive in labor camps. Korherr Report, April 19, 1943, NA/RG, NO-5194.

camp.[18] In Poland, this economically dysfunctional decision making was manifested in January 1943 when Himmler, after visiting the Warsaw Ghetto, ordered that the "so-called armament plants" there be closed by February 15, 1943, and that half of the 32,000 Jews working in them be sent to a concentration camp, and 8,000 of the Jewish laborers be murdered immediately.[19]

In this context, the change of German policy towards Russian POWs is also relevant and sheds further light on the issue at hand. By 1942, Himmler had come to appreciate the need to use Russian POWs as forced laborers, with the result that the lethal starvation policy of the first years of the war gave way to a less murderous regime. This change, necessitated by real labor shortages in the German war economy, tellingly indicates that there was no over-supply of workers available to the Reich, but just the opposite. Yet, while this acknowledgment forced an alteration in German policy with regard to Russian prisoners of war, it did not stop those in charge of deciding the fate of Jews from sending tens of thousands, even hundreds of thousands, of real and potential Jewish workers to be murdered. This included even Jews who, as we have seen, were crucial to the military effort but who were now removed and sent on to the death camps to be exterminated. Hans Frank, governor of the *Generalgouvernement*, himself lamented this situation, telling his staff that "the directive for the annihilation of the Jews comes from higher sources . . . now the order provides that the armament Jews are also to be taken away. I hope that this order, if not already voided, will be revoked, because then the situation will be even worse."[20]

Jews, whether in Poland or elsewhere, were not assessed vis-à-vis their capacity as laborers, as were members of other ethnic and national groups, nor was their destiny decided according to pre-war population theories. As evidence, I note, for example, that of the 61,098 Jews deported to Auschwitz from France, 47,976, or 78.5 percent, were sent directly to be gassed.[21] The same fate awaited Dutch Jews who began to be deported to Auschwitz on July 15, 1942. By the end of 1942, 38,571 Jews had been transported from Holland. Ultimately, over 100,000 Dutch Jews were murdered.

Seeking a justification for the decimation of Polish Jewry, German administrators and bureaucrats were correct in concluding that Jews were less productive after being ghettoized, but even in the ghettos they were still productive.[22] Indeed,

---

18 Wolf Gruner, "The Factory Action and the Events at the Rosenstrasse in Berlin: Facts and Fictions about 27 February 1943 – Sixty Years Later," *Central European History* 36.2 (2003): 192. On the arrival and gassing of these Jewish workers soon after coming to Auschwitz, see Danuta Czech, *Kalendarium der Ereignisse im Konzentrationslager Auschwitz-Birkenau: 1939–1945* (Hamburg, 1990), p. 428.
19 U. Herbert, "Forced Laborers in the Third Reich: An Overview," *International Labor and Working-Class History* 58 (Fall 2000): 202–203.
20 Hans Frank, *Das Diensttagebuch des deutschen Generalgouverneurs in Polen 1939–1945* (Stuttgart, 1975), entry dated December 9, 1942.
21 Hermann Langbein, *People in Auschwitz* (Chapel Hill, 2004), p. 58.
22 This is a complex issue that I plan to return to in a separate essay.

Frank himself recognized this fact and had therefore earlier, on March 25, 1941, proclaimed, in regard to utilizing Jewish and Polish labor, that "it is more important that we win the war than implement racial policy."[23] Again, on April 14, 1942, he asserted, with marked pragmatism: "If I want to win the war I must be an ice-cold technician. The question what will be done from an ideological-ethnic point of view I must postpone to a time after the war."[24] And on December 9, 1942, he was openly critical of the indiscriminate murder of Poland's Jews, telling his subordinates: "Not unimportant labor [was something that has] been taken from us when we lost our old trustworthy Jews . . . Clearly the labor situation is aggravated when, at the height of the war effort, an order is given to prepare Jews for annihilation."[25] Yet Frank's concerns with the practical implications of the murder of Polish Jewry went unheeded. It did not significantly matter to those ultimately directing National Socialist policy whether Jewish labor was needed at this critical juncture of the war or not. "Higher sources" had decided, for their own, very different, reasons that those Jews had to die.

Himmler, the chief Nazi figure after Hitler in deciding the fate of the Jews, well understood the implications, both actual and potential, of the choice of death over life that he was making with regard to Jewish workers, as well as the impact it would have on German industrial and armaments production. In April 1942, Oswald Pohl, who was Himmler's own appointee and confidant in matters of labor recruitment and exploitation, had written to Himmler:

> The war has brought about a change . . . Keeping people in detention for reasons of security, education, or prevention only is no longer the prime consideration. Now the economic situation is the most important factor. The value of mobilizing all prisoner labor for war needs (stepping up the manufacture of armaments) and for construction needs in the approaching peacetime is rising steadily. This realization necessitates certain measures to make the concentration camps into organizations that are suited to the economic goals, unlike the previous situation, when [the camps] were of political interest only.[26]

In June 1942, in light of this now pressing, even urgent, military-labor situation, the chief of the *Generalgouvernement*'s labor administration went so far as to agree to the following temporary compromise on the use of Jewish labor: the Jews

---

23 Frank, *Das Diensttagebuch*, p. 337.
24 *Ibid.*, p. 489.
25 *Ibid.*, entry dated December 9, 1942.
26 Cited in Bella Gutterman, *A Narrow Bridge to Life: Jewish Forced Labor and Survival in the Gross-Rosen Camp System, 1940–1945* (New York, 2008), p. 16. The full German text is reprinted in the collection of documents edited by Walter Bartel, *Buchenwald: Mahnung und Verpflichtung: Dokumente und Berichte* (Frankfurt am Main,, 1983), pp. 250–52. An English translation can be found in Noakes and Pridham, *Nazism*, vol. 4, doc. 1028, pp. 174–75.

would "not actually be exempted from SS operations but [would be left] to work for the duration of the war."[27] But neither Pohl's recommendation nor any partial compromise reached on the temporary labor service of Jews deflected the project of mass murder in a major way.

In early June, Reichsführer Himmler, in a secret meeting with SS officers in Berlin, assured his audience that: "The migration of the Jewish People will be completed within a year . . . We shall make a clean sweep [of them]."[28] And this commitment was reinforced when on July 19, 1942, while visiting Lublin, he told Higher SS Leader Friedrich-Wilhelm Krüger that almost all Jews in the *Generalgouvernement* had to be exterminated by the end of the year. Therefore, on July 22, the major deportations from the Warsaw Ghetto began.[29] In light of these plans it is clear why even Himmler's own instruction to Richard Glücks, head of concentration camp inspection (*Inspektion der Konzentrationslager*), given on January 25, 1942, following the Wannsee Conference, to make preparations for the deportation of 150,000 Jews to his camps "for major economic tasks,"[30] did not translate into keeping many Jews alive. Nor did his conversations and correspondence in February and March 1942 with Hans Kammler, head of the SS main office of Budgets and Building, regarding a massive building program in the East.[31] For Himmler and the SS, which remained primarily in charge of the final "disposal" of Jewish workers in Poland, even the critical labor situation created by the expansion and changing fortunes of the war were not cause enough to allow any significant deviation from the program of the Final Solution.

The consequential policy of excluding Jews from the work force was imposed by Krüger regarding the Jews in the *Generalgouvernement* in the summer of 1942.[32] Nevertheless, he appeared to recognize the practical necessity of delaying

---

27 Cited in Wolf Gruner, *Jewish Forced Labor under the Nazis: Economic Needs and Racial Aims, 1938–1944* (New York,, p. 259. For more on this subject, see Jan Erik Schulte, *Zwangsarbeit und Vernichtung: das Wirtschaftsimperium der SS: Oswald Pohl und das SS-Wirtschafts-Verwaltungshauptamt 1933–1945* (Paderborn, 2001); and Walter Naasner (ed.), *SS-Wirtschaft und SS-Verwaltung: das SS-Wirtschafts-Verwaltungshauptamt und die unter seiner Dienstaufsicht stehenden wirtschaftlichen Unternehmungen: und weitere Dokumente* (Düsseldorf, 1998).
28 Heinrich Himmler, *Geheimreden 1933 bis 1945 und andere Ansprachen: [mit 243 zum Teil unbekannten Bild- und Textdokumenten]* (Frankfurt am Main, 1974), p. 159.
29 Himmler's activities during late May and early June 1942 can be followed in his Day Book, Peter Witte et al. (eds.), *Der Dienstkalender Heinrich Himmlers 1941/42* (Hamburg, 1999), pp. 441–56. In addition to his visit to Lublin and meeting with Krüger, he met with Hitler seven times between May 27 and June 5.
30 TWC, vol. 5, p. 365, translation of document NO-500. This order has been analyzed by Peter Longerich, *Heinrich Himmler: A Life* (Oxford, 2011), p. 559; Wolfgang Sofsky, *The Order of Terror: The Concentration Camp*, trans. William Templer (Princeton, 1997), p. 321, n. 6; and Christopher Browning, "Jewish Workers in Poland," in his *Nazi Policy, Jewish Workers, German Killers* (Cambridge, UK, 2000), p. 59.
31 Schulte, *Zwangsarbeit und Vernichtung*, pp. 344–45.
32 Bundesarchiv, Abr Berlin, NS19/1765. This order is republished in Peter Longerich (ed.), *Die Ermordung der Europäischen Juden* (Munich, 1989), pp. 202–203. HSSPF stands for *Höhere SS-und Polizeiführer*, or Higher SS and Police Leader.

the extirpation of a segment of Polish Jewry due to their value as slave workers and, at the request of Josef Bühler for more Jewish workers, issued orders reflecting this view on May 9 and May 20. Soon thereafter, however, he demanded the end of Jewish labor camps in the *Generalgouvernement*[33] and the need for Jewish labor was again subordinated to other standards, that is, ideological, necessities which took precedence. In making this repercussive decision, Krüger was conforming to the wishes of the *Reichsführer*, who had already dictated that extermination predominate over labor in the event of any ambiguity as to the policy to be adopted towards Jewish workers. Thus, for example, in regard to the liquidation of the Pinsk Ghetto on October 27, 1942, he stipulated:

> According to my information, the ghetto in Pinsk can be regarded as the headquarters for all the bandit activity in the Pripet marshes. I therefore recommend that, despite any economic concerns you may have, you immediately dissolve and liquidate the ghetto in Pinsk. If possible 1,000 male workers are to be secured and transferred to the Wehrmacht for the construction of the wooden huts. The work of these 1,000 workers must, however, be carried out only in a closed camp under the strictest guard. If this guard cannot be provided, then these 1,000 workers should also be annihilated.[34]

This disregard for workers was also apparent in Lithuania where, despite an order from the *Reichsführer* that Jews "aged 16 to 32 who are capable of work are to be excluded from special measures until further notice,"[35] nearly all Jews were soon murdered. This is because Himmler subsequently ordered the extermination of all Lithuanian Jews, with the result that by the end of 1943, 96 percent of Lithuanian Jewry, including almost "all Jews and Jewesses aged 16 to 32 . . . capable of work," had been murdered.[36]

Even in the domain of aircraft production, which was absolutely essential to the German war effort, the hierarchy of extermination over production where Jewish workers were at issue prevailed. Thus, for example, when the Heinkel Corporation created a new plant in the *Generalgouvernement* in 1942 to increase the output of its fighter planes, it became evident by the summer of 1942, as Heinkel's representative in Berlin, Rittmeister von Pfistermeister, reported to Karl Frydag, chairman of the Airframe Main Committee, that the production schedule at the plant was not

---

33 Bundesarchiv, Abl. Berlin NS19/2462.
34 Cited in Longerich, *Heinrich Himmler*, p. 622.
35 *Ibid.*, p. 567.
36 Approximately 15 percent of Lithuanian Jewry were exempted from the order of immediate annihilation, much to the anger of Karl Jäger, the Commander of *Einsatzkommando* 3. But this cohort would also be killed by 1943. The figure of 15 percent is cited by Yisrael Gutman in his paper, "The Concept of Labor in Judenrat Policy," in *Patterns of Jewish Leadership in Nazi Europe, 1933–1945: Proceedings of the Third Yad Vashem International Historical Conference, Jerusalem, April 4–7, 1977* eds. Yisrael Gutman and Cynthia J. Haft (Jerusalem, 1979), pp. 164–65.

being met because of the deportation of Jewish workers.[37] Again, in 1943, Heinkel had to move production back to its Vienna-Schwechat factory due to a scarcity of workers, and even in Vienna it found itself short of workers to build its He 219 plane. By the summer of 1943, frustrated by the labor situation in Vienna, Heinkel again moved production of the He 219 to Poland, but here, once more, finding suitable and sufficient labor proved a significant obstacle to manufacturing of the plane.[38] Throughout the war, with relatively marginal modifications vis-à-vis the utilization of Jewish labor in 1944–45, the Reich preferred to kill Jews rather than increase its supplies of armaments, including planes.[39]

This became indisputable when on July 19, 1942, Himmler, as already noted, asserted his authority over all Jews in the *Generalgouvernement* and ordered that all ghettos in the territory be liquidated and all Jews moved to labor camps by the end of 1942. "I herewith order," he wrote to his key subordinates,

> that the resettlement of the entire Jewish population of the Government-General be carried out and completed by December 31, 1942 . . . From December 31, 1942, no persons of Jewish origin may remain within the Government-General, unless they are in the collection camps in Warsaw, Cracow, Czestochowa, Radom, and Lublin. All other work on which Jewish labor is employed must be finished by that date, or, in the event that this is not possible, it must be transferred to one of the collection camps . . . These measures are required with a view to the necessary ethnic division of races and peoples for the New Order in Europe, and also in the interests of the security and cleanliness of the German Reich and its sphere of interest. Every breach of this regulation spells a danger to quiet and order in the entire German sphere of interest, a point of application for the resistance movement and a source of moral and physical pestilence.[40]

---

37 Daniel Uziel, *Arming the Luftwaffe: The German Aviation Industry in World War II* (Jefferson, NC, 2012), p. 171.
38 *Ibid.*, pp. 172–74.
39 Christopher Browning's influential distinction, reflective of differences of opinions among Nazi bureaucrats between "attritionists" and "productionists" – which became intense with the debate over the policy of ghettoization – supports the present argument. According to Browning's typology, for ideological reasons, the attritionists placed primacy on the murder of the Jews. In contrast, the productionists, influenced by pragmatic economic considerations, sought to utilize Jews as slave labor on behalf of the severely stretched war economy. In this dispute the two main protagonists, defending the alternative positions, would be, as described above, Himmler and Speer. And these two titans would have their local surrogates who were involved in local disputes, throughout Europe. Who won? According to Browning, despite an oft-made misunderstanding of his position, it was ultimately the attritionists who gained the upper hand and their view became the dominant one that shaped National Socialist labor policy. For his full argument, see "Jewish Workers in Poland," especially the analysis on p. 59.
40 Nuremberg document NO-5574, reproduced in Tatiana Berenstein, Artur Eisenbach, Bernard Mark, and Adam Rutkowski (eds.), *Faschismus-Getto-Massenmord: Dokumentation über Ausrottung*

Through this action the *Reichsführer* was increasing the tempo of the murder of European Jewry. The temporary era of ghettos, and the economic-military contribution of ghetto production, was to be ended, as was the existence of most of European Jewry. Insofar as there were very limited exceptions to this agenda, even these were only to be short-lived, as Himmler asserted elsewhere, in "accordance with the wishes of the Führer."

When explaining the need for this extreme order Himmler left no room for ambiguity. He made no mention of matters related to economic advantage, to Lebensraum, or to an "oversupply" of workers or food shortages. Rather, consistent with his racial *Weltanschauung*, he employed the language of pseudo-biology, describing Jews, as "a source of moral and physical pestilence." The requirement that they be exterminated was not the result of an ad hoc crisis brought about by some newly arising military or economic contingency but an ontological necessity. This distinctive type of racially saturated language reflected Himmler's deepest beliefs, as revealed also in his infamous October 4, 1943, address to high-ranking Nazi officials in Poznań, in which he referred to the mass murder of the Jews of Europe as "destroying a bacillus."[41] "We do not want," he told his audience, "in the end ... to be infected by this bacillus and to die."[42] And he continually and regularly proceeded to make determinative decisions on Jews and Jewish labor, in strict conformity with this putative parasitological principle. As a result, by 1943 most Jews in the *Generalgouvernement* had been transported to death camps.[43] The crucial needs of the armaments industry[44] and the Wehrmacht[45] were, for the *Reichsführer*, secondary to the production of Jewish corpses. Though it is incontrovertible that by the end of 1942 the German war economy was straining

---

und Widerstand der Juden in Polen während des zweiten Weltkrieges (Berlin, 1960), doc. no. 229, p. 303. An English translation can be found in Yitzhak Arad, Israel Gutman, and Abraham Margaliot (eds.), *Documents on the Holocaust*, 8th ed. (Lincoln, NE, 1999), pp. 275–76.

41 TWC, vol. 29, pp. 110–73, PS-1919, "Speech by Himmler on the occasion of the SS group leader meeting in Posen, October 4, 1943." A partial English translation, which includes the material here cited, is available in Arad et al., *Documents on the Holocaust*, 8th ed., p. 345.

42 *Ibid.*

43 See Korherr Report data.

44 Ernst Heinkel, one of Germany's leading aircraft manufacturers, for example told Field Marshal Erhard Milch, head of the Air Ministry, in the fall of 1942, that one could not create new airplane manufacturing facilities in Poland because of "the extirpation [*Ausrottung*] of the Jews." Lutz Budrass, *Flugzeugindustrie und Luftrüstung in Deutschland 1918–1945* (Düsseldorf, 1998), p. 784. Still, the murder of Jews in Poland was not halted so that these potential planes, desperately needed by the Luftwaffe which was in the process of losing control of the skies over Germany and occupied Europe – and thus the war – could be built.

45 The details of the negotiations between the Wehrmacht and the SS regarding the possible use of Jewish labor can be found in the documents in Helga Grabitz and Wolfgang Scheffler, *Letzte Spuren: Ghetto Warschau, SS-Arbeitslager Trawniki – Aktion Erntefest. Fotos und Dokumente über Opfer des Endlösungswahns im Spiegel der historischen Ereignisse* (Berlin, 1988), pp. 306–15.

to maintain itself[46] and was desperate for additional workers, Himmler's – and the Third Reich's – priorities were deflected from production to extermination.

As this fateful arrangement was known to be consistent with, and in fulfillment of, Hitler's most deeply held beliefs, no one in authority in the National Socialist hierarchy dared to challenge it. Thus, for example, Göring, knowing Hitler's wishes in the matter, interceded in support of Himmler's design for the murder of the Jews and, at a meeting on August 14, 1942, told his subordinates and various assembled representatives of the armaments and military establishment: "The [genocidal] orders that have been issued [regarding Jews] are clear and hard. They are valid not only for the *Generalgouvernement* but for all occupied territories."[47] Moreover, Himmler, convinced of the absolute correctness of his position and unconcerned with any possible opposition, ordered General Wilhelm Keitel, on September 5, 1942, to replace all Jews working in the armaments industry in Poland with Poles, and required Keitel to pass on this order to his subordinates by mid-September.[48]

Although a small minority of Jews was now "selected"[49] to remain alive for exploitation as workers,[50] their fate had already been sealed by Himmler, with the concurrence of Göring and Hitler. Himmler's overriding ambition to eliminate all Jews from the labor pool engaged in the war industries was evidenced, for example, in a series of decisions he made regarding, as noted, the work force of the Warsaw Ghetto. This, the largest of all ghettos, was home to approximately 450,000 Jews at the beginning of 1942; thousands of Jews in the ghetto were involved in war-related production. Nevertheless, Himmler, through lethal actions authorized in July 1942 and September 1942, and in direct disregard of pragmatically grounded opposition to the liquidation of the ghetto from various quarters of the German bureaucracy, including the armaments ministry, dramatically reduced both the overall population and the organized work force in the ghetto. As a result, the ghetto labor force was reduced to 95,000 by the fall of 1942,[51] nearly all of whom were engaged in war production. Yet this substantial diminution was still not extensive enough to satisfy Himmler. Over the fall of 1942 and the winter

---

46 As a recent study suggests, SS armament factories were inefficient and less than maximally productive. Details can be found in Schulte, *Zwangsarbeit und Vernichtung*, pp. 216–20.
47 Speer, *Infiltration*, p. 260.
48 Gruner, *Jewish Forced Labor*, p. 263.
49 I have chosen to use the English word "selected" as a form of the German word *Selektion* because this is what the Nazis called the separation of Jews into two groups, one of which was sent to be murdered, and the other of which was utilized for labor.
50 On the conditions of Jewish laborers, see the comments of Mark Spoerer and Jochem Fleischhacker in their essay "Forced Laborers in Nazi Germany: Categories, Numbers and Survivors," *Journal of Interdisciplinary History* 33.2 (Autumn 2002): 169–204.
51 I base this figure on the population data given by Hilberg, *The Destruction of the European Jews*, 3rd ed., vol. 1, p. 261, which refers to the ghetto work force, as of July 31, 1942, as "having risen to 95,000, an employment rate that was nearing 50 percent." Hilberg cites as his source Adam Czerniaków's diary entry for that date, p. 378, in Raul Hilberg (ed.), *The Warsaw Diary of Adam Czerniaków* (New York, 1979).

of 1943 he required that the number of Jewish laborers in the ghetto be further reduced by another 40 percent and then, in April 1943, ordered that the ghetto be liquidated in its entirety and that almost all remaining ghetto workers be deported to Treblinka where they would be gassed. A small number of Jews were sent to the labor camps of Trawniki and Poniatowa, but the overwhelming majority of ghetto Jews went to their deaths. And even those few transported to Trawniki would be murdered six months later in the so-called *Erntefest* of November 2–4, 1943. Although the last 95,000 Jewish workers were certainly not a "surplus population" in any normal sense of this term, given the overall shortfall in the supply of workers at this point in the war, they were "a surplus population" according to the reigning racial criterion determining who could live and who must die.

That this racial logic was the principal factor deciding the fate of the great majority of Jewish slave laborers required to support the war economy was additionally revealed in the period between March and June 1943, during which Himmler ordered the closing of the still-extant ghettos and work camps in the *Generalgouvernement*. Though important elements in the army and those in charge of the armaments industry tried to persuade him to delay, or at least slow down, the process of liquidation and extermination, Himmler remained adamant and therefore the process continued at an accelerated pace.[52] On May 10, he openly and unashamedly explained that:

> I will not slow-down the evacuation of the rest of some 300,000 Jews in the Generalgouvernement, but rather carry them out with the greatest urgency. However much the carrying out of Jewish evacuations causes unrest at the moment, to the same degree they are the main precondition for a basic pacification of the region after their conclusion.[53]

In the districts of Radom, Lublin, and Galicia, almost all Jews, regardless of their ability to work, were deported to death camps.[54]

The most complete extermination of the local Jewish community at this point in time took place in Galicia, where, on June 30, 1943, *SS-Gruppenführer* Fritz Katzmann notified the Reichsführer that 434,329 Jews had been exterminated, all the ghettos in the region had been liquidated, and only 21,156 Jews remained in work camps supervised by the SS, where they were subject to annihilative conditions.[55]

---

52 A fuller analysis of these actions in the *Generalgouvernement* is provided by Dieter E. Pohl, *Von der "Judenpolitik" zum Judenmord: der Distrikt Lublin des Generalgouvernements, 1934–1944* (Frankfurt am Main, 1993). For a specific analysis of the events of 1942 that transformed Nazi policy from one of ghettoization to one of mass extermination, see his review, pp. 157–67.
53 Cited in Browning, "Jewish Workers in Poland," p. 82.
54 On the murder of Jewish workers in Radom, see Dieter Pohl, "Die Ermordung der Juden in Generalgouvernement," in Ulrich Herbert (ed.), *Nationalsozialistische Vernichtungspolitik, 1939–1945: Neue Forschungen und Kontroversen* (Frankfurt am Main, 1998), p. 106.
55 Known as the "Katzmann Report"; this report is available in full in the original German in *Trials of the Major War Criminals before the Nuremberg Military Tribunal, 1947–1949*, vol. 37, document

This insistence that Jewish labor be eliminated on bio-metaphysical grounds rather than on economic ones is evidenced by still other murderous actions and decisions that took place between 1941 and 1943 in Nazi-controlled Eastern Europe.[56] These additional undertakings were intended to ensure that Himmler's uncompromising solution to the Jewish Question was implemented throughout the Baltic States, Poland,[57] Belorussia, and Ukraine. Though local German officials and representatives of the German armament and other industries objected, in varying degrees, to these destructive operations,[58] the SS advanced the ideological imperative that defined their existence – to make Europe *Judenrein* – uncompromisingly. This relentless intention was evident, for example, when Hinrich Lohse, Reich Commissioner for the Ostland (the Baltic States), attempted in mid-November 1941 to stop the SS from killing Jews in his area of authority, only to be criticized by his superiors in Berlin after a complaint about his attitude was forwarded by the SS. He was told in very plain language on December 18, 1941, by Dr. Otto Bräutigam, head of the political department of the Ministry for the Eastern Territories, that "the Jewish Question has probably been clarified by now through verbal discussion. Economic considerations are to be regarded as fundamentally irrelevant in the settlement of the problem."[59]

In another Aktion, the SS in the fall of 1942 organized the gassing of thousands of Jewish metalworkers employed in Polish armaments factories and whose skills and potential value to the German war effort were obvious. Objecting to these latter actions, the local Wehrmacht leadership, headed by General Curt Ludwig

---

NO-018-L, "Report by the SS and Police Leader for the District of Galicia, June 30, 1943: Mass Killings of Jews in Galicia," pp. 391–432. The relevant numbers concerning Jews killed "or sent to" work camps in Galicia is on p. 401.

56 Although my focus is on developments in Eastern Europe, the inability of Götz Aly's explanation to adequately deal with the mass murder of West European Jewry should also be noted in this context. For it shows us that the claim that notions of modernization and economic rationality tied to the putative solution of an "oversupply of labor" was the cause of the destruction of European Jewry is not persuasive. There was no need to modernize France or Holland or Belgium or Italy or France, and in none of these states was there an economic circumstance marked by the overabundance of workers, especially in time of war and when the Third Reich was pressing millions of West Europeans into forced labor. Yet, the Jews of these West European countries were also sent by German authorities, with and without local collaboration, to be reduced to ashes in the Polish death camps. Aly cannot explain why this took place. That is to say, he cannot explain all that needs to be explained in order to provide an intellectually coherent and convincing decipherment of the Final Solution.

57 See, for example, the arguments advanced as to the need to retain Jewish labor in Poland, in the discussion that took place in Kraków in the summer of 1942, as reported in Frank, *Das Diensttagebuch*, entry for June 22, 1942. pp. 515–17.

58 See, for example, National Archives, Washington, D.C., RG 238 1104-PS, Report of District Commissar Cark in Shitsk, October 30, 1941. This report was called to my attention by Martin Dean in his book *Collaboration in the Holocaust: Crimes of the Local Police in Belorussia and Ukraine, 1941–44* (New York, 2000), p. 191.

59 Noakes and Pridham, *Nazism*, doc. 821, vol. 3, p. 1098.

Freiherr von Gienanth, noted that this policy of extermination was irrational, and he made his view known in a formal complaint to Berlin. The reaction to this appeal for a more rational labor policy was not a more "productionist" accommodation but the replacement of von Gienanth.[60]

The same non-economic rationality governing the use – and disposal – of productive Jewish men and women within the orbit of National Socialism was revealed in the murder of 45,000 Jewish workers of both sexes in the *Erntefest* massacre in Lublin, described below.[61] By then, the remnants of the Jewish population in the Lublin district, that had been home to hundreds of thousands of Jews before the war,[62] had been incarcerated in several labor camps where Jewish male and female workers were employed in producing goods for the SS and Wehrmacht. Although these men and women were still alive and working effectively for their Nazi overlords, their fate had already been decided. In accordance with the memo Himmler sent out on July 19, 1942, referred to above, the plan for the complete extermination of European Jewry had been set in motion. In November 1943, it was the turn of Jewish slave laborers in Lublin to be murdered. Therefore, Jewish workers, both male and female, in the Lublin camp were led out of their barracks and killed in nearby trenches that had been dug for this purpose.[63] This slaughter was undertaken without regard to its immediate effect, which in this case happened to be the closure of the *SS-Ostindustrie GmbH* (known as Osti), which produced war materiel and armaments. In his report to the Armaments Commission on December 29, 1943, General Maximilian Schindler observed that: "The resettlements [*sic*] of Jews from the district of Lublin have caused a number of plants to shut down."[64]

Five months after the November *Erntefest* massacre, Dr. Maximilian Horn, the WHVA officer whom Odilo Globocnik, chief of the SS in the Lublin district, had put in charge of the Lublin work camps and who had advocated a more rational

---

60 Longerich, *Holocaust*, pp. 341–42.
61 A full account of this massacre has been given by Yitzchak Arad, *Bełżec, Sobibor, Treblinka: The Operation Reinhard Death Camps* (Bloomington, IN, 1987), pp. 365–69. In addition, see Pohl, *Von der "Judenpolitik" zum Judenmord*.
62 On the slow and uneven implementation of a plan to create a ghetto in Lublin, see Pohl, *Von der "Judenpolitik" zum Judenmord*, pp. 66–68. About 50 ghettos were created in the Lublin area in late 1941 and early 1942. Most were "open" ghettos, at least initially. For more information see Tomasz Kranz, *Die Vernichtung der Juden im Konzentrationslager Majdanek* (Lublin, 2007); idem, "Lublin-Majdanek Stammlager," in W. Benz and B. Distel (eds.), *Der Ort Des Terrors*, vol. 7, *Niederhagen/Wewelsburg; Lublin-Majdanek; Arbeitsdorf; Herzogenbusch (Vught); Bergen-Belsen; Mittelbau-Dora* (Munich, 2007), pp. 33–84; idem., "Die Erfassung der Todesfälle und die Häftlingssterblichkeit im KZ Lublin," in *Zeitschrift für Geschichtswissenschaft* 55 (2007): 220–44; and Barbara Schwindt, *Das Konzentrations- und Vernichtungslager Majdanek: Funktionswandel im Kontext der "Endlösung"* (Würzburg, 2005).
63 Christopher Browning, *Ordinary Men: Reserve Police Battalion 101 and the Final Solution in Poland* (New York, 1992), pp. 138–39. Additional analyses can be found in Grabitz and Scheffler, *Letzte Spuren*, pp. 262–72.
64 Cited in Speer, *Infiltration*, p. 277.

use of Jewish labor, beginning with providing these workers with a better diet, bitterly described its consequences. In a letter dated March 13, 1944, to Oswald Pohl, whom Himmler had appointed head of the Osti enterprise in March 1943, Horn reported:

> Despite the continuous difficulties that OSTI had to overcome during construction of its plants and factories it was possible to take over and improve these industries . . . until 3 Nov. 1943, 70 German supervisors, 1,000 Poles, and 16,000 Jews were employed. On 3 Nov. 1943 all Jews were removed . . . The construction and completion of work done so far became completely valueless through the withdrawal of the Jewish labor.[65]

Moreover, as other German officials openly recognized, this now-dead cohort of Jewish laborers, which was certainly not considered by them a "surplus population," was unavailable for present and future exploitation. Therefore, a report of January 18, 1944, entitled "Wirtschaftlicher Teil der Aktion Reinhardt," summarizing the effects of the extensive decimation that had occurred among Jewish workers in the fall of 1943, noted that the promises that had been given regarding an increased supply of Jewish workers for the armaments industry could not now be kept. The *Erntefest* killings had destroyed the Jewish labor urgently required by the military. Nor had utilitarian considerations been allowed to interfere with the murderous activity in Lublin 10 weeks earlier. For everyone, including Pohl, the *Osti* chief, knew that the *Reichsführer*, with the *Führer's* support, placed a higher priority murdering Jews than he did on producing guns and shells.[66]

Reflecting on the damage done by the carnage in Lublin, Speer accurately commented that:

> The destructive action of November 3, 1943 had paralyzed "East Industry." This is also reflected in the reports of the armament's agencies. At the meeting of the Armaments Commission of November 10, 1943, [General] Schindler [Chief of the Wehrmacht's Armaments Inspectorate] reported that "great difficulties [have] emerged in the Jewish employment operation because of the recent great removals in the Lublin area. These sudden losses, without previous notification of the East Industry Company, are chiefly affecting the clothing and equipment sectors." On November 11, the diary of the Central Division of the Armaments

---

65 Nuremberg Document No. 2187, Office of Chief of Counsel for War Crimes, "Business Report II of the Ostindustrie G.m.b.H. for the year 1943, sent from Lublin on March 13, 1944 and received March 16, 1944."
66 TWC, NO-057, vol. 5, pp. 716–720. See also Robert Kuwałek, "Die Durchgangsghettos im Distrikt Lublin (u.a. Izbica, Piaski, Rejowiec und Trawniki)," in Bogdan Musial, *The Origins of "Operation Reinhard,"* pp. 197–232.

Inspection mentioned the action, while cautiously circumscribing the extermination events, as did all the other reports from armaments agencies: "Unexpected and total removal of Jewish workers from the factories of Walter C. Tobbins in Poniatowa and Schultz & Co. in Trawniki." That same day, the war diary of the Administration Division recorded a report from the Armaments Command of Warsaw, stating that "because of definitive loss of Jewish manpower, production is interrupted in both firms." The Defense Economy Leader, under the Supreme Command of the Wehrmacht, was even blunter in his report: "Major supply delays at various textile plants in Lublin district because of loss of Jewish manpower due to police actions" that were "ordered" by the SD.[67]

But none of these pressing concerns, these disabling consequences regarding war production – 10 million zloty of military orders had by now gone unfulfilled – had been powerful enough to stop the killing of Jewish men and women who could have provided the labor that would make such vital production possible. As a result, the 10,000 Jewish men and women in the Trawnicki work camp, and 14,000 in the sizable Poniatowa camp to the east of Lublin, were slaughtered in a "celebration" of the supreme Nazi principle that race is always primary.

At the nearby Majdanek slave-labor camp, established in the summer of 1941, Jewish women, who were enslaved in a special women's camp, were also murdered in large numbers as a result of the November 1943 orders. Their deaths, like the massacre in Lublin, were part of an eruption of ideologically driven violence that turned a blind eye to matters of authentic military necessity as well as practical considerations relevant to maintaining production.

Further proof that Jewish labor was ultimately seen to be without consequential value is provided by the fate of Jewish workers, male and female, who served as slave laborers in the eighty-four work camps connected to Organization Schmelt in Eastern Upper Silesia. These plants which, beginning in 1942, employed more than 50,000 Jewish skilled laborers in the manufacture of armaments, had been considered indispensable not only by the Wehrmacht but by the SS as well. In April 1942, Higher SS- and Police Leader Ernst Heinrich Schmauser had even written to Himmler to tell him how pleased he was to see the use of Jewish labor in this project because "other workers are hardly available at all anymore."[68] Nonetheless, by the late spring of 1943, following the Warsaw Ghetto uprising that broke out in mid-April, Himmler, notwithstanding Speer's protests and the substantial profits that the SS was earning from this venture, felt that he could no longer tolerate the prudent compromise that allowed Jewish men and women to temporarily remain alive as slave laborers in this enterprise and therefore ordered

---

67 Speer, *Infiltration*, pp. 276–77.
68 Cited in Sybille Steinbacher, "In the Shadow of Auschwitz: The Murder of the Jews of East Upper Silesia," in *National Socialist Extermination Policies: Contemporary German Perspectives and Controversies*, ed. Ulrich Herbert (New York, 2000), p. 291.

the closure of these work sites. *SS-Obersturmbannführer* Adolf Eichmann was put in charge of the removal of the Jews in those camps. Although some of the Jewish workers in the Organization Schmelt complex were re-routed to the concentration camp industries at Gross-Rosen[69] and Auschwitz I, and there were delays until the spring of 1944 in closing down all the Schmelt operations, most of the Jews who had been kept alive for a few months as a result of having been assigned to the Schmelt program were sent to Birkenau to be annihilated.

A report in late June 1943 prepared by an inspector for the armaments office in Breslau noted that: "Because of the removal of Jewish manpower, the lack of construction workers is quite noticeable."[70] Another assessment from Armaments Inspectorate VIIIb to Speer regarding the labor situation in light of the termination of Organization Schmelt argued that, despite Speer's need for manpower: "Taking over the Jewish camps into the administration of concentration camps will cause very great problems *because of the demanded head count of some 1,000 Jewesses and more in these camps, since in most cases it is impossible to build such large camps for these firms and employ 1,000 and more Jewesses for the firms involved*" (emphasis added).[71] Himmler had made up his mind that the importance of carrying out the Final Solution overrode all other, more pragmatic considerations. And so, between June 26, 1943, and October 8, 1943, tens of thousands of Jews who had been working productively for the Reich in Eastern Upper Silesia were deported to Auschwitz.

Korherr put the number of Jewish workers at Organization Schmelt camps in mid-1942 at 50,570. This represented approximately 27 percent of all the Jews – numbering 185,776 at this point in time – at work in the German armaments industry in the Reich and annexed territory.[72] Now, 41,600 of these men and women, were to be immolated, while 8,479 of them – 4,151 men and 4,328 women – were selected to remain alive as slave laborers in the camps that were henceforth to be taken over and controlled by the SS.[73] Those to be exterminated included Jewish men and

---

69 For a detailed examination of Gross-Rosen and all its sub-camps, see the essays in Benz and Distel, (eds.), *Der Ort des Terrors,* vol. 6, "Natzweiler, Gross-Rosen, Stutthof," pp. 191–473. This is now the most complete account. See also Hans Brenner (ed.), *Die Ausnutzung der Zwangsarbeit der Häftlinge des KL Groß-Rosen durch das Dritte Reich* (Wałbrzych, 2004).
70 Albert Speer, *The Slave State* (London, 1981), p. 285. See also critical comments on this made by military and civilian officers and reproduced in *Faschismus,* pp. 438–51.
71 Speer, *ibid.*
72 Artur Eisenbach, *Hitlerowska Polityka Zagłady Żydów* (Warsaw, 1961), p. 349. I cite from Franciszek Piper, *Auschwitz Prisoner Labor: The Organization and Exploitation of Auschwitz Concentration Camp Prisoners as Laborers* (Oświęcim, 2002), p. 231.
73 As a result of the SS takeover of the remaining Organization Schmelt Camps, from December 1943, "Auschwitz controlled new subcamps at Neu-Dachs, Jawischowitz, Eintrachthütte, Lagischa, Fürstengrube, Golleschau, Janinagrube, Sosnowitz, and Brünn. In April 1944, Auschwitz III took over Blechhammer forced-labor camp with 3,056 male and 150 female prisoners working on Oberschlesische Hydrierwerke projects. A short time later, Auschwitz also acquired the Bobrek, Gleiwitz, I, II, and III, Günthergrube, and Laurahütte, subcamps." Wolf Gruner, *Jewish Forced Labor Under the Nazis: Economic Needs and Racial Aims, 1938–1944* (New York, 2006), p. 228.

women directly involved in armaments production. For example, Jews working in the Adolf Hitler tank-building program, at several plants in different locations, were all deported to their deaths.[74] And these were followed over the next year by subsequent selections at the still-extant work camps to which the 8,479 Jews who had been protected during the 1943 Aktions had been sent, thereby further reducing the already small number of Jews connected with *Osti* that were still alive.

Then there is the example of German actions in regard to Jewish workers in the Białystok Ghetto. Efraim Barash, chairman of the Judenrat, had encouraged war-related work by the ghetto's inhabitants with considerable success. The German authorities were therefore divided over the future course of action that should be taken vis-à-vis the ghetto and its workers. Local administrators favored maintenance of the ghetto and the retention of Jews as workers at least in the short term, while the SS, under pressure from Berlin, sought to liquidate the local Jewish population in toto. Mordechai Tenenbaum-Tamaroff, leader of the Jewish resistance in Białystok,[75] wrote at the time that he had learned there was to be a postponement of the planned extirpation of all Jews in the ghetto. "Our fate," he informed his comrades,

> is supposed to be settled on Friday, when General Constantin Canaris [commander of East Prussia's security police and security services] will be back ... Klein [administrative director for the head of the civil administration], our generous protector, has become lord of the ghetto. We see in this a victory for moderate circles in the Gestapo. He maintains that "there'll be time to exterminate the Białystok Jews, even at the end – in the meantime they can slave for us."[76]

The German commissar in charge of the ghetto warned his superiors that: "a violent and instantaneous expulsion of Jewish workers from the economic process would incur serious damage to the city, above all, for the economy related to the war effort."[77] Yet, ignoring issues of productivity, the German authorities, led by the *Reichsführer*, began a series of local murders,[78] beginning with the deportation of Jewish workers from the Białystok district and ending in the liquidation of the ghetto as of August 15, 1943, and concluding on August 23, 1943.[79]

---

74 *Ibid.*, p. 65.
75 For more on Mordecai Tenenbaum-Tamaroff, see Sara Bender, *The Jews of Białystok during World War II and the Holocaust* (Waltham, 2008).
76 Cited in Trunk, *Judenrat*, p. 410.
77 The material quoted here is cited in Gustavo Corni, *Hitler's Ghettos: Voices from a Beleaguered Society, 1939–1944* (London, 2002), p. 232; and also take account of his comments on p. 240.
78 See, for example, Ilya Ehrenburg and Vasily Grossman, *The Black Book: The Ruthless Murder of Jews* (New York, 1981); on the murder of Jewish female workers from the Białystok Ghetto, see p. 244.
79 On the liquidation of the Białystok Ghetto see Arad, *Bełżec, Sobibor, Treblinka*, ch. 17, "Deportations from the Białystok General District and Ostland," and Bogdan Musial (ed.), *"Aktion*

A similar history vis-à-vis Jewish labor and the German war economy was played out in Kovno, Lithuania, and Riga, Latvia.[80] In the former, local German authorities, led by Hans Biebow and *SA-Hauptsturmführer* Fritz Jordan, encouraged the establishment of ghetto industries, promised to support them, and sought, within limits, to protect them.[81] Beginning in September 1941, Jordan, acting for the *Gebeitskomissar* of Kovno, issued 5,000 *Scheine*[82] – special work permits for Jewish artisans within the ghetto – and thousands of additional Jewish workers left it to serve as slave laborers in surrounding areas. In January 1942, sizable workshops were created within the ghetto and, in addition, hundreds of Jewish men and women were sent to Riga in February 1942 as laborers, while other Jews from Kovno were sent from the ghetto to work camps in the summer of 1943. Yet, despite the undoubted contribution of the labor of Kovno's Jews, the ghetto was subjected to a major *Aktion* on October 1943 and eliminated in July 1944.[83] Similarly, the Riga Ghetto, which, like the ghettos in Warsaw, Białystok, and Kovno, had its defenders among civilian and military authorities in Latvia, was closed by Himmler in 1943, and a segment of its Jewish workers were transferred to the Kaiserwald concentration camp[84] where they were worked to death – *Vernichtung durch Arbeit*.[85]

A further prime example of the disregard for issues of production where the fate of Jewish workers was being decided is provided by the progress of events in Brest-Litovsk.[86] The Germans directly in charge of managing this conquered city knew that Jews were necessary to the local war economy, a fact openly attested

---

Reinhardt," Der Völkermord an den Juden im Generalgouvernement 1941–1944 (Osnabruck, 2004). Musial's essay on the subject has been translated into English by William Templer, *Yad Vashem Studies*, vol. 28 (Jerusalem, 2000), pp. 113–53.

80 The full history of Jewish labor in Kovno is narrated by Christoph Dieckmann, "Das Ghetto und das Konzentrationslager in Kaunas," in *Die nationalsozialistischen Konzentrationslager: Entwicklung und Struktur*, edited by Ulrich Herbert, Karin Orth, and Christoph Dieckmann (Göttingen, 1998), pp. 439–71.

81 See, for example, information provided by Avraham Tory, *Surviving the Holocaust: The Kovno Ghetto Diary*, diary entry of September 1, 1942 (Cambridge, MA, 1990) pp. 183–84.

82 An eyewitness description of this event, and the Jews' responses, is provided by Leib Garfunkel, *The Destruction of Kovno's Jewry* [Hebrew], (Jerusalem, 1959), pp. 64–66.

83 Described more fully by Christoph Dieckmann, *Deutsche Besatzungspolitik in Litauen 1941–1944* (Gottingen, 2011).

84 The story of what happened at Kaiserwald is surprisingly complicated because of the actions of the commandant of the subcamp at the Lenta textile factory, Fritz Scherwitz. He appears to have tried to protect his Jewish workers and is thought, by some, to have had a Jewish background; see Anita Kugler, *Scherwitz: Der Judische SS-Offizier* (Cologne, 2004).

85 This struggle between Himmler and others over Jewish labor is analyzed fully in Andrej Angrick and Peter Klein, *Die "Endlösung im Ghetto Riga: Ausbeutung und Vernichtung 1941–1944* (Darmstadt, 2006).

86 From the start of their operation in Brest-Litovsk, German forces even killed Jews identified as potential laborers. For details see Edward B. Westermann, *Hitler's Police Battalions: Enforcing Racial War in the East* (Lawrence, KS, 2005), p. 176. The killings in Brest are also described by Christian Gerlach, *Kalkulierte Morde* (Hamburg, 1999), pp. 716–17.

to by the *Polizeistandortführer* of Brest, Friedrich Wilhelm Rohde. And, given the exceptional demands the war was making on the economy, one would have expected this consideration to matter, if not actually be decisive, in the formation of German policy in the region. Yet, on returning from a meeting at "the Führer's headquarters" between August 25 and 28, 1942, Erich Koch, the *Reichskommissar* for Ukraine, with the support from the *Generalkommissar* for Volhynia and Podolia, Heinrich Schoene, ordered the total extermination of the region's Jews. In reply to this demand, Rohde wrote back to Koch:

> The shortage of labor makes itself felt more and more ... Insofar as the Jewish question is one day solved in Brest, I foresee terrible economic damage resulting from a shortage of labor. When it is alleged that after the clean up of the Jewish question in Kovel orderly conditions ensued and economic life began to operate as before, this allegation is contradicted by the fact that in Kovel at the moment everything is at a standstill and the most valuable goods were left to perish, because no artisans and workers were available. The same consequences, probably in even more drastic form, would occur in Brest after settling the Jewish question, *even if a portion of the Jews remained* [*selbst auch dann, wenn ein Teil der Juden zurückbleibt*]. I will not fail to draw attention to this time and again. (Emphasis in original)[87]

Murdering the Jews of Brest was not, Rhode urgently told those in authority, wise economic policy. And his view was seconded independently by Franz Burat, *Stadtkommissar* for Brest, who wrote to his superiors that: "Although a complete resettlement of the Jews ... is desirable from the political standpoint, from the standpoint of use of labor I must unconditionally plead for the retention of the most needed artisans and manpower."[88] But this rational, economically sensible appeal, like that made by Rhode, fell mainly on deaf ears.

In mid-October 1942, Police Battalion 310, along with other *Schutzpolizei* and security police, began rounding up and shooting the Jews of Brest. Over the course of a few days, beginning on October 15 and 16, the city's ghetto was razed completely, and when the *Aktion* ended, approximately 20,000 Jews had been murdered. This included 9,000 Jews who had been employed under SS control, 2,000 of whom had been defined as "irreplaceable."

---

87 This passage is available in translation in Browning, *Nazi Policy*, p. 137. See the testimony given in TWC, vol. 37, p. 40; and Gerlach, *Kalkulierte Morde*, p. 714. A fuller picture of the unfolding of these events is provided by Thomas Sandkühler, *"Endlösung" in Galizien: Der Judenmord in Ostpolen und die Rettungsinitiativen von Berthold Beitz 1941–1944* (Bonn, 1996). He concludes that, from June 1942, the operational practice of German forces was to kill Jews without regard for their potential as workers, p. 13.
88 Browning, *Nazi Policy*, p. 138.

This record of the murder of actual and potential Jewish workers in Poland and conquered areas of the Soviet Union is a powerful refutation of theories arguing for the "rationality" of the Holocaust, whether in whole or in part. It is a convincing repudiation of the claim that pragmatism and concerns with economic matters and war production played a significant role in the framing of Nazi anti-Jewish policy. The factor nearly always dominant in the shaping and execution of National Socialist policy regarding the present and future of the Jewish People was the extreme racial principle at the heart of the Nazi state, which demanded that the Jewish People cease to exist.

UPDATE

This paper was first published in 2015 in a *Festschrift* presented to Professor Dina Porat, Emerita Professor of Holocaust Studies at Tel Aviv University.

Though the literature on all aspects of the Holocaust continues to grow dramatically, I have not seen anything published in the past three years that forces a change in the position set out in the present essay. That is, there is no new evidence that indicates that: (a) Hitler and Himmler were willing to *significantly* alter their plans for a total execution of the "Final Solution" because of the vital labor needs of the German war economy; or (b) that the utilization of a small number of Jews as slave laborers was meant to be anything but a *temporary* reprieve for those men and women so utilized; or (c) that the policy of *Vernichtung durch Arbeit* ("Extermination through Work") was not a meaningful, quite often employed, strategy that played a role in Nazi anti-Jewish labor policy.

Three substantial studies dealing with the subject of the Nazi utilization of Jewish slave labor have, however, appeared in English since 2015 and merit comment. The first by Nikolaus Wachsmann, *KL: A History of Nazi Concentration Camps* (New York, 2015) discusses in detail the use of concentration camp inmates as workers. After expertly reviewing the development of Nazi labor and extermination policy relative to Jews he concludes: "Despite all their [camps'] differences ... the ultimate aim of SS concentration camps in occupied Eastern Europe were the same. None of their registered Jewish prisoners – those who had been selected for slave labor, rather than immediate extermination – were supposed to survive in the long run."[89] In regard to the debate over the putative contradiction between the "Final Solution" and the Nazi employment of Jews as slave laborers, he writes, focused on IG Farben but extrapolatable to other major Nazi work camps and factories:

> Historians have long argued that the Holocaust highlights a sharp contradiction at the head of Nazism: despite the desperate need for forced labor to feed the German war machine, the regime still went ahead with the mass extermination of European Jewry. But for Nazi hard-liners there was no contradiction. Economics and extermination were two sides of the same coin; both were needed for victory. Winning the war required the ruthless destruction of all perceived threats *and* the mobilization of all remaining resources for the war effort. In the case of Jews judged capable of work, the authorities fused both of these aims into the policy of "annihilation through labor." Forced labor meant temporary survival for the selected Jews; but almost all of them were dead men and women walking, as far as the SS was concerned.[90]

IG Farben was an active partner in the policy of "annihilation through labor." Instead of improving prisoner provisions and the treatment of

---

89 *KL*, p. 342.
90 *Ibid.*, pp. 343–44.

the sick, the company received an assurance from the WVHA that "all weak prisoners can be deported" to be replaced by others fit for work. This was the basis for constant selections in Monowitz. They were most frequent in the camp's infirmary, where an SS doctor came about once a week to "empty the beds," as the SS called it. Walking briskly through the rooms – individual decisions often took no more than a few seconds – the physician picked out those who had already spent two or three weeks inside and others who were not expected to return to work anytime soon. In this way, thousands of prisoners – almost all of them Jews – were selected in the Monowitz infirmary and transported to Birkenau. Here, most were driven straight to the crematoria complex; as a former Birkenau block leader put it after the war, the doomed prisoners were "practically no longer alive" even before they were gassed.[91]

This is a strong confirmation, by a knowledgable student of Nazi policy, that the *Führerstaat* preferred killing Jews to employing them.

The second significant study was published by David Cesarani under the title *Final Solution: The Fate of the Jews 1933–1949* (New York, 2016). This is a wide-ranging, well-received, general analysis of Nazi anti-Jewish policy. In the course of the study, Cesarani returns, on several occasions, to the topic of Jewish slave labor and reminds his readers that, for example, in May 1942: "Himmler resolved that the Jews of Europe would be removed totally. He used the occasion of Heydrich's state funeral to tell senior officers of the SS and the policy that '[w]ithin a year we will definitely have completed the mass migration of the Jews; then no more will migrate.'" Driving home this theme Cesarani repeats the point that the *Reichsführer* was unwavering in his determination to kill Jews rather than put them to work. So, he

> ordered Krüger, "The resettlement of the entire Jewish population of the General Government should be implemented and completed by December 31, 1942." After that date no people of Jewish origin were to remain except "if they are in assembly camps in Warsaw, Krakow, Czestochowa, Radom, and Lublin. All projects that employ Jewish labour have to be completed by that date or transferred to the assembly camps." The principle of selection on the basis of usefulness, capacity for labour, was scrapped and only those Jews already in work had any chance of survival.[92]

Other than the small exception noted here, the total murder of European Jewry went on. In November 1943,

---

91 *Ibid.*, pp. 346–47.
92 David Cesarani, *Final Solution: The Fate of the Jews 1933–49*, p. 479.

there were at least 50,000 Jews in labour camps run by the SS and the German armed forces. About 15,000 were in the Poniatowa camps, mostly producing clothing for the Többens firm. The output of items destined for the German armed forces was remarkable: each week Jewish workers produced 38,000 shirts, 18,000 pieces of underwear, 6,000 caps, over 7,000 pairs of socks, more than 4,000 packs and 2,400 belts for kit. Between 8,000 and 10,000 Jews, most relocated from the Warsaw ghetto, were employed in Schultz's factories. Some 18,000 Jewish prisoners in Majdanek, including the sub-camps in and around Lublin, toiled in DAW plants repairing uniforms, reconditioning vehicle engines, and making furniture for barracks. Since March 1943, thousands had been employed by Ostindustrie, repairing aircraft and manufacturing brushes. Yet this counted for little. On 19 October 1943, Hans Frank told a meeting in Cracow that "The camps with Jews in the General Government constituted a great danger, and that the escape of the Jews from one of these camps [Sobibór] proved it." Frank invited General Schindler of the armaments inspectorate and a representative of the SS to review all the camps with an eye to their future, but Himmler pre-empted the results. He ordered Friedrich Krüger, the HSSPF in the General Government, to terminate every single one.[93]

This decision was then acted upon in the so-called *Erntefest*: "In all, the Germans... massacred 43,000 people in under 48 hours," without regard to their value as much needed laborers. Again, he explains:

Since Jews were engaged predominantly in unskilled manual labour, notably construction, there was no need to train substitutes and no cost to letting them go. In other words, the drive to employ Jews was perfectly compatible with mass murder. Exploiting them for labour before murdering them actually compensated for the cost of deporting them in the first place.

Cesarani then adds the more controversial claim that: "This procedure became known colloquially as 'annihilation through labour', although there was no comprehensive programme as such . . . The notion was applied retrospectively and inaccurately to the fate of the Jews. In actuality, work offered a lifeline to them and more would survive in labour camps than as fugitives from ghettos."[94]

This last conclusion, in particular, while not inaccurate, requires further comment. There is a good deal of scholarly confusion about how the phrase "annihilation through work" ("*Vernichtung durch Arbeit*") should be understood and

---

93 *Ibid.*, pp. 649.
94 *Ibid.*, pp. 523–24.

applied. Literally, and most narrowly, the term describes working prisoners to death on the job. This happened. But in light of the many ways that Jewish labor was employed – and destroyed – this is, as I understand the relevant realities, too restrictive an interpretation as to how the notion should be deciphered. Instead, in contradistinction to this literal meaning, I would argue that it is quite correct to use the term to refer to instances where individuals were underfed, overworked, and otherwise mistreated, to the point that they were ruled too ill or too weak to continue their backbreaking labor and, therefore, were sent from the site at which they were employed to a death camp to be murdered (or were murdered on-site). In this sense, *Vernichtung durch Arbeit* should be understood to include the *conscious and intentional* exploitation of Jewish men and women until all of their strength was gone and then, because of their depleted physical condition, they were dispatched to be annihilated. In these many cases, it was work that killed them, though gas or bullets, often at locations other than their workplace, were employed to provide the last blow.

Consider here, as paradigmatic, the work routine devised by IG Farben and utilized at its Monowitz factory. In this facility, the "average weight loss for a slave worker at Monowitz was between 6.5 and 9 pounds per week." Two doctors who studied the impact of weight loss among this pool of laborers concluded that: "the normally nourished prisoner at Buna could make up the deficiency [in caloric intake] by his own body for three months . . . the prisoners were condemned to burn up their own body weight while working and, providing no infections occurred, finally died of exhaustion."[95]

That IG Farben was literally working their Jewish slaves to death was certainly known to those who managed the plant, yet they did not alter the operation of the factory either by providing the slave laborers with more nourishment or reducing the demands that they made on them. Working these increasingly diminished camp inmates to death was both profit-producing and consistent with the ruling political-ideological imperative that had already sentenced them to extinction.

Understanding the Führer's intentions, IG Farben utilized Jewish labor at its facilities with near-total disregard for their survival. On October 28, 1942, 600 prisoners from the main camp at Auschwitz were sent to work at Monowitz, which had just opened. Approximately 70 percent of these individuals were Jews. By January 1, 1943, the total number of slave laborers at this facility had grown to 3,700, the great majority of whom were Jewish. On January 4, 1943, only three and a half months since the start of this operation, a *Selektion* was held, and almost half of the depleted and emaciated workers were dispatched to be gassed. "SS-Captain Heinrich Schwarz reviewed about 3,500 prisoners and consigned roughly half of them to a return journey to Auschwitz."[96] Thereafter, prisoners continued to be sent to the plant, and the number of unfree laborers grew to 7,200 by

---

95 NI-5847, affidavit of Berthold Epstein, March 3, 1947. Epstein had been a hospital orderly at Buna.
96 Peter Hayes, *Industry and Ideology: I. G. Farben in the Nazi Era* (New York, 1987; 2nd edition 2001).

December 1943, and 11,600 by the end of 1944. In January 1945, the last month the IG Farben worksites at Monowitz operated, the number of individuals made over into slaves numbered 10,223, 92 percent of whom were Jews.

But this sizable final population was achieved over the corpses of tens of thousands. The camp official who kept track of the fate of the camp population testified after the war that: "Those who did not drop dead were sooner or later reclaimed by the SS and gassed. Either way, they were replaced, and the cycle resumed. In this manner, some 35,000 people passed through Monowitz during 1943–4; the toll of confirmed deaths came to about 23,000, or an average of 32 per day."[97]

Nor was it only within the universe of German industry that a policy of *Vernichtung durch Arbeit* was knowingly employed by German state officials. Consider, for instance, the road building project known as DG4 in the Ukraine. The unsparing way in which this major project was organized knowingly ruined the health of those men and women who were put to work on it. And once their health was seriously impaired individuals were "*Selekt*ed" for annihilation. For those who oversaw the DG4 project, road building, organized as "extermination through work," became an integral part of the *Endlösung*.

Otto Rasch, the head of *Einsatzgruppe C* operating in Galicia, made this lack of concern with survival very clear when he suggested in August 1941 that, "until the Final Solution of the Jewish problem is achieved across the continent *the Jews can be used up* in the cultivating of swampy areas around the Pripyat, the Dnieper, and the Volga." The very distinctive phrase employed by Rasch, "Jews can be used up" in the course of carrying out the difficult tasks assigned to them, tells us that senior German officials had integrated their understanding of the work done by Jews with their commitment to the elimination of the Jewish People – the latter to be made manifest through the former – with the DG4 project being an exemplary instance of this interrelationship. In the carrying out of this massive project, the separate objectives of constructing the highway and eliminating the Jewish People were functionally combined in the way in which the building of the road was coordinated and managed.[98] Unsurprisingly, Rasch, in September, repeated this advice

---

97 NI-7967/66, affidavit by E. Schulhof, April 21, 1947, the prisoner who compiled the card catalogue of inmates at Monowitz, and NI-12070/99, affidavit by S. Budziaszek, the head physician at Monowitz, October 27, 1947. This data is drawn from P. Hayes, *Industry and Ideology*, p. 359; and Benjamin Ferencz, *Less Than Slaves: Jewish Forced Labor and the Quest for Compensation* (Bloomington, 2002), p. 30. It is estimated that a total of "no less than 10,000 prisoners" were returned to Auschwitz and "disposed of either by gassing or phenol injection into the heart" (Piotr Setkiewicz, *The Histories of Auschwitz IG Farben Werk Camps, 1941–1945* [Bloomington, 2001], pp. 159, 162). Many historians go further and put the number of these returnees from Monowitz much higher (*ibid.*, pp. 159–60). On one count, there were approximately 20,000 slave laborers shipped back to Auschwitz from Monowitz and they are estimated to have experienced a 95 percent mortality rate (*ibid.*, pp. 164–65).

98 Despite his programmatic effort to find exceptions to the rule that the Nazi authorities put economic matters second to ideological ones, Donald Bloxham concurs on this. He says of the DG4

vis-à-vis the elimination of the Jews of Ukraine.[99] In his *Weltanschauung*, the understanding of what should be done with Jewish labor had become inseparable from the goal of Jewish extirpation.

This eliminationist mentality was similarly evident in the regimen governing Jewish workers employed in Organization Schmelt. There were periodic *Selektionen* among these individuals, and those deemed unfit for further work, those "used up," were sent to Birkenau to be gassed. Though these broken men did not "die on the job," the jobs that they did, and the manner in which they were forced to do them, were the cause of their deaths.[100] Survivors of the Michal camp that was created as part of Organization Schmelt reported, for instance, that exhausted workers were sometimes sent to Heydebreck to be murdered,[101] and that spent Jewish laborers were, at other times, transported to Auschwitz.[102]

In respect of this peculiar conception of "using up" Jews through slave labor it is relevant to recall the instructions given by Oswald Pohl, head of the Nazi concentration camp system, to individual camp commandants on being informed that in the first quarter of 1942 150,000 Jews would be sent to the camps as slave laborers. They were, he advised them, to create a work routine that was to be, "in the true meaning of the word, exhaustive."[103]

Further evidence of "extermination through work" is found in situations as different as the Łódź Ghetto, the Buchenwald concentration camp, the Dora-Mittelbau camp, Dachau, Auschwitz, Gross-Rosen, and Mauthausen.

That some Jews were able to remain alive because they were selected for work was, as Cesarani notes, not a result of a policy that fell short of or compromised with the "Final Solution." Rather, this circumstance came about because the war ended too soon, i.e., before they could be "worked to death." The small number of Jews who survived through labor was an *unintended* consequence of Nazi policy and in contradiction to its planned outcome.

---

program that it shows that "at times the very process of labour was explicitly used as a method of killing Jews." *Genocide, the World War and the Unweaving of Europe* (Edgeware, UK, 2008), p. 172.

99 Wendy Lower, *Nazi Empire-Building and the Holocaust in the Ukraine* (Chapel Hill, 2007), p. 143. This order did not specifically mention Jews.

100 Discussed by Sybille Steinbacher, *Musterstadt Auschwitz: Germanisierungspolitik Und Judenmord in Ostoberschlesien Darstellungen Und Quellen Zur Geschichte Von Auschwitz* (Berlin, 2010), pp. 280–82.

101 International Military Tribunal (at Nuremberg), vol. 34, Document no. PS7401, pp. 143–44, July 22, 1946.

102 Danuta Czech, *Kalendarium der Ereignisse im Konzentrationslager Auschwitz-Birkenau 1933–1945* (Hamburg, 1989), p. 582. This was brought to my attention by W. Gruner, *Jewish Forced Labor Under the Nazis* p. 227.

103 Pohl was informed by Richard Glücks, who had been directly informed of this news by Himmler. Pohl's circular of April 30, 1942 is reprinted in *International Military Tribunal* at Nuremberg, vol. 38 (Nuremberg, 1945–46), pp. 365–66.

The third recent major study that is relevant in this context is Christian Gerlach's *The Extermination of the European Jews*.[104] He devotes an entire chapter to the topic "Forced labor, German violence and the Jews,"[105] and provides a coherent and intelligent description of these matters. As for the role specifically that labor played in saving Jewish lives, he writes:

> The process was more complex for Jews as the intensification of their use as labor was combined with intensified mass murder – not temporarily, as was the case for Soviet POWs from November 1941 to about January 1942, but continuously. This and the transfer of Jews to camps under SS control in 1943 made the strategy of many Jewish councils – trying to ensure the survival of as many Jews as possible by making them irreplaceable as workers – obsolete.... These camps were among the best options available for Jews; for other inmates they were usually the worst. Jews were worst affected, but it would be incorrect to say that their labor ability played no role in their fate under the Germans. Consequently, a few hundreds of thousands managed to survive through forced labor.[106]

But, at the same time, it must be comprehended that the survival of these Jewish slave workers was not meant to represent a deviation from the goal of making Europe *Judenrein*. Rather, survival was completely serendipitous and does not indicate any alteration in Nazi anti-Jewish ambitions.

When discussing the specific notion of *Vernichtung durch Arbeit* and its implementation, as well as the overall Nazi strategy for the utilization of Jews in the war economy, it is, of course, necessary to recognize that there were locations where this concept, this practice, did not apply. While the principle that it was not immoral to kill a Jew was the operational norm throughout Nazi-occupied Europe, and everyone connected with the Third Reich understood that it was required that all Jews should be eradicated, there were other variables that sometimes played a role in determining the mortality rates of Jewish laborers. But, this necessary recognition of diversity and complexity acknowledged, it still remains the case that in almost every significant instance in which the issue of the use of Jewish labor versus the demands of the "Final Solution" arose, the leadership of the Third Reich strongly preferred to murder Jews rather than utilize them as workers.

---

104 Christian Gerlach, *The Extermination of the European* Jews (Cambridge, UK, 2016).
105 *Ibid.*, ch. 8, pp. 184–214.
106 *Ibid.*, p. 214.

8

THE MURDER OF JEWISH CHILDREN DURING THE HOLOCAUST

I

It is a great pleasure to contribute to this *Festschrift* in honor of Irving Greenberg. A friend of 35 years, Dr. Greenberg has been one of a small group of Jewish thinkers who have seriously attempted to respond to the situation the Jewish People found themselves in after the Holocaust and the creation of the State of Israel. By "seriously" I mean not just in terms of his thinking but also in terms of trying to understand the practical, actionable, implications of these events, especially for the American Jewish community of which he has been a leader for the past three decades. Even when one disagrees with him on specific matters one cannot doubt the profound existential commitment that he has to the Jewish People and to the State of Israel. Everyone who shares these commitments owes him a debt for what he has accomplished in, and on behalf of, these two entities.

In a paper that Dr. Greenberg delivered at a major conference on Jewish-Christian relations in light of the Holocaust, held in New York City in June 1973, he cited the following testimony given at the Nuremberg trials:

> WITNESS: When the extermination of the Jews in the gas chambers was at its height, orders were issued that children were to be thrown straight into the crematorium furnaces, or into a pit near the crematorium, without being gassed first.
>
> SMIRNOV (Russian prosecutor): How am I to understand this? Did they throw them into the fire alive, or did they kill them first?
>
> WITNESS: They threw them in alive. Their screams could be heard at the camp. It is difficult to say how many children were destroyed in this way.
>
> SMIRNOV: Why did they do this?
>
> WITNESS: It's very difficult to say. We don't know whether they wanted to economize on gas, or if it was because there was not enough room in the gas chambers.[1]

---

1 In Eva Fleischner (ed.), *Auschwitz; Beginning of a New Era? Reflections on the Holocaust* (New York, 1977), pp. 9–10.

Dr. Greenberg's paper then worked out that the gas saved in killing Jewish children in this manner was "forty-five hundredth's of a cent per person," and he went on to point out: "In the summer of 1944, a Jewish child's life was not worth the two-fifths of a cent it would have cost to put it to death rather than burn it alive."[2]

In the present essay I would like to take up this topic of the murder of Jewish children by the Nazi state and attempt to provide a fuller, though still not complete,[3] accounting of what this entailed and what this meant. My interest in doing so arises from two different concerns. First, despite the enormous literature on the Holocaust – and the fact that it is commonplace when discussing the murder of European Jewry to refer to the fact that up to 1,500,000 Jewish children were killed by the Nazis – the details of these children's deaths are rarely presented in one coherent narrative focusing solely on this issue.[4] I have therefore, tried to organize this essay to be such a presentation. Second, I have been drawn to this subject by my long-standing interest regarding the issue of the Holocaust's uniqueness as an historical phenomenon.[5] In pursuing this topic it has become clear to me that the genocidal Nazi assault on Jewish children was not only a distinctive feature of the *Shoah* but also represented a singular historical event. Put simply, I believe that the obsession with the murder of Jewish children by the Third Reich represents an historical *novum*.

II

Jewish children were the threat that the Nazis feared most. Such children represented the future and directly challenged the dystopian ambition that the Nazi *Weltanschauung* aspired to – a future that would be *Judenrein*. *Reichsführer* Heinrich Himmler was very clear on this point. Speaking to a select group of SS and Wehrmacht officers he openly told them of his operating principle with regard to the murder of Jewish women and children:

> When I was forced somewhere in some village to act against partisans and Jewish commissars . . . then as a principle I gave the order to kill

---

2 *Ibid.*, p. 11.
3 This essay concentrates mainly on the murder of Jewish children in, or in connection with, the ghettos established in Eastern Europe. A relatively brief comment is also included on the extermination of Dutch and French Jewish children in order to indicate the breadth of the Nazi policy. The final section, mainly for emphasis, records details on the killing of Jewish children at Auschwitz. I do not, however, review in detail the events at the other death camps, though I mention some of these in passing, nor do I discuss the vast killing operations of the *Einsatzgruppen*. This essay, therefore, is meant only as an introduction to a very large subject.
4 There are a few discussions of this issue, but none are comprehensive. See, for example, Deborah Dwork, *Children with a Star: Jewish Youth in Nazi Europe* (New Haven, CT, 1991) and her bibliography of works on this topic.
5 For more on this concern see vol. 1 of Steven T. Katz, *The Holocaust in Historical Context* (New York, 1994). Vols. 2A and 2B of this comparative project are published under the title *The Holocaust and New World Slavery: A Comparative History* (Cambridge, UK, 2019)

the women and children of those partisans and commissars too . . . . Believe you me, that order was not so easy to give or so simple to carry out as it was logically thought out and can be stated in this hall. But we must constantly recognize what kind of primitive, primordial, natural race struggle [*Rassenkampf*] we are involved in.[6]

Children, usually spared by the victors in war and by masters in slave societies were, in the *Shoah*, considered the ultimate racial enemy. Insofar as the Aryan people were engaged in an uncompromising life and death struggle with the Jewish People, Jewish children had to be killed in order to end this world-historical racial conflict once and for all.

In the life of the ghettos of Nazi Europe this annihilatory racial dogma was made a ruling axiom. It was first institutionalized in 1941, in the reorganization of the ghetto economy by Max Bischof, head of the Third Reich's transfer agency, whose plans intentionally entailed that large numbers of Jewish children would starve to death. The reason for this outcome was that the envisioned reorganization involved the implementation of the principle: "Conditions of undernourishment could be allowed to develop without regard for the consequences,"[7] meaning that the new economic model that was now to be utilized to govern the ghettos consciously mandated starvation for a segment of the incarcerated Jewish ghetto population. And, as a result, deaths from starvation escalated in all the ghettos in the second half of 1941 and onwards. Furthermore, the new economic strategy sharply, if only temporarily, divided "productive" from "unproductive" ghetto residents. It made this distinction absolute by instituting a new food policy that called for feeding workers soup in the workshops twice a day and supplementing this soup with bread rations, as opposed to the earlier method of food distribution that allowed workers to share their rations at home with their wives and children. In this way, "unproductive" individuals, not employed in one of the ghetto's workshops, were, in effect, given a death sentence. The rate of deaths by starvation now rose to about "11 percent of the entire ghetto population when projected over a twelve-month period."[8]

As a result of this change in the food policy, Jewish children in all of the ghettos had been sentenced to death by starvation, if not killed by other means. What this meant in quantitative terms can be readily appreciated by recalling the number of Jewish children living in the ghettos. The census done in the Warsaw Ghetto in late October 1939, soon after its creation, indicated that there were 91,611

---

6 Cited from Carol Rittner and John Roth (eds.), *Different Voices: Women and the Holocaust* (New York, 1993), p. 392. The original can be found in Bradley F. Smith and Agnes F. Peterson (eds.), *Heinrich Himmler: Geheimreden 1933 bis 1945* (Frankfurt, 1974), p. 201.
7 Götz Aly and Susan Heim, *Architects of Annihilation: Auschwitz and the Logic of Destruction* (Princeton, 2002), p. 203.
8 Steven T. Katz and Steven Bayme (eds.), *Continuity and Change* (Lanham, MD, 2010), p. 169.

children under 15 years old out of a total population of 359,827 Jews. Measured as a percentage of the ghetto population, children represented 25.4 percent of the entire Warsaw Ghetto community. In Łódź, a census taken in 1940, soon after the enclosing of the ghetto, indicated there were 36,188 children under age 14 out of a total population of 157,955. In percentage terms children represented 22.9 percent of the ghetto population.[9] In Riga, in November 1941, the German census reported that there were 5,652 children under 14 years in the ghetto population of 29,602.[10] Children, therefore, represented 19 percent of the Riga ghetto community. Given these figures we can reasonably project that, except where the Jewish population had first been reduced by the action of the *Einsatzgruppen* before ghettoization occurred, most if not all the ghettos had populations in which children under 15 represented a sizable segment of the community.

Keeping this in mind one also remembers that, in addition to the ghettos already mentioned, the Białystok Ghetto had 60,000 inhabitants, the Minsk Ghetto 80,000 to 90,000 inhabitants, the Lvov Ghetto approximately 160,000 inhabitants, the Czernowitz Ghetto 62,000 inhabitants, the Kishinev Ghetto 80,000 inhabitants, and the Vilna Ghetto 60,000 to 70,000 in 1939. Together these larger ghettos had a cumulate initial population of approximately 500,000 souls, about 100,000 (or more) of whom were children. And the smaller ghettos, for example, those in Chełm (population of 14,000 in 1939), Grodno (population 22,000), Dinaburg (population 15,000 to 18,000), Radom (population of 25,000 in 1939), Drohobycz and Boryslav (which taken together had a population of 27,000), Zhitomir (population 35,000), Berdichev (population 35,000), and Kielce (population 21,000), all had substantial numbers of Jewish children who must be accounted for.[11]

And when we do account for all of these children, from both the large and small ghettos, we learn that, given Nazi policy, almost none of these hundreds of thousands of children survived the war. So, for example, in Warsaw, consistent with the ruling food policy, the death of children through starvation was a daily occurrence. And those who did not die from hunger were routinely rounded up and deported to be gassed as part of the more general destruction

---

9 For more on the fate of Jewish children in the Lodz Ghetto see my discussion on p. 155 below. In addition, see Alan Adelson (ed.), *The Diary of Dawid Sierakowiak* (New York, 1996); Lucjan Dobroszycki, *The Chronicle of the Łódź Ghetto, 1941–1944* (New Haven, CT, 1987); Alan Adelson and Robert Lapides, *Łódź Ghetto: Inside a Community Under Siege* (New York, 1989), and Isaiah Trunk, *Łódź Ghetto: A History* (Amherst, 1962; in Yiddish), trans. and ed. Robert Moses Shapiro, Introduction by Israel Gutman (Bloomington, 2006).

10 The figures on the Warsaw Ghetto are drawn from Joseph Kermish, *To Live with Honor and Die With Honor: Selected Documents on the Warsaw Ghetto* (Jerusalem, 1986), p. 137. Those on the Riga Ghetto are cited from Bernhard Press, *Judenmord in Lettland* (Berlin, 1992), p. 65.

11 I cite these statistics from Philip Friedman, "The Jewish Ghettos of the Nazi Era," in his *Roads to Extinction: Essays on the Holocaust* (Philadelphia, 1980), pp. 75, 76. This list is not exhaustive. There are many ghettos that I have not mentioned and whose populations would need to be included in a full account of the number of Jewish children in the ghettos.

of the ghetto population that began on July 22, 1942, the eve of Tisha B'Av, the Jewish day of mourning for the destruction of the First and Second Temples. Between July 22 and September 12, 1942, 265,000 Jews were deported from the Warsaw Ghetto to Treblinka. This included nearly all of the 126,300 plus children aged 19 or younger – less those who had already died – in the ghetto. Before the deportations began there were 25,759 boys in the ghetto aged 9 and under and 25,699 girls aged 9 and under. After the deportations there were only 255 boys and 243 girls under age 9 left in the ghetto. Ninety-nine percent of the young boys in the ghetto and 99.1 percent of the young girls in the ghetto had been deported and killed. For children between 10 and 19 years of age, the rate of loss was also staggeringly high. Of 35,238 boys, only 2,183, 6.2 percent, remained. Of the 39,700 girls in this age group, only 2,263, 5.7 percent, were still alive.[12] Thus, when this *Aktion* was completed almost all the ghetto children had been murdered. Those few older Jewish individuals who remained alive in Warsaw after September 12 had been exempted from death temporarily because they were needed for work in the ghetto workshops and industries.[13] The younger children had no such utilitarian value and therefore there was no reason to keep them alive.

No Jewish child, given the racial threat it represented, could be permitted to escape the Führer's demand that s/he must die. So, for example, though deemed utterly worthless but, from a racial perspective, judged to be terribly dangerous, the 192 young charges in Janus Korzak's[14] Warsaw Ghetto orphanage had to be sent to be gassed in Treblinka. "Useless eaters" – as well as future "racial criminals" – they could not be allowed to live. Wherever a Jewish child was found it had to be murdered. Mira Pizyc, in her memoir on the reduction of the Warsaw Ghetto, remembers the following incident:

> ...Another sight that freezes the blood in your veins; Behind me marches a young woman. She has a pack on her back. The German smiles a satanic grin, walks up to her, raises a whip, and lands a blow to the pack. A terrible scream erupts from the concealed child. The German grabs the pack and, together with its living contents, smashes it up against the wall. The stricken mother wants to go after her child; the executioner explodes with laughter – the scene amuses him. With a blow of the [whip's] handle, he pushes the woman, blue with agony, back into line.[15]

---

12 Israel Gutman, *The Jews of Warsaw, 1939–1943: Ghetto Underground Revolt* (Bloomington, 1982), Table 6, p. 271. The quote from Gutman is cited from *ibid.*, p. 270.
13 This data is cited from Gustavo Corni, *Hitler's Ghettos: Voices from a Beleaguered Society, 1939–1944* (London, 2002), pp. 265–75.
14 For more on this remarkable man see Janusz Korczak, *Ghetto Diary* (New Haven, CT, 1978); and Betty Lifton, *The King of Children: The Life and Death of Janusz Korczak* (New York, 1988).
15 Y. Gutman, *The Jews of Warsaw*, p. 217.

I repeat: no Jewish child from the Warsaw Ghetto could – should – be left among the living.[16]

In Łódź the pattern was similar. From the middle of January 1942, to May 15, 1942, the first round of deportations from the ghetto took place. The first train left for Chełmno on January 16, 1942. The initial group of deportees included 780 men, 853 women, and 154 children.[17] Then every day thereafter until April 2, 1942, a period of 76 consecutive days, a transport of Jews that included Jewish children left the ghetto for the Chełmno death camp to be gassed.

Between January 16 and May 15, 1942 54,990 people, including thousands of children, were sent from the Łódź Ghetto to Chełmno. To keep the remaining Jews alive Rumkowski, the Elder of the ghetto, sought to turn the ghetto into the most productive workshop in the Reich. "Work for Life" became the ruling motto of all activities. But this adopted system unavoidably entailed that "unproductive" elements within the population, such as children, had to be sacrificed. Accordingly, on September 1, in conformity with this ruling agenda, those in ghetto hospitals were rounded up. This included 320 children who were sent to Treblinka on September 2. But this was just the opening gambit. The Nazi authorities next demanded that 20,000 Jews be handed over for deportation, including all children under 10 and those over 65.[18] When these two groups were tallied they numbered 13,000, including 850 orphans from the Marysin orphanage.[19] After these September deportations the ghetto held 89,446 Jews, very few of whom were children. By July 1944, this population was reduced to 68,516 at which point, in August 1944, the ghetto was ordered closed by Himmler and the remaining 67,000 Jews (approximately),[20] including Rumkowski and his family, were sent to Auschwitz. By the end of 1944 almost no Jewish children of the 36,188 children who had been alive in Łódź in 1940 remained among the living.

In Vilna, home to between 60,000 and 70,000 Jews on the eve of World War II, the mass killings, undertaken by *Einsatzgruppe* A, began in July when 5,000 Jewish men were murdered at the pits in nearby Ponary. During August the murder of Jewish men continued. Then women and children began to be included among the victims. On September 2, 1941 when 3,700 Jews were murdered, 2,019 of them were women and 817 of them were children. At the same time, the building of a ghetto for the surviving Jews of Vilna began, and by September 7 the creation of

---

16 For more on the fate of children in the Warsaw Ghetto see Raul Hilberg, et al. (eds.), *The Warsaw Diary of Adam Czerniaków* (New York, 1982); Abraham L. Katsh et al. (eds.), Scroll of Agony: *The Warsaw Diary of Chaim A. Kaplan* (Bloomington, 1991); Emannuel Ringelblum, *Notes from the Warsaw Ghetto*, ed. Jacob Sloan (New York, 1979); and Mary Berg, *Warsaw Ghetto: A Diary*, ed. S. Shnayderman et al. (New York, 1945).
17 Figure cited from I. Trunk, *Łódź Ghetto*, p. 23.
18 *Ibid.*, pp. 238–43.
19 *Ibid.*, pp. 242, 244.
20 *Ibid.*, Table 17, p. 267.

the ghetto had been completed. It was built in two parts. In Ghetto 1 there were, after the first round of shootings, approximately 30,000 Jews, and in Ghetto 2 approximately 10,000 Jews. Another 6,000 were penned up in nearby Lukiozki. On September 10 and 11 the deportations and mass murders in the nearby woods of Ponary resumed. In their summary report of December 1, 1941, *Einsatzkommando* 3 reported: "On 12 September, 993 males, 1,670 Jewish women, and 771 children, a total of 3,334, were liquidated in Vilna."[21] On September 17 this same *Einsatzkommando* reported killing 1,271 Jews, 687 of whom were female, and 247 of whom were children.[22] On Yom Kippur, October 1, 1942, a large *Aktion* killed approximately 2,000 additional Jews, the majority of whom were women and children. On October 15 and 16, the last two days of the festival of Succot, another *Aktion* in Ghetto 2 claimed 1,146 Jewish lives, of whom 507 were women and 257 were children.[23] On October 21, Ghetto 2 was subject to its final liquidation. About 2,500 Jews were taken to Ponary and shot. Of these, 1,036 were females and 586 were children.[24]

In the larger of the two Vilna ghettos, Ghetto I, deportation began after the final liquidation of Ghetto 2. The first mass *Aktion* took place on October 24 and 25, 1941. The *Einsatzkommando* reported that on October 25 2,578 Jews were shot at Ponary of whom 1,766 were women and 812 were children. This was followed by an *Aktion* on October 29 in which 1,533 Jews were taken to Ponary and murdered. Of these, 789 were women and 362 were children. On November 6 the act was repeated; 1,341 Jews were killed at Ponary and again, women and children made up a majority of those killed. The *Einsatzgruppe* commander, reporting on the successful completion of these massacres, told this to superiors in Berlin: "The goal of the systematic cleansing operation in the Ostland was a complete purge of the Jews, in accordance with the basic Order."[25] (This excluded 15,000 Jews who were kept alive as slave laborers until late September 1943, when the Vilna Ghetto was completely liquidated. At the time of the final closing of the ghetto, 6,000 women and children were separated from the men. Of these, 1,400 to 1,700 women were sent to work as slave laborers in Estonia; the other 4,300 to 4,600 women and children were shipped to Majdanek where they were gassed. With this final *Aktion* almost no Jewish children from the famous, historic, Jewish community of Vilna remained alive).[26]

---

21 Cited from Yitzchak Arad, *Ghetto in Flames: The Struggle and Destruction of the Jews in Vilna in the Holocaust* (Jerusalem, 1980), p. 116.
22 *Ibid.*, p. 134.
23 On the Yom Kippur *Aktion*, *ibid.*, pp. 136–38; on the Succot *Aktion*, p. 141.
24 *Ibid.*, pp. 141–42.
25 The data on the *Aktionen* in the ghetto are drawn from *ibid.*, pp. 143–63. The citation from the *Einsatzkommando* report is cited from *ibid.*, p. 170.
26 *Ibid.*, pp. 431–32. For more on the Vilna Ghetto see Y. Arad, *Ghetto in Flames*; Herman Kruk, *The Last Days of the Jerusalem of Lithuania: Chronicles from the Vilna Ghetto and the Camps 1939–1944*, ed. Benjamin Harshav, trans. Barbara Harshav (New Haven, CT, 2002); and Yitskhok Rudashevski, *The Diary of the Vilna Ghetto: June 1941–April 1943* (Tel Aviv, 1973).

In Kovno, one of the first acts after the establishment of the ghetto[27] was the murder of 3,000 women and 5,400 children by *Einsatzkommandos* 3 and 11. Again in October 1941, 581 children were murdered in Kovno as part of a larger *Aktion* in which 1,608 Jews were murdered. A few days later, in connection with still another round up, 818 children were murdered (out of 1,845 Jews). On October 29, 9,200 Jews were killed at the Ninth Fort. Of these 2,920 were women and almost half, 4,273, were children.[28] On November 25, 1941, 175 Jewish children were executed by *Einsatzkommandos* led by Karl Jäger at the Ninth Fort in Kovno. This was repeated on November 29, 1941 when these same killers murdered another 152 Jewish children (and 1155 Jewish women) at the same location.[29]

The Lithuanian Jewish community numbered approximately 240,000 persons before the war. I have been unable to arrive at an exact statistical count relative to the number of Jewish children in Lithuania in 1939 on the eve of the Nazi invasion. One reasonable estimate puts the number at approximately 71,000[30] and I will adopt this number in the present context as a roughly correct tally. Based on this estimate I will suggest, given the decimation of this community that included the special targeting of Jewish children, that fewer than 2 percent of these youngsters survived the war.

In Riga (Latvia), thousands of Jewish children were also murdered by the conquering Nazis. In the first days of the occupation, according to an eyewitness:

> . . . sadistic tortures continued unabated. On Gertrude Street a group of storm troopers went up to the roof of a six-story building and from there threw Jewish children to the ground. Some official was about to order them to stop these executions. From the roof they answered him: "We are conducting scientific work here. We are testing the accuracy of the law of universal gravity." "Donnerwetter! Well said! Continue, gentleman. Science requires sacrifices."[31]

Killing Jewish children was a joke, a source of cruel humor. For these *Einsatzkommandos*, this murder of Jewish children provided a light moment of recreation, of "*sportmachen.*"

---

27 *Ibid.*, p. 288.
28 Wolfgang Benz, Konrad Kwiet, and Juergen Mattheus (eds.), *Einsatz in "ReichKommissariai Ostland": Documente Zum Volkemord im Baltikum und in Weissrussland 1941–1944* (Berlin, 1998), Table, p. 190.
29 I draw this information from Karl Jäger's report of December 1, 1941 covering the activities of *Einsatzkommando* 3 of *Einsatzgruppe* A. This report can be found in Ernst Klee et al., *The Good Old Days: The Holocaust as Seen by Its Perpetrators* (New York, 1991), pp. 46–58.
30 Jacob Lestshinsky, "Balance Sheet of Extermination," *Jewish Affairs* 1.1 (February 1, 1946): 13.
31 Ilya Ehrenberg and Vasily Grossman (eds.), *The Complete Black Book of Russian Jewry* (New Brunswick, NJ, 2002), p. 383.

This barbaric incident was followed by the shooting of a number of Jewish children in Riga on November 8, 1941. Then on November 30 and December 1, 1941 a major *Aktion* took place in the ghetto. A report detailing the event tells us:

> Toward six o'clock in the evening [on November 30] the women, children, and old men were forced out of their apartments. The police tore through the quarter in the Moscow Vorstadt. They finished off the sick on the spot. Mothers burdened with large families were left with no more than two children; the rest were shot right there . . . Groups of women and children driven from their homes were standing in the streets. They were forced to wait there until the next morning. Numb and shivering from the cold, they watched the bloodbath in horror. Toward morning the Germans began forming columns of two to three hundred people; under the armed guard of an equal number of policemen, they were sent eastward . . . No one cleared away the bodies inside the ghetto; but once the column had passed barbed wire, carts and wheelbarrows immediately joined up with it. Without giving it a second thought, the guards shot crying children and people who lagged behind; their bodies were tossed onto a cart or wheelbarrow.

A survivor of the massacre adds:

> By evening the shooting subsided . . . I decided to crawl out from under the pile of shoes . . . I heard the faint voice of a weeping child coming from the pit, where the ones who had been murdered were lying: "Mama, I'm cold . . . Why are you just lying there, Mama?" Well, I thought, what will be will be. I'll try to save the child. But the Germans beat me to it. They went up to the pit, poked around for the little boy with their bayonets, and stabbed him. One of the Germans said, "No one gets away from us alive."[32]

To make sure that this pronouncement would not be proven false, the *Einsatzkommando* conducted another, and final, round of murdering Jewish children in Riga on December 8, 1942.

So it went, ghetto by ghetto. In the Kołomyja Ghetto, in December 1941, a large number of Jewish children were selected for deportation. On one day, almost 1,000 were shipped out in cattle cars. And those few who remained were deported in the early fall of 1942. In the Šiauliai Ghetto the same pattern was repeated with children (and women) disproportionately targeted for murder in the woods of Bubjai. And those not murdered in the Lithuanian forest outside the ghetto

---

32 *Ibid.*, pp. 387, 388, 393. I note parenthetically that this *Aktion* was also the one in which the great Jewish historian, Simon Dubnow, was murdered. This is described in the same source I am quoting from, pp. 387–88.

were sent to Auschwitz to be killed. In a document left by a Jewish *Sonderkommando*, that was buried at Auschwitz and found after the war, the following report is included.

> It was winter, the end of 1944. A contingent of children were brought in. They were from Shavel, Lithuania, where German patrol cars had picked them up from their homes. In broad daylight six hundred Jewish boys, aged twelve to eighteen, were brought in wearing flimsy striped pajamas all in tatters and wearing down-at-heel shoes or wooden clogs. The children looked so handsome, so radiant, so well-built that they shone through their rags. It was the end of October 1944. They arrived in twenty-five trucks guarded by heavily armed SS men. They got out in the yard of the crematorium area. The *Kommando* leader gave an order: "Take your clothes off in the yard!" The children saw the smoke from the chimney and instantly realized that they were being led to their death. Crazed with fright, they started running around the yard, back and forth, clutching their heads. Many of them broke into frightful crying. Their wailing was terrible to hear. The *Kommando* leader and his aide hit out ferociously at the children. He whacked so hard that his wooden club broke in his hand. He got himself another club and flailed at the children's heads. Brute strength prevailed. The children, panic-stricken though they were, with death staring them in the face, undressed. Stark naked, they pressed against each other to shield themselves from the cold, but they would not go downstairs [into the gas chamber]. A bold little boy went up and begged the *Kommando* leader to spare him. He would do any kind of work, no matter how hard. The answer was a tremendous whack on the head with the club. Many of the boys darted off frantically to the Jews of the *Sonderkommando*, threw their arms around their necks, imploring: "Save me!" Others raced about the yard, naked, running from death. The *Kommando* leader called in the SS *Unterscharführer* with his rubber baton to help . . . The boys' high-pitched voices grew louder and louder in a bitter lament. Their keening carried a great distance. One was completely deafened and overcome by this desperate weeping. With satisfied smirks, without a trace of compassion, the SS men triumphantly hailed savage blows on the children and drove them into the gas chamber. On the stairs stood the *Unterscharführer*, still wielding his club and giving a murderous crack at each child. A few lone children were, all the same, still running back and forth in search of a way out. The SS men chased after them, lashing out at them and forcing them at last into the chamber. The glee of the SS men was indescribable.[33]

---

[33] Reprinted in *Aleph-Tav: Tel Aviv Review* (Spring 1975). I cite it from Azriel Eisenberg (ed.), *The Lost Generation* (New York, 1982), pp. 141–42.

In Lublin, the final roundup of Jews in the city took place on March 13–14, 1943 and included the murder of hundreds of children. In the Bialystok region, almost all the children in the smaller ghettos were sent to die in Treblinka in October and November 1942. What this meant in late 1942 and early 1943 when the liquidation of the Polish ghettos was reaching its apogee was that not all the children could be gassed on arrival. Instead, as Jankiel Wiernik, an eyewitness to what went on at Treblinka in this period, tells us:

> All through that winter small children, stark naked and barefooted, had to stand out in the open for hours on end, awaiting their turn in the increasingly busy gas chambers. The soles of their feet froze and stuck to the icy ground. They stood and cried; some of them froze to death. In the meantime, Germans and Ukrainians walked up and down the ranks, beating and kicking the victims ... One of the Germans, a man named Sepp, was a vile and savage beast, who took special delight in torturing children. When he pushed women around and they begged him to stop because they had children with them, he would frequently snatch a child from the woman's arms and either tear the child in half or grab it by the legs, smash its head against a wall and throw the body away. Such incidents were by no means isolated. Tragic scenes of this kind occurred all the time.[34]

Jewish children were worthless, even less than worthless, and the cruel manner of their death reflected this valuation.

In the large Białystok Ghetto where 60,000 Jews were incarcerated, violence against Jewish children began almost immediately after the arrival of the Nazis. On June 27, 1941 1,000 men and boys were locked in the main synagogue of the city and burnt alive.[35] Those Jewish children who remained alive in the ghetto, despite the deprivations of ghetto life, were – except for 1,260 of them – sent to their death in Treblinka on August 21, 1943. The 1,260 children of Białystok not deported to Treblinka were shipped instead to Theresienstadt. They had been saved in connection with a Nazi plan to exchange Jews for German prisoners of war in Allied hands. As part of the negotiations then in progress, Britain had agreed to take 5,000 Jews, 85 percent of whom should be Jewish children from Eastern Europe. In the end, however, the bureaucrats at *Auswärtiges Amt* decided not to finalize the deal and the 1,260 Jewish children from Białystok were sent to be murdered in Auschwitz instead.[36]

In Galicia, by mid-1942, all the Jews had been marked for death. Though 20,000 Jewish women had previously been given work passes, the time for Jewish women

---

34 Jankiel Wiernik, "A Year in Treblinka," in *The Death Camp Treblinka*, ed. Alexander Donat (New York, 1979), p. 163.
35 P. Friedman, "The Extermination of the Polish Jews," in *Road to Extinction*, p. 222.
36 See for further details of this exchange plan H. G. Adler, *Theresienstadt (1941–1943)* (Tübingen, 1960), p. 154.

to be preserved for their labor was coming to an end. Likewise, in March, 1942, as part of "March Operation," a large number of ghetto children were deported to Bełżec. By mid-June, SS Police Leader Fredrich Krüger had negotiated an expansion of Jewish murder in the region. Nearly all Jewish women and children were now to be sent to Bełżec to be gassed. All mediating arguments about economic concerns, that might be invoked to keep Jewish women and children alive, no longer had any significant weight. When the *Kreishauptmann* of Stryj remarked on the unfortunate economic effects of these *Judenaktionen* the local SS and Police Leader Fritz Katzmann brushed these reservations aside and replied that it was imperative "to get this [Jewish] pestilence under control in a very short time."[37] This "Jewish Pestilence," included over 30,000 Jewish children nearly all of whom were killed either in the nearby forest of Lesienice – the so-called "Valley of Death" in the hills northwest of Lvov – or the extremely brutal Janowska Road camp. In the final liquidation of the large Lvov Ghetto, that at its peak housed 160,000 persons, it is reported that, "the Germans murdered the children, often in the most cruel manner: they threw them alive into the fires or dashed the heads of babies against the walls and street lights." In addition, the Hitler Jugend (Nazi Youth) participated in this massacre "and held shooting practice, using Jewish children, as live targets."[38] The small number of Jewish children who survived the forced move out of the ghetto, then became part of the *sportmachen* organized at the Janowska Road camp where the SS competed to see who could, most efficiently, tear children in two or dash their brains out.[39] When the war ended, of the approximately 32,000 to 35,000 Jewish children in Lvov at the start of the war, 85 were alive.[40]

The answer to the question of whether Jewish children had to die was, ultimately, always yes. This rule was confirmed in a telling encounter that occurred in early August 1941 in Byelaya Tserkov, a small Ukrainian village 70 kilometers from Kiev, where *Sonderkommando* 4A murdered all the Jewish adults and many of the Jewish children. But, inexplicably, 90 Jewish children under the age of 5 were allowed to remain alive. When they were discovered by the Catholic military chaplain Ernst Tewers and the Protestant chaplain Gerhard Wilczek, the two men tried to save the children's lives by appealing to the *Generalstafofficer* Lieutenant-Colonel Helmut Groscurth. Groscurth was unsure what to do and, over the protests of *Oberscharführer* Jäger, the commander of the *Einsatzgruppe* A that had murdered the town's Jewish adults and who now wanted to execute these remaining youngsters, referred the case up the chain of command to Field Marshall von Reichenau, commander of the Sixth Army, and *Standartenführer* Paul

---

37 Cited from Thomas Sandkühler, "Anti-Jewish Policy and the Murder of the Jews in the District of Galicia, 1941/42," in *National Socialist Extermination Policies*, Ulrich Herbert (New York, 2000), p. 121.
38 P. Friedman, "The Destruction of the Jews of Lwów," in *Road to Extinction*, p. 298.
39 *Ibid.*, p. 311.
40 *Ibid.*, p. 317.

Blobel. After consideration, "Blobel ordered the children executed." SS Colonel Riedl, in explaining the decision to Groscurth, told the latter that, "the elimination of the Jewish women and children was a matter of urgent necessity, whatever form it took." SS *Obersturmführer* August Häfner, who carried out this sentence, recalls what happened next:

> I went out to the woods alone. The Wehrmacht had already dug a grave. The children were brought along in a tractor. I had nothing to do with this technical procedure. The Ukrainians were standing round trembling. The children were taken down from the tractor. They were lined up along the top of the grave and shot so that they fell into it. The Ukrainians did not aim at any particular part of the body. They fell into the grave. The wailing was indescribable . . . I particularly remember a small fair-haired girl who took me by the hand. She too was shot later . . . The grave was near some woods. It was not near the rifle-range. The execution must have taken place in the afternoon at about 3:30 or 4:00. It took place the day after the discussions at the *Feldkommandanten* . . . Many children were hit four or five times before they died.[41]

Blobel and Riedl knew where their duty to the Fatherland lay. And so did Häfner. Jewish children were a threat that had to be expunged "by whatever form it took."[42] The duty of German soldiers to kill Jewish children was widely obeyed. SS man Ernst Gobel reported this *Aktion* in the area of Scholochowo, in the Ukraine.

> The victims were shot by the firing-squad with carbines, mostly by shots in the back of the head, from a distance of one meter on my command. Before every salvo Täubner gave me the order – "Get set, fire!" I just relayed Täubner's command. The way this happened was that I gave the command "Aim! Fire!" to the members of the firing-squad, and then there was a crack of gunfire. Meanwhile *Rottenführer* Abraham shot the children with a pistol. There were about five of them. These were children whom I would think were aged between two and six years. The way Abraham killed the children was brutal. He got hold of some of the children by the hair, lifted them up from

---

41 Quote is taken from Ernst Klee et al., *The Good Old Days*, p. 154.
42 Here I would remind readers of Otto Ohlendorf's testimony at Nuremberg. Ohlendorf was the Commander of *Einsatzgruppe* D which killed 90,000 Jewish men, women and children. When the prosecutor asked him why he had killed Jewish children Ohlendorf replied as follows: "I believe that it is very simple to explain [such killing of children] if one starts from the fact that this order did not only try to achieve a [temporary] security but also a permanent security because for that reason the children were people who would grow up and surely being the children of parents who had been killed they would constitute a danger no smaller than that of their parents." *Proceedings of the Trials of Major War Criminals*, vol. 4, pp. 337–38.

the ground, shot them through the back of their heads and then threw them into the grave.[43]

Five young Jewish children ages six and younger were perceived as a mortal threat to the mighty Third Reich that had to be extinguished. And so, Abraham the faithful Nazi soldier, unlike the Abraham of the *Akedah*, the binding of Isaac,[44] killed these five children.

Throughout the Ukraine similar massacres occurred on both large and small scales. Whereas in Belaya Tserkov the number of Jewish women and children was relatively small, in Kamianets-Podilskyi *Einsatzgruppe* C murdered 23,600 Jewish men, women, and children between August 27 and August 30, and, as already described, 33,000 Jewish men, women, and children in Babi Yar on the edge of the large city of Kiev. By mid-October 1941, *Einsatzgruppe* C reported killing more than 100,000 Jewish men, women, and children. At the end of the war there were almost no Jewish children left alive from families that had resided either in Kamianets-Podilskyi or Kiev. And further south, *Einsatzgruppe* D, led by Otto Ohlendorf, began the genocidal elimination of the Jews in their region of operation with the murder of all the Jewish men, women and children in Nikolayev in mid-September 1941. The murder of Jewish children had by now become routine. The 454th Security Division reported: "in some places providing for Jewish children and infants who lost their parents presented some difficulties; but also in that respect a remedy has been found by the SD." As Field Marshal von Reichenau described it, these measures were the "harsh but just punishment of Jewish subhumanity" – *Jüdische Untermenschen*.[45]

The murder of the Jewish women and children of Serbia also indicate the absolute worthlessness assigned to these two groups. After nearly all the Jewish men in Serbia had been killed a concentration camp was created, primarily for Jewish women and children, in Sajmiste. At the end of 1941 it was ready to be occupied. In early 1942 approximately 7,000 women and children and 500 surviving Jewish men, along with a group of elderly Jewish men, together with 292 Gypsy women and children, were transferred to this ghetto. But their stay was very short-lived. Starting in March 1942, after liberating the Gypsy women and children, the Jewish women and children began to be gassed in gas vans sent to the camp from

---

43 Cited from Daniel Goldhagen, *Hitler's Willing Executioners: Ordinary Germans and the Holocaust* (New York, 1996), p. 401.
44 See the full biblical tale as narrated in *Genesis* 22.
45 Christopher Browning, *The Origins of the Final Solution: The Evolution of Nazi Jewish Policy* (Lincoln, NE, 2013), pp. 291–93. See also Randolph Braham, The Kamenets Podolsk and Delvidek Massacres: Prelude to the Holocaust in Hungary," *Yad Vashem Studies* 9 (1973): 133–56; and Dieter Pohl, "Schauplatz Ukraine: Der Massenmord an den Juden im Militärverwaltungsgebiet und im Reichskommissariat 1941–1943," in *Ausbeutung, Vernichtung, Öffentlichkeit: Studien zur nationalsozialistischen Verfolgungspolitik*, eds. Norbert Frei, Sybille Steinbacher, and Bernd Wagner (Munich, 2000), pp. 135–73.

Berlin for this purpose. By the end of May, 7,500 Jews, including almost all the women and children, had been murdered.[46]

In Slovakia when Eichmann began to deport the country's Jews on March 12, 1942, the first deportation, at the request of the Slovakian regime, was comprised of women and children.[47] (This mirrored the first deportation from Vienna also organized by Eichmann that consisted of 60 percent women and girls.)[48] Likewise, out of 15,000 Czech Jewish children deported to various camps only 28 survived.[49]

The abundance of evidence that testifies to the murder of Jewish children throughout Eastern Europe is overwhelming. In no specific order, I cite some of this further data. In Minsk thousands of Jewish children were murdered by *Einsatzgruppe* A in early November 1941. Defending this, and related *Aktions*, at the war's end, General Friedrich Jeckeln who headed SS units in Minsk testified that he had received an order from Himmler that stated: "all the Jews in the Ostland down to the last man [woman and child] must be exterminated."[50] In Słonim, 12,000 Jews living in the local ghetto – mostly women and children – were shot. In explaining this *Aktion* the district commissioner referred to these women and children as *Unnütze Fresser*, "useless gobblers." And promised: "Early next year [the Jews] will be rigorously checked and sorted for further reduction."[51] In the Płaszów labor camp, manned by Jewish workers from Kraków, the 300 children who still remained alive in 1943 were rounded up and deported to their death. The *Aktion* occurred to the singing of the children's song "Mammi, Rauf mir ein pferdchen" that was broadcast over loudspeakers the Nazis had set up for the occasion.[52] In one of the villages near Słonim "they chased children, women, and the elderly into a barn and set it alight."[53] In the Commissariat of Zhitomir all of the Jewish children were killed between September 1941 and January 1942. In eastern Belorussia almost every Jewish child (and woman) was murdered by the end of 1942.[54] Walter Mattner, who participated in the mass murder of Jewish

---

46 Walter Manoschek, "The Extermination of the Jews of Serbia," in *National Socialist Extermination Policies*, ed. U. Herbert, pp. 178–81.
47 Yehuda Bauer, "The Problem of Gender" in his *Rethinking the Holocaust* (New Haven, CT, 2001), p. 177.
48 Götz Aly, *Final Solution: Nazi Population Policy and the European Jews* (London, 1999), p. 168.
49 This statistic was provided by the head of the child care department of the Central Committee of Polish Jews in 1945. See *Żydowska Agencja Prasowa Bulletin*, no. 12 (November 1945). I cite it from Kiryl Sosnowski, *The Tragedy of Children under Nazi Rule* (New York, 1983), p. 73.
50 Cited from C. Browning, *The Origins of the Final Solution*, p. 305.
51 Quoted from the situation report of Gebeitskommissar Gerhard Erren, January 25, 1942 and reprinted in E. Klee et al. (eds.), *The Good Old Days*, p. 179.
52 George Eisen, *Children and Play in the Holocaust: Games Among the Shadows* (Amherst, 1988), p. 17.
53 Martin Dean, *Collaboration in the Holocaust: Crimes of the Local Police in Belorussia and the Ukraine* (New York, 2000), p. 116.
54 Christian Gerlach, "German Economic Interests, Occupation Policy, and the Murder of the Jews in Belorussia, 1941/43," in *National Socialist Extermination Policies*, ed. U. Herbert, pp. 223–224.

women and children in Mogilev, Belorussia in early October 1941, wrote home to his wife about his activities in this massacre:

> When the first truckload [of victims] arrived, my hand was slightly trembling when shooting, but one gets used to this. When the tenth load arrived, I was already aiming more calmly and shot securely at the many women, children, and infants.[55]

In the small village of Krynichno, 16 kilometers to the north of Mir, the policeman Willy Schultz, head of the squad sent to do the killing of the Jews, gathered all the Jews together in one house. He listed their names and counted them: 21 Jews. Then he "counted those under 16 . . . and wrote in his notebook: 'acht Stück bis sechzehn Jahre' – 'eight items up to age sixteen.'"[56] Jewish children, their human status denied, were things, *items*, to list. They were of no value, monetary or moral, in the eyes of their killers. Rather, having no importance, the children of Krynichno were listed so that they could be targeted to be shot. And all of these eight children were soon corpses. Again, policeman Schultz reported that 850 Jews, mostly women and children, tried to hide in the Mir Ghetto, but were captured and shot on October 2, 1942. In this orgy of violence against children with Jewish blood even half-Jewish children were rounded up and murdered. So, for example, in Izraylovka (Ukraine) the police collected 20 children of mixed parentage and murdered them in a mass grave in Ustanovka.[57] In Western Europe, too, Jewish children (and their mothers) were targeted for deportation to the death camps. The story of Anne Frank, who was arrested in August 1944, after years of hiding in the attic of 263 Prinsengrachtstelt in Amsterdam, and then was deported to, and died of disease in, Bergen Belsen should be taken as paradigmatic of Dutch Jewish children.[58] Of 140,000 Jews in Holland in 1944, approximately 112,000, some 80 percent, were killed during the war: 46,455 Jews, men, women, and children, were deported from the Westerbork concentration camp in Holland between July 1942 and February 1943. Of these, 3,500 men were sent to work as slave laborers in the Blechhammer Camp, and then later to the industrial camp at Auschwitz III-Monowitz and Gross-Rosen. Of this group, 181 men survived the war. Of the 42,915, 85 survived the war. Included in those Dutch Jews killed in Auschwitz

---

55 I cite this from C. Browning, *The Origins of the Final Solution*, p. 298. It was earlier published in German by Christian Gerlach, *Kalkulierte Morde: Die deutsche Wirtschafts und Vernichtungspolitik in Weissrussland, 1941 bis 1944* (Hamburg, 2001), pp. 588–89.
56 I cite this testimony from M. Dean, *Collaboration in the Holocaust*, p. 80.
57 *Ibid.*, p. 84. The killing in Mir that I have just cited is reported in *ibid.*, p. 92.
58 Anne Frank, *The Diary of a Young Girl: The Definitive Edition*, ed. Otto Frank and Miryam Pressler (New York, 1995). The literature on Anne Frank and her diary is enormous. For an introduction to it see: Alex Grobman, *Anne Frank in Historical Perspective* (Los Angeles, 1995); Alvin Rosenfeld, "Popularization and Memory: The Case of Anne Frank," in *Lessons and Legacies*, ed. Peter Hayes (Evanston, 1991), pp. 251–58. I cite the statistics from Jacob Presser, *Ashes in the Wind: The Destruction of Dutch Jewry*, trans. by Arnold Pomerans (London, 2010), pp. 482–83.

were thousands of Jewish children.[59] From the first 42 transports sent to Auschwitz between July 15, 1942 and December 12, 1942 it is difficult to ascertain if any of the thousands of children deported on these trains survived. For the last 29 transports sent between August 28 and December 12, 1942 "every single one of the women and children . . . was exterminated." From the first five transports sent between January 11 and February 23, 1943 carrying 3,600 persons including 800 children under 16 years, perhaps one or two of the children survived. From the nine transports sent during this six-week period in total, carrying 7,900 Jews, only seven women, and a few children survived. Of the thousands of children deported between August 24 and November 16, 1943, that included 897 children, almost none of the children survived. In all, the Nazis deported 107,000 Dutch Jews to the East, of whom only 5,450 returned.[60]

In France,[61] deportations of foreign Jews to Auschwitz began in March 1942. The deportation of French Jews began in June 1942 – by the end of 1942, 42,500 Jews had been shipped out to Auschwitz – and continued uninterrupted until the end of 1943. Then further trainloads of Jews were deported, mostly to Auschwitz, through the first half on 1944, the last shipments leaving France in July 1944. In total, 100 convoys were sent, mainly from the Drancy concentration camp outside of Paris, to Auschwitz, with a small additional number of transports to Sobibór and Majdanek and the Natzweiler-Struthof Camp near Strasbourg. These journeys involved up to 75,000 Jews.[62] Almost no one returned. In this cohort there were over 6,000 Jewish children aged below 13 years, and of these 2,000 were under the age of 6. The total of French children and adolescents who arrived in Auschwitz came to 9,800.

And, depending on the mix of local conditions and the degree of Nazi pressure to deport the Jews in the different countries of Western Europe, the Jewish population, and the number of Jewish children, was reduced in all the countries under

---

59 The full tragedy of Dutch Jewry is described by Louis Jong, *The Netherlands and Nazi Germany* (Cambridge, MA, 1990); *idem*, "The Netherlands and Auschwitz," in *Yad Vashem Studies*, 7 (1968): 39–65; Jacob Presser, *Ashes*; Bob Moore, *Victims and Survivors: The Nazi Persecution of the Jews of the Netherlands, 1940–1945* (London, 1997); and briefly by S. Friedlander, *Nazi Germany and the Jews 1939–1945* (New York, 2007), pp. 406–13. I cite the statistics on deportations from Westerbork to Auschwitz from Friedlander, p. 413. More narrow aspects of the Dutch situation have been helpfully studied by Guus Meershoek, "The Amsterdam Police and the Persecution of the Jews," in David Cesarani (ed.), *Holocaust: Critical Concepts in Historical Studies*, vol. 3 (New York, 2004), pp. 541–42; and Gerhard Hirschfeld, *Nazi Rule and Dutch Collaboration: The Netherlands under Nazi Occupation, 1940–1945* (Oxford, 1988).
60 The figure cited is drawn from the article, "The Netherlands" written by Werner Warmbrunn in *The Holocaust Encyclopedia* (New Haven, CT, 2001), p. 442.
61 The story of French Jewry has been retold by Michael Marrus and Robert Paxton, *Vichy France and the Jews* (Stanford, CA, 1995); and Renée Poznanski, *Jews in France During World War II* (Hanover, NH, 2001).
62 There is some dispute over the numbers of French Jews sent to Auschwitz. In putting this total at approximately 75,000 I follow the research of M. R. Marrus and R. O. Paxton, *Vichy France and the Jews*, p. 343.

German control, with the exception of Finland, which was technically an ally of Germany. In the West, as in the East, Jewish children were seen as future enemies by virtue of their race and, as such, had to be exterminated.

By the end of the war, in all of occupied Europe, the Nazis had killed up to 1,500,000 Jewish children under the age of 16.

On the killing of Jewish children at Auschwitz

To end this brief review on the fate of Jewish children under the Third Reich, I would remind readers of the information and statistics we possess on the extermination of Jewish children at Auschwitz.

SS physician Johann Paul Kremer, during his interrogation after the war, reported on August 19, 1947:

> As soon as a transport of people assigned to the gas chambers arrived at the railroad ramp, SS officers selected from among the new arrivals the persons who were fit for work, both men and women. The rest, including old people, all children, women with children in their arms and other persons unfit for work, were loaded onto trucks and taken to the gas chambers. I would drive all the way to the bunker with such a transport.[63]

And Rudolf Höss, commandant at Auschwitz noted in his Nuremberg testimony that "children of tender years were invariably exterminated since by reason of their youth they were unable to work."[64] Accordingly, when transports began to arrive at Auschwitz in the spring of 1942 Jewish children began to be murdered. Between April 17 and July 17, 1942, 656 older children arrived as part of a transport of 9,749 Jewish men and boys from Slovakia. By mid-1942 "the majority had died." At the same time younger Jewish children from Slovakia, both boys and girls, who arrived in Auschwitz between April and the end of October 1942 were gassed on arrival. A transmission of November 1942 to the Polish Government in Exile in London regarding Auschwitz reported that "there is a huge percentage of women's and children's clothing among the garments of those who are liquidated. In the last Jewish transport from Slovakia (200 people) there were about 80 children . . . They were poisoned in Birkenau." In the 1942 transports from Slovakia, Bratislava, Novaky, Sered, and Zilina to the camp "about one-fourth of such transports on the average, and more than one-third in particular cases" were made up of Jewish children. Altogether, it is estimated that 9,000 of the 27,000 Slovakian Jews sent to Auschwitz and gassed there were children.

Between March 27, 1942 and August 11, 1944, 71 transports carried 69,000 Jews from France to Auschwitz. The number of children and adolescents included

---

63 See here the detailed description of R. Hilberg, *The Destruction of the European Jews*, 3rd. ed. (2003), pp. 1036–1042; and Filip Muller, *Eyewitness Auschwitz: Three Years in the Gas Chambers* (New York, 1979).
64 R. Höss, *Proceedings of the Trial of Major War Criminals* (Nuremberg, 1947), vol. 11, p. 417.

in these transports, as noted above, totaled 9,800–14 percent of the aggregate. Of these 7,400 were below the age of 14. Almost every one of these children was murdered. From Holland, via Westerbork concentration camp, Jews began being deported to Auschwitz in July, 1942. In total 60,000 Dutch Jews were sent to the camp in 68 transports. An exact statistical analysis of 38 of these transports that together carried 31,661 Jews revealed that among these deportees there were 3,832 children up to age 15, and another 969 adolescents aged 16 and 17. Thus 15.5 percent of the Dutch deportees on these transports were children. Among the entire population of 69,000 Dutch Jews sent to Auschwitz, the number of children and adolescents exceeds 8,000. Very few of these children lived until the end of the war.

Between 1942 and 1944, as the "Final Solution" gained momentum, Jewish children from all over Europe were systematically isolated and shipped by cattle car to Auschwitz. From Belgium 24,906 Jews were deported, in 27 transports, to Auschwitz. Of these 4,654, or 19 percent, of those sent to die were children aged 16 or younger. From Poland it is estimated that 300,000 Jews were shipped to Auschwitz of whom 66,000, 22 percent, were children 17 or younger. As late as May 14, 1944, 300 to 400 Jewish children, the remnant of the Kraków Ghetto, arrived in Auschwitz from Płaszów. By the war's end only a few hundred, primarily older children, of this cohort of 66,000 Polish Jewish youngsters were still among the living. (More generally, from a Polish Jewish community of 3,300,000, at least 20 percent of the community, some 660,000 individuals, were children. Of these 660,000 souls only 5,000 survived the war).[65] From Yugoslavia, 10,000 Jews were sent to Auschwitz, of whom about 1,500 were children. From Germany, 2,621 of the deported 20,405 Jews were children. From Norway, 84 children and adolescents were sent to Auschwitz. Few returned. From Austria, 200 Jews, including 15 children, were sent to Auschwitz from Vienna in eight transports between March 1943 and September 1944. Additional numbers of Jews from Austria and elsewhere also came to Auschwitz via Theresienstadt beginning in October 1942. Almost all of the children in these transports were directed on arrival to the gas chambers. The data available on the transports from Theresienstadt to Auschwitz indicates that between 1942 and 1944, 46,212 Jews made this fateful journey. Of these, 3,807 were children aged 14 or younger. Almost none of them survived the camp.

In March 1943, Greek Jews began arriving at the camp. Most of these came from the great Jewish community of Salonika. But there were also deportations from the Greek islands of Korfu and Rhodes. In total, 48,633 Greek Jews were shipped to Auschwitz, including 12,000 children. All the children were gassed on arrival. In the further 1944 deportations of 3,500 Jews from Athens and Korfu and 2,500 Jews from Rhodes there were approximately 1,000 Jewish children all

---

65 This statistic was provided by the head of the child care department of the Central Committee of Polish Jews in 1945. See *Żydowska Agencja PrasowaBulletin*, 12 (November 1945). I cite it from Kiryl Sosnowski, *The Tragedy of Children under Nazi Rule*, p. 73.

of whom were gassed on arrival. Italian Jews began to arrive in Auschwitz on October 23, 1943. (This followed the overthrow of Mussolini on July 25, 1943, the surrender of the successor government led by Marshall Badoglio to the Allies, and the Nazi takeover of Italy in late July and August 1943.) Altogether 7,400 Italian Jews were deported to Auschwitz, about a quarter of whom (approximately) are estimated to have been children. And from the liquidated Lithuanian and Estonian labor camps Jews were transported to Auschwitz in the summer of 1944. In the transport of June 26, 1944 there were 1,423 people – 899 children and 524 women. On August 1, 1944 a transport from Kovno also arrived comprised solely of 120 Jewish boys aged 8 to 14. And still another transport that arrived on September 12, 1944 was made entirely of 300 boys who were liquidated on arrival.

In the final, desperate act of the *Shoah*, 437,402 Jews were deported from Hungary when the new government of Prime Minister Döme Sztójay, working directly under German control, took office on March 22, 1944. The first deportations to Auschwitz began in mid-May 1944. It is estimated that of these deportees, approximately 90,000 were children, very few of whom survived.

By war's end a total of 216,300 Jewish children and adolescents had been sent to Auschwitz. (This represented 93.4 percent of all children sent to the camp.) Of these 216,300 children, 212 adolescents and 239 children were still alive when the camp was liberated by the Russians in late January 1945.[66]

The planned, systematic, murder of all Jewish children was the most radical, distinctive, feature of the *Shoah*.[67] More than any other act of the Third Reich, it reveals the absolute, dogmatic, racial-Manichean principles at the very core of the Hitler state. As a result, the phenomenological character of the Holocaust is different from all other instances of mass murder that are known to me.

---

66 Helena Kubica, "Children and Adolescents in Auschwitz," in *Auschwitz 1940–1945: Central Issues in the History of the Camp*, vol. 2, edited by Tadeusz Iwasko, Helena Kubica, Franciszek Piper, et al. (Oświęcim, 2000), Table 4, p. 290.
67 In light of this assault on Jewish children, one can understand post-Holocaust thinkers such as Emil Fackenheim and Jonathan Sachs who have made having Jewish children after the *Shoah* a crucial *theological* issue. This is not the place to evaluate these proposals but, given the data presented in this paper, it is relevant to make note of them. For more on this matter see Emil Fackenheim, *The Jewish Return into History: Reflections in the Age of Auschwitz and a New Jerusalem* (New York, 1978), p. 48; and Jonathan Sachs, *Crisis and Covenant: Jewish Thought after the Holocaust* (Manchester and New York, 1992), pp. 44–48.

UPDATE

This essay first appeared in a *Festschrift* entitled *Continuity and Change: A Festschrift In Honor of Irving Greenberg's 75th Birthday*, which I co-edited with Dr. Steven Bayme.[68] As I have already commented on the importance of studying the fate of children in situations of communal violence and high death counts, I would only add here that, for me, the uncompromising program regarding the killing of Jewish children everywhere in occupied Europe is the core of the Holocaust, and the most compelling example of its inexhaustible evil.

---

68 Published by the University Press of America (Lanham, 2010), pp. 167–88.

9

THOUGHTS ON THE INTERSECTION OF RAPE AND *RASSENSCHANDE* DURING THE HOLOCAUST

First thoughts

Jewish women during the Holocaust, like many other women in other situations of social unrest, military conquest, slavery (both ancient and modern) and war, experienced sexual abuse and rape. In each of these historical contexts, women, and the men to whom they were linked, were essentially powerless to stop their sexual exploitation and assault. In these environments girls and women were at the mercy of men who, both because of their carnal appetites as well as their desire to express their domination, took unspeakable sexual liberties, often accompanied by violence and coercion of various sorts, with them. Not unsurprisingly, because of its intrinsic importance, the subject of sexual violence and rape has already been considered in detail by numerous historians in the different historical cases in which it is known to have occurred, as well as by a number of scholars of the *Shoah*.[1] Thus, the broad outlines of the story are known and need no retelling here. However, in the present essay I would like to return to this deeply disturbing issue in order to call attention to one highly repercussive factor that distinguishes – and is distinctive to – the rape of Jewish women during the Holocaust, yet which has not been properly appreciated in the relevant scholarly analyses. This unique aspect of the rape of Jewish women sheds light not only on the matter of sexual violence during the Holocaust but also on the more general ideological character of the Nazi assault on the Jewish People.

---

1 The sexual exploitation and rape of women has occurred in many historical instances of war and conquest. In the twentieth century alone, it was a significant element in Japanese practice during World War II where women from Korea and other countries were forced to become so-called comfort women for Japanese troops. And rape was a part of the policy of war and conquest in the military conflict in Yugoslavia, and in Rwanda in the 1990s. For more on these atrocities, see George Hicks, *The Comfort Women: Japan's Brutal Regime of Enforced Prostitution in the Second World War* (New York, 1994); Alexandra Stiglmayer (ed.), *Mass Rape: The War against Women in Bosnia-Herzegovina*, trans. Marion Faber (Lincoln, NE, 1994); and Beverly Allen, *Rape Warfare: The Hidden Genocide in Bosnia-Herzegovina and Croatia* (Minneapolis, 1996). Earlier in the twentieth century it was a significant feature in Turkish barbarities against the Armenian population of Turkey during World War I, and was a ubiquitous feature of the conquest of Germany at the end of World War II.

Here, by way of introduction, I would begin with three methodological comments. The first is that rape is a language. Within the context of the Holocaust the rape of Jewish women by German soldiers and their non-German allies is not only a sexual act but a political declaration as to the degenerate status of the Jewish victims in accordance with Nazi ideology. The action communicates that Jewish girls and women are not fully human, that they are not shielded by normal moral rules, that they stand outside police and state protection, and that they do not belong to the universe of ethical obligation that ordinarily constrains Aryan behavior.

Second, rape, when it involved a Jewish female by an Aryan man was, despite its common recurrence, in violation of the fundamental Nazi notion of *Rassenschande* (race defilement). The contravention of this essential principle, that was one of the radical foundations of the Third Reich, generated, because of the character of this National Socialist conception, unique difficulties and complications. Moreover, the problematic realities that arose as a consequence of such behavior led, necessarily, to unprecedented – and lethal – outcomes that will be discussed and analyzed below. Indeed, the Nazi belief in the need for these deadly outcomes is the central concern of this essay.

Third, as a result of my intensive study of the issue of the sexual molestation and violation of Jewish girls and women during the Holocaust I have come to believe that, while these types of acts were strictly forbidden by the most basic laws – racial and political – of the Third Reich, there was, paradoxically, something "political" about such occurrences. For the total vulnerability in which Jewish girls and women found themselves and the sexual exploitation that resulted was the outcome of more than lust and was made possible by a state that fervently held very particular notions of Jews – and of Jewish women – as racial criminals who deserved punishment and whose violation could be understood as legitimate retribution. Seen thus, the rape of Jewish girls and women was perceived, within the totality of the *Shoah*, not only as a discrete, individual, localized sexual performance, but as an assault on the collective body, the communal being, of the Jewish People. I recognize that this last observation involves speculation, and I would welcome a more extensive scholarly conversation regarding it, but the evidence relevant to this subject seems to me to be overwhelming and thus encourages this conjecture, at least for consideration as part of a larger, more complex analysis.

Instances of sexual abuse

The rape of Jewish girls and women is known to have taken place throughout the universe of the Third Reich. It took place in Germany beginning in the 1930s and spread to all the territories conquered by the Wehrmacht. Despite official military rules and the theoretically restraining effect of racial laws against miscegenation, members of the *Wehrmacht*, and other Nazi military and quasi-military groups, regularly violated Jewish women. Recent studies suggest, for example, that 50–80 percent of the SS troops and the police units that operated in Eastern

Europe were guilty of such transgressions.[2] This eastern context was, of course, radically different than that in Western Europe, but there too sexual violence accompanied Nazi military conquest and occupation.

To begin our close review of this difficult issue I would start with the sexual violence against Jewish women in Nazi labor camps where such behavior was common. In the Wolanów labor camp, for example, rape was a repeated phenomenon. Survivors recall the recurrent rape of Jewish women by German soldiers and a "holiday celebration gang rape in December 1942."[3] In the Starachowice labor camp, Ukrainians are reported to have been persistent perpetrators of sexual violence against Jewish women.[4] And in the Majówka Camp, which was part of the Starachowice complex, there are multiple testimonies referring to the public rape of a young Jewish woman by a German Camp official.[5] Neither decency nor shame, nor the law of the state, were strong enough safeguards against this obscene action. Furthermore, as Christopher Browning has accurately identified it, this sexual molestation in the sight of the entire Jewish community was both "an act of violent domination over the powerless victim" as well as "a ritual of humiliation aimed at degrading the entire camp population."[6] In this sense it was what I have described as a "political" action. At the Dessau *Arbeitslager*, Lucille Eichengreen had the following encounter: she stole some cloth to make a headscarf and then unexpectedly was discovered having done so by an SS officer. At that point:

> His left hand moved swiftly down my body. I no longer doubted that he knew my secret. My absurd vanity would be my death. My head was still in his viselike grip as his hand came to a stop between my legs. He fingered the scarf. I stopped breathing, convinced that my life was over. Suddenly he shouted into my ear, "You filthy, useless bitch! Pfui! Menstruating!" He pushed me away in disgust.[7]

So Eichengreen escaped being raped. But other women at her forced labor camp were not so fortunate. After the war, one of her fellow inmates from Dessau told her the following tale:

> A nameless, faceless SS man came every night. I feared for my life and thought it would ensure my survival in Auschwitz. I loathed him then;

---

2 So the research and conclusion of Birget Beck, "Vergewaltigung von Frauen als Kriegsstrategie im Zweiten Weltkrieg?" in *Gewalt im Krieg: Ausübung, Erfahrung und Verweigerung von Gewalt in Kriegen des 20. Iahrhunderts*, ed. Andreas Gestrich (Munster, 1996), pp. 34–40.
3 Christopher R. Browning, *Remembering Survival: Inside a Nazi Slave-Labor Camp* (New York, 2010), p. 190.
4 *Ibid.*, p. 190.
5 *Ibid.*, p. 191.
6 *Ibid.*
7 Lucille Eichengreen with Harriet Hyman Chamberlain, *From Ashes to Life: My Memories of the Holocaust* (San Francisco, 1994), p. 107.

> I knew that he was a criminal and a killer. But as the months went by, I got used to him. He kept me out of the gas chamber. He gave me food. I didn't think of the future then. I lived one day at a time. Whatever I did was my way of surviving.[8]

Always at risk, Jewish women had few defenses against such intimate intrusions.

The mention of the exploitation at the Wolanów, Starachowice, Majówka, and Dessau camps reveals just a very small fraction of the enormous number of cases of sexual abuse and rape in the world of forced labor where women's bodies were taken advantage of in multiple ways. In every camp there were those who would capitalize on the sexual availability of Jewish women. Roman Halter, a Jewish inmate at one of the work camps built near Auschwitz remembered:

> There was this big trough of disinfectant which looked like iodine and we had to submerge ourselves in that. If we didn't submerge fully, a SS would stand on you with their boots until even our heads were submerged. With the rough shaving we'd had, anyone who was cut suffered tremendously because it stung so badly. Then we were moved to showers with water. After getting uniforms, we were given numbers and then taken to our blocks. The women were not put in the women's block, but in this big block next to us. The *Kapos* and their deputies came to rape the women at night and there were terrible screams and groans coming from that block, and the husbands in our block wept because they could understand the shouts. It was a free-for-all, a sort of reward for the criminals, the German psychopaths who were sent to Auschwitz-Birkenau and who were in charge of the blocks.[9]

The nightly molestation of Jewish women, within the hearing of their husbands and brothers, by "German psychopaths" seeking uncontrolled sexual satisfaction was a powerful confirmation that the bodies of these women were there to be ravaged by whoever would take them.

Throughout the Auschwitz complex, here including the slave-labor camps created to utilize camp inmates, the rape of Jewish girls and women was an ever-present threat.[10] Cecile Klein reports that on the arrival of her transport one

---

8 *Ibid.*, p. 190.
9 Lyn Smith, *Remembering Voices of the Holocaust: A New History in the Words of the Men and Women who Survived* (New York, 2005), p. 161.
10 Na'ama Shik, based on her research of the Auschwitz death camp, has concluded that: "Although a variety of sexually abusive practices took place in the [Auschwitz] camp, rape was the exception. Because of *Rassenschande* Germans serving in the camp were forbidden to rape Jewish prisoners," see her "Infinite Loneliness: Some Aspects of the Lives of Jewish Women in the Auschwitz Camps According to Testimonies and Autobiographies Written Between 1945 and 1948," in *Lessons and Legacies VIII: From Generation to Generation*, ed. Doris Bergen (Evanston, 2008), p. 144. This is an important methodological caution that should be taken very seriously. And, of

young Jewish girl was taken off to the officers' barracks and repeatedly raped for two days. When she was brought back to the inmate huts she was "scarcely recognizable, incoherent, face and body swollen and bruised."[11] Likewise, Lauren Varon, a Greek Jewess, was raped at Auschwitz by SS men. She remembered: "all of a sudden, the door opened, and three Nazis came, and they dragged us on the floor, they violated us, sexually violated us. They smelled like beer, you know. They raped us."[12] And, similarly, "Susan," another Jewish woman who was twenty-one when she arrived at Auschwitz reported being molested by a Polish "privileged prisoner." She told an interviewer: "He grabbed and raped me."[13] Al Gordon, a Jewish man who survived Auschwitz, testified after the war:

> They (the Gestapo) wanted me to bring women to these barracks every other day because they wanted to have sex with the women. Personally, I did not go for it, but I had to do, I had to do it to survive. They gave me an order to do it. To bring a woman every other night to have sex with him . . . That is what happened. Then he would rape her, and I had

---

course, as regards the majority of Jewish women murdered at Auschwitz who went directly from the trains that brought them to the camp into the gas chambers, this conclusion is undoubtedly correct. However, the issue is more complex than Shik's claim recognizes. And this for several reasons. First of all, Shik's conclusion does not take adequate account of what happened in the labor camps associated with Auschwitz as compared to what transpired at Birkenau. Second, given the evidence and implications of other studies, it may well be that Shik overestimates the restraining effect exercised by the rule against *Rassenschande*. Lust often trumps regulations, especially in conditions like those that existed in Nazi camps, including the death camps. Third, when seeking to measure the degree to which rape occurred in Nazi camps the methodological question regarding the reluctance of survivors to publicly testify to having been raped and otherwise sexually molested becomes crucial. Shik, herself, recognizes this concern, see her remarks on pp. 148–49, but tends to play down its salience. Readers should compare her views with those of Michael Nutkiewicz who has addressed this issue in his "Shame, Guilt, and Anguish in Holocaust Survivor Testimony," *The Oral History Review* 30.1 (2003): 1–22. Nutkiewicz argues that Holocaust survivor testimony is often self-censored. Likewise, Elizabeth Baer, agreeing with this line of argument, has pointed out that "as scholars read women's memoirs more extensively not only for what they say but also for what is coded and for elisions and gaps, we have detected much more sexual violence than had been acknowledged," "Rereading Women's Holocaust Memoirs: Liana Millu's *Smoke Over Birkenau*," in *Lessons and Legacies VIII*, pp. 162–63. Baer, moreover, explicitly criticizes Jack G. Morrison, *Ravensbrück: Everyday Life in a Women's Concentration Camp, 1939–45* (Princeton, 2000), pp. 177–78, for repeating the claim that *Rassenschande* laws were "overwhelmingly obeyed." In trying to think through the issues raised by the testimonies of female Jewish survivors in relation to the question of *Rassenschande*, it is important to remember that the Aryans involved, actually or potentially, in such sexual encounters in the Nazi camps did not usually have to worry about "race pollution" as the Jewish women abused in these contexts would, as a rule, not live long enough to have children because if they became pregnant they would, almost certainly, be immediately put to death.

11 Cecile Klein, *Sentenced to Live: A Survivor's Memoir* (New York, 1988), pp. 85–86.
12 Testimony found in Yad Vashem Archive, I cite it from N. Shik, "Infinite Loneliness," p. 151.
13 Cited from Joan Ringelheim, "The Split Between Gender and the Holocaust," in *Women in the Holocaust*, eds. Dalia Ofer and Lenore J. Weitzman (New Haven, CT, 1998), p. 341.

> to take her back to her barrack. The women did not want to go, but . . . otherwise they would get killed. They would shoot them right then and there. No mercy.[14]

The mention of shooting Jewish women who would not participate in these forced sexual acts should not go unnoticed. It points beyond sexual violence to a more total violence that is *not* incidental to what occurred here. Jewish women could not only be subjected to any and all venereal appetites but, in addition, could be, and were, counted as nothing and murdered on the whim of a degenerate German policeman.

Then, too, Jewish women were incessantly exploited by fellow prisoners in positions of authority within both the main camp and its many related work camps. *Kapos* and other privileged prisoners had access to the bodies of Jewish women, and often took advantage of this access. Na'ama Shik is correct when, reflecting on these sexual assaults, she concludes: "To these men, the female Jewish prisoners ceased being 'human women' and became a wide-open bodily site that possessed signs of sex but contained no humanity."[15]

In the concentration camps incidents of rape are similarly attested. In Ravensbrück, Ruth Elias remembers:

> Drunken SS men sometimes made unexpected appearances in our block; the door would suddenly be flung open, and they would roar in on their motorcycles. Then the orchestra was ordered to play, and the SS men would sing along while they continued to drink, their mood getting ever more boisterous. Young Jewish women would be pulled from their bunks, taken away somewhere, and raped. Raping Jewish women wasn't considered Rassenschande (race defilement), therefore it was allowed. . . . I cannot describe the pitiable state of these poor women when they came back to the barracks.[16]

Sarah Moses, one of these young girls raped by two German soldiers at Ravensbrück, has recounted her experience:

> It is very difficult for me to talk about this because it was one of the most horrible of my experiences. This was in Ravensbrück. Someone came to get me, and I was given some candy, I believe. I remember being given some candy and then I was taken into a building and into a small room and, I don't remember the sequence of this but, there were two men there. And there were other people in the room, I think, but I remember two men. I was put on a table, from what I remember, or it could have been a tall bed.

---

14 Video Testimony, USC Archive, testimony of Al Gordon, TC 3:00:25–3:01:50.
15 Shik, "Infinite Loneliness," p. 151.
16 Ruth Elias, *Triumph of Hope: From Theresienstadt and Auschwitz to Israel*, trans. Margot Bettauer Dembo (New York, 1998), p. 1120.

I was very little, and it seemed that it was kind of high up from where I was. And I was very violently sexually abused, and I remember being hit, I remember crying and I wanted to get out of there. I was calling people, screaming. One thing that stands in my mind, I remember, one of them told me that they would stand me up on my head and cut me right in half.[17]

Sara Moses' age was no defense against these predators. They would satisfy their desires without regard to normal social conventions. Nor should we ignore the fact that here again there is the threat of lethal physical force in addition to the coerced debauchery.

At the Stutthof Concentration Camp the guards did whatever they liked to Jewish women and girls with impunity. This included a sadistic form of *sportmachen* that involved torture and rape. In an exceptionally disturbing narrative, the Czech Jewish woman Juliana Carpentieri (born Zelmanovich) recalled what happened to her as a teenager in the "soldiers barracks" at the camp:

> There were dogs. I don't know if they were Dober[mans] or German Shepherds. They were very, very, vicious. If they tell them to get you, they rip you apart. Because when they walk with them, they put a thing, a [muzzle] on them. So, there was a woman there which I did not know. Then they brought in a boy, I think he was about my age, he looked like my size, I should say. After that, my sister said it was a girl. So, they brought this woman and her child. They played with her (the woman), they brought in the dogs [at this point the interviewer interrupts her and asked if the woman was raped, she said yes and then continues to tell about the dogs]. One of the dogs ripped her breast out. There was blood all over. But I am telling you, if it was a boy or a girl (the child), never cried. I did not cry. Then they came to me [interviewer brings her back to the woman]. The dog ripped one breast off then the other breast and the woman passed out. I don't know what happened to the woman after they took her outside.... The child was taken out when I was taken out. Then they said to me ... But I have no chest. I was only a kid. So, they sodomized me, they raped me and then they said they were going to kill me. There were five of them. I cried out. All five of them raped me, laughing drinking.

And she added: "The child was there the whole time and watched [his mother] being raped."[18] Savagery, sadism, and the rape of a child – plus the probable murder of a woman (and mother) and the threat to kill a second child – all mingled together in this barbaric scene. Extreme sexual deviance was here manifest in a

---

17 Video Testimony, USC Archive, testimony of Sara Moses, TC 4:00:40–4:04:35. Two further video testimonies that report rapes in Concentration Camps are those of Lya Cohen who was a prisoner at the Haidari Concentration Camp in Greece, TC 1:26:50–1:30:25; and Rose Argan who was imprisoned at the Kurowice Concentration Camps in Poland, TC 3:19:10–3:22:30.
18 Video Testimony, USC Archive, testimony of Juliana Carpentieri, TC 4:19:34–4:24:48.

number of forms and the life of a Jewish woman was almost certainly forfeit to amuse five German soldiers.

At Majdanek, according to the testimony of a Polish Jewish woman from Kielce who was arrested in Warsaw while trying to pass as an "Aryan" and deported to this camp in 1943, Jewish women were raped on arrival.

> Then the next day we were taken to Majdanek . . . So then we arrived there, first to the bathing installation. Then in the bathing installation they proceeded with a selection. An SS man came – women also, men with dogs – we were completely naked, and they simply looked us over, like animals. Looked into our teeth, tested our muscles with their hands. And the dogs barked, and then some of the older women and the sick were pushed to one side. These did not come out of the bathhouse anymore. Afterward we were bathed, and we were . . .[19]

I note, too, that when this same survivor was asked: "In general to what extent did women suffer from attempts of rape or other advances by the guards?" she replied: "Officially it was prohibited. But it only appeared that way. For instance, the most beautiful girls disappeared from Majdanek."[20]

The sexual abuse of Jewish women was also a common occurrence in the ghettos as these were spaces where Jewish women lived for quite long periods of time under the watchful eye of German military and civilian authorities. So, for example, from the inception of the Warsaw Ghetto in mid-November 1940, the rape of Jewish women here imprisoned was a regular happening. In *The Black Book of Polish Jewry*, the following is reported:

> The Germans gave up the project to have the *Judenrat* establish brothels for them, but the German soldiers continually insulted and humiliated Jewish women. Many became infected with venereal diseases; many, unable to bear the moral and physical tortures, committed suicide.
>
> I. L. states in his deposition: "In February 1940 the Germans began rounding up Jewish women for forced labor. One afternoon a truck came to Solna Street in Warsaw, and Jewish women of the district were forced into it. The procedure was frequently repeated afterward. Girls would disappear for several days and come home after having been attacked. The attractive wife of a Jew on the Iron Gate Place was abducted and permitted to return home after she had been raped."
>
> Dr. S. S. of Warsaw in his affidavit of May 12, 1940 made before the Committee for Polish Jews in Jerusalem, states: "One continually hears of the raping of Jewish girls in Warsaw. The Germans suddenly enter a

---

19 Donald Niewyk (ed.), *Fresh Wounds: Early Narratives of Holocaust Survival* (Chapel Hill, NC, 1988), p. 217.
20 *Ibid.*, p. 221.

house and rape 15- or 16-year-old girls in the presence of their parents and relatives. The surgeon-gynecologists, of course keeping secret the names of their victims, state that in their practice they have many cases of girls who have been raped under similar conditions, and it is necessary to administer antitetanus injections. In one mirror-shop in Świętojerska Street there was a mass raping of Jewish girls. The Germans seized the most beautiful and most healthy girls in the streets and brought them in to pack the mirrors. After the work the girls were raped."

In the *Free Europe* pamphlet, *The Persecution of Jews*, there appears the following report: "One of the most disgusting orgies on the part of German officers took place in the house of M. Szereszewski, a well-known Warsaw Jew, in Pius Street in Warsaw." As a result of a raid carried out in Franciszkańska Street, 40 Jewish girls were dragged into the house which was occupied by the German officers. There, after being forced to drink, the girls were ordered to undress and to dance for the amusement of their tormentors. Beaten, abused and raped, the girls were not released till 3 a.m.[21]

The diverse testimonies recorded in the Black Book are paralleled in the record of Warsaw Ghetto life provided by other chronicles of the ghetto as well. Emmanuel Ringelblum, for example, in his *Notes*, refers to the case of three Jewish women who were raped on Tłomackie Street by German men.

> At 2 Tłomackie Place three lords and masters ravished some women; screams resounded through the house. The Gestapo are concerned over racial degradation – Aryans consorting with non-Aryans – but are afraid to report it.[22]

And Marek Edelman, provided the following report of the rape of a Jewish girl that took place in public before a group of other Jews:

> They waited in line and then raped her. After the line was finished, this girl left the niche and she walked across the whole gym, stumbling against the reclining people. She was very pale, naked, and bleeding, and she slouched down into a corner. The crowd saw everything, and nobody said a word. Nobody so much as moved, and the silence continued.[23]

In the Warsaw Ghetto no Jewish girl or woman, regardless of the social or communal context, was safe from sexual depredations.

---

21 Jacob Apenszlak (ed.), *The Black Book of Polish Jewry: An Account of the Martyrdom of Polish Jewry Under the Nazi Occupation* (New York, 1995), pp. 28–29.
22 Emannuel Ringelblum, *Notes from the Warsaw Ghetto: The Journal of Emmanuel Ringelblum* (New York, 1958), p. 24.
23 Hanna Krall, *Shielding the Flame: An Intimate Conversation with Dr. Marek Edelman, the Last Surviving Leader of the Warsaw Ghetto Uprising*, trans. Joanna Stasinska and Lawrence Weschler (New York, 1986), p. 44.

And much the same was true in Łódź. I will cite only one paradigmatic case that should be understood to stand for many, the rape of a Jewish teenager, the daughter of Dr. Simha Mandels, by no less a person than the leading German bureaucrat in the city, Hans Biebow, during the very last days of the existence of the city's ghetto, in late August 1944. Biebow, who had worked in the administration of the ghetto almost since its creation and had been in charge of it in its last years, felt himself free to violate this young Jewish girl. In the event Biebow's forced seduction was eventually interrupted, at which point he shot the girl he had just had sex with and fled.[24] I would highlight this last point because, once again, it calls to attention the connection between rape and murder in this context. That is, one must understand that Biebow tried to shoot the girl he had molested even though there was no physical risk to him and he certainly knew that the victim and her family would soon be sent to Chełmno to be murdered, as indeed they were.[25] And, then, one must ask at least two questions: why did Biebow do what he did? and what was at stake here? These are questions to which I shall return and try to answer in the section below entitled "The 'Final Solution' as a license to rape."

Throughout the extensive territory conquered as a result of the invasion of Russia, the rape of Jewish women was a frequent occurrence. A survivor of the massacre at Babi Yar (in Kiev) later testified:

> I shall never forget one girl; her name was Sarra, and she was about fifteen years old. It is hard to describe the beauty of this girl. Her mother was pulling at her own hair and crying out in a heart-rending voice, "Kill us together!" They killed the mother with a rifle butt. Taking their time with the girl, five or six Germans stripped her naked, but I saw nothing more than that.[26]

But one very well knows what happened, what she didn't see.

In Minsk the Nazis killed the Jew Boris Semenovich Glushkin on August 8, 1941. "The next night [German soldiers came to his home and] there was a knock at the door. The commandant came in. He demanded the wife of the executed Jew. She was crying, shaken by the terrible death of her husband; her three children were crying too. We thought they were going to kill her, but the Germans did something even more vile; they raped her right there in the yard."[27]

---

24 The exact date of this incident is uncertain. It took place sometime in August 1944 during the final days of the ghetto when there were still 68,000 Jews in Łódź. Isaiah Trunk, *Łódź Ghetto: A History*, ed. and trans. Robert Moses Shapiro (Bloomington, 2006), p. 266. Other sources mention August 28 and 29. According to Trunk, based on the testimony of other survivors of the Łódź Ghetto: "Biebow practiced his sadistic whims . . . (rapes of girls in the women's camp, savage outrages on captured Jews) " *Łódź Ghetto*, p. 269. Thus, his behavior on the occasion recounted here was not unusual.

25 Gordon J. Horwitz, *Ghettostadt: Lodz and the Making of a Nazi City* (Cambridge, MA, 2008), pp. 299–300.

26 Ilya Ehrenburg and Vasily Grossman (eds.), *The Complete Black Book of Russian Jewry*, trans. David Patterson (New Brunswick, NJ, 2002), p. 9.

27 *Ibid.*, p. 212.

In the Vilna Ghetto Herman Kruk reports that Jewish women were taken at random to serve in brothels for the occupying German troops:

"German Precision"
In front of me is an interesting document – a receipt from a Wehrmacht bordello on Wielka Pohulanka Street. The receipt of the company is written out precisely, with the names of the woman partner, the number of the room, the date, etc. Aside from German precision, we see that our former descriptions are correct. On Subocz there is an official whorehouse, which uses women who once had been snatched off the street . . .[28]

In the Dolginovo Ghetto, in Belorussia, survivor reports tell us: "Policemen raped [Jewish] girls." And a second survivor of the Belorussian ghettos, Gertrude Schneider, when asked about her experience of sexual molestation by the ghetto's non-Jewish guards replied: "The guards raped you . . . the guards were stationed outside the ghetto and walked around. They found ways to get into the ghetto and in the night looted and raped."[29] In the Radashkovichi Ghetto, according to Faina Ryzhikova-Elman, a survivor of this ghetto: "With the arrival of the Nazis . . . humiliations and outrages began from the very first days. They raped young women." In the Mglin Ghetto, local policemen and Gestapo, according to eyewitness accounts, sexually assaulted local Jewesses, while in the Mikoyanshakhar Ghetto it was German soldiers who violated local Jewish women of all ages. Again, in the Balvi Ghetto, in Latvia, local policeman ravaged Jewish girls. And in Grajewo near Białystok, Poland, during the conquest of the city in June 1941, German troops raped a large number of Jewish girls and women.[30] And so it went from ghetto to ghetto. The list of locations in the

---

28 Herman Kruk, *The Last Days of the Jerusalem of Lithuania: Chronicles from the Vilna Ghetto and the Camps, 1939–1944*, ed. Benjamin Harshav, trans. Barbara Harshav (New Haven, CT, 2002), p. 266.
29 The testimony regarding the Dolginovo Ghetto is drawn from D. B. Mel'tser and Vladimir Levin (eds.), *The Black Book with Red Pages: Tragedy and Heroism of Belorussian Jews* (Cockeysville, MD, 2005), p. 248. The second Belorussian testimony from Gertrude Schneider is cited from Esther Katz and Joan Miriam Ringelheim (eds.), *Proceedings of the Conference on Women Surviving the Holocaust* (New York, 1983), pp. 47–48, 30.
30 The quote from the testimony of Faina Ryzhikova-Elman is cited from *The Black Book with Red Pages*, p. 293. The testimony on events in Lvov is found in *The Black Book of Russian Jewry*, p. 78. That regarding Brest, *ibid.*, p. 183. That on Stavropol, *ibid.*, p. 218. And that on Riga, *ibid.*, p. 382. The relevant information on the Mglin Ghetto is drawn from Gai Miron and others (eds.), *The Yad Vashem Encyclopedia of the Ghettos During the Holocaust*, 2 vols. (Jerusalem, 2009), vol. 1, p. 463; that on Mikoyanshakhar from *ibid.*, vol. 1, p. 472; that on the Balvi Ghetto from *ibid.*, vol. 1, p. 16. In effect, Jewish girls and women were vulnerable wherever they were situated within Nazi occupied Europe. The sexual vulnerability of Jewish women and girls is testified to in many eyewitness accounts: see, for example, Etty Hillesum, *An Interrupted Life: The Diaries of Etty Hillesum, 1941–1943* (New York, 1983); Charlotte Delbo, *None of Us Will Return*, trans. John Githens (New York, 1968); *idem, Auschwitz and After*, trans. Rosette C. Lamont (New Haven, CT, 1995); Fania Fenelon, *Playing for Time*, trans. Marcell Routier (New York, 1977); Adina Blady-Szwajgier, *I Remember Nothing More: The Warsaw Children's Hospital and the Jewish Resistance*, trans. Tasja Darowska and Danusia Stok (New York, 1992); Liana Millu, *Smoke over Birkenau*,

occupied Soviet territory in which the rape of defenseless Jewish girls and women occurred,[31] almost certainly involving thousands of instances, is nearly endless.[32]

But this terrible history, with its innumerable victims and immeasurable quantities of suffering, while essential to an understanding of the Holocaust, is not the main point of this essay – to which we must now turn our attention.

---

trans. Lynne Sharon Schwartz (Philadelphia, 1991); Alicia Appleman-Jurman, *Alicia: My Story* (New York, 1988); Isabella Leitner, *Fragments of Isabella: A Memoir of Auschwitz*, ed. Irving A. Leitner (New York, 1978); and Gerda Weissman Klein, *All But My Life* (New York, 1957; reprinted New York, 1997). See also the relevant excerpts in *Different Voices: Women and the Holocaust*, eds. John K. Roth and Carol Rittner (New York, 1993). Additional material of relevance is found in Rochelle G. Saidel, "The Jewish Victims of Ravensbrück Camp," in *Lessons and Legacies VII: The Holocaust in International Perspective*, ed. Dagmar Herzog (Evanston, 2006), pp. 210–15; and *idem*, *The Jewish Women of Ravensbrück Concentration Camp* (Madison, 2004).

31 For more on the sexual experience of Jewish women during the Holocaust see: Myrna Goldenberg, "Memoirs of Auschwitz Survivors: The Burden of Gender," in *Women in the Holocaust*, ed. Dalia Ofer and Lenore J. Weitzman, pp. 327–39; Brana Gurewitsch, *Mothers, Sisters, Resisters: Oral Histories of Women who Survived the Holocaust* (Tuscaloosa, AL, 1998), pp. 95–218; Nechama Tec, *Resilience and Courage: Women, Men, and the Holocaust* (New Haven, CT, 2003); Judith Tydor Baumel, *Double Jeopardy: Gender and the Holocaust* (London, 1998), pp. 67–99; Elizabeth R. Baer and Myrna Goldenberg, *Experience and Expression: Women, the Nazis, and the Holocaust* (Detroit, 2003); Sybil Milton, "Women and the Holocaust: The Case of German and German-Jewish Women," in *Different Voices*, eds. J. K. Roth and C. Rittner, pp. 229–30; and Margarete Buber-Neumann, *Prisonniere de Staline et d'Hitler*, translated from German by Alan Brossat (Paris, 1988), pp. 19–27 and passim. The original title of this work was, *Als Gefangene bei Stalin und Hitler: Eine Welt im Dunkel* (Stuttgart, 1958). In addition, on the closely related subject of Jewish and other women being forced to serve in Nazi bordellos, consult Christa Schulz, "Weibliche Hafdinge aus Ravensbriick in Bordellen der Mannerkonzentrationslager," in *Frauen in Konzentrationslagern: Bergen-Belsen, Ravensbrück*, eds. Claus Fullberg-Stolberg and others (Bremen, 1994), pp. 135–46; and Reinhild Kassing and Christa Paul, "Bordelle in deutschen Konzentrationslagern," *Krampfader-Kasseler Frauenzeitung*, 6.1 (1990): 26–31. It should be added that sexual perversions of all sorts are a part of this tale. Trudy Claycomb Grubbs, for example, gave this report:

> A German soldier, a sergeant or something kept looking at me. When we were supposed to go back to the [cattle] car, he said no, you go up front. My heart stood still because I did not know what was going to happen. I was . . . by that time I was a stinking Jude. I smelled, I was not . . . but at the same time there was the fear because the look that he had was not . . . you see as a child, a child knows the first time a man looks at you that way. Fortunately, he must have had a breast fetish because he just kept playing with my breasts. I guess it would still be considered a sexual ah . . . he did it until my nipples were bleeding. I was so sore, and he kept that up for hours. He finally let me go into the cattle car.(Video Testimony, USC Archive, testimony of Trudy Claycomb Grubbs, TC3:10:04–3:12:20).

32 In the archives of the United States Holocaust Museum one can find, for example, testimony, given in Yiddish, about the rape of Rayzel Goldman in Gombin (Gąbin) and of Etka Iliart in Płońsk. Similarly, in Mir, Jewish girls were raped by Belorussian policemen who then murdered them, sometime before or on November 9, 1941. In Poczajów, in the Ukraine, twenty Jewish girls were forced into a brothel for Germans. I found the record of these crimes through a cursory review of a small portion of the archival holdings at the Holocaust Museum during 2011–2012 when I had the good fortune to be the Shapiro Senior Fellow at the Museum. I am confident that many other instances could – and will be – found in the future by other researchers working in the enormous archival collection that has been assembled in Washington.

Rape, *Rassenschande*, and murder

Much of the experience of rape and sexual violence undergone by Jewish women during the *Shoah* was, of course, in many fundamental ways, similar in kind to the sexual exploitation of women in other contexts of war, conquest, and subjugation over the centuries.[33] However, during the *Shoah*, such abusive carnal behavior also regularly involved two further factors that complicate this comparability and that suggests that there are distinctive features of real importance regarding the issue of rape and sexual violation during the *Shoah* that should not go unnoticed and unanalyzed.

The first of the two factors to which I here allude relates to the natural, reproductive, consequences of acts of rape. Customarily, the rapists in the various contexts of war, colonial domination, and slavery do not concern themselves with the consequences of their criminal activities.[34] They are not interested in the children

---

[33] One might even go further and conclude that the sort of sexual misdeeds here described can be found not only in the *Shoah* but also in all societies in which the political domination of one group over another has existed. This commonality recognized, the point that I am trying to explore in this essay, and that seems to me to be distinctive about what happened to Jewish women during the Holocaust, is that the "crime" of *Rassenschande* entailed the need to murder the Jewish women who had been raped. This is not to ignore the fact that women in other contexts who were raped were also murdered. It is, however, to suggest that in other contexts there was no obligation on the part of the rapist to carry out such a murder, i.e., the act, though equally immoral to those acts that occurred during the *Shoah*, was not ideologically driven, as was the case in Nazi-dominated Europe.

[34] This needs to be qualified in regard to New World black slavery insofar as some masters were concerned with the reproduction of slave children, seen as "cash crops" that added to the masters' wealth. In connection with slavery, women who had children, even as a consequence of rape, were valued as "good breeders." For more on this last issue see, for example, the testimony of former slaves recorded in George Rawick (ed.), *The American Slave: A Composite Autobiography*, 19 vols. (Westport, CT, 1973–76), vol. 4, p. 1203; vol. 8, p. 1241; and vol. 11, p. 300, all of which indicate that "good breeders" were highly valued. Likewise, Marli Frances Weiner reminds us that:

> Being a "breed 'omans" was advantageous to Hector Godbold's Africa-born grandmother after the apparently frequent efforts she made to run away: "If dey catch her, dey didn' never do her no harm." Not all "breeding women" were targets of the sexual advances of white men, nor were all forced to accept husbands of their owners' choice. But just as all black women recognized that they were vulnerable to the advances of white men, so they knew that they and their children were economic assets for slaveholders(*Mistresses and Slaves: Plantation Women in South Carolina, 1830–80* [Urbana, IL, 1998], p. 136).

Additionally, Charles L. Perdu, Jr., Thomas E. Barden, and Robert K. Phillips (eds.), *Weevils in the Wheat: Interviews with Virginia Ex-Slaves* (Charlottesville, 1976), p. 161, record the testimony of a slave who recalled that, "the masters were very careful about a good breedin' woman. If she had five or six children, she was rarely sold." And see also, among many other contemporary sources, Frances Anne Kemble, *Journal of a Residence on a Georgian Plantation in 1838–1839* (New York, 1863), edited and with an introduction by John A. Scott (New York, 1961), pp. 201, 238, 269, 362. A fuller analysis of the many issues raised by sexual relations between master and slave woman, including its economic implications, will be found in my *The Holocaust and New World Slavery* (New York, 2019).

who will be born as a result of these coerced sexual relationships.[35] Alternatively, Jewish women who were raped during the Holocaust in the coarse, brutal, manner described above or who were taken by Nazi officers and officials as lovers in a less savage way were not permitted to have children. Indeed, biological reproduction, the bringing into being of a child with half-Jewish blood as a consequence of these sexual relationships, was the great fear. And, according to the ruling ideological imperatives, it had to be completely avoided. In principle and practice the Third Reich opposed the birth of any child with a Jewish mother.

The second factor concerns what, according to the law of the Third Reich, was the deadly serious crime of *Rassenschande* (racial defilement, i.e., racial pollution). This crime involved all sexual relationships between Aryans and Jews whether the relationship was consensual or not. Already in the 1920s Hitler made a fetish of sexual relations between Jews and non-Jews and spoke of these acts as "infecting our national ethnic body by blood poisoning."[36] From this point on this notion remained a fixed principle in the National Socialist pantheon of racial values and was prominently incorporated in the Nuremberg Laws of September 1935. *The Law for the Protection of German Blood and Honor* made sexual relations between a Jew and non-Jew a prosecutable offense. According to this legislation "Extramarital intercourse between Jews and subjects of the state of German or related blood is forbidden." The crime was to be "punished with a prison sentence with or without hard labor."[37] That the Hitler State took the law on race defilement seriously is indicated by the roughly 2,000 cases brought to courts under this statute between 1935 and 1945. By 1939 the average sentence for those found guilty of this grave offense was four to five years. During the war years the crime of *Rassenschande* could mean a death sentence.[38] For German soldiers, and particularly *Wehrmacht* officers and those in the SS, it was seen as an especially

---

35 This indifference, for example, marked much of the sexual history of the Spanish and Portuguese empires in the New World. And it was present in many other colonial contexts.

36 Adolf Hitler, "Forsetzung," January 23, 1928, cited in *Reden, Schriften, Anordnungen: Februar 1925 bis Januar 1933*, eds. Barbel Dusik et al., 3 vols. (Munich, 1994), vol. 2, pt. 2, document 222, p. 646; and *idem*, "Der Kampf der einst die Ketten bricht," in *idem*, vol. 3, pt. 1, document 50, p. 238. For more on this central issue of "Race Hygiene" and maintaining the purity of German blood see Hans-Walter Schmuhl, *Rassenhygiene, Nationalsozialismus, Euthanasie* (Gottingen, 1987); Robert Proctor, *Racial Hygiene: Medicine Under the Nazis* (Cambridge, MA, 1988); and Lars Renssmanns, "Antisemitismus und 'Volksgesundheit,' Zu ideologiehistorische bindungslinien im politischen Imaginaren und in der Politik," in *Medizin und Verbrechen: Festschrift zum 60. Geburtstag von Walter Wuttke*, ed. Christoph Kopke (Ulm, 2001), pp. 44–82.

37 This legislation is cited from Yitzhak Arad, Yisrael Gutman, and Abraham Margaliot (eds.), *Documents on the Holocaust: Selected Sources on the Destruction of the Jews of Germany and Austria, Poland, and the Soviet Union* (Lincoln, NE, 1981; revised edition, 1999), pp. 78–79.

38 Further analysis of this subject is provided by Patricia Szobar, "Telling Sexual Stories in the Nazi Courts of Law: Race Defilement in Germany, 1933 to 1945," *Journal of the History of Sexuality* 11.1–2 (2002): 131–63. The statistics on the number of prosecutions for "race defilement" and the nature of the sentences meted out by the German courts here cited are drawn from this essay.

heinous offense.[39] And the worst possible outcome of such criminal liaisons was that the Jewish women involved would become pregnant and, thereby, threaten to continue the implacable, unavoidable race war between Aryans and Jews. Thus, if the Jewish women implicated in inter-racial relations became pregnant they (and their fetuses) had to be murdered by the men who were the fathers of their children (or by their comrades in arms).

Here we begin to see clearly the singular linkage between sex and murder already mentioned. In the racial universe created by National Socialism, sex, with a distinctive emphasis on nonconsensual sex – rape – had a meaning and significance beyond the physical and the biological. For it was the most basic conduit, the means, by which normative values – transmitted through race – became incarnated in time and space. Put simply, the rise and fall of nations, and all the social, economic, and political phenomena that attended and contributed to this cycle, were, in the first instance necessarily dependent on the race of those who comprised the social order. Therefore, miscegenation – including forced sexual relations – defined as *Rassenschande*, was more than a personal matter; it determined the very future of nations and the unfolding of historical events.

As a result, Jewish women impregnated by an Aryan man, had, in theory and all too often in practice, to die. So, for example, the rule in Nazi brothels in which Jewish women, in contradistinction to the normal pattern in such brothels,[40] were

---

[39] The SS established strict rules for the marriage of SS men on December 31, 1931. All proposed marriages by SS men had to be approved by a special office (named the *Rasse-und Siedlungshauptamt der SS*), established within the SS by Himmler that dealt with issues of the racial purity of the corps. This ideal of racial purity then was carried over to cover all sexual atrocities by members of the SS. Further details can be found in R. Proctor, *Racial Hygiene*, p. 137.

[40] The Wehrmacht established such brothels for its men. And testimony given at the postwar I.G. Farben trial indicates that this company did likewise, though the nationality and religion of the women forced to serve in this facility are unspecified. I thank Professor Peter Hayes for this information on the practices of the I.G. Farben Corporation. Insofar as the instructions issued by the Army are concerned we have, for example, a circular from the German Military Supreme Command sent on January 27, 1943, that took up the prevention of venereal disease in military brothels that included the instruction that "Jewesses are to be excluded" from work in these brothels. *Oberkommando der Wehrmacht*, signed by a Dr. Handloser, to various OKH/S, January 27, 1943. I cite this document from Doris L. Bergen, "Sexual Violence in the Holocaust: Unique and Typical?" in *Lessons and Legacies VII*, p. 186. However, Bergen suggests: "That order implies an admission that Jewish women had not always been excluded from forced labor in Nazi brothels" (p. 186). Most of the larger concentration camps such as Dachau, Mauthausen, Sachsenhausen, and Buchenwald had bordellos. Such institutions also existed in a number of forced labor camps. In these locations both German soldiers and, at times, even "privileged" prisoners were allowed to utilize the services of the women brought to serve as prostitutes. The details of these arrangements are described by Wolfgang Sofsky, *The Order of Terror: The Concentration Camp*, trans. William Templer (Princeton, 1997), p. 151. For more on this see Erika Buchmann, *Frauen im Konzentrationslager* (Berlin, 1959), Christl Wickert "Tabu Lagerbordell: Vom Umgang mit der Zwangsprostitution nach 1945," in *Gedeichtnis und Geschlecht. Deutungsmuster in Darstellungen des nationalsozialistischen Genozids*, eds. Insa Eschebach, Sigrid Jacobeit, and Silke Wenk (Frankfurt, 2002), pp. 41–58; Nanda Herbermann, *The Blessed Abyss: Inmate #6582 in Ravensbrück Concentration Camp for Women*, eds. Hester Baer and Elizabeth Baer, trans. Hester Baer

forced to service German men sexually was that if any, or all, of these individuals, became pregnant, they were murdered. Likewise, this "precautionary" action was the common practice throughout the network of Nazi forced labor and concentration camps. Consider here the evidence from the Skarżysko-Kamienna labor camp in the Radom District of Poland that is significant in itself as well as representative of a more general pattern. In all three divisions of this camp that produced munitions for HASAG, the sexual exploitation of Jewish women was to be found. But when manager Walter Glaue in Werk B impregnated the Jewess Bella Sperling, he had her murdered on the probably trumped up charge of sabotage.[41] Again, when the affair between Hugo Ruebesamen, the foreman of the *Werkzeugbau* department, and a beautiful Jewess slave laborer who worked under his supervision was noticed by the plant supervisor the woman was sent to the SS headquarters at Radom and never heard from again.[42] In January 1943, when the *Werkschutz* commander Fritz Bartenschlager had several high-ranking SS officers to dinner, he ordered three Jewish women brought to his quarters where they were first raped then murdered.[43] And this because these SS men were frightened to their foundations that these Jewish women would become pregnant and so to forestall any possibility of this they were required to kill them. Furthermore, they knew that Himmler, independently of the matter of pregnancy, might have had them shot for the stark, open, racial offense they had committed that evening.[44]

The murderous actions of these three SS men, moreover, were in no way unusual. Milla Doktorczyk, who was a slave laborer at the Skarżysko-Kamienna camp, remembered the fate of her friend Hochma Eisenberg.

> My friend, she was working alongside me in Skarżysko. One beautiful girl, tall and slim, a beauty . . . Came one time, a German, he took her away from the machine. They raped her a couple of times, everybody,

---

(Detroit, 2000); Christa Schikorra, *Kontinuiteiten der Ausgrenzung: "Asoziale" Häftlinge des Frauen-Konzentrationslagers Ravensbrück* (Berlin, 2006); *idem*, "Prostitution weibli-cher KZ-Häftlinge als Zwangsarbeit: Zur Situation 'asozialer' Häftlinge im Frauen-KZ Ravensbrack," *Dachauer Hefte*, 16 (2000): 112–24; Insa Meinen, Wehrmacht und Prostitution wiihrend des Zweiten Weltkriegs im besetz-ten Frankreich (Bremen, 2002); Christa Paul, *Zwangsprostitution: Staatlich errichtete Bordelle im Nationalsozialismus* (Berlin, 1994); Christa Schulz, "Weibliche Häftlinge aus Ravensbrück in den Bordellen der Mannerkonzentrationslager," in *Frauen-Konzentrationslagern: Bergen-Belsen, Ravensbrück*, eds. Claus Füllberg-Stolberg and others (Bremen, 1994), pp. 135–46; and Reinhild Kassing and Christa Paul, "Bordelle in Deutschen Konzentrationslagern," in *Krampfader-Kasseler Frauenzeitung* 1 (1991): 26–31.

41 Felicja Karay, "Women in the Forced-Labor Camps," in *Women in the Holocaust*, eds. Dalia Ofer and Lenore J. Weitzman, pp. 289–90, 71; Witold Chrostowski, *Extermination Camp Treblinka* (London, 2004), p. 45.

42 *Ibid.*, p. 290.

43 *Ibid.*, pp. 290–91.

44 There was, for example, an SS court investigation against SS officers who had raped Jewish women in Warsaw. See the document on this case in the Bundesarchiv NS7/1147, pp. 230–303; and USHMM RG-68.051M.

and then they killed her. Her name was Hochma Eisenberg. I will never forget that. They raped her in the middle, one after another one, and they killed her. (did you see that?) I could not look. (did they do this in front of everybody?) Yes, they did. They took her to the office. It was in the middle of the factory and everybody was around it in the factory. We could see it. She was beautiful, 14 or 15 years old. Tall, slim, dark hair. I have not seen a beauty since then like that. They took her away, into the office, took off her clothes . . . there were maybe 4 or 5 of them. One after another. Then they killed her and threw her out.[45]

And when asked if this murder was an isolated incident, Doktorczyk replied: "There were many incidents like that."[46]

Charles Feldman, another survivor of this camp, gave this detailed testimony:

There was a German, a *Volkdeutsch*, Kelleran, he was a hunch back, a sadist because he was crippled. He spoke sort of Jewish . . . he was terrible. In Skarżysko he was doing all kind of brutal things. Like, for instance, he used to take a Jewish policeman and take out a woman and told her to lie down on a bench and he (the Jewish policeman) should lie down on her and make love to her. And everyone who passes by to stop and to watch it. Such a sadistic thing. He took a girl from time to time and did with her whatever he wanted and then would dump her. It was a well with water. He dumped her. He did all kinds of such nasty things. In Skarżysko Kamienna they were picking out all the beautiful girls. There was a man called Bartenschlager. He was the main man from the inside. He used to pick the most beautiful, nicest girls, they should do the jobs in their house. He used them for himself. They never came back.[47]

In this and prior testimonies cited in this section of the present essay, sexual assault always ends in the murder of the victims (as do a number of the reports and testimonies cited in the first section). There is a deadly fatalism involved in these forced seductions that separate them from common acts of sexual violence and transforms them into unusual, enacted, rituals of extirpation.

The history of the Skarżysko-Kamienna camp reveals that "commanders chose the most beautiful young women of each newly arrived transport as personal 'housemaids.'" (Almost all these women were later killed.) In one specific instance:

When Paul Kiessling, camp commander at Werk C in 1942, tired of his "maid," he sent her to Hans Schneider, Werkschutz commander at Werk

---

45 Video Testimony, USC Video Archive, testimony of Milla Doktorczyk, TC 2:26:45–2:28:19.
46 *Ibid.*
47 Video Testimony, USC Video Archive, testimony of Charles Feldman, TC 5:23:00–5:24:50.

A. Schneider discovered that the woman was pregnant and dispatched her to the "shooting range."[48]

Given his principles, both racial and prudential, Hans Schneider believed he had no other choice.

A Jewess who survived this same camp testified right after the end of the war:

> And then I was off to a labor camp, to Skarżysko, a camp for Jews only who worked in an ammunition factory . . . There was a German foreman by the name of Krause, the most terrible in the factory. When Krause would go by, even the machinery would run differently. Sometimes he would get drunk, pick a few women and rape them, and later they were shot so that there would be no "race pollution."[49]

Rassenschande, and its potential corrupting racial consequences, could not be tolerated. In consequence once this deed had been committed the violated Jewish women had to be murdered to prevent future racial degeneration. The striking result of this policy should not go unremarked for it produced the following bizarre situation: sexual relations with a Jewish woman was defined as a major criminal offense against the state and the Volk, but murdering Jewish women was not a crime at all. Instead it was seen to be a necessary public health measure.

Nor, on the testimony of the last-cited Jewish survivor of Skarżysko, was the foreman Krause alone in his practice of combining rape and homicide. For there was, as she remembered, "a well-known SS [officer at the camp who] did the same thing."[50] And had she known what we know she could have gone still further and argued that in camps of every type Nazi officials and guards took advantage of their power, not least in the realm of sexual predation and murder. At the Bruss-Sophienwalde Concentration Camp in Poland Paula Neyman observed the following incident.

> There was a girl who had a boyfriend and found herself pregnant. Willie Shultz, he was not an SS but an ex Wehrmacht army man. But he was injured, and he was, for good service, given to be commandant of a camp. He was not bestial, he never personally ever beat anybody up terribly. To me, he used to joke and said I could do anything, but don't let yourself get caught. She (the pregnant girl) decided she was going to tell him that she was pregnant and maybe he would give her some better work. I begged

---

48 F. Karay, "Women in the Forced Labor Camps," p. 291.
49 D. Niewyk (ed.), *Fresh Wounds*, p. 221. To understand this testimony properly, readers need to know that the Nuremberg Laws of September 15, 1935, defined *Rassenschande* as a crime. According to this legislation: "Extramarital intercourse between Jews and subjects of the state of German or related blood is forbidden." The crime is to be "punished with a prison sentence with or without hard labor" (clause 5.2).
50 *Ibid.*

her not to, he is only German. One day, when the transport was going back to Stutthof, she was told not to go to work. We hid her under the straw. We had more straw where the head went. So, we took away the straw, we put her like a mock pillow and we covered her with blankets . . . The Germans ran around long enough, the truck was waiting, they found her. They dragged her out, four young Germans. Each one had a leg, or an arm and they threw her on the snow. And there was some work kommando coming back about midday. They made everybody watch. Most of them were under 25 maybe 20. And in full view, more than just the four Germans, I don't remember, six or eight, but enough, raped that pregnant girl. And then, they picked her up like a sack of potatoes, again each carrying an extremity and threw her on the truck. She was never heard of.[51]

There was here no respect for this woman's pregnancy, and the pressing concern with regard to her fetus was that it not survive. By law and ideology this woman was held to subhuman and outside of the circle of moral obligation. Her deeply offensive, highly threatening, sexual misadventure and pregnancy needed to be made an example of, and her life and the life of her unborn child extinguished. There could be no compromise on, no mediation over, such a fundamental violation of the iron law of race. Accordingly, the six or eight German soldiers who raped her, and then dispatched her to be murdered, were not seen by their comrades as sexual beasts. Instead, the rapists saw themselves and were seen by those they served with as warriors doing their duty in defending the Third Reich's racial first principles.

From the Janowska Road camp we have this testimony:

A few days later a truck with twenty-four women in it stops in front of our gate. The driver has been told to wait there for a further order from the Untersturmführer, who is due to arrive any minute. Suddenly we hear shots, and then the truck turns around and drives away in the direction of the remaining fireplace. After about half an hour a Schupo comes to our quarters and orders the fire chief, his assistant, and four carriers to report for duty. In a quarter of an hour they return, having tossed the women into the fire. From the Schupos we later find out what had happened to the women. There were twenty-four girls between the ages of seventeen and twenty in the truck. They were the prettiest ones in the concentration camp. Last night the SS in the camp had had a big party. They had brought these twenty-four girls to the affair, a thing that is strictly forbidden. The girls were there all night. In the morning, to rid themselves of any witnesses, the SS men brought them to the "sands."[52]

Once again, sex and death were inseparably intertwined for Jewish women and the German men who raped them. The orgy of the night before in which these

---

51 Video Testimony, USC Archive, testimony of Paula Neyman, TC 3:19:30–3:22:07.
52 Leon Weliczker Wells, *The Death Brigade: The Janowska Road* (New York, 1978), pp. 189–90.

beautiful young women had been forced to participate had to be followed by their execution the next morning. Their rape could be overlooked, not reported, if they were executed to assure that there would be no Jewish issue from the sexual acts that had been performed on their bodies. The operational definition of what was criminal in this context was not rape but Jewish continuity and reproduction. Therefore, murdering these Jewish women had the effect of eliminating the crime of fornicating with a Jewess. The racial purity of the German state had, in a perfectly satisfactory way, been protected, despite the initial serious transgression of these men. It was assured by the sacrifice of these twenty-four young Jewish women on the fire. The modern moloch that was National Socialism would have its blood offerings. Through them, it would protect the health of its racial community. This was a justified maximal defense against the most menacing crime, the most destabilizing sin, racial pollution.

The same macabre choreography between sexual offenses and murder was present in the ghettos. A former resident of the Warsaw Ghetto has testified that she regularly saw a young SS officer come to the house of pretty young Jewish women, rape the women, and then shoot them. She remembered, "He always came prepared with a horse-drawn hearse."[53] Another ghetto survivor recalled that

> ... [the Gestapo head] Reisener [sic] ... found my niece, [my] husband's brother's daughter. She looked like a young Elizabeth Taylor. He took her out of the ghetto. He loved her. We thought he was going to kill her. He was a good-looking man. During [the] second Aktion, he knew he wasn't allowed to live with a Jewish girl. He knew she was going to be killed. He took her to the train. He killed her before she would go to Auschwitz...[54]

And still another survivor, from a town near Warsaw, has left a report: "At night the Germans would force their way into Jewish homes and rape women and girls... Some of the girls, those of the more educated type, would be taken by the Germans to their barracks where they were raped and killed."[55]

Sara Dickerman, a survivor of the Opatów Ghetto, has left the following testimony:

> We came near the shul [synagogue] on (gives the name of the street – in the Beitigasse). Right across [from] the shul there was an entrance, I remember, where we used to go through to another street, to the Shul-

---

53 Cited from Joan Ringelheim, "Women and the Holocaust: A Reconsideration of Research," in *Feminism and Community*, eds. Penny A. Weiss and Marilyn Friedman (Philadelphia, 1995), pp. 320–54.

54 Cited from Jonathan C. Friedman, *Speaking the Unspeakable: Essays on Sexuality, Gender, and Holocaust Survivor Memory* (Lanham, MD, 2002), p. 56. Max Glauben, another survivor of the Warsaw Ghetto, has reported in his testimony regarding ghetto life: "My mom's sister was taken out and supposedly raped and killed," Eric Sterling (ed.), *Life in the Ghettos During the Holocaust* (Syracuse, 2005), p. 99. Similar testimonies will be found in other survivor memoirs.

55 This testimony is reproduced in J. Apenszlak et al. (eds.), *The Black Book of Polish Jewry*, p. 9.

gasse. A German came, he took away my little sister, and I said: please, I am older than her. Please let her go. I am going to do whatever you ask from me. He gave me ah . . . he smacked me in the face, grabbed my little sister, and started to undress her right in the front. He grabbed her there, he raped her. When she came out, you could see the blood was still running. He called me, to stay in front of her and told me: now are you going to be quiet? So, I say yes. So I thought that's finished. He pulled out the gun. He killed her right in front of me (interviewee is overcome with emotion and is crying very hard at this point). I am sorry (for crying). It is very hard. She was beautiful, and she was kind. It is very hard (still crying). I am so sorry (for crying). How could be he be so cruel! Oy Gotinyu. Should have killed me instead. I was the oldest one (continues to cry). I saw some Poles, men. They were standing and laughing.[56]

There were, as one sees, variations within the dominant design, but most produce a similar ending: the liquidation of the Jewish girl or woman who had been raped. Life and the reproduction of Jewish life were outcomes that were not permitted by the ruling system.

In the ghettos and camps established within the captured territory of the Soviet Union German venereal appetites and German racial dogmas were the same as those in Warsaw and Kielce. Gertrude Schneider has provided the following testimony regarding SS Officer Krauser, the German Commandant in charge of her Belorussian ghetto.

[Krauser] loved young, pretty girls. He did. When he liked you, that was it, you got a better kommando. Since he made the law, he was above and beyond Rassenschande which means the racial sin that a German and a Jew could not have intercourse. He had one girlfriend. She was a beautician before the war. He made a beauty salon for her in the ghetto. She was Olly Adler and she was breathtakingly beautiful. I don't care what beauties you see here, she was so striking that when she walked into the ghetto and he saw her, he actually fell apart right on the spot. She knew what kind of an effect she had on men. She had a sister whom I knew quite well. Neither sister survived . . . [they were killed].[57]

Even "breathtakingly beautiful" Jewish women had, after use, to be murdered. One can, of course, explain the rape of particularly attractive women without recourse to ideology but the explanation of their murder, which is counter-intuitive, needs a further explanation. And we find it in the governing circumstance that reveals that evidently SS Officer Krauser and the Jewish woman Oily Adler were, evidently, not "above and beyond" the claims, and demands, of *Rassenschande*.

56 Video Testimony, USC Video Archive, testimony of Sara Dickerman, TC 2:13:10–2:17:10.
57 E. Katz and J. M. Ringelheim (eds.), *Women Surviving The Holocaust*, p. 48.

Other examples: at the Jewish collective farm in Zelenopolye a 16-year-old girl named Rakhil "was raped and then shot."[58] During the *Aktion* in the Lvov Ghetto a survivor recalled: "the unrestrained representatives of the 'master race' did not spare a single woman during this campaign. They raped and murdered the women or threw them into burning houses."[59] In Brest, the Jew Osher Moiseevich Zisman tells us: "I saw the Germans herd young girls into a shed next to the mass graves and rape them before then shooting them. I heard one girl crying out for help; she punched the German in the snout, and in return, they buried her alive."[60] In Riga, the officers of the Wurttemberg-Baden Grenadier regiment "were having a drinking bout. They brought in dozens of young Jewish girls to join them in their orgy, forced them to strip naked, drink, and sing songs. Many of the poor girls were raped and then taken into the courtyard and shot."[61] In the Mstislavl Ghetto, on October 15, 1941, German soldiers raped a large number of Jewish girls and women and then eliminated them.[62] And in the Mir Ghetto Belorussian police raped and then killed Jewish girls just before the general massacre of November 9, 1941.

Again, in Butrimonys, Lithuania – 46 miles south of Kovno – the Germans arrived as conquerors on June 23, 1941. The running of the town was then turned over to Lithuanian nationalist allies of the Germans. And a police force of local Lithuanians was formed under the command of Leonardas Kasperiunas. One of Kasperiunas' lieutenants named Prams Senavaitis temporarily saved a Jewish girl, described as "exceptionally beautiful," from being immediately murdered, so that she could become his sexual slave. But, under German domination, no permanent exclusion from the law that all Jewish women must die was possible and therefore he shot his beautiful Jewess five months later in mid-November. Nor was this lethal criminal action by Kasperiunas unusual. The record shows that he used many Jewish women to satisfy his lusts and then, as required, murdered them.[63] Likewise, in the camp at Tulchin in the Ukraine, that was administered during the war by Romania and annexed to Transnistria in early

---

58 I. Ehrenburg and V. Grossman (eds.), *The Black Book*, p. 42.
59 *Ibid.*, p. 78.
60 *Ibid.*, p. 221.
61 *Ibid.*, p. 302.
62 On the rape and murder in the Mstislavl Ghetto, see G. Miron et al. (eds.), *The Yad Vashem Encyclopedia of Ghettos*, vol. 1, p. 502.
63 Olga Zabludoff and Lily Poritz Miller (eds.), *If I Forget Thee: The Destruction of the Shtetl Butrimantz* (Washington, D.C., 1998), pp. 33, 49. See also Yad Vashem Archive Document E 146–2–8. For more on Butrimonys see: Leib Garfunkel (ed.), *Lithuanian Jewry*, vol. 4, *The Holocaust 1941–1945* (Tel Aviv, 1984) [Hebrew]; Nathan Cohen, "The Destruction of the Jews of Butrimonys as Described in a Farewell Letter from a Local Jew," *Holocaust and Genocide Studies* 4.3 (1989): 357–75; "Butrimonys," in *Pinkas ha-kehilot Latviyah ve-Estonyah: Entsiklopedyah shel ha.yishuvim ha-Yehudim le-min hivasdam ve-'ad le-ahar sho'at milhemet ha-'olam ha-sheniyah*, ed. Dov Levin and Yosef Rosin (Jerusalem, 1996), p. 163; and Alfonsas Eidintas, *Jews, Lithuanians and the Holocaust* (Vilnius, 2003), pp. 297–98. Published eyewitness testimonies can be found in: Rima Dulkinieth and Kerry Keys (eds.), *Su adata Sirdyje: Getu it koncentra-cijos stovyklu kalinii atsiminimai (With a Needle in the Heart: Memoirs of Former Prisoners of Ghettos and Concentration Camps)* (Vilnius, 2003), pp. 214–15; and Laurence Rees, *The Nazis: A Warning from History* (London, 1997), pp. 182–86.

September 1941, the camp commandant "the infamous Petekau ... asked each night for two Jewish virgins" who were then killed.[64] As an ally of National Socialist Germany Petekau needed to be above racial suspicion and to set an example regarding what the appropriate fate of Jewish women was. In his case, as in too many others that we have seen, this meant raping Jewish girls and women and then extirpating them.

Even at Sobibór, the Nazis feared the consequences of sexual relations with Jewish women. A survivor of Sobibór has recorded the following incident:

> The Germans selected musicians and established a small orchestra, which would play on Sundays. More than once we were forced to dance to its music. And sometimes, when transports arrived, the orchestra would be called to play, to the wonder of the people in the transport. A cabaret singer – from Holland or France – also arrived at the camp, and she sang in many languages. Sometimes all the Germans would gather, the orchestra would play, and the singer would sing. Her voice was pure and deep, and she sang plaintive songs, and although I didn't understand their words, they made my tears catch in my throat. This was the first time I had ever heard someone sing in a performance and I was enchanted by her, but it seemed that others were also enchanted, as at the end of each song our applause was joined by the applause of the Germans as well. After a short while, the singer was taken to the Lazarett and we never heard her voice again. It was said that one of the Germans got too close to her, but the Germans couldn't permit this, so she was killed.[65]

Talent may lead to temporary sexual relations, but it provided no grant of exemption from the absolute rule that sexual relations with a Jewish woman must be followed by her murder.

In the small town of Busk, in Galicia, about 1,900 Jews were gathered together in a ghetto after the town was occupied on July 1, 1941, by German military forces. The ghetto survived until May 21, 1943 when it was liquidated. During the liquidation German security forces with the aid of Ukrainian policemen, while exterminating all the other residents, kept thirty Jewish girls alive to satisfy their sexual appetites. When the girls became pregnant, a condition that was intolerable to the German "*Übermenschen*" who had impregnated them, the rapists called in the security police from Sokol to take the life of these girls in the forest five kilometers away.[66] Although it was the German soldiers and their Ukrainian partners

---

64 The Jewish Black Book Committee, *The Black Book: The Nazi Crime Against the Jewish People* (New York, 1946), p. 164.
65 Dov Freiberg, *To Survive Sobibor* (New York, 2007), p. 255.
66 I owe this information on the Busk Ghetto to Dr. Martin Dean. For more on Busk see the *Yizhkor* book entitled *Sefer Busk; Le-zekher Ha-kehila She-harva*, ed. Abraham Shayari (Haifa, 1965); and Patrick Desbois, *Porteur de mimoires: Sur les traces de la Shoah par balles* (Neuilly-sur-Seine, 2007), pp. 237–87. There is, in addition, one memoir by a survivor, Thomas T. Hecht, *Life, Death, Memories* (Charlottesville, VA, 2002).

who had violated the law against inter-racial sex, it was the Jewish women who had been forced into having carnal relations with these men who had to die. The persistent connection here emphasized between sexual relations and murder is, of course, a hypothesis, though, as evidenced, built on a good deal of relevant testimony and other credible evidence. It seeks to call attention to an empirical relationship that existed and to explain it. At the same time, in offering this argument, I am aware that, as indicated by the incidents recounted in the section entitled "Instances of sexual abuse" of this essay, not every rape of a Jewish woman eventuated in a murder. However, it does appear, on the basis of what we do know, to have repeatedly happened; to have occurred often enough to be more than an individual action, or an accident – or the invention of the present author; and to represent the instantiation of a shared understanding that became incarnate in a compelling socio-ethical belief that was actively present in the community of the killers. It therefore, if not an illusion, must be accounted for.

The "Final Solution" as a license to rape

In the discussion just concluded the concentration was on the connection created between sexual relations and murder because of the law of *Rassenschande*. Here I would briefly point out that this relationship also ran, as it were, in an inverted manner, that is, the requirement that all Jewish women be eliminated became a license for Germans, and their allies, to rape Jewish women. In cases where this happened, ideology, that is, the fateful decision to create genocide, here meaning the knowledge that the Jewish women to be assaulted would soon be corpses, created sexual opportunity.

Four examples will make this clear.

(1) In Kovno, Jewish women, awaiting their death, who were held prisoner in the Seventh Fort were not spared the degradation of being raped and then shot. Avraham Tory recorded in his diary for August 4, 1941:

> The gray fortress barracks, permanently dank, which until recently was brimming over with Jewish women and children rounded up together, has already been emptied. Night after night the Lithuanian henchmen would proceed to select their victims: the young, the pretty. First, they would rape them, then torture them, and finally murder them. They called it "going to peel potatoes."[67]

(2) During an *Aktion* in the Minsk Ghetto, on March 2, 1941, German soldiers chose to embellish their butchery with a slightly novel twist.

---

[67] Avraham Tory, *Surviving the Holocaust: The Kovno Ghetto Diary* (Cambridge, MA, 1990), p. 24. Other incidents of rape were reported by the Jewish Police in Kovno. See, for example, USHMMA Acc 1998 A. 0073 (from Central State Archive 973–2–46 and 47).

The "operatives" were ordered to pick out the prettiest women. I hid and watched how they were led to the cemetery. The deathly pale Jewish beauties were going to meet their deaths. The Nazis entertained themselves. They ordered the policemen to bring the husbands to their wives to say farewell. The husbands were shot first. Then they raped the women and shot them.[68]

(3) The destruction of Jewish women from the Minsk Ghetto was not a new German sport invented in 1944. Ever since Minsk had been taken by the Wehrmacht and accompanying Einsatzgruppen in 1941 Jewish women had been subjected to a myriad of sexual torments and deadly actions. So, for example, M. I. Brudner, who was a resident in the Minsk Ghetto testified as follows:

In 1942, before my very eyes, Gottenbach shot nine people because they had exchanged their things for foodstuffs with Russians. They were executed publicly in the square without trial or investigation. During the execution, Gottenbach ordered the victims to blindfold each other. The Germans excelled in using anything in search of an occasion for destruction. Gottenbach went around the ghetto and gathered the prettiest girls. After they were raped, he killed them.[69]

(4) Jewish girls being deported from Budapest to Auschwitz in the spring of 1944 were raped by the German soldiers policing their travel to the death camp. Annamarie Sokoly recollected:

We fell asleep and the next thing I knew, my mother . . . we heard a big noise and my mother, pulling toward me, we hear they are breaking the stall at the door. Breaking in, we saw a group of German soldiers. They were completely drunk. They were screaming and hollering and looking with the flashlights looking at all the faces of the people who were there. My mother made a very fast movement and laid on the top of me. And I heard screaming, screaming of the girls who were with us. I could hear my mother screaming and crying: don't take her don't take her. What happened, the German soldiers picked out only the younger ones, 13, 14, 15 or maybe 16-year-old girls and they took them away. We heard their screams. We heard their cries. We heard the mothers cry. We never saw them again (she stops talking for a moment and is crying). They raped them. Whatever happened to them after, we never found out. My mother saved my life laying on top of me."[70]

In the eyes of their molesters, these young Jewish girls were not only sexually available but, and ultimately more significant, they had no right to live. The

---

68 Testimony of the Jewish woman Ellen Marbina of Minsk. Cited from D. B. Meltser and V. Levin (eds.), *The Black Book with Red Pages*, p. 167.
69 Testimony of M. I. Brudner given on July 18, 1944. Cited from *ibid.*, p. 171.
70 USC Video Archive, video testimony of Annamarie Sokoly, TC 4:08:10–4:10:40.

German soldiers on the train knew the terrible secret of what would happen to these *Untermenschen* when they arrived at the ramp at Birkenau and so felt no compunction about despoiling them as they liked and then guaranteeing that their criminal actions would have no untoward consequences. They were well aware that in this context the ideological made possible the carnal, that because these Jewesses were on their way to being gassed, they could be raped.

Even in the shadow of the gas chambers or, perhaps more correctly, precisely in the shadow of the gas chambers, the rape – and then murder – of Jewish women took place. This odious action represented, to those who took part in it, a confirmation of the function of the death camps: Jewish women were not governed by the normal ethical reciprocities that usually existed between human beings. In this sense, these sexual violations, followed by the extermination of the victims – and done with the full knowledge that the victims were about to be exterminated – were "political" acts in the sense described above. The racial-metaphysical principles of the Hitler state not only make these rapes possible but justify them. And they, in turn, reconfirm these principles. The National Socialist regime's insistence that Jewish women are *Untermenschen*, less than human beings, is here given concrete affirmation. The individuals who raped these women may well not have thoughts about their actions in such sophisticated "symbolic" categories, but the camp context in which they worked and that made their transgressions possible had been constructed so as to allow just such mocking sexual interventions. Witold Chrostowski, who had been a prisoner at Treblinka, tells us:

> Women, Polish and Ukrainian, helped in the camp with cooking and washing the dishes. There were about 50 of them. Sometimes, from a group of the Jewish women who were to be exterminated, the prettiest would be selected and forced to participate in orgies organized in the camp. After a few days or weeks, such girls went to the gas chambers and new ones were selected from transports.[71]

A last word

The contentions and arguments in this article have not been fully worked out. They represent, rather, the first effort to decipher and account for the evidence of what I take to be distinctive aspects of the rape and sexual molestation of Jewish girls and women during the Holocaust. It seems unquestionable to me that this evidence, taken as a collective whole, is, indeed, singular in nature, but I could be wrong on this. It may be that other scholars can show that similar behavior existed in other historical cases of mass murder. If so, then the thesis of the present essay will have to be given up. But for now, the challenge is not to offer hasty judgments nor to make snap-decisions on too limited evidence but, rather, to do the serious research work of gathering together and comparing relevant material, and then thinking through the core issues that this subject raises.

---

71 Witold Chrostowski, *Extermination Camp Treblinka* (London, 2004), p. 45.

UPDATE

The study of sexual crimes committed in the course of war that are, in addition, integral to occasions of "genocide,"[72] and that were common in the Holocaust, has become a significant area of study and research. Especially prominent in the newer literature is a concentration on the primitive depravity evident in Rwanda and the heinous crimes committed during the Civil War in Yugoslavia. During the latter conflict it is estimated that between 20,000 and 50,000 women were raped, mostly by Serbian forces.[73] It is quite clear, however, that Serbians and Hutus have no monopoly over these sorts of dehumanizing acts – the vile phenomenon of rape and the carnal abuse of defenseless women is a near universal phenomenon. This given reality has finally come to be recognized as legally significant in contemporary post-war tribunals. In fact, the crime of rape has now been accepted as a separate, punishable act under international law.[74] So, for instance, beginning with the International Criminal Tribunal for Rwanda (ICTR) in 1998, individuals like Jean-Paul Akayesu were found guilty of assisting in and overseeing the rape of Tutsi women. The tribunal found that rape "constitutes genocide in the same way as any other act as long as they were committed with the specific intent to destroy in whole or in part, a particular group, targeted as such."[75]

I applaud the research and the new sensibility that led to this legal development. The sexual victimization of women in whatever circumstance, and the employment of rape as a political-military strategy, is appalling and altogether unacceptable.

Significant recent publications that address the issue of sexual violation include: Amy Randall (ed.), *Genocide and Gender in the Twentieth Century: A Comparative Survey* (London, 2015); Samuel Totten (ed.), *Plight and Fate of Women During and Following Genocide* (London, 2009); Anne-Marie de Brouwer, Charlotte Ku, Renee Romkens, and Larissa van den Herik (eds.),

---

72 On this subject see the studies cited at the bottom of this page and the top of p. 197. In addition consult: Beverly Allen, *Rape Warfare: The Hidden Genocide in Bosnia-Herzogovina and Croatia* (London, 1996); Roger Smith, "Women and Genocide: Notes on an Unwritten History," *Holocaust and Genocide Studies* 8.3 (Winter, 1994): 315–334; Kelly Askin, "Prosecuting Wartime Rape and Other Gender-Related Crimes under International Law: Extraordinary Advances, Enduring Obstacles," *Berkeley Journal of International Law* 21.2 (2003); Anne-Marie de Brouwer, *Supranational Criminal Prosecution of Sexual Violence: The ICC and the Practice of the ICTY and the ICTR* (Antwerp, 2005); and Mark Ellis, "Breaking the Silence: Rape as an International Crime," *Case Western Reserve Journal of International Law* 38 (2006/2007): 232–235.

73 The evidence that bears on these acts has been reviewed by the contributors to Alexandra Stiglmayer (ed.), *Mass Rape: The War Against Women in Bosnia-Herzogovina*, trans. Marion Faber (Lincoln, NE, 1994); and again by R. Charli Carpenter, *Forgetting Children Born of War* (New York, 2010). I cite the number of rapes that took place in Yugoslavia from Elisa Von Joeden-Forgey, "Gender and Genocide," in *The Oxford Handbook of Genocide Studies*, ed. Donald Bloxham and A. Dirk Moses (Oxford, 2010), p. 70.

74 On this issue see the interesting essay by Doris Buss, "Making Sense of Genocide, Making Sense of Law: International Criminal Prosecutions of Large-Scale Sexual Violence," in *Genocide and Gender in the Twentieth Century*, ed. Amy Randall (London, 2015), pp. 277–97.

75 ICTR, Prosecutor v. A. Kayesu, Case No. IT-96–4-T, 731.

Sexual Violence as an International Crime: Interdisciplinary Approaches (Cambridge, UK, 2013); the anthology edited by Adam Jones, *Gendercide and Genocide* (Nashville, 2004); the essays included in Rosemary Gartner and Bill McCarthy (eds.), *The Oxford Handbook of Gender, Sex, and Crime* (New York, 2014), pp. 690–707; and Nicola Henry, *War and Rape: Law, Memory and Justice* (London, 2013).

In light of the subject of this essay, I would here expand our conversation to include not only rape – and its linkage to murder in the world of the Third Reich – but also the topic of miscegenation that will illuminate the significance of this subject in additional important ways. This is because it deals with the issue of reproduction and the birth – not the murder – of children under terrible circumstances – a reality seen in many historical contexts where forced sexual relationships occurred. In other words, to just consider the matter of rape and to ignore its consequences is to decipher only part of the relevant story.

In light of this unintended consequence of sexual exploitation, an important question arises in relation to the analysis of genocide and the deconstruction of mass crimes: what is the significance of miscegenation relative to cases to which one seeks to attach the term "genocide"?

Regarding our interest in comparative history, we need to consider that the issue of race mixing, known in Spanish as *mestizaje*, is particularly relevant. Not only does it bear on the demographic history of the aboriginal peoples of the Americas, but it also relates to the equally relevant issues of morality, theology, and ontology as these normative categories were incarnated in Spanish America. Consider, in relation to these ethical and metaphysical concerns, that in the Third Reich sexual relations between a Jew and an Aryan, identified as *Rassenschande*, was a major crime because it was said to directly "pollute" Aryan blood. In contrast, Spain, both through the actions of the Crown and teachings of the Church, accepted, and in some instances even encouraged, race mixing.

Then, too, beyond the normative considerations, the diverse and extensive material on the rampant pattern of inter-racial sexual relationships, that was the norm rather than the exception in colonial Spanish America, raises intricate methodological issues relative to a consideration of Spanish state policy in the New World. In particular, miscegenation casts a large shadow over the accuracy of the accusation that a program of *physical* genocide was at work in this setting. For while this pattern of racial mixing in this colonial circumstance entailed an ethnocidal component, i.e., it involved the, at least partial, eradication of the pre-conquest aboriginal culture, it ran counter to the logic of physical genocide. Miscegenation, after all, produces children who are part Indian, and enlarges the overall population. It represents a genetic dialectic through which two groups have sexually come together, whether willingly or unwillingly, to form a third. As a result, the two original biological forms gave way to a new and different form. This hybrid biological reality does not necessarily represent a higher form à la the Hegelian notion of *das Aufheben*, a negation that produces an advance, but it is certainly an act that creates a new type of identity that retains elements of its origin. Miscegenation is thus a process of amalgamation that promotes a form of native survival in a transmuted form.

Seen from the perspective of the indigenous peoples – continually subjected to violence and exploitation – race mixing, ironically, became one of the modes through which "Indianness," understanding this term both culturally and racially, made an effort to survive. The indigenous peoples gained a future, in an odd and unexpected fashion, by way of this sexual activity. Miscegenation, therefore, needs to be understood not as negation or extinction but, rather, as a form of retention and transition. The native women, "who had babies, who struggled so that their fathers would recognize them, free them if they were slaves, provide for them, perhaps provide them with some education – these women were making possible the survival of their own kind over a long period. They were refusing to die."[76]

The making of a new people, or peoples, bred of Spaniards and Indians began immediately after Columbus's first landfall. Straightaway the Conquistadors took local women as concubines (both willingly and against their will),[77] raped Indian women,[78] and were given native women as gifts by local *caciques* as a sign of friendship and welcome.[79] Pedro Simón tells of the gift of 100 young women to Don Pedro de Heredia by the *Cacique* of Cipacuá, "all so good looking, charming, beautiful and smiling that we called the town Las Hermosas."[80]

This sexual intermingling created, in large measure, the majority of the present population of Latin America. A 2010–2012 census gives us a clear picture of the impact that racial mixing has had on the current demographic profile of the region. Stretching from Mexico to the tip of South America, *mestizos* are, in spite of the enormous European emigration of the last two centuries, the largest ethnic group. They represent about 47 percent of the total population, while whites account for 32.5 percent, and the Amerindian peoples make up 6.7 percent of the total community. These numbers, in effect, report and reflect a history of extraordinary race mixing in Spanish America. More than 500 years of miscegenation has produced a population that for all of Ibero-America is nearly half *mestizo* (about 227.5 million), and 5.3 percent *mulatto* (white mixed with black – almost

---

76 Solange Alberro, "Beatriz de Padila: Mistress and Mother," in *Struggle and Survival in Colonial America*, eds. Gary Nash and David Sweet (Berkeley, 1981), p. 256.
77 Mentioned, for example, in Bernal Diaz's report of the conquest of Tepoztlán in 1512 (*Historia verdadera de la conquista de la Nueva España* [Buenos Aires, 1955], p. 360); of Tenochtitlán, *ibid.*, pp. 427–29; and of Tetzcoco, *ibid.*, p. 351. In all of these cases, and others, he refers to the taking of "good spoils, generally with very good women specimens" (*ibid.*, p. 351).
78 Repeated by Las Casas on which see S, Lyman Tyler, *Two Worlds: The Indian Encounter with the European 1405–1505* (Salt Lake City, 1988), p. 156.
79 Described briefly, particularly in terms of its political significance, by Magnus Mörner, *Race Mixture in the History of Latin America* (Boston, 1967), pp. 23–24.
80 Pedro Simón, *Tercera noticia historial de las conquistas de tierra firma en las Indias Occidentales* (Madrid, 1961), pp. 39f.

30 million). Accordingly, any and all analysis of the history of colonial and later Spanish America, including the long centuries of depredation, spoliation, violation, religious conversion, ethnocide, assimilation, and loss of life, must take account of sexuality, racial-intermixing and the resultant production of a vast population, rather than its extermination. Contrary to Nazi laws regarding *Rassenschande*, sexual mixing between peoples does not necessitate murder but, rather, the embrace of a new model of being human.

A similar circumstance applies in the history of New World Slavery. Sex between masters, overseers, and slaves was common and produced a large community of mixed-race children who had, at a minimum, economic value.[81]

---

[81] For a full accounting of this phenomenon see my *The Holocaust and New World Slavery*, 2 vols. (Cambridge, 2019).

10

IRVING GREENBERG ON HISTORY AND *HALAKHA*: THE IMPLICATIONS OF THE HOLOCAUST

I Introductory comments

I am delighted and honored to participate in this volume dealing with the thought of Rabbi Irving (Yitz) Greenberg. Rabbi Greenberg and I have been friends for decades and I have been a dialogue partner and friendly critic of certain aspects of his theological views during this time. Though I have found central features of his theological reflections problematic I have seen his work continually grow and mature in depth and now believe that he should be recognized as a theologian of the first rank.

In reading Greenberg's work, one cannot but be impressed with his broad erudition and command of the history of Jewish thought. He moves seamlessly from the biblical, through the rabbinic and medieval eras, and then on to the modern period and the *Shoah* and its implications. Moreover, his exegetical sensitivity and insight into particular texts and issues is exceptional. In his explanations and discussions well-known biblical and rabbinic passages often acquire a new clarity and deep meaning, while his critiques of specific theological positions, e.g., of Reform Judaism and the Haredi version of Orthodox Judaism, are often remarkably insightful.

It is also a testimonial to Rabbi Greenberg's seriousness and the authenticity of his search for truth that he is willing to reconsider dubious ideas present in his own earlier studies, for example, the idea of a "voluntary covenant" and "moment faith."

II Exegesis of the main claim

Though Greenberg's views have continued to evolve, his basic theoretical model remains what I would call "Greenbergian Hegelianism." By this I mean that, like Hegel, Greenberg is a devoted student of the significance of history, in his case Jewish history, or, the history of the Jewish People, and is committed to arguing for the significance of this historical experience vis-à-vis theological truth and reflection. One could, therefore, fairly say that his work is an investigation of the theological meaning of the movement of Jews through time. It begins with the Patriarchs and the historical narratives of the Torah, focused on the Exodus from Egypt and the revelation of the Law at Sinai, continues with probing reflections on the destruction of the First and Second Temples and the Jewish People's responses thereto, moves forward through the medieval period with informed commentary on Maimonides and the medieval halakhists and kabbalists, and then takes us into the modern period beginning with the expulsion from Spain in 1492, from Portugal in 1496, and the emergence of the Jewish community of Safed in the sixteenth century. He then intelligently reviews the era of revolutionary modernity beginning with the French Revolution and explores the significance of the previously unthinkable possibility of Jews becoming citizens of the nation states in which they lived. Finally, this long historical narrative climaxes in the two monumental and revolutionary events of the twentieth century: the *Shoah* and the recreation of a Jewish commonwealth in the Land of Israel.

For Greenberg, like Hegel, this historical narrative moves essentially in one progressive direction – albeit with acknowledged detours and backsliding, the Holocaust being the most notable. And, for Greenberg, central to his explanation of this upward direction is the traditional theological notion of *brit* = covenant. On his reading of the movement of history, the covenant contributes to the perfection of the world. It provides a paradigm of what life should be like, and how one might go about achieving this ideal state of social and communal existence that has as its goal the fundamental transformation of human existence. For this reason, Judaism is best described as a "hope" that has as its central ambition the improvement and ultimate perfection of what it is to be human. Most importantly, this covenant is defined by Greenberg as a partnership "between God and man" entered into by both partners without coercion, i.e., made by both man and God "as a free choice."

However, despite the fundamental phenomenological structure of the covenant, the pattern of God's relationship to Israel, as manifest in historical reality, changes in fundamental ways over time. In the biblical era God is present, visible, and directly intervenes in a powerful way into history. So, for example, the dramatic revelation of the Divine will in the Exodus from Egypt and the conquest of the Land of Israel under Joshua. Also, after the conquest of the Land of Israel and the establishment of the Davidic monarchy, the presence of God was felt in the First Temple with immediacy and an overwhelming sense of awe. The mystery of the Holy of Holies, and the meaning that the sacrificial cult carried, conveyed a profound sense of the presence of the Divine within the community of the People of Israel. In contrast, after the destruction of the First Temple in 586 B.C.E., and Israel's return from the Babylonian exile in 538 B.C.E., and then the construction of the Second Temple (which traditionally is dated to have begun in 516 B.C.E.) the situation had changed. The Second Temple did not carry the same transcendental weight, and the sense of the Almighty's immediate reality was less intense. Greenberg also notes that in the Second Temple period, during which time the story of Esther occurs, the *Book of Esther* does not mention God. God has become less apparent, less visible, and now appears in Jewish history less directly, more obliquely, than had been the case earlier.

After the destruction of the Second Temple in 70 C.E. the Divine becomes even more remote and appears less concerned to manifest His overt power in the flow of history. Now the sages and the People of Israel assume a more active role in responding to the destruction of the Second Temple and in taking fundamental steps to assure the continued vitality and meaningfulness of their religious tradition. This is evident, most especially, in the foundational role played by the rabbis of the Talmudic era who led the Jewish People without new and direct Divine revelation. Hence the profound difference in style and content between rabbinic and prophetic leadership.

But history did not end in 70 C.E. nor in the post-70 exile. Rather, as Greenberg argues, the *tzimtzum*, the "contraction," of God's public and obvious role in Jewish (and world) history, continued to increase during the Middle Ages and climaxed in our time with the Holocaust. Nevertheless, in spite of His hiddenness, there always remains what Greenberg describes as a sustaining presence of God in history. In effect, the metaphysical paradox working itself out within the unfolding of history is that, as God becomes more hidden, God comes closer to men and women. Thus, even though rabbinic Judaism does not depend for its continuity on direct revelatory moments it creates a way of life in which the Jewish People still sense the Divine reality.

The essential insight that Greenberg would here emphasize is that God becomes more "hidden" in history not because He is actually absent or because humans are becoming more alienated from the transcendent but, rather, because men and women have responded to their historical experience by becoming more mature and aware of their own capacities for altering the world. Thus, they can relate to God with independence and integrity rather than as passive, mute, frightened creatures. In actuality, in a dialectical movement shared together by God and Israel, the transcendental withdrawal of God is inextricably linked with what Greenberg sees as the growing level of (human) responsibility; of men and women taking responsibility for themselves and their world. This growing maturity and taking of responsibility is, moreover, to be recognized not as the disconfirmation of the covenant but rather as its fulfillment.

This drama, revealed in the "evolution" of history, leads to Greenberg's well-known and seductive schema that, in the Bible and biblical era, "God was the senior partner," in the rabbinic era "an equal partner," and in the modern era "a junior partner." As Greenberg has written in an as-yet-unpublished manuscript:

> Out of respect for humans, God calibrates the elements of force and limits coercion in the encounter. God wants humans to grow into full capacity, i.e., to want the good for its own sake and to seek it without pressure or punishment. God wants humans to join in the task of *tikkun olam* out of love for God (and God's vision) and love of fellow humans (and wanting the best for them). The degree of Divine visibility and intervention

is greater at the beginning to get humans' attention and to motivate them to take on covenant and responsibility. As they develop more, the Divine role is "reduced" – really, reconfigured – to operate as role modeling: it is to be experienced as persuasion and education and less as command or authority.

What is particularly important about this evolutionary metaphysical deconstruction of the history of Israel (and the nations) is that it carries with it a demand for normative reevaluations and ethical reconsiderations. It is not just that history evolves that is significant but that human beings and human societies do so as well. Thus, for example, in his exegesis of the biblical rules governing the institution of slavery, and in his review of the status of women and the rules of marriage in the Mishna, Greenberg explains that these rules were interpreted and reinterpreted by the *Tannaim* (sages of the Mishna) and later scholars in ways that were increasingly sensitive to the existential and ethical implications carried by these issues. In this way they showed that they understood the need for more equal and ethical readings of these societal norms. This obligation to continually re-study and reinterpret the Torah's regulations continues into our own time. As history unfolds and the Jews mature they are called upon, are obligated, to look ever more deeply into the moral core of their religious-halakhic traditions. And most essentially, after the *Shoah* we live in a situation where, as Greenberg wrote in an early essay: "The Holocaust challenges the claims of all the standards that compete for modern man's loyalties."[1]

What Greenberg's analysis takes away from this theological explanation of Jewish history is that men and women are now challenged to do better morally, i.e., to be more responsible for ourselves, for others, for the People of Israel, and for humanity in general. Therefore, Greenberg's historical/metaphysical decipherment concludes by making profound moral demands. His "progressive" historical narrative, in which God finally, in our time, becomes the "junior partner," entails that not only is *God* not visibly active in historical events but also that men and women are wholly, or nearly wholly, responsible for what occurs in history. They are most definitely responsible for all social and ethical norms. Accordingly, all inherited teachings and orthodoxies require reexamination in accordance with our modern, elevated, social, and ethical sensibilities.

These telling observations and entailments about our relation to inherited normative demands and values are, self-evidently, exceedingly consequential, especially for those who would retain some form of orthodoxy – in our case, Orthodox Judaism. They force us to address directly the foundational Jewish subjects of the Torah and *Halakha*. We will return to these cardinal issues in our critical reflections below.

---

1 "Cloud of Smoke, Pillar of Fire: Judaism, Christianity, and Modernity After the Holocaust," in *Auschwitz: Beginning of a New Era?*, ed. Eva Fleischner (New York, 1977), p. 213.

III Critical reflections

There is something fundamentally persuasive about Greenberg's historical "model." It is hard to deny that history, including Jewish history, both as an empirical matter as well as a phenomenological philosophical datum, appears to have moved over time to higher and higher levels of ethical sensitivity, increased humanitarian concern, more developed concepts of human equality, and more capacious notions of human and societal freedom. And as Greenberg so persuasively recounts and deconstructs this history, this is exactly what God wanted. God is the ultimate guarantor of this process of liberation and its main booster. Moreover, and for our present discussion a matter of considerable significance, Greenberg perceives this positive "advance" as being not only desirable but also relatively "frictionless" over against Orthodox Jewish belief.

But are matters quite so simple? Is this covenantal progress as deciphered by Greenberg so conceptually (and existentially) benign? Is the concept of *brit* = covenant so flexible and non-judgmental, so malleable and approving? Is all of this remarkable change and "advance" to be experienced solely, or even mainly as, in Greenberg's words, "persuasion and election" and less as communal command or authority.

To help clarify these interrelated theological questions, and others that flow naturally, even necessarily, from them, I would raise five critical issues for reflection. In raising these specific questions I am especially concerned to interrogate Greenberg's view that the Holocaust carries implications for the *Halakha*. That is, I note Greenberg's basic, repercussive argument that the *Halakha* should change in light of the "Final Solution."

Issue 1: In an age of "autonomy" in which Jews are the "senior partner" in their covenantal relationship with God, and fidelity to the covenant is defined as "the transformation of history" and "a hope," is the *Halakha* still binding? Two linked queries are here relevant:

(a) *Does the Halakha possess authority, even, in keeping with Jewish tradition, **absolute** authority?* I begin with this question because I hold the view that there is only one important question in religious matters, both conceptual and existential, and that question is: Who or what has authority? Once this inquiry is resolved everything else moves smoothly forward. If the *Halakha* still has authority then many things follow. If it does not, then many other, very different, things follow. In the present instance, in light of Greenberg's theological claims, it thus needs to be asked: For Jews to live a "covenantal life," must they live according to traditional, authoritative, halakhic rules, or are these rule "negotiable," possessing no binding authority?

(b) In the modern era a second, related question needs also to be confronted, namely: *Even if one posits the continued salience of Halakha, must the Halakha of today be essentially monolithic?* That is, must the *Halakha* be governed, as in the past, by a specific set of men who possess the requisite rabbinical knowledge and whose rulings are all made within the traditional halakhic circle, i.e., in a fundamentally monolithic form (though with differences of opinion), or, after modernity, Auschwitz and the recreation of the State of Israel, can – even must – the *Halakha* be pluralistic?

The crucial existential-theological dilemma raised by these questions is that if the answer to our first question is "No, *Halakha* is not *the* religious Jewish authority," then we are no longer thinking and living religiously within an Orthodox circumstance. Alternatively, if the *Halakha is* the authority then we are not in a realm in which God is a "junior partner." Certainly the *Halakha* is decided by human beings, but in such a way that the halakhic authorities claim direct Divine sanction and authority. I recognize that this very complex issue – i.e., the nature of the halakhic process and how it operates – needs much more analysis than can be offered here. However, readers need to ponder this both in this context and more generally. Moreover, by definition, it is not inconsequential that the *Halakha* is meant to severely circumscribe human autonomy.

If, however, we *are* living in an age where human agency and the *tzimtzum* of God are paramount, can we declare, with authority, that Reform, Reconstructionist and Conservative religious formulations – whether described by their adherents as *Halakha* or not – are to be rejected? But if these non-Orthodox forms of Jewish practice and *Halakha are* acceptable, i.e., are legitimated as the religious equal of Orthodox interpretation and practice, then the Orthodox position has no superior claim to truth, nor are its rule-making procedures more authoritative than those of other groups. Indeed, in this scenario, Judaism has become a smorgasbord of spiritual options.

At this juncture I would also note that Greenberg, if I understand his view correctly, wants to reply to this cluster of methodological concerns that modern pluralism in religious matters, i.e., *Halakha*, is *not* a radical break with the logic and tradition of covenant but is, rather, its natural outgrowth and "transformation." This makes good sense given that he wants, despite all talk of evolution, change, diversity, and pluralism, to maintain an "Orthodox" position. But here the very complex term "transformation" needs close examination. For when is "X becomes Y" considered to be an act, a process, of transformation, and when is it something different, even radically different? Put another way, when is the concept, the process, of transformation conceptually and actionably legitimate, and when is it a term that in fact serves to represent discontinuous change?

Issue 2: Greenberg, with great sophistication, turns to the interpretation of history, to history itself, to substantiate and verify his covenantal vision of the evolution of the Jewish spirit through time. It is this subtle and well informed reading that is the foundation for his normative judgments, both halakhic and non-halakhic. It needs, however, to be appreciated that while he talks of empirical events as the test of his view, and claims that history confirms his understanding of the meaning of history, the deconstruction and interpretation of Israel's history for both halakhic and non-halakhic purposes is not a simple matter of reading the historical record "as it is." Rather, it is a very complex situation based on assumptions and structural conceptions. Accordingly, the meaning of Jewish history is the outcome of diverse interpretive rules and intricate hermeneutical techniques. Vis-à-vis *Halakha*, this means that drawing halakhic conclusions from historical experience is not a simple nor a direct procedure. So, for example, on the basis of the Holocaust experience, Greenberg draws the strong halakhic conclusion that the *Halakha* needs to change, to become more just and equitable in certain ways, in response to what the Holocaust was, especially the ethnic and gender principles upon which it was predicated.

But the Lubavitcher Rebbe, the Munkatcher Rebbe, and the Haredi world read this history very differently. For them, the empirical historical event of the Holocaust is proof certain that the Jews were being punished for violating the *Halakha*, and the correct response to the death camps is, therefore, meticulous traditional halakhic observance, not the "transformation" of the *Halakha*. Again, Greenberg's revered teacher, Rav Joseph Soloveitchik, while not endorsing the traditional view of *mipnei chataeinu* (because of our sins) as the "explanation" of the Holocaust, also demanded the maintenance and perpetuation of the halakhic tradition with little change. He certainly would not endorse changes in the *Halakha* because of the *Shoah*.

Furthermore, to take a very different example, Richard Rubenstein "read" the empirical event of the murder of six million Jews as "proving" *leth din ve leth dayan* (there is neither justice nor judge). That is, the *Shoah* is proof that the *Halakha*, though of sociological and communal significance à la Mordechai Kaplan, has no ontological standing. I would also recall in passing that the German Protestant, Pastor Dean Gruber, who was Richard Rubenstein's theological discussion partner, thought that it was theologically correct to understand the murder of a million Jewish children by the forces of the Hitler state as a contemporary verification of the historical-theological claim that Jews were to be eternally punished for the first-century crime of deicide. Alternatively, the Catholic Church has, since Vatican II, rejected this time-honored Christian belief. Getting at the "meaning" of history is no simple thing.

Issue 3: In a related though different way, relative to the deconstruction and conceptualization of historical experience, I would ask another question that bears centrally on the theological-covenantal interpretation of modern Jewish history: *Where is God relative to the creation and maintenance of the State of Israel?* Does it make sense to claim that the state is *reshit zemichat geulateynu* (the beginning of the dawn of our redemption), as it is described in the standard prayer for the State of Israel, in any traditional sense? In relation to this seminal topic one can talk about God as a "junior partner" and the obvious role of human activity in the creation and maintenance of the State of Israel. But if one chooses to do so what do such assertions really mean? Why not just talk of human enterprise and activity in this historical happening? Given the revised conception of God as "hidden" and "contracted" (*tzimtzum*), what does the invocation of God add to the description and explanation of events? For God to be understood to have played some truly meaningful role in this dramatic adventure we need more than a claim that God's *tzimtzum* is a sign of His presence. On what criteria, empirical and otherwise, do we decide to include God in the necessary description of the relevant details that make up this narrative? And on what criteria do we decide to simply leave God out of the description as He appears to provide no added agency or influence. Can it be that to talk about *tzimtzum* here is only to speak of one's own faith rather than to make claims that are theologically or historically significant?

Issue 4: Returning directly to thinking about the status and value of the *Halakha* in our time relative to Greenberg's schema, it is apposite, in light of the changes that have occurred in the modern era, to ask whether the *Reform* Jews might not be right. Did they not do what Greenberg asks that we all do, i.e., measure the *Halakha* by a meta-halakhic ethical norm, in their case Kantian morality, and adjust Jewish practice accordingly?

Here one must acknowledge that Greenberg appears to have the weight of moral sensitivity – and it is a significant weight – on his side. Modern ethical norms do, on occasion, require halakhic changes given the record of the past. However, at this juncture we encounter a truly vexing issue. Who is the ultimate arbiter of the moral domain? (And, fundamentally related, of the religious domain?) I note that the original conference at which an earlier version of this essay was presented was held in the United Kingdom, still a member of the European Union at that point, and that the European Union has, in various ways, objected to circumcision as barbaric and "incompatible with modern European ethical values." The same type of "moral" objection to Jewish Orthodox practice has also arisen in many European countries relative to *kashrut*. In addition, the question of "who is a Jew" became an issue in Britain not long ago relative to admission to Jewish day schools. So we are confronted by a very real, very immediate, moral challenge: should Jews abandon *brit mila* and *kashrut*, and revise the classical, normative definitions of "who is a Jew" because these practices are not thought to be ethical by European civilization in 2016 (or since)?

In this context, the very complicated matter of the relationship of *Halakha*, morality, and sociology becomes relevant, even inescapable. For when is change truly warranted and when is it merely a capitulation to sociological pressures? I remind readers that changing the *Halakha* is, at least in theory, altogether different from changing human social conventions or political constitutions. The transcendental claims made for the Torah as Divine revelation, and for the Torah as the source of the *Halakha*, raise difficult issues about how one interprets the Torah, how one draws laws from it, how one goes about making alterations in the law (*Halakha*), and what limits exist vis-à-vis making such changes. The Torah *sh'be'al pe* (the Oral Tradition) does acknowledge, however carefully, sociological phenomena but it does not recognize sociological forces as ultimate.

Issue 5: Every theological proposition and every theological position has logical and metaphysical implications and involves specific theological "costs." Which is to recognize in this context that the key issue raised directly and profoundly by Greenberg's evolutionary theology is not only what it offers that is insightful, original, and persuasive, but also what it denies, makes difficult, and brings into doubt. That is to say, Greenberg is free, especially in our post-Holocaust age, to redefine "God" (and other foundational concepts) as he wishes. But, having redefined God (and other basic theological concepts) he must attend to the myriad conceptual and metaphysical consequences of having done so. So, for instance, one must inquire, what happens to the traditional "God of Judaism" in his revisionist theological schema?

Specifically, what conceptual and ontological corollaries flow from conceiving of God as a "junior partner"? And are these implications, that I assume will be significant, acceptable, in particular, to Orthodox Jews, or is their cost, i.e., what they entail, too high? Consider, for instance, what the costs are if God is now a "junior partner" relative to such cardinal notions as reward and punishment, God as the underwriter and enforcer of morality, the character of Torah law, the meaning of Revelation, the idea of *mitzvoth*, the understanding of redemption, and other eschatological notions. Is God as a "junior partner" capable of being the guarantor of moral rules? Is He capable of insuring the ultimate messianic fulfillment that Greenberg repeatedly discusses? The deep structure of Jewish messianism is meant to guarantee that in the end good triumphs and evil is defeated, and that there is a moral balance in creation. Can a God who is a "junior partner" be responsible for, and guarantee, this outcome? And can a "junior partner" be the source of authority sufficient for the demands of the regimen of *mitzvoth*?

Again, when the Divine is defined as, and perceived as, a "junior partner," is sin still a viable, meaningful idea, or is it now only a metaphor of a sort? Does God "save" both personally and communally? What becomes of *Yom Kippur* when God is a "junior partner?" Does the whole cycle of the *asseret yomei teshuvah* (the Ten Days of Repentance), culminating in our fasting and self-debasement on Yom Kippur, make any sense if men and women are now the "senior partner"? What sense does it make to pray for forgiveness, redemption and life from a "junior partner"? Why think that the traditional practices of *teshuva, tefillah*, and *tzedakah* (repentance, prayer, and charity) that are central to the rituals of Yom Kippur, will have any power to "avert the *gezerah*" (the evil decree), or even why we should think them necessary when interrelating with a "junior partner?"

More generally, we all know that the term *mitzvah*, commandment, derives its meaning, its power, from the belief that the *mitzvot* are grounded in the will of a Divine Commander. Can God as a "junior partner" still be a *metzaveh*, a Commander? Or do both the concepts of "commander" and "commandment" become, in our age, just metaphors that remind us of a past that is no more?

In addressing the meaning of concepts like *mitzvot* and revelation it is, moreover, apposite to remind ourselves that while Greenberg's comments on the changing context in which people "hear God's revelation" are certainly correct and raise a fundamental point, at the same time one has to be aware that there is always a competing dialectic vis-à-vis God's revelation. Which is to say, we do not want to claim that we hear God's voice, that God speaks to us, only in conformity with *our* "context" and norms, because this would be to relativize and reduce God's voice to our hearing. One should always think of God's revelation as potentially or actually challenging our context and as possibly speaking to us in an unfamiliar voice that calls into question the assumptions and values of our own time.

IV Conclusion

Rabbi Greenberg has many elemental and consequential things to teach us. His work is, despite my critical questions, profound and repercussive. But it is not yet complete.

UPDATE

The present paper was written for a special seminar, organized by the Center for Jewish Studies at Oxford University in the summer of 2014, on the thought of Rabbi Irving (Yitz) Greenberg. The essays from the conference have been edited by Miri Freud-Kandel, Steven Bayme, and Adam Ferziger and published under the title *The Road Not Taken: Yitz Greenberg and Modern Orthodox Judaism* (Boston, 2019). The purpose of the conference was to examine critically Greenberg's radical theological position. My paper focused on his provocative view of the relationship between Torah and historical development, and especially the implicit and explicit implications that he draws from the Holocaust. This topic has a long history and has been central to Jewish thought from the rabbinic period on. In the modern era, especially the period after Jewish emancipation began at the end of the eighteenth century, it became the dominant and determinate issue in the debates that led to the creation of Reform Judaism, the *Wissenschaft des Judentums* that in turn led to the creation of Conservative Judaism, and Neo-Orthodoxy. After all of the heated discussions and fierce debates over the past 200 years, one would have thought that just about everything worth saying on the subject had already been said. But, in fact, Yitz Greenberg found a new way of organizing the philosophy of Jewish history and its meaning.

Included in Greenberg's refashioning and explanation of the movement of Jewish history are, as must be the case for all authentic Jewish thought, explicit recommendations as to how his views should be understood to impact the meaning and authority of the *Halakha* (Jewish law). In Greenberg's case, these proposals for interpreting and applying the *Halakha* in our time, i.e., after the Holocaust, assume a radical form. Though Greenberg was trained as an Orthodox rabbi and has lived his public life as an influential Orthodox communal leader and his personal life as a modern Orthodox Jew, his refashioning of the demands of the *Halakha* directly challenge the normative presuppositions of Orthodox Judaism. So, for example, he advocates alterations in the understanding of basic Jewish theological concepts, most notably the idea of Covenant, elevates the role of human autonomy in matters of religion, and offers recommendations regarding practical theological issues, such as the status of women and the relationship to Christianity after Auschwitz, that are departures from tradition. Above all, he has emphasized the need to revise the *Halakha* to conform to *our* moral sensibilities in areas like sexuality, gender equality, political power, and the relationship that should exist between people of different faiths.

As readers will have already learned, Rabbi Greenberg and I have been friends for nearly fifty years. But I first encountered him as his critic – indeed I have been his most outspoken and persistent critic for four decades – rather than as a disciple. I believe his work is often highly original and profound and his reinterpretation of classical texts and ideas remarkably insightful, but, as explained in the present essay, I do not think he has resolved all the serious puzzles and problems to which his work gives rise. Nor do I find his methodological procedures always valid and defensible.

Moreover, the Jewish tradition's classical sources are complex, and interpreting them in a coherent manner is a difficult matter. Take, for example, that Jews usually explain that when God offered the Torah to Israel at Sinai, after the other nations had already rejected it, the Jewish People responded: *"Na'aseh ve'nishma"* – "we will do and we will listen" (see *Exodus* 24:7, *Mekhilta Yitro* 5, and *Sifre Deuteronomy* 34.3). That is, the Jewish People freely accepted the obligations that the Torah imposed. And, not surprisingly, Greenberg's emphasis on human autonomy follows this well-worked theme. But what about the very different tale told in the Babylonian Talmud, *Tractate Shabbat* 88a. Here God addresses Israel at Sinai and says, "If you accept the Torah it will be well with you, if not, this spot will be your burial [ground]." So the issue of free choice versus authority is turned on its head. And with this sharp reversal the key question becomes – to put the issue in classical theological terms – is the *Halakha* heteronomous? I think so, and I believe that Orthodox Judaism has traditionally thought so and continues to think so. Thus, for the sages of all ages, from the Mishnaic era (before 200 C.E.) onward, the commandments of the Torah, and those derived from the Torah, are obligatory (what philosophers refer to as deontological in character), and normative, i.e., they establish what is permissible and what is forbidden.

Then there is Greenberg's profound but not unproblematic exposition of Jewish history into three "ages," and his deep belief that Judaism is a "historical religion." For both the Jewish tradition and Greenberg, history is not understood as a secular, linear, non-teleological phenomenon. Its origin and purpose is powered forward by God, both through the natural order and by a series of non-natural events like those that took place during the Exodus and at Mount Sinai, and through the destruction of the First and Second Temples and Israel's exile. From the perspective of the Jewish tradition these happenings are not explicable solely by way of immanent causation. Now Greenberg, and many other modern Jewish thinkers, want to extend this history to include the Holocaust and the creation of the State of Israel. These events too are seen to reflect Divine intervention. But the matter of God's "causation" of events is very difficult, if not impossible, to sort out. Consider that the Satmar Rebbe and other ultra-Orthodox sages reject the theological interpretation of these events offered by Greenberg. To resolve the disagreement, and to decide who is right and who is wrong, we require valid criteria by which to judge the matter, but we lack these necessary criteria. Neither the Satmar Rebbe (R. Yoel Teitelbaum) nor Rabbi Greenberg have much to offer by way of persuasive criteria. But then how do we know that these events, that are undoubtedly exceptional, have transcendental significance and that Greenberg's demands that we make halakhic changes predicated on these historical developments is theologically justified? Conversely, the same epistemological difficulty confronts R. Teitelbaum's strong theological pronouncements. As outsiders to the Satmar community we need reasons to accept the Rebbe's claims, but no sound (non-midrashic) reasons were ever provided.

Like Greenberg and most modern Jewish thinkers, I agree that historical events over the millennia have caused fundamental changes in the shape and practice of

Judaism. After 70 C.E., living in *Galut* (exile), without the Temple in Jerusalem, alterations in Jewish life were necessary. Changes like the leadership of the community passing from priests to sages, the center of worship moving from the Temple to synagogues, and the refashioned emphasis on "portable" *mitzvot* like *kashrut*, *Shabbat*, and family purity laws were all required if Judaism were to survive in its new circumstances. However, at one and the same time, the structure of rabbinic tradition tells me that emphasizing history and historical change, as modern Jewish movements, as their scholarly defenders do, somehow misses, and distorts, the tradition.

I would observe that the Mishnah, redacted *after* the destruction of the Second Temple and conceived as a guide to authentic Jewish living without the Temple, and addressed to a Jewish People increasingly to be found outside the Land of Israel, is organized around six topics (*sedarim* – orders of content), none of which deal explicitly with history, historical events, historical change, or historical justifications for halakhic alterations. The Mishnaic Orders of: (1) Agriculture (*zeraim*); (2) Appointed Times (*Mo'ed*) including Rosh Hashanah and Yom Kippur that have *no* historical associations; (3) Women (*Nashim*) with its emphasis on marriage (*Kiddushin*) and divorce (*Gittin*), along with *Ketubot* (marriage contracts) and *yebamot* (the status of women who lose their husbands without children); (4) Damages (*Nezikin*) dealing with financial issues; (5) Holiness (*Kodashim*) that investigates the laws and practices of the sacrificial order of the Temple, even after its destruction; and (6) Purities (*Taharot*) that focuses on defining the concept of ritual cleanliness and ways of purifying unclean objects, all essentially deal with the foundational issues that define most of Jewish thought and practice in ways that are conceptual and metaphysical, not historical. Even after the shattering historical event of 70 C.E., the loss of Jewish sovereignty, and the movement of Jewish life to the diaspora, the sages have little to say about history and its significance. The Mishnah, for instance, has nothing to say about the rise of Christianity, the details of the Bar Kochba revolt (132–135 C.E.), or the Roman Empire in which the *Tannaim*, the teachers of the Mishnah, lived. And the Jerusalem Talmud, redacted at the end of the fifth century C.E., and the Babylonian Talmud, redacted in the sixth century, tell us nothing about the transformation of the Roman Empire into a Christian state. The only thing that one finds regarding Christianity (*Notzrim*) are a few polemical tales about Jesus. All this suggests that we need to rethink the relationship between the "revealed" (Torah) and the "historical," and that we need to come to an agreement over the method by which we decide whether revelation or historical (and sociological) experience has priority and authority.

In contrast to the emphasis on historical development that dominates modern scholarship in the areas of both rabbinics and history, I would remind readers of what the distinguished Israeli historian, Jacob Katz, pointed out regarding the dialectic of continuity and change with regard to *Halakha* in the medieval era (particularly relating to the work of the Tosaphists [medieval Talmudic commentators]):

> If conditions of existence had any power to break down the barriers of prohibitions, surely many of the major elements of Halakhah that lim-

ited the Jew's Lebensraum during the Middle Ages would have been uprooted. They imposed restrictions on what he could eat and drink, forbade him to engage in economic activities a good many days each year, and these restrictions remained firmly entrenched despite the pressures of existence. One cannot but ask, therefore, where were the limits of Halakhah flexibility, which of the restrictive precepts were easily pushed aside, which of them maintained their resistance even under conditions of pressure, and so on?[2]

What Katz's observation brings to notice is that explaining halakhic status and change is difficult and in some ways even counter-intuitive.

I do not know how to arrange all of these sociological and theological pieces. Nor can I fit together, in one coherent line of halakhic developments, the way in which history and *Halakha* are seen to come together in Rabbeinu Tam and the Tosaphists,[3] then Maimonides' *Mishneh Torah*, followed by Joseph Karo and the many post-medieval sages. However, these authoritative sources tell me that "history" is not a simple explanatory category in Jewish life and thought. Nor is it an uncomplicated, straightforward, matter to decide what specific changes need to be made in the *Halakha* because of historical developments. The *Zeitgeist* is clearly not unimportant, but how to work with it, and when to work against it, is one of the most difficult challenges facing Jewish thinkers in every age.

Because I do not know how to resolve these theological and conceptual conundrums, I carry on talking together with Greenberg about the meaning of such fundamental Judaic ideas as Torah, revelation, commandments, the idea of a commander, covenant, redemption, messianism, and salvation. Together we both continue to puzzle over the unavoidable question of what takes precedence when morality and revelation come into conflict; to ask whether "messianism" is only a metaphor for progress; to ponder the consequences of talking about a broken covenant between God and Israel; about what it means to talk of God as a "junior partner." Does a "junior partner" "punish and reward"? These are very big questions to which neither Yitz Greenberg nor I have any conclusive answers.

---

2 Jacob Katz, *Introduction to Halacha and Kabbalah* (Jerusalem, 1986), pp. 2–3 [Hebrew].
3 See here Ephraim Urbach, *The Tosaphists* (Jerusalem, 1980) [Hebrew].

11

EXPLORING THE CONCEPT OF *KOL YISRAEL AREVIM ZEH L'ZEH*

I

Kol Yisrael Arevim, the complex and many sided ideal that Jews are responsible for one another, is a pillar of traditional Jewish thought. It is a concept that involves a variety of obligations, and, over the centuries, has accumulated diverse understandings of what the concept of obligation itself entails. Furthermore, it has come to be appreciated as a broad category that involves moral, psychological, ontological, and metaphysical implications.

The exact phrase "*Kol Yisrael Arevim Zeh L'Zeh*," originated with Rashi, the great medieval French exegete. In his commentary on the Torah, when glossing the biblical verse in *Leviticus* 26:37: "They will stumble, each man over his brother as if from a sword," Rashi explains, employing a non-literal, midrashic, hermeneutical style of interpretation that the verse means that:

עונו של זה

"through the sins of another"

לכל ישראל

"for all Israel"

ערבי זה לזה

"are guarantors for one another."

That is, all Israel is bound together as a community and the sin and corruption of a part of the community will affect the status of the entire collective. Thus, the usual rendering that "all Israelites have responsibility for all other Israelites." Rashi, when framing this interpretation, certainly knew the explanation provided in the *Mekhilta* of the Sinai covenant provided by Rabbi Yehuda Ha-Nasi: "I am the Lord, your God [*Exodus* 20:2]. This tells the merit of Israel. When they stood at Sinai to receive the Torah . . . they pledged themselves each for the other" (*Mekhilta de Rabbi Ishmael, Yitro* 5). And he was undoubtedly familiar with the statement in T.B. *Sanhedrin* 27 that the verse in *Leviticus* 26 "And they shall stumble one upon another" means "one [will stumble] through the sin of the other, which teaches that all are sureties for one another. There, the reference [in *Leviticus* 26] is such as to have the power to restrain [their fellowman from evil] but did not." (See also *Sifra, Bechukotai* 2:7.)

Accordingly, the *peshat*, the simple meaning, of the text in *Leviticus*, is, as summarized by Rabbi Bachya ben Asher in his *Commentary on the Torah*, that the Israelites "disregarded their reciprocal responsibility and this was their undoing."

But this interpretation immediately raises a host of fundamental theological, philosophical and ethical questions. Like all things biblical and rabbinic it implicates us in a spider-like web of meaning(s) in which each individual element is supported, and requires support from, all the other elements in the architectonic design of the whole. That is, to deconstruct both the literal and midrashic exegesis of the original biblical phrase we need to ask and answer three questions: (1) what is the meaning of the notion of "responsibility" (*ahariout*), (2) where does the notion of mutual responsibility come from, and (3) within Jewish tradition what are its grounds? From where does it receive its authority? And, again, how far does it extend in controlling and directing Jewish ethical behavior?

Before proceeding I must note that answering these, and related questions, that arise vis-à-vis our privileged text provided by Rashi, is not a straightforward exegetical or philosophical matter. And this because, in spite of the popularity of the observation that "*Kol Yisrael Arevim Zeh L'Zeh*," there is very little discrete discussion of it in the long history of Jewish thought. Other than a few glosses by later biblical commentators, who know Rashi's reading, it almost never appears as a distinctive idea that is analyzed separately, by itself, by later philosophical, kabbalistic or ethical commentators. Therefore, I have had to construct that spider's web of reinforcing parts just referred to, from which the notion takes its full meaning and gains its repercussive significance.

In the Torah, the source of ethical obligation, within the community of Israel, lies in three interconnected concepts. The first is the collective nature of the covenant between God and Israel; the second emerges from the obligation, the commandment, to love one another. And the third is the "election of Israel."

The covenant is first established between God and the Patriarchs and then, most fully, between God and Israel after the Exodus from Egypt. It forges a shared reality that, by its very nature, establishes a sense of kinship, of "family," and fosters a feeling of solidarity among all Jews. By its nature, it is capacious and without temporal limits. The relationship that it establishes between God and Israel is "eternal." As God tells the People of Israel at Sinai: "It is not with you alone that I create this Covenant and this oath [of obedience], but with those who are standing with us this day before the Lord, our God, and with those who are not us today ... secret things belong to the Lord, our God, but that which had been revealed is for us and our children forever to carry out the words of the Torah" (*Deuteronomy* 29:13, 18). At a minimum, it engenders what Rav Joseph Soloveitchik labeled a "Covenant of Fate," and, at a maximum, creates a shared "Covenant of Destiny."

It is against this foundational context that Maimonides, quite remarkably, defined a heretic as someone who is indifferent to the wellbeing of the People of Israel (in *Hilchot Teshuvah*, 3:11). The experience at Sinai ties all Israel together and then binds their communal self into a compact with the Almighty. The covenant relates primarily to Israel not Israelites, and the responsibility of maintaining it with fidelity is a shared one. The entire Jewish People benefits from appropriate societal behavior, and the entire Jewish People suffers – all Israel – suffers from individual sins that disturb or violate the joint obligation. That is, the covenant entails, at its core, mutual responsibility. Israel is elected as "a kingdom of priests and a holy nation," not a group of individuals some of whom do the right and some of whom do the wrong things, with each person being judged accordingly.

The behavior of Moses, in two different incidents, makes this clear. In the first, reported in *Exodus* 2:11–17, Moses intercedes for a slave and the text speaks of his intercession on behalf of "his beaten brethren." Moses understands he has an *a priori* moral obligation to the other Jew even though he is a Prince and the other individual is a slave. He knows that he is responsible for his "brethren" and must choose to act.[1] In the second episode, Moses encounters God after the sin of the golden calf. An angry God had told Moses that he was soon to destroy Israel and begin a new nation from Moses. But Moses, fully aware of the people's colossal wrongdoing and the legitimacy of the divine intention, nevertheless, replies to God's offer as follows:

> Now it came to pass on the next day that Moses said to the people, "You have committed a great sin. So now I will go up to the Lord; perhaps I can make atonement for your sin." Then Moses returned to the Lord and said, "Oh, these people have committed a great sin, and have made for themselves a god of gold! Yet now, if You will forgive their sin – but if not, I pray, blot me out of Your book which You have written." [*Exodus* 32:30–32]

For Moses, God's plan is unacceptable and he will not be party to it. Being a member of *Am Yisrael*, the People of Israel, means showing ultimate concern for the others in the community even when they have fallen short of their obligations. For the leader of the nation, the values operating in this context go beyond strict justice, and demand recognition of the interdependence of all Israelites. In the course of making this choice, Moses reminds God of His moral obligations to the Patriarchs, and, at the same time, lives up to his responsibility to insure the future of the Jewish People.

From this episode also derives the *Midrash* that compares Noah, Abraham, and Moses as ethical models. Noah did not plead for his fellow human beings and was therefore inferior to Abraham who pled for the righteous at Sodom. However, Abraham was inferior to Moses because while he did challenge God's severe judgment

---

1 This is to employ the midrashic mode of analysis on the content of this the biblical tale.

against Sodom, he pled *only* for the righteous. In comparison Moses pleads for the sinners who danced around the golden calf and links his future to theirs.

The notion of covenantal responsibility appears throughout the Torah. One finds, for example, that in discussing false teachers (*Deuteronomy* 13:12), Israel is told, "All Israel shall hear, and fear." The threat such individuals pose is not primarily to individuals but, rather, to the wellbeing of the national community. Again, in response to those who violate the covenant, the Torah demands that they shall be killed first by the witnesses against them and then "the hand of the entire people afterward, and you shall destroy evil from your midst" (*Deuteronomy* 17:7). Every Israelite is answerable for the maintenance of the "contract" between God and Israel. These are highly challenging obligations but God makes high demands. Later this principle of interdependence will become the normative assumption that justifies the critique of Israel's behavior by the Prophets. The prophet is both a member of the nation and a severe critic from within it in the name of the maintenance of its integrity.

Likewise, in the case of the rebellious son, the Torah commands: "All the men of his city shall pelt him with stones and he shall die; and you shall remove evil from your midst; and all Israel shall hear, and they shall fear" (*Deuteronomy* 21:21). Israel is a collective enterprise. As such there must be a concern by all its members for the effect of the behavior of individual members of the community. Hence, the obligation that the nation "sweep out evil from your midst," lest evil consume the nation." (*Deuteronomy* 13:6, 17:7, and 19:19). Though this rule was not enforced, it, nevertheless, reflects the high bar God ideally sets for the behavior of His covenantal partner.

The themes of mutual accountability and Israel's inescapable connectedness again finds expression in, and through, the event recounted in Chapter 7 of the *Book of Joshua*. Here we read:

> The Israelites were unfaithful in regard to the devoted things; Achan son of Karmi, the son of Zimri, the son of Zerah, of the tribe of Judah, took some of them. So the Lord's anger burned against Israel. [*Book of Joshua* 7:1]

And as a result:

> The Lord said to Joshua, "Stand up! What are you doing down on your face?" [*Book of Joshua* 7:10]

> Israel has sinned; they have violated my covenant, which I commanded them to keep. They have taken some of the devoted things; they have stolen, they have lied, they have put them with their own possessions. [*Book of Joshua* 7:11]

> That is why the Israelites cannot stand against their enemies; they turn their backs and run because they have been made liable to destruction. I will not be with you anymore unless you destroy whatever among you is devoted to destruction. [*Book of Joshua* 7:12]

God declares not that Achan has sinned but that "Israel has sinned." Israel, defined by a collective integrity, was held liable for not preventing Achan's crime and, after the fact, for not punishing it, thereby becoming an accomplice.

A self without concern for others, a social order that does not respond to evil in its midst, even if it otherwise dedicates itself to its own religious virtuosity, is, in actuality, a transgressor who betrays the fundamental imperative of the Torah and Jewish life. In the lived social and political drama of communal existence, Jews are not allowed to be "bystanders." The "bystander" is not, as is often mistakenly believed, neutral but an ally of those who do evil. Moses is Moses because he comes down from Sinai to join in the national experience and to share in the fate of Israel. So, too, the later prophets do not flee their social environments. Instead they remain firmly within them and make severe demands upon them.

The second foundational principle that mandates our mutual ethical concern is the biblical command *v'ahavta l're'ekka kamokha*, "love your neighbor as yourself: I am the Lord" (*Leviticus* 19:18). This verse, found almost exactly in the middle of the Torah as if to emphasize its centrality, demands that we be other-directed. Egotism is the source of sin and selfishness – what the sages identified as *middot sedom*, the ethics of Sodom. Ezekiel reminds us of this when he exhorts Israel: "Behold, this was the inequity of thy sister Sodom . . . it did not strengthen the hand of the poor and needy" (16:49). While, drawing on this tradition, T.B. *Ketubot* 68a, teaches: "He who closes his eyes against charity is like an idolater." In contrast, love is always directed toward another – one unique being encountering another unique being and responding to their need. As Martin Buber noted, love means responsibility for the other.

This ethical norm, that should define our relationship with one another, is expressed in such biblical laws as those of the Jubilee Year and the rules governing the Israelite slave (*Deuteronomy* 15:13; and *Leviticus* 25:42). The Israelite whose impoverishment leads to voluntary enslavement is to be shown respect and accorded freedom after six years. According to the demand put forward in *Exodus* 21:2: "If you buy a Jewish bondsman he shall work for six years; and in the seventh he shall go free, for no charge." Even if he refuses, he is to be liberated. According to the rabbinic interpretation of the phrase (verse 5) "he shall serve [him] forever" should be understood until the Jubilee Year. There must be an end to degradation and subjugation for the Israelite slave for he, too, belongs rightfully *within* the national association.

The Torah, likewise, instructs us:

> At the end of every three years, bring all the tithes of that year's produce and store it in your towns, so that the Levites (who have no allotment or inheritance of their own) and the aliens, the fatherless and the widows who live in your towns may come and eat and be satisfied, and so that the Lord your God may bless you in all the work of your hands. [*Deuteronomy* 14:28–29]

"Loving one's neighbor" means insuring that everyone in the community is fed. Looking after the welfare of all members of society, whatever class they belong to, reflects our primordial interconnectedness, and is a non-negotiable obligation. As Maimonides observed: "We have never seen nor heard of an Israelite community that does not have a charity fund" (*Mishnah Torah, Law of Gifts to the Poor* 9.3). This involvement, not the indifference of the modern autonomous self, is obligatory for every Jew. Drawing on the ruling in the *Baba Batra* 8b, Maimonides even concludes that the *Beth Din*, the community court, "may take from a person what it is proper for that person to give. It may [also] pawn possessions for purposes of charity, even on the eve of the Shabbat." Moreover, *tzedaka* must be provided, according to the *Halakha*, in a way that preserves the dignity of the recipient. This, as much as the giving itself, is what defines a just and decent society.

Similarly, the Jubilee Year (*Leviticus* 25:8–24, and *Deuteronomy* 15:1–11) demands that all debts be canceled and all sales of land over the previous 49 years be annulled. "And ye shall hallow the fiftieth year and proclaim liberty throughout the land unto all the inhabitants thereof . . . ye shall return every man to his possessions, and ye shall return every man to his family." The purpose of this practice is to eliminate economic inequity by recreating the original fair division of the land. If enacted there would be no rich and no poor.

These, and all similar rules, are predicated on the duty that one must "love your fellow as yourself." We must take on the assignment to protect others, even to protect them against themselves, against their weaknesses, mistakes and inadequacies. There are, in these various ethical prescriptions, elements of prudence and pragmatism but ultimately, as is the case in our love of self, these initiatives are not grounded in utilitarian concerns. Moreover, we can never legitimately say, "This is not my affair." Or, "I have no stake in this and, hence, no responsibility for what occurs." One must *always* respond to the needs of others; especially, in the repeated language of the Torah, to the widow, the stranger, and the orphan. And one must work towards creating a society in which the political, economic, and social institutions promote this inclusive goal.

The third root concept that is salient to understanding the notion of "*Kol Yisrael Arevim*" is that of the "election" of the Jewish People. There has been much debate, over the centuries, regarding the interpretation of the concept of "election" and the very claim has had many critics, both inside and outside the Jewish community. Mordecai Kaplan, for example, argued for its elimination from the Jewish theological universe in his early theological writings, and Richard Rubenstein has done so more recently. Both thinkers reject the idea as too narrow and self-centered. However, the main interpretation that has been given to this central biblical doctrine in rabbinic tradition is that "election" means responsibility *not* privilege. Duty not pride. As Deuteronomy encourages: "You shall do the good and the right" (6:18). And with regard to this command I am reminded that it repeats the description for his covenant with Abraham in *Genesis* 18:19, where God says: "I have chosen [Abraham] so that he will direct his children and his household after him to keep the way of the Lord by doing what is right and just."

The "election" of Israel, independent of our individual autonomous choices, assigns a unique and unavoidable ethical and theological charge on those who belong to the nation of Israel. *Exodus* describes the special character of Israel: "you shall be a kingdom of priests and a holy nation" (19:5–6). And *Leviticus* explains this as follows: "the entire community of the people of Israel [shall] be holy for I the Lord your God am holy" (5:2). And at least a large part of what this means is explained when the Bible tells us that "God supreme . . . shows no favor and takes no bribes, but upholds the cause of the fatherless and the widow, and loves the stranger, providing him with food and clothing" (*Deuteronomy* 10:17–18).

Being "chosen" entails high ethical standards and imposes demanding moral goals that have dramatic consequences. In the words of the Prophet Amos: "You only have I known of all the families of the earth, therefore I will punish you for your inequities" (3:2). While Jeremiah exhorts:

> Thus says the Lord: Do justice and righteousness, and deliver from the hand of the oppressor him who has been robbed. And do no wrong or violence to the resident alien, the fatherless, and the widow, nor shed innocent blood in this place. For if you will indeed obey this word, then there shall enter the gates of this house kings who sit on the throne of David, riding in chariots and on horses, they and their servants and their people. But if you will not obey these words, I swear by myself, declares the Lord, that this house shall become a desolation. [*Jeremiah* 22:3–5]

Being Israel requires that, individually and collectively, Jews and the Jewish People pursue the wellbeing of others and social justice. This demand, this obligation, is inescapable. Its inescapability is the core of the essential meaning of being an *am segulah*, of "being elected." This is not a volunteer assignment. In answer to Cain's question: "Am I my brother's keeper?" the answer is emphatically "yes" (*Genesis* 4:9). Thus, the answer Rabbi Akiva once gave to a Roman who asked him: "Why does your God, who is the God of the poor, not feed the poor?" Akiva aptly replied: "So we can escape damnation."

Importantly, this notion of *Arevim Zeh L'Zeh* has strong halakhic, i.e., legal, implications. Consider, for example, besides the more usual daily legal principles governing social and economic justice, the rule, that was so important in premodern times, regarding the absolute responsibility of all Jewish communities to redeem Jews taken as captives and slaves (*pidyon shvuim*). Joseph Karo in his authoritative *Shulchan Aruch* (*Yoreh Deah* 252:1,3), instructs us:

> Redeeming captives takes precedence over sustaining the poor and clothing them, and there is no commandment more important than redeeming captives . . . every moment that one delays redeeming captives where it is possible to do so quickly, one is like a person who sheds blood.

If funds are limited, this requirement has priority over almost all other obligations. A Jewish community is required to help other Jews in distress, even if this means assisting someone unknown to them or from a distant land. And they must do this even when it will disadvantage other pressing local needs.[2]

Let me summarize the relationship that must exist between moral obligations and the halakhic process by citing two great authorities on the requirements that must govern the process of legal decision making. First there are the instructions given by Ramban (Rabbi Moses ben Nachman, the thirteenth century Spanish sage) as a comment on, and explanation of, the verse in *Deuteronomy* 6:18 "do what is right and good in the sight of the Lord." This "refers," he tells us, "to compromise and conduct beyond the requirements of the law (*lifnim mishurat ha-din*) . . . now God says that, with respect to what He has not [explicitly] commanded, you should take heed to do the right and the good" (*Commentary on the Torah, Deuteronomy* 6:18). This should be understood to mean that the *posek*, the halakhic decisor is enjoined not to decide the cases that come to him according to the standard of the religious elite and the most pious in the community. Rather, he is to rule so that his decision does not impose unnecessarily strict burdens on the mass of the community. And second, and a remark of decisive importance, when Rabbi Haim Brisk (1853–1918) was asked by his students what the primary responsibility of a rabbi was, he replied: "To redress the grievances of those who are abandoned and alone, to protect the dignity of the poor, and to save the oppressed from the hands of the oppressor."[3]

How deep our responsibility for others is can be seen, according to the *Halakha*, in the legal requirement (T.B. *Berakhot*) that even the High Priest, who, as a general rule, is commanded to avoid the dead, must attend to the burial of a corpse on Yom Kippur, if there is no one else to undertake this task. This is known as an act of *hesed shel emet* ("mercy of truth"). The usual, elevated, ritual rules that apply to maintaining the purity of the High Priest are here set aside. The fact that the High Priest is the central actor in the Temple service on Yom Kippur, is of secondary significance. All that matters is our unshakable commitment to our fellowman. "Come and hear," the ancient sages taught, "great is human dignity, since it overrides a negative percept of the Torah" (repeated in T.B. *Menachot* 37B). Furthermore, this norm is a corollary of the still more encompassing halakhic category of *kevod ha' beriot*, the imperative that we be concerned with the intrinsic value of all human beings.

Applying this understanding the sages instructed (in T.B. *Moed Katan*, 27B), that in order to show our common humanity in a final act of concern for others, everyone should be buried in a shroud of the sort that is available to all men and women, so as to not embarrass the poor.

---

2 I would note, for example, that when destitute Jews in the Ottoman Empire were unable to pay the taxes imposed on all Jews by the state, rich Jews paid these taxes so as to prevent their poor brethren being pulled into debt slavery.
3 Joseph Soloveitchik, *Halakhic Man* (Philadelphia, 1983), p. 91.

To grasp a still more complete insight in to the full meaning of *Arevim Zeh L'Zeh* it is also of interest to note that not only halakhists but medieval Jewish philosophers, while highly valuing contemplation, emphasized the priority of moral action as the primary Jewish obligation. Thus, one finds Abraham Ibn Daud, after reflecting on the speculations of philosophers, and works like Aristotle's *Nicomachean Ethics*, observing that: "the reason of all philosophy is proper conduct [vis-à-vis others]" (*ha-Emunah ha-Ramah*, Introduction, p. 4). And his fellow medieval rationalist, Joseph Ibn Tzaddik arguing, in a very Jewish reading of the proper role of philosophy, that philosophy is meant: "to lead one to know the Creator, but the fruit and effect of its teachings is to cause one to emulate according to one's ability the Creator's moral qualities (*Olam Katan*, p. 64). As the Almighty is selflessly concerned with us, we must be selflessly concerned with others.

Maimonides, the greatest of the medieval Jewish thinkers, though he generally adopts Aristotle's view that ethics is to be understood as a precondition for the ultimate human end, the life of contemplation (*Nicomachean Ethics*, book 10, 7–8, 1177A-1179A), demurs from endorsing this hierarchical order when discussing the biblical term *hesed* that means, depending on the context, "love," "kindness," or "loving kindness" (see his *Commentary* on *Peáh* 1:1). In this context he repeatedly makes clear the primary "responsibility Jews have to one another." Consider, as paradigmatic, his instructions regarding the proper behavior relative to festive meals on holidays:

> ... while one eats and drinks himself, it is his duty to feed the stranger, the orphan, the widow, and other poor and unfortunate people, for he who locks the doors to his courtyard and eats and drinks with his wife and family, without giving anything to eat and drink to the poor and the bitter in soul – his meal is not a rejoicing in a divine commandment but rejoicing in his own stomach. Rejoicing of this kind is a disgrace to those who indulge in it, as Scripture says, *And I will spread dung upon your faces, even the dung of your sacrifices.* [*Malachi* 2:3]

Again, he tells us that when instructing a convert to Judaism, the convert's teachers must inform the proselyte "of the transgressions involved in the law of gleanings, forgotten sheaves, the corner of the [*peáh*], and the poor man's tithe [*ma'aser oni*]" (*Issure Biáh*, XIV,2). These are essential rules that bind Jews to each other.

In the *Guide for the Perplexed*, Maimonides insists that acts of *hesed* are not to be done to repay an obligation or in order to acquire indebtedness and future gain. Instead, they are to be done only out of one's sense of responsibility, that is they should be the product of love. Imitating God, we must love other human beings with whom we share the divine image, "*be'tzelem elohim*." As God creates the world and takes a self-imposed duty for it without self-interest, we must do likewise.

Complementarily, there is the challenging ethical idea drawn by the kabbalists from the act of the creation. Just as God, through the act of *tzimtzum*, divine contraction, made space for creation, so we, too, following His example – *v'halachta be'drachav* ("walking in His ways") – need to make room for, and recognize the needs of, others. Moreover, this obligation that demands that we be answerable for the other is asymmetrical, i.e., it does not depend on the reciprocal behavior of the other or their correct or incorrect behavior.[4]

II

It is significant that the Torah commands us to both "love God" – "love the Lord thy God with all thy heart and with all thy soul, and with all thy might" (*Deuteronomy* 6:5) – and to love our fellow human beings. Both require our taking responsibility. Love of heaven is, as the rabbis put it, "manifest through adhering to the rules regarding the rejection of idolatry and acting for the sake of heaven." It is instantiated through the many, most usually ritualistic, acts that occur "*ben Adam le'makom*," between human beings and heaven. And these assuredly make heavy and continuous demands. However, the command to "love our fellowmen" is still more demanding. Loving God, who is perfect, is relatively easy. Alternatively, loving our fellowmen, who are often mean-spirited and miserable, is far more difficult. But this is the law. In following this commandment, we engage the world and attempt to make a positive difference within it. This, of course, is the great challenge: to take responsibility for the other who is not oneself, whose self is decidedly independent and different, yet whose being, as a human being, makes an absolute demand to which one is obligated to respond. "*Arevim Zeh L'Zeh*" means that the other makes me responsible for them.

The concept of "*Arevim*" entails many things. It denotes that we are required to acknowledge the pain of the other, and to be concerned with their suffering, to seek to help them in their despair. Furthermore, it requires that we help them to establish and maintain their self-esteem. To refuse to hear the pained cry of the other is immoral. As Isaiah demanded: "thou seest the naked, that thou cover him; and that thou hide not thyself from thine own flesh" (58:7). The suffering of others irrevocably obligates us. In the words of the Prophet, we are instructed in God's name: "Learn to do good. Seek justice. And vindicate the oppressed. Uphold the rights of the orphan, defend the cause of the widow" (1:17). In T.B. *Ta'anit* we learn that Moses was known to say: "Seeing that the people of Israel suffer, I suffer with them." (Parenthetically, it is relevant to observe that this is said of God by the sages: "I am with them in their suffering.")

---

4 The notion of *Arevim Zeh L'Zeh* is not only central to halakhists, philosophers, and kabbalists. At a still more basic level of Jewish spirituality and religious obligation it needs to be recognized that Jewish prayer is usually framed in the plural, i.e., we pray not, or even primarily, for ourselves, but rather, for the entire "Knesset Yisrael." In addition, the normative organization of prayer involves a *minyan*, a group of ten men, representative of the entire community.

This is not to introduce some comforting theodicy that "explains" suffering. Neither appeals to *yissurin shel ahavah* (affections of love), nor the doctrine of vicarious suffering after *Isaiah* 53, nor theological "explanations" that invoke *Job* or the *Akedah* (binding of Isaac) can provide adequate explanations. In fact, to introduce theodicy is to hide, to seek to avoid, the reality of the too-real suffering. The demand of "*Arevim*" is to be compassionate, not to provide false explanations of why others are in pain. The reality of pain and suffering transcend the false promises of theodicy.

III

In that this lecture is the closing event in a conference on Jewish behavior during the Holocaust it is not inappropriate to add that these ethical and existential considerations, the morality of other-directness and the concern with the welfare of the community, were fully in evidence in the halakhic decisions made by the sages in the ghettos of World War II. In this unprecedented context the *poskim* (decisors) knew their *responsa* must be based on the needs of the inquirer. Their obligation was not only, or even primarily, to get the decision right halakhically – though they always tried very diligently and honorably to do this – but rather to meet the living, pressing, needs of the question-askers. As one sees from the answers they gave to the questions they were asked, it is clear that they gave priority to lightening the burden of their fellow Jews.

Though the *teshuvot*, rabbinic *responsa*, we possess from the war years are relatively few in number, those that have survived indicate a profound awareness of the unprecedented situation that the Jewish People, and the individual questioner were in. Therefore, in their replies, the rabbinic sages of the period took it upon themselves, as best they could, to alleviate the religious burdens the faithful carried by suggesting the most practical and "lenient" course of action possible. Consider the following four *responsa*.

1. The first of these deals with the issue of contraception by Jewish women:

    On 20 Iyar 5702–May 7, 1942–the evildoers issued an edict that if a Jewish woman were found pregnant they would kill her. I was asked whether Jewish women in the ghetto might utilize contraceptives to avoid pregnancy and the concomitant risk of death.
    Response: I ruled that because there was an absolute danger to their lives if the defiling evildoers should discover them pregnant, women might use contraceptive devices before intercourse.

2. The second "response", given by Rabbi Ephraim Oshry in the Kovno Ghetto, involves the possibility of a Jew serving as a cook on the Sabbath:

    I ruled that [the questioner] was allowed to cook on Shabbos, because the alternative of slave labor in the airfield on Shabbos was no less a desecration of the Sabbath than the cooking. In neither case would he be desecrating the Sabbath willfully, but solely out of compulsion. It was therefore preferable that he work in the kitchen [on Shabbos] because there he would get enough food to eat. I allowed him to eat the black soup that he himself would cook on Shabbos because it is not forbidden to eat the product of Shabbos labor where one eats it to preserve life.

3. The third, again the work of Rav Oshry, provided the following ruling about eating on Yom Kippur:

> Jewish laborers came to me in the pre-Yom Kippur days of 5702 – late September 1941 – and asked if they might be permitted to eat the soup since their lives would ultimately be endangered if they did not eat it.
> **Response**: Medical experts maintained that it was impossible for the person to survive with the nutrition then available to the Jews. The laborers' lives were certainly in danger; famine is an extremely agonizing, drawn-out way to die. I ruled that they might eat the soup now because of the eventual danger to their lives. The rabbi of Kovno, the *gaon* Rav Avrohom DovBer Shapira, concurred with me.

4. Finally, we have the following, interesting, *teshuva* from Rabbi Katriel Tchorsh, writing in Tel Aviv *after* the end of the war, that deals with our responsibility to the dead in the "world above":

> **Question:** Is one who had not relatives who perished in the Holocaust also obligated to say Kaddish for the martyrs, or should one say Kaddish only if he had relatives who perished?
> **Response:** Obviously it is understood that just as each individual is obligated to join with the community and share the grief, so also is each individual obligated to do something for the spirits and souls of the departed. We find that the Kaddish has great importance, and we are obligated to [say] it for parents and relatives (Sh. AR. YD 376:4, according to the Rema). So also, is every person obligated to add to the purity of the many souls of the entire house of Israel.

This last ruling, linked to the essential concept of caring for the dead, among which one finds the obligation to say *Kaddish*, is based on the general obligation to perform acts of kindness. R. Tchorsh cites as his authority R. Moses Isserles (the *Rema*, sixteenth-century Kraków), but he also certainly knew the ruling of Maimonides [MT *Evel* 14:1]) who wrote:

It is a positive rabbinical precept to visit the sick, to console mourners, to accompany the corpse, etc. It is true kindness that we practice with the dead, for there is not selfish calculation of accepting anything from the dead in exchange, and we do it only for the sake of the obligation to practice kindness. This is sufficient to establish the significance and precious value of saying the Kaddish even for the deceased person who is not a family relative. Therefore, it is clear to us that no Jew anywhere should refrain from practicing kindness to the dead, and it is each Jew's duty to join in saying Kaddish in memory of the dead and for the elevation of their soul.

This is a maximal representation of the principle "*Kol Yisrael Arevim*." One's obligation extends to Jews who have died no less than to Jews with whom one lives.

IV

Beyond the ethical demands of caring and the responsibility that we bear to those who suffer and are in need, the principle of *Arevim* – that I will here translate as "those we have responsibility for" – in addition, raises the crucial issue of *justice*. "*Kol Yisrael*," "All Israel," carries the communal implication that we must create a just society in which the rights of all are guaranteed and protected. Our obligation requires that the laws, practices, and institutions of Jewish society be equitable and "blind." "You shall not recognize persons in justice" (*Deuteronomy* 16:19). Accordingly, Moses instructs Israel, as they were about to enter the Land of Israel: "Judges and officials you shall appoint for yourself in your cities. They shall rule the people with just justice, justice shall you pursue." Indeed, this is the required precondition of Israelite society in the land of Israel. It is only on the basis of creating a just society that, as the Torah teaches: "you may occupy the land that the Lord is giving you" (*Deuteronomy* 16:20). The concept of the "holiness" (*kedushah*) of the Land of Israel is inseparable from justice. Hence, Isaiah insists that: "The Holy God is sanctified through justice" (*Mikdash be' Bedakah* 5:16).

This entails creating state institutions that have as their purpose the protection of the rights of everyone in the society. These institutions must embody the values of altruistic responsibility and respect the dignity of all those who appeal to them. They must limit violence and coercion, delimit and constrain the preferences of the strong and rich, and ensure that Jewish society protects and is fair to every member of the community. Injustice represents the manifest failure to honor the principle of "*Kol Yisrael Arevim*." As we read of Solomon in *I Kings* 3:28: "All Israel heard the judgment that the King rendered. They saw that the wisdom of God was within him, to do justice," "*La-asot mishpat*." And to guarantee this outcome the King, like all state institutions, must be subordinate to the law, and is to be judged by its statutes and ordinances.

V

To conclude, I would like to call to attention a few of the many consequential examples of *Kol Israel Arevim* that took place during the Holocaust. I would begin by recalling the existence of "self-help efforts": the creation of orphanages, hospitals and schools; the special collections for children; and the communal support of the elderly. Almost everyone was starving in the ghettos, yet the community organized itself to share the little that it had.

Second, I would remind everyone of the intense debates that went on between the heads of the *Judenräte* and the leaders of the underground and resistance movements in various locations, during which the *Judenräte* members warned the primarily young resistance fighters that their actions could bring reprisals to those who remained behind in the ghettos. And this argument often succeeded in dissuading those who wanted to flee the ghetto, in spite of the personal consequences this had for them. This exact circumstance is described in the *Pinkas Shavli* (the records of the Shavli Ghetto). On February 5, 1943, a meeting was held between the Jewish underground and the ghetto leaders to discuss ghetto-wide armed resistance. In the course of this meeting it became clear that the plan to escape, that involved flight to the Soviet partisans operating in the not-too-distant marshlands of northern Lithuania, would mean leaving the women, children, and the elderly who remained in the ghetto completely exposed and vulnerable. In consequence, the majority of the young Jews present, moved by this appeal to "*Kol Yisrael Arevim*," decided that they could not so endanger the other ghetto residents and so the plan was abandoned.[5]

Similar debates went on in other ghettos as well. In Vilna Zelig Kalmanovich, one of the intellectual leaders of the community, wrote: "The attempt to arm is the result of irresponsibility."[6] And in this he was supported by the head of the ghetto, Jacob Gens. As a result, though there was an organized resistance, no revolt broke out inside the ghetto. And this same moral confrontation took place in the Silesian ghettos of Będzin and Sosnowiec headed by Moshe Merin, as well as in Lwów and in Bielorussia. Regarding the outcome of these tense life and death dialogues Shalom Cholawsky reports that: "Collective responsibility was the chief constraint to Jewish resistance in the ghettos."[7]

Third, one needs to remember the heroic actions of the Kovno Ghetto Jewish Police. The Nazis arrested the entire Jewish Police force on March 27, 1944 and tortured its members to get them to reveal the hiding places of Jews in the ghetto, but none of the policemen betrayed their fellow Jews. Here the responsibility of *Kol Yisrael Arevim* was taken with ultimate seriousness which resulted in all of these policemen – including the head of the Police, Moshe

---

5 Eliezer Yerushalmi (ed.), *Pinkas Shavli* (Jerusalem, 1958), p. 315.
6 Zelig Kalmanovich, "A Diary of the Nazi Ghetto in Vilna," *YIVO Annual*, vol. 8 (1953), pp. 9–81.
7 Shalom Cholawsky, *The Jews of Bielorussia during World War II* (Amsterdam, 1998), p. 136.

Levin and his lieutenants Yehuda Supovitz and Itka Grinberg – being killed in the Ninth Fort.

Of course, such moral courage and faithful solidarity on behalf of their fellow Jews was not always the rule for Jewish Ghetto Police. In Warsaw, for example, relations between the ghetto police and the resistance movement were bad. And, so, too, in the Łódź Ghetto. In these, and comparable contexts, one understands that the profound desire to live encouraged immoral actions, like those perpetuated by the ghetto police in Warsaw and Łódź. To honor the principle of selfless ethical action in the midst of the Holocaust called for exceptional moral integrity. Yet, remarkably, one finds numerous instances of dedication unto death. The principle of *Kol Israel Arevim* was neither altogether absent nor devoid of influence during the Holocaust, and we should not allow it to go unnoticed.

Fourth, it is incumbent on us not to forget the acts of Jewish leaders like Itzhak Wittenberg, head of the Communist underground forces in Vilna, who committed suicide when the Nazis required that he hand himself over and promised the destruction of the entire ghetto if he did not meet their demand. Wittenberg could have tried to find safety, or fled, but he understood how perilous this would be for the ghetto community. His private interests were sacrificed out of his profound sense of responsibility for the protection of the remaining Jews of Vilna.[8] And this concern with protecting the Vilna Ghetto community arose a second time when Jacob Gens, the head of the Jewish Council, was ordered on September 14, 1943 to report to the Gestapo headquarters. Though he was warned what awaited him if he came as ordered, he delivered himself to the police fearing a reprisal against the ghetto if he did not appear. Gens was shot at 6:00 p.m. the same day.

Fifth, we cannot fail to mention the extraordinary behavior of Janusz Korczak, the author of widely read children's books, and the unbreakable bond that he had with the children he looked after in an orphanage that he headed in the Warsaw Ghetto. All he was concerned with was their welfare, even choosing to go with them to their annihilation rather than allow himself to be smuggled to safety. He would not compromise his boundless concern for them out of self-interest, though he was encouraged to do so by the Polish Underground. He submitted to the merciless Nazi demands without attempting any evasion, because of his fidelity to his wards.

Then there was the exceptional heroism of doctors and nurses in the many ghettos located throughout Nazi-occupied Europe. Dr. Adina Szwajger-Blady gave the

---

8 Discussed in N. N. Shneidman, *Jerusalem of Lithuania: The Rise and Fall of Jewish Vilnius: A Personal Perspective* (Oakville, 1998), pp. 440–41. See also Eric Sterling, "The Ultimate Sacrifice: The Death of Resistance Hero Yitzhak Wittenberg and the Decline of the United Partisan Organization," in *Resisting the Holocaust*, ed. Ruby Rohrlich (Oxford, 1998), pp. 59–76; and Zila Rosenberg-Amit, *Not to Lose the Human Face* (Tel Aviv, 1990), pp. 46–49 [Hebrew].

following testimony regarding what occurred during the final phase of the liquidation of the Warsaw Ghetto. At this point in time, early 1943, the hospitals were being cleared and their patients, including sick children, were being rounded up and sent to Treblinka. Responding to this circumstance, she took ultimate responsibility for those in her care:

> I asked Mira what we should do, and she said: "Help them, surely." So we helped them, too. And by the window there was this woman, swollen from starvation and suffering from circulatory insufficiency, and she kept looking at us pleading with her eyes. She was the last one we gave an injection to . . . So when I left the room, I held out my hand and got two large containers of morphine. We didn't say a word to each other, just squeezed each other's hand, I think. I took the morphine upstairs. Dr. Margolis was there, and I told her what I wanted to do. So, we took a spoon and went to the infants room. And just as, during those two years of real work in the hospital, I bent over the little beds, so now I poured this last medicine in those tiny mouths. Only Dr. Margolis was with me. And downstairs there was screaming because the Szaulis and the Germans were already there, taking the sick from the wards to the cattle trucks. After that we went to the older children and told them that this medicine was going to make their pain disappear. They believed us and drank the required amount from the glass. And then I told them to undress, get into bed and sleep. So they lay down and after a few minutes – I do not know how many – but the next time I went into the room, they were asleep. And then I don't know what happened after that.[9]

VI Conclusion

The *Shoah* tested the claims of *Kol Yisrael Arevim Zeh L'Zeh* more profoundly than any prior event or experience in Jewish history. In the ghettos, forced labor camps, and death camps Jews were called upon to live up to the demands of covenantal responsibility, the idea of "love of neighbor," and the implications of "election." Not surprisingly, these ethical claims were not always met. There were, in spite of the normative precepts that everyone knew to exist, uncountable acts of selfishness, repeated manifestations of cruel indifference, both small and large instances of rancid corruption. The Jewish Councils were, in certain times and places, less than perfect. The Jewish Police, in the many ghettos, often took

---

[9] Adina Szwajger-Blady, *I Remember Nothing More: The Warsaw Children's Hospital and the Jewish Resistance* (New York, 1992), pp. 52–57.

advantage of their positions to protect themselves and their own. There were Jewish informers and *kapos*. And all too many Jews and Jewish communities were passive while all sorts of Jewish individuals, at all levels of wealth, influence, and power, took unfair advantage of their neighbors. But these severe and significant failures notwithstanding, and in no way diminishing their relevance, I am still inclined to judge that the majority of Jewish communities of Europe generally acted with courage, dignity, and an abiding sense of obligation that flowed from their instinctive sense of *Kol Yisrael Arevim Zeh L'Zeh.*

UPDATE

This essay was originally delivered on December 18, 2014, as the closing lecture at a conference entitled "All of Israel are Responsible for One Another," held in Jerusalem at Yad Vashem, the Israel Holocaust Museum. It has not been previously published but will be included in the forthcoming conference volume. Since its presentation in Jerusalem I have not encountered any new literature that would require me to alter the views I expressed in 2014. This is not surprising as almost all of the sources I drew on in my lecture were taken from the classical canon of rabbinic literature, and this has not changed, nor has our reading of it. Accordingly, there is no need to "update" the essay.

12

THINKING ABOUT JEWISH RESISTANCE DURING THE HOLOCAUST

I

Of all the sensitive and difficult subjects related to the Jewish side of the *Shoah* one, in particular, is of exceptional significance: the highly controversial, issue of Jewish resistance during the war. This subject, though much discussed, is, in actuality, little understood, much distorted, and widely misrepresented. Therefore, it needs to be re-examined and the relevant material and evidence correctly – and fairly – set out. In this essay I will attempt to begin to do just this based on the authentic historical record.

In the course of my analysis in this essay I will not discuss, in detail or at any length, particular occasions of resistance, e.g., the Warsaw Ghetto Uprising, or the resistance in Białystok, or Jewish partisan activity, or the uprisings at the death camps, though I will briefly summarize these phenomena in the last section of this essay. Rather, drawing primarily on the original sources of the war years, written by those who were caught up in this unprecedented catastrophe, I will try to explore, as a first step in revising our understanding of this crucial matter, what one needs to know, what topics must be taken into account, in order to engage in a serious and legitimate discussion of this complex topic.

II

To begin to enter into a serious, meaningful, conversation of our subject we must start by recalling a number of basic facts about the changing context and unfolding chronology.

As to context, I begin with the response of German Jewry to Hitler's accession to power in 1933. Almost immediately German Jewry organized itself and tried to resist the new order in essential ways. Between 1933 and 1938, individuals like Martin Buber and Leo Baeck organized a wide program of spiritual resistance. In September 1935, in the shadow of the Nuremberg laws, Rabbi Baeck, the head of the German-Jewish community, rejecting collective inaction, formulated a prayer to be read in all synagogues that encouraged Jews to remember who they were.[1] The prayer spoke of Jewish history as a "history of spiritual greatness and spiritual dignity."[2] Martin Buber, who became the director of the Adult Jewish Education Center created in 1933 by the *Reichsvertretung der Deutschen Juden* (The Reich Representation of German Jews), described his task as "shap[ing] a society that can hold fast, overcome, and preserve the spark [of Jewishness]."[3] And, on the level of daily life, the community created schools, soup kitchens, medical organizations, and social services. At the same time, Orthodox religious groups organized religious services, continued to teach Torah, and carried on with the practice of *shechitah* (kosher slaughtering) at great risk, as all of these things were forbidden by the Third Reich.

There was also a large emigration of Jews from Germany, beginning in 1933, and then from Austria after the *Anschluss* (the 1938 annexation). Of the total of 700,000 Jews resident in these two countries, 410,000 managed to emigrate. By 1941, 300,000 German Jews had left the country. About 60,000 individuals in this cohort, due to the increased activity of the various Zionist organizations in Germany, went to Palestine before Britain closed the doors to the country.[4] And 10,000 Jewish children found safety in Britain as a result of the *Kindertransport* program. By 1939, 83 percent of Jews under 24 years had left Germany. Of those who remained in the country after 1939, about 10,000 Jews tried to save themselves, in the midst of Nazi society, by finding hiding places.[5] Of these, 5,000 who found refuge in Berlin came to be known as "U-boats" (submarines).[6] Of these

---

1 "Prayer composed by Rabbi Leo Baeck for all Jewish communities in Germany for the eve of the Day of Atonement, October 10, 1935, in Yitzhak Arad, Israel Gutman, and Abraham Margaliot, trans. Lea Ben Dor, *Documents on the Holocaust: Selected Sources on the Destruction of the Jews of Germany and Austria, Poland, and the Soviet Union* (Lincoln, NE, 1999), pp. 87–88. I wrote the new Introduction to this volume.

2 Raul Hilberg, *The Destruction of the European Jews*, 3rd ed., 3 vols. (New Haven, CT, 2003), vol. 3, p. 1031.

3 Yitzchak Mais, David Engel, and Eva Fogelman (eds.), *Daring to Resist: Jewish Defiance in the Holocaust* (New York, 2007), p. 12.

4 Jeffrey Herf, *The Jewish Enemy: Nazi Propaganda During World War II and the Holocaust* (Cambridge, MA, 2006) puts the figure for total emigration of German Jews to Mandate Palestine at 60,000 between 1933 and 1939 (p. 74); and see also Hagit Lavsky, "German Jewish Interwar Migration in a Comparative Perspective: Mandatory Palestine, the United States, and Great Britain," in *Ethnicity and Beyond, Theories and Dilemmas of Jewish Group Demarcation*, ed. Eli Lederhendler (New York, 2011), especially Table 6, p. 122, "Jewish Emigration from Nazi Germany to Palestine, 1933–1941." It puts the number in 1941 at 53,200.

5 Marion Kaplan, *Between Dignity and Despair: Jewish Life in Nazi Germany* (New York, 2008), p. 203. She cites a figure "between 10,000 and 12,000." Jürgen Matthäus, "Evading Persecution," in *Jewish Life in Nazi Germany: Dilemmas and Responses*, eds. Francis R. Nicosia and David Scarse (New York, 2010), p. 48, mentions that "an estimated 10,000 Jews in Germany and Austria had taken the illegal route, but most of them did not survive."

6 Eric Johnson and Karl Heinz-Reuband, *What We Knew: Mass Murder and Everyday Life in Nazi Germany, An Oral History* (Cambridge, MA, 2005), p. 336: "Although most Jews who went underground did not survive in the end, many did. In Berlin alone, about fourteen-hundred of the

10,000 Jews, some 3,000 survived the war.[7] As late as February 1942, 50 Jewish scouts, boys and girls, celebrated *Tu B'Shvat*,[8] while a year later, in 1943–44, the *Chug Chalutzi*, the Zionist circle, was still actively organizing hiding places for young Jews in Berlin, and smuggling other Jews to Switzerland.[9] German and Austrian Jews were hardly passive in their own defense after Hitler became Chancellor in 1933.

Parenthetically, but not irrelevant, it is also to be remembered that not only German and Austrian Jews left their homes to find refuge. In this connection one needs to take account of:

- the 300,000 Polish Jews who fled to the Soviet Union;
- the 40,000 Jews came to the U.S. in 1930s – despite severe difficulties in receiving visas;
- the 40,000 French Jews who crossed into Spain and Switzerland and, who, in addition, saved 12,000 Jewish children through the OSE network;
- the 1,600 Dutch Jews who escaped to Britain; and the Norwegian and Danish Jews who found refuge in Sweden during the war.

The oft-repeated claim that European Jews did little or nothing to save themselves is, as this data reveals, simply false. It is true that they could have done more, but why they did not – or why many of their efforts were unsuccessful, which is a separate subject – is a complicated matter that I will try to explain as this essay proceeds.

At this juncture, i.e., at the start of our analysis, it is necessary, prior to anything else, to explore the meaning of "resistance" in this specific context and the particular criteria by which it is to be established. Now, before proceeding to an analysis of the complicated story of Jewish resistance during the war years (1939–45), it is necessary to take note of certain facts.

(1A) First of all, one must be clear about what one is measuring: that is, is one judging effort or outcome. Being unsuccessful is not the equivalent of an absence of effort. Failure is not the equivalent of passivity. For example, in Riga there was an active underground group that was planning armed resistance but before they could act they were betrayed. Likewise, the resistance movement in the infamous

---

estimated five thousand Jews who went underground were still alive when the war ended . . . For the entire Reich, an estimated ten to fifteen thousand Jews went underground, of whom between three and five thousand survived." Discussed also by Walter Laqueur, *Geboren in Deutschland: Der Exodus der jüdischen Jugend nach 1933* (Munich, 2000), p. 79.

7 Using Kaplan's estimate of a 25 percent survival rate would put the number of survivors in the region of 2,500–3,000.
8 Yitzchak Mais, et al. (eds.), *Daring to Resist, Jewish Resistance in the Holocaust* (New York, 2007), p. 33.
9 Chana Schütz, "In Spite of Everything: Zionists in Berlin," in *Jews in Nazi Berlin: From Kristallnacht to Liberation*, eds. Chana Schütz, Beate Meyer, and Hermann Simon (Chicago, 2009), pp. 122–43.

Janowska Road camp outside Lvov was informed on before it could act. And there were failures in execution – not intent and organization – in the Vilna, Białystok, Baranowicze, and Stolin ghettos. In all these locations there was a genuine attempt to create a meaningful resistance to Nazi rule, but all of these undertakings failed.

(1B) Raul Hilberg concluded, based only on outcomes, that, "measured in German casualties Jewish armed resistance shrinks into insignificance."[10] But, given the existing military circumstances, this is to use the wrong criteria. Which is to say, that one needs to decide, when making such judgments, whether the criteria for evaluation include only matters like:

i. the number of Nazis killed;
ii. or alternatively, the number of Jews saved; Tuvia Bielski, who saved 1200 Jews in Byelorussia said: "If I had the choice of killing dozens of Germans or saving one Jew, I would save the Jew";[11]
iii. and do we weigh in only the strictly military significance of an action or must one also take into account the non-military impact and meaning of an action?
iv. then, too, do we only credit as significant physical resistance or, given the singular situation of the Jews in the universe of the Third Reich, must we also acknowledge, and give adequate recognition to, acts of non-physical (spiritual) resistance?
v. and if we do, how do we evaluate their meaning?
vi. and does the intention of the action matter? An Auschwitz survivor testified after the war: "Oppression as violent as that under which we lived provoked resistance. Our entire existence in the camp was marked by it. When laborers at the spinning wheels dared to slacken their working pace . . . when we . . . passed letters from one camp to another . . . it was resistance."[12]

(1C) Third, whatever standard one employs to evaluate the matter of resistance, it must be remembered that the victory against the occupier almost always comes about because of major outside intervention. In World War II, it resulted from the military success of the U.S. and its Allies; in World War I, it came about from the Allied victory over Germany, Austro-Hungary and Turkey (a fact relevant and relative to the Armenian massacres); in 1994 it was outside intervention in Rwanda that brought about the end of the Hutu killings of the Tutsis; in the Sudan it was the consequence of action by the United Nations; in Yugoslavia success came as a result of the actions of an international consortium; and in Cambodia the terror of the Khmer Rouge came only to an end as a consequence of the successful

---

10 Raul Hilberg,, *The Destruction of the European Jews*, vol. 3, p. 1031.
11 Moshe Barach, *Attestation – In the Ghettos and Forests of Byelorussia* (Tel-Aviv, 1981), p. 172 [Hebrew].
12 Terrence des Pres, *The Survivor: An Anatomy of Life in the Death Camps* (New York, 1977), p. 125.

invasion of the Vietnamese military. Thus, to take the measure of internal forms of resistance, to judge their success and meaning, requires the correct, realistic perspective.

(1D) Beyond matters of definition, at least eleven other structural factors need to be recognized as influencing the possibility and reality of Jewish resistance. The most basic of these elements was the degree of Nazi control in a given territory. This varied from country to country within occupied Europe and directly affected the situation of both Jews and non-Jews – and the degree to which resistance could be organized. What was possible in Denmark was not possible in Ukraine or Lithuania.

(2) In addition, one must to take into account the significance of geography. Did the terrain in and around a locale provide places to escape to and to hide in? For instance, there were nearby forests in Minsk and Kovno, but no natural safe havens in Warsaw or Vilna, where the ghettos were situated in the center of each city. Because of the landscape, flight was more possible in Belorussia or the western Ukraine than in Łódź, Lublin or Budapest. In Eastern Volhynia, 3,000 Jews from the Tuczyn Ghetto fled to the forest, and 2,000 survived. Altogether, approximately 50,000 Jews fled to the forest of Western Belorussia and about 8,000 survived until the end of the war.[13] Likewise, in Western Europe, interpreting the concept of geography more broadly, Jews who lived in occupied countries that bordered Switzerland and/or Spain had a better chance of escape and many undertook such difficult journeys, often on foot.

(3) Nor should we forget that it takes time to organize, plan and execute resistance. But most of the ghettos were created in late 1940 and 1941, in a period before the "Final Solution" had been agreed upon, and then, quite soon after, were liquidated in 1942 and early 1943. In the captured parts of the Soviet Union, many ghettos only existed for a few months.

(4) The course of the war significantly affected non-Jewish resistance. Thus, most non-Jewish resistance in France, Poland, Slovakia, and Yugoslavia only appeared in 1943 and 1944, after El Alamein in the Fall of 1942, the major defeat at Stalingrad in the winter of 1942–43, and the advances of Allied troops in North Africa and Eastern Europe. And the major uprising in Poland came only in 1944 when German forces were in retreat. Jews in the ghettos, work camps, and death camps, however, were not able to take advantage of these developments in the same way as non-Jewish resistance movements. Thus, one must be careful not to judge what Jews did and did not do by comparison to the behavior of the other national resistance movements.

(5) Non-Jewish resistance efforts had outside help from groups and governments. Jewish resistance groups had essentially no outside help from any quarter.

(6) Contrary to widely circulated and passionately believed claims of organized Jewish international conspiracies, the reality was that the 9,000,000 Jews

---

13 Shlomo Spector, "The Mass Flights and Jewish Resistance," in *Major Changes within the Jewish People in the Wake of the Holocaust*, ed. Israel Gutman (Jerusalem, 1996), p. 376.

in Europe were deeply divided by nationality, class, education, politics, religion, and language. No effective centralized, international Jewish leadership existed. The Jewish community across the European continent, in its totality, had no common goals or agenda. Bundists and Communists linked their future with the larger non-Jewish society, though the Bund was created to take into account the special punishing situation of the Jews in Eastern European societies. Zionists rejected all the possible changes proposed to improve the Jewish situation within European states as not being viable, long-term solutions to the problems of both Jews and Judaism. Reform Jews had discarded the claim that Jews were a nation, and pursued a policy that was dictated by an ideology that asserted that Jews were German and Austrian citizens of "mosaic persuasion." As to the solution of the "Judenfrage," much of the Jewish proletariat sought to migrate to Britain and, in much greater numbers, to America and other locations in the Western hemisphere. And still other Jews, if in relatively small numbers, advocated and pursued conversion to Christianity, while an ever increasing number endorsed assimilation. These substantive divisions continued to exist during the war years and in the ghettos. Thus, in the Warsaw Ghetto, the Revisionist Zionists, Betar, refused to join the Communist leftist resistance movement until late in the war. In the Białystok Ghetto the community was fractured by the division between Revisionists, Zionists, Communists, and Bundists.[14] Accordingly, it was only in the last period of the history of the Białystok Ghetto that a united resistance that included the Zionists, Communists, and Bundists was created. Similarly, Herman Kruk, a leader of the Bund in Vilna, recorded in his diary on June 12, 1943:

> If not for the specific tragic situation in which the ghetto finds itself, none of our group would have agreed to cooperate with the Revisionists, Shomrim [Zionists] and Comm[unists]. Not wanting to remain isolated, we, too, were forced to join the FPO (United Partisan Organization). Naturally, the Reds took over the institution. They harnessed the partners in the supposed organized self-defense while turning it into a fortress of their own. Having no alternative, our group swallowed all that.[15]

Conversely, Orthodox Jews, led by the *Agudat Yisrael* party, generally did *not* join armed resistance in any of the ghettos. Some Hasidim and Haredim (ultra-Orthodox) even saw active physical resistance as a sinful reaction to the *Shoah* which they interpreted as just Divine punishment that required *zaddik ha-Din* (acknowledgment of Divine justice).[16]

(7) It needs also to be appreciated that it was difficult to be a resister. In contradistinction to what one had been taught throughout one's entire life, one was now

---

14 See David Wdowinski, *And We Are Not Saved* (New York, 1963), pp. 79–80
15 Herman Kruk, *The Last Days of the Jerusalem of Lithuania: Chronicles from the Vilna Ghetto and the Camps, 1939–1944*, ed. Benjamin Harshav (New Haven, CT, 2002), p. 561.
16 See the ultra-Orthodox sources translated in Steven Katz et al. (eds.), *Wrestling with God: Jewish Theological Responses During and After the Holocaust* (New York, 2007), Part I.

encouraged to participate in illegal activity, and join in acts of theft, fraud, and even murder. Moreover, resistance, however noble as an ideal, was not widely supported by either Jews or non-Jews because of the fear of reprisals.

(8) In thinking about Jewish resistance one has to constantly and accurately keep in mind, and to triangulate it with, the evolution of the formulation of the *Endlösung* ("Final Solution"). It must be understood that in the first two years of the war, 1939–41, there was, in spite of the mistaken claims of distinguished scholars like Lucy Dawidowicz, no genocidal policy in force against the Jews.[17] Therefore, we cannot fault Jews for not being aware of, and failing to respond to such a policy. Until late 1941 to early 1942, even the Nazi leadership was not agreed on what to do with the Jews. There were important divisions at the highest levels of the Third Reich on this topic, e.g., between Himmler and the senior SS and the Army High Command. Today we look back at this history with a full awareness of what was to happen. As this extraordinarily difficult circumstance was actually lived, things were more ambiguous and uncertain. Against the widespread view that Hitler had already advocated for the total extermination of European Jewry in *Mein Kampf* (1923), the facts of the matter are otherwise. It was only in connection with the invasion of Russia in late 1941 and subsequently, when the first mass killing operations of the *Einsatzgruppen* took place in the East, that the decision on the total extermination of European Jewry was taken. This means that the Jews of Poland, Lithuania, and Latvia, who had been ghettoized beginning in early 1940 – the first ghetto having been created in Łódź in April 1940 – did not know, and could not foresee that a policy of total annihilation was to become the operational blueprint for Nazi anti-Jewish actions. I will return to the consequences of this fact below.

(9) Even as late as 1943 there was a disbelief in the official circles of the free world that the Hitler state had decided to annihilate all the Jews in the territories under their control. For example, Jan Karski, the representative of the Polish underground, came to Washington to bring news of the murder of the Jewish People. He was met with skepticism in many quarters. When he told Felix Frankfurter in Washington about Auschwitz, Frankfurter replied: "I do not deny what you say but I cannot believe it."[18] In consequence, what might have been done to assist with Jewish resistance was not done.

---

17 Lucy Dawidowicz, "The Jews in Hitler's Mental World," in her *The War Against the Jews, 1939–1945* (New York, 1975; reprinted New York, 1986), pp. 3–22
18 Roger Moorehouse, *Berlin at War* (New York, 2010), describes the encounter:

> The same phenomenon was witnessed when the Polish underground courier Jan Karski travelled to Washington, D.C., in the summer of 1943, to present his evidence of the Holocaust to a group of American Jewish leaders. After he finished his testimony – which included his own eyewitness account of life in the Warsaw Ghetto and the murders taking place at the Izbica transit camp – Karski was addressed by Justice Felix Frankfurter of the America Supreme Court: "Mr. Karski, he said, "I am unable to believe you." When a Polish diplomat then interjected and asked whether Mr. Frankfurter was calling Mr. Karski a liar, Justice Frankfurter clarified his response, replying: I did not say this young man is lying. I said I am unable to believe him. There is a difference." (p. 175)

(10) The Catholic Church in Poland and Eastern Europe as well as the Orthodox Church in Russia were all decidedly unsympathetic to Jews. And the question of Pius XII and the Vatican is still a subject of intense debate.

(11) Lastly, it must be remembered that Jewish relations with non-Jews in almost all local areas were invariably bad. Indeed local reactions were often, if not usually hostile. In consequence, Jewish resisters and resistance fighters got little, if any, support from their neighbors. Consider the following country by country circumstances:

(A) **Poland**. There was no significant support for Jewish resistance activities provided by Polish society at large, or individual Polish resistance groups, especially the largest of them the Home Army (AK, *Armia Krajowa*). Even before and during the Warsaw Ghetto Uprising (the first such uprising in Nazi-occupied Europe) little in the way of help and arms were provided to the Jewish underground. I would add that the "official" AK's underground press *never once*, throughout the entire course of the war, asked Poles to help Jewish partisans.[19] As decisive evidence of this hostility one recalls, in particular, the horrific events of July 10, 1941 in Jedwabne where Poles, without Nazi assistance, murdered the 1,600 Jews who lived in the town.[20] And this was *not* an isolated case.[21] There were similar murders of this kind throughout Poland. Antisemitism, with heroic exceptions,[22] was the norm in wartime Poland.[23] So we find that the *Armia Krajowa* did not accept Jews into its units, and some AK units actively hunted and killed Jews who were in hiding.[24] In

---

19 This attitude also manifest itself during and after the Warsaw Ghetto Uprising. See Simha Rotem, *Memoirs of a Warsaw Ghetto Fighter* (New Haven, CT, 1994).
20 Jan Gross, *Neighbors: The Destruction of the Jewish Community of Jedwabne, Poland* (Princeton, 2001).
21 According to the Institute of National Remembrance Commission for the Prosecution of Crimes Against the Polish Nation, established by the Polish government in December 1998, there were, in total, 23 villages, aside from Jedwabne, where the local populations killed their Jewish neighbors.
22 This is most definitely indicated by the number of Polish men and women who have been honored as "Righteous Among the Nations" by Yad Vashem. Poland has the highest number of such individuals. Many of the Righteous were individuals but some belonged to Żegota, the Polish Council to Aid Jews affiliated with the Polish Underground State, that was active between 1942 and 1945 in German-occupied Poland. A sympathetic description of Żegota's activity has been recently set out in Bartosz Heksel and Katarzyna Kocik, *Code Name Żegota: The Hidden Aid* (Kraków, 2017).
23 One must, in fairness, note that the Nazis imposed the death penalty on Poles who in any way assisted Jews. We have a number of examples where the Nazis acted on this principle.
24 See Shmuel Krakowski, *The War of the Doomed: Jewish Armed Resistance in Poland, 1942–1944*, trans. Orah Blaustein (New York, 1984), originally published in Hebrew as *Lehimah Yehudit be-Folinneged ha-Natsim, 1942–1944* (Jerusalem, 1977). More recent discussions of Jewish-Polish relations during the war include three important books by Jan Grabowski: *The Polish Police: Collaboration in the Holocaust* (Washington, D.C., 2017); *Hunt for the Jews: Betrayal and Murder in German Occupied Poland* (Bloomington, 2011); *Rescue for Money: Paid Helpers in Poland: 1939–1945* (Jerusalem, 2008); and his collaborative study, written with Barbara Engelking and Dariusz Libionka, *Dalej jest noc: Losy Żydów w wybranych powiatach okupowanej Polski*, 2 vols. (Warsaw, 2018), soon to be published in an abbreviated English version by the USHMM as *Next is the Night: Fate of Jews in Selected Counties in Occupied Poland*.

1943 the AK issued an order to kill "Jewish bandits" who were said to be robbing food from Poles.[25]

(B) **Ukraine.** In the Ukraine, nationalist groups were violently anti-Jewish and frequently Ukrainians rounded up and killed Jews. In consequence, we are not surprised to learn that Ulas Samchuk, editor of the newspaper *Volhyn*, who was fully aware of the mass murder of the Jews that was being carried out by the *Einsatzgruppen* and Order Police with the help of many Ukrainians, wrote: "The element that has settled in our cities, whether it is Jews or Poles who were brought here from outside the Ukraine, must disappear completely from our cities."[26] And Jews did disappear. Almost all the Jews in the Western Ukraine, and most of the Jews in the Eastern Ukraine were extirpated, often with the assistance of local police and militia units.

(C) **Lithuania, Latvia, and Estonia.** In these Baltic States, the local populations were fervently antisemitic, and assisted in the murder of the resident Jewish populations. In Lithuania, *before* the arrival of the *kommando* units of *Einsatzgruppe A* in late June and early July 1941, pogroms had already been initiated by native Lithuanian groups. According to reliable testimonies, pogroms occurred in at least forty locations. In Latvia, a nationalist unit, known as the Arajs Kommando, named after its leader Viktor Arajs, that numbered about 500 men, played a major role in killing the Jews of Riga in the Bikernieki forest outside the city, as well as in the provincial areas of the county. It is estimated that as many as 30,000 Jews were killed by these *Kommandos*. In addition, many local police units joined the killing of Jews, and over 2,000 Latvians served with the Nazi S.D. (Security Service) in anti-Jewish actions.

(D) **Romania, Hungary, and Slovakia.** Here, the local governments were official allies of the Third Reich, and the local populations supported the pro-German policy of their governments. In Romania (until 1943) and Slovakia these policies were essentially exterminationist in design. In Hungary the demand to kill Jews came from Berlin and was organized by Adolf Eichmann after his arrival in Budapest. At the same time, however, Eichmann only brought a small number of Germans with him, in March 1944, and depended on the assistance of Hungarian police – with the support of the new national government that came into office on March 22 1944 – to carry out the last great cataclysm of the Holocaust.

(E) **Russia.** Stalin was indifferent to the fate of the Jews being murdered by the *Einsatzgruppen*. In thirty-three public speeches that he gave during the war he mentioned the Jews only once, and then it was to play down their situation and to play up the fact that the Slavic people were the true targets of Nazi murders. More generally, the murder of Jews as Jews was almost never mentioned in Soviet state reports. Accordingly, one finds that an editorial and

---

25 *Rescue Attempts During the Holocaust: Proceedings of the Second Yad Vashem International Historical Conference*, eds. Israel Gutman, and Efraim Zuroff (Jerusalem, 1977), p. 341.
26 *Vohyn*, September 1, 1941; cited from Shmuel Spector, "The Jews of Volhynia and their Reaction to Extermination," *Yad Vashem Studies* 15 (1983): p. 160.

announcement by the Extraordinary Commission about the murders in Kiev and Babi Yar in 1943 said:

> During the German occupation of Kiev ... over 195,000 citizens, whose only guilt was being Soviet people, were killed ... at Babi Yar, they threw new-born children into the ravine and buried them alive, together with their killed and wounded parents ... On September 29, 1941, the Hitlerite bandits rounded up thousands of peaceful Soviet citizens to the corner of Melnik and Dokterev streets and led them to Babi Yar where they took away from them their valuables and shot them.[27]

One can see that there is no mention in this report of the defining nature of this extraordinary massacre: all of the victims at Babi Yar were Jews.

As late as March 24, 1944, when asked to condemn the murder of Hungarian Jewry, Stalin refused. As has been correctly pointed out:

> After the German occupation of Hungary, when the Hungarian Jews faced deportation and extermination, President Roosevelt published a warning to Germany and its satellites. He condemned the wholesale systematic murder of the Jews and stressed the "determination that none who participate in these acts of savagery go unpunished." This declaration was broadcast by radio to the people and governments of German-dominated Europe and millions of leaflets were dropped by allied planes. The State Department asked the Soviet Union to express its support of this declaration because of its influence in Romania and Hungary and on the fate of Jews there. The Soviet Union refused, responding that it was not only the Jews, but also the Russian people, who were facing extermination, and therefore no efforts should be made on behalf of one group.[28]

In trying to decipher this desperate situation in Eastern Europe that worked against Jewish resistance efforts it needs, furthermore, to be recognized that many Jews in this region dressed differently, usually spoke Yiddish instead of the local language, and that Jewish men were circumcised. In consequence, for most Jews "passing" as a non-Jew among the gentile population was generally impossible.[29] And for assimilated Jews who did speak the local language and did dress like the

---

27 *Pravda*, March 1, 1944, cited from Yitzhak Arad, "The Holocaust as Reflected in the Soviet Russian Language Newspapers in the Years 1941–1945," in *Why Didn't the Presses Shout? American & International Journalism during the Holocaust*, ed. Robert Moses Shapiro (New York, 2003), p. 210.
28 *Nova Renascença* 18.68–71 (1998): 455.
29 "Passing" is very specifically discussed in Lenore Weitzman, "Living on the Aryan Side in Poland: Gender, Passing, and the Nature of Resistance," in *Women in the Holocaust*, eds. Dalia Ofer and Lenore Weitzman (New Haven, CT, 1998), pp. 187–222.

local population, there were always and everywhere those willing to betray them for a pack of cigarettes or some vodka. Assimilated Jews were subject to blackmail until their financial resources ran out and then they were betrayed.

(F) **Western Europe.** Even in Western Europe conditions were not propitious. In Holland, because of the Anne Frank story, we have largely come to think of the valorous actions of the Dutch resistance and the safeguarding of Jews. Anne and her family were hidden for two years by Christian friends, but were eventually betrayed and deported. Anne, whose diary was found after the war, died in Bergen-Belsen. Anne's story of protection, however, is misleading as a significant proportion of Dutch men joined the SS, and "the number of Dutch Nazi collaborators during World War II exceeded the number of those active in the resistance, even if one does not include in the first category [of collaborators] the unknown number of those who stole Jewish property."[30] The Netherlands, in fact, had the highest number of *Waffen* SS volunteers in Western Europe on a *pro rata* population basis, and there was widespread collaboration by ordinary people who became members of the NSB, the Dutch Nazi Party. Moreover, the Dutch Civil authorities and the Dutch police were sympathetic to the Nazi anti-Jewish program. Chief Constable Tulp of the Amsterdam Police was a committed Nazi sympathizer and supporter.[31] Nor it should be forgotten that Anne Frank and her family were betrayed by a Dutch neighbor. Similarly, in France, the Vichy regime was led by antisemites and their position was reinforced by anti-Jewish collaborators throughout the country. As the war progressed, and knowledge of the extermination of the Jews grew – and was everywhere more apparent – antisemitic attitudes, paradoxically, grew more and more intense in France, as well as in all of Europe.[32] As a consequence of this near universal hostility, armed Jewish resistance in France had very great difficulty gaining local (and international) support.

---

30 Manfred Gerstenfeld, "Wartime and Postwar Dutch Attitudes Toward the Jews: Myth and Truth," *Jerusalem Letter/Viewpoints*, 15 August 1999, Jerusalem Center for Public Affairs.

31 Guus Meershoeck, "The Amsterdam Police and the Persecution of the Jews," in *The Holocaust and History: The Known, the Unknown, the Disputed, and the Reexamined*, ed. Michael Berenbaum and Abraham Peck (Bloomington, 2008), pp. 284–300. For more on this issue consult: Gerhard Hirschfeld, *Nazi Rule and Dutch Collaboration: The Netherlands under German Occupation, 1940–1945* (Oxford, 1998); Joseph Michman, "Changes in the Attitude of the Dutch toward the Jews on the Eve of the Holocaust," in *Studies in the History of Dutch Jewry*, ed. Joseph Michman (Jerusalem, 1975) [Hebrew], vol. 3, pp. 247–62; *idem*, "Planning for the Final Solution Against the Backdrop of Developments in Holland in 1941," *Yad Vashem Studies* 17 (1986): 145–80; J. Blom, "The Persecution of Jews in the Netherlands: A Comparative Western European Perspective," *European History Quarterly* 19.3 (July 1989): 333–51; and Leni Yahil, *The Holocaust: The Fate of European Jewry, 1932–1945* (New York, 1990), pp. 391–93.

32 See the full tale as retold by Robert Paxton and Michael Marrus in *Vichy France and the Jews* (Stanford, 1995). Despite Vichy's proactive collaboration with the Nazis, about 80 percent of French Jews survived the Holocaust thanks to assistance from the general population and the Catholic and Protestant Churches. France is also one of the few countries where the Jewish resistance (OSE) was successful in saving 12,000 Jewish children. See Mordecai Plaidel, *Saving One's Own: Jewish Rescuers During the Holocaust* (Philadelphia, 2017), chap. 7, pp. 201–64.

(G) **Britain**. British policy, in spite of Churchill's personal sympathies, was essentially to do nothing to assist Jews or Jewish resistance groups. Consider, for example, the failure of the Brand mission in May 1944. Joel Brand, a Jew, was sent by Himmler to negotiate with the Allies for 10,000 trucks in exchange for one million Jews. When he reached British-controlled Egypt, he was imprisoned by the British officials in charge, and no negotiations were undertaken. There is a widespread, but disputed, claim that when Lord Moyne, representing British authority in Egypt, was reminded that such negotiations could lead to saving a million Jewish lives, he replied, conscious of the British blockade of Jewish emigration to Palestine: "And what will I do with these million Jews?"[33] Then, there was the incident precipitated by the SS *Struma*. This ship with 769 Jewish refugees, including 70 Jewish children, was denied permission to land in Palestine, despite two months of negotiations between the Jewish Agency and British mandatory officials. The ship was detained in Turkey and then sank in the Black Sea. Two people survived.[34] Again, in 1943, the British government agreed publicly to allow 29,000 Jewish children from Bulgaria, Romania, and elsewhere to enter Palestine under the 75,000 limits on Jewish emigration set by the 1939 White Paper. But in private, as we now know from the opening of British government archives, the British government did everything it could to block the travel of these children. In the end, none of the 29,000 came. Almost all were killed.[35]

(H) **United States**. American attitudes were no different. In 1942, the *Auschwitz Document* describing the gassing of Jews was smuggled out and passed on to the Allies. The Americans kept it secret for months before passing it on to Gerhard Reigner of the World Jewish Congress in Switzerland. And, after some time, the U.S. State Department asked its Swiss mission not to pass on any more "private messages." In this context, the decisive fact was the control of State Department immigration policy by the antisemite Breckenridge Long. He instructed all American Embassies and consulates to: "Delay, delay and delay, when Jews come in

---

33 Cited from Shlomo Aronson, *Hitler, the Allies, and the Jews* (Cambridge, UK, 2004), p. 229. Aronson notes in his footnote to this quote "See Joel Brand, *In the Mission of the Sentenced to Death* (Tel Aviv, 1956), p. 155 (in Hebrew)." This is available in an English version translated by Alex Weissberg, *Advocate for the Dead – The Story of Joel Brand* (London, 1958), p. 167. In this essay Brand wrote that the person who exclaimed "And what shall I do with a million Jews" was not Moyne but another British official. On British policy in its totality consult Bernard Wasserstein, *Britain and the Jews of Europe, 1939–1945* (London, 1999).
34 The ship originated in Constanta, Romania. When it arrived in Istanbul's harbor it waited for two months, anticipating disembarkation for Palestine, and eventually it was towed out of the harbor when an explosion ripped open its hull. This series of events has been discussed by Anna Porter, *Kasztner's Train: The True Story of an Unknown Hero of the Holocaust* (Vancouver, 2007), pp. 55–56; R. Hilberg, *The Destruction of the European Jews*, vol. 2 p. 840; and Douglas Frantz and Catherine Collins, *Death on the Black Sea: The Untold Story of the Struma and World War II's Holocaust at Sea* (New York, 2003).
35 Itamar Levin, *His Majesty's Enemies: Great Britain's War Against Holocaust Victims and Survivors*, pp. 11–12, analyzes this failure.

asking for visas, even if they already have numbers and fit inside the quotas."[36] (Parenthetically, I note that the neighbor of the U.S. to the north, Canada, adopted a similar policy. Early in 1939 an unidentified immigration official was asked how many Jews should be allowed into the country during the time of Nazi persecution. He replied: "None is too many.")[37]

In sum, these eleven issues represent a long and formidable list of factors to keep in mind, but all of them are relevant when one attempts to decipher the issue of Jewish resistance during the Holocaust. They collectively define the existential and political circumstances in which Jews and Jewish communities found themselves. Together they created the controlling context in which Jews made their decisions and undertook resistance – and other – action.

Now that they have been set out, if only briefly and schematically, we can begin to properly understand that the mounting of resistance by Jews and Jewish groups was a monumental task that needs to be judged by criteria appropriate to its phenomenological reality.

III Ghettos 1940–45

To begin our review of the concrete forms that Jewish resistance took let us consider the history of the Polish, Lithuanian, and Latvian ghettos in which millions of Jews lived and died.

After the Nazi victories in Poland beginning in September 1939, and the conquest of the Baltic States in June and July 1941, the Jewish populations in these areas – 3,000,000 in Poland alone – were forcibly ghettoized. Living conditions were horrific. Consider:

> *Food* – the official shipment of food into the ghetto allowed, on average, for fewer than 300 calories a day, per person; thus, starvation soon became the main problem.[38]
>
> *Disease* – soon began to appear in many forms, especially dysentery.
>
> *Fuel* – despite the harshness of Polish (and Baltic) winters no fuel was allowed into the ghettos.[39]
>
> *Terrible sanitary conditions* – 95 percent of houses in the Łódź ghetto had no toilets or running water; Irena Liebman, a resident of the Łódź ghetto, wrote in her diary:
>
> > The ghetto. Tiny, narrow streets. Little houses without conveniences. A well in the backyard. A refuse dump infested with rats. A stinking

---

36 This outrage is described by David Wyman in his classic study *The Abandonment of Jews: America and the Holocaust* (New York, 1998).
37 See on Canada's immigration policies during this era, Irving Abella and Harold Troper, *"None Is Too Many": Canada and the Jews of Europe 1933–1948* (Toronto, 1983).
38 Discussed in greater detail below in the context of the Warsaw ghetto.
39 Isaiah Trunk, *Łódź Ghetto: A History*, ed. and trans. Robert Moses Shapiro (Bloomington, 2006), pp. 124–25.

toilet full of melting snow, impossible to use. A leaking roof, dilapidated walls. One little room and a small kitchen for seven people.[40]

This became the typical condition in all the ghettos. In particular, the absence of heating meant that the pipes froze and broke, making toilets inoperable in those homes that had indoor plumbing. And the absence not only of fuel but of clean water meant that both filth and germs multiplied.

Fear and brutality – were the order of the day.

However, between the spring of 1940 and the summer of 1941, Nazi policy governing the management of the ghettos was not yet genocidal. Therefore, the *Judenräte*, the leadership of the ghetto councils created by the Nazis, made decisions accordingly. When, in 1942, they came to realize that all Jews were marked for extermination, they were already trapped in a context that was purposely designed to mislead them, and rendered their efforts at survival largely meaningless.

Relative to the judgments of the *Judenräte* one must also take into consideration that:

(a) The behavior of the *Judenräte* and its members was not monolithic as the research of Aharon Weiss[41] and Isaiah Trunk unequivocally shows.[42] It varied during the *Shoah*, especially as the war wore on and the membership of the councils changed. There were councils that cooperated with the underground and did not take a stand against the eventual outbreak of physical resistance and there were those that unwaveringly opposed such actions. For example, Moshe Merin in Będzin and Sosnowiec vigorously opposed the organization of physical resistance, while the opposite was the case in Minsk. And there were many councils that were split over this cardinal issue and were uncertain how to proceed. Then, too, there were council leaders who absolutely refused to cooperate with the German authorities in sending Jews out of the ghetto. They were usually murdered and replaced by more cooperative individuals. Three out of four council heads in Lvov were murdered by the Nazis, while two were killed in Minsk, and two in Vilna.[43] There were those like Adam Czerniaków in Warsaw who drew a line at deporting children, and took his own life when he was ordered to cross it. Then there was Mordechai Chaim Rumkowski, who did deport children from the Łódź Ghetto because he sincerely believed that it would keep the other tens of thousands

---

40 Alan Adelson and Robert Lapides (eds.), *Lodz Ghetto: Inside a Community Under Siege* (New York, 1989), p. 35.
41 Abraham Weiss, The Relations Between the Judenrat and the Jewish Police, www.yadvashem.org/odot_pdf/Microsoft%20Word%20-%203224.pdf
42 Isaiah Trunk, *Judenrat: The Jewish Councils in Eastern Europe* under *Nazi Occupation* (Lincoln, NE, 1996).
43 Yitzhak Arad, *The Holocaust in the Soviet Union* (Lincoln, NE, 2009), p. 479.

of Jews in the Łódź ghetto alive – who he believed would be saved by the approaching Soviet army. When the Łódź Ghetto was finally liquidated in August 1944 there were still approximately 70,000 Jews alive in it. Had the Red Army accelerated their advance they would have changed the fate of the (non-Jewish) Warsaw Uprising that broke out on August 1 and lasted until October 2, 1944, and perhaps the fate of the 70,000 Jews still alive in the *Litzmannstadt* (Łódź) Ghetto.

(b) The actions of the councils provide an extraordinary example of unintended consequences. They all sought to preserve the Jewish People and to provide a route that would allow for Jewish survival. Due to the context in which they were trapped, by forces over which they had no control or almost no control, their actions – contrary to their intentions – helped those who sought to actualize the "Final Solution." So the controversy over how to judge their actions still continues in scholarly circles (see point d) below).

(c) Jews would have been, and were, pursued to death with and without the help of the councils. The deaths of 1.5 million Jews by the *Einsatzgruppen*, with essentially no intervention by *Judenräte* is proof enough of this. This should be kept in mind when reflecting on Hannah Arendt's extreme and unnuanced condemnation of the councils.[44]

(d) All of the councils understood that their obligation was to keep as many Jews as possible – and the Jewish People – alive. They therefore overwhelmingly made the fateful and *very* controversial decision to support a policy of "work for life." They would consciously transform the ghettos into work sites producing necessary articles for the *Wehrmacht*, and by doing so they thought that they would, at least, keep "productive" Jews among the living. And, in fact, this strategy kept several hundred thousand Jews alive until 1944 in Łódź, Radom, and a number of other locations. However, this policy meant that the councils had to sacrifice some Jews in order to save other Jews. The elderly, the ill, and the young who did not work in the ghettos were, as the Nazis defined them, "useless eaters," and defenseless against deportation to the death camps. With the two-sided implications of this policy of saving some by sacrificing others. With this in mind, Jakob Gens, the Elder of the Vilna Ghetto, felt justified in telling a group of intellectuals in the ghetto: "Should I, Jakob Gens, survive, I will leave the ghetto soiled, with blood on my hands. But I will go before a Jewish court and declare: I have done everything to save more and more of the ghetto's Jews and to bring them to freedom."

(e) Finally, I note that, while there has been much legitimate criticism of the councils, in many locations like Białystok, Kovno, and Minsk, there was close cooperation between the official leadership of the ghettos and the Jewish underground.

There is still much more to say about the ghetto experience and Jewish resistance, both relative to the behavior and judgments of the *Judenräte* as well as independently of them, but I will limit myself to six observations. First of all, not all Jews

---

44 Hannah Arendt, *Eichmann in Jerusalem: A Report on the Banality of Evil* (New York, 1963).

were young, single, and healthy. This was a decisive factor. While young Jews could sometimes escape the ghettos to join the partisans, most of the ghetto inhabitants were physically unable to do this. In consequence, young Jews often remained to help their parents and grandparents or younger siblings, or wives and children. This meant that for those who chose to remain in the ghettos and forego joining the partisans, their behavior, no less than those who left for the forest, was heroic. We know, for example, from the *Pinkas Shavli*, that in the Šiauliai Ghetto a meeting of the community leaders was held on February 5, 1943, to discuss organizing ghetto-wide armed resistance. In the course of the discussion it became clear that this plan, involving flight to the Soviet partisans operating in the marshlands of northern Lithuania, would mean leaving behind women, children, and the elderly. The majority of those present felt they could not do this, and the plan was abandoned.[45]

Abba Kovner, the famous partisan leader of the Vilna Ghetto underground, tells us in his *Scrolls of Testimony*:

> And Sha'ul looked after his mother. And he built her a *maline* in a secret place under the garbage and contrived an entrance with great skill and ingenuity. And his mother went down there, together with three *agunot* and a young cripple, and they stayed there all the time. He took them down the few necessities of life. And they lived there and were saved. And Sha'ul said to himself: Now I know why I left the partisan dugout, my commander and my comrades, and came back to the ghetto. If I had come here just for this moment, it would have been sufficient.[46]

After the war, when Kovner was acclaimed as a heroic example of a Jewish resistance fighter, he asked: "Am I a hero in Israel? Or have I betrayed my mother?"[47]

Second, there was a well justified fear of Nazi reprisals in response to Jews fleeing the ghetto and joining partisan groups or carrying out acts of armed resistance. To the Führer state, Jews were, *a priori*, enemies whose lives were worthless. Therefore, murdering Jews as retribution for things that other Jews did – and even for things Jews did not do – was a constant possibility, regularly exercised. One paradigmatic case in point is that the Germans justified the taking of the lives of over 30,000 Jews at Babi Yar as a reprisal for Russian air raids on Ukraine. Likewise, in Serbia, the army officer in charge ordered 100 Jews killed for every German soldier murdered by the partisans. And in Vilna, on July 22, 1943, a group of Jews escaped the ghetto and on their way to join partisans met a group of German soldiers. In the ensuing battle several Jews were killed and two were taken prisoner. The next day,

---

45 See Eliezer Yerushalmi, *Pinkas Shavli* (Jerusalem, 1958), p. 315. This is also commented on in Isaiah Trunk, *Judenrat: The Jewish Councils of Eastern Europe Under Nazi Occupation* (New York, 1927; reprinted Lincoln, NE, 1996), p. 454–55; and Meir Grubsztein (ed.), *Jewish Resistance During the Holocaust* (Jerusalem, 1971) pp. 203–209.
46 Abba Kovner, *Scrolls of Testimony* (Philadelphia, 2001), pp. 74–75.
47 Cited from Y. Mais, et al. (eds.), *Daring to Resist*, p. 135.

the Gestapo Chief, Nuegebauer, ordered the families of the men who had been shot or captured to be arrested. In the middle of the night thirty-two Jews were rounded up and taken out to the pits of Ponary where they were murdered. After this an article appeared in the *Geto Yedies* (the "News of the Ghetto") of August 1, 1943, saying: "The responsibility [for the deaths] is upon those who separated themselves from the ghetto community . . . in this way they are putting in danger the existence of the whole ghetto and first of all the lives of their dear ones."[48] What the right course of action in this circumstance was is still a subject of intense debate.

When considering the significance of anti-Jewish reprisals one must take into account not only the possibility of reprisals against individuals but also the possibility of lethal retaliation being taken against entire ghettos. Possessing a profound sense of collective responsibility,[49] the *Judenräte* were always concerned with the likely imposition of collective retribution if armed resistance and flight occurred. In many cases the leaders, therefore, concluded that the preferred moral action was *not* to resist.

I would here add, to emphasize the seriousness with which the councils took both the notion of collective responsibility and the need to forestall collective reprisals, another similar case where the concern for the ghetto as a whole decided the issue against overt physical resistance.

> A witness who belonged to a youth group in Międzyrzec (Volhynia), reports that a group in the town had organized itself to escape. Knowing, however, that the whole ghetto would be made responsible for the escape of a small group, they decided to seek the advice of the Judenrat chairman, Isaiah Rubenstein, who, they knew, could be entrusted with a secret. Rubenstein's answer was something like this: "Believe me, I would escape together with you, but how can one abandon the ghetto to its fate? You will escape, and the next day the Germans will come and kill everybody; your families will suffer, as well. It would be a different thing if all of us could escape. You will save your lives, perhaps, but your parents and everybody else remaining in the ghetto will become innocent victims." The witness adds: "These words were convincing enough. It was clear to us that the responsibility was too great, that perhaps it would be criminal to endanger the lives of the rest of the Jews. Anyhow, those were strange times. One did not know what was right and what was wrong."[50]

---

48 *Geto Yedies*, no. 5, August 1, 1943. Cited from Isaiah Trunk, "The Attitude of the Judenrats to the Problems of Armed Resistance Against the Nazis," in *The Catastrophe of European Jewry: Antecedents – History – Reflections*, eds. Yisrael Gutman and Livia Rothkirchen (Jerusalem, 1976), p. 424.
49 This issue is analyzed more fully in the essay "Exploring the concept of *Kol Yisrael Arevim Zeh L'Zeh*," Chapter 11 in this volume, pp. 228–230.
50 Cited from I. Trunk, "The Attitude of the Judenrats to the Problems of Armed Resistance Against the Nazis," p. 431.

I am not sure that 75 years later we can do any better in deciding what was right and what was wrong.

Vladka Meed, a survivor of the Warsaw Ghetto, wrote after the war that even when the leaders of the Jewish Council in this largest of the ghettos learned of the killings in Vilna they were unwilling, for fear of its consequences, to support an all-out uprising.

> The Jewish leaders did not want to assume the responsibility of risking the lives of those who still hoped to survive. The prevailing opinion still was that no more than 60,000 or 70,000 would be deported and that the rest would survive. Under the circumstances how could anyone find it in his heart to jeopardize the lives of the entire Warsaw Ghetto for the sake of active resistance.[51]

When we think of resistance we must again ask the same questions that the members of the *Judenräte* did, and put ourselves in their near-impossible position. Across the decades the moral dilemmas remain ambiguous and the resolution of the existential conundrums to which they point becomes no more transparent.

In Vilna, Jakob Gens, head of the Council, was in contact with the main underground group, the *Fareynikte Partizaner Organizatsye*, but cautioned against provocations or precipitous action lest it bring retribution and ruin to the entire ghetto.[52] With this in mind, when he was ordered on September 14, 1943 to report to the headquarters of the security police, although he was warned of what awaited him, he delivered himself to the police fearing an *Aktion* against the ghetto in its entirety. Gens was shot at 6:00 p.m. the same day.[53]

Lest anyone think that this concern with severe retaliation for acts of resistance was a mere rationalization for inaction, or a sign of cowardice, let me recall one example that speaks powerfully to this issue:

> In Dolhynov, a small township in Byelorussia, with 3,000 Jewish inhabitants, a resistance group was formed in late 1941 under the leadership of Yakov Segalchik and Leib Mintzel. Searching in the forest for Soviet partisans, they were caught by the Byelorussian policemen and Germans, beaten up, and tortured. At night, with the help of an iron bar, they broke the barred windows of their cells, and escaped into the ghetto . . . On the following day, March 15, 1942, the Dolhynov Judenrat leader, Nyumka

---

51 Vladka Meed, *On Both Sides of the Wall: Memoirs from the Warsaw Ghetto* (New York, 1979), p. 69.
52 N. N. Shneidman, *Jerusalem of Lithuania* (Oakville, 1998), pp. 72–91.
53 Yitzhak Arad, *Ghetto in Flames: The Struggle and Destruction of the Jews of Vilna in the Holocaust* (Jerusalem, 1980), p. 425. There is some disagreement on the date of this event: Meir Dworzecki "gives a version according to which Gens was shot at Gestapo headquarters on September 15, 1943" (I. Trunk, "The Attitude of the Judenrats to the Problems of Armed Resistance Against the Nazis," p. 442).

Rayer, was told by the Nazis that all of Dolhynov's Jews would be killed if the two resisters did not come forward. The two escapees could not be found. On March 17, 1,540 Dolhynov Jews were murdered . . .[54]

Having read widely in the secondary literature on resistance it is obvious to me that this cardinal issue of the threat of Nazi retaliation and retribution has been seriously underestimated by students of the Holocaust, and underestimated, in particular, vis-à-vis the subject of resistance.

Third, the leadership of the councils was generally operating under two mistaken assumptions. The first was that Nazism was like prior antisemitism. Therefore, it was rational to give the Nazis what they wanted in order to "buy time" and preserve life. Furthermore, they thought that Jewish cooperation might improve Nazi behavior and, in consequence, better Jewish living standards. But this understanding of the situation radically misconceived Nazi intentions. The second mistake that the councils made was rooted in the false analogy that they drew between the situation of the Jews in the ghettos and the logic of black New World slavery. That is to say, the Jews knew that, as a historical matter, masters do not kill their slaves. They therefore believed that Jews who worked and, thereby, became valuable slave labor would survive the war. They did not know that Himmler and Hitler had decreed that no Jews were to ultimately survive. What the Third Reich wanted from the Jewish People was not their labor but their dead bodies.[55]

Fourth, the Nazis purposely misled the *Judenräte*. For example, Adam Czerniaków, the head of the *Judenrat* in Warsaw Ghetto, wrote in his diary on July 20, 1942:

> In the morning at 7:30 [I am] at the Gestapo. I ask Mende how much truth there was in the rumors. He replied that he had heard nothing. I turned to Brandt; he also knew nothing. When asked whether it *could* happen, he replied that he knew of no such scheme. Uncertain, I left his office. I proceeded to his chief, *Kommissar* Böhm. He told me that this was not his department but Hoeheman [Hohmann] might say something about the rumors. I mentioned that according to rumor, the deportation is to start tonight at 7:30. He replied that he would be bound to know something if it were about to happen. Not seeing any other way out, I went to the deputy chief of Section III, Scherer. He expressed his surprise hearing the rumor and informed me that he too knew nothing about it. Finally, I asked whether I could tell the population that their fears were groundless. He replied that I could and that all the talk was *Quatsch* and *Unsinn* [utter nonsense] . . . I ordered Lejkin to make the public announcement through the precinct police stations. I drove

---

54 I drew this from Yehuda Bauer, *A History of the Holocaust* (New York, 1982), pp. 248–49.
55 See the more complete discussion of this matter in the essay "Extermination trumps production," Chapter 7 in this volume, pp. 121–149.

to Auerswald. He informed me that he reported everything to the SS *Polizeiführer*. Meanwhile, First went to see Jesuiter and Schlederer, who expressed their indignation that the rumors were being spread and promised an investigation.[56]

But Czerniaków had been repeatedly misled. All of these German replies to his questions were lies. On the day he engaged in these many conversations the SS unit that was to carry out the mass deportations was already in Warsaw. The deportations began three days later on July 22, 1942.

Another example: in April 1943, Jacob Gens, head of the *Judenrat* in Vilna, was told that 5,000 people would be deported to Kovno to work. The Jews were assembled, but as Itzhak Rudashevski recorded in his diary of April 5, 1943, these Jews "were not taken to Kovno as promised." Instead they were taken to the killing pits at Ponary and shot.

And a third example: Efraim Barash, the vice-chairman of the Białystok *Judenrat*, met, on one occasion with Chaika Grossman, a member of the ghetto's *Ha-Shomer Ha-Za'ir* Zionist youth group. In the course of the meeting they discussed the murder of the Jews of Vilna at Ponary. According to Grossman's Hebrew memoir, Barash said to her: "I don't believe that what happened in Vilna will happen in Białystok. I know the Germans, and they won't dare to behave in such a way . . . If they get such orders, they will let me know. They won't apply the Vilna method here; they need us."[57] He was completely convinced that the Nazi war machine needed Jewish labor. He had been told this lie after the early February 1943 deportations, when 30,000 Jews still remained in the Białystok ghetto, and it seemed convincingly rational to him. Moreover, on February 19, the local Nazi police commander came to Barash and told him that he foresaw no further deportations and that the Jews still alive in the ghetto would, in all likelihood, survive until "the end of the war."[58] But none of this was true. It was intended misinformation spread to keep the Jews quiescent and productive for the time being. On August 16, 1943, under Globocnik's direct command, and in conformity with Himmler's orders, the Białystok Ghetto was liquidated and all of its surviving residents, including Barash, were sent to be murdered at Treblinka and Majdanek.[59]

Note that when the Jews of Warsaw and Vilna were convinced of the certainty of the uncompromising Nazi genocidal plan they revolted. Which is to appreciate the obvious: knowledge is important to resistance. It was only when the

---

56 Adam Czerniaków, *The Warsaw Diary of Adam Czerniaków: Prelude to Doom*, eds. Raul Hilberg, Stanislaw Staron, and Josef Kermisz (New York, 1979), pp. 382–83.
57 Saul Friedländer, *The Years of Extermination: Nazi Germany and the Jews, 1939–1945* (New York, 2007), p. 531.
58 Chaika Grossman, *Anshe ha-mahteret* (Tel Aviv, 1965), p. 77 and p. 199; this memoir is now available in English as *The Underground Army: Fighters of the Białystok Ghetto*, ed. Sol Lewis (New York, 1987).
59 S. Friedländer, *The Years of Extermination*, p. 529.

underground in Warsaw learned of the murder of the Jews of Vilna at Ponary that they planned for an uprising. As Tzivia Lubetkin, a leader of the ŻOB (Jewish Fighting Organization), wrote in her memoirs: "Our feeling was that Vilna was the beginning of total annihilation."[60] In Vilna itself, Abba Kovner, in his famous speech of December 31, 1941, called for open resistance because he knew that: "All those taken away from the ghetto never come back. All the roads of the Gestapo lead to Ponary. And Ponary is death."[61]

But such reliable information was not always obtainable, and the little that was known was often too fragmentary to serve as the basis of concerted, collective, action. One thinks here especially of Łódź where, unlike the leaders in Vilna and Warsaw, Rumkowski and the Council were essentially cut off from outside news, that is, news of total annihilation. In consequence, there was no physical resistance in the Łódź Ghetto. And to keep the secret, the Germans went through the charade of permitting the Jews being deported from Łódź to their death to change ghetto money into German marks – something otherwise forbidden – in order to foster the illusion that the Jews were being transported to other work camps.[62] It is, therefore, necessary for us to ask, before we make any final judgments, would a rational person risk his or her life and, possibly, the life of their entire community if they (mistakenly) believed, based on the false information the enemy purposely fed them, that they would survive the war as a result of their "needed" labor?

Fifth, in Warsaw, on the eve of the ghetto revolt, the Jewish underground had only one machine gun and fifty or sixty pistols that they bought from the Polish underground plus a small amount of ammunition. Once the fighting started they received an additional twenty rifles.[63] In contrast, non-Jewish partisan groups could be, and often were, supplied with weapons by parachute drops, a possibility not available to Jews confined to the ghettos. By the end of the war the Jewish underground was the only anti-Nazi underground/partisan group in occupied Europe that received *no* weapons, with the exception of the small supplies just noted, from an outside source.[64]

In attempting to evaluate the degree and impact of Jewish resistance one needs, moreover, to know that in many locations armed non-Jewish resistance was organized by the remnants of the national army. This was the case in Russia, in Serbia (where the partisans were brought under the leadership of Mikhailovich's

---

60 Tzivia Lubetkin, *In the Days of Destruction and Revolt* (Israel, 1981), p. 85; and see also Yitzchak Zuckerman, *A Surplus of Memory: Chronicle of the Warsaw Ghetto Uprising* (Berkeley, 1993), pp. 148–58.
61 N. N. Shneidman, *The Three Tragic Heroes of the Vilna Ghetto*, p. 48.
62 Lucjan Dobroszycki, *The Chronicle of the Łódź Ghetto, 1941–1944* (New Haven, CT, 1984), p. xix.
63 This at a time when the Polish underground had a large supply of weapons. I. Trunk, "The Attitude of the Judenrats to the Problems of Armed Resistance against the Nazis," p. 439.
64 Yitzhak Arad, "Jewish Armed Resistance in Eastern Europe: Its Characteristics and Problems," in *The Catastrophe of European Jewry*, eds. Israel Gutman and Livia Rothkirchen, p. 499.

Chetniks) and in Greece where the resistance was commanded by General Zerva. And, complementarily, the Americans parachuted operational troops to the French "Maquis" in 1944, and the Russians did the same in Poland, Slovakia and a number of other locations. None of this type of support existed, or was made available, for Jewish resisters. There was no national (or international) Jewish army or government to send assistance to Jews in the ghettos and death camps. The token efforts of the Zionist leadership, best known through the parachuting of three Jews into Eastern Europe in 1942–43, and a further 32, including Hannah Senesh,[65] between March and September 1944, is proof of the feeble, almost completely nonexistent nature of such Jewish aid. (Of the thirty-two Jews from Palestine who were dropped in 1944, twelve were captured and seven of them were executed).[66]

Sixth, Jewish Resistance, as compared to non-Jewish resistance, was undertaken on the assumption of almost certain death. Here is the full appeal written by Mordecai Tamarov-Tennenbaum, head of the underground resistance movement in the Białystok ghetto, to the remaining ghetto residents:

BROTHER JEWS!

Agonizing days are upon us. We are not only threatened with yellow armbands, hate, perfidy, insult and humiliation, now death itself is hanging over us. Our wives, children, mothers and fathers, brothers and sisters, have been sent to their death before our very eyes. Thousands have been led to their doom and thousands more will follow . . . In these days that decide whether we live or die we issue the following appeal: first, I would have you know that five million European Jews have already been killed by Hitler and his executioners. Barely ten percent of the Jews in Poland are still alive. More than two million Polish Jews have been subjected to every conceivable form of torture in Chełmno, Belsen, Oświęcim, Treblinka, Sobibór, and other death camps . . . I assure you that whoever is taken from the ghetto is going to his death!. . . Have no faith in the Gestapo's tempting propaganda based on alleged deportees' letters. These are the brazen lies that pave the way to the giant crematoria and the burial pits in the heart of the Polish forests; all of you are doomed to die.

We have nothing to lose!

Do not deceive yourself that work will save you. The first "action" will be followed by a second, the second by a third – right to the last Jew! The

---

65 This mission has been described by Marie Syrkin, *Blessed is the Match: The Story of Jewish Resistance* (Philadelphia, 1947); and Judith Baumel, "The Parachutists' Mission from a Gender Perspective," in *Resisting the Holocaust*, ed. R. Rohrlich, pp. 95–114, who provides more complete information on the women who participated in these parachute drops organized by the British. Her work covers Hannah Senesh who was dropped into her native Hungary, Haviva Reik who parachuted into Slovakia, and Sara Braverman who was sent to Romania.

66 Y. Arad, "Jewish Armed Resistance in Eastern *Europe*, pp. 490–518.

division of the ghetto into different categories is nothing but a perfidious enemy manoeuvre to ease their task by sowing false illusions among us.

JEWS!

Our destination is Treblinka. There we shall be gassed, then burnt like mad beasts. Do not go like lambs to the slaughter! We may be too weak to save ourselves, but we are strong enough to defend our honour as Jews and as human beings, strong enough to show the world that even though we are in chains, we are not conquered . . . Do not go meekly to your death. Fight for your lives to your last breath. Stand up to your slaughterers with your teeth and nails, with axes and knives, with vitriol and iron bars. Extort from them blood for blood, a life for a life. Do you intend hiding in rat holes while they take away your nearest and dearest to humiliation and death? Will you sell your wives, your children and parents, and your souls for a few more weeks of abject slavery? Rather let us ambush the enemy, kill him, seize his weapons; let us oppose the murderers and if need be let us die heroically and gain immortality by our death.

We have nothing to lose but our honor!

Let us not sell our lives cheaply! Let us avenge the annihilated communities! When you leave your house set fire to it! Set fire to the factories, demolish them! Do not allow our assassins to be our beneficiaries as well!. . . Young Jews, follow the example of generations of Jewish fighters and martyrs, the doers and the dreamers, the pioneers and the builders. Arm yourselves and fight! Hitler will lose the war. Slavery and oppression will be wiped out, leaving the world purged and purified. With such a radiant future before you why die like dogs! Escape to the forests and join the partisans. But do not flee from the ghetto unarmed for you will certainly perish. Do your duty by your country, opposing the destruction of the ghetto and escape with arms to the forest. All you have to do is seize one weapon from every German in the ghetto.

Be strong and courageous.[67]

The assumption of death that is central to Tenenbaum's appeal is crucial because it points to the fact that a small, subjugated, militarily defenseless population, acting rationally, would not risk open military resistance unless all illusions had been shattered, and it was certain that there was no escaping extermination. At the same time, it means that such action came too late, i.e., it came only after many, or even most, Jews had already been killed and the Nazis' plans were all too clear.

---

67 Cited from Lucien Steinberg, *Not as a Lamb: The Jews Against Hitler* (Farnborough, UK, 1974), pp. 250–51. See also Reuben Ainsztein, "The Bialystok Ghetto Revolt," in *They Fought Back: The Story of Jewish Resistance in Nazi Europe*, ed. Yuri Suhl (New York, 1967), pp. 136–43.

IV *Einsatzgruppen* murder of Jews

1.5 million Jews were killed by the *Einsatzgruppen*, the special Nazi killing squads, and their local helpers, that operated, alongside the *Wehrmacht*, in Russia. Immediately upon the Nazi invasion of the Soviet Union on June 22–23, 1941, the *Einsatzgruppen* began their program of mass executions.

There was almost no meaningful resistance to these deadly actions. But lest this fact be misinterpreted, and the Jews of the Soviet Union be accused of "going like sheep to the slaughter," a number of fundamental realities relative to the work of these specially created murder squads must be confronted. Among these factors are:

A) Nothing like these mass murders, i.e., mass murder solely for the purpose of mass murder, had occurred previously since the start of World War II, two years earlier. Therefore, the Jews of Russia could not have predicted them, nor prepared for them.

B) The Soviet regime intentionally kept information about these murder squads from being widely disseminated so that the Nazis preoccupation with the murder of the Jewish population would slow down the German advance, and permit non-Jews more time to organize their escape.

C) The policy creating the *Einsatzgruppen* was a military secret, closely guarded among the German forces.

D) The lightning speed of the Nazi conquest meant that the Jews of the western borderlands of the Soviet Union and the Baltic States had *no* time to create organized armed resistance to the deadly assault against them. The invasion found not only the Jews unprepared but also eventuated in the complete rout of the Soviet army. In the first few months of the Nazi offensive the *Wehrmacht* captured five million Soviet prisoners of war.

E) The Jewish communities had no idea, and could not possibly have had an idea, of what was awaiting them as the *Einsatzgruppen* represented a novum in military warfare. That this was the case becomes strikingly evident when one studies the behavior of the Jews leading up to the massacre at Babi Yar on the outskirts of Kiev in September 1941, and during the initial murderous sweep of the killing units through the Jewish communities of Vilna, Kovno, Riga, and Minsk. Therefore, in light of these defining conditions, it is absurd to talk of a Jewish *failure* to resist the *Einsatzgruppen*.

V Acts of resistance

Despite everything that has been said about the many obstacles that stood in the way of Jewish resistance, the historical record makes it plain that Jews did resist in many ways and many places. Before describing this resistance, however, there is a crucial definitional issue, already referred to above, that must be explained more fully. In that the Nazi assault against Jewry involved defining Jews as *untermenschen* who belonged to a lower species, as well as murdering them, the definition of "resistance" needs to be broad enough to include any act that "resisted" the program of dehumanization, as well as those acts that attempted to oppose the program of extermination. In consequence, Jewish resistance includes both what can be called "spiritual resistance," that is, acts that defy the dehumanization of the Jew, as well as acts that meet the criterion of "physical resistance."

(A) **Spiritual Resistance.** "Spiritual resistance" included a wide range of issues and values. Among them was the maintenance of Jewish dignity, the demonstration that Jews were part of the human family, and the living out of Judaism's ethical ideals. Recognizing the nature of the enemy's onslaught on the very being of the Jew, i.e., the Nazi claim that Jews were parasites and vermin, every act of Jewish dignity and ethical correctness was, in effect, an act of disconfirmation and, in a meaningful way, an act of resistance. And such actions occurred in all the ghettos, in all the work camps, and in all the death camps.

I will not, because this essay is already too long, describe these acts in detail. Instead, I will only provide a brief listing of the various individual and communal educational, religious, and charitable, forms that such resistance took. To be included in this inventory are:

1. Putting on *tefillin* even in the death camps.[68]
2. Studying Torah.
3. Lectures on all sorts of subjects, e.g., in Vilna, in the summer of 1942, Eliezer Goldberg gave a course of lectures on classical Jewish history,[69] while in this same year Moshe Illitzky gave a lecture on "Jewish Humor under all Conditions."[70]
4. Attempts to maintain a diet consistent with the kosher food laws.
5. The singing of Yiddish songs.
6. The formation of choral societies, e.g., the 50-member group in Vilna organized by *B'rit Ivrit*,[71] and a similar group created in Łódź.
7. The formation in the Vilna and Łódź ghettos[72] of musical conservatories. The one in Vilna had over 100 students.
8. The organization of religious services on Yom Kippur – and despite the rampant hunger many Jews fasted on this holy day. (It should be added that the Nazis, as already briefly noted, often made a special effort to abuse and mock Jews on the Holidays, e.g., on Purim, 1942, the Nazis hung 10 Jews in

---

68 Examples of this are cited in Yitzhak Arad, *Belzec, Sobibor, Treblinka: The Operation Reinhard Death Camps* (Bloomington, 1987), p. 217. In Bełżec prisoners managed to acquire *tefillin* and prayer shawls and to meet in order to say *Kaddish* for the dead. *Kaddish* was also said in Sobibór. Irving Rosenbaum, *The Holocaust and Halakhah* (New York, 1976), pp. 77–78, provides still other examples of the presence of *tefillin* in the camps.
69 Joseph Rudavsky, *To Live with Hope, to Die with Dignity* (Lanham, MD, 1987), p. 52.
70 *Ibid.*, p. 55.
71 *Ibid.*, p. 61.
72 "Music in the Holocaust," *Encyclopedia of the Holocaust*, 4 vols., ed. Israel Gutman (New York, 1990), vol. 2, p. 1023.

Zduńska-Wola, a small town 30 miles from Łódź;[73] There was also an intentional *Aktion* on Shavuot, 1942; and in 1944, Mengele chose the eve of Yom Kippur to kill a group of Jewish boys at Auschwitz.)[74]

9. The holding of Passover *Seders*. Listen to this tragic but luminescent story of Rabbi Raphael from Salonika, Rabbi Nathan Cassuto of Florence, and Gonda Redlich, "the Czech pioneer youth," who together celebrated Passover "in the seventh block of the largest death camp the Germans had set upon the soil of occupied Poland. 'The seventh,' *di zibele* in the argot of the inmates of Auschwitz-Birkenau, was the block for the sick, the last stop before the furnaces."[75]

> All night, in the faintest whisper, they had been telling the story of the Exodus from Egypt. With their legs hanging down from their bunks, they repeated by heart what they could remember, helping each other out; they had also begun by blessing the two wafers, a kind of matzah that they had prepared well ahead, fearfully and in great secrecy, "bread of affliction" in every sense. They tasted nothing else, despite the gnawing hunger, and drank only the four measured sips of water they had set aside, no more; then they placed their elbows on their knees and began to sing the traditional songs . . . Gonda held his chin in his bandaged hand. The others covered their sunken, unshaven cheeks. They could hardly be said to be singing,

---

73 Martin Gilbert, *The Holocaust: A History of the Jews of Europe during the Second World War* (New York, 1987), p. 297. Gilbert also describes several additional instances of violence on Purim – for example, in Minsk, on Purim, the Germans ordered the *Judenrat* to hand over 5,000 Jews, and when the Jewish Council refused to do so German and Belorussian police came into the ghetto and seized the children resident in a nursery and buried them alive. The Germans then continued their destruction in Minsk and killed another 5,000 Jews.

74 Gerald Posner and John Ware, *Mengele: The Complete Story* (New York, 1986) pp. 49–50, have reproduced the testimony of a witness named Kleinman at the Adolf Eichmann trial. On the eve of Yom Kippur:

> All of a sudden, a tremble passed through the parade ground like an electric current. Dr. Mengele appeared on his bicycle. He put his hands behind his back; his lips as usual were tightly closed...He went to the center of the parade ground, lifted his head so he could survey the whole scene, and then his eyes landed on al little boy around fifteen years old, perhaps only fourteen years old. I remember his face very well. He was blonde, very thin and very sunburnt. His face had freckles. He was standing in the first line when Mengele approached him and asked him, "How old are you?" The boy shook and said, "I'm eighteen years old." I saw immediately that Dr. Mengele was furious, and he started shouting, "I'll show you. Get me a hammer and some nails and a plank." A deathly silence prevailed on the parade ground... Mengele approached a tall boy...in the first row. He put the boy near the goalpost and gave orders to nail the plank above the boy's head so that it was like the letter "L" only in reverse. Then he ordered the first group to pass under the board. The first group of boys started going in single file...We had no explanations. We understood that the little ones who did not reach the board, who were not tall enough, would be taken to their death. (*ibid.*, p. 51)

75 A. Kovner, *Scrolls of Testimony*, p. 116.

for only their lips moved soundlessly. Even so, it was clear from the movement of their bodies that each sang a different tune.[76]

And then Rabbi Cassuto addressed his comrades:

In every generation a Jew has seen himself the sum of all previous generations. Our forefathers did not hand down to us their personal experiences, or not that alone; what we received from them was the story of the people and the individual. It is the whole story that to this day has shaped our character. Perhaps each of us here and now is charged with the holy duty of hearing what happened to the others, not only to himself, so that when the time comes, whoever of us survives will be able to serve as a mouthpiece for the many, "for we bear witness before You"; and if we cannot be the sum of everything our people have undergone under Nazi rule, we can be the sum of this block in Birkenau . . . so let us make this night a night of vigil; before we depart for the darkness of oblivion, let us share our knowledge, something we have never done till now. Let each of us place his story in the safe keeping of his companion's memory and, God willing, the last of us fated to survive will be the first to write the scrolls of testimony for his generation. And let us say this to our brothers in the blocks and they shall do likewise. His penetrating remarks were heard in total simplicity, entering their hearts like good news.[77]

10. The use of underground radios.[78]
11. The publication of Jewish newspapers. In total, both in and out of the ghettos, Jewish groups published tens of thousands of pages of material[79] that provided a Jewish voice, a Jewish narrative, over against the dominant, authoritarian, assertions of the Hitler state.
12. The establishment in Vilna of a publishing office that collected literary and musical material for publication after the war.
13. The rescue of Jewish books and religious artifacts in Vilna and elsewhere.

---

76 *Ibid.*
77 *Ibid.*, p. 117.
78 Table 9.2 in *What We Knew*, eds. Eric Johnson and Karl-Heinz-Reuband, provides data from a survey that inquires into the illegal activity among Jewish survivors. It reveals that 26 percent of Jews who left Germany between 1933 and 1939 listened to illegal radio broadcasts, and 39 percent of Jews who were still in Germany after 1939 listened to illegal radio broadcasts, p. 292.
79 I. Trunk, *Judenrat*, p. 537 reports that: "According to incomplete information, approximately fifty underground publications in Yiddish, Polish, and Hebrew were issued in Warsaw between 1940 and April 1943 by almost all political parties. Literary and historical anthologies and books under titles such as *Martyrdom and Heroism, and the Paris Commune* (both in Yiddish), and others were published. The incomplete list of Bund publications alone contains thirteen titles with a total of 180,000 typewritten pages."

14. The organization of soup kitchens in ghettos – that also became illegal education centers for children. Children numbering 35,000 were educated at these soup kitchens.[80]
15. The smuggling of food into the ghettos that was crucial in providing enough sustenance food to keep at least a segment of those caught up in the walls of the ghettos alive. The Nazis, not caring if the Jews died of starvation – in fact planning for just this eventuality – only allowed 220 calories per person per day into the Warsaw Ghetto.[81].
16. The creation of ghetto hospitals.
17. The maintenance of a secret library in the Vilna Ghetto.[82]
18. The daily coming together of 600 illegal *minyanim* (prayer quorums) in the Warsaw Ghetto.[83]
19. The creation of schools and the giving of academic lectures. There were, for example, 50,000 children aged between 5 and 12 years in the Warsaw ghetto. Of these, 10,000 went to one of 16 elementary schools.[84] (Warsaw had 16 elementary schools, 3 secular/Yiddish schools, 3 Zionist/Tarbut schools, 5 Orthodox schools, 4 non-aligned schools that taught in Polish, and 1 Yid-

---

80 *The Black Book of Polish Jewry: An Account of the Martyrdom of Polish Jewry Under the Nazi Occupation*, eds. Jacob Apenszlak, Jacob Kenner, Isaac Lewin, and Moses Polakiewicz (New York, 1943), p. 47.
81 Emmanuel Ringelblum, *Polish-Jewish Relations During the Second World War*, edited by Joseph Kermish and Shmuel Krakowski (New York, 1976), pp. 74–75, n. 16: "according to the 'Oneg Shabbat' research, 'The energy value, in calories, of food supplied on ration-cards in 1941 amounted to only 220 calories per head per day; about 19 percent of the quantity to keep someone alive and capable of working.'"; Yisrael Gutman, *The Jews of Warsaw, 1939–1943: Ghetto, Underground, Revolt* (Bloomington, 1982), p. 66, cites a lower estimate, drawn from a Polish source, of 184 calories. A contemporary estimation "of 12,164 persons under the age of sixteen in Warsaw calculated that 52 to 60 percent of them suffered from marked undernourishment and emaciation." J. Apenszlak, et al. (eds.), *The Black Book of Polish Jewry*, pp. 185–86.
82 H. Kruk, *The Last Days of the Jerusalem of Lithuania*, chronicles the creation and maintenance of the library in Vilna. Rachilė Kostanian-Danzig, *Spiritual Resistance in the Vilna Ghetto* (Vilnius, 2002) also discusses the Vilna ghetto library. And see on the heroic effort to preserve Jewish books and religious artifacts in Vilna David Fishman, *The Book Smugglers: Partisans, Poets and the Race to Save Jewish Treasures from the Nazis* (Lebanon, N.H., 2017)
83 Emmanuel Ringelblum, *Notes from the Warsaw Ghetto: The Journal of Emmanuel Ringelblum*, edited and translated by Jacob Sloan (New York, 1958), p. 47.
84 Y. Gutman *The Jews of Warsaw*, p. 84: "In October 1941 the schools were reopened by official permission, and at first six schools operated in the children's shelters . . . the number of schools increased during the first (and last) official school year in the ghetto, and at the end of the 1941/42 school year, nineteen schools were fully or partially operational with 5,700 pupils enrolled . . . In all, about 7,000 of the 50,000 children of school age were engaged in studying in the ghetto." For more on this matter see Debórah Dwork, *Children With a Star: Jewish Youth in Nazi Europe* (New Haven, 1991), pp. 179–88; the article on "Education and Science," in Barbara Engelking and Jacek Leociak, *The Warsaw Ghetto: A Guide to the Perished City* (New Haven, 2009), pp. 343–66; and *The Ghetto Anthology: A Comprehensive Chronicle of the Extermination of Jewry in Nazi Death Camps and Ghettos in Poland*, edited by Roman Mogilanski (Los Angeles, 1985), p. 48, that reports that: "By the end of 1942, only 7000 out of *50000 children* had access to public education."

dish-Hebrew school.) In addition, there were several high schools in the Łódź and Vilna ghettos.[85]

20. The establishment of ORT (Association for the Promotion of Skilled Trades) vocational training programs. These schools taught their students to be locksmiths, carpenters, tinsmiths, and tailors. And in secret they offered instruction in chemistry, pharmacy, nursing, mechanics, electronics, art, accounting, and horticulture.
21. The presentation of plays and musical reviews. In Vilna and Łódź there were symphony orchestras with forty members. A piano was smuggled, piece by piece, into the Vilna Ghetto.
22. The holding of poetry readings.
23. The organization of literary contests with judges and prizes.
24. The remarkable activities of Emmanuel Ringelblum's *Oneg Shabbat* group of intellectuals. In their work we witness Jews writing the history of the *Shoah* as a form of resistance.[86]
25. The life and death efforts to provide safety and affection to the children in ghetto orphanages. Janusz Korczak's orphanage in the Warsaw Ghetto was the most famous of these institutions but it was only one of many such homes. And his heroism was matched by other doctors and nurses working in such institutions, both in Warsaw and other ghettos.[87]
23. The loyalty of the Kovno 140, Jewish Police who refused to betray the ghetto resistance organization and were killed as a consequence.[88]

This inventory, long as it is, is still not complete. But it conveys the efforts and courage of the Jews, mainly – but not only – in the ghettos, to confirm their humanity.

(B) **Physical resistance**. The record of physical acts of Jewish resistance by Jews is better known than the many activities that I have described as "spiritual." Therefore, and because of the constraints imposed by the essay format, I will only very briefly summarize these many heroic initiatives that took place in a variety of different contexts throughout occupied Europe.

(1) **Partisan activity**. In all the major countries controlled by the Nazis, from Italy, Holland, Germany, Belgium, and the Netherlands in the west, to Yugoslavia, Poland, Lithuania, the Ukraine, Byelorussia, Czechoslovakia, and the Soviet Union in the east, Jews joined non-Jewish partisan groups and also formed wholly Jewish partisan groups. Jews were, for instance, leaders within Italian partisan

---

85 I. Trunk, *Judenrat*, p. 217.
86 The work of this group has been described, with great insight, by Samuel Kassow, *"Who Will Write Our History?" Rediscovering a Hidden Archive from the Holocaust* (Bloomington, 2009).
87 The full history is retold by Betty Lifton, *The King of Children: The Life and Death of Janusz Korczak* (New York, 1988); and in Janusz Korczak's own *Ghetto Diary* (New York, 1978). See also the evidence provided in the essay on *Kol Yisrael Arevim Zeh L'zeh* in this volume.
88 L. Steinberg, *Not as a Lamb*, p. 245.

units, in the French underground, in which Jews made up approximately 20 percent of the membership,[89] in Belgium where the actions of Jewish partisans saved many lives, and in the various groups active in Poland.

(2) **Armed resistance in the ghettos.** As for armed resistance in the ghettos, everyone is familiar with the story of the Warsaw Ghetto uprising in April 1943. Against a military force sent to liquidate the ghetto, the remnants of the Jewish population, with no food and little in the way of arms, held out against the Nazis for almost three weeks. But it is essential to know that physical resistance was not restricted to the Warsaw Ghetto. There was, though too often unknown, organized physical resistance in many other ghettos. The first such action happened in the Nieśwież Ghetto on July 21, 1942.[90] This was then followed by uprisings in the Tuczyn Ghetto[91] and the small Lachwa Ghetto.[92] These ghettos were set on fire and the Jews in them fled to the nearby forests. There was, in addition,

---

[89] Robert Wistrich, *Hitler and the Holocaust* (New York, 2004), has pointed out that: "In France, Jews at one stage represented more than 15 percent of the resistance forces, more than twenty times their proportion of the total population. Their role in positions of leadership and command as well as in rank and file of the resistance was outstanding. Half the founders of *Libération* were Jews, and they were almost 20 percent of the members of the National Committee, the highest institution of the French underground. The founder of the Franc Tireurs et Partisans in the Paris region in 1942–1943 was a Jew, as were a disproportionate number of those who rallied to Charles de Gaulle's Free French forces in London." (p. 83). And consult also, on Jewish participation in the French Resistance, Ruby Rohrlich (ed.), *Resisting the Holocaust* (Oxford, 1998), p. 23. More generally, Wistrich observes that: "If we also consider the heroism and skill of the more than half a million Jewish soldiers in the ranks of the Red Army, as well as the distinguished service of more than seven hundred thousand Jews in the British and American armies (not to mention other Allied forces), then the military contribution of Jews to the defeat of Nazi Germany was by no means negligible. Approximately 10 percent of world Jewry (1.6 million out of 16 million) actually fought in the war, including the thirty-five thousand Palestinian Jews who volunteered for the Jewish Brigade in the British Army" (p. 84).

[90] I. Trunk, *Judenrat*, pp. 470–72; *idem.*, "The Attitude of the Judenrats to the Problem of Armed Resistance Against the Nazis," pp. 442, 444; *idem.*, *Fighters Among the Ruins* [Hebrew] (Jerusalem, 1988); and L. Steinberg, *Not as a Lamb*, p. 185.

[91] Y. Suhl (ed.), *They Fought Back*, contains a narrative regarding the Tuczyn ghetto revolt as pieced together by Mendel Mann, "The Revolt in the Tuczyn Ghetto," pp. 168–71.

[92] L. Steinberg, *Not as a Lamb*, describes the resistance in the Lachwa ghetto in August of 1942, "the first known case of organized physical resistance" (p. 184). Once the Jews of Lachwa realized that their fate was to be the same as that of the Jews in the neighboring community of Mikaszewice, which had been liquidated, they turned to the leader of their organized resistance movement, Icchak Rochczyn, and supported his call for an open revolt. Knowing that they could not defeat the Germans, Rochczyn decided that "At least [by fighting] they could make sure that as many of their assassins as possible would die with them and [something] would have been done to restore the dignity of the Jewish people" (pp. 183–84). Makeshift weapons such as axes, knives, iron bars, pitchforks, and clubs were used in addition to the single automatic weapon that the resistance was able to obtain. When the ghetto population discovered that pits were being dug in the vicinity, the signal was given, on August 27, for the attack. The Resistance set fire to the ghetto, Rochczyn succeeded in decapitating one German before he was killed, and the Germans fled. Several hundred Jews succeeded in reaching the surrounding forests, after which they faced attacks by Ukrainian soldiers and peasants. Only a handful survived.

armed resistance in the Mir Ghetto in 1942; in the Białystok Ghetto in August 1943; in the Słonim Ghetto, where the *Judenrät* was active in helping form the resistance; in the Kletzk Ghetto where 1,200 Jews escaped to the forest and 600 of these Jews survived; and in the Goldicher Ghetto where 1,200 Jews fled and joined the partisans. In Kovno, Haim Yellin, with the aid of the *Judenrät*, created an underground that organized escapes from the ghetto.[93] And when, as already noted, 140 Kovno ghetto police were taken prisoner by the Nazis and pressured for information on the ghetto underground they refused to betray their fellow Jews in spite of the fact that they knew they would be shot. In the Minsk Ghetto, the underground smuggled up to 10,000 Jews to freedom in the nearby forests, and up to 6,000 of these Jews survived the war.[94] In the Częstochowa Ghetto, in 1943, two armed Jewish youth groups and members of the workers' council fought the Nazis. One of these groups was trapped and murdered; one survived. And in the Tarnów Ghetto there was an open armed revolt in 1943. In total, the available evidence tells us that there were at least sixty-one ghettos that had some form of armed Jewish resistance.

(3) **Armed resistance in concentration and labor camps.** There were rebellions of different sorts in the many concentration and work camps. We know about acts of resistance at the Kruszyna concentration camp, the Krychów concentration camp, the Lublin camp, and the Kopernik camp at Minsk-Mazowiecki, as well as at Sachsenhausen.

(4) **Armed resistance in the death camps.** Most remarkably, there were uprisings at Sobibór in May 1942; in Treblinka on August 2, 1943; and in Auschwitz (Birkenau) on October 6–7, 1944. The Auschwitz uprising was led by the 451 Jewish *Sonderkommando* – those terribly fated young Jewish men who were chosen by the Nazis to work in the gas chambers and crematoria. This group managed to smuggle in gunpowder, with the help of Jewish women who worked as slave laborers in the factories at Buna and Monowitz, and used the powder they obtained to blow up one of the crematoria. This deed ended gassings at Auschwitz and, as a result, up to 60,000 Jews were still alive when the Camp was emptied by the Nazis and the infamous "Death Marches" of January 1945 took place. The camp was liberated by the Soviet army on January 27, 1945. And, at the same time,

---

93 *Ibid.,* p. 24.
94 Barbara Epstein, *The Minsk Ghetto, 1941–1943: Jewish Resistance and Soviet Internationalism* (Berkeley, 2008) discusses how the Minsk ghetto was unique in that a resistance movement emerged inside and outside the ghetto that included both Byelorussians and Jews. She tells us that:

> No one knows for sure how many Jews from the Minsk ghetto survived to join partisan units, but they certainly numbered in the thousands, and some estimate as many as 10,000 from a ghetto whose population was approximately 100,000 at its height…In the Minsk ghetto… there was no effort to mobilize an internal revolt. Instead, the main aim of the underground movement was to send as many Jews to the forest as possible to join the growing Soviet-aligned partisan movement. Flight to the partisans also became the aim of large numbers of ghetto Jews who did not belong to the underground; in effect, it became the major strategy of resistance of the ghetto as a whole. (p. 13)

there was an uprising at Chełmno (Kulmhof). These death camp revolts, by men and women who were starving, sick and pulverized by overwork and physical abuse, are the maximal expression of Jewish resistance. In environments in which all social and ethical norms had been upended and replaced by an extreme ethic based on uncompromising racial criteria that reduced *"der Jude"* to the status of sub-human vermin, the Jews retained their dignity, and were willing, against all odds, to fight, to the death, for it.

VI A few brief comparative observations in conclusion

The comparative remarks that I am about to make are not offered, and should not be misunderstood, as criticism of the non-Jewish groups to which I will make reference. Rather, they are introduced into this analysis as further data that should be factored into any adequate decipherment of, and judgment regarding, Jewish behavior during the *Shoah*.

The first cohort, whose behavior can, if done with care, be appropriately compared to that of the Jews, is the assemblage of 7.5 million non-Jewish forced laborers working in the German war economy.[95] These workers were not, of course, under sentence of death and so their situation was radically different from that of the Jews, hence my caution about this comparison. Yet, even allowing for all due difference in their lived situation, it is not without relevance to note that there was no organized resistance of any kind among these millions of forced laborers.

The second group of interest, whose actions might shed light on Jewish behavior, comprises the various underground movements in the different countries of Europe. Most of these undergrounds were, quite rightly, fearful of reprisals and did very little active, armed resisting until late in the war when the Germans were on the run. So one finds, for instance, that on February 5, 1941, the leadership of the Polish underground in London received the following report from General Stefan Grot-Rowecki, the leader of the Polish underground forces in Poland: "Active warfare against the Nazis can take place in our country only when the German people will be broken by military defeats, hunger and propaganda."[96] Following this advice, the Polish underground did not rise up in Warsaw until August 1, 1944, when the Soviet army was only a few miles from the capital. Likewise, in Slovakia, the national underground only openly rebelled in August 1944 when the Soviet army was already on Slovakian territory.[97] The Czechs revolted in Prague only on May 4, 1945, when Hitler had already committed suicide and the Third Reich was about to surrender to the Allies.[98] (One needs to remember that the

---

95 See details in Ulrich Herbert, "Labor as Spoils of Conquest, 1933–1945," in *Nazism and German Society, 1933–1945*, ed. David Crew (New York, 1994); and his longer study *A History of Foreign Labor in Germany, 1880–1980: Seasonal Workers, Forced Laborers, Guest Workers* (Ann Arbor, 1990).
96 Armia Krajowa, *Polskie Siły Zbrojne w Drugiej Wojnie Światowej* (London, 1951), vol. 3, pp. 172–83. I cite this from Y. Arad, "Jewish Armed Resistance in Eastern Europe," p. 492.
97 *Ibid.*
98 *Ibid.*

Czech underground had been paralyzed by the reprisals in Lidice following the assassination of Heydrich on May 27, 1942).[99]

Indeed, in Eastern Europe, the only significant partisan activity – other than that carried on in Yugoslavia by Tito – was undertaken in the western part of the Soviet Union where the partisan groups were organized and armed by the Soviet army, and operated as an official part of the Soviet army.[100]

The third group consists of the millions of non-Jewish concentration camp inmates. As with conscripted non-Jewish labor, their situation was, as a rule and by design, different from that of the Jews in both concentration and death camps. Nonetheless, their treatment, in many camps, was horrible and lethal. Large numbers of non-Jewish concentration camp inmates died from overwork, hunger, disease, and cruelty. Yet, there was no organized armed resistance by these tens of thousands of non-Jewish camp inmates in any of the concentration camps.

Fourth, the non-Jewish group that is the most significant for comparative purposes vis-à-vis Jewish conduct, is the 5.7 million Soviet POWs.[101] These men were, like the Jews, starved, beaten, dehumanized, and murdered. Of the 5.7 million Soviet prisoners of war, approximately 3.5 million would die in Nazi camps. Unlike the Jews, however, these individuals had been trained to fight. In addition, they were single men without families – wives, children, grandparents – to worry about, and they had a command structure that was led by seasoned officers. Yet, despite these "advantages" – and keeping in mind the terribly brutal treatment that they received – there was almost no organized resistance among these millions of military men.[102]

---

99 *Ibid.*
100 *Ibid.*
101 Christian Streit provides the following summary regarding the fate of these Russian prisoners of war: "Between 22 June 1941 and the end of the war, roughly 5.7 million members of the Red Army fell into German hands. In January 1945, 930,000 were still in German camps. A million at most had been released, most of whom were the so-called "volunteers" (*Hilfswillige*) for (often compulsory) auxiliary service in the Wehrmacht. Another 500,000, as estimated by the Army High Command, had either fled or been liberated. The remaining 3,300,000 (57.5 percent of the total) had perished," "Soviet Prisoners of War in the Hands of the Wehrmacht," in *War of Extermination: The German Military in World War II 1941–1944*, eds. Hannes Heer and Klaus Naumann (New York, 2000), pp. 80–81; Streit's larger German language study dealing with this same issue is entitled *Keine Kameraden. Die Wehrmacht und die sowjetischen Kriegsgefangenen 1941–1945* (Stuttgart, 1978). *The Oxford Companion to World War II*, eds. Ian Dear and Michael Foot (Oxford, 2001) summarizes the debate on these numbers as follows: "Historians also debate the overall figure of Soviet POW who died while they were under the armed forces' control. These numbers range from 1.68 million to at least 2.53 million and up to 3.3 million, out of a total of 5.7 million prisoners taken between 1941 and 1945" (p. 368).
102 They did participate, however, in the uprising at Sobibór. Here the leader of the Jewish resistance, numbering some 300 men, was Lieutenant Alexander Pechersky, a captured Russian officer. He had arrived at the camp with a small contingent of other Russian POWs in a transport of Jews from the Minsk Ghetto in September 1943, five weeks before the revolt. However, it is important to understand that his role was not representative of a specifically organized action by a distinct bloc of Soviet POWs as compared to a more general uprising of Jewish camp inmates. Thus,

This information about the deportment of the Russian POWs is not reported in order to criticize them for, I would argue, their passivity under the conditions in which they were incarcerated, is exactly what one would, and should, expect. Initially subject to intentional starvation and savagery, and always underfed and severely mistreated, it is completely understandable that these men did not have the will to rebel.

Yet, it is exactly this significant recognition that leads me to my final judgment: in light of this comparative diverse material, what is so striking about Jewish resistance in its totality, is not that there was too little as is regularly claimed, but rather, that there was so much.[103]

---

regarding this context, it is necessary to know that planning for resistance at the camp was already in the works under the leadership of Leon Feldhendler who had been the head of the *Judenrat* in Żółkiew (Galicia). For more on the uprising at Sobibór see Y. Arad, *Belzec, Sobibor, Treblinka*; Miriam Novitch (ed.), *Sobibór, Martyrdom and Revolt: Documentation and Testimonies* (New York, 1980); and Chris Webb, *Sobibor Death Camp: History, Biographies, Remembrance* (Stuttgart, 2017).

103 This paper was previously unpublished. It was revised for inclusion in this volume. Therefore there is no need to update it.

13

ELIE WIESEL: THE MAN AND HIS LEGACY*

I

Elie Wiesel died on July 2, 2016, bringing to an end a remarkable life. He was born in the small town of Sighet, at that time part of Romania, on September 30, 1928. His father, Shlomo, was a traditional Jew who made his living as a local merchant. He was known for his "intelligence, his perspicacity, and his kindness." Yet, late in life Elie would describe his relationship with his father as difficult and distant: "I never really knew my father . . . The truth is I knew little of the man I loved most in the world."[1] His mother, Sarah Feig, was a pious woman, the daughter of a Vizhnitz Hasid, who presided over the household. There were four children in the family, Eliezer, was the third youngest and the only boy. A bright youngster, he received a traditional orthodox education dominated by Talmudic study. And like his friends, he was also deeply interested to study Kabbalah. He would later recall:

> I met with my master of mysticism every evening. Under his vigilant eye three of us decided to venture into the Pardes, the orchard of forbidden knowledge. We began our quest for the absolute by fasting on Mondays and Thursdays. We would stay at the House of Study until midnight, poring over the Sefer Yetzirah (which is attributed to Rabbi Yehuda Hachasid) and the writings of Rabbi Hayyim Vital, favorite disciple of the founder of Lurianic mysticism. I was insatiable. Captivated by the dazzling theories of creation: the shattering of the vessels, the emanations of first light, the scattered sparks. How could the purity of the beginning be recovered? How to liberate the Lord, prisoner of Himself and of our own actions? How to join the first breath to the last, to master the source and that which overflows? For an adolescent thirsting

---

* I would like to thank Rabbi Josef Polak and Dr. Yoel Rappel, both of whom were close friends of Elie Wiesel, for reading and commenting on this essay in draft.

1 The description of the relationship with his father is cited from *All Rivers Run to the Sea: Memoirs, Vol. 1, 1928–1969* (New York, 1995), pp. 3 and 6.

for knowledge and dreams there is nothing more romantic and alluring than the Kabala.[2]

Had World War II not intervened to change his life totally, Wiesel probably would have become, as he told me, a teacher of Talmud. His mother's ambition for him was the rabbinate or a medical degree.

During the first years of the war the Jews of Sighet were sheltered from Nazi violence by virtue of the fact that Hungary had taken over the area of Romania in which Sighet was located. In consequence, Wiesel and his family were protected from deportation, like all the Jews of Hungary, until the spring of 1944. At that point in time the Hungarian Arrow Cross government that had come to power in October 1944 agreed to the deportation of the country's Jews, who represented the last surviving major Jewish community in occupied Europe that was still intact. Eichmann arrived in Budapest in March 1944 and, with the help of a contingent of Germans and the full cooperation of the Hungarian government, began the massive deportations of Hungarian Jewry. In a period of 56 days, from May 15 to July 8, 1944, 437,402 Jews were deported to the Death Camps, and especially to Auschwitz-Birkenau. Of those Jews who arrived at Auschwitz-Birkenau, approximately 90 percent were exterminated immediately, and 10 percent were "selected" for slave labor.

Wiesel, at age 15, found himself in the minority cohort. He was assigned to the nearby Buna-Monowitz industrial complex where, despite the terrible conditions, he survived the last year of the war. In January 1945, as the Russian army approached the camp, those Jews still among the living were sent on the infamous "death march" towards Germany. Many of those who were forced to make this brutal trek died along the way. But the young Wiesel managed to finish the journey and, a starving skeleton, found himself at Buchenwald. At war's end, in the spring of 1945, he had lost both his parents and his younger sister, Tsiporah, to whom he was deeply attached, while his two older sisters had, like him, survived as slave laborers.

Immediately following the surrender of Germany, Wiesel was sent, along with some 426 other Jewish youngsters, to Normandy, to a home for refugee children provided by the L'Oeuvre de Secours aux Enfants (OSE), a French Jewish organization that during the war rescued, and after the war helped, Jewish refugee children. France would now become his home and French his literary language. His deep appreciation for the reception he received in France, and his affection for its culture, were to be among the defining features of his adult personal and intellectual life. His books were nearly always written in French, though he also wrote in Hebrew and Yiddish, and later in English. Indeed, the first version of his most famous and iconic work, *Night*, was originally written in Hebrew, then Yiddish, and was entitled *Un Di Velt Hot Geshvign* (*The World Remained Silent*).

2 *Ibid.*, p. 34.

In France, life slowly regained its normality. Elie studied the language, went to the equivalent of high school, began to write, became a student of literature at the Sorbonne, and, importantly, continued to study Talmud with a very mysterious Lithuanian Talmudic genius named Rav Mordechai Shushani. Oral tradition reports that Shushani knew thirty languages and could quote by heart the whole of the Talmud and Zohar. It is about Shushani that Wiesel wrote: "I owe my constant drive to question, my pursuit of mystery that lies within knowledge, and of the darkness hidden within light," and that, "What I know is that I would not be the man I am, the Jew I am, had not an astonishing, disconcerting vagabond accosted me one day to inform me that I understood nothing."[3] Later in life, Wiesel, as the very loyal student that he was, sought to re-establish contact with Shushani, who was then living in South America, in order to offer financial help, but without success. Wiesel later expressed his gratitude in an essay entitled "The Death of My Teacher."

To support himself, Wiesel worked for a small wage as a choir master. He loved music – he had played the violin as a boy – and this was an interest that stayed with him throughout his adult life. He was a friend to many of the leading musical figures of our times. On one occasion I recall his telling me to call Yitzhak Pearlman and YoYo Ma to come and play at a conference in his honor at Boston University. His passion for music found its most public manifestation in a concert at the 92nd Street Y in New York City in 1992, where he performed as a soloist guest conductor with the National Jewish Chorale. In addition, he acted as Cantor in his New York City orthodox synagogue on Tisha Be'Av, on the eve of Yom Kippur, and on the holiday of Simchat Torah, which also coincided with his birthday.

In 1948, on the eve of the founding of the State of Israel, Wiesel volunteered for the Haganah but was rejected because of his physical condition. In 1949 he made his first visit to Israel. He later described the journey as, "like reliving . . . childhood dreams."[4] However he did not stay in Israel – it is uncertain why – and he returned to Paris. In January 1952 he went by ship in search of psychological and spiritual tranquility in India, but, overwhelmed by the poverty and "an immeasurable, unnamable suffering,"[5] he returned once again to Paris. In Paris he made new friends, was deeply influenced by French existentialist thought, and in 1954 began to write the Yiddish version of his Auschwitz experiences. All through his lifetime his close connections with French intellectuals were important to him and this affection was reciprocated by many in French intellectual and political

---

3 *All Rivers Run to the Sea*, pp. 128, 130. See his entire description of this relationship, pp. 121–30. For more on Shushani see Jeffrey Mehlman, "The Mozart of the Talmud," in *Agni* 76 (2012): 220–29. Mehlman records a conversation with Emmanuel Levinas at Johns Hopkins University in 1973 during which Levinas said: "Believe me, Mehlman, I who studied with Heidegger, can tell you that next to Shushani Heidegger was *nothing*!" (p. 221). And see also Wiesel's reminiscence in *All Rivers Run to the Sea*, p. 124.
4 *All Rivers Run to the Sea*, p. 181.
5 "Recalling Swallowed-Up Worlds," *The Christian Century* 98.19 (May 27, 1981): 610–11.

circles, including Francois Mitterrand, his friend for many years, who became the President of the nation in 1981. Wiesel regularly returned to the French capital throughout the 1980s and 1990s to participate in major events, many held at the Élysée Palace.

In the late 1940s he began publishing newspaper articles and in 1950 he became the Paris correspondent for the Israeli paper *Yediot Ahronot*. In 1955 he was asked to become their representative in America. This brought him to New York City in 1956 where he made his home for the next sixty years. Here, despite a serious car accident in 1956 that caused forty-eight fractures and kept him in a wheel chair for a year, he began to write columns in Yiddish on cultural matters for the *Forverts*, and was befriended by Rabbi Wolfe Kelman, an influential presence at the Jewish Theological Seminary, and the Executive Vice-President of the Rabbinical Assembly. Through him, Wiesel became a devoted "student" of the great Talmudist Saul Lieberman and a close friend of Abraham Joshua Heschel who he later described as, "a sort of older brother to me."[6] In addition, the Seminary became the academic home of his childhood friend from Sighet, David Weiss Halivni, also an Auschwitz survivor, and to whom Wiesel now became very close. It was Kelman who arranged for him to address a Rabbinical Convention of the Conservative Movement where he deeply impressed his rabbinical audience. As a result, he received a long list of invitations to speak in synagogues and thus became known to the American Jewish community. To the end of his life he expressed his indebtedness to these seminary figures, especially Lieberman.[7] I vividly remember his sobbing phone call to me on the day Lieberman died on an airplane en route to Israel.

The French publication of *Night*, under the title *La Nuit*, occurred in 1958. It was based on the much longer, 825-page, Yiddish version (printed in Buenos Aires in 1956). Elie had shortened and made it into a more readable and available work at the urging of the well-known French intellectual Francois Mauriac, a Catholic author who had won the Nobel Prize for literature. Mauriac wrote a Foreword to the book, introducing it to the French reading public. Over the years some critics have alleged that this transformation involved creating events and scenes that had not actually taken place. Elie was deeply stung by these criticisms; he told me he could identify every person and incident in *Night*. There had been no liberties taken. One of the great ironies connected with this famous publication is that Wiesel's royalties were, and remained, minimal. Being very anxious to see his work in print, he signed a very one-sided contract with the book's French publishers, Les Éditions de Minuit, a fact he laughed at many times in private conversation. In 1960 the book was translated into English and became an international phenomenon. It has since been translated into thirty languages, with a new English translation by his wife Marion in 2006. It has been read by millions and has had a

---

6 Elie Wiesel and Philippe-Michael De Saint-Cheron, *Evil and Exile* (Notre Dame, IN, 1990), p. 162.
7 See Wiesel's comments on Professor Lieberman in *All Rivers Run to the Sea*, p. 105.

remarkable and varied history. For example, it has been the required "Book of the Year" in the Chicago schools, and the "Book of the Month" of the Oprah Winfrey Book Club (2006).

However famous Wiesel now became, his experience at Auschwitz defined and haunted him:

> Never shall I forget that night, the first night in camp, which has turned my life into one long night, seven times cursed and seven times sealed. Never shall I forget that smoke. Never shall I forget the little faces of children, whose bodies I saw turned into wreaths of smoke beneath the blue sky . . . never shall I forget these things, even if I am condemned to live as long as God Himself. Never.[8]

This was his literal nightmare that compelled him to tell the story. To allow the memory of the Death Camps to fall into oblivion would be, in his view, the ethical equivalent of murdering the victims twice. "The urgent obligation to bear witness remains constant. It is quite simple, a witness who does not give his or her witness may be considered a false witness."[9] But being a witness is a very difficult thing. Testifying is a very heavy burden to bear because reminding others of what was is often not welcome. In *Five Biblical Portraits*, when retelling the event of Elijah's passing on the mantle of prophecy to Elisha, he has the great prophet say:

> And now we understand Elijah's parting words to Elisha: You want your powers to be twice as great as mine? If you see me go away how to look, how to participate in all events, if you know how to face pain and despair and go beyond them, and if later you will be capable of telling about them, your wish will be granted: you will have my powers and yours as well. And you will need them, I am your master but you are the survivor. I thought I was alone, and I was – and still am – but now you are with me and you too will be alone, you already are. You will speak and you will need great strength and good fortune to make yourself heard . . . you will tell of the fire that has carried me away from you, and the others will refuse to believe you. And I feel sorry for you. You will speak a few will listen, fewer will understand, and still fewer will agree. I feel sorry for you, Elisha, my young friend – for what you are seeing now, no one will ever see. And yet, the first that will carry me away will not stay with me; I will stay with you. Forever.[10]

---

8 Elie Wiesel, *Night* (New York, 1982), p. 32. The new translation by Marion Wiesel was published by Hill and Wang (New York, 2006).
9 On the subject of witnessing see: Elie Wiesel, "Why I Write," in Alvin H. Rosenfeld and Irving Greenberg (eds.), *Confronting the Holocaust: The Impact of Elie Wiesel* (Bloomington, 1978), p. 201; and idem, *One Generation After* (New York, 1972), p. 174.
10 Elie Wiesel, *Five Biblical Portraits* (Notre Dame, IN, 1986), pp. 28–29.

Throughout the 1960s, Wiesel's reputation continued to grow. Along with the expanding influence of *Night*, he carried on his other journalistic activities, including covering the Eichmann trial in 1961, and became a key mediator between Israeli and American Jews, especially in the period leading up to and away from the Six Day War in June, 1967, and a leader in the struggle to liberate Soviet Jewry. In the mid-1960s he traveled twice to the Soviet Union and chronicled his experiences in his book, *The Jews of Silence: A Personal Report on Soviet Jewry*, published in 1966, which exposed the restrictions on Jews imposed by the Soviet government. The book became an instant sensation and energized a world-wide campaign to free Soviet Jewry, at the head of which was Wiesel.

In 1969 Elie married Marion Rose, a French Jewish woman, and in 1972 their only son, Elisha, was born. Saul Lieberman officiated at their wedding in Jerusalem, and Marion was now to become an important translator of Wiesel's work from French into English.

From 1966 to 1990, Wiesel devoted himself to the cause of Soviet Jewry, speaking throughout the world on behalf of the Jews of the Soviet Union. Emphasizing their desire to remain Jews, and insisting on the moral obligation of Jews in the West to help them achieve this goal, he worked tirelessly in pursuit of this cause. He was successful, in particular, in making this an initiative that western democratic governments became involved in. During these years, until 1990, no other issue consumed his time as much as this one. In private conversation he told me how he would visit Lod airport in Israel to watch Russian *olim* arrive in Israel in the early morning as the fulfillment of a dream, as the completion of an obligation. On one occasion he confided that of all the activities he had been involved in he was proudest of this work and, if he could be remembered for only one thing, he would like it to be his involvement in this campaign.

Wiesel's work on behalf of Soviet Jewry, because of the public and political way he went about it, did not meet with universal approval. Among those who disagreed, and who counted most to Wiesel, was the Lubavitcher Rebbe, Menachem Mendel Schneerson, with whom he had begun to forge a close and affectionate bond. In his memoir, *All Rivers Run to the Sea* and, again, in his collection *Against Silence* he talks of this friendship:

> The fourth chapter of *Gates of the Forest* is about Brooklyn, the *Farbrengen*, and my idealized image of a Hasidic Rebbe, the Lubavitcher Rebbe. I describe how we met, how I came to the *Farbrengen*. I describe our first conversation which lasted hours. At one point, I asked him point blank, "Rebbe, how can you believe in God after the Khourban?" He looked at me and said, "And how can you not believe after the Khourban?" Well, that was a turning point in my writing, that simple dialogue.[11]

---

11 *All Rivers Run to the Sea*, p. 402; and *Against Silence: The Voice and Vision of Wiesel*, edited by Irving Abrahamson, 3 vols. (New York, 1985), vol. 3, p. 63.

But on the issue of the approach to be taken vis-à-vis Soviet Jewry they disagreed fundamentally. Lubavitch was, by the 1960s, already extremely active in the Soviet Union – today they dominate Jewish life in Russia – but they purposely worked in a quiet manner that was meant to keep them out of the news. The Rebbe, therefore, disapproved of Wiesel's very public campaign. When, in the end, the Soviet Union allowed its Jews to leave because of the world-wide pressure that had been brought to bear in the very public fight to allow the emigration of Soviet Jewry, the Rebbe wrote to Wiesel praising him and telling him that he had been right, while the Rebbe had been wrong. In the life of both men this was a unique experience.

Closer to home, Wiesel formed a close friendship with another rising star in the American Jewish community, Rabbi Irving (Yitz) Greenberg. Greenberg, an orthodox rabbi, with a doctorate in American history from Harvard, was reaching out to the leadership of American Jewry with an optimistic message that was validating the work of the Jewish Federations. Greenberg emphasized four values: the meaningfulness, even sanctity, of communal activity; support for Israel; a new, controversial, theological response to the Holocaust; and the need for the Jewish leadership to become more Jewishly literate. In the late 1960s he moved from Yeshiva University, where he had become a controversial figure, to the City College of New York where he became Director of the Program in Jewish Studies. Realizing Wiesel's teaching gifts Greenberg invited him to join his faculty as a Distinguished Professor in 1972. In addition, in 1974, Greenberg and Wiesel, together with Rabbi Stephen Shaw, created an organization called the National Jewish Resource Center (which in 1985 changed its name to The National Jewish Center for Learning and Leadership, and most recently has evolved into CLAL, headed by R. Irwin Kula), in order to advance the objectives just noted. Under this organizational umbrella Greenberg, Wiesel, and others – including myself – lectured to all sorts of Jewish groups across the country, from Federations to synagogues and even on Wall Street to early breakfast study sessions.

In 1976 President John Silber of Boston University, one of the most controversial figures in American higher education, heard Wiesel lecture in New York City. He was deeply impressed and immediately offered Wiesel the Andrew Mellon Chair at Boston University. Wiesel accepted and thus began a career of 36 years of teaching in Boston, to where he commuted from New York City (with dinner each week with the Silbers). During these years he taught thousands of undergraduates, a number of doctoral students, and gave three public lectures each fall that drew approximately 1,500 listeners on each occasion. These public lectures became so popular that when President Silber eliminated the expensive intercollegiate football program at Boston University, he explained that Wiesel's lectures drew a larger audience than did the football team.

Wiesel was by now a world figure. The publication of a continual stream of books and articles on many issues and themes including the Bible, the Talmud, and Hasidism now became a major feature in both the Jewish and Christian cultural and religious scene. Among the main publications of this extraordinarily fertile period in

Wiesel's intellectual life were: *Souls on Fire* (1972), *Messengers of God* (1975), *Four Hasidic Masters* (1978), *Somewhere a Master* (1982), *Five Biblical Portraits* (1986), *Sages and Dreamers* (1991), and *Wise Men and Their Tales* (2003), and also included a wide range of essays which were collected together in a three-volume set entitled *Against Silence* (1985). There was also a steady stream of fiction: *Dawn* (1961), *The Accident* (1962, later republished as *Day*, based on its original French title), *The Town Beyond the Wall* (1962), *The Gates of the Forest* (1964), *A Beggar in Jerusalem* (1968), *The Oath* (1973), *Zalman, or the Madness of God* (1974), *The Testament* (1980), *Twilight* (1987), and *The Forgotten* (1992). The earliest of these works dealt with the aftermath of the Holocaust, but after his third novel, beginning with *The Town Beyond the Wall* (1962), Wiesel moved to the wider canvas of Jewish history and human experience. But whatever the specific subject of these later publications, at the core of his work was always the issue of suffering, the question of meaning/meaninglessness, the search for God and justice, and the need to witness to "what cannot really be described." Deeply self-aware, he described what he was attempting to do with this cryptic remark: "I try to communicate silence with words."[12]

He also repeatedly emphasized that more than honorable intentions were required of all of us: men and women must take responsibility and act. "We must admit the obsession, the overall dominating theme of responsibility, that we are responsible for one another."[13] Thus Wiesel insisted: "Man can't afford to wait for God's decision to send the Messiah because his life hangs in the balance,"[14] Likewise, the rabbi turned madman in Wiesel's *Zalman, or the Madness of God* demandingly teaches that: "God requires of man not that he live, but that he choose to live. What matters is to choose . . . at the risk of being defeated"[15]

These were profound themes and critics and ordinary readers alike were enthralled by Wiesel, both as a consummate storyteller in the tradition of the *Maggid* and as an interpreter of the Jewish tradition. But amidst his re-readings of the classical Jewish material there was always a post-Holocaust sensibility. "Let him who wants fervor not seek it on mountain places [i.e., Sinai], rather let him stop and search among the ashes."[16] As such, with the interest in the *Shoah* continually expanding in America and Europe, his novels became regular reading assignments in many religion, philosophy, and ethics classes throughout the world. And his work began to attract an increasing number of scholarly studies and doctoral dissertations – today these number well over 100 in a wide variety of languages.

The earliest of these secondary works began to appear in the 1970s. Alvin Rosenfeld and Irving Greenberg edited an influential collection of essays by a

---

12 "Why I Write," in *From the Kingdom of Memory: Reminiscences* (New York, 1990), p. 14.
13 Harry James Cargas in *Conversation with Elie Wiesel* (New York, 1976), p. 17.
14 *Ibid.*, p. 62. See Wiesel's narrative in *The Gates of the Forest*, pp. 32–33, 225: "Whether or not the Messiah comes doesn't matter: we'll manage without him. We shall be honest and humble and strong, and then he will come, he will come every day, thousands of times every day."
15 *Ibid.*, p. 53
16 *Souls on Fire*, p. 71.

number of distinguished scholars entitled *Confronting the Holocaust: The Impact of Elie Wiesel* (1978), and Harry James Cargas edited a second collection entitled *Responses to Elie Wiesel: Critical Essays by Major Jewish and Christian Scholars* (1978). The latter publication began a long and rich stream of studies by Christian theologians on Wiesel's work, such as Robert McAfee's influential *Elie Wiesel: Messenger to all Humanity* (1989), and saw Wiesel's influence spread among notable Christian thinkers such as A. Roy Eckhardt and Alice Eckhardt, Eugene Fisher, Franklin Littell, Johann Baptist Metz, Reinhold Boschki and John Roth. This flow of doctoral theses and critical appraisals by scholars of many religious traditions has continued down to the collection created to celebrate Wiesel's 80th birthday, *Jewish Literary and Moral Perspectives* (2013), edited by Alan Rosen and myself. And there is no doubt that there will now be a new, extended, round of scholarly appraisals and appreciations following his death.

What is particularly notable in Wiesel's own, very long, list of publications is that the great majority do not deal with the Holocaust. Instead, drawing heavily on the French existentialists – he was especially taken with, and influenced by, the work of Albert Camus – he reinterpreted classical Jewish sources, beginning with the Bible, in a powerful and immediate way. In particular, he tried to argue, through stories and speeches rather than formal philosophical or theological works, for the need to empathetically participate in and alleviate the suffering of others, a theme whose emphasis he shared with another great Jewish post-war intellectual, Emmanuel Levinas.

As he grew older, he increasingly came to terms with God. His youthful, innocent faith shattered by the Death Camps, Wiesel had written in *Night*: "The Eternal, Lord of the universe, the All-Powerful and Terrible was silent,"[17] And had pointedly asked: "Where is God now? Where is He? Here He is – He is hanging here on this gallows."[18] Again, in his 1962 work *Day*, he wrote:

> Yes, God needs man. Condemned to eternal solitude, he needs man only to use him as a toy to amuse himself . . . Man prefers to blame himself for all possible sins and crimes rather than conclude that God is capable of the most flagrant injustice . . . I still blush every time I think of the way God makes fun of human beings, his favorite toys.[19]

This theme of betrayal by Heaven was continued in the 1979 play, *The Trial of God*. Here, the Divine is put on trial.

> He annihilated Shamgorod and you want me to be for Him? I can't. If He insists upon going on with His methods, let Him – but I won't say Amen.

---

17 *Night*, p. 31.
18 *Ibid.* (New York, 1972), p. 76.
19 Elie Wiesel, *Day* (first published in English in 1962 as *The Accident*). I cite this quote from the reprint edition, *Night Dawn, Day* (Northvale, NJ, 1985), p. 239. This novel was first published in French (*Le Jour*) in 1961 and in English in 1962.

> Let Him crush me, I won't say Kaddish. Let Him kill us all, I shall shout and shout that it's His fault. I'll use my last energy to make my protest known. Whether I live or die, I submit to Him no longer.[20]

This theologically challenging event, which Wiesel sets in the Ukraine in 1649, was based on an actual trial that had taken place at Auschwitz.

In effect, in the decades after Auschwitz, Wiesel could not live with God, and he could not live without Him.

> God's final victory, my son, lies in man's inability to reject Him. You think you're cursing Him, but your curse is praise; you think you're fighting Him, but all you do is open yourself to Him; you think you're crying out your hatred and rebellion, but all you're doing is telling Him how much you need His support and forgiveness.[21]

However much one tried to believe, all religious commitment had been "broken." What religious faith now remained available had to be rebuilt from the fragments of the tradition that had been shattered by the Death Camps. "Perhaps someday someone will explain how, on the level of man, Auschwitz was possible; but on the level of God it will remain forever the most disturbing of mysteries."[22]

By the 1980s, however, his attitude, while never uncritical and never without a note of protest – and always involving the unresolved question of where was God at Auschwitz – became less confrontational, less hostile. Indeed, he told me that he would like his words that are quoted inside the United States Holocaust Memorial Museum: "Never shall I forget those flames which consumed my faith forever" (*Night*, p. 32), to be removed and replaced by something less skeptical. In a 1997 *New York Times* piece he wrote to God: "In my testimony, I had written harsh words, burning words, about your role in our tragedy . . . Let us make up, Master of the Universe. In spite of everything that happened? Yes, in spite. Let us make up for the child in me. It is unbearable to be divorced from you so long."[23]

---

20 *The Trial of God: (as it was held on February 25, 1649 in Shamgorod)* (New York, 1979), p. 133.
21 *The Gates of the Forest* (New York, 1966), p. 33.
22 *One Generation After* (New York, 1970), p. 67.
23 *New York Times*, October 2, 1997. In *Souls on Fire* Wiesel made this crucial point: "Jewish tradition allows man to say anything to God, provided it be on behalf of man. Man's inner liberation is God's justification. It all depends on where the rebel chooses to stand. From inside his community, he may say everything. Let him step outside, and he will be denied this right. The revolt of the believer is not that of the renegade; the two do not speak in the name of the same anguish" (*Souls on Fire*, p. 111). And in *All Rivers Run to the Sea* he made his most mature statement on the issue of God: "I have never renounced my faith in God. I have risen against His justice, protested His silence and sometimes His absence, but my anger rises up within faith and not outside it . . . I have always aspired to follow in the footsteps of my father and those who went before him . . . it is permissible for man to accuse God, provided it be done in the name of faith in God (*All Rivers Run to the Sea*, p. 84).

In 1979 President Carter, for his own political reasons, appointed Wiesel to be the Chair of the President's Commission on the Holocaust. This led to his 1980 appointment as the founding Chairman of the United States Holocaust Memorial Council which turned out to be a difficult and contentious assignment. And Wiesel, angry at the political aspects of the undertaking, resigned his chairmanship, although later he became the main figure associated with the museum.

In 1985 fate thrust him into the public arena in a new and dramatic way. It was announced that he was to be honored by President Ronald Reagan with the Congressional Gold Medal of Achievement. The ceremony was to take place at the White House on April 19, 1985, the 42nd anniversary of the Warsaw Ghetto Uprising. But bestowing this honor on Wiesel was not quite innocent. President Reagan had become embroiled in an international controversy sparked by his having accepted an invitation from German Chancellor Helmut Kohl to participate in a wreath laying ceremony at Bitburg's military cemetery where SS men were buried. I believe that Reagan had hoped to use the medal ceremony to deflect what was becoming a loud chorus of criticism of his acceptance of Kohl's invitation. But he was to be surprised by Wiesel's words during his acceptance speech at the ceremony: "That place, Mr. President, is not your place. Your place is with the victims of the SS."

These words reverberated in America, Europe, and Israel: Wiesel was now seen as an unparalleled moral force in the contemporary world. In 1986 he was awarded the Nobel Peace Prize. The Nobel citation explained the reason for his selection: "His message is one of peace, atonement and human dignity. His belief that the forces fighting evil in the world can be victorious is a hard-won belief." On that occasion, Wiesel told his audience:

> That is why I swore never to be silent whenever and wherever human beings endure suffering and humiliation . . . apartheid is, in my view, as abhorrent as antisemitism. To me, Andrei Sakharov is as much of a disgrace as Joseph Begun's imprisonment. As is the denial of the "Solidarity" trade union and denial of Lech Walesa's right to dissent and Nelson Mandela's interminable imprisonment . . . as long as one dissident is in prison, our freedom will not be true.[24] (Nobel Acceptance Speech, December 10, 1986)

The Nobel Prize money went into a foundation that Wiesel created to help those in need, most of the funds going, over the years, to help Ethiopian Jewish children in Israel. In connection with such charitable actions Wiesel purposely kept a low profile. Yet it should be said in his memory that this was just one of a very large number of good deeds done for many, in private. He supported the yeshiva of his very close childhood friend, R. Menashe Klein, in Israel almost

---

24 Nobel Acceptance Speech, December 10, 1986. Reprinted in *From the Kingdom of Memories: Reminiscences* (Summit Books: New York, 1990), pp. 232–36.

single-handedly, found extra funds for graduate students, aided organizations and publications he felt were important, and lent his name and influence to a myriad of good causes. The Madoff scandal (revealed in 2008) almost destroyed both his personal resources and those of the Wiesel Foundation. And Madoff was the only man I ever heard Wiesel effectively curse. Fortunately, following the scandal, a portion of this money was clawed back and returned to the Wiesel Foundation.

After winning the Nobel Prize Wiesel became even more engaged as an activist on the world stage. He tirelessly attempted to assist and mediate in circumstances of war and oppression wherever he felt it was necessary. As he explained in his Nobel Prize speech: "We must always take sides. Neutrality helps the oppressor, never the victim. Silence encourages the tormentor, never the tormented. When human lives are endangered, when human dignity is in jeopardy, national borders and sensitivities become irrelevant." In truth, however, this was not a completely new role for him. Already in 1966, he had actively taken up the cause of Biafra.[25] Then in 1975, during a trip to South Africa, he spoke out against the apartheid regime.

> You feel ashamed when you look inside their dwellings, when you glance at their faces. It is man within you, white man, who feels himself reduced to shame. You lower your eyes so as not to see South Africa.
>
> You want to do something. You know that something ought to be done – and quickly. But you also know that you are powerless. Too much misery has been built up here over too many years. There has been too much suffering, too much injustice. Might it still be possible to act, to make a fresh start? That is difficult to believe. One is imbued with a feeling of finality. Too late, it is too late.
>
> What strikes one about apartheid is its pettiness, as well as its cruelty. Those restaurants for blacks and whites. Those separate hospitals. Those separate buses. Those separate lavatories. An injured white and an injured black must not be carried together in the same ambulance. Either one or the other, but not together.
>
> It is impossible not to protest; impossible at one and the same time to believe in Judaism and to pass over in silence an ideology based on considerations of color. We are against racism by tradition and by definition.[26]

In 1976, Wiesel wrote a Preface to a book by Richard Arens that focused on the persecution of the Ache Indians of Paraguay.[27] He also went to Thailand to protest the murderous action of Pol Pot's Khmer Rouge regime, a visit he movingly

---

25 See his 1970 reprint, "Biafra the End," in *A Jew Today* (New York, 1979), pp. 29–30.
26 "Dateline: Johannesburg," pp. 52 and 54, in *A Jew Today* (New York, 1979), pp. 52–55.
27 *Genocide in Paraguay*, (Philadelphia, 1976).

recounted in an essay "A Plea for the Boat People";[28] traveled to Nicaragua to speak on behalf of the Miskito Indians who were being badly mistreated by the leftist Sandinistas;[29] and undertook a journey to Argentina in defense of Jacobo Timerman who had been accused of disloyalty and jailed by the right-wing civic-military dictatorship that took over control of the country in 1976. (See Timerman's well-known book, *Prisoner Without a Name, Cell Without a Number*, chronicling his imprisonment.) Nor did Wiesel stop protesting the crimes of the Soviet Union against its Jewish citizens.

And, from a distance, he raised his voice over the murder that was taking place in Chile, South Africa, Rwanda, the former Yugoslavia, and Darfur. At the opening dedication of the U.S. Holocaust Memorial Museum Wiesel, just returned from a trip to war-torn Yugoslavia, told President Clinton: "Mr. President, I cannot not tell you something. I cannot sleep [since my visit to Yugoslavia]. We must stop the bloodshed in that country . . . Something, something must be done."[30] A few months later President Clinton finally acted.

He befriended the Dalai Lama and protested on his behalf against Chinese actions in Tibet. In private conversation, as in public statements, he expressed particular admiration for the Dalai Lama who he considered a visionary figure. He publicly supported the Armenian account of their suffering in World War I. His door was always open to those who protested against tyranny and oppression. He told me that the day his very serious heart problems were discovered in 2012, and his doctors demanded that he come in immediately for what turned out to be a quintuple bypass operation, he asked his physicians for a brief postponement of his surgery to later in the day because he had a group of Iranian opposition figures coming to see him. His activism caused occasional criticism and embroiled him in political controversy – e.g., over the Iraq war which he supported publicly – with parts of the Israeli left that wanted him to become involved in their activities, and later with President Obama over Iran, a subject on which he was exceptionally passionate and outspoken, but he believed that he was consistent in the positions he struck, including vis-à-vis Israel and the Palestinians.[31]

Wiesel's activism also included major involvement in almost every major Holocaust-related scholarly and political initiative in North America, Europe and Israel. As regards the last, and especially to be noted, was his active participation in the affairs of Yad Vashem, Israel's official Holocaust Remembrance Center and Archive. He served as Vice Chair of the Yad Vashem Council for a number

---

28 Irving Abrahamson (ed.) *Against Silence*, vol. 1, in his *The Kingdom of Memory* and in his memoir *And the Sea is Never Full*, pp. 89–90.
29 See his recollection in *And the Sea is Never Full*, pp. 91–94.
30 Cited in an *Associated Press* news story entitled "Black Hole in History: 50 Years after Holocaust Museum Dedicated," April 23, 1993.
31 See his anguished open letter "To a Young Palestinian Arab" (1970) and his comments in *And the Sea is Never Full*, p. 125. Note also his comments in Elie Wiesel and Michaël de Saint Cheron, *Evil and Exile* (Notre Dame, IN, 1990), pp. 21–22.

of years and was also instrumental in helping to create the American Friends of Yad Vashem. He worked closely with the Yad Vashem leadership, beginning with Professor Yitzchak Arad, in order to ensure cooperation between the United States Holocaust Museum and the already established World Center in Jerusalem.

It was not for nothing that Wiesel received 140 honorary doctorates from universities all over the world and at least 200 major prizes of various sorts. Or that he was asked by the Prime Minister of Sweden to be the Honorary Chair of the Stockholm Conference on Conscience and Humanity that led to the creation of the International Holocaust Remembrance Alliance, now comprising thirty-one countries with several more about to join. This is now the major organization in the world that supports Holocaust remembrance and education and that works against all forms of Holocaust denial and contemporary antisemitism. Or that he was invited to chair the International Commission on the Holocaust in Romania (2003). And that he was twice offered the presidency of Israel and given an honorary knighthood by Queen Elizabeth in London.

Here it needs to be emphasized that Wiesel was a man with not only a very strong sense of moral obligation, but also a man with an iron will. It is not widely known, but now should be, that he was for many years, as already mentioned, a friend of French President Francois Mitterrand. Yet, when it became known that Mitterrand's behavior during World War II included some very dubious actions, Wiesel asked him to publicly apologize. Mitterrand declined this request as "unbecoming" for the President of France. At which point Wiesel ended all relations with him. Mitterrand repeatedly attempted to renew the friendship – I was in his office one morning when Mitterrand called and Elie refused to take it – but Wiesel was adamant on the need for an apology and the two never re-established their friendship. Again, when Prime Minister Netanyahu failed to keep a commitment he had made to Wiesel, their relations became distant. Earlier, he had become critical of President Carter and ended his association with him and his advisors. Then too, one cannot but wonder at the courage that it took to rebuke President Reagan publicly, and to speak truth to power in the case of President Clinton.

Elie's strong will was also manifest on a number of occasions related to Israel. I believe that the security and wellbeing of Israel were his most profound commitments, for example, when in 1991 Iraq fired rockets into Israel, Wiesel, who had just returned from a visit to the country, turned around and went back to be with the People of Israel during this dangerous time. Yet, he rejected an invitation to become the President of Israel. When I strongly encouraged him to accept this offer as a remarkable culmination of his personal journey, he said that he felt "he could do more good representing Israel in his private capacity," and was unmovable from this decision. Again: despite his support of President Obama, he courageously wrote an open letter to the President in 2010 asking him not to pressure Israel over the issue of the settlements and Jerusalem. "For me, the Jew that I am," wrote Wiesel, "Jerusalem is above politics." And then, regardless of his reservations about Prime Minister Netanyahu, he strongly and openly supported Netanyahu's address before the U.S. Congress, making the trip to Washington and sitting in the Congress' gallery during the speech. Lastly, it should also be recognized that he repeatedly and courageously criticized Iran even though he believed that he was a possible target of Iranian assassins.

II

Though Wiesel is inseparably and forever linked to issues arising from the interpretation of the Holocaust, it is also important to appreciate his wide and very serious Jewish learning. His studies of the classical Hebrew canon, even though almost always presented through stories and retellings of biblical, Talmudic, and Hasidic tales, show a profound, if highly personal, lifelong relationship with this material. His rendering of biblical stories is a composite of a close reading of the text filtered through midrashic commentary, Talmudic Aggadot, medieval exegetes like Rashi, Rambam, and Ibn Ezra, Kabbalistic renderings, and Hasidic revisions, all of which were re-imagined as a consequence of his post-Holocaust sensibilities. The end product of this complex hermeneutical process resulted in an often-fascinating retelling of a biblical story, now with certain features of its composition highlighted for pedagogical and moral emphasis. Thus Adam is conceived, in Wiesel's own self-image, "after the fall as a broken man . . . One part of him yearned for God, the other for an escape from God."[32] The tale of Cain and Abel is interpreted as the first human conflict that eventuates in genocide.[33] The *Akedah*, the binding of Isaac, is deciphered as the paradigm of the *Shoah*: "the crusades, the persecutors, the slaughterers, the catastrophes, the massacres by word and the liquidations by fire – each time it was Abraham leading his son to the altar, to the holocaust all over again."[34] As he explains:

> That is why the theme and term of the *Akeda* have been used, throughout the centuries, to describe the destruction and disappearance of countless Jewish communities everywhere . . . Of all the Biblical tales, the one about Isaac is perhaps the most timeless and relevant to our generation. We have known Jews who like Abraham, witnessed the death of their children; who, like Isaac, lived the *Akeda* in their flesh; and some who went mad when they saw their father disappear on the altar, with the altar, in a blazing fire whose flames reached into the highest of heavens.[35]

Isaac and Jacob are revisited and imaged by Wiesel as existentialist heroes. Moses appears in many forms in Wiesel's tales and stories and is described not only as the incomparable Jewish hero who fights with both Israel and God but also as a "madman," "the first link in this dynasty of madmen . . . [the] king of clowns, the

---

32 *Messengers of God*, pp. 5–7.
33 *Ibid.*, pp. 37–40.
34 *Messengers of God*, pp. 95–97.
35 *Ibid.*, p. 95.

prophetic fool free to do anything."[36] Then, too, there is the towering figure of Jeremiah who, like Wiesel, wrote after catastrophe. "Jeremiah appeals to us as a writer, a modern chronicler, above all, his obsessions are ours . . . he transmitted only what he received – and so do we . . . We are proud of him. The world was not worthy of his tears. Or ours." And always there is Job who makes repeated appearances throughout Wiesel's writings. "I prefer," Wiesel has written, "to take my place on the side of Job who chose questions not answers, silence not speeches."[37]

The same interpretive schema, built out of a continuation of personal experience and extensive learning, is at work in Wiesel's retelling of rabbinic stories. Fascinated by their complexity, ambiguity, contradiction, and the fact that they allowed for multiple meanings, the Talmudic tales awed and occupied his imagination from childhood. Focusing not on the legal (halakhic discussions) that form the core of the Talmud, but instead on the lives and teachings of individual sages, he goes in search not of ritual exactitude or correct jurisprudential understanding but, rather, of more personal, more human meaning:

> Each master is singular, enriching, in his own manner, the Talmudic universe. Sometimes without knowing one another, except through their learning, they challenged and defied one another, contradicted one another, only to find themselves reconciled, appeased in the end . . . To follow these masters is to love them. It is to provoke in us a taste and a passion for study.[38]

Take as an example of his method – and his normative concerns – the following tale of Rabbi Akiva's martyrdom about which he writes:

> I am mystified by Rabbi Akiva's passivity during his [final] agony. He seems to have welcomed suffering and death. Rather than rebel and turn his pain into an existential insurrection, his punishment into an act of supreme protest, he decided to submit and pray. Rather than formulate the question of all questions – that of the role of divine justice in human anguish – he answered it. And for some time, I did not like his answer. As much as I admired and revered Rabbi Akiva, a hero of many dreamers, I could not help but set him as a martyr who was attracted by martyrdom . . . The fact that countless generations of victims and martyrs have claimed kinship with Rabbi Akiva has made the problem even more acute, more

---

36 *Legends of Our Time*, pp. 81, 82.
37 On Jeremiah see *Five Biblical Portraits*, pp. 97–128; the material quoted is from pp. 123, 127. Wiesel also spoke of Job in his Nobel Lecture, reprinted in *From the Kingdom of Memory*, p. 248. Here he refers to Job as, "our ancestor . . . our contemporary." On Job, as here quoted, see *Legends of Our Time*, p. 221; *Messenger of God*, p. 232; and see also *The Town Beyond the Wall*, p. 52.
38 *Wise Men and their Tales: Portraits of Biblical, Talmudic, and Hasidic Masters* (New York, 2003), p. 290.

challenging. Who knows? Had he spoken up, had he revealed his anger, had he protested what was happening to him, his fate – and ours – might have taken a different course . . . I remember the nocturnal processions of Jewish families walking toward death – it seems that they, too, like Rabbi Akiva, were offering themselves to the altar. It seems that they, too, had given up on life – as he had, many of them with Shema Israel on their lips . . . Why didn't Rabbi Akiva opt for defiance? Why didn't he proclaim his love of life up to the very moment it was taken away from him? Why didn't he weep instead of rejoice? Didn't he consider that to die willingly for one's faith could – eventually – be interpreted as an element of weakness in that faith? What kind of law is the law that brings suffering and cruelty upon those who serve it with all their might and with all their soul?[39]

Combined together in this text, both as a commentary and meditation, are some of the most elemental questions that consumed Wiesel through his post-Holocaust life and that are relevant to all those who, like him, try to think about the perplexing nature, the vexing implications and the uncertain meaning, of the Holocaust: Did the Jews go like sheep to the slaughter? Was this the result of Jewish tradition? Should not the Jews have resisted their murderers? Or did they offer forms of resistance? And how can God and His Torah mandate this path? As Irving Greenberg has noted: God should not obligate Jews to take on a "suicide mission."

Of the martyr Rabbi Ishmael, Wiesel writes:

> What he told us – what he taught us – is as follows: Yes, I could destroy the world, and the world, ruled by cynicism and hatred, deserves to be destroyed; but to be a Jew is to have all the reasons in the world to destroy, and not to destroy. To be a Jew is to have all the reasons in the world to hate the executioners and not to hate them. To be a Jew is to have all the reasons in the world to mistrust prayer and faith and humanity and power and beauty and truth and language – and yet not to do so. To be a Jew is to continue using words when they heal, and silence when it redeems mankind.[40]

This was a lesson Wiesel repeatedly emphasized, not to seek vengeance, not to hate, not to destroy. "There are all the reasons in the world not to trust man, not to trust history, not to trust civilization, not even to believe in God," he wrote, "And yet we must be capable of refuting all these reasons and go on believing in man, in mankind, in language, in poetry and in friendship – in friendship above all."[41]

---

39 Elie Wiesel, *Sages and Dreamers* (New York, 1991), p. 226. This tale was highlighted by Rabbi Joseph Polak in his paper, "Wiesel and Rabbi Akiva," in *Elie Wiesel: Jewish Literary and Moral Perspectives*, edited by Steven T. Katz and Alan Rosen (Bloomington, 2013), pp. 31–32.
40 *Sages and Dreamers*, p., 223.
41 I. Abrahamson (ed.), *Against Silence*, vol. 3, p. 295.

Again Wiesel, employing the Talmudic tale to work out his own post-Holocaust doubts and struggles, says of Rabbi Tarfon:

> I love Rabbi Tarfon. I love him, although I do not always understand him. I fail to understand why the defeat of Judah, the tragedy of the destruction of Jerusalem and its temple play almost no role in his teaching. Was he trying to tell us that silence too can be a response to extreme suffering? And that some secrets, protected by silence, must remain inviolate."[42]

What Wiesel is really asking through this questioning exegesis is: how should we speak of Auschwitz? Should we speak of Auschwitz at all?[43] Is it true that, "by saying things, one betrays them; by telling the story, one distorts it. Thus, it would perhaps be better to remain silent."[44] Alternatively, why not speak of Auschwitz? Wiesel well understands the paradox of his insistence on ineffability combined with his overwhelming sense that he *must* tell the tale. Unable not to remain silent he describes himself as a messenger: "I have received the words and in combining them I am simply fulfilling the function of a messenger, which to me is as important as that of the storyteller. In fact, the storyteller is only important as a messenger. I am communicating what I have received. I'm passing it on."[45]

Then there are Wiesel's several, very well-known, books of Hasidic tales. Intimately familiar with Hasidism since childhood, the grandson of a devout Hasid, Wiesel loved these stories. He first heard them as a young boy from his grandfather who was "a devout follower of the Rabbi of Vizhnitz." Wiesel recalled that:

> he was the embodiment of Hasidic creative force and fervor . . . A cultured and erudite man, an avid reader of the Bible and of the Rashi and Ramban commentaries, and especially of the work of Rabbi Haim ibn Attar, my grandfather was fascinated with the Midrash, with the works of the Musar – a movement founded in Lithuania to foster the teaching of Jewish values and ethics – and with Hasidic literature. He maintained a perfect balance between his quest for the sacred and the exigencies of daily life. He was a whole being . . . He told stories too. Stories of miracle-makers, of unhappy princes and just men in disguise. It is to him

---

42 *Ibid.*, p. 223, and then *Wise Men and Their Tales*, p. 223.
43 At the first meeting of the President's Commission on the Holocaust, held on February 15, 1979, Wiesel told the assembled audience: "In its scope and incommensurable magnitude, its sheer weight of numbers, by its mystery and silence, the Holocaust defies anything the human being can conceive of or aspire to" (USHMM Institutional Archives, Records of the Chairman – Elie Wiesel, 1978–1980, Box 17, Accession No. 1997–0/3). He also said: "We stress the uniqueness of the events."
44 Elie Wiesel, "Why I Write," in *Confronting the Holocaust: The Impact of Elie Wiesel*, edited by Irving Greenberg and Alvin Rosenfeld (Indiana University Press: Bloomington, 1978, p. 201).
45 Wiesel's comment, reprinted in Henry Kaufmann and Gene Koppel, *Elie Wiesel: A Small Measure of Victory: An Interview* (Tucson, 1974), p. 14.

I owe everything I have written on Hasidic literature. The enchanting tales of Rebbe Nahman of Bratslav, the parables of the Rebbe of Kotzk, the sayings of the Rebbe of Rizhin, and the witticisms of the Rebbe of Ropshitz: he knew them all and he taught me to savor them . . . I felt exhilarated, inspired, and enriched from moment to moment, from tale to tale. "I will never forget these stories," I told him, and he answered, "That's why I'm telling them to you. So they won't be forgotten."[46]

To retell these tales is to keep faith with his grandfather and the Jewish People. As Wiesel writes of the Hasidim of Zanz and Sadegora, who both danced with their rebbes together one Shavuot in Zanz, despite the theological differences: "After all, once upon a time they all stood at Sinai, together, to receive the same law. They? They alone? No. All of us."[47] But as revised by Wiesel, the tales are no longer stories of wonder workers and the miracles they performed. Now their meanings are more ambiguous, even obscure and have been altered. Quoting the tale of R. Yisrael of Rizhin, Wiesel reminds his readers, as did the Rebbe, "O Lord, King of the Universe, have mercy! The secret of the Baal Shen Tov's ritual of fire and his prayers for salvation are long forgotten. Here I stand before you, unable even to find the place in the forest. All I can do is tell the story. And this must be sufficient."[48]

Wiesel understood that for the true Hasid these tales, told by their master, were magical and were told in anticipation of redemption. And there is no doubt that something of this spirit remained with Wiesel who personally identified with Hasidism. A connection he made explicit: "When asked about my Jewish affiliation, I identify myself as a Hasid. Hasid I was, Hasid I remain." It is, therefore, no surprise that Wiesel retells these stories with great affection, though now touched by, transmuted by, the experience of the *Shoah*. He emphasizes neither their ritualistic nor their technical kabbalistic elements but, rather, the this-worldly struggles of their heroes, the *zaddikim*. For Wiesel they represent the singularity, the isolation, of the man of faith – a theme also prevalent in his biblical interpretations of Adam, Cain, Hagar, Abraham, Jacob, Joseph, Moses, and the Prophets for whom life is simultaneously a search and a struggle. He explains in *Souls on Fire* that, "We are never alone. Yet, we have never been so alone. Nor so silent. Only our cry has not been heard."[49] Even God is lonely: "Only God is truly and irreducibly alone." Wiesel's *homo religious* is, like Rav Soloveitchik's, a "lonely man of faith."

Wiesel's *zaddikim* are, of course, pious and observant, and fully located in the mystical and folkloric context of eastern European Jewry before the Holocaust that was saturated with holy men (and women) capable of performing magical deeds. But nonetheless, they are, in his retellings, subtly refashioned as modern existentialist heroes who create meaning, who give life purpose, in a world of "brokenness."

---

46 *All Rivers Run to the Sea*, p. 42.
47 The tale of Zanz is cited from *Wise Men and Their Tales* (New York, 2003), p. 315.
48 Wiesel appended this tale of R. Israel of Rizhin at the end of *The Gates of the Forest*.
49 *Souls on Fire*, p. 201.

So, for example, after citing a tale connected with Rebbe Pinchas of Koretz, he tells us: "A good story in Hasidism is not about miracles, but about friendship and hope – the greatest miracles of all." Hasidism is no longer about the theurgical power of the *mitzvah* or the liberation of "sparks" (*nitzozot*) of holiness from their physical imprisonment but, instead, is about the everyday, the concrete struggles that life throws up in front of men and women. About the here and now. After retelling the history of the conflict between the Kotzker Rebbe and his student, Reb Mordechai Yosef Leiner of Izbica, Wiesel chose to end his history lesson with the true story of the Izbica's fifth-generation descendent, Rabbi Shmuel-Shlomo of Radzin:

> ... in a ghetto near Sobibor, [R. Shmuel-Shlomo] rose against the Germans and the Judenrat with powerful appeals to armed resistance and combat. . . . "Give me fifty men," he told his disciples. "I will be their leader. We shall fight. We shall set the ghetto on fie and stop the killers and the murderers: silence is dangerous, silence means consent, consent means complicity . . ." His pleas went unheeded. When he was finally apprehended by a German officer in 1942, he spat in the German's face. He was executed. And buried in the Jewish cemetery.[50]

Lastly, relative to Wiesel's vision of the meaning of Judaism past, present, and future, the remaking of the theme of messianic hope, a repeated subject in his writings and public lectures, requires comment for it was central to Wiesel's analysis, to his vision, of the human – and specifically the Jewish – drama. Recalling R. Pinchas of Koretz, Wiesel explains: "To be Jewish is to link one's fate to the Messiah – to that of those who are waiting for the Messiah." However, this is no simple matter for Wiesel's invocation of the messianic, while it does not deny the literal, traditional messianic hope, nor the redemptive remaking of history that is central to Maimonides' vision, it also includes another, more personal level of meaning. Accordingly, he retells a tale of R. Pinchas as follows:

> Basing myself on the Talmudic saying that if all men repented, the Messiah would come, I decided to do something about it. I was convinced I would be successful. But where was I to start? The world is so vast. I shall start with the country I know best, my own. But my country is so very large. I had better start with my town. But my town, too, is large. I had best start with my street. No: my home. No: my family. Never mind, I shall start with myself.[51]

So the messianic drama is immediate and personally demanding. It begins with the self, not the cosmic order. But even with pure intentions, the most sincere

---

50 The tale of R. Shmuel-Shlomo of Radzin is told in *Sages and Dreamers*, p. 421.
51 The tale of R. Pinchas of Koretz appears in Souls *on Fire*, pp. 134–35.

subjective commitments, one may not be able to move the world towards redemption for the messianic hope must now be refracted through Auschwitz. And when we view the matter from this perspective we understand that: "If the Messiah does not hurry he may be too late, there will be no one left to save." And even if he hurries, the Messiah's journey will be difficult because "the smoke of the crematoria has obscured His way."[52]

III

Before concluding, I would like to say another brief word about Elie Wiesel's large literary corpus that I have been unable to do justice to in this essay. I believe that all of these works were, in one way or another, at least in part, Elie's effort to speak for those gassed in the Death Camps and those shot by the *Einsatzgruppen*. As he confesses: "The dead never leave me." His work thus represents his attempt to give memory a central place in the experience of future generations; they were his way of struggling with the dead while existing among the living. "I owe the dead my memory. I am duty bound to serve as their emissary," Wiesel notes in *From the Kingdom of Memory*. "Why do I write? To wrest those victims [of the Holocaust] from oblivion. To help the dead vanquish death."[53] There is, of course, something profoundly paradoxical about such writing when one sets it over against Wiesel's insistence that words do not satisfactorily describe Auschwitz. Elie was well aware of this. Reflecting on this contradiction he observes: "Perhaps what we tell about what happened and what really happened has nothing to do, one with the other." Instead, "the moment it is told it turns into betrayal."

IV

If I may be allowed a few remarks of a more personal nature. It was not easy to be Elie Wiesel. He was never free from his past, and in the lived present he was often overwhelmed by the evil that continues to be so appallingly evident in our world. One of my most intense memories is the 50th Commemoration of the liberation of Auschwitz. Elie and I were both part of the official visitor's delegation. After the ceremonies we walked through the camp with the elderly Chief Rabbi of Poland who was also a camp survivor. He told us how he would get up early each morning to run to a nearby hut to trade a portion of his bread ration for a chance to put on a pair of *tefillin* that had been smuggled into the bunk. Elie and I were both profoundly moved by the story and Elie, in particular, became very

---

52 *Gates of the Forest*, p. 32. Again, in the concluding passages of *The Fifth Son* (London, 1986), we read: "The Messiah may well come too late ... Never mind, I shall wait nonetheless" (p. 219).

53 "Why I Write," in *From the Kingdom of Memory*, pp. 16 and 21. Wiesel reused this essay, which originally appeared in *Confronting the Holocaust* (as noted in notes 9 and 44). In this second appearance of the piece he changed the word "wrench" in the translation of the original essay's last sentence (p. 206) to "wrest" (p. 21).

quiet and sad. And so we walked for quite a while in silence. On other occasions, when we learned of new and horrific tragedies all over the globe and tried to digest their implications, he would say in private conversation: "We have learned nothing." But he took great consolation from his family, the State of Israel, and his teaching. He was a consummate teacher who was sincerely concerned with his students, and they adored him. Awed initially, they came to see in him a mentor who was interested in them beyond the exams and seminar questions. In a quiet way he did many kindnesses for his students, especially his graduate students. He also always welcomed and helped young scholars who were seeking his advice, wherever they came from.

Inside and outside the university world he was sought after day and night by all sorts of (non-student) individuals and groups, as a result of which he was very cautious about strangers. He once told me that he received at least ten invitations and requests every day. These included, after his exceptional encounter with President Reagan, regular meetings with American presidents. He would frequently sit with Hilary Clinton at her husband's "State of the Union" address and was invited to the White House by George W. Bush, and then by President Obama. The latter asked him to lunch one day when he was having difficulties with the American Jewish community over issues related to Israel. The next day I asked him what it was like to have lunch at the White House. He replied: "You cannot eat while the President is talking, and you can't eat while you are responding, so it's not much of a lunch."

He also had his limitations. On one occasion, at a fundraising dinner for the United States Holocaust Memorial Museum, he saw that he was to be seated between billionaire Sheldon Adelson, the Las Vegas casino owner, and Robert Kraft, the owner of the highly successful New England Patriots football team (of the U.S. National Football League). He rushed over to me and said: "I know nothing of casinos or football. You must come and sit at our table so it is not a night of silence."

There were those who were critical of him, and many who did not understand the good reason for his reserve and reticence. And there were those who were jealous. In Israel, in particular, there was consistent criticism, driven first and foremost by his decision to live in America, while among survivors there were those who resented his success. But if he knew you, if he trusted you, if he respected you, he was a remarkable, generous, and caring friend. His willingness to help was unlimited. No matter where he was in the world he would return a phone call, answer a question, write a letter, help raise funds – though, in fact, he hated fundraising.

He was curious about all things Jewish, a great listener when one had information or a tale to tell. Whenever I returned from the regular meetings of the International Holocaust Remembrance Alliance that, as noted above, he had played a role in creating, he was always eager to hear my reports of what took place, where difficulties had arisen, and the way forward that had been decided. He always offered advice and help if needed. He had strong opinions on who the "good guys" and who the "bad guys" were, and was always willing, if he felt it necessary, to make the good fight. He knew everyone. He was close to Kofi Anan, the General Secretary of the United Nations, and I remember an interesting dinner we had together one night in New York City. The connection to Kofi he used wisely, but very carefully, to advance Jewish and Israeli interests at the U.N. He was close to Vaclav Havel (President of Czechoslovakia) and was thoughtful enough to send Havel a note introducing me to him when I was due to be in Prague for a meeting dealing with Holocaust reparations. Then, too, the leaders of the political world called regularly. I remember being in the midst of conversations in his office at Boston University when, on a number of occasions, his secretary would interrupt to tell him that there was a call from Angela Merkel, or Benjamin Netanyahu, or Vaclav Havel, or the Swedish Prime Minister.

His archive at Boston University contains nearly one million items, including tens of thousands of personal letters. This represents, I am told, a larger archive than David Ben-Gurion left in Sde Boker. He was an expert on fine chocolate, and wonderful company wherever we were together around the world. He always strongly conveyed the sense that you mattered to him and he valued your friendship. He will be greatly missed – by myself and many, many others.

UPDATE

Elie Wiesel died on July 2, 2016. As the author of *Night* and the winner of the Nobel Peace Prize, he had become the most well-known of all Holocaust survivors. Soon after his passing, Dr. David Silberklang, the editor of *Yad Vashem Studies*, the journal of Israel's Holocaust museum and archive, knowing of my long and close friendship with Elie, asked me to write an essay reflecting on Elie's extraordinary life and career for the journal. The present essay, which first appeared in December 2016,[54] is the result.

When I started to write this piece it proved, contrary to my initial expectations, to be a difficult assignment. I had known Elie since the 1970s, and came to Boston University in 1996, where he had been teaching for approximately twenty years, to direct a new Jewish Studies Center that was to be named after him. From then on we worked closely together on a regular basis. Hence, I grew to know Elie very well and very much wanted to convey in this essay something of his very special human qualities without being sentimental, sycophantic, or dishonest. Others will have to judge how close I came to achieving these several goals.

Since his death, Elie has been remembered by countless friends and acquaintances, including President Barack Obama and Prime Minister Benjamin Netanyahu, and criticized by a few individuals who carried a grudge against him because they have personal agendas that he did not support. In September 2017, a major international conference, attended by many well-known Jewish and non-Jewish figures, was held in his memory in Oradea, Romania, and in Sighet, Elie's home town. The climax of the event was a candlelight march in his memory on the Sunday night of the conference by today's non-Jewish Sighet population. Dressed in traditional local costumes, the assembled individuals walked from the house in which Elie was raised – that now serves as a museum telling his life story – to the town train station from which he was deported to Auschwitz. At the official ceremony organized at the station a plaque was unveiled that indicated that the station had been renamed after him. On this occasion, as I marched to the station, I could only think of how much the world and the Jewish People – and I – have lost a special friend.

---

54 "Elie Wiesel: The Man and his Legacy," *Yad Vashem Studies* 44.2 (December 2016): 11–42.

14

THE ISSUE OF CONFIRMATION AND DISCONFIRMATION IN JEWISH THOUGHT AFTER THE *SHOAH*

Karl Popper has taught modern thinkers that in assessing the truth of a proposition it is necessary to state the conditions under which the proposition would not be true. Since Popper's initial work on this issue, it has become clear that the matter is not as straightforward as he, with his specific philosophical, logical, and scientific assumptions, thought – and that there are deep problems connected with establishing the truth of a proposition by recourse to the conditions that would disconfirm it. However, the Popperian legacy in this regard, if I might so refer to it, is not without importance, especially in relationship to theological discourse and the analysis of theodicy. That is, theologians and philosophers of religion need to pay close attention to the logical matters of confirmation and disconfirmation when they attempt to answer questions regarding divine justice – and this nowhere more so than when Jewish thinkers attend to the issue of theodicy after Auschwitz.

In this essay I would like to critically review some of the efforts that have been made in this arena as a first step towards trying to think our way forward to a more substantial and defensible Jewish theological response to the *Shoah*.

To make clear what is at stake in this discussion, I will begin by reconstructing the position of the well-known Jewish "Death of God" theologian Richard Rubenstein. Rubenstein has been criticized severely within the Jewish intellectual community, but his effort raises elementary theological and metaphysical questions with clarity and directness. Rubenstein's position can be summed up in three words: "God is dead." The logic that has driven him to utter these three extraordinarily powerful words can be put in the following syllogism: (1) God, as He is conceived of in the Jewish tradition, could not have allowed the Holocaust to happen; (2) the Holocaust did happen. Therefore (3), God as he is conceived of in the Jewish tradition does not exist.

This seemingly straightforward argument is the basis upon which Rubenstein has felt compelled to reject the God of history and hence the God of Jewish tradition. The radical negation represented by this position is of the utmost seriousness for modern Jewish (and non-Jewish) thought, even if one finally dismissed it as out of place in a Jewish context, as some naive critics have done.[1] It does raise

---

[1] It should be mentioned at the start of this paper, in the clearest possible terms, that my criticism of Rubenstein is intended to be *strictly* philosophical and *not* ad hominem. *I* wish to dissociate myself *totally* from those critics who, rather than discuss Rubenstein's ideas, have abused the man. No

a real, if frightening, possibility about the "meaning of Auschwitz," i.e., that there is no meaning to history. History is a random, arbitrary series of events that are unrelated either to a transcendental order or to a context of absolute meaning or value. In *After Auschwitz*,[2] Rubenstein stated this contention articulately:

> When I say we live in the time of the death of God, I mean that the thread uniting God and man, heaven and earth has been broken. We stand in a cold, silent, unfeeling cosmos, unaided by any purposeful power beyond our own resources. After Auschwitz what else can a Jew say about God? . . . I see no other way than the "death of God" position of expressing the void that confronts man where once God stood.[3]

Philosophically this challenge to belief, generated from the consideration of the implications of Auschwitz, is both interesting and more problematic than it at first appears. Let me note, specifically, before saying anything else, that rather than accept Israel's sinfulness as the justification for the Holocaust or see it as some inscrutable act of divine wrath or fiat, the vision of which appears to blaspheme against the loving God of the Jewish tradition and the entire meaning of Jewish covenantal existence, the radical theologian takes the difficult step in denying both poles of the divine-human dialectic, thereby destroying the traditional theological encounter altogether. There is no God and there is no covenant with Israel:

> If I believed in God as the omnipotent author of the historical drama and Israel as His chosen People, I had to accept [the] . . . conclusion that it was God's will that Hitler committed six million Jews to slaughter. I could not possibly believe in such a God nor could I believe Israel is the chosen people of God after Auschwitz.[4]

The second element emerging out of, as well as essential to, the "Death of God" view putatively grounded in the Holocaust experience is equally fundamental. It concerns nothing less than the way one views Jewish history, its continuities and discontinuities, its "causal connectedness" and interdependencies. By raising the issue of how one evaluates Jewish history and what hermeneutic of historic meaning one need adopt, I mean to bring into focus the fact – and it is a fact – that

---

instances of such abuse will be singled out for citation here, but those familiar with the literature will recognize this as an all-too-prevalent, and odious, element in the critical response to Rubenstein's position. Let me add in connection with the present essay that Professor Rubenstein has taken the criticism offered by me over the years in a most generous spirit and has become a valued friend.

2 *After Auschwitz* (Indianapolis, IN, 1966). This is Rubenstein's earliest and most important collection of material dealing with the Holocaust and its implications. This paper will primarily deal with Rubenstein's views as presented in this work, which I take to be his most significant statement on the theological implications of this theme.

3 *After Auschwitz*, p. 49.

4 *Ibid.*, p. 47.

the radical theologian sees Jewish history too narrowly, i.e., focused solely in and through the Holocaust. He takes the decisive event of Jewish history to be the death camps. But this is a distorted image of Jewish experience, for there is a pre-Holocaust and post-Holocaust Jewish reality that must be considered in dealing with the questions raised by the Nazi epoch. These questions touch the present Jewish situation as well as the whole of the Jewish past. One cannot make the events of 1933–45 intelligible in isolation. To think, moreover, that one can excise this block of time from the flow of Jewish history and then, by concentrating on it, extract the "meaning" of *all* Jewish existence is more than uncertain,[5] no matter how momentous or demonic this time may have been.

Jews went to Auschwitz and suffered and died at Auschwitz through no specific fault of their own: their crime was their Jewishness. The Nuremberg laws extracted from the 1933–45 generation the price of their parents', grandparents', and great-grandparents' decision to have Jewish children. This, if nothing else, forces us to widen our historic perspective when we try to comprehend what happened in Nazi Germany. When one tries to understand the "grandparents" of the death camp generation one will find that their actions are likewise unintelligible without following the historic chain that leads backwards into the Jewish millennial past. The same rule also applies in trying to fathom the historic reality of the murderers and their inheritance. The events of 1933–45 were the product of the German and Jewish past; to decode this present we must enter into that past.

This recognition of a pre-Holocaust and post-Holocaust Israel forces two considerations upon us. The first is the very survival of the Jewish People despite their "sojourn among the nations." As both Fredrick the Great and Karl Barth are reported to have said, "the best proof of God's existence is the continued existence of the Jewish people." Without entering into a discussion of the metaphysics of history, let this point just stand for further reflection, i.e., that the Jews survived Hitler, and Jewish history did not end at Auschwitz. Secondly, and equally if not more directly significant, is the recreation after Auschwitz of a Jewish state, the Third Jewish Commonwealth in the Land of Israel.[6] This event, too, is remarkable in the course of Jewish existence. Logic and conceptual adequacy require that if in our discussion of the relation of God and history we want to give theological weight to the Holocaust, then we *must* also be willing to attribute *theological* significance to the state of Israel. Just what weight one assigns to each of these events, and then again to events in general, in constructing a theological reading of history is an extraordinarily complex theoretical issue, about which there is need

---

5 Those who would deal with the Holocaust need to master not only Holocaust materials but also the whole of Jewish history. This point has been well made by Eliezer Berkovits in his *Faith after the Holocaust* (New York, 1973). To obtain some idea of what is involved in such a mastery of Jewish history, readers are referred to Salo Baron's magisterial *Social and Religious History of the Jews*, 18 vols. (New York, 1952–83), and especially to his extraordinary notes.

6 On Rubenstein's appreciation of the state of Israel see, for example, his essay "The Rebirth of Israel in Jewish Theology" in *After Auschwitz*.

for much discussion, and which allows for much difference of view. Still, it is clear that any final rendering of the "meaning of Jewish history" that values in its equation only the negative factors of the Nazi Holocaust or it and previous holocausts is, at best, arbitrary. If one wants to make statements about God's presence (or in this case absence) in Jewish history as a consequence of Auschwitz then one must also, in all theological and existential seriousness, consider the meaning of His presence (or absence) in Jewish history as played out in Jerusalem. If it makes sense to talk theologically at all – an open question – about God's presence and absence, His existence and nonexistence, and to judge these matters on the basis of what happened to the Jews of Europe in some sort of negative natural theology, then it is equally meaningful and logical – *and theologically* – necessary to consider what the events in *Eretz Yisroel* since 1945 tell us about His reality and ours.

To his credit, Rubenstein does appreciate that the state of Israel is of consequence, even momentous consequence, but he insists on treating it as *theologically* independent from Auschwitz so that no positive linkage in some larger rendering of Jewish experience is possible; nor can we posit what in traditional idiom would be termed "redemptive" significance to this national rebirth. Rather, the renaissance of Jewish life in its ancestral homeland is seen by Rubenstein, consistent with his own principles, as the clearest manifestation of the post-1945 rejection of the God of history by Jews and their return to a natural, land-related, nontheistic life.

However, despite Rubenstein's interesting working through of this event in his own terms, his interpretation of the situation will not do, for it is clear that from a logical point of view it is methodologically improper to construct a phenomenology of historical reality that gives weight only to the negative significance of "evil" without any attempt to balance it against the positive significance of the "good" we encounter in history. History is too variegated to be understood only as good or evil; the alternating rhythms of actual life reveal the two forces as interlocked and inseparable. For our present concerns, the hermeneutical value of this recognition is that one comes to see that Jewish history is neither conclusive proof of the existence of God (because of the possible counterevidence of Auschwitz) nor, conversely, is it proof of the nonexistence of God (because of the possible counterevidence of the state of Israel as well as the whole three-thousand-year historic Jewish experience). Rubenstein's narrow focus on Auschwitz reflects an already decided theological choice based on certain normative presuppositions and a compelling desire to justify certain conclusions. It is not a value-free phenomenological description of Jewish history.

Before I leave this argument, it should be made absolutely clear that it is not being asserted that the state of Israel is compensation for Auschwitz, nor that Auschwitz is the "cause," in a theological or metaphysical sense, of the creation of the Jewish state, as many simplistic historical and theological accounts, offered for all kinds of mixed reasons, have asserted. Whatever relation does exist between Holocaust Europe and the state of Israel is far more ambiguous and many sided than a simple causal or compensatory schema would explain. The argument as presented, however, is a reminder that the state of Israel is an event – one might,

I think, even legitimately say a "miracle," if that term means anything at all – at least equal to if not more important than Auschwitz in Jewish theological terms; it must be respected as such.

There is an unspoken but implied, highly influential premise in Rubenstein's argument concerning the relation of God and history. This hidden premise relates to what is well known as the "empiricist theory of meaning" made famous by A. J. Ayer in *Language, Truth and Logic* and then given a more particularly significant theological twist by Anthony Flew in his "falsifiability challenge." This was first expressed in the widely discussed "University Discussion" reprinted in *New Essays in Philosophical Theology*.[7] Space prohibits an extended review of this most aggressive challenge to religious belief, which in any case is familiar enough if not always completely understood, but its implicit use in the "Death of God" argument must at least be called into the open, for it is the employment of this thesis that provides much of the initial rigor of the radical theologian's challenge. I am not sure whether Rubenstein's employment of this notion is intentional or indirect, but its presence and significance for Rubenstein is nonetheless real. He at least tacitly accepts the basic premise of the "empiricist falsifiability thesis,"[8] i.e., that propositions about God are to be straightforwardly confirmed or disconfirmed by appeal to empirical events in the world. It is only the result of the at-least implicit adoption of this empirical principle, or something very close to it, that allows Rubenstein to judge that "God is dead," for it is only on the basis of some such norm that the conditions of the Holocaust can become the empirical test case for the existence or nonexistence of God. In effect Rubenstein argues as follows: if there is too much evil in the world (putting aside the problem of how one would measure this for the moment and recognizing that this subject is never dealt with by Rubenstein), then God, as conceived in the Jewish tradition, cannot exist. At Auschwitz there was such evil and God did not step in to stop it; thus God does not exist. Hence the traditional theological notions based upon such a belief in God are decisively falsified by an appeal to this empirical evidence.

Respecting this challenge as an important one that is often too lightly dismissed by theologians, and respecting Rubenstein's employment of it as an authentic existential response to an overwhelming reality, I nonetheless would point out that the empirical falsifiability challenge is not definitive one way or the other in theological matters and thus cannot provide Rubenstein (or others) with an unimpeachable criterion for making the negative theological judgments that he seeks to advance regarding the nonexistence of God. The falsifiability thesis allows one *decisively* neither to affirm not to disaffirm God's presence in history, for history provides evidence both for and against the nonexistence of God on empirical verificationist

---

7 See Anthony Flew's essay in *New Essays in Philosophical Theology* (London, 1964). For a useful introduction to the enormous literature generated by this issue see Raeburne Heimbeck's *Theology and Meaning* (London, 1969), especially his bibliography and notes.
8 On the "verification principle" see the sources given in R. Heimbeck, *Theology and Meaning*.

grounds, i.e., there is both good and bad in history. Moreover, the very value of the empirical criteria turns, on the one hand, on what one considers to be empirical verificationist evidence, i.e., on what one counts as empirical or experiential, and on the other, on whether the empirical verificationist principle is, in itself, philosophically coherent, which it appears not to be. Again, here too the state of Israel is a crucial "datum" (and solidly empirical) that the radical theologian must consider when framing his falsifiability equation. This is to observe that someone might challenge the critic with this counterclaim: "Yes, the assertion of God's existence does not depend on what happens in history. Among the events of history is not only Auschwitz but also the creation of the state of Israel. Whereas the former event is evidence against the 'God hypothesis,' the latter is evidence in its favor." Neither position is decisively provable – but both are equally meaningful,[9] as well as equally unprovable.

Again, the Jew (or a Christian theologian like Karl Barth) might respond to the falsifiability challenge by returning to the first historical argument discussed above – i.e., Auschwitz is not decisive evidence for or against God's existence – and meet the empiricist critic head on by rephrasing the nature of the empiricist challenge itself. That is, he could argue that he accepts the challenge in general terms but offers different specific empirical conditions by which to decide the matter one way or the other. For example, he stipulates as the decisive falsifying condition the complete elimination of Jews from history, which was, in fact, Hitler's goal through his "Final Solution." Here we have a straightforward, if theologically enormous, claim: the existence of God is inseparably related to the existence of the Jewish People (a claim not too distanced from that actually made in at least some classical Jewish sources). If the Jewish People are destroyed, then we will agree that God does not exist. This is certainly a falsifiable thesis, i.e., the Jewish People *logically* are removable from history. What happens to the empiricist challenge at this point? This question seems especially challenging given that the hypothetical argument constructed can be construed, at least according to a certain quite respectable theological ideology, as a close analogue to what actually transpired in twentieth-century Europe.

What this second counter-example, as well as the argument advanced above about the presence of both good and evil in history, suggests is that Rubenstein has too easily accepted a form of the empiricist theory of meaning and verification. Though this theory is obscure at best, and ultimately philosophically indefensible, Rubenstein has made this, or something like it, a foundation stone of his entire enterprise without a sufficient degree of epistemological self-consciousness regarding its philosophical accuracy or logical adequacy. In his invocation of this procedure, he has sought to adopt a clear and indisputable method of reaching

---

9 Readers must not confuse "verification" and "meaning" – the essential error made by A. J. Ayer. Nor should they confuse "meaning" and "falsification," which is a common distortion of Karl Popper's extremely interesting and widely influential views. See Popper's own discussion of this matter in his *Conjectures and Refutations* (London, 1963).

theological conclusions, the appeal of such clarity and decisiveness being obvious. But the seductiveness of this stratagem is more illusory than real, for the empirical verificationist criterion achieves its putative precision and rigor only by illegitimately reducing the complex to the simple and the ambiguous to the transparent. Thus its results are a caricature of the situation.

Before I move on, it should be registered that despite my criticism of Rubenstein's formulation of the empiricist issue as logically inadequate, his intentions are well directed, namely, he wants to find nonapologetic, nonhomiletical, nonsubjective ways to talk meaningfully about covenantal existence or, rather, its nonexistence, after the Holocaust and in light of what the Holocaust has to teach us. But, alternatively, what also needs to be recognized is that his frontal assault on the questions involved, which use various forms of empiricist verificationist instruments, is not successful; other ways to get at the root of the problem need to be found.

At the other theological extreme from Rubenstein's work stands the well-known theological efforts of Emil Fackenheim. To sketch the salient features of his position is not too difficult. It has its roots, on the one hand, in a desire to do two radically opposite things, and, on the other, it emerges out of a need to hold two radically alternative possibilities in dialectical tension, wishing to surrender neither. The two radically opposite claims he wants to maintain are that: (1) the Holocaust is unique; but (2) it does not lead to a denial of the existence of God à la Rubenstein. The dialectic he wishes to affirm is that (1) the Holocaust is without "meaning"; and yet (2) out of Auschwitz the commanding voice of the Living God of Israel is heard. This complex structure is necessitated by the concern not to do injustice to the martyrs of the death camps, nor to speak against God. It recognizes, indeed insists upon, the awesome nature of the Holocaust and its "unique" significance for theology, yet it also demands that this event be located within the structures of theistic belief rather than be allowed to break these structures apart in an irreparable manner that would mark the end of religion in any traditional sense.

Fackenheim, like Richard Rubenstein and most other "Holocaust theologians," rejects categorically any attempt to give a causal explanation of the Holocaust in terms of any "answer" borrowed from traditional theodicy. Auschwitz is *not* punishment for sin; it is *not* divine judgment; it is *not* moral education à la Job: "Behold, happy is the man whom God reproves . . . He delivers the afflicted by their affliction and opens their ear by adversity" (*Job* 5:17; 36:15). As Franklin Sherman has correctly noted, the Jobean view has merit but only up to a point, for "when [a man's] humanity begins to be destroyed, as was the case in the concentration camps, then it is fruitless to talk of the ennoblement of character."[10] The Holocaust is also inconceivable as an "affliction of love" (*yissurin shel ahavah*)[11] and unjustifiable on the grounds of any doctrine of progress or of a Spinoza-like

---

10 Franklin Sherman, "Speaking of God after Auschwitz," *Worldview* (Sept. 1974): 27.
11 On this classical rabbinic doctrine see, for example, Saadiah Gaon, *Emunot ve Deot* 5:3.

dictum of *sub specie aeternitatis*. In short, no good reason can be advanced to explain or defend Auschwitz. No theodicy seems able to vindicate the time-honored normative view of God's absolute goodness in the face of the Holocaust. Thus, as a consequence, as Fackenheim honestly acknowledges, God Himself is called into question, nothing less.

Yet, unlike those who at this crucial juncture try God and find Him wanting, thus concluding His nonexistence, Fackenheim insists that God does exist and that He is still present in history despite the crematoriums. Though it is enormously difficult to believe in God after the Kingdom of Night, it is precisely a continued belief that must be the response to the challenge of Auschwitz. Though we cannot, and this is an absolute "cannot," fathom why God allowed Auschwitz and why He did not intervene to end the Holocaust, we must affirm that He was present even there, even at Auschwitz, and that He continues to be present still as the Lord of History.

This demand is first and foremost made as an affirmation of faith, of faith in the Kierkegaardian sense of holding fast to that which is objectively uncertain. Indeed, this stance owes much to Kierkegaard, the patriarch of modern religious existentialism. The conceptual link connecting Kierkegaard and Fackenheim is primarily the dialogical teaching of Martin Buber. To the extent that metaphysics or theology is employed in support of his account, Fackenheim draws heavily on Buber's philosophy of I-Thou. This dependence on Buber is clearly seen, for example, in Fackenheim's most sustained attempt to respond to the Holocaust, the lectures published in *God's Presence in History*. In this monograph he accepts, in its general specifications, the Buberian doctrine of I-Thou as the model for Jewish openness to the reality of the living God and therefore his own attempt to construct a post-Holocaust Jewish theology. Thus, he eschews all proofs for the existence of God, beginning instead with the presumption that God does exist. He accepts the Buberian dictum that God cannot be proven, He can only be met. Consequently, he argues that only from within the circle of faith can one "hear" the Eternal Thou (Buber's terminology for God) and respond accordingly. Developing this claim, Fackenheim, like Buber, insists that God reveals Himself in history in personal encounters with the Jews and Israel, but this revelation of divine presence, though it can happen everywhere and at all times, is not subject to external criteria of verification or objectivity.[12] God does not show Himself decisively to those who would not "hear" the voice. The I-Thou encounter has its own rhythm and any attempt to form it into improper objective categories (I-It language, to use Buber's terminology) destroys its character and silences its message. Accordingly,

---

12 See Martin Buber, *I and Thou* (New York, 1958). For a critique of this position see my essay "Martin Buber's Epistemology," in *idem, Post-Holocaust Dialogues* (New York, 1983), pp. 1–51. That the Buberian account is not without its serious philosophical and theological difficulties, which may undermine it, is not unknown to Fackenheim. See in this connection his essay "Buber's Doctrine of Revelation," in *The Philosophy of Martin Buber*, eds. Paul Schilpp and Maurice Friedman (La Salle, IL, 1967).

the Fackenheim who hears "a commanding voice from Auschwitz" is the Fackenheim who already stands *within* the covenantal affirmation.[13]

Working from this base, Fackenheim asserts that we witness God's presence in history in the continued experience of the people of Israel throughout its existence, and this in two ways. The first of these ways Fackenheim calls the "root experiences"[14] of the people of Israel; the second he describes as "epoch making events."[15] The former are creative, extraordinary, historical happenings that are of a decisive and formative character such that they continue to influence all future "presents" of the Jewish People. These events are of such a magnitude that they continue to legislate as normative occasions to every future generation of the nation. For example, the Exodus is an historical movement that is relived every Passover and whose power affects each subsequent generation, continually revealing through this yearly reenactment the saving activity of God.[16] In this way these past "root experiences" are lived through as "present reality" and the Jew of every age is "assured that the past saving God saves still."[17] In contrast, "epoch making events" are not formative for Jewry's collective consciousness; rather, they are historical occasions that challenge the "root experiences" to answer to new and often unprecedented conditions. The destruction of the First and Second Temples are, for example, such events. These occurrences test the foundations of Jewish life, i.e., the saving and commanding God of the Exodus and Sinai, but do not shatter them, as the continued existence of the Jewish People testifies. This traditional interpretive pattern has theretofore always shown enough elasticity and resiliency to absorb and survive any and all catastrophes that threatened its fundamental structure.

But what of Auschwitz? Can it be assimilated to this older midrashic model? To this question Fackenheim answers an unreserved "Yes." Even Auschwitz does not destroy the "root experiences" of Israel's faith; God is present even in the Kingdom of Night, commanding Israel still from within the very eye of the Holocaust itself. This extreme reply to the unprecedented circumstances of Auschwitz is the essential response of Fackenheim and those who would follow his lead. The Jew cannot, dare not, must not, reject God. Auschwitz itself is revelatory, commanding, and we must learn to sense what God would reveal to us even there.

What is the commanding word, which Fackenheim, in a now-famous phrase, has called the 614th commandment, which is heard at Auschwitz? "Jews are forbidden to hand Hitler posthumous victories!"[18] After Auschwitz Jews are under a

---

13 See Emil Fackenheim, *Quest for Past and Future* (Bloomington, IN, 1968), p. 10.
14 See Emil Fackenheim, *God's Presence in History* (New York, 1970), pp. 8 ff.
15 See *ibid.*, pp. 16 ff.
16 Thus, the traditional rabbinic dictum that every Jew at the Passover Seder should participate in the event with the sense that *he* or *she* was personally redeemed from Egypt, i.e., it is not just a commemoration of a past, concluded, event.
17 Emil Fackenheim, *God's Presence in History*, p. 11.
18 *God's Presence in History*, p. 84, repeated from Emil Fackenheim's earlier essay, "Jewish Faith and the Holocaust," *Commentary*. 46.2 (August, 1968): 30–36.

sacred obligation to survive; Jewish existence is itself a holy act; Jews are under a duty to remember the martyrs; Jews are, as Jews, forbidden to despair of redemption, or to become cynical about the world and humanity, for to submit to cynicism is to abdicate responsibility for the here and now and to deliver the future into the hands of the forces of evil. And above all, Jews are "forbidden to despair of the God of Israel, lest Judaism perish."[19] Hitler's demonic passion was to eradicate Israel from history. For the Jew to despair of the God of Israel as a result of Hitler's monstrous actions would be, ironically, to do Hitler's work and to aid in the accomplishments of Hitler's goal. The voice that speaks from Auschwitz demands above all that Hitler win no posthumous victories, that no Jew do what Hitler could not do. The Jewish will for survival is natural enough, but Fackenheim invests it with transcendental significance. Precisely because others would eradicate Jews from the earth, Jews are commanded to resist annihilation. Paradoxically, Hitler makes Judaism after Auschwitz a necessity. To say "no" to Hitler is to say "yes" to the God of Sinai; to say "no" to the God of Sinai is to say "yes" to Hitler.

Since 1945 every person who has remained a Jew has, from Fackenheim's perspective, responded affirmatively to the commanding voice of Auschwitz.

Yet this is only half of the traditional ideology of Judaism, for the God of biblical faith is *both* a commanding and a saving God. The crossing of the Red Sea is as much a part of Jewish history as is the revelation at Sinai: both are "root experiences." Fackenheim has made much of the commanding presence of Auschwitz, but where is the saving God of the Exodus? Without the crossing of the Red Sea there can be no Sinai. Fackenheim knows this. He is also aware that to talk of a God of deliverance, no matter how softly, no matter how tentatively, after the Holocaust is problematical when God did not work His kindness there and then. To even whisper about salvation after Treblinka and Majdanek is already to speak as a person of faith, not as a seeker, and even then one can only whisper. The continued existence of the people of Israel, however, and most specifically the establishment and maintenance of the state of Israel, forces Fackenheim to risk speaking of hope and the possibility of redemption. The destruction of European Jewry and the state of Israel are, for him, inseparably tied together; what the former seems to deny, the latter, at least tentatively, affirms. For Fackenheim, the state of Israel is living testimony to God's continued presence in history. Through it the modern Jew witnesses a reaffirmation of the "root experience" of salvation essential to the survival of Jewish faith.[20]

Fackenheim argues for Jewish survival first and foremost on the positive basis of the presence of God in Jewish history and the ever-contemporary possibility of

---

19 *Ibid.*, 84. Here Fackenheim spells out the implication of these "commandments" in some detail; see pp. 85–92.
20 See here Fackenheim's essay, read at the conference held at St. John the Divine in New York City and printed in Eva Fleischer (ed.), *Auschwitz: Beginning of a New Era* (New York, 1977), pp. 205–17. See also his more recent work, which increasingly emphasizes the significance of the state of Israel. These newer essays are collected in *The Jewish Return into History* (New York, 1980).

I-Thou encounter between God and humanity. Only from this absolute ontological presupposition, which he borrows from Martin Buber, do the other corollaries of Fackenheim's account, including that of not giving Hitler a "posthumous victory," flow. To ignore this elemental feature of his thought, i.e., his dialogical ontology, or to read him differently is to misread him altogether.

This essential clarification of Fackenheim's view is, however, not a vindication of it. A serious difficulty remains; to phrase it differently, this schema needs to be criticized for the right reasons. Perhaps foremost among these reasons is the largely uncritical acceptance of Buber's dialogical affirmations. Buber's metaphysical structure – indeed, his entire account of I-Thou relation and the nature and meaning of revelation – involves philosophical deficiencies that ultimately render it of little, if any, help in constructing a significant and viable metaphysics of history. His position is quite simply unworkable as the basis of an intelligent account of God's relation to humanity and history. Its weakness is that it provides intuitions where serious and well-formed conceptual articulation is required.[21] Thus, whereas Buber's teachings are called in to provide the broad schematic metaphysical basis for the "614th commandment," its own internal philosophical deficiencies will not allow it to adequately fill this role.

Buber's dialogical thinking is incapable of dealing in any meaningful and sustainable fashion with real history, the presence of evil in the world, or the category of revelation, the very philosophical-cum-theological categories particularly relevant here. Fackenheim's considerable insight into history, and more particularly the nuances of the philosophy of history, in fact, comes more from his in-depth study of Hegel[22] than his discipleship in the school of dialogue. The difficulty is that Hegel and Buber do not easily mix; they are certainly not integratable. Buber was, in large part, reacting to Hegel's historicism; in his flight from Hegel he seems to have run away from history, despite his best intentions and disclaimers,[23] altogether.

Related to this flight from history, though grounded in independent metaphysical presuppositions, was Buber's inability to deal with evil. His feeble, bewildered

---

21 See my essay "Martin Buber's Epistemology: A Critical Appraisal," *International Philosophical Quarterly* 21.2 (June 1981): 133–58. Fackenheim's appreciation of Buber's position is to be found in his *God's Presence in History*, in his contribution to *The Philosophy of Martin Buber*, and in his collected essays, *Quest for Past and Future* (Bloomington, IN, 1968).

22 See his outstanding study of Hegel, *The Religious Dimensions of Hegel's Thought* (Bloomington, IN, 1967), and his important essay "Hegel's Understanding of Judaism," in *Encounters between Judaism and Modern Philosophy* (New York, 1973). Note also the Hegelian influence in several essays in *The Jewish Return into History*.

23 Buber would not agree. He saw his treatment of Judaism as emphasizing the historical in comparison, for example, with the system of his friend Franz Rosenzweig, or again, of the older Hermann Cohen. However, despite his genuine attempt to make history matter, to do it justice, his dialogical mode of thought essentially eliminated this possibility from satisfactorily actualizing itself in his work. I have briefly noted the reasons for this in the essay on Buber's epistemology cited in note 21 above.

response to the Holocaust is testimony to this. One is struck by the very paucity even of attempts to deal with what had happened to Jews in his generation, an event in which up to 1938 he had played so dramatic and heroic a role.[24] One can well appreciate Buber's silence, but this silence must be allowed to count against the adequacy of dialogical thought as a way of meeting the problem of evil more generally[25] and of the Holocaust in particular. *Eclipse of God*, the title of Buber's volume of essays[26] written, in part, as a response to Auschwitz, is a metaphor that itself needs to be explained, that cries out for, demands, explication and content. In and of itself it hides more than it reveals; it evades more than it illuminates. Yet Buber had no real illumination to offer in these matters, nor will he assist others – e.g., Fackenheim – just here where the theological going is roughest.

Lastly, Buber's prescription for contentless revelation, while setting out to protect revelation from its modern critics, turns back upon itself and devours its own substance. I-Thou encounter is in the end an incoherent model for the revelatory moment. As such it *cannot* serve as the theoretical model for Fackenheim's own attempt to reconstruct a viable analysis of revelation, certainly not of a meaningful, content-full revelation like his 614th commandment. The lapses in Buber's redescription of revelation are logically insuperable; they deny the very possibility of coherence to all who rely upon it – Fackenheim, unfortunately, included.[27]

A further word about the connection, or rather, impossibility of a connection, between Buber's dialogical, contentless revelation and Fackenheim's 614th commandment is required. How does one get from the former to the latter? On Buber's *I and Thou* account, the 614th commandment could only be a "human response" to the divine presence, *not* – and this negation is nonnegotiable in Buber's thinking – the imperative of the divine. If this is so, however, what universal status does it have? Buber's personalist summary of what he takes revelation to be, in part 3 of *I and Thou*, specifically rules out anything issuing from revelation that "can be held above all men's heads." Only the "I" partner of the encounter is commanded, if "commanded" is still even a meaningful concept in this setting, especially given

---

24 On Buber's role in the life of German Jewry under the Nazis, see Hans Kohn's biography *Martin Buber: Sein Werk und Seine Zeit, 1880–1930; Nachwort 1930–1960*, ed. Robert Weltsch (new edition, Köln, 1961). See also the article by Ernst Simon in the *Leo Baeck Yearbook*, vol. 1 (1956) entitled "Jewish Adult Education in Nazi Germany as Spiritual Resistance," pp. 68–104; and Ernest Wolf, "Martin Buber and German Jewry," *Judaism* 1 (1952): 346–52.

25 On Buber's handling of the problem of evil see Maurice Friedman, *The Life of Dialogue* (Chicago, 1976); Greta Schaeder, *The Hebrew Humanism of Martin Buber* (Detroit, 1973). For criticism see Nahum Glatzer, *Baeck-Buber Rosenzweig Reading the Book of Job* (Leo Baeck Memorial Lecture, No. 10) (New York, 1966); Paul Edwards, *Buber and Buberism* (Lawrence, KS, 1970); and William Kaufmann, *Contemporary Jewish Philosophers* (New York, 1976). It should be noted that Edwards and Kaufmann's critiques are too simplistic in some important respects and hence must be read with care.

26 Martin Buber, *Eclipse of God* (New York, 1957).

27 For a more detailed analysis of Buber's views, see my papers referred to above, as well as my paper "Martin Buber's Theory of Revelation," read at the Sixth World Congress of Jewish Studies (Jerusalem, 1976).

Buber's acceptance of a Kantian embargo on heteronomous norms. This being so, however, how can this personalist, nonuniversalist model become the *urgrund* for a 614th commandment of any kind, particularly as from Buber's perspective the original 613 commandments have lost their commanding resonance?[28]

Discussion of the content of revelation brings us back to Fackenheim's sketch of the 614th commandment with the requirement that we put several additional questions to it. Passing over, for the present, the contradiction of there being any content to revelation on Buberian grounds, we must ask, what exactly does Fackenheim mean by the term "commandment"? In the older, traditional theological vocabulary of Judaism, it meant something God actually "spoke" through Moses, and through the sages in elaboration thereon, to the people of Israel. Fackenheim, however, would reject this literal meaning in line with his dialogical premises. But then what does "commanded" here mean? It would seem the word has only an analogical or metaphorical sense in this case, but if so, what urgency and compelling power does it retain? Fackenheim would, correctly, reject the just-mentioned option of analogy or metaphor, but if these are rejected, and the literal meaning is denied, what, we ask again, remains?

There emerges a curious "double think" in this position. On the one hand, the word "commandment" (and like terms, e.g., "revelation," "salvation," "redemption") are used because they have a content we all know from the biblical account. On the other hand, the literalness of the biblical witness is denied, leaving the intelligibility of these terms, both in their original biblical and in their modern employments, obscure. This, in term, leads to two corollaries. The first of these relates back to a line of thought mentioned briefly above. When I ask Professor Fackenheim whether his 614th commandment is revelation as the Torah was believed to be revelation – i.e., *Halakhah l'Moshe m'Sinai*, in the traditional formula – the answer must, I believe, be no: God did not "speak these things." They are, rather, a human response to Auschwitz, but a human awakening, even be it to Auschwitz, is religious anthropology rather than revelation as this term has heretofore been understood. Alternatively, to redefine the term "revelation" dialogically merely achieves similar, unsatisfactory results by a slightly different route. Which is to ask: is the 614th commandment revelation or only our talk *about* revelation?

At this juncture I would also stand one of our major objections to Richard Rubenstein[29] on its head and apply the inverted critique to Fackenheim. Whereas the radical theologians seem naively to rely on an empiricist criterion of falsifiability and meaning, Fackenheim seems to go to the other extreme, avoiding direct

---

28 On this sensitive issue see Arthur A. Cohen's "Revelation and Law: Reflections on Martin Buber's View on Halakah," *Judaism* 1 (July 1952): 250–56; and Marvin Fox, "Some Problems in Buber's Moral Philosophy," in *The Philosophy of Martin Buber*, pp. 151 ff. See also Eliezer Berkowitz, *Major Themes in Modern Philosophies of Judaism* (New York, 1974), pp. 68–137.

29 See the article "Richard Rubenstein, the God of History, and the Logic of Judaism," in my *Post-Holocaust Dialogues: Critical Studies in Modern Jewish Thought* (New York, 1983), pp. 174–204, for more on this issue as it applies to his position.

confrontation with empirical evidence to such an extent that all discussion and evaluation becomes irrelevant. Though Fackenheim does not state his doctrine in these terms, his demand that one must stand within the faith circle in order to understand the propositions of the religious person leads inexorably to this conclusion. This final cul-de-sac is arrived at partly consciously and partly as a legacy of his Buberian, and more generally existentialist, inheritance. The particularly significant implication of this stance is to make it difficult to see what would be allowed to count against the 614th commandment by its advocates. Under what circumstances would they admit either that "God is dead" or, less extremely, that at least He had broken His covenant with Israel, thereby rendering Jewish belief either irrelevant or foolish after Auschwitz?

In his essay "Elijah and the Empiricists,"[30] Fackenheim attempts to respond to this challenge by engaging and overcoming the empiricist polemic presented in the well-known "University Discussion" and earlier by A. J. Ayer.[31] He notes that Judaism and Christianity must be treated differently in terms of this issue, the former being, in his view, more open to history and hence disconfirmation. He, in fact, goes so far as to offer this significant counterclaim:

> Unlike the Christian eschatological expectation, the Jewish is at least in part falsifiable by future history ... Sophisticated philosophers have overlooked this possibility at a time when even ordinary Jewish believers are unable to overlook it. After Auschwitz, it is a major question whether the Messianic faith is not already falsified – whether a Messiah who would come, and yet did not come, has become a religious impossibility.
> Falsification is not, in any case, unimaginable.[32]

In support of this bold assertion he then, in good philosophical fashion, constructs the following example to indicate the conditions under which Jewish belief would be falsified. "Imagine," he writes,

> a small band of Jewish believers as the sole survivors of a nuclear holocaust. Imagine them to be totally certain that no human beings have survived anywhere else, and that they themselves and their children are inexorably doomed. They are not faced with a repetition of Noah's flood but rather with the end of history. Of the destiny of individual souls, the whole picture is not yet in sight. But the whole picture of history is already seen, and it refutes the Jewish eschatological hope concerning it. The suffering to which Jews have exposed themselves by remaining

---

30 Emil Fackenheim, *Encounters*, pp. 7–30.
31 "University Discussion," in *New Essays in Philosophical Theology*, ed. Anthony Flew and Alasdair MacIntyre (London, 1966); and A. J. Ayer, *Language, Truth, and Logic* (London, 1936); several subsequent revised editions.
32 Emil Fackenheim, *Encounters*, p. 20.

a people is already seen to have been pointless. (This is true at least of suffering radical enough to have remained pointless in pre-Messianic history.) Precisely insofar as it holds fast to history, Jewish faith risks falsification by history.[33]

This case appears to go a long way towards actually setting forth an at least *in-principle*[34] situation in which Jewish faith, Fackenheim's faith, would be decisively disproven. It is true that the case is implausible and hence loses some of its force as a consequence, but, essentially, Fackenheim is attempting to meet the conceptual challenge with a philosophical response. But now he hedges and all that had been gained is lost. Seemingly worried by the possibility of falsification that has been allowed into the discussion, he feels constrained to add:

> Let us return to the example of the survivors of nuclear catastrophe. Exactly what part of their faith is refuted? That God exists? No. That He loves us? To the extent to which it holds fast to actual history, Jewish faith has in any case long qualified any such sweeping and simplistic affirmation. Some evils in history may be only apparent, such as deserved punishment. Not all historical evils are apparent – history is unredeemed. Jewish faith cannot say why history is unredeemed, why God "hides His face," or is, as it were, temporarily without power, and in any case restrains the Messiah from coming. This does not, however, either refute Jewish faith nor deprive it of content, so long as the promised coming of the Messiah can still be expected. It is this promise, and it alone, that would be falsified by a catastrophic end of human history.[35]

This exposition is full of interest, for it now appears that, in contradistinction to the possibility of falsifying Jewish belief, i.e., the existence of the Jewish God, this is not the case. God's reality is untouched even by this hypothetical worst-case scenario, as is also, it seems, the more particular doctrine of God's love for us. Both are not, we are instructed, disconfirmed.

What then is disconfirmed? Only the Jewish Messianic doctrine. And what implications flow from this?

> How would a Jewish believer respond to this falsification? He could of course at long last surrender his age-old stubbornness, and accept

---

[33] *Ibid.*, p. 21.
[34] It is now recognized that the verification/falsification challenge must usually be carried on in the language of *in-principle*, i.e., future possibilities, rather than actual disconfirming instances. Of course, this weakens the challenge first laid down by Ayer as subsequent editions of *Language, Truth, and Logic* clearly demonstrate. But this diminution of the challenge was the only way to retain its intelligibility. Whether it is intelligible even in this weaker form is an open question.
[35] *Ibid.*, p. 21.

his faith as having been, all along, a mere hypothesis, now falsified. But then he should have let go of his stubbornness long ago, for the hypothesis had, after all, always been most improbable. The authentic Jewish believer would take a different course. He has in any case spent his life *working* for the coming of the divine kingdom, as well as waiting for it. He would now cite the divine commandment to do this work against God Himself, would refuse to abandon what God either chose to abandon or could not help abandoning and spend his last hours on earth beating swords into plowshares . . . It is a telling proof of anti-Judaic bias that contemporary empiricists treating the subject of falsifiability of religious faith have wholly overlooked the possibility of citing God against God Himself. This possibility appears even in the New Testament, for Jesus asks why God has forsaken him. In the Jewish Bible the theme is everywhere. Abraham cites God against God. So does Job. So do most of the prophets. Elijah at Mount Carmel would have done likewise had the necessity arisen. What if the heavenly fire had devoured the sacrifice of the priests of Baal, rather than his own? We have already seen what Elijah would not have done: accept the "hypothesis" that Baal "control[s] the physical world." It has now emerged what he *would* have done. He would have lamented that, already forsaken by men, he was now forsaken by *Adonai* as well – and continued to do His work, alone.[36]

In the final reckoning even the imagined catastrophe makes no real difference to Jewish belief. The Jew in Fackenheim's formulation continues, as it were, as if nothing had occurred. The recommended course of action – "citing God against God" – is particularly odd, for it is the very presence of God that is at stake. Whence comes the certitude about God's existence, *in the face of tragedy*, that allows such dispute, such dialogue, to continue? The only answer is that, in the last accounting, *nothing is* allowed to count against God's being there. Despite appearances, the falsification challenge has not been met; it has, rather, been sidestepped. All is in the end as it was in the beginning.

As a consequence, though Fackenheim is sincerely concerned to do more justice to the concatenation of Jewish history than he believes his rivals do, going so far as to assert that "authentic Jewish theology cannot possess the immunity I once gave it, *for its price is an essential indifference* to all history between Sinai and the messianic days,"[37] he seems finally to replace an authentic encounter with temporal events with a transhistorical faith that is impervious to the actual happenings of the world historical. Neither history not logic in the end seem able, by definition, to provide possible counterevidence to the Fackenheim thesis. This does not make

36 *Ibid.*, pp. 21–22.
37 *Return*, p. 52.

the thesis false, but it does make it a special type of metaphysical claim that is less interesting, certainly less rigorous and probing, than it at first appears to be.

Consider now the very traditional theological position of Eliezer Berkovits. One could pick at the edges of Berkovits's position at length, but the center of his argument turns on his advocacy of a traditional free will theodicy. Therefore, one can cut to the heart of the matter by turning directly to a scrutiny of his presentation of this defense. Taking his cue from the biblical doctrine of *hester panim* ("the Hiding Face of God"), Berkovits claims that God's hiddenness is required for the human being to be a moral creature. God's hiddenness brings into being the possibility for ethically valent human action, for by "absenting" Himself from history He creates the reality of human freedom that is necessary for moral behavior. For human good and human evil to be real possibilities God has to respect the decisions of humankind and be bound by them. Among the necessary corollaries of this ethical autonomy is that God has to abstain from reacting immediately to immoral deeds, and certainly from acting in advance to suppress them. But it is just here that the fundamental paradox emerges: for a moral humanity to exist, freedom must exist, yet it is the nature of freedom that it is always open to the possibility of abuse.

The corollary of this, as Berkovits understands the situation, is that "while He [God] shows forbearance with the wicked, He must turn a dead ear to the anguished cries of the violated."[38] Consequently, the paradoxical reality that flows from this divine circumstance is that humanity is impossible if God is strictly just, while if God is loving beyond the requirements of strict justice there will be human suffering and evil: "One may call it the divine dilemma that God's *erek apayim*, His patiently waiting countenance to some is, of necessity, identical with His *hester panim*, His hiding of the countenance, to others."[39] Auschwitz is a paradigmatic instantiation of this truth.

What is one to say to this argument? The first thing is that in the face of the *Shoah* this millennia-old theodicy is as coherent as any of those, new or old, that has been proposed, even if not fully convincing. The second thing is that Berkovits reveals his mature theological intuition by opting for this gambit as his "response." The third is that the many dramatic, intensely moving, examples of Jewish heroism in the face of Nazism that Berkovits cites in his studies do help advance a case for the existence of evil as a possibility that must be allowed by God in order for there to be true human freedom – and also for the reality of evil as an ingredient in the generation of certain "goods," for example, love and compassion, fidelity and courage. Granting all this, however, two pressing difficulties remain. With regard to human autonomy, and while recognizing its two-sidedness all the more because of Berkovits's discussion of Jewish heroism in the camps and elsewhere, an ancient enquiry reasserts itself: "Could not God, possessed of

---

38 *Faith*, p. 106.
39 *Ibid.*, p. 107.

omniscience, omnipotence, and absolute goodness, have created a world in which there was human freedom but no evil?" And secondly, "even if certain 'goods' are generated by overcoming or in response to evil, couldn't God either have allowed the production of these goods without so much evil, or, more radically still, wouldn't it be preferable if there were no such goods given the evil (and suffering) needed to produce them?" Let us examine each of these questions in turn.

The issue as to whether God could have created a world in which people always freely choose to do good has been given a particularly tight formulation by J. L. Mackie. In a well-known article in *Mind* he commented:

> I should query the assumption that second order evils are logically necessary accompaniments of freedom. I should ask this: if God has made men such that in their free choices they sometimes prefer what is good and sometimes what is evil, why could he not have made men such that they always freely choose the good? If there is no logical impossibility in a man's freely choosing the good on one, or on several, occasions, there cannot be a logical impossibility in his freely choosing the good on every occasion. God was not, then, faced with a choice between making innocent automata and making beings who, in acting freely, would sometimes go wrong: there was open to him the obviously better possibility of making beings who would act freely but always go right. Clearly, his failure to avail himself to this possibility is inconsistent with his being both omnipotent and wholly good.[40]

Many theologians and philosophers have replied to Mackie's challenge, the most cogent counter being Alvin Plantinga's. For our present purposes, I am prepared to admit his general conclusion, which I cite at length.

The Free Will Defense vindicated

Put formally, the Free Will Defender's project is to show that

(1) God is omniscient, omnipotent, and wholly good

is consistent with

(2) There is evil.

What we have seen (in a previous argument) is that

---

40 J. L. Mackie, "Evil and Omnipotence," originally published in *Mind* 44.254 (1955). Reprinted in Linwood Urban and Douglas Walton (eds.), *The Power of God* (New York, 1978), pp. 17–31, this quote is from page 27. A similar position has also been advanced by Anthony Flew, "Divine Omnipotence and Human Freedom," in *New Essays in Philosophical Theology* (New York, 1955), ch. 8. A counterargument has been provided by, among others, Ninian Smart, "Omnipotence, Evil, and Supermen," *Philosophy* 36.137 (1961). Smart's position has in turn been criticized by H. J. McCloskey, *God and Evil* (The Hague, 1974), 103–105.

(3) It was not within God's power to create a world containing moral good, but no moral evil

is possible and consistent with God's omnipotence and omniscience. But then it is clearly consistent with (1). So we can use it to show that (1) is consistent with (2). For consider:

(1) God is omnipotent, omniscient, and wholly good
(3) It was not within God's power to create a world containing moral good without creating one containing moral evil; and
(4) God created a world containing moral good.

These propositions are evidently consistent – i.e., their conjunction is a possible proposition. But taken together they entail

(2) There is evil.

For (4) says that God created a world containing moral good; this together with (3) entails that He created one containing moral evil. But if it contains moral evil, then it contains evil. So (1), (3), and (4) are jointly consistent and entail (2); hence (1) is consistent with (2); hence set A is consistent. Remember: to serve in this argument (3) and (4) need not be known to be true, or likely on our evidence, or anything of the sort; they need only be consistent with (1). Since they are, there is no contradiction in set A; so the Free Will Defense appears to be successful.[41]

Berkovits provides nothing logically comparable to Plantinga's reasoning, but I am willing[42] to allow Plantinga's analysis to stand in defense of Berkovits's championing of the free will position, recognizing that Berkovits would endorse both Plantinga's procedure and his conclusion.

However, this vindication pushes us another step, and here I demur from Plantinga's and Berkovits's position. For the problem now becomes: "could not God have created a world in which there was human freedom but less evil (as compared to no evil)?" Again Plantinga (and by inference Berkovits) answers "no" to this

---

41 Alvin Plantinga, *God, Freedom, and Evil* (New York, 1974), pp. 54–55. I have revised the numbering of the various propositions in this argument, Plantinga's numbering being different because part of a larger thesis, e.g., my number (2) is his (3), my (3) his (35), my (4) his (36).

42 I have technical philosophical reservations regarding Plantinga's argument. Given our present concern, however, we need not take them up here. For the sorts of issues that are relevant to a discussion of Plantinga's views see J. E. Tomberlin and F. McGuiness, "God, Evil, and the Free Will Defense," in *Religious Studies* 13 (1977): 455–75, which is critical of Plantinga's position. This paper has, in turn, been replied to by Del Ratzsch, "Tomberlin and McGuiness on Plantinga's Free Will Defense," *International Journal for the Philosophy of Religion* 12.4 (1981): 75–95; and by Robert Burch, "The Defense of Plenitude against the Problem of Evil," *International Journal for the Philosophy of Religion* 12.1 (1981): 29–38; and *idem*, "Plantinga and Leibniz's Lapse," *Analysis* 39.1 (Jan. 1979): 24–29. This should be taken as only a sample of the extensive secondary literature generated by Plantinga's important, if not fully convincing, work.

question[43] for, according to his analysis of the Free Will Defense, given genuine freedom, God cannot control the amount of evil in the world. But this "no" is not convincing, for the quantity of sheer gratuitous evil manifest during the Holocaust goes beyond anything that seems logically or metaphysically necessary for the existence of human freedom and beyond the bounds of "toleration" for an omnipotent, omniscient, and just God. One has only to recognize that given the belief in miracles, which Berkovits shares,[44] one miracle, even a "small" one, could have reduced some of the tragedy of the *Shoah* without canceling the moral autonomy of the murderers. Thus, it is logically conceivable and requires no great feat of the imagination to imagine a world in which there was less evil.

As to the second question, it increasingly seems to me that it would have been preferable, morally preferable, to have a world in which "evil" did not exist, at least not in the magnitude witnessed during the *Shoah*, even if this meant doing without certain heroic moral attributes or accomplishments. That is to say, for example, though feeding and caring for the sick or hungry is a great virtue, it would be far better if there were no sickness or hunger and hence no need for such care. The price is just too high. This is true even for the much exalted value of freedom itself. For we recognize the need to limit freedom where evil consequences are concerned, for example, we allow convicts to be incarcerated so that they will not cause further evil, we limit the right to cry "fire" in a crowded theater, we curtail the right to molest children, and the list goes on. Which is to recognize, as these examples indicate, that freedom is properly subordinated to the prevention of suffering and other undesirable consequences. In respect of the *Shoah* such a limitation on freedom would have clearly been preferable to the results of freedom run riot, whatever limited instances of good the evil of Auschwitz engendered.

At this juncture some might want to object that my refutation of the Free Will Defense and its attendant call to limit freedom in the face of the death camps has not confronted the truly radical implication of my own contention regarding autonomy and its restraints. This is because to suggest controlling free will would mean not only overriding the rights of individuals to do certain particular things, as in the examples just given, but also overcoming the basis for freedom altogether. This clarification rightly recognizes that free will is not equivalent to liberty of action, being more fundamental and at the same time a necessary condition of morality. In reply, however, it seems cogent to advance the reservations introduced above, if with modification. Better to introduce limits, even limits on that freedom of the will requisite to moral choice, than to allow Auschwitz. Here it is salient to recognize that free will is not, despite a widespread tendency to so understand it, all of one piece. One can limit free will in certain aspects, that is, with respect, for example, to specific types of circumstances, just as one constrains

---

43 *Ibid.*, pp. 55 ff.
44 On this issue of miracles and its relevance see the argument below.

action in particular ways. For instance, a person can have a phobia about X that does not impair that person's unrestrained power of decision in regard to Y. Such a case reveals that the call to limit free will does not necessarily mean its total elimination but rather its powerful curtailment by, in our present content, a divine intelligence under conditions such as those that reigned supreme during the Holocaust. Consider, too, that God could have created a humankind that, while possessing free will, nonetheless also had a proportionately stronger inclination for the good and a correspondingly weaker inclination to evil. He could also have endowed us with a greater capacity for moral education. Neither of these alterations in the scheme of things would have obviated the reality of free will, though they would have appreciably improved humankind's moral record, perhaps even to the point of significantly reducing the moral evil done to the innocent by a Hitler.

Much of my disquiet with this whole line of theological defense lies in my somewhat different mode of reasoning about morality. In contradistinction to the habitual way of conceiving the problem of freedom's relation to morality – that is, no volitional autonomy, no morality – one can and should turn the issue around and argue that if one has no, or small amounts of, evil to contend with, free will is less necessary because those virtues generated through its exercise, e.g., concern, love, etc., are not required in the same way. Macrocosmically, morality is a good not least because it helps us make our way in an evil world; eliminate or lessen the evil we encounter and the need for morality – and freedom – declines correspondingly.

From this angle of vision it becomes clear that the Jobean thesis usually developed in this connection, that is, the view that suffering creates higher goods and in addition trains one's character, requires another look. It has been asserted that

> the value judgment that is implicitly being invoked here [in the Jobean thesis] is that one who has attained to goodness by meeting and eventually mastering temptations, and thus by rightly making responsible choices in concrete situations, is good in a richer and more valuable sense than would be one created *ab initio* in a state either of innocence or of virtue. In the former case, which is that of the actual moral achievements of mankind, the individual's goodness has within it the strength of temptations overcome, a stability based upon an accumulation of right choices, and a positive and responsible character that comes from the investment of costly personal effort.[45]

This contention is not without interest as long as Job stays alive. But as a response to Auschwitz Job is not the right model, for unlike Job of old, the Jews in the death

---

45 John Hick, *Evil and the God of Love* (London, 1966), pp. 255–56. A similar argument is advanced by Gordon Kaufman in his *God the Problem* (Cambridge, MA, 1972), pp. 171–200. Berkovits is explicitly sensitive to the disanalogy involved in the Job metaphor per se (see *Faith*, 67–70), though he uses the same argument in a more general way.

camps were not protected from destruction. Therefore, the Jobean defense of tragedy, of suffering as the occasion for growth and overcoming, has little relevance to the Holocaust.

The incremental conception is simply too naive, too optimistic. It emphasizes the position value of evil as an aid to the growth and manifestation of goodness, but it ignores altogether the more telling fact that wickedness of the magnitude and quality unloosed by Nazism not only, or even primarily, increased our opportunities to display courage and love but even more – and essentially – destroyed forever such possibilities for six million Jews, including the all too many Jewish children whose youthful potential was never to be realized. Still more, the logic of this incremental thesis leads, if followed to its end, to an untenable conclusion. It suggests that good comes from, or in response to, evil, and that without evil there would be no heroism, no giveness, no love. The greater the malevolence, the greater the heroism. The significance of Berkovits's constant invocation of instances of truly extraordinary moral heroism in the face of Nazi brutality turns on this contention. Yet the irony here is this: if an increase in the diabolic is defended by recourse to the greater good it produces, i.e., more heroism is generated by Nazism than by a lesser plague, then the proper goal to be desired is a still greater Holocaust (God forbid) that would, by this line of reasoning, make for still more courage and fortitude. Thus, if killing six million Jews caused a corresponding amount and kind of virtue, killing twelve million will produce, say, twice the amount and a still higher quality of moral nobility. But surely this is all wrong. The recognition of its absurdity forces us to acknowledge the inherent deficiency of the incremental thesis as exposed by the reality of the *Shoah*.

There is still another moral objection to this incremental line of reasoning. One can contend that selfless love or forgiveness, or faith and fortitude, are unavailable without the corruption to which they are a reaction, but even if one makes this case, which in itself is not an easy case to make, it does not justify the evil per se. To argue the contrary is to suggest that the Nazis were helping Jews be virtuous and were assisting Jews in their ethical development. Likewise, is it morally acceptable to suggest that Jewish children should suffer disease and starvation, death by fire and by gas, so that others might have an opportunity to care for or comfort them? As to the children themselves, what sort of standard is involved? What moral improvement was achieved when Janus Korczak's orphans, and countless others like them, died in the ghettos and crematoriums? Their deaths contradicted that very freedom and moral autonomy that are at the base of the Free Will Defense. God's goodness is also impugned in the face of such barbarities. He, so the position contends, gave humankind freedom because He is gracious and compassionate, loving and concerned, but here His care for Nazis and for their freedom meant a total absence of solicitude for their victims.

The Free Will Defense becomes still more difficult to maintain when employed as a Jewish theodicy. The reason for this increase in complexity is the necessity of relating the Free Will Defense, as drawn in a more general philosophical way, with the God idea of Judaism, i.e., the God of the Bible who is known to perform miracles in the face of overwhelming evil. Hence, it is a case not only of trying to decipher, in some theologically neutral sense, the world God set out to create but, rather, of understanding Jewishly why, given the exaggeratedly high cost of human freedom, God did not once again, as He had in the past, step into the flow of events and say: "Enough."

Berkovits is theologian enough to be aware that this is a serious objection and he tries to meet it:

> Man can only exist because God renounces the use of his power on him. This, of course, means that God cannot be present in history through manifest material power. Such presence would destroy history. History is the arena for human responsibility and its product. When God intervenes in the affairs of men by physical might as, for instance, in the story of Exodus, we speak of a miracle. But the miracle is outside of history; in it history is at a standstill.[46]

But this is an evasion, for the critical challenge simply needs to be rephrased: why, if God performed a miracle and entered history at the Exodus, did He show such great self-restraint at Auschwitz? Wasn't Auschwitz far worse than Egypt, Pharoah far more humane than Hitler? Given that history did not end because of the miracles connected with the Exodus, why would a miracle at Auschwitz now "destroy history"? Given Berkovits's biblically rooted faith this line of defense is not plausible.

Then, too, if God did not intervene in the *Shoah*, even if one might still thereafter be able to defend His power by recourse to a Berkovits-like argument regarding divine self-restraint, what happens in such an equation to God's love? Is a God who allows such total freedom, who does not act when human freedom takes on an apocalyptic character of frenzied sadism, still worthy of respect and admiration? Of being worshipped? In aid of the Free Will Defense Berkovits might be able to argue with cogency that "God cannot as a rule intervene whenever man's use of freedom displeases him."[47] But surely Auschwitz is not a mere "whenever"; it was a time that demanded just such interference.

A further corollary of Berkovits's teaching is also worthy of mention. He recognizes that for all its logical suggestiveness the Free Will Defense is not convincing.[48] Therefore, he feels compelled to add, "all this does not exonerate God for

---

46 *Faith*, p. 109. Berkovits's preference for the term "miracle" is both correct and misleading. That is, we can grant the term and the correctness of its usage, but this does not solve anything. The issue merely becomes why God did not perform a miracle.
47 *Ibid.*, p. 105.
48 In his book, *With God in Hell* (New York, 1978), Berkovits elaborates on this weakness at some length. In addition to the appeal to a "hereafter" he refers to three other Jewish "responses" to

all the suffering of the innocent in history . . . there must be a dimension beyond history in which all suffering finds its redemption through God. This is essential to the faith of a Jew."[49] This well-worked proposal is tantamount to a confession that human freedom extorts too high a price; as a result, the traditional "crutch" of an afterlife is introduced without any justification to bolster the classical metaphysical and moral structure under pressure.

This otherworldly appeal, however, is less than adequate to the task. Besides the elemental difficulty of the absence of any legitimation being given for this belief in the hereafter, the fact is that what this suggestion translates into is an appeal for compensation. God wrongs humankind and then tries to make up to it for the unjustifiable evil done. But just as we reject such compensatory actions as lesser goods in human relations, how much more so does it seem unworthy of God. It is this moral disquiet that makes the conclusion of the Book of Job so unsatisfactory and that makes it more unsatisfactory still in the case of victims of the *Shoah*. God may "redeem" the suffering, but it seems morally preferable that there should be no evil to redeem. Berkovits is right; this argument does not exonerate God.

There is also a deep irony in all this relating to the heart of the free will thesis. If there is a heaven where one resides in bliss without the tensions and difficulties caused by freedom of choice, why did God not create such an earth without freedom of choice and all of its terrible consequences? That is, if heaven is better than earth even without human autonomy, why wouldn't a similarly structured earth, one in which Auschwitz would be impossible, be likewise good? And if so, i.e., if this is a legitimate question to ask, the whole Free Will Defense falls.[50]

Berkovits's theodicy rests on the thesis, integral to the free will position, that God's "absence" is the real proof of His "presence"[51] – that in His "self-control" we are "introduced to a concept of Divine mightiness that consists in self restraint."[52] God's presence in history must be sensed as hiddenness and His hiddenness must be read as the sign of His presence. God reveals His power in the world by curbing His power so that humanity, too, might be powerful.

---

buttress the free will argument. They are the *Akedah*, the "Exile of the Shechinah," and the "Suffering Servant" motif. I shall not discuss Berkovits's treatment of these themes as they do not seem to me to advance appreciably the logic of the argument. Readers are referred to *With God in Hell*, pp. 124 ff., for Berkovits's presentation.

49 *Faith*, p. 136. This, of course, is a standard proposal often made in the past by theists. See, .e.g., Kant's moral theism as developed in a number of his works, and C. A. Campbell's *On Selfhood and Godhood* (London, 1959), among many other instances of this defense.

50 The possible counterargument some might advance, that heaven is good because it is earned by good deeds, would not be relevant in the case I present. This is because the causal mechanism whereby one gets to heaven does not account for, and is a different matter from, heaven's intrinsic goodness. Heaven is good per se not because this is where righteous souls ascend to. Rather, righteous souls ascend to heaven because it is good.

51 This position has also been adopted by Irving (Yitz) Greenberg through, in all likelihood, Berkovits's influence.

52 *Faith*, p. 109.

> That man may be, God must absent himself; that man may not perish in the tragic absurdity of his own making, God must remain present. The God of history must be absent and present concurrently. He hides his presence. He is present without being indubitably manifest; he is absent without being hopelessly inaccessible. Thus, many find him even in his "absence"; many miss him even in his presence. Because of the necessity of his absence, there is the "Hiding of the Face" and suffering of the innocent; because of the necessity of his presence, evil will not ultimately triumph; because of it, there is hope for man.[53]

This suggestion is neither original nor without its fascination. However, in light of the Holocaust it becomes necessary not only to advocate this thesis but also to ask anew, how and when is God's restraint of His omnipotence to be interpreted differently from His lack of omnipotence? How in fact and in logic do we know there really is an omnipotent God who is exercising self-restraint at a staggering human cost rather than allowing this evidence of "self-restraint" to be construed as data for either the nonexistence of God or at least God's nonomnipotence as advocated, for example, by a platonic Whiteheadian "process" theism?

If the nonpresence, nonpower, noninvolvement of God proves His presence, His power, and His involvement, then by a similar demonstration we could "prove" all sorts of entities and attributes into existence.

There is, however, another aspect to Berkovits's presentation of this theme that is more intriguing and that in fairness must be taken up. For he does not merely refer to God's "hiddenness" and "presence" in the abstract but rather gives these notions flesh by tying them to a seminal, traditional, Jewish theological claim relating to God's involvement with the Jewish People. According to this account, the true and enduring witness to God's ultimate power over history is the Jewish People. In Israel's history we see both God's "presence" and His "hiddenness." The continued existence of Israel despite its long record of suffering – "if God is powerless, God's people will be powerless"[54] – is the greatest single testimony, the most impressive proof that God is active in history despite his "hiddenness."[55] The Nazis, according to Berkovits, recognized this, and their slaughter of Jews was an attempt to slaughter the God of history. They intuited, even as Israel sometimes fails to, that God's reality in our world is necessarily linked to the fate of the Jewish People.

> That the Jewish people has withstood all the barbarous attacks upon it, that it has been able to maintain itself in the midst of deadly enemies, bespeaks the presence of another kind of power, invisibly playing its part in the history of men. The survival of the Jew, his capacity for revival

---

53 *Ibid.*, p. 107.
54 *Faith*, p. 124.
55 *Ibid.*, pp. 109 ff., for Berkovits's views on Israel in history.

after catastrophes such as had eliminated mighty nations and empires, indicate the mysterious intrusion of a spiritual dimension into the history of man. The more radical rebellion against the world of the spirit, the greater the hatred against the Jew. The Final Solution was not only to eliminate the Jewish people from history, but through the destruction of Israel it was meant to finalize the defeat of that mysterious spiritual force against which the rebellion was directed. The Nazis were quite correct in believing that if they did not succeed in the elimination of the "Jewish influence" upon world history, they would also fail in their plans for world conquest. No matter what they said in their official propaganda, they sensed the mysterious nature of that influence, the presence of a hiding God in history.[56]

As such, Jewish existence per se stands as prophetic testimony against the moral degeneracy of people and nations: it is a mocking proclamation in the face of all human idolatry and witnesses to the final judgment of history by a moral God.

For myself, I find much in this analysis suggestive for, like Berkovits, I too wonder at Israel's continued existence. Jewish history defies all theories, usually being the "exception" that cracks open all generalizations put forward as historical laws. This much I feel able to say with philosophical probity. To say more than this is to speak in the language of faith, which, even if one shares it, or rather, precisely because one shares it, one can only witness to it rather than argue about it. I see no way of convincing anyone that Israel is God's people or that, as Judah Halevi described it over a thousand years ago, Israel is the "heart" of the nations. While I, like Berkovits, find Israel's very survival[57] *the* strongest evidence both of its transhistorical vocation and the existence of divine providence, this affirmation, once offered, cannot be demonstrated.

The same judgment applies to the two additional themes of importance educed by Berkovits from God's "powerlessness." The first is that the Jewish People manifest a qualitatively different type of historical existence than other nations, that Israel lives in "faith history," the nations in "power history."[58] The second is that the state of Israel reveals God's "saving Presence."

> For the Jew, for whom Jewish history neither begins with Auschwitz nor ends with it, Jewish survival through the ages and the ingathering of the exiles into the land of their fathers after the Holocaust proclaim God's holy presence at the very heart of his inscrutable hiddenness. We recognized in it the hand of divine providence because it was exactly what, after the Holocaust, the Jewish people needed in order to survive.

---

56 *With God in Hell*, p. 83.
57 Having said this I should also say that I disagree with Berkovits's further remarks on the interaction of Jewish vs. non-Jewish history in *Faith*, pp. 111–12.
58 *Ibid.*

Broken and shattered in spirit even more than in body, we could not have been able to continue on our Jewish way through history without some vindication of our faith that the "Guardian of Israel neither slumbers nor sleeps." The state of Israel came at a moment in history when nothing else could have saved Israel from extinction through hopelessness. It is our lifeline to the future.[59]

Of course, Berkovits recognizes that this "lifeline" does not answer the agonizing questions of theodicy with logical decisiveness,[60] but he believes it gives hope to those who would share in such hope that they will be answered in God's future redemptive acts.

I accept Berkovits's contention that each of these themes reveals an authentic insight – yet each can be embraced, if embraced at all, only with one's critical eyes wide open. By this I mean that both of these are metaphysical claims that depend primarily on "faith" and are not subject – nor has Berkovits produced any evidence to the contrary – to either logical demonstration or verification of any stringent sort. This is not to say that they are false; indeed, I do not see how one could adjudicate whether they are "false" in a simple true/false sense. Rather, it is to indicate what type of propositions these are. Once it is recognized what sort of metaphysical statements they are, one also comes to recognize that one could not produce any argument or data that would disconfirm them. Nor can I imagine under what circumstances Berkovits would reject any or all of them. Contrariwise, it is not evident how Berkovits, having stated his theological credo, could do anything to persuade a sceptic. Certainly he could not charge the sceptic with any logical error or self-contradiction for failing to give his consent to any of these claims, nor could the sceptic be indicted for holding fast to his objection to what is demonstrably an inadequate metaphysical position per se, for neither of these corollaries necessarily flow from rejecting Berkovits's claims. Conversely, the sceptic cannot charge Berkovits with logical or metaphysical error – his propositions are well formed, intelligible, and Jewishly fertile, even if they are not confirmable.[61] This "stalemate" is, of course, if properly understood, to Berkovits's credit in that he has formulated several important theological theses that, even if they are "faith" statements, are suggestive in a Jewish theological context after Auschwitz. One can claim neither more nor less for them.

Having deciphered Berkovits's account, let me briefly take up the position of Arthur A. Cohen as set out in his book *The Tremendum*. I do so here because like Berkovits he endorses a version of the Free Will Defense, though in a totally

---

59 *Ibid.*, p. 134. On the meaning of the rebirth of the state of Israel see also *ibid.*, pp. 144–69; and *Crisis and Faith* (New York, 1976), pp. 159 ff.
60 *Ibid.*, pp. 136 ff.
61 The positivists' erroneous conflation of meaning and verification must be recognized and avoided. Again, Karl Popper's views on "disconfirmation" and the nature of scientific propositions must not be misapplied, as Popper himself acknowledges, to metaphysical propositions.

different, very radical, metaphysical context. Cohen now situates his Free Will Defense in what is essentially a Whiteheadian process position that argues for what Cohen calls a "dipolar" account of God.

The subtle intention that lies behind this transformative redescription of God is twofold. On the one hand it seeks to assure the reality of human freedom and hence to facilitate a simultaneous reemployment of a sophisticated version of a free will theodicy. On the other hand, and reciprocally, it redefines the transcendent nature of God's being such that He is not directly responsible for the discrete events of human history and hence cannot be held responsible for the *Shoah* or other acts of human evil. This is a very intriguing two-sided ontological strategy. Our question therefore must be, does Cohen defend it adequately? If so, at what theological price?

Let us begin to explore these questions by deciphering Cohen's second thesis as to God's redefined role in history. The clearest statement of Cohen's revised God idea in respect of divine accountability for the *Shoah* comes in his discussion of God's putative silence and what Cohen takes to be the mistaken tradition-based expectation of miraculous intervention.

> The most penetrating of *post-tremendum assaults* upon God has been the attack on divine silence. Silence is surely in such a usage a metaphor for inaction: passivity, affectlessness, indeed, at its worst and most extreme, indifference and ultimate malignity. Only a malign God would be silent when speech would terrify and stay the fall of the uplifted arm. And if God spoke once (or many times as scripture avers), why has he not spoken since? What is it with a God who speaks only to the ears of the earliest and the oldest and for millennia thereafter keeps silence and speaks not? In all this there is concealed a variety of assumptions about the nature and efficacy of divine speech that needs to be examined. The first is that the divine speech of old is to be construed literally, that is, God actually spoke in the language of man, adapting speech to the styles of the Patriarchs and the Prophets, and was heard speaking and was transmitted as having spoken. God's speech was accompanied by the racket of the heavens so that even if the speech was not heard by more than the prophetic ear, the marks and signals of divine immensity were observed. As well, there is the interpretive conviction that God's speech is action, that God's words act. Lastly, and most relevantly to the matter before us, God's speech enacts and therefore confutes the projects of murderers and tyrants – he saves Israel, he ransoms Jews, he is forbearing and loving. God's speech is thus consequential to the historical cause of justice and mercy. Evidently, then, divine silence is reproof and punishment, the reversal of his works of speech, and hence God's silence is divine acquiescence in the work of murder and destruction.[62]

---

62 *Ibid.*, pp. 136 ff.

As opposed to this older view, Cohen recommends an alternative:

> Can it not be argued no less persuasively that what is taken as God's speech is really always man's hearing, that God is not the strategist of our particularities or of our historical condition but rather the mystery of our futurity, always our posse, never our acts? If we can begin to see God less as the interferer whose insertion is welcome (when it accords with our needs) and more as the immensity whose reality is our prefiguration, whose speech and silence are metaphors for our language and distortion, whose plenitude and unfolding are the hope of our futurity, we shall have won a sense of God whom we may love and honor, but whom we no longer fear and from whom we no longer demand.[63]

In response to this reconstruction of the God idea, four critical observations are in order. First, it need not be belabored that there *is* truth in the proposition that "what is taken as God's speech is really always man's hearing."[64] But at the same time, it is only a half-truth as stated. For our hearing the word of revelation does not create "God's speech" – this would be illusion and self-projection. Certainly, we can *mis*hear God, or not hear at all what there is to hear – but these qualifications do not erase the dialogical nature of divine speech, i.e., the requirement that there be a speaker as well as a hearer. And if revelation requires this two-sidedness, then we have to reject Cohen's revisionism because it fails to address the full circumstance of the reality of revelation and God's role in it. Alternatively, if Cohen's description is taken at face value, revelation as such disappears, in any meaningful sense, from the theological vocabulary, for what content can we ultimately give to "man's hearing" as revelation? And, specifically, from a Jewish point of view, anything recognizable as Torah and *mitzvot* would be negated altogether.

Secondly, this deconstruction of classical theism and its substitution by theological dipolarity fails to deal with the problem of divine attributes. Is God still God if He is no longer the providential agency in history? Is God still God if He lacks the power to enter history vertically to perform the miraculous? Is such a dipolar absolute still the God to whom one prays, the God of salvation? Put the other way round, Cohen's divinity is certainly not the God of the covenant,[65] nor again the God of Exodus Sinai, not yet again the God of the Prophets and the *Churban Bayit Rishon* (Destruction of the First Temple) and the *Churban Bayit Sheni (Destruction of the Second Temple)*. Now, none of these objections, which point to Cohen's failure to account for the very building blocks of Jewish theology, count *logically*

---

63 *Ibid.*, p. 97.
64 *Ibid.*, p. 97.
65 Cf. here my comments on Yitzchak Greenberg's redefinition of God and his notion of a "voluntary covenant" in my essay "'Voluntary Covenant': Irving Greenberg on Faith after the Holocaust," in *Historicism, the Holocaust, and Zionism: Critical Studies in Modern Jewish Thought and History*, ed. Steven T. Katz (New York, 1992), pp. 225–50.

against Cohen's theism as an independent speculative exercise. However, they do suggest that Cohen's God is *not* the God of the Bible and Jewish tradition and that if Cohen is right – indeed, particularly if Cohen is right – there is no real meaning left to Judaism and to the God idea of Jewish tradition. Cohen's deconstruction in this particular area is so radical that it sweeps away the biblical and rabbinic ground of Jewish faith and allows the biblical and other classical evidence to count not at all against his own speculative metaphysical hypotheses.

The dipolar ontological schema is certainly logically neater and sharper than its "normative" biblical and rabbinic predecessor, but one questions whether this precision has not been purchased at the price of adequacy, i.e., at the price of an inadequate grappling with the multiple evidences and variegated problems that need to be addressed in any attempt, however bold, to fashion a defensible definition and description of God and His relations to humankind. Logical precision must not be achieved too easily, nor given too high a priority, in the sifting and sorting, the phenomenological decipherment and rearranging, of God's reality and our own.

Thirdly, is the dipolar, noninterfering God "whom we no longer fear and from whom we no longer demand" yet worthy of our "love and honor?"[66] This God seems closer, say, to Plato's *Demiurgos* or perhaps closer still to the innocuous and irrelevant God of the Deists. Such a God does not count in how we act, nor in how history devolves or transpires. After all "God is not," Cohen asserts, "the strategist of our particularities or of our historical condition." But if this is so, if God is indeed so absent from our life and the historical record, what difference is there for us between this God and no God at all? Again, is such a God, who remains uninvolved while Auschwitz is producing its corpses, any more worthy of being called a "God whom we may love," especially if this is His metaphysical essence, than the God of tradition?"[67] A God who we can only see as the "immensity whose

---

66 *Ibid.*, p. 97.
67 It is worth comparing Cohen's present description and understanding of the divine as dipolar with his comments made in conversation with Mordecai Kaplan over the idea of God in Kaplan's reconstructionism. This exchange is published in the volume *If Not Now, When?* (New York, 1973). There Cohen offered:

> I think it also implies a rather fundamental distinction within the tradition between God as creator and God as revealer. One of the things I particularly love in Rosenzweig's discussion of the reality of God in his *The Star of Redemption* is the recognition that the distinction between God the creator and God the revealer is rather too sharp in traditional theology. The assumption that the creating God is not also a revealing God and that the revealing God is not also a creating God at one and the same time is mistaken. The God who brought the people of Israel out of the land of Egypt to be their God was not only revealing himself to the people and calling the people to himself, convoking the people as the object of the act, but at the same time was exhibiting an undisclosed aspect of himself. The notion in classical theology (which I dislike as much as you do) that God *is being* alone, *ens entissimus*, and that history is somehow oppositive to the divine nature; that God concedes to history, condescends himself to it, seems to me meaningless and defeating. God needs history. God needs his creatures. God as creator requires as much the thing that he creates as he does the capacity to create. The creation of the

reality is our prefiguration," while rhetorically provocative, will not advance the theological discussion, for it provides negations and evasions just where substantive analysis is required.

Lastly, this proposed metaphysical reconstruction is not founded upon any direct phenomenological procedure per se. Though fashioned in response to the *Shoah*, belief in such a dipolar God requires just as great a "leap of faith" – maybe an even greater one as it lacks the support of the Jewish past – as do the theistic affirmations of the tradition. Phenomenologically, it is difficult to discern why one would move in the direction of dipolar theism, given the negativity of the *Shoah*, unless one were committed at a minimum to theism, if not dipolar theism, to start with. Cohen is correct that both Schelling and Rosenzweig begin "by *assuming* that human natures are created and therefore dependent upon the operative analogue of divine nature."[68] But why should we, or he, begin with this assumption – especially given his negation of much of the theistic inheritance that both Schelling and Rosenzweig retained, even if not always consciously? It is surely not enough to introduce this as an argument from authority, i.e., to hold this view on the claimed authority of Schelling and Rosenzweig; some better reason(s) for even introducing the dipolar God into the present conversation is required but remains always absent.

The second major aspect of Cohen's account turns on what I have called his revised free will theodicy. He advances the familiar thesis that God gave humankind freedom as an integral part of creation and, of necessity, this freedom can be variously misused, ergo the *tremendum*.

> The bridge that I have, not casually but I fear insubstantially, cast over the abyss is one that sinks its pylons into the deep soil of human freedom and rationality, recognizing no less candidly now than before that freedom without the containment of reason returns to caprice and reason without the imagination of freedom is supineness and passivity.[69]

In response to this proposal two reservations must be entered. The first is evoked by the particular form that the reconstructed Cohenian version of this classic theodicy takes. The second concerns itself with the Free Will Defense in its generality.

It is not clear why we need dipolar theism to produce the Free Will Defense, or that the defense is any more or any less sound in a dipolar than a traditional

---

universe and the giving of the Torah are part of the same continuum of self-expression. God's nature demands self-expression as profoundly as his creatures demand it.

Cohen's presentation here seems more satisfying and closer to the reality of Jewish views of God than his statement in his new work. It is instructive to follow the whole of Cohen's debate with Kaplan. Also of interest is a comparison of his present views as to the nature of God with those voiced in his earlier *The Natural and Supernatural Jew* (New York, 1962).

68 *The Tremendum: A Theological Reinterpretation of the Holocaust* (New York, 1981), p. 90. The emphasis of "assuming" has been added.
69 *Ibid.*, p. 94.

theistic context. That is, given Cohen's metaphysical dependence on Kabbalah and Schelling it is hard to see why or how their thinking makes any effective difference to the correctness, or otherwise, of the free will position. Cohen, in attempting to justify recourse to these sources in this context, i.e., in relation to the reality of authentic human freedom, criticizes traditional theism, what he chooses to call "fundamental theism," for holding that "God [is] respondent to extremity, the greater the human need the greater the certainty of his assistance, with the result that human life denies its essential freedom returning to ethical passivity and quietism in which everything is compelled to be God's direct work."[70]

But this criticism is inaccurate and establishes a "straw man" to be demolished by Cohenian dipolarity. "Fundamentalist" theologians have championed the Free Will Defense as vigorously and as "successfully" as Cohen; see, for example, Eliezer Berkovits's theological response to the Holocaust.[71] Contra Cohen, the pressing, gnawing problematic for the "fundamentalist" does not arise from the side of human freedom but rather from the belief in a saving God, a belief radically challenged by the Holocaust. That is to say, the "fundamentalist" knows the evil of humankind to be a striking challenge to its elemental doctrine(s) regarding the character of the Creator. In comparison, Cohen's position is specifically structured in such a way as to avoid having to grapple with this extreme difficulty. Indeed, this is the very reason for his particular theological reconstruction, i.e., the world's evil does not, cannot, impinge in a dipolar system upon God's being or status. But while this metaphysical redescription succeeds in solving, or dissolving, certain tensions – not allowing the evil of the world to count against God – it raises others of equal or greater force, especially regarding the divine attributes, in particular, those relating to the categories of omnipotence and omniscience. Of course, Cohen wants to redefine these cardinal attributes; this is, if I understand his call for a renewal of a kabbalistic Schelling model of Creation-Revelation aright, exactly what he intends. But in the process, does his dipolar God still remain Godlike? Or has Cohen actually capitulated to those critics who deny God's meaningful reality, by whatever name, while attempting to make a virtue of this covert capitulation?

Then, too, the moral dimension of theodicy remains to be dealt with even after Cohen's ontological reconstructions, if for something of a new reason. For the moral or, rather, amoral corollary of the dipolar schematization of God is deeply disquieting. Cohen's dipolar God appears, of necessity, morally indifferent to human suffering and historical acts of evil,[72] factors of no small consequence, for, in the end, the most sensitive as well as the most telling objections to theodicy arise from the side of the ethical.

---

70 *Ibid.*, p. 96.
71 Compare in particular Eliezer Berkovits, *Faith after the Holocaust* (New York, 1973) and *With God in Hell* (New York, 1978). See also my critical discussion of Berkovits's views in *Post-Holocaust Dialogues*, pp. 268–86, as well as earlier in this essay, pp. 307–315.
72 For more on the issue of the relation of God and history see below.

I have already analyzed the logical weaknesses inherent in attempting to meet the theological problems raised by the *Shoah* through recourse to the free will argument. Though this analysis needs to be modified in certain specific respects given the total construction of Cohen's theodicy, the general negative conclusion there argued that this defense is inadequate to the immense task at hand applies in the case of the *tremendum* as well.

Here I would also add another word about Cohen's view of the connection between God and history. That is, Cohen recognizes that his programmatic reconstruction impacts upon the fundamental question of God's relation to history. In explicating his understanding of this vexing relationship, he writes, "God and the life of God exist neither in conjunction with nor disjunction from the historical, but rather in continuous community and nexus. God is neither a function nor a cause of the historical nor wholly other and indifferent to the historical."[73] If God then is unrelated to the historical in any of these more usual ways, as "neither a function nor a cause," how then is He present, i.e., not "wholly other and indifferent," and what difference does He make in this redefined and not wholly unambiguous role? Cohen tells us:

> I understand divine life to be rather a filament within the historical, but never the filament that we can identify and ignite according to our requirements, for in this and all other respects God remains God. As filament, the divine element of the historical is a precarious conductor always intimately linked to the historical, its presence securing the implicative and exponential significance of the historical and always separate from it, since the historical is the domain of human freedom.[74]

But this advocacy of an "implicit" but noncausal nexus will not do.

In the final reckoning, this impressionistic articulation of the problem must collapse in upon itself, for at some level of analysis the reciprocal notions of "causality" and "function" cannot be avoided. One can talk lyrically of God as a "filament" and a "conductor" in history as if these were not causal or connective concepts, but upon deeper probing it will be revealed that they are. For talk of God as "filament" and "conductor" to retain its coherence – for it not to evaporate into empty metaphor – we have to know what it means to refer to God as a "filament," as a "conductor," no matter how precarious the theological reconstruction. To rescue these instrumental concepts from complete intellectual dissolution we need also to know something of how God is present in the world in these ways. What evidence can we point to in defense of these images?[75] For example, and deserving of a concrete answer, are the questions: What of God is conducted? His

---

73 Cohen, *The Tremendum*, p. 97.
74 *Ibid.*, pp. 97–98.
75 Here, that is, we raise issues as to meaning and related, but separate, questions as to verification, i.e., not conflating the two but asking about both.

love? Grace? Salvation? And if so, how? Wherein, against the darkness of the *tremendum*, do we experience His love, His grace, His salvation?" To anticipate this objection as well as to attempt to deflect it by arguing that God is a "filament" but "never the filament that we can identify"[76] is a recourse to "mystery"[77] in the obfuscatory rather than the explanatory sense. For as explanation it means simply, "I claim God is somehow present or related to history but don't ask me how." Alternatively, to come at this thesis from the other side, the analogies of "filament" and "conductor" are disquieting as analogues of the relation of God and history because they so strongly suggest passivity and inertness. If they are the proper analogues for God's activity or presence in history, all our earlier concrete concerns about maintaining the integral vitality of Judaism resurface. For the God of creation, covenants, Sinai, and redemption is altogether different, i.e., qualitatively, metaphysically, and morally other, then a "conductor" or "filament."

Given the dispassionate, disinterested, amoral nature of Cohen's deity, it is not surprising that the conclusion drawn from this descriptive recasting of God's role in "community and nexus" is, vis-à-vis the *Shoah*, finally, trivial (in the technical sense).

> Given these assumptions, it would follow that the *tremendum* does not alter the relation of God to himself, nor the relation in which God exists to the historical, nor the reality of creation to the process of eternal beginning within God, but it does mean that man not God renders the filament of the divine incandescent or burns it out. There is, in the dialect of man and God amid history, the indispensable recognition that man can obscure, eclipse, burn out the divine filament, grounding its natural movement of transcendence by a sufficient and oppository chthonic subscension. It is this which is meant by an *abyss* of the historical, the demonic, the *tremendum*.[78]

That the Holocaust makes no different to God's relation to Himself we can grant *in principle* for the purposes of this analysis. And, logically and structurally, i.e., ontologically, we can allow for the purposes of argument Cohen's conclusion that "the *tremendum* does not alter the relation in which God exists to the historical." But, if we grant both these premises, it is necessary to conclude, contra Cohen, that the *tremendum* is not, and *in principle* could not be, a theological problem. It is, on its own premises, irrelevant to God's existence, irrelevant to God's relation to history, and, on these criteria, irrelevant to God's relation to humankind whatever humankind's relation to God.

---

76 *Ibid.*, pp. 97 ff.
77 See my paper on the "Logic and Language of Mystery," in *Christ, Faith, and History*, eds. Stephen Sykes and John Clayton (Cambridge, UK, 1972), pp. 239–62, for a fuller criticism of this common theological gambit.
78 Cohen, *The Tremendum*, p. 98.

The *tremendum* is seen by Cohen to be crucially relevant to humanity's recognition of a creator, but this is anthropology, for it perceives the *tremendum* only as a human event with no consequences for God other than our indifference to Him. And our indifference does not appear to matter in any transcendental sense, for God apparently does not make any response to it. This is the logic of the free will position driven to its "nth" degree – to a degree that makes God all but irrelevant. This remarkable implication flows, ironically, from Cohen's consummate attempt to redefine and reconstruct the theological landscape in order to *protect the viability of some* (not the traditional) *God idea* in the face of the *tremendum*, an end it accomplishes through the total disconnection of God and the *tremendum*.

The last thinker whose work needs mention in this context is Irving (Yitz) Greenberg. Greenberg has argued that as a result of the Holocaust the covenant between God and Israel is voluntary. The *Shoah* marks a new era in which the Sinaitic covenant was shattered. Thus, if there is to be any covenantal relationship at all today it must assume new and unprecedented forms.[79] In this context Greenberg insists that the covenant always implied further human development. The natural outcome of the covenant is full human responsibility. "In retrospect," he argues, paraphrasing A. Roy Eckardt:

> It is now clear that the divine assignment to the Jews was untenable. In the Covenant, Jews were called to witness to the world for God and for a final perfection. After the Holocaust, it is obvious that this role opened the Jews to a total murderous fury from which there was no escape. Yet the divine could not or would not save them from this fate . . . Therefore, morally speaking, God must repent of the covenant, i.e., do Teshuvah for having given his chosen people a task that was unbearable cruel and dangerous within having provided for their protection. Morally speaking, then, God can have no claims on the Jews by dint of the Covenant.[80]

What this means is that the covenant can no longer be commanded, nor can it be subject to a serious external enforcement. It cannot be commanded because morally speaking – covenantally speaking – one cannot *order* another to step forward

---

79 The five articles by Greenberg I will be concerned with in this section are (1) "Cloud of Smoke, Pillar of Fire: Judaism, Christianity, and Modernity after the Holocaust," in *Auschwitz: Beginning of a New Era?* ed. Eva Fleischner (New York, 1977), pp. 1–55 (hereafter cited as "Cloud"); (2) "Judaism and History: Historical Events and Religious Change," in *Ancient Roots and Modern Meanings*, ed. Jerry V. Dillen (New York, 1978), pp. 43–63 (hereafter cited as JH); (3) "New Revelations and New Patterns in the Relationship of Judaism and Christianity," *Journal of Ecumenical Studies* (Spring 1979): 249–67; (4) "The Transformation of the Covenant" (not yet published); and (5) "The Third Great Cycle in Jewish History," printed and circulated by the National Jewish Resource Center (New York, 1981), 44 pages (hereafter TGC).
80 TGC, p. 23. Here it is to be noted that in this paragraph Greenberg is paraphrasing a remark by A. Roy Eckardt. Yet, despite this undoubted influence, there may be some significant differences between Eckardt's position and Greenberg's over the final understanding of this seminal issue.

to die. One can give an order like this to an enemy, but in moral relationship I cannot demand from another that he/she give up his/her life. I can ask for it or plead for it – but I cannot order it. To put it again in Elie Wiesel's words: "When God gave us a mission, that was all right. But God failed to tell us that it was a suicide mission."[81] Moreover, after the horrors of the *Endlösung*, nothing God could threaten for breach of the covenant would be frightening, hence the covenant cannot be enforced by the threat of punishment any longer.[82]

Out of this complex of considerations, Greenberg pronounces the fateful judgment: *The Covenant is now voluntary!* After Auschwitz Jews have, quite miraculously, chosen to continue to live Jewish lives and collectively to build a Jewish state, the ultimate symbol of Jewish continuity, but these acts are, now, the result of the free choice of the Jewish People.

> I submit that the covenant was broken but the Jewish people, released from its obligations, chose voluntarily to take it on again and renew it. God was in no position to command anymore but the Jewish people was so in love with the dream of redemption that it volunteered to carry on with its mission.[83]

The consequence of this voluntary action transforms the existing covenantal order. First Israel was a junior partner, then an equal partner, and now, after Auschwitz, it becomes

> the senior partner in action. In effect, God was saying to humans: you stop the Holocaust. You bring the redemption. You act to insure: never again. I will be with you totally in whatever you do, wherever you go, whatever happens but you must do it.[84]

---

81 *Ibid.*, p. 23.
82 *Ibid.*, pp. 23–24.
83 *Ibid.*, p. 25.
84 *Ibid.*, p. 27. Because of the significance of this doctrine and its apparent radicalness, it is important that we understand Greenberg's position correctly. In correspondence with this author he has given the following explication that I quote in full:

> It is true that I go on to describe "the shattering of the Covenant" and "the Assumption of the Covenant." However, in light of this whole essay the human taking charge, i.e., full responsibility for the covenant is God's calling to them. "If the message of the destruction of the Temple was that the Jews were called to greater partnership and responsibility in the covenant, then the Holocaust is an even more drastic call for total Jewish responsibility for the covenant" (TGC, p. 36). The more I reflected upon this insight, I grew more and more convinced that this third stage was an inevitable and necessary state of the covenant. The covenant always intended that humans ultimately must become fully responsible. In retrospect, the voluntary stage is implicit in the covenantal model from the very beginning. Once God self-limits out of respect for human dignity, once human free will is accepted, the ultimate logic is a voluntary covenant. (Personal correspondence from Dr. Greenberg to the author, January 3, 1989)

In turn, Israel's voluntary acceptance of the covenant and continued will to survive suggest three corollaries. First, they point, if obliquely, to the continued existence of the God of Israel. By creating the state of Israel, by having Jewish children, Israel shows that "covenantal hope is not in vain."[85]

Secondly, and very importantly, in an age of autonomy rather than coercion, living Jewishly under the covenant can no longer be interpreted monolithically, i.e., only in strict halakhic fashion. A genuine Jewish pluralism,[86] a Judaism of differing options and interpretations, is the only legitimate foundation in the age of Auschwitz. Orthodox observance no less than Reform, Conservative, or "secular" practices are freely adopted – none can claim either automatic authority or exclusive priority in the contemporary Jewish world.[87]

Thirdly, and repeating a theme sounded several times in earlier essays, Greenberg offers that

> the urgency of closing any gap between the covenantal methods and goals is greater in light of the overwhelming countertestimony of evil in this generation. The credibility of the Covenant is so troubled and so hanging in the balance that any internal element that disrupts or contravenes its affirmations must be eliminated. So savage was the attack on the images of God that any models or behavior patterns within the tradition that demean the image of God of people must be cleansed and corrected at once.[88]

A note of caution in pushing this dramatic statement of a "voluntary covenant" too far is, however, now required because of Greenberg's, further, mediating remarks on this provocative thesis. He writes: "We are at the opening of a major new transformation of the covenant in which Jewish loyalty and commitment manifests itself by Jews taking action and responsibility for the achievement of its goals. This is not a radical break with the past. In retrospect, this move is intrinsic in the very concept of covenant."[89] And Greenberg goes on:

> The Rabbis [of the Talmud] put forth Purim, with its hidden, human agency and flawed redemption, as the new redemptive model to which

---

85 TGC, p. 30.
86 See *ibid.*, p. 33. For further adumbration of Greenberg's position on pluralism and its many implications, cf. also his essay "Toward a Principled Pluralism," *Perspectives* (National Jewish Center for Learning and Leadership, New York, March 1986).
87 These ideas are more fully described in TGC, pp. 37ff. For Greenberg this means that it is God's will that humans take full responsibility for the outcome of the covenant. Such a grant of autonomy entails that even if the actual policy decisions reached and acted upon are erroneous, the error is, in some real sense, a legitimate error within the broader confines of the covenant rather than a wholly illegitimate form of religious behavior.
88 *Ibid.*, pp. 37–38. See also pp. 16ff.
89 TGC, p. 18.

> the Jews gave assent in upholding the covenant. *Today we can say that the covenant validated at Purim is also coercive, for then the genocide was foiled, and it is less binding in a world that saw Hitler's murder of six million Jews.* [emphasis original]

In responding to the many genuinely interesting philosophical and theological positions Greenberg has advanced, one feels, to begin, a certain unease that one has not quite captured his meaning completely. The source of this disquiet lies not only in the limits of one's own understanding but also in Greenberg's imprecise use of essential terms and ideas. Such elemental terms as "revelation," "messianic," "messianism," "history," "redemption," "real," "secular," and "religious" are all used in a multiplicity of ways, aimed at a spectrum of differently informed listeners, and all are employed (perhaps in part intentionally) without any precise definitions being offered. Then again, his work suffers from a certain lack of logical rigor. This is evident both in the construction of particular arguments as well as in certain underlying architectonic features of Greenberg's thought as a whole. The most notable of these lapses, which is present so consistently that it should be seen as a structural flaw, is located in his hermeneutical overemployment of the notions "dialectic" and "dialectical" and in his unsatisfactory usage of the interrelated notion of "paradox." Merely holding, or claiming to believe, two contradictory propositions simultaneously is not a fruitful theological procedure.

Greenberg offers two seminal criteria of verification for theological discourse in our time. The first criterion is strikingly powerful in its directness and simplicity. It states: "No statement, theological or otherwise, should be made that would not be credible in the presence of burning children."[90] The second criterion, more philosophically sculpted and no doubt shaped in response to the positivist verificationist challenge, reads as follows:

> Faith is not pure abstractions, unaffected or unshaken by contradictory events; is subject to "refutation." Yet it is not simply empirical either. A purely empirical faith would be subject to immediate refutation, but in fact the people of Israel may continue to testify in exile and after defeat. It may see or hope beyond the present moment to the redemption which will inevitably follow. Thereby, it continues to testify despite the contradiction in the present moment. In fact, when the redemption comes, it will be all the greater proof of the assertions of faith and of the reliability of God's promises because it will overcome the present hopeless reality. On the other hand, if redemption never came or if Israel lost hope while waiting for redemption, then the status quo would win and Jewish testimony would come to an end. Thus, faith is neither a simple product of history nor insulated from history. It is a testimony anchored in history,

---

90 "Cloud," p. 23.

in constant tension with it, subject to revision and understanding as well as to fluctuation in credibility due to the unfolding events.[91]

While modern Jewish philosophers have tended to ignore the all-important challenge raised by requests for verification, here Greenberg, astutely as well as courageously, meets it head on. The question to be put to him, however, is whether his two formulations are adequate as principles of verification.

Begin with the first formulation. It does not set out a straightforward empirical criterion. Empirical evidence will neither simply confirm it nor, as it is phrased in the negative, simply disconfirm it. There is no empirical statement with which it is incompatible. That is, it is not, finally, a statement of an empirical sort. But this need not matter *decisively*, for it is not put as an empirical criterion; rather, its appeal is to the broader category of "credibility," and many things are credible that are not empirical. In this way, the task before us transforms itself into showing that "credible" is not used trivially, but this is a far more ambiguous and uncertain task than at first appears to be the case. Consider, for example, the remarks of the German Protestant pastor Dean Grueber that had such a profound impact on Richard Rubenstein.[92] The dean honestly held that Jewish children died for the crime of deicide committed by their first-century ancestors. Such "good" Christian theology was obviously "credible" to the dean in the face of the Holocaust. Likewise, Satmar Hasidim and other right-wing Orthodox Jews who continue to account for the Holocaust through recourse to the doctrine of "for our sins we are punished" (*mipnei chata'eynu*), remembering, for example, the terrible fate of the children of Jerusalem of old recounted in *Lamentations*, which is credited to "our sins," also believe that their propositions are "credible." It thus becomes evident that *credible* is not a self-explanatory category of judgment. What is credible to Dean Grueber and the Satmar Rebbe is *incredible* to Greenberg, and the dispute between them is not resolved by appeal to the criterion Greenberg has established, as it would be were it a viable criterion. It turns out that what is "credible" depends on one's prior theological commitments, the very issue at stake. Accordingly, the argument becomes circular.

Consider now the second, more formal, criterion. It is attested to be falsifiable, "subject to refutation," yet it is not, at the same time, a "simply empirical" proposition. The two conditions of "refutation" established are (a) "redemption never comes"; or (b) "if Israel lost hope while waiting for redemption, then the status quo would win." The first criterion appears, at least in what has been called a "weak" sense, to be empirically verifiable – i.e., it states a specific empirical condition under which it would, in principle, be disconfirmed. However, the established thesis is inadequate as a criterion because it turns on the temporal notion "never comes." Logically, we could not make any use of this norm until world history ended, in redemption or otherwise. At any time prior to the end of history

---

91 JH, p. 47.
92 On the details of this encounter see R. Rubenstein's article in *After Auschwitz*, pp. 47–58.

an appeal could be made to "wait a minute more," hence putting off the empirical disconfirmation indefinitely. It certainly is not, contra Greenberg, a "testimony anchored in history" in any strong sense, as immediate and available historical evidence, e.g., the obscene reality of the death camps, is deflected by appeal to the end that never is.

The second condition offered is of more interest. But it, too, is not sufficient for two reasons. First, the continued and continuing status of Israel's faith qua subjective affirmation is not a logical or ontological warrant for any proposition regarding "God's mighty acts in history," Greenberg's claim to the contrary notwithstanding. What is disconfirmed "if Israel loses hope" is, of course, Israel's faith – i.e., the strength of its commitment – but the ontological content of the commitment is unaffected. Propositions such as "there is a God," or "God redeems," or "history reveals a loving providence" are neither confirmed by Israel's faith nor disconfirmed by Israel's apostasy.

Given the weak verification procedures proposed by Greenberg, his advocacy of faith in God after the *Shoah* would seem compatible with any empirical set of conditions. That is, there seems no empirical state of affairs that is actually incompatible with theism, especially Greenberg's particular expression of theism.

II

This review of several major theological positions formulated as responses to the Holocaust reveals both the creativity and the limits of Jewish thought after the *Shoah*. Analyzing each of these positions individually and then comparing and contrasting them in their totality, has made it evident that no (single or multiple) way has been found to provide meaningful criteria of confirmation and disconfirmation in our theological discourse. And, as a corollary, no real advance has been made relative to the absolutely fundamental questions of theodicy.

Accordingly, we need to begin to think about the essential theological issues all over again *from the beginning* if we are to advance the argument concerning Jewish belief after Auschwitz in a satisfactory way.

UPDATE

This essay was written in connection with two conferences organized by the Memorial Foundation for Jewish Culture. Both were held in Ashkelon, in 1999 and 2001 respectively. I was one of the conveners, together with Professor Eliezer Schweid of the Hebrew University. The particular subject of the present paper was "provoked" by what I saw, and still see, as works put forward as Jewish philosophy, or more loosely, Jewish thought – and specifically Jewish philosophical responses to the Holocaust – that do not possess the technical philosophical coherence required in order for them to make arguments that are acceptable. In writing this paper, I was drawing on my own understanding of what philosophy was about, i.e., the formulation and presentation of convincing logical arguments about any given subject, and how that subject should be pursued. That is to say, the content of the paper was not about theological or metaphysical speculation or "opinions."

In my view philosophical work must have a healthy respect for the laws of logic and language, a coherent understanding of the meaning and significance of contradictions and paradoxes, and needs to avoid abusing and misusing essential terms like "God," "revelation," and "covenant." These methodological first principles reflect my own training that has been heavily influenced by five years (1967–72) at Cambridge University where I did my doctoral studies and wrote my doctoral thesis on Martin Buber. In this world center of so-called analytical philosophy – that had been the academic home of G. F. Moore, Bertrand Russell, Ludwig Wittgenstein, and their heirs – I studied with such major figures as Bernard Williams and John Wisdom, and my doctorate had been supervised by Elizabeth Anscombe, who was Wittgenstein's disciple, translator and literary executor, and Donald MacKinnon, a distinguished philosopher of religion.

Two reminiscences will help describe the prevailing outlook regarding what philosophy was understood to be in this academic context. In a discussion regarding existentialism, which was an extremely popular and influential philosophical movement in the decades following World War II, with a large following up until the 1980s – one that included Buber and other major figures like Paul Tillich, Martin Heidegger, Karl Jaspers, and Jean-Paul Sartre – I was told by Professor A. J. Ayer at Oxford that, "existentialism is nothing but a misuse of the verb 'to be.'" What he meant was that such well-known books as Martin Heidegger's famous *Sein Und Zeit* (in English, *Being and Time*) and Jean Paul Sartre's *Being and Nothingness* – that talked about the "meaning" of being – were just examples of confused, often empty, rhetoric. Rather than being profound, they represented little more than a radical misuse of logic and language. This highly dismissive observation was very relevant vis-à-vis my own work, as my doctoral thesis, focusing on Buber's "philosophy of dialogue" (made famous by his 1923 book *I and Thou*), shared this philosophical denigration of contemporary continental philosophy. In consequence, it reflected an only somewhat less hostile attitude toward Buber than Ayer did to existentialism in general.

The second incident occurred during the oral defense of my doctoral thesis. Professor Emmanuel Levinas had come to Cambridge from Paris to be my external examiner.[93] After about an hour of intense questions and answers regarding Buber and other major figures in modern Jewish thought, Levinas, a leading phenomenologist who had studied in Germany with Heidegger and who was part of the circle of existentialist thinkers in Paris, obviously exasperated at my severe deconstruction of Buber's dialogical philosophy, asked me: "Doesn't Buber ask all the right questions?", to which I replied with far too much arrogance: "Yes, but he gives all the wrong answers." At which point Levinas, with a very dramatic French gesture, put his arms out and said, "Finis." He was clearly very unhappy with my probing of Buber's philosophical writings from a technical, unforgiving, logical point of view. Despite this he kindly approved my thesis, as I discovered three months later by way of a telegram sent by Professor Donald Mackinnon that reached me at Dartmouth College where I was beginning my teaching career. Included in the telegram was advice, passed along from Levinas, suggesting that I "tone down" my criticism when I published my views.[94]

In the present essay I have critically examined the theological and philosophical claims advanced by Richard Rubenstein, Emil Fackenheim, Eliezer Berkovits, Arthur Cohen, and Irving (Yitz) Greenberg who were, and largely remain, the key Jewish intellectuals who, from 1966 to the present, have dominated the debate regarding the theological significance of the murder of European Jewry.

Since the late 1980s I have increasingly moved away from research in the field of the philosophy of religion except for my ongoing work on comparative mysticism.[95] However, insofar as I am aware of recent developments over the past three decades in the area of theological and philosophical responses to the Holocaust, there has been no serious response to my challenge calling for more rigorous philosophical standards when approaching this basic topic. Michael Morgan's *Beyond Auschwitz: Post-Holocaust Jewish Thought in America* (New York, 2001), is essentially an exercise in exegesis that paraphrases the positions of the thinkers he is reviewing. Serious, independent, philosophical and theological reflection is largely absent. This does not mean that Morgan's study does not add new facts to the discussion – it does. But what it does *not* add is any significant new understanding of the arguments being considered. Zachary Braiterman's *(God) After Auschwitz: Tradition and Change in Post-Holocaust Jewish Thought*[96] deals with literary as well as more narrowly defined theological issues, especially on the

---

93 Because of a mix-up related to the time of the beginning of Yom Kippur my defense actually took place in a hotel at Heathrow airport so that I could fly out immediately after the defense.

94 Readers can catch a glimpse of my unfavorable view of Buber's work in a paper I published on the subject: "Martin Buber's Epistemology," *International Philosophical Journal* (June 1981); reprinted in my *Post-Holocaust Dialogues*, pp. 1–51. I have never published the thesis in its entirety

95 See the titles of five of my books on this subject in the Introduction to this volume, p.___, n.3

96 Zachary Braiterman, *(God) After Auschwitz: Tradition and Change in Post-Holocaust Jewish Thought* (Princeton, 1998), p. 11

subject of theodicy and what he calls "anti-theodicy." In so doing he adds information to the debate, telling his readers:

> I remain deeply indebted to Steven Katz's *Post-Holocaust Dialogues* – undoubtedly the single most important example of critical scholarship in the field. In this seminal text, Katz applied a closely reasoned philosophical analysis to the claims posed by post-Holocaust thinkers. While relying on Katz, my own study includes a "literary" dimension that he left unexplored. Rhetoric simply inundates the literature. Under "rhetoric" I include hyperbolic slogans, polemical overkill, rhetorical overstatement, and gross over-interpretation expressed with the intention to shock readers, foment resistance, rally solidarity and carve out new theological identities.[97]

He then faithfully carries out this project. But his work, while not without interest, is not cutting edge philosophically.

The same can be said about most of the numerous essays written on individual figures, the most prominent of whom still appears to be Emil Fackenheim. The majority of these studies fail to offer any original reframing of the central issues, or any new form of organizing and deconstructing the relevant sources and questions. Two works, however, do distinguish themselves with original theological formulations. The first of these is Melissa Raphael's *The Female Face of God in Auschwitz: A Jewish Feminist Theology of the Holocaust*, published in 2003. This is a thoughtful effort that creatively attempts to think about post-Holocaust theology in a new, and decidedly radical, way. She describes her purpose in writing the book as follows:

> Steven Katz is right that Auschwitz "will not yield to any conceptual oversimplification." Using gender as a category of analysis will neither explain nor solve the Holocaust. But as at least a corrective to the almost universal scholarly assumption that women's Holocaust experience tells us something important about Nazi savagery but not about God, it will show that much that is theologically significant about women's experience has been overlooked in the production of post-Holocaust theology and in exclusively masculine models of divine agency during the period in question.[98]

Raphael accomplishes a number of her goals. The work, however, is not philosophical in a narrow sense, being more of an exposition of basic theological themes from a feminist perspective. Hence, it essentially ignores the technical logical and methodological questions raised in the present essay.

The second study is David Weiss Halivni's *Breaking the Tablets: Jewish Theology After the Shoah*, published in 2007. Halivni, a friend of many decades, is one

---

97 *Ibid.*
98 Melissa Raphael, *The Female Face of God in Auschwitz: A Jewish Feminist Theology of the Holocaust* (London, 2003), p. 2.

of the great Talmudic scholars of our age and his knowledge of Jewish sources from all periods of Jewish history is encyclopedic. But the theological courage that Halivni reveals in his reformulations of Jewish prayer and study after Auschwitz, though undoubtedly both provocative and profound, is far removed from the arguments and concerns of philosophers.

Two additional books that are relevant here I will just mention as I have a personal connection to both. The first is a collection of new essays entitled, *The Impact of the Holocaust on Jewish Theology* (New York, 2005) that I edited and from which the present paper is drawn. The second, titled *Ethics and Suffering since the Holocaust: Making Ethics "First Philosophy" in Levinas, Wiesel and Rubenstein* (New York, 2016), is an interesting and learned study by Ingrid Anderson who was my doctoral student at Boston University. Therefore, while I have a high regard for this study, I will resist evaluating it further.

In concluding these "afterthoughts" on "Confirmation and Disconfirmation," I would go back to A. J. Ayer's views, most famously expressed in his *Language, Truth and Logic*, published in 1936 under the influence of the Vienna positivists. He, and the positivists, made a serious mistake in equating verification and meaning. Propositions like Ayer's Verification Principle itself can have meaning without being verified or verifiable. However, at the same time, verification is not something that Jewish theologians can, or should, do without.

15

JEWISH THEOLOGIANS RESPOND TO THE HOLOCAUST

I

In this essay the main Jewish theological responses – for the most part excluding those voiced in the ultra-Orthodox and Hasidic world – will be described and briefly critiqued.

The responses come mainly in two forms. The first set primarily draws upon and recycles explanatory models that have their roots in the Bible. That is, they employ explanations that were first offered in the Bible in response to the perennial questions of theodicy and human suffering. Now, in the aftermath of the Holocaust, these varied traditional "solutions" are again appealed to, with modifications, to provide an understanding of the interaction of God and man and God and Israel. The second set of responses is composed of new answers that attempt to reconfigure the theological landscape in various original ways in light of the profound theological difficulties engendered by the existence of *Einsatzgruppen* (Hitler's murder squads in Eastern Europe) and the death camps. Given the importance of these positions, some old, some new, it will be of help to readers, especially those just beginning their study of these issues, if each is described individually with its main conceptual features highlighted. Let us begin with an examination of the six biblical models, starting with the famous event of the *Akedah*, "the binding of Isaac."

The Akedah: The binding of Isaac

The biblical narrative in *Genesis* 22:2, which reports the "binding of Isaac" by his father, Abraham, in anticipation of his being sacrificed in fulfillment of God's command, is often appealed to as a possible paradigm for interpreting the Holocaust. Such a theological move is well grounded in Jewish tradition, especially given its use in the medieval Hebrew martyrologies of the Crusader and post-Crusader period (late eleventh and twelfth centuries), during which the biblical event of the *Akedah* became the prism through which the horrific Jewish medieval experience became refracted and was made "intelligible" to Jews of that era.[1]

---

1 For more on these medieval texts see: Shlomo Eidelberg, trans., *The Jews and the Crusaders: The Hebrew Chronicles of the First and Second Crusades* (Madison, WI, 1977). For further discussion,

Now again, after the Holocaust, this religious model is used to describe the victims of Hitler's crusade to make the world *Judenrein*, free of Jews. The great appeal of this decipherment lies in its imputation to the dead of heroism and unwavering religious faith. Their deaths are not due to sin or to any imperfection on their part, nor are they the consequence of any violation of the covenant. Rather, they are the climactic evidence of the Jews' unwavering devotion to the faith of their fathers.

This response to the Holocaust is not without its intellectual and emotional appeal. Yet readers should carefully evaluate its claims, and the analogies upon which it rests, before concluding that it supplies a full, or even partial, "answer" to Auschwitz and Treblinka. Students need to think hard about just how exact the parallel between the *Akedah* and the Holocaust is. For example, in the *Akedah*, it is Abraham who is commanded to kill the son he loves. In the Holocaust, Hitler kills the Jews he hates. This murder creates no emotional or ethical "problem" for him; he is more than happy to carry it out.

Job

The biblical Book of *Job*, the best-known treatment of theodicy in the Hebrew Bible, naturally presents itself as a second possible model for decoding the Holocaust. For example, Martin Buber, Eliezer Berkovits, and Robert Gordis have all discussed its relevance in the context of post-Holocaust Jewish theology. That this should be the case is not surprising for Job provides an inviting paradigm in that Job's suffering is caused not by his sinfulness but rather by his righteousness – perceived by Satan as a cause for jealousy. Moreover, the tale ends on a "happy" note: Job is rewarded by God for his faithfulness with a double blessing. On a deeper level, of course, the issues are far more problematic and their meaning ambiguous. Thus, the ultimate meaning of the book is unclear and much argued about and its applicability to the Holocaust – especially insofar as Satan is not allowed to kill Job, unlike the victims of the Holocaust – is much contested.

The "suffering servant"

One of the most influential biblical doctrines framed in response to the "problem of evil" is that of the "suffering servant."[2] Given its classic presentation in the *Book of Isaiah* (especially chapter 53), the suffering servant doctrine suggests that the righteous vicariously suffer and atone for the wicked and, in some mysterious

---

see Jacob Katz, *Exclusiveness and Tolerance* (London, 1961), pp. 82–92; and Moses Shulvass, "Crusaders, Martyrs, and the Marranos of Ashkenaz," in his *Between the Rhine and the Bosphorus: Studies and Essays in European Jewish History* (Chicago, 1964), pp. 1–14.

2 In Christian tradition, the "suffering servant" is Jesus.

way, allay God's wrath and judgment, thereby making the continuation of history possible.

According to the majority of traditional Jewish interpreters, the "suffering servant" is the nation of Israel,[3] the people of the covenant, who suffer with and for God in the midst of the evil of creation. As God is long suffering with His creation, so Israel, God's people, must be long suffering. In this, they mirror the Divine in their own reality and, while suffering for others, make it possible for creation to endure. Moreover, through this act of faithfulness the guiltless establish a unique bond with the Almighty. As they suffer for and with Him, He suffers their suffering, shares their agony, and comes to love them in a special way for loving Him with such fortitude and without limit.

This theme has been enunciated in Jewish theological writings emanating from the Holocaust era itself, as well as in post-Holocaust sources. One finds it in the teachings of Hasidic rebbes as well as Conservative thinkers such as Abraham Joshua Heschel, and Orthodox thinkers, like Eliezer Berkovits.

It should also be noted that one contemporary Jewish theologian in particular has gone beyond the traditional framework and used the suffering servant idea to construct an elaborate, very novel, reading of the Holocaust. For Ignaz Maybaum, a German Reform rabbi who survived the war in London, the pattern of the suffering servant is the paradigm of Israel's way in history. First in the "servant of God" in *Isaiah*, then in the Jew Jesus, and now at Treblinka and Auschwitz, God uses the Jewish People to address the world and to save it: "They died though innocent so that others might live." According to this decipherment of the Holocaust, the perennial dialectic of history is God's desire that the gentile nations come close to Him, while they resist this call. Therefore, the special God-given task, the "mission" of Israel, is to foster and facilitate this relationship between God and the nations. It is they who must make God's message accessible in terms that the gentile nations will understand and respond to. But what language, what symbols, will speak to the nations? Not that of the *Akedah* in which Isaac is spared and no blood is shed but rather, and only, that of the crucifixion, i.e., a sacrifice in which the innocent die for the guilty, where some die vicariously so that others might live.

The theological deconstruction of the Holocaust using the suffering servant model can thus be seen to be interesting as well as challenging. Readers, however, must pause and carefully examine the plausibility of this response – and in particular Maybaum's unique rendering of this doctrine – before concluding that it supplies the needed explanation for the murder of European Jewry. And this not least because they need to ask questions about the logic of the suffering servant thesis (i.e. the notion of vicarious suffering) *itself.*

---

3 For more on the different classical Jewish interpretations of the theme of the suffering servant in Isaiah 53, see Samuel R. Driver and Adolf Neubauer (eds.), *The 53rd Chapter of Isaiah according to Jewish Authors*, 2 vols. (Oxford, 1876–1877; reprint, New York, 1969).

Hester Panim: *"God hides His face"*

The Bible, in wrestling with the problem of human suffering, appeals in a number of places to the notion of *Hester Panim*: "The hiding of the face of God." This concept has two meanings. The first, in *Deuteronomy* 31:17–18 and later in *Micah* 3:4, is a causal one that links God's "absence" from the unfolding historical events to human sin: God turns away from the sinner. The second sense, found most notably in a number of psalms (e.g., *Psalms* 44, 69, 88, and variants in, e.g., *Psalms* 9, 10, 13; see also *Job* 13:24), does not relate God's absence to sin but, instead, suggests human despair and confusion – and even protest – over His "disappearance" for no reason that can be discerned. Here mankind stands "abandoned" for reasons that are unknown and unfathomable.

In applying this unusual doctrine to the Holocaust, modern theologians – for example, Martin Buber, Joseph Soloveitchik, Zvi Kolitz, and Eliezer Berkovits – are attempting to do three things: (a) To vindicate the Jewish People, i.e., the death camps are not the consequence of sin and do not represent Divine punishment; (b) to remove God as the direct cause of the evil, i.e., the Holocaust is something men did to other men, women, and children; and (c) to affirm the reality and ever-saving nature of the Divine despite the empirical evidence to the contrary. The first two points need no further explanation; the third does. With regard to this line of reasoning, one must understand that the notion of *Hester Panim* is not merely or only about the absence of God but rather, at least in specific contexts, entails a more complex exegesis of Divine Providence stemming from an analysis of the ontological nature of the Divine. In such instances God's absence, *Hester Panim*, is a necessary, active condition of His saving mercy. His "hiddenness" is the obverse of His "long-suffering" patience with sinners, that is, being patient with sinners means allowing sin.

Then too, within the larger mosaic of human purpose, *Hester Panim* is dialectically related to the fundamental character of human freedom without which human beings would not be the potentially majestic beings Judaism envisions them to be. It needs also to be recognized that this challenging notion is, at one and the same time, a proclamation of a deep religious faith.

For some, the creation of the State of Israel following so closely upon the Holocaust is proof that God will not forever "hide His face."

The theological claim that God hides His face undoubtedly speaks eloquently to the religious confusion of the post-Holocaust situation. But students should beware of accepting it too easily as an answer to the horror of the Nazi period for, among other things, it appeals to a mystery, God's hiddenness, to solve the mystery represented by the evil of the *Shoah*.

Mipnei Chataeynu: *"Because of our sins we are punished"*

In biblical and later Jewish (rabbinic) sources, the principal explanation for human suffering was sin. According to this view, there was a balance – established by God – in the universal order that was inescapable: Good brought forth blessing;

sin brought retribution (see, for example, *Deuteronomy* 28). Both on the individual and the national level, the law of cause and effect, sin and grief, operated. In our time, this doctrine, given its undoubted theological pedigree, has been reused by a number of theologians, especially those of a more traditional bent, and by certain rabbinic sages, to account for the Holocaust. The Hasidic (Satmar) Rebbe, Joel Teitelbaum, for example, puts this claim forward clearly and with certitude: "[S]in is the cause of all suffering."[4]

Harsh as it is, the argument that Teitelbaum (and others who share this view) make is that Israel sinned "grievously" and God, after much patience and hope of "return," finally "cut off" the generation of the wicked. It needs to be noted explicitly that the majority of Jewish thinkers who have wrestled with the theological implications of the *Shoah* have rejected this line of analysis.

Two critical questions immediately arise in pursuing the application of this millennia-old doctrine to the contemporary tragedy of the Holocaust. The first is: What kind of God would exact such retribution? This crucial theological issue requires close and careful reflection. Second, of what sin could Israel be guilty to warrant such retribution? Here the explanations vary depending on one's perspective. All the justifications and explanations of this position,[5] however, must be treated with great suspicion. Readers need to reflect on the two fundamental questions raised above when deciding whether or not this response, which blames the victims for their own destruction, is plausible and represents a claim that they wish to endorse.

The burden of human freedom: The "Free Will Defense"

Among the theological and philosophical traditions that have been concerned to uphold God's justice despite the manifest evil in the world, none has an older or more distinguished lineage than that known as the "Free Will Defense." According to this argument, human evil is the ever-present possibility entailed by the reality of human freedom. If human beings are to have the potential for majesty they must, conversely, have an equal potential for corruption; if they are to be capable of acts of authentic morality, they must be capable of acts of authentic immorality. Applying this consideration to the events of the Nazi epoch, the *Shoah* becomes a case of man's inhumanity to man, the extreme misuse of human freedom. At the same time, such a position, with its emphasis on human actions, does not call into

---

4 *Va'Yoel Moshe*, 3 vols. (Brooklyn, NY, 1959, 1960, 1961), Introduction, vol. 1, p. 5 [Hebrew].
5 For a critique of Teitelbaum's views, see Norman Lamm, "The Ideology of *Naturei Karta* according to the Satmar Version," *Tradition* 12.2 (Fall 1971): 38–53; Allan L. Nadler, "Piety and Politics: The Case of the Satmar Rebbe," *Judaism* 31.2 (Spring 1982): 135–52; and Zvi Jonathan Kaplan, "Rabbi Joel Teitelbaum, Zionism, and Hungarian Ultra-Orthodoxy," *Modern Judaism* 24.2 (May 2004): 165–78. For a very different Orthodox view see Joseph Soloveitchik, *Fate and Destiny: From the Holocaust to the State of Israel*, ed. Walter Wurzburger (Hoboken, 1992). His famous earlier essay, first written in Hebrew and published in 1961 under the title "Kol Dodi Dofek" ("The voice of my beloved knocks"), appears in English in this 1992 volume.

question God's goodness and solicitude for it is man, not God, who perpetrates genocide. God observes these events with his unique Divine pathos, but in order to allow human morality to be a substantively real thing, He refrains from intercession, even though His patience results in human suffering.

This defense has been advocated by a number of post-Holocaust thinkers. The two most notable presentations of this theme are found in Eliezer Berkovits' *Faith after the Holocaust* and Arthur A. Cohen's *The Tremendum*. And in both cases, as well as in the work of other thinkers, it advances a powerful theological position. But, for all its significance, it does not fully answer the problem, for God is, in some ultimate sense, still responsible for creation. Thus, in the past, He is said to have intervened in history, e.g., at the Exodus from Egypt, but this type of intervention seems altogether absent in the case of the Holocaust.[6]

II

The first six theological positions that have been analyzed have all been predicated upon, and are the extension of, classical Jewish responses to national tragedy. In the last four decades, however, a number of innovative, more radical, responses have been proposed by contemporary post-Holocaust thinkers. Six, in particular, merit serious attention.

Auschwitz: A new revelation

The first of these emerges from the work of Emil Fackenheim, who has contended that the Holocaust represents a new revelation. Rejecting any account that analyzes Auschwitz as *mipnei chataeynu* (because of our sins), Fackenheim, employing a Buberian model of dialogical revelation[7] – i.e., revelation as the personal encounter of an I with the Eternal Thou (God) – urges Israel to continue to believe despite the moral outrage of the *Shoah*. God, on this view, is always present in Jewish history, even at Auschwitz. We do not, and cannot, understand what He was doing in the death camps, nor why He allowed them, but we must insist that He was there. Equally, if not more significant, God commands Israel from the death camps as He did from Sinai. The essence of this commanding voice, what Fackenheim has called the "614th commandment" is "Jews are forbidden to hand Hitler posthumous victories." That is, Jews are under a sacred obligation to survive. After the death camps, Jewish existence itself is a holy act. And most important, Jews are "forbidden to despair of the God of Israel, lest Judaism

---

6 This response has been deconstructed much more fully in chapter 14 above: "The issue of confirmation and disconfirmation in Jewish thought after the *Shoah*."
7 This refers to Martin Buber's theory of revelation most famously presented in his classic work *I and Thou*, first published in German in 1923.

perish." The voice that speaks from Auschwitz demands that no one assist Hitler to win posthumous victories.

To fully evaluate this interesting, highly influential response to the *Shoah*,[8] a detailed analysis of a sort that is beyond our present possibilities is required. Nevertheless, it needs to be stressed that the main line of critical inquiry into Fackenheim's position must center on the dialogical (Buberian) notion of revelation and the related idea of commandment, as that traditional notion is here employed. One needs to ask Fackenheim: (a) How do historical events like the Holocaust become "revelatory"? (b) What exactly does he mean by the term "commandment"? And, as a related question, one needs to ask whether one wants to make reaction to Hitler the main reason for continued Jewish existence.

The covenant broken: A new age

A second contemporary thinker who has urged continued belief in the God of Israel, though on new terms, is Irving (Yitz) Greenberg. For Greenberg, all the old truths and certainties, all the old commitments and obligations, have been destroyed by the Holocaust. Moreover, simple faith is now impossible. The Holocaust ends the old era of Jewish covenantal existence and ushers in a new and different one. Greenberg explains his radical view in this way. There have been three major periods in the history of Israel, and in each the idea of covenant has meant something different. The first is the biblical era. What characterizes this first covenantal stage is the asymmetry of the relationship between God and Israel. The biblical encounter may be a covenant but it is clearly a covenant in which "God is the initiator, the senior partner, who punishes, rewards, and enforces the punishment if the Jews slacken."[9]

The second phase"[10] in Jewish history and in the development of the meaning of covenant is marked by the destruction of the Second Temple by Rome in 70 C.E. The meaning adduced from this catastrophic event by the rabbinical sages of the era was that now Jews must take a more equal role in the covenant and become true partners with the Almighty. The destruction of 70 C.E. signaled the initiation of an age in which God would be less manifest, though still present.

This brings us to what is decisive and radical in Greenberg's ruminations, what he has termed the "third great cycle in Jewish history," which has come about as a consequence of the Holocaust. The *Shoah* marks a new era in which the Sinaitic covenantal relationship has been shattered, and thus a new and unprecedented form of covenantal relationship – if there is to be any covenantal relationship at all – must now come into being to take its place.

---

8 Fackenheim sets out his position at length in his *God's Presence in History* (New York, 1970), pp. 84–92.
9 *The Third Great Cycle of Jewish History* (New York, 1981), p. 6.
10 To be dated approximately 150 B.C.E., i.e. beginning with the Hasmonean state, to 600 C.E.

What this means, Greenberg argues, is that the covenant

> can no longer be commanded and subject to a serious external enforcement. It cannot be commanded because morally speaking – covenantally speaking – one cannot order another to step forward to die. One can give an order like this to an enemy, but in a moral relationship I cannot demand the giving up of one's life. I can ask for it or plead for it – but I cannot order it.

Out of this interconnected set of considerations, Greenberg pronounces the fateful judgment: The Jewish covenant with God is now voluntary! Jews have, quite miraculously, chosen to continue to live Jewish lives and collectively to build a Jewish state, the ultimate symbol of Jewish continuity, but these acts are, after Auschwitz, the result of the free choice of the Jewish People. After the Holocaust, Israel, vis-à-vis God, has become the "senior partner in action."

Greenberg's reconstruction of Jewish theology after the Holocaust presents a creative reaction to the unprecedented evil manifest in the death camps. Whether his position is theologically convincing, however, turns on (a) the correctness of his reading of Jewish history; and (b) the meaning and status of key concepts, such as "covenant," "revelation," "commandment," and the like, in his radically revisionist interpretation of what Judaism has been and now is. For example, can the covenant made at Sinai be broken? And can a new "voluntary covenant" really take its place? (On the issue of *Halakha* see also essay 10 above).

A redefinition of God

An influential school in modern theological circles known as "process theology," inspired by the work of Alfred North Whitehead and Charles Hartshorne, has argued that the classical understanding of God has to be dramatically revised – not least in terms of our conception of His power and direct, causal involvement in human affairs – if we are to construct a coherent theological position. According to those who advance this thesis, God exists, but the old-new difficulties raised by the problem of theodicy for classical theistic positions arise precisely because of an inadequate description of the Divine, i.e., one that mis-ascribes to Him attributes of omnipotence and omniscience that He does not possess.

Arthur A. Cohen, in his *The Tremendum: A Theological Interpretation of the Holocaust*,[11] has advanced the fullest, most detailed version of this redefinitional strategy, while defending it as the most appropriate way to respond to the theological challenges posed by the Holocaust. After arguing for the enormity of the

---

11 (New York, 1981).

Shoah, i.e., its uniqueness and its transcendence of any "meaning," Cohen suggests that the way out of the theological dilemma that the death camps pose for classical Jewish thought is to rethink whether "national catastrophes are compatible with our traditional notions of a beneficent and providential God."[12]

For Cohen, the answer is that they are not. Against the traditional view that, given its understanding of God's action in history, asks "how could it be that God witnessed the Holocaust and remained silent?" he would redefine God as not being a direct causal agent in human affairs, and thereby, eliminate the theological tension created by what he labels the *tremendum*.

But this deconstruction of classical theism and its substitution by what Cohen terms "theological dipolarity" creates its own theological difficulties. For instance, one needs to ask: Is "God" still God if He is no longer the providential agency in history? Is "God" still God if He lacks the power to enter history vertically to perform the miraculous? Is such a "dipolar" God still the God to whom one prays, the God of salvation?

Like Arthur Cohen, Hans Jonas has also suggested that the proper theological response to the Holocaust is to redefine the concept of God. In contradistinction to classical theological claims that the Divine is perfect and unchanging, he proposes both that God suffers along with humankind and that through His relation with men and women He "becomes." At the same time: "God emerges in time instead of possessing a completed being that remains identical with itself throughout eternity." God has been altered by – "temporalized" by – His relationship with others and, in the process, has become open to human suffering, which causes Him to suffer and to care. However, Jonas contends that human action is required to perfect the world. "God has no more to give: It is man's now to give to Him."[13]

A third redefinition of God has been proposed represented by Melissa Raphael. In an intriguing argument, she suggests that during and after the Holocaust the correct way to decipher the action of the Divine is through the model of "God as mother" rather than through the inherited traditional idea of "God as father." The patriarchal notion of God as almighty and omniscient is simply incompatible with what happened in the death camps. Yet, faced with this jarring fact, one need not give up belief in God altogether. Rather, one should refashion one's understanding of God in the image of a caring, suffering, loving – but not omnipotent – mother.

Raphael's proposed revision is undoubtedly suggestive, but there remains the fundamental theological question: Will the concept of "God as mother" be able to answer all the problematic metaphysical and ethical conundrums produced by the "Final Solution" better, i.e., both more inclusively and more conclusively, than prior patriarchal accounts of the Divine?[14]

---

12 *The Tremendum*, p. 50.
13 Jonas set out his view in his speech on the occasion of receiving the Leopold Lucas Prize from the University of Tubingen in 1984. This was published by the university in the form of a booklet.
14 Raphael's full position is contained in her *The Female Face of God in Auschwitz: A Jewish Feminist Theology of the Holocaust* (London, 2003).

God is dead

It is natural that many should have responded to the horror of the Holocaust with unbelief. How, such individuals quite legitimately ask, can one continue to believe in God when God did nothing to halt the demonic fury of Hitler and his minions? Such skepticism usually takes a nonsystematic, almost intuitive form: "I can no longer believe." However, one contemporary Jewish theologian, Richard Rubenstein, has provided a formally structured "death of God" theology as a response to the *Shoah*. In Rubenstein's view, the only honest response to the death camps is the rejection of God, "God is dead," and the open recognition of the meaninglessness of existence. For Rubenstein, all theological "rationalizations" of the Holocaust pale before its enormity and the only reaction that is worthy is the rejection of the entire inherited Jewish theological framework: There is no God and no covenant with Israel.

Humankind must, after Auschwitz, turn away from transcendental myths and face its actual existential situation honestly. This means that if there are to be any values, individuals must fashion and assert these values; in response to history's meaninglessness, human beings must create and project what meaning there is to be.

Had Rubenstein merely asserted the death of God, his would not be a Jewish theology. What makes it "Jewish" are the implications he draws from his radical negation with respect to the people of Israel. It might be expected that the denial of God's covenantal relation with Israel would entail the end of Judaism and so the end of the Jewish People as a meaningful collective. From the perspective of traditional Jewish theology, this would certainly be the case. Rubenstein, however, again inverts our ordinary perception and argues that with the death of God, the existence of "peoplehood," of the community of Israel, is all the more important. Now that there is nowhere else to turn for meaning, Jews need each other all the more in order to create meaning: "[I]t is precisely because human existence is tragic, ultimately hopeless, and without meaning that we treasure our religious community."[15] Though Judaism has to be "demythologized," i.e., it has to renounce all of its traditional metaphysical doctrines as well as its normative claim to a unique "chosen status," at the same time it paradoxically gains heightened importance in the process.

Rubenstein's position is certainly challenging; however it is not free of philosophical and theological difficulties. Students need, for example, to evaluate his criteria and method. That is, they have to ask whether the question of God's existence or nonexistence is subject to empirical confirmation, as Rubenstein believes. Again, if historical events like the Holocaust count against God's existence, do positive events like the creation of the State of Israel count as evidence for God's existence? Asking these questions, we begin to see that judging God's existence or nonexistence is no simple matter.

---

15 *After Auschwitz* (Indianapolis, 1966), p. 68.

An ethical demand

Emmanuel Levinas and Amos Funkenstein reject, in different ways and for different metaphysical reasons, the classical theologies and theodicies that would defend God and His justice in spite of the gas chambers and crematoriums. And both urge that rather than upholding theological doctrines that have been rendered "indefensible" by the Holocaust – what Levinas in a telling phrase describes as "useless suffering"[16] – the primary, absolute demand of our post-Holocaust era is the defense of the ethical obligation that human beings owe to one another.

While not denying the existence of God, Levinas stresses that the fundamental human requirement after Auschwitz is caring for the Other. Likewise, Funkenstein advances the primacy of the ethical as the appropriate response to the *Shoah* while also arguing for a more negative theological position that denies the existence of God.[17]

This position, i.e., the requirement that we first pay attention to ethics for, at Auschwitz, we saw what the disregard of the ethical permits, is appealing but raises, in turn, a number of deep, interrelated questions: What is the ground of the ethical? What is the source of ethical obligation? Who or what is the guarantor of the value of the ethical? To propound *a priori* the primacy of the ethical is merely to stipulate the conclusion, not to prove it.

Mystery and silence

In the face of the abyss, the devouring of the Jewish People by the dark forces of evil incarnate, recourse to the God of mystery and the endorsement of human silence are not unworthy options. There are, however, two kinds of silence, two kinds of employment of the God of mystery. The first is closer to the attitude of the agnostic: "I cannot know," and hence all deeply grounded existential and intellectual wrestling with the enormous problems raised by the *Shoah* are avoided. The second is the silence and mystery to which the Bible points in its recognition of God's elemental otherness. This is the silence that comes after struggling with God, after reproaching God, after feeling His closeness or His painful absence. This silence, this mystery, does not attempt to diminish the tragedy by a too quick, too gauche answer yet, having followed reason to its limits, it recognizes the limits of reason. One finds this attitude more commonly expressed in the literary and personal responses to Auschwitz by survivors than in technical works of theology. For example, it is preeminent in the work of Elie Wiesel and André Schwarz-Bart, as well as in the poetry of Nellie Sachs.

---

16 "Useless Suffering," in *The Provocation of Levinas*, ed. Robert Bernasconi and David Wood (London, 1988), p. 159.
17 Amos Funkenstein put forward his views in his essay "Theological Interpretations of the Holocaust," in *Unanswered Questions: Nazi Germany and the Genocide of the Jews*, ed. François Furet (New York, 1989), pp. 275–303.

Yet, silence, too, can be problematic for if employed incorrectly, or too casually, or too universally, as a – or the – theological response to the *Shoah*, it removes the Holocaust from history and all post-Holocaust human experience. And by doing so, it may produce the unintended consequence of making the Holocaust irrelevant. If the generations that come after Auschwitz cannot speak of it, and thus cannot raise probing questions as a consequence of it, then it becomes literally meaningless to them.[18]

III Conclusion

The death camps and *Einsatzgruppen* do challenge – even while they do not necessarily falsify – traditional Jewish theological claims. However, just what this challenge ultimately means remains undecided.

---

[18] More extensive criticism of many of the views described in this essay can be found in "The issue of confirmation and disconfirmation in Jewish thought after the *Shoah*," Chapter 14 in this volume. Selections of the work of the thinkers here discussed can be found in Steven T. Katz, Shlomo Biderman, and Gershon Greenberg (eds.), *Wrestling with God: Jewish Theological Responses during and after the Holocaust* (New York, 2007).

UPDATE

In the last three decades the serious discussion of Jewish theology after, and in response to, the Holocaust has become less central and less vibrant, both inside both the academy and the synagogue. Nonetheless, thinkers like Melissa Raphael in her *The Female Face of God in Auschwitz: A Jewish Feminist Theology of the Holocaust* (London, 2003), and Rabbi Jonathan Sacks, the former Chief Rabbi of Great Britain, especially in his *Tradition in an Untraditional Age: Essays in Modern Jewish Thought* (London, 1990), and *Crisis and Covenant: Jewish Thought after the Holocaust* (London, 1992), have added further layers of some consequence to the complex discussion.

I have offered lengthy critiques of the theological positions of almost all of the significant Jewish thinkers who have contributed to the discussion of this issue in two previous collections of essays. In the first of these, *Post-Holocaust Dialogues: Critical Studies in Modern Jewish Thought* (New York, 1982), there are long and detailed deconstructions of the efforts of Richard Rubenstein, Eliezer Berkovits, Emil Fackenheim, and Ignaz Maybaum. In the second, *Historicism, the Holocaust and Zionism: Critical Studies in Modern Jewish History and Thought* (New York, 1993), the work of Irving Greenberg and Arthur Cohen is probed. To date I have not written at length about responses to the Holocaust articulated by Emmanuel Levinas, Hans Jonas, Amos Funkenstein, or Joseph Soloveitchik.

In reflecting on the theological debate that has gone on since the 1960s, primarily by non-Orthodox thinkers, it is now clear to me that the one area of important Jewish responses that I, and most of the others involved in this dialogue, have ignored at our cost are the contributions that have come from the ultra-Orthodox world. The presentations made by these traditional sages are significant, not least because they are closely in touch with – and their views are deeply informed by – authentic Jewish sources and tradition. Thus were I now to write a comprehensive review of Jewish theological responses after Auschwitz, I would include analyses of figures like Kalonymous Kalman Shapira, author of the *Esh Kodesh* (*Holy Fire*), who preached, wrote and was murdered in the Warsaw Ghetto; Yissachar Teichtal, author of *Eim Habanim Semehah* (*A Happy Mother's Children*) that was published in the midst of the Holocaust in December 1943; Shlomoh Zalman Unsdorfer, whose sermons were written in Bratislava, Slovakia, in 1943 and published after the war in a translation into Hebrew from Yiddish under the title *Siftei Shlomoh* (*The Lips of Shlomoh*, Brooklyn, 1972); and the teachings of both Yosef Yitzchak Schneersohn, the Lubavitcher Rebbe during the war, and his successor, Menachem Mendel Schneersohn, after the war.

These are difficult works to decipher, and especially to decipher sympathetically, because they were written from within a very special, ultra-Orthodox universe of thought that is predicated on theological assumptions that are foreign, and often very critically responded to, by those outside of this distinctive community. In addition, they presume a good deal of Jewish learning, an understanding of midrashic motifs, a knowledge of *Halakha*, and an intimate familiarity with kabbalistic theory that most modern academics, and non-Orthodox thinkers more broadly, do not possess. All of these ultra-Orthodox "responses" assume the ultimacy of, and the ever-new meanings to be discovered within, the Torah. They all unquestioningly accept the traditional notion that the Torah in its entirety, except for the last few verses of Deuteronomy that tell of Moses' death, was revealed by God at Sinai. They never question the notion of the authority of the rabbinic tradition, i.e., the claim of *"halakha l'Moshe mi'Sinai"* ("the law given to Moses at Sinai"). Moreover, these works do not conform to any familiar model of academic, systematic theology. Nevertheless, as I have studied them more deeply over the past three decades, I now realize that they represent a unique repository of Jewishly learned, very diverse and multi-faceted, religious (and political) positions.

Among the contributors to this erudite literature were Hasidic masters of the stature of the Satmar Rebbe, Yoel Teitelbaum; two Lubavitcher Rebbes, *mitnagdim* ("opponents" of Hasidism) like R. Elhanan Wasserman; and *mussarniks* (disciples of the ethical school of R. Israel Salanter). Many of these works lean heavily on eschatological and apocalyptic themes and put considerable emphasis on the unique character of the People of Israel. And precisely because they raise such classical themes their claims and interpretations are, for the most part, absent in studies by more "modern" thinkers. For myself, while I find it difficult to endorse much of their *Weltanschauung*. The anti-Reform, anti-Zionist, and anti-modernist claims made by many of these authors are, for me, no more valid today than they were when I first came across them decades ago in the yeshiva world. I have, however, come to appreciate the depth and conceptual diversity represented by their varied claims and explanations. Reading the material that comprises this corpus provides much thoughtful, challenging and not-usual *theological* material to reflect on. Collectively, it requires us – and this is one of the great values of this potpourri of ideas – to have a broader *theological* imagination and a more richly conceived metaphysical schema.

As I have not been persuaded by any of the explanations and responses given to date, I remain committed to the view that there is no "correct" theological explanation or response to Auschwitz. At the same time, I now see that the epistemological and metaphysical issues that one must here wrestle with are even more complex than I appreciated in years past.

INDEX

Akiva, Rabbi: 221, 282–3
Aly, G.: 118, 123n7, 133n52, 134n56, 152n7, 164n48; on Jewish labor 121
Anti-Semitism: 58n5–6, 61n19, 102–3, 114, 116–9, 184n36, 251; *Adversus Judaeos tradition 115*; Church 2, 21
Arendt, H.: xvi–xvii, 247; on Auschwitz and the *Gulag* 57, 61n18, 247; *see also* Eichmann, A.
Armenian massacre: 2, 4–5, 12n20, 22–3, 236; conversion of 10, 116; refugees 11–2, 12n20, 116
Auschwitz: xv, 13–7, 13n21, 23, 25–6, 39, 63, 64n28, 66, 67n47, 73, 87, 99, 102, 122n5, 126n18, 138n72, 146, 147n97, 148n100–2, 150n1, 151n3, 152n7, 166n59, 167–9, 174n10, 276, 294–6, 296n10, 298–300, 300n20, 304, 307, 313, 316, 325n79, 327n92, 330, 332, 332n96, 333n98, 336, 340, 342n14, 344, 345, 347
Australia: 92n7; aborigines 2
Ayer, A. J.: 295, 296n9, 304, 305n34, 331, 334; *see also* faith after Auschwitz

Berkovits, E.: 293n5, 307, 309–0, 311n45, 312–7, 322n71, 340, 293n5, 313n45; *see also* faith after Auschwitz.
Białystok Ghetto: 12 307, 309–3, 139n78–9, 140, 153, 160, 238, 247, 252n58;
 Efraim Barash, elder of *Judenräte* 139;
 Mordechai Tenenbaum, resistance leader 139n75, 233, 236, 254, 255n67; slave labor in 139, 252
Biebow, H.: 140; Lodz Ghetto 180, 180n24
Birkenau: 126n18, 167, 174, 174n10, 181, 196, 258–9, 268; armed resistance 263;

murder of Jewish children 16; Murder of Jewish Labor 138, 144, 148
Bloxham, D.: xvii, 25, 94n13, 103, 103n37, 104–7, 107n98, 147n98, 197n73
Brest-Litovsk Ghetto: 140, 140n86; Koch, E. 141; Rhode, F. W. 141
Browning, C.: 94, 94n13, 135n53, 135n63, 163n45, 164n50, 165n55, 173, 173n3; on Jewish labor 128n30, 130n39, 141n88
Buber, M.: 219, 233–4, 298, 298n12, 301, 301n21, 301n23, 302n24–5, 301–3, 331–2, 332n94, 340, 340n7
Buchenwald concentration camp: 127n26, 185n40, 268; and Jewish labor 148

Cambodia: 3–4, 18, 34, 48–9, 50n48, 51–3, 52n53, 53n54, 236; Buddhist monks, persecution of 51, 53
Catholic Church: 3; during the Holocaust 240, 243n32; in the New World 113, 119–20, 198; Vatican II 207
Cesarani, D.: on Final Solution 94n13, 144, 144n92; on Jewish labor 144–5, 148
China: 18; Civil War 2, 2n2
Churchill, W.: 6, 6n6, 244
Cohen, A.: 317–0, 320n67, 321–5, 340, 343; *see also* faith after Auschwitz
Columbus, C.: xvii, 199
Constantinople: 8, 12
Covenant: 169n67, 201, 211, 331; between God and Israel 99, 102, 202–7, 214–8, 220, 230, 292, 297, 299, 304, 319, 319n65, 324–8, 326n84, 336–7, 341–2, 344, 347
Crusaders: 3, 281, 335n1

349

INDEX

Czerniaków, A.: 132n51; killing of Jewish children 155n16, 246; misled by Nazis 251–2, 252n56
Częstochowa: 130, 144, 263

Dachau concentration camp: 64, 148, 185, 185n40
death camps: xv, 16, 63, 64n28, 87n35, 105, 118, 122, 196, 237, 254, 257, 257n68, 263, 265, 268, 271, 275–6, 287, 293, 297, 310, 330, 335, 338, 340, 342–4, 346; *see also* Auschwitz; Bełżec 71, 122, 122n5, 161, 257n68; Chełmno 71, 122, 124, 155, 180, 254, 264; Majdanek 137, 145, 156, 166, 178, 252, 300; Sobibór, 139n79, 145, 166, 193, 193n65, 254, 257n68, 263, 265n102; Treblinka 14, 39, 56, 63, 64n28, 69, 71, 139n79, 154–5, 160, 160n34, 186n41, 196, 196n71, 252, 254–5, 263, 265n102, 300, 336–7, 344
Dora-Mittelbau camp: 148

Eckhardt, A.: 275
Eckhardt, R.: 275
Eichmann, A.: xviin5, 13, 87n36, 118, 124n12, 138, 164, 241, 247n44, 258n74, 268, 272
election of Israel: 216, 221; Kaplan M. on 207, 220, 320n87; Rubenstein R. on xvii, 102, 112, 207, 220, 291, 291n1, 292, 292n2, 293n6, 294–7, 303, 329, 329n92, 332, 334, 344, 347

Fackenheim, E.: 169n67, 297–300, 300n20, 300–6, 333, 340–1; *see also* faith after Auschwitz
faith after Auschwitz: Ayer, A. J. 295, 296n9, 304, 305n34, 331, 334; Berkovits, E. 293n5, 307, 312–3, 314–5, 316–7, 316n57, 322, 322n71, 337–8; Buber, M. 182, 219, 233–4, 298, 298n12, 301–2, 301n21, 301n23, 302n24–5, 302n27, 303, 303n28, 332, 332n94, 340n7; Cohen, A. on redefinition of God 303n28, 317–25, 320n67, 324n78, 332, 340, 342–3, 347; Fackenheim, E. on 82n22, 297–305, 298n12, 299n13–5, 299n17–8, 300n19–20, 301n21, 332–3, 340–1; and Free Will Defense 308, 310, 309n42, 312, 314, 317–8, 321–2, 339; Job 225, 282, 282n37, 311–2, 331, 336; Rubenstein, R. on 102, 207, 291–2, 295, 297, 303n29, 344; *see also* Wiesel, E.
France: 3, 243, 243n32, 262n89; deportations from 25, 123, 126, 134, 166–7, 166n61–2
Frankfurter, F.: 239, 239n18
Free Will Defense: *see* faith after Auschwitz

Galut: 213
Genocide: concept of xiii–iv, xvi–vii, xviin10, 2–3, 2n2, 6n7, 7n9, 8n11, 10, 12n20, 15, 21–3, 23n44–6, 24n47, 37, 39, 43, 45–6, 49, 51–2, 52n53, 54–6, 55n62–3, 61, 71, 91, 91n3–5, 93, 111–2, 115, 119, 194, 197, 197n72, 197n74; Kuper, L. on xvii, 22; Midlarsky, M. on 23, 23n44, 25; United Nation Genocide Convention 23, 90n2, 91n6, 92, 92n9–10, 96
Gerlach, C.: 118, 140n86, 141n87, 165n55, 167n63; on Jewish labor 149, 149n104, 164n54
Germany: 58, 58n6, 61, 121,123, 264n95, and Leo Baeck 233, 234n1, 234n5–6; and Martin Buber 302
Globocnik, O.: 122n5, 135, 252
God: and Covenant 99, 102, 169n67, 202–6, 211, 214–8, 220, 292, 304, 319, 319n65, 325–7, 326n84, 337, 341–2, 344, 347; hidden nature of 203, 207, 269, 295, 307, 314–6, 338; as "Junior Partner" 203–4, 206–7, 209, 214, 326; kabbalistic view of 214n2, 223, 322, 348; and mitzvot 209, 319; and repentance 209; and revelation 102, 202–3, 208–10, 213–4, 298, 298n12, 300–3, 319, 328, 331, 341
Greece: 11, 25, 55, 177n17, 254; deportations from 25
Greenberg, I.: 150–1, 210–12, 214, 273, 319n65, 325–7, 325n-79–80, 326n84, 327n87, 328–2, 341–2; *see also Halakha*
Gross Rosen concentration camp: 138, 138n69, 165; murder of Jews 127n26, 148
Gulag: 4, 13–5, 13n21, 15n25, 15n32, 19–20, 22, 25, 57–8, 62–71, 66n42, 70n53, 75, 86, 86n32; children in 16–8, 26n55, 73, 74n1, 76, 79, 83–4, 87–8, 88n38; kulaks in 26, 30, 32, 52; sexual activity in 15–6

350

INDEX

Halakha: 204, 303, 347; and history 207, 213–4; Greenberg, I. on 205–7, 211; Teitelbaum, J., Rabbi on 339, 339n5
HASAG: 186; *see also* Częstochowa; Radom
Heissmeyer K., Dr.: medical experiments at Neuengamme 80–1; medical experiments at Bullenhusendamm 81
Herbert U.: 121, 124n13, 126n19, 133n54, 137n68, 140n80, 161n37, 164n46, 164n54, 264n95; *Historikerstreit* 57n2, 121n2
Hilberg, R.: xvi, xvin4, 67n43, 124, 124n11, 132n51, 155n16, 234n2, 236, 236n10, 244n34, 252n56
Himmler H.: 122n5, 128n28–30, 131n41, 145, 152n6, 185n39, 186, 239, 251; on ghettos 118, 125–6, 130, 133, 155, 164, 252; on Jewish labor 66, 125, 125n15, 132, 137, 140n85, 143; view of Jews 5, 68, 105, 122, 122n5, 125–6, 128–9, 131–2, 134–5, 138, 144, 151
Holodomor: 52, 54–6, 56n69, 88n37; *see also* Ukraine
Hungary: 11, 163n45, 241, 254n65, 268; deportation of Jews 169, 242, 268

Jewish children: 17, 55, 80, 82–4, 88, 103, 152, 157, 160, 162–3, 162n42, 169n67, 170, 207, 234–5, 244, 277, 293, 312, 327, 329; in death camps 39, 80, 83, 155, 164, 167–9; in occupied Eastern European ghettos 81, 84, 84n24, 151n3, 152, 153n9, 153n11, 156, 157–8, 160–1, 163–5; in occupied Western Europe 39, 165–8, 235, 243n32
Jewish labor: Frank, H. on 126–7, 134n57; in *Generalgouvernement* 122, 125, 125n15, 127–9, 133n34; Glücks, R. on 128; Greiser, A. on 124; for Heinkel corporation 129, 131n44; Korherr, R. report on 122, 123n6, 125n17, 138; Krüger, F-W. on 128–9, 144; in Lublin 130, 135–7, 144–5; Pohl, O. on 125, 125n15, 127–8, 136, 148; at Radom 130, 133n54, 144, 247
Jewish resistance: during the Holocaust xvi, 228–9, 233, 235–239, 240n24, 243n32, 245, 248, 249n48, 262, 286; and Adam Czerniaków 155n16, 246, 251–2, 252n56; analogy to slavery 112, 255; armed resistance in concentration camps 263; armed resistance in death camps 263; *see also* Treblinka, Auschwitz, Sobibór; armed resistance in labor camps 263–4; Bundists and 238; communists and 238; and *Einsatzgruppen* 256; emigration as 234–5; and Gens, J. 228, 250; *see also Judenräte*; in Germany 233; in ghettos 228–9, 233, 236, 238, 245–50; and Russian POWs 265n102; spiritual resistance 233, 236, 257, 260n82, 302n24; weapons 253, 262n92
Jewish Women: xvi, 95n15, 103, 105, 151, 161–2, 225; in concentration camps 177; in death camps 161, 163, 196, 263; in ghettos 156–7, 163, 195; in labor camps 137, 173; rape and 16, 171–4, 174n10, 176–81, 181n30, 182n31, 183–6, 183n33, 185n40, 186n44, 188–96; *see also Rassenschande*
Job: 225, 282, 282n37, 311–2, 331, 336; *see also* faith after Auschwitz
Joshua: 202, and book of 218, 270
Judaism after the Holocaust: 102n34, 169n67, 204n1, 293n5, 300, 319n65, 322n71, 325, 336, 340, 342–3, 346n18, 347; *Akedah* – binding of Isaac 163, 225, 281, 313n48, 335–7; God is dead 291, 295, 305, 344; *Hester Panim* ("God hides His face") 307, 338; *Mipnei Chataeynu* ("because of our sins") 338, 340; redefinition of God 319n65, 342; Suffering Servant (Isaiah, ch. 53) 314n48, 336–7, 337n3
Judenräte: xvii, 228, 246–7, 249–51; Ephraim Barash, Elder of the Białystok Ghetto 139, 252; Międzyrzec Ghetto 249; Vilna Ghetto 228–9, 246–7, 250, 252; Warsaw Ghetto 246, 250–1; *see also* Czerniaków, A.

Karski, J.: 239, 239n18
Khmer Rouge: 48–9, 52–4, 52n53, 236, 278; Kampuchea 3–4, 27, 48–9, 49n44, 50, 50n47–8 *see also* Cambodia
Kierkegaard, S.: xv, 298
Kiev: 79, 242, 256; Jewish children 84, 161, 163, 242
Kol Yisrael Arevim: concept of xiii, 215–6, 220, 227–8, 230–1, 249n49, 261n87; and collective responsibility during the Holocaust 228, 249; halakhic

significance of 224; Janusz Korczak 229, 261, 312; Talmud on 212;
Kolyma: 13, 17, 59n13, 60n17, 65n36, 67, 67n44, 67n46, 67n48, 68n50, 69, 74n1 *see also* Gulag and Stalin
Kovno Ghetto: 140, 157, 169, 194n67, 228, 261, 263; rape of Jewish women 194; slave labor 140, 140n80–2
Kulaks: 27–8, 29n3, 30–2, 52–3, 59, 68, 71, 88, 113, 116; and agricultural collectivization 26–7, 29, 71 see *also* Stalin

Lengyel, O.: 16, 16n35
Levinas, E.: 269n3, 275, 332, 345
Lewin, M.: xiv, 27n1, 28n2, 31n7–8, 60n17
Lipper, E.: 17, 17n36, 18n39, 74n1.
Lithuania: 140, 156n26, 157, 241, 250n52, 261; murder of Jews 25, 129, 129n36, 158–9, 169, 181n28, 192, 192n63, 194, 229n8, 238n15, 241
Lodz Ghetto: 153n9, 155n17, 180n25, 246n40 *see also* Biebow, H.; and Jewish labor 140
Lublin District: 122n5, 128n29, 130, 133, 133n52, 135–7, 136n65–6, 160, 237, 263; Jewish ghettos in 128, 135n62; Jewish labor camps in 135–7, 144–5

Maimonides: 202, 214, 286; action vs. contemplation 223; *Guide for the Perplexed* 223; on charity 220; responsibility for other Jews 217, 223, 226
mass murder: 26n55, 32, 39, 43, 52–3, 59n13, 67, 91, 91n3–4, 92n9, 95n17, 116, 128, 131, 149, 196; dialectic within 32, 115–6, 119
Mauthausen concentration camp: 148, 185n40
Maybaum, I.: on Christian theology 337, 347
Messiah/messianism: 209, 214, 274, 274n14, 286–7, 287n52, 304–5, 328
Mishnah: 220; six orders of 213; *Tannaim* 204, 213; time of composition 213
Moses: 224, 285, 303, 348; and sinners 217–9; character of 217, 281; ethics of 217, 219, 227
Moses A. D.: xvii, 94n13, 98–103, 98n23, 100n26, 101n33, 106–7, 106n42, 109, 113, 197n73

New World Indians: 2–4, 21, 88n37, 112, 120, 199, 278–9; death from disease 112; New World slavery xvii, xvii-n9, xvii-n11, 13n22, 14n23, 64n29, 88n37, 90n1, 109, 112, 151n5, 183n34, 251
Nolte, E.: 12–3, 57, 57n3

"Organization Schmelt:" 137–8, 138n73, 148

Pakistan/Bangladesh: 49; tribal wars 3, 95n17
Pascal, B.: xv
Pol Pot: 48–9, 49n44, 50n48, 52–3, 52n53, 278 *see also* Khmer Rouge; Chandler, D. 52, 52n52
Poland: 25, 118, 128n30, 237, 240, 240n22, 240n24, 242n29, 245, 254, 261, 264; murder of Jews 25, 121–3, 135n63, 188, 234n1, 240n20, 254, 260n84
Poniatowa: Jews at 133, 137, 145
principle of mediation: 4, 51, 68, 116, 189

Rassenschande: xiii, 172, 174n10, 183n33, 184, 188, 188n49, 194, 198
Rubenstein, R.: 291–2, 293n6, 294–6, 303n29, 332, 344, *see also* faith after Auschwitz; election of Israel
Russian POWs: 265n102; diets 266; labor 126
Rwanda: 3, 18, 112, 116, 171n1, 197, 279; and genocide 23, 97–8, 98n21–2; Hutu 23, 34, 236; Tutsi 23, 34, 97, 197, 236

Schneerson, M. Rabbi: 272
Shain, M.: 110, 119
Shapira, K.: 347
Smyrna: 12; *see also* Armenian massacre
Soloveitchik, J. Rabbi: 207, 222, 285, 338, 339n5, 347; on covenant 216
Solzhenitsyn, A.: 14–5, 14n25, 15n32, 35n16, 58n8, 59n11, 59n13, 60n17, 65 74n1, 75, 75n3–4, 75n7, 76, 76n8, 79, 83n23; *see also Gulag*
Spanish Empire: xvii, 198; conquistadors 4, 199
Speer, A.: 66n41, 122n3, 125, 125n14, 132n47, 135n64, 137n67, 138n70–1; on Jewish labor 66, 125n15, 130n39, 136–8
Stalin: 14, 17 , 22, 25–7, 26n55, 29, 31n6, 33, 41–5, 52–3, 54n59, 55n62–3, 58–9, 59n12, 58n15, 60n17, 61–4, 63n25–6,

INDEX

64n31, 66–8, 70, 71n55–6, 72n59, 75n3, 78n12, 115–6, 241–2; and agricultural collectivization 26, 29–31, 71, 71n56; and Ukraine 21, 26–7, 26n56, 29n3, 31n3, 33n10, 34–5, 34n11, 34n14, 36n17, 36n19, 37–8, 40, 53–4, 56, 56n66, 56n69, 116; and Kolyma 13, 17, 59n13, 60n17, 65n36, 67, 67n44–6, 67n48, 68n50, 69, 74; and minorities 27, 40, 42–3, 42n31, 47–8, 52, 71, 116
Stannard, D.: xvii, xvii-n11, 95n15, 112
Stone, D.: xvii, 25, 26n55, 53n54, 55n63, 70n54, 91n4, 96n20, 102–3, 102n35, 107, 109

Teichtal, Y.: 347
Teitelbaum, Y., Rabbi: 212, 339, 339n5
Tertullian: xv
Tory, A.: Kovno Ghetto 140n81, 194, 194n67
Trawniki: 135n66; Jewish labor 131n45, 133, 137
Turkey: 4, 7–9, 11–2, 18, 22–5, 115–6, 171n1, 236, 244; Ottoman Empire 5, 8n10, 22–6, 25n52, 112, 115, 222n2; Van, revolt in 5, 7–8, 12; World War I 4, 6–9, 12n20, 18, 22, 115, 171n1, 279; Young Turks 6, 22, 25, 112, 115

Ukraine: 26, 26n56, 33–5, 33n912–4, 34n11–4, 56n67, 58n9, 147–8, 148n99, 163, 164n53, 182n32, 241; Conquest, R. on 32, 34n14, 35n15, 36n17, 36n20, 37n22, 38n23, 39, 57; death of children 38n23–25; Holodomor 52, 54–6, 56n69, 88n37; Stalin and 21, 27, 36–8, 36n19, 53, 56, 56n66
uniqueness of the Holocaust: xvi, 2, 2n4, 4, 9, 21–3, 36–8, 54–6, 70, 73, 86n32, 88, 90, 92n7, 93–5, 98, 100, 107, 109, 111, 115, 117–8, 120, 151, 169; Bauer, Y. on 91n5, 94–5, 94n12–3, 100, 102; Bloxham, D. on xvii, 94n13, 103–7, 103n37, 109; Moses, A. D. on xvii, 94n13, 98–102, 106, 106n42, 107, 109, 113; Snyder, T. on 94, 94n12; Stone, D.

on xvii, 53n54, 91n4, 97, 102, 102n35, 107, 109
United States: 22, 113, 119, 234n4, 244; immigration to 11; Reigner Telegram 244
United States Holocaust Memorial Museum: 22, 125n16, 182n32, 276–7, 279–80, 279n30, 288; *see also* Wiesel E.

Vernichtung durch Arbeit (extermination through work): 121n2, 128n27, 128n31, 132n46, 133n54, 135n62, 140, 140n85, 143, 145–7, 149
Versailles Treaty: 58
Vilna Ghetto: 153, 155–6, 156n21, 156n26, 228n6, 253n61, 257n6; Kruk, H. 156n26, 181, 181n28, 238, 238n15, 260n82; resistance in 228–9, 236, 248, 250, 250n53, 252–3
Von Gienanth, C. L. F.: on Jewish labor 135

Warsaw Ghetto: 56, 153–4, 155n16, 178–9, 179n22–3, 190, 229–30, 233, 238, 239n18, 240, 250, 253, 253n60, 260, 260n83, 262, 277; Czerniaków, A. 132n51, 155n16, 246, 251–2, 252n56; Ringelblum, E. 155n16, 179, 179n22, 260n83; labor in 126, 130, 132, 137, 144
Wiesel, E.: 99–101, 111, 267; childhood 268–9; and Clinton, W. J. President 279–80; concern for Israel 269, 280, 288–9; deportation 268; Hasidism 273, 284–6; *Jews of Silence* 272; *Night* 268, 270, 271n8, 272, 275, 275n17, 276, 290; Nobel Prize 277–8, 290; and Obama, B. President 279, 288, 290; on God 272, 274–6, 281; and Russian Jewry 272–3; and Schneerson, M., Lubavitcher Rebbe 272; United States Holocaust Memorial Museum 276, 288;
witch craze: 112–4
Wolfson, H.: xiv

Yugoslavia: 168, 171, 197, 261, 265, 279

Zhitomir: 82, 153; Jewish children 81, 164

353